Cumulative Chapter Vocabulary Lists for Wheelock's Latin

Richard A. LaFleur and Brad Tillery

— Second Edition —

Bolchazy-Carducci Publishers, Inc.
Wauconda, Illinois USA

Editor: Laurie Haight Keenan
Cover Design: Adam Phillip Velez

Cumulative Chapter Vocabulary Lists for Wheelock's Latin

Richard A. LaFleur & Brad Tillery
Second Edition

Published by Bolchazy-Carducci Publishers, Inc.

Bolchazy-Carducci Publishers, Inc.
1000 Brown Street
Wauconda, Illinois 60084
www.bolchazy.com

Printed in the United States of America
2022
by Publishers' Graphics

ISBN 978-0-86516-770-4

The full, unabbreviated Wheelock Latin-English vocabulary entry is given for each word, i.e., all principal parts for verbs (even regular first-conjugation verbs are spelled out), the complete nominative and genitive case forms for nouns, etc., and all with full English meanings; macrons as well as accents are included for all Latin words; each entry is followed by a number in parentheses indicating the Wheelock chapter in which the word is introduced.

These lists have a wide range of uses, but perhaps the most valuable are (a) as a handy resource for student review—studying for a test that covers through Chapter 10 will be much expedited by simply using the Chapter 10 list in this book; and (b) as a convenient reference for instructors writing cumulative vocabulary quizzes or composing Latin sentences and passages for translation on tests and classroom exercises—no longer will you need to flip back and forth through the pages of preceding chapters to check on whether a particular word has already been introduced or not.

Thanks are due to family and friends who tolerated our evening and weekend "leaves of absence" while we labored on this project, to Joseph Stanfiel, who assisted with the typing and compilation of a prototype of these lists while a graduate student at UGA, to Martha Wheelock and Deborah Wheelock Taylor for their constant support, and to the good folks at Bolchazy-Carducci Publishers—in particular our editor Laurie Haight Keenan and production manager Jody Cull—for appreciating the merits of this and our other *Wheelockiana* and generously sharing their expertise in order to make these materials even more useful than they might otherwise have been.

RICHARD A. LAFLEUR, University of Georgia
BRAD TILLERY, North Oconee High School

"He studied Latin like the violin, because he liked it."
Robert Frost, *The Death of the Hired Man*

CUMULATIVE VOCABULARY LISTS
for
WHEELOCK'S LATIN

by
RICHARD A. LAFLEUR
University of Georgia

BRAD TILLERY
North Oconee High School, Oconee County, Georgia

— SECOND EDITION —

Wheelock's Latin is THE CLASSIC introductory Latin course, widely used in colleges and high-schools, as well as by independent learners, throughout the U.S. and abroad. A host of ancillary materials support the program, including the *Workbook for Wheelock's Latin; Scribblers, Sculptors, and Scribes: A Companion to* WHEELOCK'S LATIN *and Other Introductory Textbooks;* the *Vocabulary Cards and Grammatical Forms Summary for Wheelock's Latin;* the 4-CD audio package *Readings from Wheelock's Latin;* online audio and an online *Teacher's Guide;* Dale Grote's *Comprehensive Guide to Wheelock's Latin;* Groton and May's *38 Latin Stories;* and the intermediate text *Wheelock's Latin Reader.* For details and ordering information, be sure to visit each of these websites: www.bolchazy.com, www.wheelockslatin.com, and www.harpercollins.com.

An early version of these *Cumulative Vocabulary Lists* was developed for use at the University of Georgia with the 5th Edition of *Wheelock's Latin.* Over the years the lists proved so helpful to our own students and faculty alike that it was decided to reorganize and produce a more elaborate, updated set to accompany the textbook's 7th edition, and to make this resource available to Latin teachers and students throughout the country.

The book contains 40 lists, corresponding to the 40 chapters in *Wheelock's Latin.* Each list contains ALL the vocabulary items introduced in the book up through that particular chapter; e.g., the Chapter 25 list contains all nouns, pronouns, adjectives, etc., in Wheelock's chapter vocabularies for Chapters 1–25, grouped together and sorted by part of speech. Nouns are listed first and categorized by declension, with all first-declension nouns given first, in alphabetical order, then all second-declension nouns in alphabetical order, followed by third-, fourth-, and fifth-declension nouns, and finally indeclinable nouns; pronouns are listed next; then adjectives, categorized into first/second-declension, third-declension, and indeclinables, with each category in alphabetical order; verbs appear next, with categories including, each in alphabetical order, the four regular conjugations, as well as irregular, deponent, and defective verbs; next come adverbs; then conjunctions; prepositions; interjections; idioms; prefixes; suffixes; and finally numerals. Again, each chapter list contains all items introduced in that and all preceding chapters (except that such incomplete items as **mē,** introduced in Chapter 1, are deleted from the lists once the full form set has been introduced—i.e., **mē** is dropped from the Chapter 11 and subsequent lists, since the full declension of **ego, meī** is presented in Chapter 11 and thus included under **ego** in the Chapter 11–40 lists); the Chapter 40 list, of course, contains all of the nearly 900 entries appearing in Wheelock's 40 chapters.

Chapter 1

Noun
níhil - nothing

Pronouns
mē - me, myself
quid - what

Verbs
1st Conjugation
ámō, amā́re, amā́vī, amā́tum - to love, like
cṓgitō, cōgitā́re, cōgitā́vī, cōgitā́tum - to think, ponder, consider, plan
cōnsérvō, cōnservā́re, cōnservā́vī, cōnservā́tum - to preserve, conserve, maintain
dō, dáre, dédī, dátum - to give, offer
érrō, errā́re, errā́vī, errā́tum - to wander; err, go astray, make a mistake, be mistaken
laúdō, laudā́re, laudā́vī, laudā́tum - to praise
sérvō, servā́re, servā́vī, servā́tum - to preserve, save, keep, guard
vócō, vocā́re, vocā́vī, vocā́tum - to call, summon

2nd Conjugation
dḗbeō, dēbḗre, dḗbuī, dḗbitum - to owe; ought, must, should
móneō, monḗre, mónuī, mónitum - to remind, advise, warn
sálvē, salvḗte - hello, greetings
sálveō, salvḗre - to be well, be in good health
térreō, terrḗre, térruī, térritum - to frighten, terrify
válē, valḗte - good-bye, farewell
váleō, valḗre, váluī, valitū́rum - to be strong, have power; be well
vídeō, vidḗre, vī́dī, vī́sum - to see; observe, understand

Adverbs
nōn - not
saépe - often

Conjunction
sī - if

Idiom
amā́bō tē - please

Chapter 2

Nouns

1st Declension

fā́ma, fā́mae (f) - rumor, report; fame, reputation (2)
fṓrma, fṓrmae (f) - form, shape; beauty (2)
fortū́na, fortū́nae (f) - fortune, luck (2)
ī́ra, ī́rae (f) - ire, anger (2)
naúta, naútae (m) - sailor (2)
pátria, pátriae (f) - fatherland, native land, (one's) country (2)
pecū́nia, pecū́niae (f) - money (2)
philosóphia, philosóphiae (f) - philosophy (2)
poéna, poénae (f) - penalty, punishment (2)
poḗta, poḗtae (m) - poet (2)
pórta, pórtae (f) - gate, entrance (2)
puélla, puéllae (f) - girl (2)
rósa, rósae (f) - rose (2)
senténtia, senténtiae (f) - feeling, thought, opinion, vote, sentence (2)
vī́ta, vī́tae (f) - life; mode of life (2)

Indeclinable

níhil - nothing (1)

Pronouns

mē - me, myself (1)
quid - what (1)

Adjectives

antī́qua, antī́quae - ancient, old-time (2)
mágna, mágnae - large, great; important (2)
méa, méae - my (2)
múlta, múltae - much, many (2)
túa, túae - your *(sing.)* (2)

Verbs

1st Conjugation

ámō, amā́re, amā́vī, amā́tum - to love, like (1)
cṓgitō, cōgitā́re, cōgitā́vī, cōgitā́tum - to think, ponder, consider, plan (1)
cōnsérvō, cōnservā́re, cōnservā́vī, cōnservā́tum - to preserve, conserve, maintain (1)
dō, dáre, dédī, dátum - to give, offer (1)
érrō, errā́re, errā́vī, errā́tum - to wander; err, go astray, make a mistake, be mistaken (1)
laúdō, laudā́re, laudā́vī, laudā́tum - to praise (1)
sérvō, servā́re, servā́vī, servā́tum - to preserve, save, keep, guard (1)
vócō, vocā́re, vocā́vī, vocā́tum - to call, summon (1)

2nd Conjugation

dḗbeō, dēḗre, dḗbuī, dḗbitum - to owe; ought, must, should (1)
móneō, monḗre, mónuī, mónitum - to remind, advise, warn (1)
sálvē, salvḗte - hello, greetings (1)
sálveō, salvḗre - to be well, be in good health (1)
térreō, terrḗre, térruī, térritum - to frighten, terrify (1)
válē, valḗte - good-bye, farewell (1)
váleō, valḗre, váluī, valitū́rum - to be strong, have power; be well (1)
vídeō, vidḗre, vī́dī, vī́sum - to see; observe, understand (1)

Irregular

est - is (2)

Adverbs

nōn - not (1)
saépe - often (1)

Conjunctions

et - and; even (2)
et . . . et - both . . . and (2)
sed - but (2)
sī - if (1)

Preposition

síne (+abl.) - without (2)

Interjection

ō - O!, Oh! (2)

Idioms

amā́bō tē - please (1)
poénās dáre - to pay the penalty (2)

Chapter 3

Nouns

1st Declension

agrícola, agrícolae (m) - farmer (3)
amíca, amícae (f) - friend (female) (3)
fā́ma, fā́mae (f) - rumor, report; fame, reputation (2)
fḗmina, fḗminae (f) - woman (3)
fī́lia, fī́liae (f) - daughter (3)
fṓrma, fṓrmae (f) - form, shape; beauty (2)
fortū́na, fortū́nae (f) - fortune, luck (2)
ī́ra, ī́rae (f) - ire, anger (2)
naúta, naútae (m) - sailor (2)
pátria, pátriae (f) - fatherland, native land, (one's) country (2)
pecū́nia, pecū́niae (f) - money (2)
philosóphia, philosóphiae (f) - philosophy (2)
poéna, poénae (f) - penalty, punishment (2)
poḗta, poḗtae (m) - poet (2)
pórta, pórtae (f) - gate, entrance (2)
puélla, puéllae (f) - girl (2)
rósa, rósae (f) - rose (2)
sapiéntia, sapiéntiae (f) - wisdom (3)
senténtia, senténtiae (f) - feeling, thought, opinion, vote, sentence (2)
vī́ta, vī́tae (f) - life; mode of life (2)

2nd Declension

áger, ágrī (m) - field, farm (3)
amī́cus, amī́cī (m) - friend (male) (3)
fī́lius, fī́liī (m) - son (3)
númerus, númerī (m) - number (3)
pópulus, pópulī (m) - the people, a people, a nation (3)
púer, púerī (m) - boy; boys, children *(pl.)* (3)
vir, vírī (m) - man, hero (3)

Indeclinable

níhil - nothing (1)

Pronouns

mē - me, myself (1)
quid - what (1)

Adjectives

antī́quus (m), antī́qua (f) - ancient, old-time (2)
avā́rus (m), avā́ra (f) - greedy, avaricious (3)
mágnus (m), mágna (f) - large, great; important (2)
méus (m), méa (f) - my (2)
múltus (m), múlta (f) - much, many (2)
paúcī (m), paúcae (f) - few, a few (3)
Rōmā́nus (m), Rōmā́na (f) - Roman (3)
túus (m), túa (f) - your *(sing.)* (2)

Verbs

1st Conjugation

ámō, amā́re, amā́vī, amā́tum - to love, like (1)
cṓgitō, cōgitā́re, cōgitā́vī, cōgitā́tum- to think, ponder, consider, plan (1)
cōnsérvō, cōnservā́re, cōnservā́vī, cōnservā́tum - to preserve, conserve, maintain (1)
dō, dáre, dédī, dátum - to give, offer (1)
érrō, errā́re, errā́vī, errā́tum - to wander; err, go astray, make a mistake, be mistaken (1)
laúdō, laudā́re, laudā́vī, laudā́tum - to praise (1)
sátiō, satiā́re, satiā́vī, satiā́tum - to satisfy, sate (3)
sérvō, servā́re, servā́vī, servā́tum - to preserve, save, keep, guard (1)
vócō, vocā́re, vocā́vī, vocā́tum - to call, summon (1)

2nd Conjugation

dḗbeō, dēbḗre, dḗbuī, dḗbitum - to owe; ought, must, should (1)
hábeō, habḗre, hábuī, hábitum - to have, hold, possess; consider, regard (3)
móneō, monḗre, mónuī, mónitum - to remind, advise, warn (1)
sálvē, salvḗte - hello, greetings (1)
sálveō, salvḗre - to be well, be in good health (1)
térreō, terrḗre, térruī, térritum - to frighten, terrify (1)
válē, valḗte - good-bye, farewell (1)
váleō, valḗre, váluī, valitū́rum - to be strong, have power; be well (1)
vídeō, vidḗre, vī́dī, vī́sum - to see; observe, understand (1)

Irregular

est - is (2)

Adverbs

hódiē - today (3)
nōn - not (1)
saépe - often (1)
sémper - always (3)

Conjunctions

et - and; even (2)
et . . . et - both . . . and (2)
sed - but (2)
sī - if (1)

Prepositions

dē (+abl.) - down from, from; concerning, about (3)
in (+abl.) - in, on (3)
síne (+abl.) - without (2)

Interjection

ō - O!, Oh! (2)

Idioms

amā́bō tē - please (1)
poénās dáre - to pay the penalty (2)

Chapter 4

Nouns

1st Declension

agrícola, agrícolae (m) - farmer (3)
amíca, amícae (f) - friend (female) (3)
cúra, cúrae (f) - care, attention, caution, anxiety (4)
fáma, fámae (f) - rumor, report; fame, reputation (2)
fémina, féminae (f) - woman (3)
fília, fíliae (f) - daughter (3)
fórma, fórmae (f) - form, shape; beauty (2)
fortúna, fortúnae (f) - fortune, luck (2)
íra, írae (f) - ire, anger (2)
magístra, magístrae (f) - schoolmistress, teacher, mistress (4)
móra, mórae (f) - delay (4)
naúta, naútae (m) - sailor (2)
pátria, pátriae (f) - fatherland, native land, (one's) country (2)
pecúnia, pecúniae (f) - money (2)
philosóphia, philosóphiae (f) - philosophy (2)
poéna, poénae (f) - penalty, punishment (2)
poéta, poétae (m) - poet (2)
pórta, pórtae (f) - gate, entrance (2)
puélla, puéllae (f) - girl (2)
rósa, rósae (f) - rose (2)
sapiéntia, sapiéntiae (f) - wisdom (3)
senténtia, senténtiae (f) - feeling, thought, opinion, vote, sentence (2)
víta, vítae (f) - life; mode of life (2)

2nd Declension

áger, ágrī (m) - field, farm (3)
amícus, amícī (m) - friend (male) (3)
básium, básiī (n) - kiss (4)
béllum, béllī (n) - war (4)
cōnsílium, cōnsíliī (n) - plan, purpose, counsel, advice, judgment, wisdom (4)
dṓnum, dṓnī (n) - gift, present (4)
exítium, exítiī (n) - destruction, ruin (4)
fílius, fíliī (m) - son (3)
magíster, magístrī (m) - schoolmaster, teacher, master (4)
númerus, númerī (m) - number (3)
óculus, óculī (m) - eye (4)
offícium, offíciī (n) - duty, service (4)
ṓtium, ṓtiī (n) - leisure, peace (4)
perículum, perículī (n) - danger, risk (4)
pópulus, pópulī (m) - the people, a people, a nation (3)
púer, púerī (m) - boy; boys, children *(pl.)* (3)
remédium, remédiī (n) - cure, remedy (4)
stúltus, stúltī (m)- a fool (4)
vir, vírī (m) - man, hero (3)

Indeclinable

níhil - nothing (1)

Pronouns

mē - me, myself (1)
quid - what (1)

Adjectives

antíquus, antíqua, antíquum - ancient, old-time (2)
avárus, avára, avárum - greedy, avaricious (3)
béllus, bélla, béllum - pretty, handsome, charming (4)
bónus, bóna, bónum - good, kind (4)
hūmā́nus, hūmā́na, hūmā́num - pertaining to man, human; humane, kind; refined, cultivated (4)
mágnus, mágna, mágnum - large, great; important (2)
málus, mála, málum - bad, wicked, evil (4)
méus, méa, méum - my (2)
múltus, múlta, múltum - much, many (2)
párvus, párva, párvum - small, little (4)
paúcī, paúcae, paúca - few, a few (3)
Rōmā́nus, Rōmā́na, Rōmā́num - Roman (3)
stúltus, stúlta, stúltum - foolish (4)
túus, túa, túum - your *(sing.)* (2)
vḗrus, vḗra, vḗrum - true, real, proper (4)

Verbs

1st Conjugation

ádiuvō, adiuvā́re, adiū́vī, adiū́tum - to help, aid, assist; to please (4)
ámō, amā́re, amā́vī, amā́tum - to love, like (1)
cṓgitō, cōgitā́re, cōgitā́vī, cōgitā́tum- to think, ponder, consider, plan (1)

cōnsérvō, cōnservā́re, cōnservā́vī, cōnservā́tum - to preserve, conserve, maintain (1)
dō, dáre, dédī, dátum - to give, offer (1)
érrō, errā́re, errā́vī, errā́tum - to wander; err, go astray, make a mistake, be mistaken (1)
iúvō, iuvā́re, iū́vī, iū́tum - to help, aid, assist; to please (4)
laúdō, laudā́re, laudā́vī, laudā́tum - to praise (1)
sátiō, satiā́re, satiā́vī, satiā́tum - to satisfy, sate (3)
sérvō, servā́re, servā́vī, servā́tum - to preserve, save, keep, guard (1)
vócō, vocā́re, vocā́vī, vocā́tum - to call, summon (1)

2nd Conjugation
dḗbeō, dēbḗre, dḗbuī, dḗbitum - to owe; ought, must, should (1)
hábeō, habḗre, hábuī, hábitum - to have, hold, possess; consider, regard (3)
móneō, monḗre, mónuī, mónitum - to remind, advise, warn (1)
sálvē, salvḗte - hello, greetings (1)
sálveō, salvḗre - to be well, be in good health (1)
térreō, terrḗre, térruī, térritum - to frighten, terrify (1)
válē, valḗte - good-bye, farewell (1)
váleō, valḗre, váluī, valitū́rum - to be strong, have power; be well (1)
vídeō, vidḗre, vī́dī, vī́sum - to see; observe, understand (1)

Irregular
sum, ésse, fúī, futū́rum - to be, exist (4)

Adverbs

hódiē - today (3)
nōn - not (1)
saépe - often (1)
sémper - always (3)

Conjunctions

et - and; even (2)
et . . . et - both . . . and (2)
sed - but (2)
sī - if (1)

Prepositions

dē (+abl.) - down from, from; concerning, about (3)
in (+abl.) - in, on (3)
síne (+abl.) - without (2)

Interjection

ō - O!, Oh! (2)

Idioms

amā́bō tē - please (1)
poénās dáre - to pay the penalty (2)

Chapter 5

Nouns

1st Declension

adulēscéntia, adulēscéntiae (f) - youth, young manhood; youthfulness (5)
agrícola, agrícolae (m) - farmer (3)
amíca, amícae (f) - friend (female) (3)
cúlpa, cúlpae (f) - fault, blame (5)
cū́ra, cū́rae (f) - care, attention, caution, anxiety (4)
fā́ma, fā́mae (f) - rumor, report; fame, reputation (2)
fḗmina, fḗminae (f) - woman (3)
fī́lia, fī́liae (f) - daughter (3)
fṓrma, fṓrmae (f) - form, shape; beauty (2)
fortū́na, fortū́nae (f) - fortune, luck (2)
glṓria, glṓriae (f) - glory, fame (5)
ī́ra, ī́rae (f) - ire, anger (2)
magístra, magístrae (f) - schoolmistress, teacher, mistress (4)
móra, mórae (f) - delay (4)
naúta, naútae (m) - sailor (2)
pátria, pátriae (f) - fatherland, native land, (one's) country (2)
pecū́nia, pecū́niae (f) - money (2)
philosóphia, philosóphiae (f) - philosophy (2)
poéna, poénae (f) - penalty, punishment (2)
poḗta, poḗtae (m) - poet (2)
pórta, pórtae (f) - gate, entrance (2)
puélla, puéllae (f) - girl (2)
rósa, rósae (f) - rose (2)
sapiéntia, sapiéntiae (f) - wisdom (3)
senténtia, senténtiae (f) - feeling, thought, opinion, vote, sentence (2)
vī́ta, vī́tae (f) - life; mode of life (2)

2nd Declension

áger, ágrī (m) - field, farm (3)
amī́cus, amī́cī (m) - friend (male) (3)
ánimī, animṓrum (m) - high spirits, pride, courage (5)
ánimus, ánimī (m) - soul, spirit, mind (5)
bā́sium, bā́siī (n) - kiss (4)
béllum, béllī (n) - war (4)
caélum, caélī (n) - sky, heaven (5)
cōnsílium, cōnsíliī (n) - plan, purpose, counsel, advice, judgment, wisdom (4)
dṓnum, dṓnī (n) - gift, present (4)
exítium, exítiī (n) - destruction, ruin (4)
fī́lius, fī́liī (m) - son (3)
magíster, magístrī (m) - schoolmaster, teacher, master (4)
númerus, númerī (m) - number (3)
óculus, óculī (m) - eye (4)
offícium, offíciī (n) - duty, service (4)
ṓtium, ṓtiī (n) - leisure, peace (4)
perī́culum, perī́culī (n) - danger, risk (4)
pópulus, pópulī (m) - the people, a people, a nation (3)
púer, púerī (m) - boy; boys, children *(pl.)* (3)
remédium, remédiī (n) - cure, remedy (4)
stúltus, stúltī (m) - a fool (4)
vérbum, vérbī (n) - word (5)
vir, vírī (m) - man, hero (3)

Indeclinable

níhil - nothing (1)
sátis - enough (5)

Pronouns

mē - me, myself (1)
quid - what (1)
tē - you, yourself *(sing.)* (5)

Adjectives

antī́quus, antī́qua, antī́quum - ancient, old-time (2)
avā́rus, avā́ra, avā́rum - greedy, avaricious (3)
béllus, bélla, béllum - pretty, handsome, charming (4)
bónus, bóna, bónum - good, kind (4)
hūmā́nus, hūmā́na, hūmā́num - pertaining to man, human; humane, kind; refined, cultivated (4)
lī́ber, lī́bera, lī́berum - free (5)
mágnus, mágna, mágnum - large, great; important (2)
málus, mála, málum - bad, wicked, evil (4)
méus, méa, méum - my (2)
múltus, múlta, múltum - much, many (2)
nóster, nóstra, nóstrum - our, ours (5)
párvus, párva, párvum - small, little (4)
paúcī, paúcae, paúca - few, a few (3)
púlcher, púlchra, púlchrum - beautiful, handsome; fine (5)
Rōmā́nus, Rōmā́na, Rōmā́num - Roman (3)
sā́nus, sā́na, sā́num - sound, healthy, sane (5)

stúltus, stúlta, stúltum - foolish (4)
túus, túa, túum - your *(sing.)* (2)
vérus, véra, vérum - true, real, proper (4)

Indeclinable
sátis - enough, sufficient (5)

Verbs
1st Conjugation
ádiuvō, adiuvā́re, adiū́vī, adiū́tum - to help, aid, assist; to please (4)
ámō, amā́re, amā́vī, amā́tum - to love, like (1)
cḗnō, cēnā́re, cēnā́vī, cēnā́tum - to dine (5)
cṓgitō, cōgitā́re, cōgitā́vī, cōgitā́tum - to think, ponder, consider, plan (1)
cōnsérvō, cōnservā́re, cōnservā́vī, cōnservā́tum - to preserve, conserve, maintain (1)
cúlpō, culpā́re, culpā́vī, culpā́tum - to blame, censure (5)
dō, dáre, dédī, dátum - to give, offer (1)
érrō, errā́re, errā́vī, errā́tum - to wander; err, go astray, make a mistake, be mistaken (1)
iúvō, iuvā́re, iū́vī, iū́tum - to help, aid, assist; to please (4)
laúdō, laudā́re, laudā́vī, laudā́tum - to praise (1)
sátiō, satiā́re, satiā́vī, satiā́tum - to satisfy, sate (3)
sérvō, servā́re, servā́vī, servā́tum - to preserve, save, keep, guard (1)
súperō, superā́re, superā́vī, superā́tum - to be above, have the upper hand, surpass; overcome, conquer (5)
vócō, vocā́re, vocā́vī, vocā́tum - to call, summon (1)

2nd Conjugation
dḗbeō, dēbḗre, dḗbuī, dḗbitum - to owe; ought, must, should (1)
hábeō, habḗre, hábuī, hábitum - to have, hold, possess; consider, regard (3)
máneō, manḗre, mā́nsī, mā́nsum - to remain, stay, stay behind, abide, continue (5)
móneō, monḗre, mónuī, mónitum - to remind, advise, warn (1)
remáneō, remanḗre, remā́nsī, remā́nsum - to remain, stay, stay behind, abide, continue (5)
sálvē, salvḗte - hello, greetings (1)
sálveō, salvḗre - to be well, be in good health (1)
térreō, terrḗre, térruī, térritum - to frighten, terrify (1)
válē, valḗte - good-bye, farewell (1)
váleō, valḗre, váluī, valitū́rum - to be strong, have power; be well (1)
vídeō, vidḗre, vī́dī, vī́sum - to see; observe, understand (1)

Irregular
sum, ésse, fúī, futū́rum - to be, exist (4)

Adverbs
crās - tomorrow (5)
héri - yesterday (5)
hódiē - today (3)
nōn - not (1)
quándō - when (5)
saépe - often (1)
sátis - enough, sufficiently (5)
sémper - always (3)
tum - then, at that time; thereupon, in the next place (5)

Conjunctions
et - and; even (2)
et . . . et - both . . . and (2)
ígitur - therefore, consequently (5)
sed - but (2)
sī - if (1)

Prepositions
dē (+abl.) - down from, from; concerning, about (3)
in (+abl.) - in, on (3)
própter (+acc.) - on account of, because of (5)
síne (+abl.) - without (2)

Interjection
ō - O!, Oh! (2)

Idioms
amā́bō tē - please (1)
poénās dáre - to pay the penalty (2)
sī quándō - if ever (5)

Suffix
-ne – interrogative suffix attached to the first word of a sentence, typically the verb or another word on which the question hinges, to introduce a question whose answer is uncertain (5)

Chapter 6

Nouns

1st Declension

adulēscéntia, adulēscéntiae (f) - youth, young manhood; youthfulness (5)
agrícola, agrícolae (m) - farmer (3)
amī́ca, amī́cae (f) - friend (female) (3)
cúlpa, cúlpae (f) - fault, blame (5)
cū́ra, cū́rae (f) - care, attention, caution, anxiety (4)
déa, déae (f) - goddess (6)
discípula, discípulae (f) - learner, pupil, student (female) (6)
fā́ma, fā́mae (f) - rumor, report; fame, reputation (2)
fḗmina, fḗminae (f) - woman (3)
fī́lia, fī́liae (f) - daughter (3)
fṓrma, fṓrmae (f) - form, shape; beauty (2)
fortū́na, fortū́nae (f) - fortune, luck (2)
glṓria, glṓriae (f) - glory, fame (5)
īnsídiae, īnsidiā́rum (f) - ambush, plot, treachery (6)
ī́ra, ī́rae (f) - ire, anger (2)
magístra, magístrae (f) - schoolmistress, teacher, mistress (4)
móra, mórae (f) - delay (4)
naúta, naútae (m) - sailor (2)
pátria, pátriae (f) - fatherland, native land, (one's) country (2)
pecū́nia, pecū́niae (f) - money (2)
philosóphia, philosóphiae (f) - philosophy (2)
poéna, poénae (f) - penalty, punishment (2)
poḗta, poḗtae (m) - poet (2)
pórta, pórtae (f) - gate, entrance (2)
puélla, puéllae (f) - girl (2)
rósa, rósae (f) - rose (2)
sapiéntia, sapiéntiae (f) - wisdom (3)
senténtia, senténtiae (f) - feeling, thought, opinion, vote, sentence (2)
vī́ta, vī́tae (f) - life; mode of life (2)

2nd Declension

áger, ágrī (m) - field, farm (3)
amī́cus, amī́cī (m) - friend (male) (3)
ánimī, animṓrum (m) - high spirits, pride, courage (5)
ánimus, ánimī (m) - soul, spirit, mind (5)
bā́sium, bā́siī (n) - kiss (4)
béllum, béllī (n) - war (4)
caélum, caélī (n) - sky, heaven (5)
cōnsílium, cōnsíliī (n) - plan, purpose, counsel, advice, judgment, wisdom (4)
déus, déī (m) - god (6)
discípulus, discípulī (m) - learner, pupil, student (male) (6)
dṓnum, dṓnī (n) - gift, present (4)
exítium, exítiī (n) - destruction, ruin (4)
fī́lius, fī́liī (m) - son (3)
Graécus, Graécī (m) - a Greek (6)
líber, líbrī (m) - book (6)
magíster, magístrī (m) - schoolmaster, teacher, master (4)
númerus, númerī (m) - number (3)
óculus, óculī (m) - eye (4)
offícium, offíciī (n) - duty, service (4)
ṓtium, ṓtiī (n) - leisure, peace (4)
perī́culum, perī́culī (n) - danger, risk (4)
pópulus, pópulī (m) - the people, a people, a nation (3)
púer, púerī (m) - boy; boys, children *(pl.)* (3)
remédium, remédiī (n) - cure, remedy (4)
stúltus, stúltī (m) - a fool (4)
tyránnus, tyránnī (m) - absolute ruler, tyrant (6)
vérbum, vérbī (n) - word (5)
vir, vírī (m) - man, hero (3)
vítium, vítiī (n) - fault, crime, vice (6)

Indeclinable

níhil - nothing (1)
sátis - enough (5)

Pronouns

mē - me, myself (1)
quid - what (1)
tē - you, yourself *(sing.)* (5)

Adjectives

antī́quus, antī́qua, antī́quum - ancient, old-time (2)
avā́rus, avā́ra, avā́rum - greedy, avaricious (3)
béllus, bélla, béllum - pretty, handsome, charming (4)
bónus, bóna, bónum - good, kind (4)
Graécus, Graéca, Graécum - Greek (6)
hūmā́nus, hūmā́na, hūmā́num - pertaining to man, human; humane, kind; refined, cultivated (4)
lī́ber, lī́bera, lī́berum - free (5)
mágnus, mágna, mágnum - large, great; important (2)
málus, mála, málum - bad, wicked, evil (4)
méus, méa, méum - my (2)
múltus, múlta, múltum - much, many (2)

nóster, nóstra, nóstrum - our, ours (5)
párvus, párva, párvum - small, little (4)
paúcī, paúcae, paúca - few, a few (3)
perpétuus, perpétua, perpétuum perpetual, lasting, uninterrupted, continuous (6)
plḗnus, plḗna, plḗnum - full, abundant, generous (6)
púlcher, púlchra, púlchrum - beautiful, handsome; fine (5)
Rōmā́nus, Rōmā́na, Rōmā́num - Roman (3)
sálvus, sálva, sálvum - safe, sound (6)
sā́nus, sā́na, sā́num - sound, healthy, sane (5)
secúndus, secúnda, secúndum - second; favorable (6)
stúltus, stúlta, stúltum - foolish (4)
túus, túa, túum - your *(sing.)* (2)
vḗrus, vḗra, vḗrum - true, real, proper (4)
véster, véstra, véstrum - your *(pl.)* (6)

Indeclinable
sátis - enough, sufficient (5)

Verbs

1st Conjugation
ádiuvō, adiuvā́re, adiū́vī, adiū́tum - to help, aid, assist; to please (4)
ámō, amā́re, amā́vī, amā́tum - to love, like (1)
cḗnō, cēnā́re, cēnā́vī, cēnā́tum - to dine (5)
cṓgitō, cōgitā́re, cōgitā́vī, cōgitā́tum - to think, ponder, consider, plan (1)
cōnsérvō, cōnservā́re, cōnservā́vī, cōnservā́tum - to preserve, conserve, maintain (1)
cúlpō, culpā́re, culpā́vī, culpā́tum - to blame, censure (5)
dō, dáre, dédī, dátum - to give, offer (1)
érrō, errā́re, errā́vī, errā́tum - to wander; err, go astray, make a mistake, be mistaken (1)
iúvō, iuvā́re, iū́vī, iū́tum - to help, aid, assist; to please (4)
laúdō, laudā́re, laudā́vī, laudā́tum - to praise (1)
sátiō, satiā́re, satiā́vī, satiā́tum - to satisfy, sate (3)
sérvō, servā́re, servā́vī, servā́tum - to preserve, save, keep, guard (1)
súperō, superā́re, superā́vī, superā́tum - to be above, have the upper hand, surpass; overcome, conquer (5)
tóllerō, tolerā́re, tolerā́vī, tolerā́tum - to bear, endure (6)
vócō, vocā́re, vocā́vī, vocā́tum - to call, summon (1)

2nd Conjugation
dḗbeō, dēbḗre, dḗbuī, dḗbitum - to owe; ought, must, should (1)
hábeō, habḗre, hábuī, hábitum - to have, hold, possess; consider, regard (3)
máneō, manḗre, mā́nsī, mā́nsum - to remain, stay, stay behind, abide, continue (5)
móneō, monḗre, mónuī, mónitum - to remind, advise, warn (1)
remáneō, remanḗre, remā́nsī, remā́nsum - to remain, stay, stay behind, abide, continue (5)
sálvē, salvḗte - hello, greetings (1)
sálveō, salvḗre - to be well, be in good health (1)
térreō, terrḗre, térruī, térritum - to frighten, terrify (1)
válē, valḗte - good-bye, farewell (1)
váleō, valḗre, váluī, valitū́rum - to be strong, have power; be well (1)
vídeō, vidḗre, vī́dī, vī́sum - to see; observe, understand (1)

Irregular
póssum, pósse, pótuī - to be able, can, could, have power (6)
sum, ésse, fúī, futū́rum - to be, exist (4)

Adverbs

crās - tomorrow (5)
héri - yesterday (5)
hódiē - today (3)
íbi - there (6)
nōn - not (1)
nunc - now, at present (6)
quándō - when (5)
quā́rē - because of which thing *(lit.)*; therefore, wherefore, why (6)
saépe - often (1)
sátis - enough, sufficiently (5)
sémper - always (3)
tum - then, at that time; thereupon, in the next place (5)
úbi - where, when (6)

Conjunctions

et - and; even (2)
et . . . et - both . . . and (2)
ígitur - therefore, consequently (5)
sed - but (2)
sī - if (1)

Prepositions

dē (+abl.) - down from, from; concerning, about (3)
in (+abl.) - in, on (3)
própter (+acc.) - on account of, because of (5)
síne (+abl.) - without (2)

Interjection

ō - O!, Oh! (2)

Idioms

amā́bō tē - please (1)
poénās dáre - to pay the penalty (2)
sī quándō - if ever (5)

Suffixes

-ne – interrogative suffix attached to the first word of a sentence, typically the verb or another word on which the question hinges, to introduce a question whose answer is uncertain (5)
-que - and *(enclitic conjunction; appended to the second of two words to be joined)* (6)

Chapter 7

Nouns

1st Declension

adulēscéntia, adulēscéntiae (f) - youth, young manhood; youthfulness (5)
agrícola, agrícolae (m) - farmer (3)
amíca, amícae (f) - friend (female) (3)
cúlpa, cúlpae (f) - fault, blame (5)
cū́ra, cū́rae (f) - care, attention, caution, anxiety (4)
déa, déae (f) - goddess (6)
discípula, discípulae (f) - learner, pupil, student (female) (6)
fā́ma, fā́mae (f) - rumor, report; fame, reputation (2)
fḗmina, fḗminae (f) - woman (3)
fī́lia, fī́liae (f) - daughter (3)
fṓrma, fṓrmae (f) - form, shape; beauty (2)
fortū́na, fortū́nae (f) - fortune, luck (2)
glṓria, glṓriae (f) - glory, fame (5)
īnsídiae, īnsidiā́rum (f) - ambush, plot, treachery (6)
ī́ra, ī́rae (f) - ire, anger (2)
líttera, lítterae (f) - a letter of the alphabet (7)
lítterae, litterā́rum (f) - a letter (epistle), literature (7)
magístra, magístrae (f) - schoolmistress, teacher, mistress (4)
móra, mórae (f) - delay (4)
naúta, naútae (m) - sailor (2)
pátria, pátriae (f) - fatherland, native land, (one's) country (2)
pecū́nia, pecū́niae (f) - money (2)
philosóphia, philosóphiae (f) - philosophy (2)
poéna, poénae (f) - penalty, punishment (2)
poḗta, poḗtae (m) - poet (2)
pórta, pórtae (f) - gate, entrance (2)
puélla, puéllae (f) - girl (2)
rēgī́na, rēgī́nae (f) - queen (7)
rósa, rósae (f) - rose (2)
sapiéntia, sapiéntiae (f) - wisdom (3)
senténtia, senténtiae (f) - feeling, thought, opinion, vote, sentence (2)
térra, térrae (f) - earth, ground, land, country (7)
vī́ta, vī́tae (f) - life; mode of life (2)

2nd Declension

áger, ágrī (m) - field, farm (3)
amícus, amícī (m) - friend (male) (3)
ánimī, animṓrum (m) - high spirits, pride, courage (5)
ánimus, ánimī (m) - soul, spirit, mind (5)
bā́sium, bā́siī (n) - kiss (4)
béllum, béllī (n) - war (4)
caélum, caélī (n) - sky, heaven (5)
cōnsílium, cōnsíliī (n) - plan, purpose, counsel, advice, judgment, wisdom (4)
déus, déī (m) - god (6)
discípulus, discípulī (m) - learner, pupil, student (male) (6)
dṓnum, dṓnī (n) - gift, present (4)
exítium, exítiī (n) - destruction, ruin (4)
fī́lius, fī́liī (m) - son (3)
Graécus, Graécī (m) - a Greek (6)
líber, líbrī (m) - book (6)
magíster, magístrī (m) - schoolmaster, teacher, master (4)
númerus, númerī (m) - number (3)
óculus, óculī (m) - eye (4)
offícium, offíciī (n) - duty, service (4)
ṓtium, ṓtiī (n) - leisure, peace (4)
perī́culum, perī́culī (n) - danger, risk (4)
pópulus, pópulī (m) - the people, a people, a nation (3)
púer, púerī (m) - boy; boys, children *(pl.)* (3)
remédium, remédiī (n) - cure, remedy (4)
stúltus, stúltī (m) - a fool (4)
tyránnus, tyránnī (m) - absolute ruler, tyrant (6)
vérbum, vérbī (n)- word (5)
vir, vírī (m) - man, hero (3)
vítium, vítiī (n) - fault, crime, vice (6)

3rd Declension

ámor, amṓris (m) - love (7)
cármen, cárminis (n) - song, poem (7)
cī́vitās, cīvitā́tis (f) - state, citizenship (7)
córpus, córporis (n) - body (7)
hómō, hóminis (m) - human being, man (7)
lábor, labṓris (m)- labor, work, toil; a work, production (7)
mṓrēs, mṓrum (m) - habits, morals, character (7)
mōs, mṓris (m) - habit, custom, manner (7)
nṓmen, nṓminis (n) - name (7)
pāx, pā́cis (f) - peace (7)
rēx, rḗgis (m) - king (7)
témpus, témporis (n) - time; occasion, opportunity (7)
úxor, uxṓris (f) - wife (7)
vírgō, vírginis (f) - maiden, virgin (7)
vírtūs, virtū́tis (f) - manliness, courage; excellence, character, worth, virtue (7)

Indeclinable
níhil - nothing (1)
sátis - enough (5)

Pronouns

mē - me, myself (1)
quid - what (1)
tē - you, yourself *(sing.)* (5)

Adjectives

antī́quus, antī́qua, antī́quum - ancient, old-time (2)
avā́rus, avā́ra, avā́rum - greedy, avaricious (3)
béllus, bélla, béllum - pretty, handsome, charming (4)
bónus, bóna, bónum - good, kind (4)
Graécus, Graéca, Graécum - Greek (6)
hūmā́nus, hūmā́na, hūmā́num - pertaining to man, human; humane, kind; refined, cultivated (4)
lī́ber, lī́bera, lī́berum - free (5)
mágnus, mágna, mágnum - large, great; important (2)
málus, mála, málum - bad, wicked, evil (4)
méus, méa, méum - my (2)
múltus, múlta, múltum - much, many (2)
nóster, nóstra, nóstrum - our, ours (5)
nóvus, nóva, nóvum - new; strange (7)
párvus, párva, párvum - small, little (4)
paúcī, paúcae, paúca - few, a few (3)
perpétuus, perpétua, perpétuum perpetual, lasting, uninterrupted, continuous (6)
plḗnus, plḗna, plḗnum - full, abundant, generous (6)
púlcher, púlchra, púlchrum - beautiful, handsome; fine (5)
Rōmā́nus, Rōmā́na, Rōmā́num - Roman (3)
sálvus, sálva, sálvum - safe, sound (6)
sā́nus, sā́na, sā́num - sound, healthy, sane (5)
secúndus, secúnda, secúndum - second; favorable (6)
stúltus, stúlta, stúltum - foolish (4)
túus, túa, túum - your *(sing.)* (2)
vḗrus, vḗra, vḗrum - true, real, proper (4)
véster, véstra, véstrum - your *(pl.)* (6)

Indeclinable
sátis - enough, sufficient (5)

Verbs

1st Conjugation
ádiuvō, adiuvā́re, adiū́vī, adiū́tum - to help, aid, assist; to please (4)
ámō, amā́re, amā́vī, amā́tum - to love, like (1)
cḗnō, cēnā́re, cēnā́vī, cēnā́tum - to dine (5)
cṓgitō, cōgitā́re, cōgitā́vī, cōgitā́tum- to think, ponder, consider, plan (1)
cōnsérvō, cōnservā́re, cōnservā́vī, cōnservā́tum - to preserve, conserve, maintain (1)
cúlpō, culpā́re, culpā́vī, culpā́tum - to blame, censure (5)
dō, dáre, dédī, dátum - to give, offer (1)
érrō, errā́re, errā́vī, errā́tum - to wander; err, go astray, make a mistake, be mistaken (1)
iúvō, iuvā́re, iū́vī, iū́tum - to help, aid, assist; to please (4)
laúdō, laudā́re, laudā́vī, laudā́tum - to praise (1)
nécō, necā́re, necā́vī, necā́tum - to murder, kill (7)
sátiō, satiā́re, satiā́vī, satiā́tum - to satisfy, sate (3)
sérvō, servā́re, servā́vī, servā́tum - to preserve, save, keep, guard (1)
súperō, superā́re, superā́vī, superā́tum - to be above, have the upper hand, surpass; overcome, conquer (5)
tólerō, tolerā́re, tolerā́vī, tolerā́tum - to bear, endure (6)
vócō, vocā́re, vocā́vī, vocā́tum - to call, summon (1)

2nd Conjugation
aúdeō, audḗre, aúsus sum - to dare (7)
dḗbeō, dēbḗre, dḗbuī, dḗbitum - to owe; ought, must, should (1)
hábeō, habḗre, hábuī, hábitum - to have, hold, possess; consider, regard (3)
máneō, manḗre, mā́nsī, mā́nsum - to remain, stay, stay behind, abide, continue (5)
móneō, monḗre, mónuī, mónitum - to remind, advise, warn (1)
remáneō, remanḗre, remā́nsī, remā́nsum - to remain, stay, stay behind, abide, continue (5)
sálvē, salvḗte - hello, greetings (1)
sálveō, salvḗre - to be well, be in good health (1)
térreō, terrḗre, térruī, térritum - to frighten, terrify (1)
válē, valḗte - good-bye, farewell (1)
váleō, valḗre, váluī, valitū́rum - to be strong, have power; be well (1)

vídeō, vidḗre, vī́dī, vī́sum - to see; observe, understand (1)

Irregular

póssum, pósse, pótuī - to be able, can, could, have power (6)

sum, ésse, fúī, futū́rum - to be, exist (4)

Adverbs

crās - tomorrow (5)

héri - yesterday (5)

hódiē - today (3)

íbi - there (6)

nōn - not (1)

nunc - now, at present (6)

quándō - when (5)

quā́rē - because of which thing *(lit.);* therefore, wherefore, why (6)

saépe - often (1)

sátis - enough, sufficiently (5)

sémper - always (3)

tum - then, at that time; thereupon, in the next place (5)

úbi - where, when (6)

Conjunctions

et - and; even (2)

et . . . et - both . . . and (2)

ígitur - therefore, consequently (5)

sed - but (2)

sī - if (1)

Prepositions

dē (+abl.) - down from, from; concerning, about (3)

in (+abl.) - in, on (3)

post (+acc.) - after, behind (7)

própter (+acc.) - on account of, because of (5)

síne (+abl.) - without (2)

sub (+abl. w/ verbs of rest ***or*** **+acc. w/ verbs of motion)** - under, up under, close to, down to/into, to/at the foot of (7)

Interjection

ō - O!, Oh! (2)

Idioms

amā́bō tē - please (1)

poénās dáre - to pay the penalty (2)

sī quándō - if ever (5)

Suffixes

-ne – interrogative suffix attached to the first word of a sentence, typically the verb or another word on which the question hinges, to introduce a question whose answer is uncertain (5)

-que - and *(enclitic conjunction; appended to the second of two words to be joined)* (6)

Chapter 8

Nouns

1st Declension

adulēscéntia, adulēscéntiae (f) - youth, young manhood; youthfulness (5)
agrícola, agrícolae (m) - farmer (3)
amī́ca, amī́cae (f) - friend (female) (3)
cṓpia, cṓpiae (f) - abundance, supply (8)
cṓpiae, cōpiā́rum (f) - supplies, troops, forces (8)
cúlpa, cúlpae (f) - fault, blame (5)
cū́ra, cū́rae (f) - care, attention, caution, anxiety (4)
déa, déae (f) - goddess (6)
discípula, discípulae (f) - learner, pupil, student (female) (6)
fā́ma, fā́mae (f) - rumor, report; fame, reputation (2)
fḗmina, fḗminae (f) - woman (3)
fī́lia, fī́liae (f) - daughter (3)
fṓrma, fṓrmae (f) - form, shape; beauty (2)
fortū́na, fortū́nae (f) - fortune, luck (2)
glṓria, glṓriae (f) - glory, fame (5)
īnsídiae, īnsidiā́rum (f) - ambush, plot, treachery (6)
ī́ra, ī́rae (f) - ire, anger (2)
líttera, lítterae (f) - a letter of the alphabet (7)
lítterae, litterā́rum (f) - a letter (epistle), literature (7)
magístra, magístrae (f) - schoolmistress, teacher, mistress (4)
móra, mórae (f) - delay (4)
naúta, naútae (m) - sailor (2)
pátria, pátriae (f) - fatherland, native land, (one's) country (2)
pecū́nia, pecū́niae (f) - money (2)
philosóphia, philosóphiae (f) - philosophy (2)
poéna, poénae (f) - penalty, punishment (2)
poḗta, poḗtae (m) - poet (2)
pórta, pórtae (f) - gate, entrance (2)
puélla, puéllae (f) - girl (2)
rēgī́na, rēgī́nae (f) - queen (7)
rósa, rósae (f) - rose (2)
sapiéntia, sapiéntiae (f) - wisdom (3)
senténtia, senténtiae (f) - feeling, thought, opinion, vote, sentence (2)
térra, térrae (f) - earth, ground, land, country (7)
victṓria, victṓriae (f) - victory (8)
vī́ta, vī́tae (f) - life; mode of life (2)

2nd Declension

áger, ágrī (m) - field, farm (3)
amī́cus, amī́cī (m) - friend (male) (3)
ánimī, animṓrum (m) - high spirits, pride, courage (5)
ánimus, ánimī (m) - soul, spirit, mind (5)
bā́sium, bā́siī (n) - kiss (4)
béllum, béllī (n) - war (4)
caélum, caélī (n) - sky, heaven (5)
cōnsílium, cōnsíliī (n) - plan, purpose, counsel, advice, judgment, wisdom (4)
déus, déī (m) - god (6)
discípulus, discípulī (m) - learner, pupil, student (male) (6)
dṓnum, dṓnī (n) - gift, present (4)
exítium, exítiī (n) - destruction, ruin (4)
fī́lius, fī́liī (m) - son (3)
Graécus, Graécī (m) - a Greek (6)
líber, líbrī (m) - book (6)
magíster, magístrī (m) - schoolmaster, teacher, master (4)
númerus, númerī (m) - number (3)
óculus, óculī (m) - eye (4)
offícium, offíciī (n) - duty, service (4)
ṓtium, ṓtiī (n) - leisure, peace (4)
perī́culum, perī́culī (n) - danger, risk (4)
pópulus, pópulī (m) - the people, a people, a nation (3)
púer, púerī (m) - boy; boys, children *(pl.)* (3)
remédium, remédiī (n) - cure, remedy (4)
stúltus, stúltī (m) - a fool (4)
tyránnus, tyránnī (m) - absolute ruler, tyrant (6)
vérbum, vérbī (n)- word (5)
vir, vírī (m) - man, hero (3)
vítium, vítiī (n) - fault, crime, vice (6)

3rd Declension

ámor, amṓris (m) - love (7)
cármen, cárminis (n) - song, poem (7)
Cícerō, Cicerṓnis (m) - (Marcus Tullius) Cicero (8)
cī́vitās, cīvitā́tis (f) - state, citizenship (7)
córpus, córporis (n) - body (7)
frā́ter, frā́tris (m) - brother (8)
hómō, hóminis (m) - human being, man (7)
lábor, labṓris (m)- labor, work, toil; a work, production (7)
laus, laúdis (f) - praise, glory, fame (8)
lībértās, lībertā́tis (f) - liberty (8)
mṓrēs, mṓrum (m) - habits, morals, character (7)
mōs, mṓris (m) - habit, custom, manner (7)

nṓmen, nṓminis (n) - name (7)
pāx, pā́cis (f) - peace (7)
rátiō, ratiṓnis (f) - reckoning, account; reason, judgment, consideration; system; manner, method (8)
rēx, rḗgis (m) - king (7)
scrī́ptor, scrīptṓris (m) - writer, author (8)
sóror, sorṓris (f) - sister (8)
témpus, témporis (n) - time; occasion, opportunity (7)
úxor, uxṓris (f) - wife (7)
vírgō, vírginis (f) - maiden, virgin (7)
vírtūs, virtū́tis (f) - manliness, courage; excellence, character, worth, virtue (7)

Indeclinable
níhil - nothing (1)
sátis - enough (5)

Pronouns

mē - me, myself (1)
quid - what (1)
tē - you, yourself *(sing.)* (5)

Adjectives

antī́quus, antī́qua, antī́quum - ancient, old-time (2)
avā́rus, avā́ra, avā́rum - greedy, avaricious (3)
béllus, bélla, béllum - pretty, handsome, charming (4)
bónus, bóna, bónum - good, kind (4)
Graécus, Graéca, Graécum - Greek (6)
hūmā́nus, hūmā́na, hūmā́num - pertaining to man, human; humane, kind; refined, cultivated (4)
lī́ber, lī́bera, lī́berum - free (5)
mágnus, mágna, mágnum - large, great; important (2)
málus, mála, málum - bad, wicked, evil (4)
méus, méa, méum - my (2)
múltus, múlta, múltum - much, many (2)
nóster, nóstra, nóstrum - our, ours (5)
nóvus, nóva, nóvum - new; strange (7)
párvus, párva, párvum - small, little (4)
paúcī, paúcae, paúca - few, a few (3)
perpétuus, perpétua, perpétuum perpetual, lasting, uninterrupted, continuous (6)
plḗnus, plḗna, plḗnum - full, abundant, generous (6)
púlcher, púlchra, púlchrum - beautiful, handsome; fine (5)
Rōmā́nus, Rōmā́na, Rōmā́num - Roman (3)
sálvus, sálva, sálvum - safe, sound (6)
sā́nus, sā́na, sā́num - sound, healthy, sane (5)
secúndus, secúnda, secúndum - second; favorable (6)
stúltus, stúlta, stúltum - foolish (4)
túus, túa, túum - your *(sing.)* (2)
vḗrus, vḗra, vḗrum - true, real, proper (4)
véster, véstra, véstrum - your *(pl.)* (6)

Indeclinable
sátis - enough, sufficient (5)

Verbs

1st Conjugation
ádiuvō, adiuvā́re, adiū́vī, adiū́tum - to help, aid, assist; to please (4)
ámō, amā́re, amā́vī, amā́tum - to love, like (1)
cḗnō, cēnā́re, cēnā́vī, cēnā́tum - to dine (5)
cṓgitō, cōgitā́re, cōgitā́vī, cōgitā́tum- to think, ponder, consider, plan (1)
cōnsérvō, cōnservā́re, cōnservā́vī, cōnservā́tum - to preserve, conserve, maintain (1)
cúlpō, culpā́re, culpā́vī, culpā́tum - to blame, censure (5)
dēmṓnstrō, dēmōnstrā́re, dēmōnstrā́vī, dēmōnstrā́tum to point out, show, demonstrate (8)
dō, dáre, dédī, dátum - to give, offer (1)
érrō, errā́re, errā́vī, errā́tum - to wander; err, go astray, make a mistake, be mistaken (1)
iúvō, iuvā́re, iū́vī, iū́tum - to help, aid, assist; to please (4)
laúdō, laudā́re, laudā́vī, laudā́tum - to praise (1)
nécō, necā́re, necā́vī, necā́tum - to murder, kill (7)
sátiō, satiā́re, satiā́vī, satiā́tum - to satisfy, sate (3)
sérvō, servā́re, servā́vī, servā́tum - to preserve, save, keep, guard (1)
súperō, superā́re, superā́vī, superā́tum - to be above, have the upper hand, surpass; overcome, conquer (5)
tólerō, tolerā́re, tolerā́vī, tolerā́tum - to bear, endure (6)
vócō, vocā́re, vocā́vī, vocā́tum - to call, summon (1)

2nd Conjugation
aúdeō, audḗre, aúsus sum - to dare (7)
dḗbeō, dēbḗre, dḗbuī, dḗbitum - to owe; ought, must, should (1)

dóceō, docḗre, dócuī, dóctum - to teach (8)
hábeō, habḗre, hábuī, hábitum - to have, hold, possess; consider, regard (3)
máneō, manḗre, mā́nsī, mā́nsum - to remain, stay, stay behind, abide, continue (5)
móneō, monḗre, mónuī, mónitum - to remind, advise, warn (1)
remáneō, remanḗre, remā́nsī, remā́nsum - to remain, stay, stay behind, abide, continue (5)
sálvē, salvḗte - hello, greetings (1)
sálveō, salvḗre - to be well, be in good health (1)
térreō, terrḗre, térruī, térritum - to frighten, terrify (1)
válē, valḗte - good-bye, farewell (1)
váleō, valḗre, váluī, valitū́rum - to be strong, have power; be well (1)
vídeō, vidḗre, vī́dī, vī́sum - to see; observe, understand (1)

3rd Conjugation
ágō, ágere, ḗgī, ā́ctum - to drive, lead, do, act; pass, spend *(life or time)* (8)
díscō, díscere, dídicī - to learn (8)
dū́cō, dū́cere, dū́xī, dúctum - to lead; consider, regard; prolong (8)
gérō, gérere, géssī, géstum - to carry; carry on, manage, conduct, wage, accomplish, perform (8)
scrī́bō, scrī́bere, scrī́psī, scrī́ptum to write, compose (8)
tráhō, tráhere, trā́xī, tráctum - to draw, drag; derive, acquire (8)
víncō, víncere, vī́cī, víctum - to conquer, overcome (8)

Irregular
póssum, pósse, pótuī - to be able, can, could, have power (6)
sum, ésse, fúī, futū́rum - to be, exist (4)

Adverbs

crās - tomorrow (5)
héri - yesterday (5)
hódiē - today (3)
íbi - there (6)
nōn - not (1)
númquam - never (8)
nunc - now, at present (6)
quándō - when (5)
quā́rē - because of which thing *(lit.)*; therefore, wherefore, why (6)
saépe - often (1)
sátis - enough, sufficiently (5)
sémper - always (3)
támen - nevertheless, still (8)
tum - then, at that time; thereupon, in the next place (5)
úbi - where, when (6)

Conjunctions

dum - while, as long as, at the same time that; *or* until *(+subjunctive)* (8)
et - and; even (2)
et . . . et - both . . . and (2)
ígitur - therefore, consequently (5)
sed - but (2)
sī - if (1)

Prepositions

ad (+acc.) - to, up to, near to (8)
dē (+abl.) - down from, from; concerning, about (3)
ex , ē (abl.+) - out of, from, from within; by reason of, on account of ; of *(after cardinal numerals)* (8)
in (+abl.) - in, on (3)
post (+acc.) - after, behind (7)
própter (+acc.) - on account of, because of (5)
síne (+abl.) - without (2)
sub (+abl. w/ verbs of rest *or* +acc. w/ verbs of motion) - under, up under, close to, down to/into, to/at the foot of (7)

Interjection

ō - O!, Oh! (2)

Idioms

amā́bō tē - please (1)
grā́tiās ágere (+dat.) - to thank someone; to give thanks to (8)
poénās dáre - to pay the penalty (2)
sī quándō - if ever (5)

Suffixes

-ne – interrogative suffix attached to the first word of a sentence, typically the verb or another word on which the question hinges, to introduce a question whose answer is uncertain (5)
-que - and *(enclitic conjunction; appended to the second of two words to be joined)* (6)

Chapter 9

Nouns

1st Declension

adulēscéntia, adulēscéntiae (f) - youth, young manhood; youthfulness (5)
agrícola, agrícolae (m) - farmer (3)
amíca, amícae (f) - friend (female) (3)
cṓpia, cṓpiae (f) - abundance, supply (8)
cṓpiae, cōpiā́rum (f) - supplies, troops, forces (8)
cúlpa, cúlpae (f) - fault, blame (5)
cū́ra, cū́rae (f) - care, attention, caution, anxiety (4)
déa, déae (f) - goddess (6)
discípula, discípulae (f) - learner, pupil, student (female) (6)
fā́ma, fā́mae (f) - rumor, report; fame, reputation (2)
fḗmina, fḗminae (f) - woman (3)
fī́lia, fī́liae (f) - daughter (3)
fṓrma, fṓrmae (f) - form, shape; beauty (2)
fortū́na, fortū́nae (f) - fortune, luck (2)
glṓria, glṓriae (f) - glory, fame (5)
īnsídiae, īnsidiā́rum (f) - ambush, plot, treachery (6)
ī́ra, ī́rae (f) - ire, anger (2)
líttera, lítterae (f) - a letter of the alphabet (7)
lítterae, litterā́rum (f) - a letter (epistle), literature (7)
magístra, magístrae (f) - schoolmistress, teacher, mistress (4)
móra, mórae (f) - delay (4)
naúta, naútae (m) - sailor (2)
pátria, pátriae (f) - fatherland, native land, (one's) country (2)
pecū́nia, pecū́niae (f) - money (2)
philosóphia, philosóphiae (f) - philosophy (2)
poéna, poénae (f) - penalty, punishment (2)
poḗta, poḗtae (m) - poet (2)
pórta, pórtae (f) - gate, entrance (2)
puélla, puéllae (f) - girl (2)
rēgī́na, rēgī́nae (f) - queen (7)
rósa, rósae (f) - rose (2)
sapiéntia, sapiéntiae (f) - wisdom (3)
senténtia, senténtiae (f) - feeling, thought, opinion, vote, sentence (2)
térra, térrae (f) - earth, ground, land, country (7)
victṓria, victṓriae (f) - victory (8)
vī́ta, vī́tae (f) - life; mode of life (2)

2nd Declension

áger, ágrī (m) - field, farm (3)
amī́cus, amī́cī (m) - friend (male) (3)
ánimī, animṓrum (m) - high spirits, pride, courage (5)
ánimus, ánimī (m) - soul, spirit, mind (5)
bā́sium, bā́siī (n) - kiss (4)
béllum, béllī (n) - war (4)
caélum, caélī (n) - sky, heaven (5)
cōnsílium, cōnsíliī (n) - plan, purpose, counsel, advice, judgment, wisdom (4)
déus, déī (m) - god (6)
discípulus, discípulī (m) - learner, pupil, student (male) (6)
dṓnum, dṓnī (n) - gift, present (4)
exítium, exítiī (n) - destruction, ruin (4)
fī́lius, fī́liī (m) - son (3)
Graécus, Graécī (m) - a Greek (6)
líber, líbrī (m) - book (6)
lóca, locṓrum (n) - places, region (9)
lócī, locṓrum (m) - passages in literature (9)
lócus, lócī (m) - place; passage in literature (9)
magíster, magístrī (m) - schoolmaster, teacher, master (4)
mórbus, mórbī (m) - disease, sickness (9)
númerus, númerī (m) - number (3)
óculus, óculī (m) - eye (4)
offícium, offíciī (n) - duty, service (4)
ṓtium, ṓtiī (n) - leisure, peace (4)
perī́culum, perī́culī (n) - danger, risk (4)
pópulus, pópulī (m) - the people, a people, a nation (3)
púer, púerī (m) - boy; boys, children *(pl.)* (3)
remédium, remédiī (n) - cure, remedy (4)
stúdium, stúdiī (n) - eagerness, zeal, pursuit, study (9)
stúltus, stúltī (m) - a fool (4)
tyránnus, tyránnī (m) - absolute ruler, tyrant (6)
vérbum, vérbī (n) - word (5)
vir, vírī (m) - man, hero (3)
vítium, vítiī (n) - fault, crime, vice (6)

3rd Declension

ámor, amṓris (m) - love (7)
cármen, cárminis (n) - song, poem (7)
Cícerō, Cicerṓnis (m) - (Marcus Tullius) Cicero (8)
cī́vitās, cīvitā́tis (f) - state, citizenship (7)
córpus, córporis (n) - body (7)
frā́ter, frā́tris (m) - brother (8)

hómō, hóminis (m) - human being, man (7)
lábor, labṓris (m)- labor, work, toil; a work, production (7)
laus, laúdis (f) - praise, glory, fame (8)
lībértās, lībertā́tis (f) - liberty (8)
mṓrēs, mṓrum (m) - habits, morals, character (7)
mōs, mṓris (m) - habit, custom, manner (7)
nṓmen, nṓminis (n) - name (7)
pāx, pā́cis (f) - peace (7)
rátiō, ratiṓnis (f) - reckoning, account; reason, judgment, consideration; system; manner, method (8)
rēx, rḗgis (m) - king (7)
scrī́ptor, scrīptṓris (m) - writer, author (8)
sóror, sorṓris (f) - sister (8)
témpus, témporis (n) - time; occasion, opportunity (7)
úxor, uxṓris (f) - wife (7)
vírgō, vírginis (f) - maiden, virgin (7)
vírtūs, virtū́tis (f) - manliness, courage; excellence, character, worth, virtue (7)

Indeclinable
níhil - nothing (1)
sátis - enough (5)

Pronouns

hic, haec, hoc - this; the latter; he, she, it, they (9)
ílle, ílla, íllud - that; the former; the famous; he, she, it, they (9)
íste, ísta, ístud - that of yours, that; such (as you have, as you speak of); *sometimes with contemptuous force, e.g.,* that despicable, that wretched (9)
mē - me, myself (1)
quid - what (1)
tē - you, yourself *(sing.)* (5)

Adjectives

áliī . . . áliī - some . . . others (9)
álius, ália, áliud - other, another (9)
álter, áltera, álterum - the other (of two), second (9)
antī́quus, antī́qua, antī́quum - ancient, old-time (2)
avā́rus, avā́ra, avā́rum - greedy, avaricious (3)
béllus, bélla, béllum - pretty, handsome, charming (4)
bónus, bóna, bónum - good, kind (4)
Graécus, Graéca, Graécum - Greek (6)
hūmā́nus, hūmā́na, hūmā́num - pertaining to man, human; humane, kind; refined, cultivated (4)
lī́ber, lī́bera, lī́berum - free (5)
mágnus, mágna, mágnum - large, great; important (2)
málus, mála, málum - bad, wicked, evil (4)
méus, méa, méum - my (2)
múltus, múlta, múltum - much, many (2)
neúter, neútra, neútrum - not either, neither (9)
nóster, nóstra, nóstrum - our, ours (5)
nóvus, nóva, nóvum - new; strange (7)
nū́llus, nū́lla, nū́llum - not any, no, none (9)
párvus, párva, párvum - small, little (4)
paúcī, paúcae, paúca - few, a few (3)
perpétuus, perpétua, perpétuum perpetual, lasting, uninterrupted, continuous (6)
plḗnus, plḗna, plḗnum - full, abundant, generous (6)
púlcher, púlchra, púlchrum - beautiful, handsome; fine (5)
Rōmā́nus, Rōmā́na, Rōmā́num - Roman (3)
sálvus, sálva, sálvum - safe, sound (6)
sā́nus, sā́na, sā́num - sound, healthy, sane (5)
secúndus, secúnda, secúndum - second; favorable (6)
sṓlus, sṓla, sṓlum - alone, only, the only (9)
stúltus, stúlta, stúltum - foolish (4)
tṓtus, tṓta, tṓtum - whole, entire (9)
túus, túa, túum - your *(sing.)* (2)
ū́llus, ū́lla, ū́llum - any (9)
ū́nus, ū́na, ū́num - one, single, alone (9)
úter, útra, útrum - either, which (of two) (9)
vḗrus, vḗra, vḗrum - true, real, proper (4)
véster, véstra, véstrum - your *(pl.)* (6)

Indeclinable
sátis - enough, sufficient (5)

Verbs

1st Conjugation
ádiuvō, adiuvā́re, adiū́vī, adiū́tum - to help, aid, assist; to please (4)
ámō, amā́re, amā́vī, amā́tum - to love, like (1)
cḗnō, cēnā́re, cēnā́vī, cēnā́tum - to dine (5)
cṓgitō, cōgitā́re, cōgitā́vī, cōgitā́tum- to think, ponder, consider, plan (1)
cōnsérvō, cōnservā́re, cōnservā́vī, cōnservā́tum - to preserve, conserve, maintain (1)

cúlpō, culpā́re, culpā́vī, culpā́tum - to blame, censure (5)
dēmṓnstrō, dēmōnstrā́re, dēmōnstrā́vī, dēmōnstrā́tum to point out, show, demonstrate (8)
dō, dáre, dédī, dátum - to give, offer (1)
érrō, errā́re, errā́vī, errā́tum - to wander; err, go astray, make a mistake, be mistaken (1)
iúvō, iuvā́re, iū́vī, iū́tum - to help, aid, assist; to please (4)
laúdō, laudā́re, laudā́vī, laudā́tum - to praise (1)
nécō, necā́re, necā́vī, necā́tum - to murder, kill (7)
sátiō, satiā́re, satiā́vī, satiā́tum - to satisfy, sate (3)
sérvō, servā́re, servā́vī, servā́tum - to preserve, save, keep, guard (1)
súperō, superā́re, superā́vī, superā́tum - to be above, have the upper hand, surpass; overcome, conquer (5)
tólerō, tolerā́re, tolerā́vī, tolerā́tum - to bear, endure (6)
vócō, vocā́re, vocā́vī, vocā́tum - to call, summon (1)

2nd Conjugation
aúdeō, audḗre, aúsus sum - to dare (7)
dḗbeō, dēbḗre, dḗbuī, dḗbitum - to owe; ought, must, should (1)
dóceō, docḗre, dócuī, dóctum - to teach (8)
hábeō, habḗre, hábuī, hábitum - to have, hold, possess; consider, regard (3)
máneō, manḗre, mā́nsī, mā́nsum - to remain, stay, stay behind, abide, continue (5)
móneō, monḗre, mónuī, mónitum - to remind, advise, warn (1)
remáneō, remanḗre, remā́nsī, remā́nsum - to remain, stay, stay behind, abide, continue (5)
sálvē, salvḗte - hello, greetings (1)
sálveō, salvḗre - to be well, be in good health (1)
térreō, terrḗre, térruī, térritum - to frighten, terrify (1)
válē, valḗte - good-bye, farewell (1)
váleō, valḗre, váluī, valitū́rum - to be strong, have power; be well (1)
vídeō, vidḗre, vī́dī, vī́sum - to see; observe, understand (1)

3rd Conjugation
ágō, ágere, ḗgī, ā́ctum - to drive, lead, do, act; pass, spend *(life or time)* (8)
díscō, díscere, dídicī - to learn (8)
dū́cō, dū́cere, dū́xī, dúctum - to lead; consider, regard; prolong (8)
gérō, gérere, géssī, géstum - to carry; carry on, manage, conduct, wage, accomplish, perform (8)
scrī́bō, scrī́bere, scrī́psī, scrī́ptum to write, compose (8)
tráhō, tráhere, trā́xī, tráctum - to draw, drag; derive, acquire (8)
víncō, víncere, vī́cī, víctum - to conquer, overcome (8)

Irregular
póssum, pósse, pótuī - to be able, can, could, have power (6)
sum, ésse, fúī, futū́rum - to be, exist (4)

Adverbs
crās - tomorrow (5)
héri - yesterday (5)
hódiē - today (3)
íbi - there (6)
nímis, nímium - too, too much, excessively; *(in a positive sense, esp. with adjectives and adverbs)* exceedingly, very (9)
nōn - not (1)
númquam - never (8)
nunc - now, at present (6)
quándō - when (5)
quā́rē - because of which thing *(lit.)*; therefore, wherefore, why (6)
saépe - often (1)
sátis - enough, sufficiently (5)
sémper - always (3)
támen - nevertheless, still (8)
tum - then, at that time; thereupon, in the next place (5)
úbi - where, when (6)

Conjunctions
dum - while, as long as, at the same time that; *or* until *(+subjunctive)* (8)
énim - for, in fact, truly (9)
et - and; even (2)
et . . . et - both . . . and (2)
ígitur - therefore, consequently (5)
sed - but (2)
sī - if (1)

Prepositions

ad (+acc.) - to, up to, near to (8)
dē (+abl.) - down from, from; concerning, about (3)
ex, ē (abl.+) - out of, from, from within; by reason of, on account of ; of *(after cardinal numerals)* (8)
in (+acc.) - into, toward; against (9)
in (+abl.) - in, on (3)
post (+acc.) - after, behind (7)
própter (+acc.) - on account of, because of (5)
síne (+abl.) - without (2)
sub (+abl. w/ verbs of rest ***or*** **+acc. w/ verbs of motion)** - under, up under, close to, down to/into, to/at the foot of (7)

Interjection

ō - O!, Oh! (2)

Idioms

amā́bō tē - please (1)
grā́tiās ágere (+dat.) - to thank someone; to give thanks to (8)
nōn sṓlum . . . sed étiam - not only . . . but also (9)
poénās dáre - to pay the penalty (2)
sī quándō - if ever (5)

Suffixes

-ne – interrogative suffix attached to the first word of a sentence, typically the verb or another word on which the question hinges, to introduce a question whose answer is uncertain (5)
-que - and *(enclitic conjunction; appended to the second of two words to be joined)* (6)

Chapter 10

Nouns

1st Declension

adulēscéntia, adulēscéntiae (f) - youth, young manhood; youthfulness (5)
agrícola, agrícolae (m) - farmer (3)
amíca, amícae (f) - friend (female) (3)
amīcítia, amīcítiae (f) - friendship (10)
cṓpia, cṓpiae (f) - abundance, supply (8)
cṓpiae, cōpiā́rum (f) - supplies, troops, forces (8)
cúlpa, cúlpae (f) - fault, blame (5)
cū́ra, cū́rae (f) - care, attention, caution, anxiety (4)
déa, déae (f) - goddess (6)
discípula, discípulae (f) - learner, pupil, student (female) (6)
fā́ma, fā́mae (f) - rumor, report; fame, reputation (2)
fḗmina, fḗminae (f) - woman (3)
fī́lia, fī́liae (f) - daughter (3)
fṓrma, fṓrmae (f) - form, shape; beauty (2)
fortū́na, fortū́nae (f) - fortune, luck (2)
glṓria, glṓriae (f) - glory, fame (5)
hṓra, hṓrae (f) - hour, time (10)
īnsídiae, īnsidiā́rum (f) - ambush, plot, treachery (6)
ī́ra, ī́rae (f) - ire, anger (2)
líttera, lítterae (f) - a letter of the alphabet (7)
lítterae, litterā́rum (f) - a letter (epistle), literature (7)
magístra, magístrae (f) - schoolmistress, teacher, mistress (4)
móra, mórae (f) - delay (4)
nātū́ra, nātū́rae (f) - nature (10)
naúta, naútae (m) - sailor (2)
pátria, pátriae (f) - fatherland, native land, (one's) country (2)
pecū́nia, pecū́niae (f) - money (2)
philosóphia, philosóphiae (f) - philosophy (2)
poéna, poénae (f) - penalty, punishment (2)
poḗta, poḗtae (m) - poet (2)
pórta, pórtae (f) - gate, entrance (2)
puélla, puéllae (f) - girl (2)
rēgī́na, rēgī́nae (f) - queen (7)
rósa, rósae (f) - rose (2)
sapiéntia, sapiéntiae (f) - wisdom (3)
senténtia, senténtiae (f) - feeling, thought, opinion, vote, sentence (2)
térra, térrae (f) - earth, ground, land, country (7)
vía, víae (f) - way, road, street (10)
victṓria, victṓriae (f) - victory (8)
vī́ta, vī́tae (f) - life; mode of life (2)

2nd Declension

áger, ágrī (m) - field, farm (3)
amī́cus, amī́cī (m) - friend (male) (3)
ánimī, animṓrum (m) - high spirits, pride, courage (5)
ánimus, ánimī (m) - soul, spirit, mind (5)
bā́sium, bā́siī (n) - kiss (4)
béllum, béllī (n) - war (4)
caélum, caélī (n) - sky, heaven (5)
cōnsílium, cōnsíliī (n) - plan, purpose, counsel, advice, judgment, wisdom (4)
déus, déī (m) - god (6)
discípulus, discípulī (m) - learner, pupil, student (male) (6)
dṓnum, dṓnī (n) - gift, present (4)
exítium, exítiī (n) - destruction, ruin (4)
fī́lius, fī́liī (m) - son (3)
Graécus, Graécī (m) - a Greek (6)
líber, líbrī (m) - book (6)
lóca, locṓrum (n) - places, region (9)
lócī, locṓrum (m) - passages in literature (9)
lócus, lócī (m) - place; passage in literature (9)
magíster, magístrī (m) - schoolmaster, teacher, master (4)
mórbus, mórbī (m) - disease, sickness (9)
númerus, númerī (m) - number (3)
óculus, óculī (m) - eye (4)
offícium, offíciī (n) - duty, service (4)
ṓtium, ṓtiī (n) - leisure, peace (4)
perī́culum, perī́culī (n) - danger, risk (4)
pópulus, pópulī (m) - the people, a people, a nation (3)
púer, púerī (m) - boy; boys, children *(pl.)* (3)
remédium, remédiī (n) - cure, remedy (4)
stúdium, stúdiī (n) - eagerness, zeal, pursuit, study (9)
stúltus, stúltī (m) - a fool (4)
tyránnus, tyránnī (m) - absolute ruler, tyrant (6)
vérbum, vérbī (n) - word (5)
vir, vírī (m) - man, hero (3)
vítium, vítiī (n) - fault, crime, vice (6)

3rd Declension

ámor, amṓris (m) - love (7)
cármen, cárminis (n) - song, poem (7)
Cícerō, Cicerṓnis (m) - (Marcus Tullius) Cicero (8)
cī́vitās, cīvitā́tis (f) - state, citizenship (7)
córpus, córporis (n) - body (7)
cupíditās, cupiditā́tis (f) - desire, longing, passion; cupidity, avarice (10)
frā́ter, frā́tris (m) - brother (8)
hómō, hóminis (m) - human being, man (7)
lábor, labṓris (m)- labor, work, toil; a work, production (7)
laus, laúdis (f) - praise, glory, fame (8)
lībértās, lībertā́tis (f) - liberty (8)
mṓrēs, mṓrum (m) - habits, morals, character (7)
mōs, mṓris (m) - habit, custom, manner (7)
nṓmen, nṓminis (n) - name (7)
pāx, pā́cis (f) - peace (7)
rátiō, ratiṓnis (f) - reckoning, account; reason, judgment, consideration; system; manner, method (8)
rēx, rḗgis (m) - king (7)
scrī́ptor, scrīptṓris (m) - writer, author (8)
senéctūs, senectū́tis (f) - old age (10)
sóror, sorṓris (f) - sister (8)
témpus, témporis (n) - time; occasion, opportunity (7)
tímor, timṓris (m) - fear (10)
úxor, uxṓris (f) - wife (7)
vḗritās, vēritā́tis (f) - truth (10)
vírgō, vírginis (f) - maiden, virgin (7)
vírtūs, virtū́tis (f) - manliness, courage; excellence, character, worth, virtue (7)
volúptās, voluptā́tis (f) - pleasure (10)

Indeclinable

níhil - nothing (1)
sátis - enough (5)

Pronouns

hic, haec, hoc - this; the latter; he, she, it, they (9)
ílle, ílla, íllud - that; the former; the famous; he, she, it, they (9)
íste, ísta, ístud - that of yours, that; such (as you have, as you speak of); *sometimes with contemptuous force, e.g.,* that despicable, that wretched (9)
mē - me, myself (1)
quid - what (1)
tē - you, yourself *(sing.)* (5)

Adjectives

áliī . . . áliī - some . . . others (9)
álius, ália, áliud - other, another (9)
álter, áltera, álterum - the other (of two), second (9)
antī́quus, antī́qua, antī́quum - ancient, old-time (2)
avā́rus, avā́ra, avā́rum - greedy, avaricious (3)
beā́tus, beā́ta, beā́tum - happy, fortunate, blessed (10)
béllus, bélla, béllum - pretty, handsome, charming (4)
bónus, bóna, bónum - good, kind (4)
Graécus, Graéca, Graécum - Greek (6)
hūmā́nus, hūmā́na, hūmā́num - pertaining to man, human; humane, kind; refined, cultivated (4)
lī́ber, lī́bera, lī́berum - free (5)
mágnus, mágna, mágnum - large, great; important (2)
málus, mála, málum - bad, wicked, evil (4)
méus, méa, méum - my (2)
múltus, múlta, múltum - much, many (2)
neúter, neútra, neútrum - not either, neither (9)
nóster, nóstra, nóstrum - our, ours (5)
nóvus, nóva, nóvum - new; strange (7)
nū́llus, nū́lla, nū́llum - not any, no, none (9)
párvus, párva, párvum - small, little (4)
paúcī, paúcae, paúca - few, a few (3)
perpétuus, perpétua, perpétuum perpetual, lasting, uninterrupted, continuous (6)
plḗnus, plḗna, plḗnum - full, abundant, generous (6)
púlcher, púlchra, púlchrum - beautiful, handsome; fine (5)
Rōmā́nus, Rōmā́na, Rōmā́num - Roman (3)
sálvus, sálva, sálvum - safe, sound (6)
sā́nus, sā́na, sā́num - sound, healthy, sane (5)
secúndus, secúnda, secúndum - second; favorable (6)
sṓlus, sṓla, sṓlum - alone, only, the only (9)
stúltus, stúlta, stúltum - foolish (4)
tṓtus, tṓta, tṓtum - whole, entire (9)
túus, túa, túum - your *(sing.)* (2)
ū́llus, ū́lla, ū́llum - any (9)
ū́nus, ū́na, ū́num - one, single, alone (9)
úter, útra, útrum - either, which (of two) (9)
vḗrus, vḗra, vḗrum - true, real, proper (4)
véster, véstra, véstrum - your *(pl.)* (6)

Indeclinable
sátis - enough, sufficient (5)

Verbs

1st Conjugation
ádiuvō, adiuvā́re, adiū́vī, adiū́tum - to help, aid, assist; to please (4)
ámō, amā́re, amā́vī, amā́tum - to love, like (1)
cḗnō, cēnā́re, cēnā́vī, cēnā́tum - to dine (5)
cṓgitō, cōgitā́re, cōgitā́vī, cōgitā́tum- to think, ponder, consider, plan (1)
cōnsérvō, cōnservā́re, cōnservā́vī, cōnservā́tum - to preserve, conserve, maintain (1)
cúlpō, culpā́re, culpā́vī, culpā́tum - to blame, censure (5)
dēmṓnstrō, dēmōnstrā́re, dēmōnstrā́vī, dēmōnstrā́tum to point out, show, demonstrate (8)
dō, dáre, dédī, dátum - to give, offer (1)
érrō, errā́re, errā́vī, errā́tum - to wander; err, go astray, make a mistake, be mistaken (1)
iúvō, iuvā́re, iū́vī, iū́tum - to help, aid, assist; to please (4)
laúdō, laudā́re, laudā́vī, laudā́tum - to praise (1)
nécō, necā́re, necā́vī, necā́tum - to murder, kill (7)
sátiō, satiā́re, satiā́vī, satiā́tum - to satisfy, sate (3)
sérvō, servā́re, servā́vī, servā́tum - to preserve, save, keep, guard (1)
súperō, superā́re, superā́vī, superā́tum - to be above, have the upper hand, surpass; overcome, conquer (5)
tólerō, tolerā́re, tolerā́vī, tolerā́tum - to bear, endure (6)
vócō, vocā́re, vocā́vī, vocā́tum - to call, summon (1)

2nd Conjugation
aúdeō, audḗre, aúsus sum - to dare (7)
dḗbeō, dēbḗre, dḗbuī, dḗbitum - to owe; ought, must, should (1)
dóceō, docḗre, dócuī, dóctum - to teach (8)
hábeō, habḗre, hábuī, hábitum - to have, hold, possess; consider, regard (3)
máneō, manḗre, mā́nsī, mā́nsum - to remain, stay, stay behind, abide, continue (5)
móneō, monḗre, mónuī, mónitum - to remind, advise, warn (1)
remáneō, remanḗre, remā́nsī, remā́nsum - to remain, stay, stay behind, abide, continue (5)
sálvē, salvḗte - hello, greetings (1)
sálveō, salvḗre - to be well, be in good health (1)
térreō, terrḗre, térruī, térritum - to frighten, terrify (1)
válē, valḗte - good-bye, farewell (1)
váleō, valḗre, váluī, valitū́rum - to be strong, have power; be well (1)
vídeō, vidḗre, vī́dī, vī́sum - to see; observe, understand (1)

3rd Conjugation
ágō, ágere, ḗgī, ā́ctum - to drive, lead, do, act; pass, spend *(life or time)* (8)
dī́cō, dī́cere, dī́xī, díctum - to say, tell, speak; name, call (10)
díscō, díscere, dídicī - to learn (8)
dū́cō, dū́cere, dū́xī, dúctum - to lead; consider, regard; prolong (8)
gérō, gérere, géssī, géstum - to carry; carry on, manage, conduct, wage, accomplish, perform (8)
scrī́bō, scrī́bere, scrī́psī, scrī́ptum to write, compose (8)
tráhō, tráhere, trā́xī, tráctum - to draw, drag; derive, acquire (8)
víncō, víncere, vī́cī, víctum - to conquer, overcome (8)
vī́vō, vī́vere, vī́xī, vī́ctum - to live (10)

3rd Conjugation -iō
cápiō, cápere, cḗpī, cáptum - to take, capture, seize, get (10)
fáciō, fácere, fḗcī, fáctum - to make, do, accomplish (10)
fúgiō, fúgere, fū́gī, fugitū́rum - to flee, hurry away; escape; go into exile; avoid, shun (10)

4th Conjugation
aúdiō, audī́re, audī́vī, audī́tum - to hear, listen to (10)
invéniō, invenī́re, invḗnī, invéntum - to come upon, find (10)
véniō, venī́re, vḗnī, véntum - to come (10)

Irregular
póssum, pósse, pótuī - to be able, can, could, have power (6)
sum, ésse, fúī, futū́rum - to be, exist (4)

Adverbs

crās - tomorrow (5)
héri - yesterday (5)
hódiē - today (3)
íbi - there (6)
nímis, nímium - too, too much, excessively; *(in a positive sense, esp. with adjectives and adverbs)* exceedingly, very (9)
nōn - not (1)
númquam - never (8)
nunc - now, at present (6)
quándō - when (5)
quā́rē - because of which thing *(lit.);* therefore, wherefore, why (6)
saépe - often (1)
sátis - enough, sufficiently (5)
sémper - always (3)
támen - nevertheless, still (8)
tum - then, at that time; thereupon, in the next place (5)
úbi - where, when (6)

Conjunctions

dum - while, as long as, at the same time that; *or* until *(+subjunctive)* (8)
énim - for, in fact, truly (9)
et - and; even (2)
et . . . et - both . . . and (2)
ígitur - therefore, consequently (5)
quóniam - since, inasmuch as (10)
sed - but (2)
sī - if (1)

Prepositions

ad (+acc.) - to, up to, near to (8)
cum (+abl.) - with (10)
dē (+abl.) - down from, from; concerning, about (3)
ex, ē (abl.+) - out of, from, from within; by reason of, on account of ; of *(after cardinal numerals)* (8)
in (+acc.) - into, toward; against (9)
in (+abl.) - in, on (3)
post (+acc.) - after, behind (7)
própter (+acc.) - on account of, because of (5)
síne (+abl.) - without (2)
sub (+abl. w/ verbs of rest *or* **+acc. w/ verbs of motion)** - under, up under, close to, down to/into, to/at the foot of (7)

Interjection

ō - O!, Oh! (2)

Idioms

amā́bō tē - please (1)
grā́tiās ágere (+dat.) - to thank someone; to give thanks to (8)
nōn sṓlum . . . sed étiam - not only . . . but also (9)
poénās dáre - to pay the penalty (2)
sī quándō - if ever (5)

Suffixes

-ne – interrogative suffix attached to the first word of a sentence, typically the verb or another word on which the question hinges, to introduce a question whose answer is uncertain (5)
-que - and *(enclitic conjunction; appended to the second of two words to be joined)* (6)

Chapter 11

Nouns

1st Declension

adulēscéntia, adulēscéntiae (f) - youth, young manhood; youthfulness (5)
agrícola, agrícolae (m) - farmer (3)
amī́ca, amī́cae (f) - friend (female) (3)
amīcítia, amīcítiae (f) - friendship (10)
cṓpia, cṓpiae (f) - abundance, supply (8)
cṓpiae, cōpiā́rum (f) - supplies, troops, forces (8)
cúlpa, cúlpae (f) - fault, blame (5)
cū́ra, cū́rae (f) - care, attention, caution, anxiety (4)
déa, déae (f) - goddess (6)
discípula, discípulae (f) - learner, pupil, student (female) (6)
fā́ma, fā́mae (f) - rumor, report; fame, reputation (2)
fḗmina, fḗminae (f) - woman (3)
fī́lia, fī́liae (f) - daughter (3)
fṓrma, fṓrmae (f) - form, shape; beauty (2)
fortū́na, fortū́nae (f) - fortune, luck (2)
glṓria, glṓriae (f) - glory, fame (5)
hṓra, hṓrae (f) - hour, time (10)
īnsídiae, īnsidiā́rum (f) - ambush, plot, treachery (6)
ī́ra, ī́rae (f) - ire, anger (2)
líttera, lítterae (f) - a letter of the alphabet (7)
lítterae, litterā́rum (f) - a letter (epistle), literature (7)
magístra, magístrae (f) - schoolmistress, teacher, mistress (4)
móra, mórae (f) - delay (4)
nātū́ra, nātū́rae (f) - nature (10)
naúta, naútae (m) - sailor (2)
pátria, pátriae (f) - fatherland, native land, (one's) country (2)
pecū́nia, pecū́niae (f) - money (2)
philosóphia, philosóphiae (f) - philosophy (2)
poéna, poénae (f) - penalty, punishment (2)
poḗta, poḗtae (m) - poet (2)
pórta, pórtae (f) - gate, entrance (2)
puélla, puéllae (f) - girl (2)
rēgī́na, rēgī́nae (f) - queen (7)
rósa, rósae (f) - rose (2)
sapiéntia, sapiéntiae (f) - wisdom (3)
senténtia, senténtiae (f) - feeling, thought, opinion, vote, sentence (2)
térra, térrae (f) - earth, ground, land, country (7)
vía, víae (f) - way, road, street (10)
victṓria, victṓriae (f) - victory (8)
vī́ta, vī́tae (f) - life; mode of life (2)

2nd Declension

áger, ágrī (m) - field, farm (3)
amī́cus, amī́cī (m) - friend (male) (3)
ánimī, animṓrum (m) - high spirits, pride, courage (5)
ánimus, ánimī (m) - soul, spirit, mind (5)
bā́sium, bā́siī (n) - kiss (4)
béllum, béllī (n) - war (4)
caélum, caélī (n) - sky, heaven (5)
cōnsílium, cōnsíliī (n) - plan, purpose, counsel, advice, judgment, wisdom (4)
déus, déī (m) - god (6)
discípulus, discípulī (m) - learner, pupil, student (male) (6)
dṓnum, dṓnī (n) - gift, present (4)
exítium, exítiī (n) - destruction, ruin (4)
fī́lius, fī́liī (m) - son (3)
Graécus, Graécī (m) - a Greek (6)
líber, líbrī (m) - book (6)
lóca, locṓrum (n) - places, region (9)
lócī, locṓrum (m) - passages in literature (9)
lócus, lócī (m) - place; passage in literature (9)
magíster, magístrī (m) - schoolmaster, teacher, master (4)
mórbus, mórbī (m) - disease, sickness (9)
númerus, númerī (m) - number (3)
óculus, óculī (m) - eye (4)
offícium, offíciī (n) - duty, service (4)
ṓtium, ṓtiī (n) - leisure, peace (4)
perī́culum, perī́culī (n) - danger, risk (4)
pópulus, pópulī (m) - the people, a people, a nation (3)
púer, púerī (m) - boy; boys, children *(pl.)* (3)
remédium, remédiī (n) - cure, remedy (4)
stúdium, stúdiī (n) - eagerness, zeal, pursuit, study (9)
stúltus, stúltī (m) - a fool (4)
tyránnus, tyránnī (m) - absolute ruler, tyrant (6)
vérbum, vérbī (n) - word (5)
vir, vírī (m) - man, hero (3)
vítium, vítiī (n) - fault, crime, vice (6)

3rd Declension

ámor, amṓris (m) - love (7)
cáput, cápitis (n) - head; leader; beginning; life; heading; chapter (11)
cármen, cárminis (n) - song, poem (7)
Cícerō, Cicerṓnis (m) - (Marcus Tullius) Cicero (8)
cívitās, cīvitā́tis (f) - state, citizenship (7)
cṓnsul, cṓnsulis (m) - consul (11)
córpus, córporis (n) - body (7)
cupíditās, cupiditā́tis (f) - desire, longing, passion; cupidity, avarice (10)
frā́ter, frā́tris (m) - brother (8)
hómō, hóminis (m) - human being, man (7)
lábor, labṓris (m)- labor, work, toil; a work, production (7)
laus, laúdis (f) - praise, glory, fame (8)
lībértās, lībertā́tis (f) - liberty (8)
mṓrēs, mṓrum (m) - habits, morals, character (7)
mōs, mṓris (m) - habit, custom, manner (7)
nḗmō, nūllíus, nḗminī, nḗminem, nū́llō, nū́llā (m *or* f) - no one, nobody (11)
nṓmen, nṓminis (n) - name (7)
pāx, pā́cis (f) - peace (7)
rátiō, ratiṓnis (f) - reckoning, account; reason, judgment, consideration; system; manner, method (8)
rēx, rḗgis (m) - king (7)
scríptor, scrīptṓris (m) - writer, author (8)
senéctūs, senectū́tis (f) - old age (10)
sóror, sorṓris (f) - sister (8)
témpus, témporis (n) - time; occasion, opportunity (7)
tímor, timṓris (m) - fear (10)
úxor, uxṓris (f) - wife (7)
vḗritās, vēritā́tis (f) - truth (10)
vírgō, vírginis (f) - maiden, virgin (7)
vírtūs, virtū́tis (f) - manliness, courage; excellence, character, worth, virtue (7)
volúptās, voluptā́tis (f) - pleasure (10)

Indeclinable

níhil - nothing (1)
sátis - enough (5)

Pronouns

égo, méī - I (11)
hic, haec, hoc - this; the latter; he, she, it, they (9)
ídem, éadem, ídem - the same (11)
ílle, ílla, íllud - that; the former; the famous; he, she, it, they (9)
is, éa, id - this, that; he, she, it (11)
íste, ísta, ístud - that of yours, that; such (as you have, as you speak of); *sometimes with contemptuous force, e.g.,* that despicable, that wretched (9)
mē - me, myself (1)
quid - what (1)
tē - you, yourself *(sing.)* (5)
tū, túī - you *(sing.)* (11)

Adjectives

áliī . . . áliī - some . . . others (9)
álius, ália, áliud - other, another (9)
álter, áltera, álterum - the other (of two), second (9)
amícus, amíca, amícum - friendly (11)
antíquus, antíqua, antíquum - ancient, old-time (2)
avā́rus, avā́ra, avā́rum - greedy, avaricious (3)
beā́tus, beā́ta, beā́tum - happy, fortunate, blessed (10)
béllus, bélla, béllum - pretty, handsome, charming (4)
bónus, bóna, bónum - good, kind (4)
cā́rus, cā́ra, cā́rum - dear (11)
Graécus, Graéca, Graécum - Greek (6)
hūmā́nus, hūmā́na, hūmā́num - pertaining to man, human; humane, kind; refined, cultivated (4)
líber, líbera, líberum - free (5)
mágnus, mágna, mágnum - large, great; important (2)
málus, mála, málum - bad, wicked, evil (4)
méus, méa, méum - my (2)
múltus, múlta, múltum - much, many (2)
neúter, neútra, neútrum - not either, neither (9)
nóster, nóstra, nóstrum - our, ours (5)
nóvus, nóva, nóvum - new; strange (7)
nū́llus, nū́lla, nū́llum - not any, no, none (9)
párvus, párva, párvum - small, little (4)
paúcī, paúcae, paúca - few, a few (3)
perpétuus, perpétua, perpétuum perpetual, lasting, uninterrupted, continuous (6)
plḗnus, plḗna, plḗnum - full, abundant, generous (6)
púlcher, púlchra, púlchrum - beautiful, handsome; fine (5)
Rōmā́nus, Rōmā́na, Rōmā́num - Roman (3)
sálvus, sálva, sálvum - safe, sound (6)
sā́nus, sā́na, sā́num - sound, healthy, sane (5)
secúndus, secúnda, secúndum - second; favorable (6)

sṓlus, sṓla, sṓlum - alone, only, the only (9)
stúltus, stúlta, stúltum - foolish (4)
tṓtus, tṓta, tṓtum - whole, entire (9)
túus, túa, túum - your *(sing.)* (2)
ū́llus, ū́lla, ū́llum - any (9)
ū́nus, ū́na, ū́num - one, single, alone (9)
úter, útra, útrum - either, which (of two) (9)
vḗrus, vḗra, vḗrum - true, real, proper (4)
véster, véstra, véstrum - your *(pl.)* (6)

Indeclinable
sátis - enough, sufficient (5)

Verbs

1st Conjugation
ádiuvō, adiuvā́re, adiū́vī, adiū́tum - to help, aid, assist; to please (4)
ámō, amā́re, amā́vī, amā́tum - to love, like (1)
cḗnō, cēnā́re, cēnā́vī, cēnā́tum - to dine (5)
cṓgitō, cōgitā́re, cōgitā́vī, cōgitā́tum- to think, ponder, consider, plan (1)
cōnsérvō, cōnservā́re, cōnservā́vī, cōnservā́tum - to preserve, conserve, maintain (1)
cúlpō, culpā́re, culpā́vī, culpā́tum - to blame, censure (5)
dēmṓnstrō, dēmōnstrā́re, dēmōnstrā́vī, dēmōnstrā́tum to point out, show, demonstrate (8)
dō, dáre, dédī, dátum - to give, offer (1)
érrō, errā́re, errā́vī, errā́tum - to wander; err, go astray, make a mistake, be mistaken (1)
iúvō, iuvā́re, iū́vī, iū́tum - to help, aid, assist; to please (4)
laúdō, laudā́re, laudā́vī, laudā́tum - to praise (1)
nécō, necā́re, necā́vī, necā́tum - to murder, kill (7)
sátiō, satiā́re, satiā́vī, satiā́tum - to satisfy, sate (3)
sérvō, servā́re, servā́vī, servā́tum - to preserve, save, keep, guard (1)
súperō, superā́re, superā́vī, superā́tum - to be above, have the upper hand, surpass; overcome, conquer (5)
tólerō, tolerā́re, tolerā́vī, tolerā́tum - to bear, endure (6)
vócō, vocā́re, vocā́vī, vocā́tum - to call, summon (1)

2nd Conjugation
aúdeō, audḗre, aúsus sum - to dare (7)
dḗbeō, dēbḗre, dḗbuī, dḗbitum - to owe; ought, must, should (1)
dóceō, docḗre, dócuī, dóctum - to teach (8)
hábeō, habḗre, hábuī, hábitum - to have, hold, possess; consider, regard (3)
máneō, manḗre, mā́nsī, mā́nsum - to remain, stay, stay behind, abide, continue (5)
móneō, monḗre, mónuī, mónitum - to remind, advise, warn (1)
remáneō, remanḗre, remā́nsī, remā́nsum - to remain, stay, stay behind, abide, continue (5)
sálvē, salvḗte - hello, greetings (1)
sálveō, salvḗre - to be well, be in good health (1)
térreō, terrḗre, térruī, térritum - to frighten, terrify (1)
válē, valḗte - good-bye, farewell (1)
váleō, valḗre, váluī, valitū́rum - to be strong, have power; be well (1)
vídeō, vidḗre, vī́dī, vī́sum - to see; observe, understand (1)

3rd Conjugation
ágō, ágere, ḗgī, ā́ctum - to drive, lead, do, act; pass, spend *(life or time)* (8)
dī́cō, dī́cere, dī́xī, díctum - to say, tell, speak; name, call (10)
dī́scō, dī́scere, dídicī - to learn (8)
dū́cō, dū́cere, dū́xī, dúctum - to lead; consider, regard; prolong (8)
gérō, gérere, géssī, géstum - to carry; carry on, manage, conduct, wage, accomplish, perform (8)
intéllegō, intellégere, intellḗxī, intellḗctum - to understand (11)
míttō, míttere, mī́sī, míssum - to send, let go (11)
scrī́bō, scrī́bere, scrī́psī, scrī́ptum to write, compose (8)
tráhō, tráhere, trā́xī, tráctum - to draw, drag; derive, acquire (8)
víncō, víncere, vī́cī, víctum - to conquer, overcome (8)
vī́vō, vī́vere, vī́xī, vī́ctum - to live (10)

3rd Conjugation -iō

cápiō, cápere, cḗpī, cáptum - to take, capture, seize, get (10)

fáciō, fácere, fḗcī, fáctum - to make, do, accomplish (10)

fúgiō, fúgere, fū́gī, fugitū́rum - to flee, hurry away; escape; go into exile; avoid, shun (10)

4th Conjugation

aúdiō, audī́re, audī́vī, audī́tum - to hear, listen to (10)

invéniō, invenī́re, invḗnī, invéntum - to come upon, find (10)

séntiō, sentī́re, sḗnsī, sḗnsum - to feel, perceive, think, experience (11)

véniō, venī́re, vḗnī, véntum - to come (10)

Irregular

póssum, pósse, pótuī - to be able, can, could, have power (6)

sum, ésse, fúī, futū́rum - to be, exist (4)

Adverbs

béne - well, satisfactorily, quite (11)

crās - tomorrow (5)

étiam - even, also (11)

héri - yesterday (5)

hódiē - today (3)

íbi - there (6)

nímis, nímium - too, too much, excessively; *(in a positive sense, esp. with adjectives and adverbs)* exceedingly, very (9)

nōn - not (1)

númquam - never (8)

nunc - now, at present (6)

quándō - when (5)

quā́rē - because of which thing *(lit.)*; therefore, wherefore, why (6)

saépe - often (1)

sátis - enough, sufficiently (5)

sémper - always (3)

támen - nevertheless, still (8)

tum - then, at that time; thereupon, in the next place (5)

úbi - where, when (6)

Conjunctions

aútem - however; moreover (11)

dum - while, as long as, at the same time that; *or* until *(+subjunctive)* (8)

énim - for, in fact, truly (9)

et - and; even (2)

et . . . et - both . . . and (2)

ígitur - therefore, consequently (5)

néque, nec - and not, nor (11)

néque . . . néque, nec . . . nec - neither . . . nor (11)

quod - because (11)

quóniam - since, inasmuch as (10)

sed - but (2)

sī - if (1)

Prepositions

ad (+acc.) - to, up to, near to (8)

cum (+abl.) - with (10)

dē (+abl.) - down from, from; concerning, about (3)

ex, ē (abl.+) - out of, from, from within; by reason of, on account of; of *(after cardinal numerals)* (8)

in (+acc.) - into, toward; against (9)

in (+abl.) - in, on (3)

post (+acc.) - after, behind (7)

própter (+acc.) - on account of, because of (5)

síne (+abl.) - without (2)

sub (+abl. w/ verbs of rest *or* **+acc. w/ verbs of motion)** - under, up under, close to, down to/into, to/at the foot of (7)

Interjection

ō - O!, Oh! (2)

Idioms

amā́bō tē - please (1)

grā́tiās ágere (+dat.) - to thank someone; to give thanks to (8)

nōn sṓlum . . . sed étiam - not only . . . but also (9)

poénās dáre - to pay the penalty (2)

sī quándō - if ever (5)

Suffixes

-ne – interrogative suffix attached to the first word of a sentence, typically the verb or another word on which the question hinges, to introduce a question whose answer is uncertain (5)

-que - and *(enclitic conjunction; appended to the second of two words to be joined)* (6)

Chapter 12

Nouns

1st Declension

adulēscéntia, adulēscéntiae (f) - youth, young manhood; youthfulness (5)
agrícola, agrícolae (m) - farmer (3)
amíca, amícae (f) - friend (female) (3)
amīcítia, amīcítiae (f) - friendship (10)
Ásia, Ásiae (f) - Asia (12)
cṓpia, cṓpiae (f) - abundance, supply (8)
cṓpiae, cōpiā́rum (f) - supplies, troops, forces (8)
cúlpa, cúlpae (f) - fault, blame (5)
cū́ra, cū́rae (f) - care, attention, caution, anxiety (4)
déa, déae (f) - goddess (6)
discípula, discípulae (f) - learner, pupil, student (female) (6)
fā́ma, fā́mae (f) - rumor, report; fame, reputation (2)
fḗmina, fḗminae (f) - woman (3)
fī́lia, fī́liae (f) - daughter (3)
fṓrma, fṓrmae (f) - form, shape; beauty (2)
fortū́na, fortū́nae (f) - fortune, luck (2)
glṓria, glṓriae (f) - glory, fame (5)
hṓra, hṓrae (f) - hour, time (10)
īnsídiae, īnsidiā́rum (f) - ambush, plot, treachery (6)
ī́ra, ī́rae (f) - ire, anger (2)
líttera, líterae (f) - a letter of the alphabet (7)
lítterae, litterā́rum (f) - a letter (epistle), literature (7)
magístra, magístrae (f) - schoolmistress, teacher, mistress (4)
médica, médicae (f) - doctor, physician (female) (12)
móra, mórae (f) - delay (4)
nātū́ra, nātū́rae (f) - nature (10)
naúta, naútae (m) - sailor (2)
patiéntia, patiéntiae (f) - suffering; patience, endurance (12)
pátria, pátriae (f) - fatherland, native land, (one's) country (2)
pecū́nia, pecū́niae (f) - money (2)
philosóphia, philosóphiae (f) - philosophy (2)
poéna, poénae (f) - penalty, punishment (2)
poḗta, poḗtae (m) - poet (2)
pórta, pórtae (f) - gate, entrance (2)
puélla, puéllae (f) - girl (2)
rēgī́na, rēgī́nae (f) - queen (7)
rósa, rósae (f) - rose (2)
sapiéntia, sapiéntiae (f) - wisdom (3)
senténtia, senténtiae (f) - feeling, thought, opinion, vote, sentence (2)
térra, térrae (f) - earth, ground, land, country (7)
vía, víae (f) - way, road, street (10)
victṓria, victṓriae (f) - victory (8)
vī́ta, vī́tae (f) - life; mode of life (2)

2nd Declension

áger, ágrī (m) - field, farm (3)
amī́cus, amī́cī (m) - friend (male) (3)
ánimī, animṓrum (m) - high spirits, pride, courage (5)
ánimus, ánimī (m) - soul, spirit, mind (5)
ánnus, ánnī (m) - year (12)
bā́sium, bā́siī (n) - kiss (4)
béllum, béllī (n) - war (4)
caélum, caélī (n) - sky, heaven (5)
cōnsílium, cōnsíliī (n) - plan, purpose, counsel, advice, judgment, wisdom (4)
déus, déī (m) - god (6)
discípulus, discípulī (m) - learner, pupil, student (male) (6)
dṓnum, dṓnī (n) - gift, present (4)
exítium, exítiī (n) - destruction, ruin (4)
fī́lius, fī́liī (m) - son (3)
Graécus, Graécī (m) - a Greek (6)
líber, líbrī (m) - book (6)
lóca, locṓrum (n) - places, region (9)
lócī, locṓrum (m) - passages in literature (9)
lócus, lócī (m) - place; passage in literature (9)
magíster, magístrī (m) - schoolmaster, teacher, master (4)
médicus, médicī (m) - doctor, physician (male) (12)
mórbus, mórbī (m) - disease, sickness (9)
númerus, númerī (m) - number (3)
óculus, óculī (m) - eye (4)
offícium, offíciī (n) - duty, service (4)
ṓtium, ṓtiī (n) - leisure, peace (4)
perículum, perículī (n) - danger, risk (4)
pópulus, pópulī (m) - the people, a people, a nation (3)
prīncípium, prīncípiī (n) - beginning (12)
púer, púerī (m) - boy; boys, children *(pl.)* (3)
remédium, remédiī (n) - cure, remedy (4)
stúdium, stúdiī (n) - eagerness, zeal, pursuit, study (9)
stúltus, stúltī (m) - a fool (4)

tyránnus, tyránnī (m) - absolute ruler, tyrant (6)
vérbum, vérbī (n)- word (5)
vir, vírī (m) - man, hero (3)
vítium, vítiī (n) - fault, crime, vice (6)

3rd Declension

aduléscēns, adulēscéntis (m *or* f) - young man *or* woman (12)
ámor, amṓris (m) - love (7)
Caésar, Caésaris (m) - Caesar (12)
cáput, cápitis (n) - head; leader; beginning; life; heading; chapter (11)
cármen, cárminis (n) - song, poem (7)
Cícerō, Cicerṓnis (m) - (Marcus Tullius) Cicero (8)
cī́vitās, cīvitā́tis (f) - state, citizenship (7)
cṓnsul, cṓnsulis (m) - consul (11)
córpus, córporis (n) - body (7)
cupíditās, cupiditā́tis (f) - desire, longing, passion; cupidity, avarice (10)
frā́ter, frā́tris (m) - brother (8)
hómō, hóminis (m) - human being, man (7)
lábor, labṓris (m)- labor, work, toil; a work, production (7)
laus, laúdis (f) - praise, glory, fame (8)
lībértās, lībertā́tis (f) - liberty (8)
mā́ter, mā́tris (f) - mother (12)
mṓrēs, mṓrum (m) - habits, morals, character (7)
mōs, mṓris (m) - habit, custom, manner (7)
nḗmō, nūllī́us, nḗminī, nḗminem, nū́llō, nū́llā (m *or* f) - no one, nobody (11)
nṓmen, nṓminis (n) - name (7)
páter, pátris (m) - father (12)
pāx, pā́cis (f) - peace (7)
rátiō, ratiṓnis (f) - reckoning, account; reason, judgment, consideration; system; manner, method (8)
rēx, rḗgis (m) - king (7)
scrī́ptor, scrīptṓris (m) - writer, author (8)
senéctūs, senectū́tis (f) - old age (10)
sóror, sorṓris (f) - sister (8)
témpus, témporis (n) - time; occasion, opportunity (7)
tímor, timṓris (m) - fear (10)
úxor, uxṓris (f) - wife (7)
vḗritās, vēritā́tis (f) - truth (10)
vírgō, vírginis (f) - maiden, virgin (7)
vírtūs, virtū́tis (f) - manliness, courage; excellence, character, worth, virtue (7)
volúptās, voluptā́tis (f) - pleasure (10)

Indeclinable

níhil - nothing (1)
sátis - enough (5)

Pronouns

égo, méī - I (11)
hic, haec, hoc - this; the latter; he, she, it, they (9)
ī́dem, éadem, ídem - the same (11)
ílle, ílla, íllud - that; the former; the famous; he, she, it, they (9)
is, éa, id - this, that; he, she, it (11)
íste, ísta, ístud - that of yours, that; such (as you have, as you speak of); *sometimes with contemptuous force, e.g.,* that despicable, that wretched (9)
mē - me, myself (1)
quid - what (1)
tē - you, yourself *(sing.)* (5)
tū, túī - you *(sing.)* (11)

Adjectives

acérbus, acérba, acérbum - harsh, bitter, grievous (12)
áliī . . . áliī - some . . . others (9)
álius, ália, áliud - other, another (9)
álter, áltera, álterum - the other (of two), second (9)
amī́cus, amī́ca, amī́cum - friendly (11)
antī́quus, antī́qua, antī́quum - ancient, old-time (2)
avā́rus, avā́ra, avā́rum - greedy, avaricious (3)
beā́tus, beā́ta, beā́tum - happy, fortunate, blessed (10)
béllus, bélla, béllum - pretty, handsome, charming (4)
bónus, bóna, bónum - good, kind (4)
cā́rus, cā́ra, cā́rum - dear (11)
Graécus, Graéca, Graécum - Greek (6)
hūmā́nus, hūmā́na, hūmā́num - pertaining to man, human; humane, kind; refined, cultivated (4)
lī́ber, lī́bera, lī́berum - free (5)
mágnus, mágna, mágnum - large, great; important (2)
málus, mála, málum - bad, wicked, evil (4)
méus, méa, méum - my (2)
múltus, múlta, múltum - much, many (2)
neúter, neútra, neútrum - not either, neither (9)
nóster, nóstra, nóstrum - our, ours (5)
nóvus, nóva, nóvum - new; strange (7)
nū́llus, nū́lla, nū́llum - not any, no, none (9)
párvus, párva, párvum - small, little (4)
paúcī, paúcae, paúca - few, a few (3)

perpétuus, perpétua, perpétuum perpetual, lasting, uninterrupted, continuous (6)
plḗnus, plḗna, plḗnum - full, abundant, generous (6)
púlcher, púlchra, púlchrum - beautiful, handsome; fine (5)
Rōmā́nus, Rōmā́na, Rōmā́num - Roman (3)
sálvus, sálva, sálvum - safe, sound (6)
sā́nus, sā́na, sā́num - sound, healthy, sane (5)
secúndus, secúnda, secúndum - second; favorable (6)
sṓlus, sṓla, sṓlum - alone, only, the only (9)
stúltus, stúlta, stúltum - foolish (4)
tṓtus, tṓta, tṓtum - whole, entire (9)
túus, túa, túum - your *(sing.)* (2)
ū́llus, ū́lla, ū́llum - any (9)
ū́nus, ū́na, ū́num - one, single, alone (9)
úter, útra, útrum - either, which (of two) (9)
vḗrus, vḗra, vḗrum - true, real, proper (4)
véster, véstra, véstrum - your *(pl.)* (6)

Indeclinable
sátis - enough, sufficient (5)

Verbs

1st Conjugation
ádiuvō, adiuvā́re, adiū́vī, adiū́tum - to help, aid, assist; to please (4)
ámō, amā́re, amā́vī, amā́tum - to love, like (1)
cḗnō, cēnā́re, cēnā́vī, cēnā́tum - to dine (5)
cṓgitō, cōgitā́re, cōgitā́vī, cōgitā́tum- to think, ponder, consider, plan (1)
cōnsérvō, cōnservā́re, cōnservā́vī, cōnservā́tum - to preserve, conserve, maintain (1)
créō, creā́re, creā́vī, creā́tum - to create (12)
cúlpō, culpā́re, culpā́vī, culpā́tum - to blame, censure (5)
dēmṓnstrō, dēmōnstrā́re, dēmōnstrā́vī, dēmōnstrā́tum to point out, show, demonstrate (8)
dō, dáre, dédī, dátum - to give, offer (1)
érrō, errā́re, errā́vī, errā́tum - to wander; err, go astray, make a mistake, be mistaken (1)
iúvō, iuvā́re, iū́vī, iū́tum - to help, aid, assist; to please (4)
laúdō, laudā́re, laudā́vī, laudā́tum - to praise (1)
nécō, necā́re, necā́vī, necā́tum - to murder, kill (7)
sátiō, satiā́re, satiā́vī, satiā́tum - to satisfy, sate (3)
sérvō, servā́re, servā́vī, servā́tum - to preserve, save, keep, guard (1)
súperō, superā́re, superā́vī, superā́tum - to be above, have the upper hand, surpass; overcome, conquer (5)
tólerō, tolerā́re, tolerā́vī, tolerā́tum - to bear, endure (6)
vócō, vocā́re, vocā́vī, vocā́tum - to call, summon (1)

2nd Conjugation
aúdeō, audḗre, aúsus sum - to dare (7)
dḗbeō, dēbḗre, dḗbuī, dḗbitum - to owe; ought, must, should (1)
dóceō, docḗre, dócuī, dóctum - to teach (8)
hábeō, habḗre, hábuī, hábitum - to have, hold, possess; consider, regard (3)
máneō, manḗre, mā́nsī, mā́nsum - to remain, stay, stay behind, abide, continue (5)
móneō, monḗre, mónuī, mónitum - to remind, advise, warn (1)
remáneō, remanḗre, remā́nsī, remā́nsum - to remain, stay, stay behind, abide, continue (5)
sálvē, salvḗte - hello, greetings (1)
sálveō, salvḗre - to be well, be in good health (1)
térreō, terrḗre, térruī, térritum - to frighten, terrify (1)
válē, valḗte - good-bye, farewell (1)
váleō, valḗre, váluī, valitū́rum - to be strong, have power; be well (1)
vídeō, vidḗre, vī́dī, vī́sum - to see; observe, understand (1)

3rd Conjugation
ágō, ágere, ḗgī, ā́ctum - to drive, lead, do, act; pass, spend *(life or time)* (8)
āmíttō, āmíttere, āmī́sī, āmíssum - to send away; lose, let go (12)
cádō, cádere, cécidī, cāsū́rum - to fall (12)
dī́cō, dī́cere, dī́xī, díctum - to say, tell, speak; name, call (10)
díscō, díscere, dídicī - to learn (8)

dū́cō, dū́cere, dū́xī, dúctum - to lead; consider, regard; prolong (8)
gérō, gérere, géssī, géstum - to carry; carry on, manage, conduct, wage, accomplish, perform (8)
intéllegō, intellégere, intellḗxī, intellḗctum - to understand (11)
míttō, míttere, mī́sī, míssum - to send, let go (11)
scrī́bō, scrī́bere, scrī́psī, scrī́ptum to write, compose (8)
tráhō, tráhere, trā́xī, tráctum - to draw, drag; derive, acquire (8)
víncō, víncere, vī́cī, víctum - to conquer, overcome (8)
vī́vō, vī́vere, vī́xī, vī́ctum - to live (10)

3rd Conjugation -iō
cápiō, cápere, cḗpī, cáptum - to take, capture, seize, get (10)
fáciō, fácere, fḗcī, fáctum - to make, do, accomplish (10)
fúgiō, fúgere, fū́gī, fugitū́rum - to flee, hurry away; escape; go into exile; avoid, shun (10)

4th Conjugation
aúdiō, audī́re, audī́vī, audī́tum - to hear, listen to (10)
invéniō, invenī́re, invḗnī, invéntum - to come upon, find (10)
séntiō, sentī́re, sḗnsī, sḗnsum - to feel, perceive, think, experience (11)
véniō, venī́re, vḗnī, véntum - to come (10)

Irregular
póssum, pósse, pótuī - to be able, can, could, have power (6)
sum, ésse, fúī, futū́rum - to be, exist (4)

Adverbs

béne - well, satisfactorily, quite (11)
crās - tomorrow (5)
díū - long, for a long time (12)
étiam - even, also (11)
héri - yesterday (5)
hódiē - today (3)
íbi - there (6)
nímis, nímium - too, too much, excessively; *(in a positive sense, esp. with adjectives and adverbs)* exceedingly, very (9)
nōn - not (1)
númquam - never (8)
nunc - now, at present (6)
nū́per - recently (12)
quándō - when (5)
quā́rē - because of which thing *(lit.)*; therefore, wherefore, why (6)
saépe - often (1)
sátis - enough, sufficiently (5)
sémper - always (3)
támen - nevertheless, still (8)
tum - then, at that time; thereupon, in the next place (5)
úbi - where, when (6)

Conjunctions

aútem - however; moreover (11)
dum - while, as long as, at the same time that; *or* until *(+subjunctive)* (8)
énim - for, in fact, truly (9)
et - and; even (2)
et . . . et - both . . . and (2)
ígitur - therefore, consequently (5)
néque, nec - and not, nor (11)
néque . . . néque, nec . . . nec - neither . . . nor (11)
quod - because (11)
quóniam - since, inasmuch as (10)
sed - but (2)
sī - if (1)

Prepositions

ad (+acc.) - to, up to, near to (8)
cum (+abl.) - with (10)
dē (+abl.) - down from, from; concerning, about (3)
ex, ē (abl.+) - out of, from, from within; by reason of, on account of; of *(after cardinal numerals)* (8)
in (+acc.) - into, toward; against (9)
in (+abl.) - in, on (3)
post (+acc.) - after, behind (7)
prō (+abl.) - in front of, before, on behalf of, for the sake of, in return for, instead of, for, as (12)
própter (+acc.) - on account of, because of (5)
síne (+abl.) - without (2)
sub (+abl. w/ verbs of rest *or* **+acc. w/ verbs of motion)** - under, up under, close to, down to/into, to/at the foot of (7)

Interjection

ō - O!, Oh! (2)

Idioms

amā́bō tē - please (1)
grā́tiās ágere (+dat.) - to thank someone; to give thanks to (8)
nōn sṓlum . . . sed étiam - not only . . . but also (9)
poénās dáre - to pay the penalty (2)
sī quándō - if ever (5)

Suffixes

-ne – interrogative suffix attached to the first word of a sentence, typically the verb or another word on which the question hinges, to introduce a question whose answer is uncertain (5)

-que - and *(enclitic conjunction; appended to the second of two words to be joined)* (6)

Chapter 13

Nouns

1st Declension

adulēscéntia, adulēscéntiae (f) - youth, young manhood; youthfulness (5)
agrícola, agrícolae (m) - farmer (3)
amíca, amícae (f) - friend (female) (3)
amīcítia, amīcítiae (f) - friendship (10)
Ásia, Ásiae (f) - Asia (12)
cṓpia, cṓpiae (f) - abundance, supply (8)
cṓpiae, cōpiā́rum (f) - supplies, troops, forces (8)
cúlpa, cúlpae (f) - fault, blame (5)
cū́ra, cū́rae (f) - care, attention, caution, anxiety (4)
déa, déae (f) - goddess (6)
discípula, discípulae (f) - learner, pupil, student (female) (6)
dīvítiae, dīvitiā́rum (f. pl.) - riches, wealth (13)
fā́ma, fā́mae (f) - rumor, report; fame, reputation (2)
fḗmina, fḗminae (f) - woman (3)
fī́lia, fī́liae (f) - daughter (3)
fṓrma, fṓrmae (f) - form, shape; beauty (2)
fortū́na, fortū́nae (f) - fortune, luck (2)
glṓria, glṓriae (f) - glory, fame (5)
hṓra, hṓrae (f) - hour, time (10)
īnsídiae, īnsidiā́rum (f) - ambush, plot, treachery (6)
ī́ra, ī́rae (f) - ire, anger (2)
líttera, lítterae (f) - a letter of the alphabet (7)
lítterae, litterā́rum (f) - a letter (epistle), literature (7)
magístra, magístrae (f) - schoolmistress, teacher, mistress (4)
médica, médicae (f) - doctor, physician (female) (12)
móra, mórae (f) - delay (4)
nātū́ra, nātū́rae (f) - nature (10)
naúta, naútae (m) - sailor (2)
patiéntia, patiéntiae (f) - suffering; patience, endurance (12)
pátria, pátriae (f) - fatherland, native land, (one's) country (2)
pecū́nia, pecū́niae (f) - money (2)
philosóphia, philosóphiae (f) - philosophy (2)
poéna, poénae (f) - penalty, punishment (2)
poḗta, poḗtae (m) - poet (2)
pórta, pórtae (f) - gate, entrance (2)
puélla, puéllae (f) - girl (2)
rēgī́na, rēgī́nae (f) - queen (7)
rósa, rósae (f) - rose (2)
sapiéntia, sapiéntiae (f) - wisdom (3)
sententia, senténtiae (f) - feeling, thought, opinion, vote, sentence (2)
térra, térrae (f) - earth, ground, land, country (7)
vía, víae (f) - way, road, street (10)
victṓria, victṓriae (f) - victory (8)
vī́ta, vī́tae (f) - life; mode of life (2)

2nd Declension

áger, ágrī (m) - field, farm (3)
amī́cus, amī́cī (m) - friend (male) (3)
ánimī, animṓrum (m) - high spirits, pride, courage (5)
ánimus, ánimī (m) - soul, spirit, mind (5)
ánnus, ánnī (m) - year (12)
bā́sium, bā́siī (n) - kiss (4)
béllum, béllī (n) - war (4)
caélum, caélī (n) - sky, heaven (5)
cōnsílium, cōnsíliī (n) - plan, purpose, counsel, advice, judgment, wisdom (4)
déus, déī (m) - god (6)
discípulus, discípulī (m) - learner, pupil, student (male) (6)
dṓnum, dṓnī (n) - gift, present (4)
exítium, exítiī (n) - destruction, ruin (4)
fáctum, fáctī (n) - deed, act, achievement (13)
fī́lius, fī́liī (m) - son (3)
Graécus, Graécī (m) - a Greek (6)
líber, líbrī (m) - book (6)
lóca, locṓrum (n) - places, region (9)
lócī, locṓrum (m) - passages in literature (9)
lócus, lócī (m) - place; passage in literature (9)
magíster, magístrī (m) - schoolmaster, teacher, master (4)
médicus, médicī (m) - doctor, physician (male) (12)
mórbus, mórbī (m) - disease, sickness (9)
númerus, númerī (m) - number (3)
óculus, óculī (m) - eye (4)
offícium, offíciī (n) - duty, service (4)
ṓtium, ṓtiī (n) - leisure, peace (4)
perī́culum, perī́culī (n) - danger, risk (4)
pópulus, pópulī (m) - the people, a people, a nation (3)
prīncípium, prīncípiī (n) - beginning (12)
púer, púerī (m) - boy; boys, children *(pl.)* (3)

remédium, remédiī (n) - cure, remedy (4)
sígnum, sígnī (n) - sign, signal, indication; seal (13)
stúdium, stúdiī (n) - eagerness, zeal, pursuit, study (9)
stúltus, stúltī (m) - a fool (4)
tyránnus, tyránnī (m) - absolute ruler, tyrant (6)
vérbum, vérbī (n)- word (5)
vir, vírī (m) - man, hero (3)
vítium, vítiī (n) - fault, crime, vice (6)

3rd Declension
adulḗscēns, adulēscéntis (m *or* f) - young man *or* woman (12)
ámor, amṓris (m) - love (7)
Caésar, Caésaris (m) - Caesar (12)
cáput, cápitis (n) - head; leader; beginning; life; heading; chapter (11)
cármen, cárminis (n) - song, poem (7)
Cícerō, Cicerṓnis (m) - (Marcus Tullius) Cicero (8)
cī́vitās, cīvitā́tis (f) - state, citizenship (7)
cṓnsul, cṓnsulis (m) - consul (11)
córpus, córporis (n) - body (7)
cupíditās, cupiditā́tis (f) - desire, longing, passion; cupidity, avarice (10)
frā́ter, frā́tris (m) - brother (8)
hómō, hóminis (m) - human being, man (7)
lábor, labṓris (m)- labor, work, toil; a work, production (7)
laus, laúdis (f) - praise, glory, fame (8)
lībértās, lībertā́tis (f) - liberty (8)
mā́ter, mā́tris (f) - mother (12)
mṓrēs, mṓrum (m) - habits, morals, character (7)
mōs, mṓris (m) - habit, custom, manner (7)
nḗmō, nūllī́us, nḗminī, nḗminem, nū́llō, nū́llā (m *or* f) - no one, nobody (11)
nṓmen, nṓminis (n) - name (7)
páter, pátris (m) - father (12)
pāx, pā́cis (f) - peace (7)
rátiō, ratiṓnis (f) - reckoning, account; reason, judgment, consideration; system; manner, method (8)
rēx, rḗgis (m) - king (7)
scrī́ptor, scrīptṓris (m) - writer, author (8)
senéctūs, senectū́tis (f) - old age (10)
sóror, sorṓris (f) - sister (8)
témpus, témporis (n) - time; occasion, opportunity (7)
tímor, timṓris (m) - fear (10)
úxor, uxṓris (f) - wife (7)
vḗritās, vēritā́tis (f) - truth (10)
vírgō, vírginis (f) - maiden, virgin (7)
vírtūs, virtū́tis (f) - manliness, courage; excellence, character, worth, virtue (7)
volúptās, voluptā́tis (f) - pleasure (10)

Indeclinable
níhil - nothing (1)
sátis - enough (5)

Pronouns

égo, méī - I (11)
hic, haec, hoc - this; the latter; he, she, it, they (9)
ī́dem, éadem, ídem - the same (11)
ílle, ílla, íllud - that; the former; the famous; he, she, it, they (9)
ípse, ípsa, ípsum - myself, yourself, himself, herself, itself, *etc.*, the very, the actual (13)
is, éa, id - this, that; he, she, it (11)
íste, ísta, ístud - that of yours, that; such (as you have, as you speak of); *sometimes with contemptuous force, e.g.,* that despicable, that wretched (9)
quid - what (1)
quísque, quídque, cuiúsque, cuíque - each one, each person, each thing (13)
súī - himself, herself, itself, themselves (13)
tū, túī - you *(sing.)* (11)

Adjectives

acérbus, acérba, acérbum - harsh, bitter, grievous (12)
áliī . . . áliī - some . . . others (9)
álius, ália, áliud - other, another (9)
álter, áltera, álterum - the other (of two), second (9)
amī́cus, amī́ca, amī́cum - friendly (11)
antī́quus, antī́qua, antī́quum - ancient, old-time (2)
avā́rus, avā́ra, avā́rum - greedy, avaricious (3)
beā́tus, beā́ta, beā́tum - happy, fortunate, blessed (10)
béllus, bélla, béllum - pretty, handsome, charming (4)
bónus, bóna, bónum - good, kind (4)
cā́rus, cā́ra, cā́rum - dear (11)
dóctus, dócta, dóctum - taught, learned, skilled (13)
fortūnā́tus, fortūnā́ta, fortūnā́tum - lucky, fortunate, happy (13)
Graécus, Graéca, Graécum - Greek (6)
hūmā́nus, hūmā́na, hūmā́num - pertaining to man, human; humane, kind; refined, cultivated (4)
lī́ber, lī́bera, lī́berum - free (5)

mágnus, mágna, mágnum - large, great; important (2)
málus, mála, málum - bad, wicked, evil (4)
méus, méa, méum - my (2)
múltus, múlta, múltum - much, many (2)
neúter, neútra, neútrum - not either, neither (9)
nóster, nóstra, nóstrum - our, ours (5)
nóvus, nóva, nóvum - new; strange (7)
nū́llus, nū́lla, nū́llum - not any, no, none (9)
párvus, párva, párvum - small, little (4)
paúcī, paúcae, paúca - few, a few (3)
perpétuus, perpétua, perpétuum perpetual, lasting, uninterrupted, continuous (6)
plḗnus, plḗna, plḗnum - full, abundant, generous (6)
púlcher, púlchra, púlchrum - beautiful, handsome; fine (5)
Rōmā́nus, Rōmā́na, Rōmā́num - Roman (3)
sálvus, sálva, sálvum - safe, sound (6)
sā́nus, sā́na, sā́num - sound, healthy, sane (5)
secúndus, secúnda, secúndum - second; favorable (6)
sṓlus, sṓla, sṓlum - alone, only, the only (9)
stúltus, stúlta, stúltum - foolish (4)
súus, súa, súum - his own, her own, its own, their own (13)
tṓtus, tṓta, tṓtum - whole, entire (9)
túus, túa, túum - your *(sing.)* (2)
ū́llus, ū́lla, ū́llum - any (9)
ū́nus, ū́na, ū́num - one, single, alone (9)
úter, útra, útrum - either, which (of two) (9)
vḗrus, vḗra, vḗrum - true, real, proper (4)
véster, véstra, véstrum - your *(pl.)* (6)

Indeclinable
sátis - enough, sufficient (5)

Verbs

1st Conjugation
ádiuvō, adiuvā́re, adiū́vī, adiū́tum - to help, aid, assist; to please (4)
ámō, amā́re, amā́vī, amā́tum - to love, like (1)
cḗnō, cēnā́re, cēnā́vī, cēnā́tum - to dine (5)
cṓgitō, cōgitā́re, cōgitā́vī, cōgitā́tum- to think, ponder, consider, plan (1)
cōnsérvō, cōnservā́re, cōnservā́vī, cōnservā́tum - to preserve, conserve, maintain (1)
créō, creā́re, creā́vī, creā́tum - to create (12)
cúlpō, culpā́re, culpā́vī, culpā́tum - to blame, censure (5)
dēmṓnstrō, dēmōnstrā́re, dēmōnstrā́vī, dēmōnstrā́tum to point out, show, demonstrate (8)
dō, dáre, dédī, dátum - to give, offer (1)
érrō, errā́re, errā́vī, errā́tum - to wander; err, go astray, make a mistake, be mistaken (1)
iúvō, iuvā́re, iū́vī, iū́tum - to help, aid, assist; to please (4)
laúdō, laudā́re, laudā́vī, laudā́tum - to praise (1)
nécō, necā́re, necā́vī, necā́tum - to murder, kill (7)
sátiō, satiā́re, satiā́vī, satiā́tum - to satisfy, sate (3)
sérvō, servā́re, servā́vī, servā́tum - to preserve, save, keep, guard (1)
stō, stā́re, stétī, státum - to stand, stand still *or* firm (13)
súperō, superā́re, superā́vī, superā́tum - to be above, have the upper hand, surpass; overcome, conquer (5)
tólerō, tolerā́re, tolerā́vī, tolerā́tum - to bear, endure (6)
vócō, vocā́re, vocā́vī, vocā́tum - to call, summon (1)

2nd Conjugation
aúdeō, audḗre, aúsus sum - to dare (7)
débeō, dēbḗre, dḗbuī, dḗbitum - to owe; ought, must, should (1)
dóceō, docḗre, dócuī, dóctum - to teach (8)
hábeō, habḗre, hábuī, hábitum - to have, hold, possess; consider, regard (3)
máneō, manḗre, mā́nsī, mā́nsum - to remain, stay, stay behind, abide, continue (5)
móneō, monḗre, mónuī, mónitum - to remind, advise, warn (1)
remáneō, remanḗre, remā́nsī, remā́nsum - to remain, stay, stay behind, abide, continue (5)
sálvē, salvḗte - hello, greetings (1)
sálveō, salvḗre - to be well, be in good health (1)
térreō, terrḗre, térruī, térritum - to frighten, terrify (1)
válē, valḗte - good-bye, farewell (1)

váleō, valḗre, váluī, valitū́rum - to be strong, have power; be well (1)

vídeō, vidḗre, vī́dī, vī́sum - to see; observe, understand (1)

3rd Conjugation

ágō, ágere, ḗgī, ā́ctum - to drive, lead, do, act; pass, spend *(life or time)* (8)

álō, álere, áluī, áltum - to nourish, support, sustain, increase; cherish (13)

āmíttō, āmíttere, āmī́sī, āmíssum - to send away; lose, let go (12)

cádō, cádere, cécidī, cāsū́rum - to fall (12)

dī́cō, dī́cere, dī́xī, díctum - to say, tell, speak; name, call (10)

dī́ligō, dīlígere, dīlḗxī, dīlḗctum - to esteem, love (13)

díscō, díscere, dídicī - to learn (8)

dū́cō, dū́cere, dū́xī, dúctum - to lead; consider, regard; prolong (8)

gérō, gérere, géssī, géstum - to carry; carry on, manage, conduct, wage, accomplish, perform (8)

intéllegō, intellégere, intellḗxī, intellḗctum - to understand (11)

iúngō, iúngere, iū́nxī, iū́nctum - to join (13)

míttō, míttere, mī́sī, míssum - to send, let go (11)

scrī́bō, scrī́bere, scrī́psī, scrī́ptum to write, compose (8)

tráhō, tráhere, trā́xī, tráctum - to draw, drag; derive, acquire (8)

víncō, víncere, vī́cī, víctum - to conquer, overcome (8)

vī́vō, vī́vere, vī́xī, vī́ctum - to live (10)

3rd Conjugation -iō

cápiō, cápere, cḗpī, cáptum - to take, capture, seize, get (10)

fáciō, fácere, fḗcī, fáctum - to make, do, accomplish (10)

fúgiō, fúgere, fū́gī, fugitū́rum - to flee, hurry away; escape; go into exile; avoid, shun (10)

4th Conjugation

aúdiō, audī́re, audī́vī, audī́tum - to hear, listen to (10)

invéniō, invenī́re, invḗnī, invéntum - to come upon, find (10)

séntiō, sentī́re, sḗnsī, sḗnsum - to feel, perceive, think, experience (11)

véniō, venī́re, vḗnī, véntum - to come (10)

Irregular

póssum, pósse, pótuī - to be able, can, could, have power (6)

sum, ésse, fúī, futū́rum - to be, exist (4)

Adverbs

ánte (+acc.) - before, previously (13)

béne - well, satisfactorily, quite (11)

crās - tomorrow (5)

díū - long, for a long time (12)

étiam - even, also (11)

héri - yesterday (5)

hódiē - today (3)

íbi - there (6)

nímis, nímium - too, too much, excessively; *(in a positive sense, esp. with adjectives and adverbs)* exceedingly, very (9)

nōn - not (1)

númquam - never (8)

nunc - now, at present (6)

nū́per - recently (12)

ṓlim - once (upon a time), long ago, formerly; some day, in the future (13)

quándō - when (5)

quā́rē - because of which thing *(lit.)*; therefore, wherefore, why (6)

saépe - often (1)

sátis - enough, sufficiently (5)

sémper - always (3)

támen - nevertheless, still (8)

tum - then, at that time; thereupon, in the next place (5)

úbi - where, when (6)

Conjunctions

aútem - however; moreover (11)

dum while, as long as, at the same time that; *or* until *(+subjunctive)* (8)

énim - for, in fact, truly (9)

et - and; even (2)

et . . . et - both . . . and (2)

ígitur - therefore, consequently (5)

nam - for (13)

néque, nec - and not, nor (11)

néque . . . néque, nec . . . nec - neither . . . nor (11)

quod - because (11)

quóniam - since, inasmuch as (10)

sed - but (2)

sī - if (1)

Prepositions

ad (+acc.) - to, up to, near to (8)

ánte (+acc.) - before *(in place or time)*, in front of (13)

cum (+abl.) - with (10)

dē (+abl.) - down from, from; concerning, about (3)

ex, ē (abl.+) - out of, from, from within; by reason of, on account of ; of *(after cardinal numerals)* (8)
in (+acc.) - into, toward; against (9)
in (+abl.) - in, on (3)
per (+acc.) - through; by *(with reflexive pronoun)* (13)
post (+acc.) - after, behind (7)
prō (+abl.) - in front of, before, on behalf of, for the sake of, in return for, instead of, for, as (12)
própter (+acc.) - on account of, because of (5)
síne (+abl.) - without (2)
sub (+abl. w/ verbs of rest *or* **+acc. w/ verbs of motion)** - under, up under, close to, down to/into, to/at the foot of (7)

Interjection

ō - O!, Oh! (2)

Idioms

amā́bō tē - please (1)
grā́tiās ágere (+dat.) - to thank someone; to give thanks to (8)
nōn sṓlum . . . sed étiam - not only . . . but also (9)
poénās dáre - to pay the penalty (2)
sī quándō - if ever (5)

Suffixes

-ne – interrogative suffix attached to the first word of a sentence, typically the verb or another word on which the question hinges, to introduce a question whose answer is uncertain (5)
-que - and *(enclitic conjunction; appended to the second of two words to be joined)* (6)

Chapter 14

Nouns

1st Declension

adulēscéntia, adulēscéntiae (f) - youth, young manhood; youthfulness (5)
agrícola, agrícolae (m) - farmer (3)
amī́ca, amī́cae (f) - friend (female) (3)
amīcítia, amīcítiae (f) - friendship (10)
áqua, áquae (f) - water (14)
Ásia, Ásiae (f) - Asia (12)
cṓpia, cṓpiae (f) - abundance, supply (8)
cṓpiae, cōpiā́rum (f) - supplies, troops, forces (8)
cúlpa, cúlpae (f) - fault, blame (5)
cū́ra, cū́rae (f) - care, attention, caution, anxiety (4)
déa, déae (f) - goddess (6)
discípula, discípulae (f) - learner, pupil, student (female) (6)
dīvítiae, dīvitiā́rum (f. pl.) - riches, wealth (13)
fā́ma, fā́mae (f) - rumor, report; fame, reputation (2)
fḗmina, fḗminae (f) - woman (3)
fī́lia, fī́liae (f) - daughter (3)
fṓrma, fṓrmae (f) - form, shape; beauty (2)
fortū́na, fortū́nae (f) - fortune, luck (2)
glṓria, glṓriae (f) - glory, fame (5)
hṓra, hṓrae (f) - hour, time (10)
īnsídiae, īnsidiā́rum (f) - ambush, plot, treachery (6)
ī́ra, ī́rae (f) - ire, anger (2)
líttera, lítterae (f) - a letter of the alphabet (7)
lítterae, litterā́rum (f) - a letter (epistle), literature (7)
magístra, magístrae (f) - schoolmistress, teacher, mistress (4)
médica, médicae (f) - doctor, physician (female) (12)
móra, mórae (f) - delay (4)
nātū́ra, nātū́rae (f) - nature (10)
naúta, naútae (m) - sailor (2)
patiéntia, patiéntiae (f) - suffering; patience, endurance (12)
pátria, pátriae (f) - fatherland, native land, (one's) country (2)
pecū́nia, pecū́niae (f) - money (2)
philosóphia, philosóphiae (f) - philosophy (2)
poéna, poénae (f) - penalty, punishment (2)
poḗta, poḗtae (m) - poet (2)
pórta, pórtae (f) - gate, entrance (2)
puélla, puéllae (f) - girl (2)
rēgī́na, rēgī́nae (f) - queen (7)
Rṓma, Rṓmae (f) - Rome (14)
rósa, rósae (f) - rose (2)
sapiéntia, sapiéntiae (f) - wisdom (3)
senténtia, senténtiae (f) - feeling, thought, opinion, vote, sentence (2)
térra, térrae (f) - earth, ground, land, country (7)
túrba, túrbae (f) - uproar, disturbance; mob, crowd, multitude (14)
vía, víae (f) - way, road, street (10)
victṓria, victṓriae (f) - victory (8)
vī́ta, vī́tae (f) - life; mode of life (2)

2nd Declension

áger, ágrī (m) - field, farm (3)
amī́cus, amī́cī (m) - friend (male) (3)
ánimī, animṓrum (m) - high spirits, pride, courage (5)
ánimus, ánimī (m) - soul, spirit, mind (5)
ánnus, ánnī (m) - year (12)
bā́sium, bā́siī (n) - kiss (4)
béllum, béllī (n) - war (4)
caélum, caélī (n) - sky, heaven (5)
cōnsílium, cōnsíliī (n) - plan, purpose, counsel, advice, judgment, wisdom (4)
déus, déī (m) - god (6)
discípulus, discípulī (m) - learner, pupil, student (male) (6)
dṓnum, dṓnī (n) - gift, present (4)
exítium, exítiī (n) - destruction, ruin (4)
fáctum, fáctī (n) - deed, act, achievement (13)
fī́lius, fī́liī (m) - son (3)
Graécus, Graécī (m) - a Greek (6)
líber, líbrī (m) - book (6)
lóca, locṓrum (n) - places, region (9)
lócī, locṓrum (m) - passages in literature (9)
lócus, lócī (m) - place; passage in literature (9)
magíster, magístrī (m) - schoolmaster, teacher, master (4)
médicus, médicī (m) - doctor, physician (male) (12)
mórbus, mórbī (m) - disease, sickness (9)
númerus, númerī (m) - number (3)
óculus, óculī (m) - eye (4)
offícium, offíciī (n) - duty, service (4)
ṓtium, ṓtiī (n) - leisure, peace (4)
perī́culum, perī́culī (n) - danger, risk (4)
pópulus, pópulī (m) - the people, a people, a nation (3)

prīncípium, prīncípiī (n) - beginning (12)
púer, púerī (m) - boy; boys, children *(pl.)* (3)
remédium, remédiī (n) - cure, remedy (4)
sígnum, sígnī (n) - sign, signal, indication; seal (13)
stúdium, stúdiī (n) - eagerness, zeal, pursuit, study (9)
stúltus, stúltī (m) - a fool (4)
tyránnus, tyránnī (m) - absolute ruler, tyrant (6)
vérbum, vérbī (n)- word (5)
vir, vírī (m) - man, hero (3)
vítium, vítiī (n) - fault, crime, vice (6)

3rd Declension
adulḗscēns, adulēscéntis (m *or* f) - young man *or* woman (12)
ámor, amṓris (m) - love (7)
Caésar, Caésaris (m) - Caesar (12)
cáput, cápitis (n) - head; leader; beginning; life; heading; chapter (11)
cármen, cárminis (n) - song, poem (7)
Cícerō, Cicerṓnis (m) - (Marcus Tullius) Cicero (8)
cī́vitās, cīvitā́tis (f) - state, citizenship (7)
cṓnsul, cṓnsulis (m) - consul (11)
córpus, córporis (n) - body (7)
cupíditās, cupiditā́tis (f) - desire, longing, passion; cupidity, avarice (10)
frā́ter, frā́tris (m) - brother (8)
hómō, hóminis (m) - human being, man (7)
iūs, iū́ris (n) - right, justice, law (14)
lábor, labṓris (m)- labor, work, toil; a work, production (7)
laus, laúdis (f) - praise, glory, fame (8)
lībértās, lībertā́tis (f) - liberty (8)
mā́ter, mā́tris (f) - mother (12)
mṓrēs, mṓrum (m) - habits, morals, character (7)
mōs, mṓris (m) - habit, custom, manner (7)
nḗmō, nūllī́us, nḗminī, nḗminem, nū́llō, nū́llā (m *or* f) - no one, nobody (11)
nṓmen, nṓminis (n) - name (7)
ōs, ṓris (n) - mouth, face (14)
páter, pátris (m) - father (12)
pāx, pā́cis (f) - peace (7)
rátiō, ratiṓnis (f) - reckoning, account; reason, judgment, consideration; system; manner, method (8)
rēx, rḗgis (m) - king (7)
scrī́ptor, scrīptṓris (m) - writer, author (8)
senéctūs, senectū́tis (f) - old age (10)
sóror, sorṓris (f) - sister (8)
témpus, témporis (n) - time; occasion, opportunity (7)
tímor, timṓris (m) - fear (10)
úxor, uxṓris (f) - wife (7)
vḗritās, vēritā́tis (f) - truth (10)
vírgō, vírginis (f) - maiden, virgin (7)
vírtūs, virtū́tis (f) - manliness, courage; excellence, character, worth, virtue (7)
volúptās, voluptā́tis (f) - pleasure (10)

3rd Declension I-Stem
ánimal, animā́lis (n) - a living creature, animal (14)
ars, ártis (f) - art, skill (14)
aúris, aúris (f) - ear (14)
cī́vis, cī́vis (m *or* f) - citizen (14)
máre, máris (n) - sea (14)
mors, mórtis (f) - death (14)
nū́bēs, nū́bis (f) - cloud (14)
pars, pártis (f) - part, share; direction (14)
urbs, úrbis (f) - city (14)
vī́rēs, vī́rium (f. pl.) - strength (14)
vīs, vīs (f) - force, power, violence (14)

Indeclinable
níhil - nothing (1)
sátis - enough (5)

Pronouns
égo, méī - I (11)
hic, haec, hoc - this; the latter; he, she, it, they (9)
ī́dem, éadem, ídem - the same (11)
ílle, ílla, íllud - that; the former; the famous; he, she, it, they (9)
ípse, ípsa, ípsum - myself, yourself, himself, herself, itself, *etc.,* the very, the actual (13)
is, éa, id - this, that; he, she, it (11)
íste, ísta, ístud - that of yours, that; such (as you have, as you speak of); *sometimes with contemptuous force, e.g.,* that despicable, that wretched (9)
quid - what (1)
quísque, quídque, cuiúsque, cuíque - each one, each person, each thing (13)
súī - himself, herself, itself, themselves (13)
tū, túī - you *(sing.)* (11)

Adjectives
acérbus, acérba, acérbum - harsh, bitter, grievous (12)
áliī . . . áliī - some . . . others (9)
álius, ália, áliud - other, another (9)
álter, áltera, álterum - the other (of two), second (9)
amī́cus, amī́ca, amī́cum - friendly (11)

antíquus, antíqua, antíquum - ancient, old-time (2)
avárus, avára, avárum - greedy, avaricious (3)
beátus, beáta, beátum - happy, fortunate, blessed (10)
béllus, bélla, béllum - pretty, handsome, charming (4)
bónus, bóna, bónum - good, kind (4)
cárus, cára, cárum - dear (11)
dóctus, dócta, dóctum - taught, learned, skilled (13)
fortūnátus, fortūnáta, fortūnátum - lucky, fortunate, happy (13)
Graécus, Graéca, Graécum - Greek (6)
hūmánus, hūmána, hūmánum - pertaining to man, human; humane, kind; refined, cultivated (4)
líber, líbera, líberum - free (5)
mágnus, mágna, mágnum - large, great; important (2)
málus, mála, málum - bad, wicked, evil (4)
méus, méa, méum - my (2)
múltus, múlta, múltum - much, many (2)
neúter, neútra, neútrum - not either, neither (9)
nóster, nóstra, nóstrum - our, ours (5)
nóvus, nóva, nóvum - new; strange (7)
núllus, núlla, núllum - not any, no, none (9)
párvus, párva, párvum - small, little (4)
paúcī, paúcae, paúca - few, a few (3)
perpétuus, perpétua, perpétuum perpetual, lasting, uninterrupted, continuous (6)
plénus, pléna, plénum - full, abundant, generous (6)
púlcher, púlchra, púlchrum - beautiful, handsome; fine (5)
Rōmánus, Rōmána, Rōmánum - Roman (3)
sálvus, sálva, sálvum - safe, sound (6)
sánus, sána, sánum - sound, healthy, sane (5)
secúndus, secúnda, secúndum - second; favorable (6)
sólus, sóla, sólum - alone, only, the only (9)
stúltus, stúlta, stúltum - foolish (4)
súus, súa, súum - his own, her own, its own, their own (13)
tótus, tóta, tótum - whole, entire (9)
túus, túa, túum - your *(sing.)* (2)
úllus, úlla, úllum - any (9)
únus, úna, únum - one, single, alone (9)
úter, útra, útrum - either, which (of two) (9)
vérus, véra, vérum - true, real, proper (4)
véster, véstra, véstrum - your *(pl.)* (6)

Indeclinable
sátis - enough, sufficient (5)

Verbs

1st Conjugation
ádiuvō, adiuváre, adiúvī, adiútum - to help, aid, assist; to please (4)
ámō, amáre, amávī, amátum - to love, like (1)
appéllō, appelláre, appellávī, appellátum - to speak to, address (as), call, name (14)
cénō, cēnáre, cēnávī, cēnátum - to dine (5)
cógitō, cōgitáre, cōgitávī, cōgitátum- to think, ponder, consider, plan (1)
cōnsérvō, cōnserváre, cōnservávī, cōnservátum - to preserve, conserve, maintain (1)
créō, creáre, creávī, creátum - to create (12)
cúlpō, culpáre, culpávī, culpátum - to blame, censure (5)
dēmónstrō, dēmōnstráre, dēmōnstrávī, dēmōnstrátum to point out, show, demonstrate (8)
dō, dáre, dédī, dátum - to give, offer (1)
érrō, erráre, errávī, errátum - to wander; err, go astray, make a mistake, be mistaken (1)
iúvō, iuváre, iúvī, iútum - to help, aid, assist; to please (4)
laúdō, laudáre, laudávī, laudátum - to praise (1)
mútō, mūtáre, mūtávī, mūtátum to change, alter; exchange (14)
nécō, necáre, necávī, necátum - to murder, kill (7)
sátiō, satiáre, satiávī, satiátum - to satisfy, sate (3)
sérvō, serváre, servávī, servátum - to preserve, save, keep, guard (1)
stō, stáre, stétī, státum - to stand, stand still *or* firm (13)
súperō, superáre, superávī, superátum - to be above, have the upper hand, surpass; overcome, conquer (5)
tólerō, toleráre, tolerávī, tolerátum - to bear, endure (6)

vī́tō, vītā́re, vītā́vī, vītā́tum - to avoid, shun (14)
vócō, vocā́re, vocā́vī, vocā́tum - to call, summon (1)

2nd Conjugation

aúdeō, audḗre, aúsus sum - to dare (7)
dḗbeō, dēbḗre, dḗbuī, dḗbitum - to owe; ought, must, should (1)
dóceō, docḗre, dócuī, dóctum - to teach (8)
hábeō, habḗre, hábuī, hábitum - to have, hold, possess; consider, regard (3)
máneō, manḗre, mā́nsī, mā́nsum - to remain, stay, stay behind, abide, continue (5)
móneō, monḗre, mónuī, mónitum - to remind, advise, warn (1)
remáneō, remanḗre, remā́nsī, remā́nsum - to remain, stay, stay behind, abide, continue (5)
sálvē, salvḗte - hello, greetings (1)
sálveō, salvḗre - to be well, be in good health (1)
téneō, tenḗre, ténuī, téntum - to hold, keep, possess; restrain (14)
térreō, terrḗre, térruī, térritum - to frighten, terrify (1)
válē, valḗte - good-bye, farewell (1)
váleō, valḗre, váluī, valitū́rum - to be strong, have power; be well (1)
vídeō, vidḗre, vī́dī, vī́sum - to see; observe, understand (1)

3rd Conjugation

ágō, ágere, ḗgī, ā́ctum - to drive, lead, do, act; pass, spend *(life or time)* (8)
álō, álere, áluī, áltum - to nourish, support, sustain, increase; cherish (13)
āmíttō, āmíttere, āmī́sī, āmíssum - to send away; lose, let go (12)
cádō, cádere, cécidī, cāsū́rum - to fall (12)
cúrrō, cúrrere, cucúrrī, cúrsum - to run, rush, move quickly (14)
dī́cō, dī́cere, dī́xī, díctum - to say, tell, speak; name, call (10)
dī́ligō, dīlígere, dīlḗxī, dīlḗctum - to esteem, love (13)
dísco, díscere, dídicī - to learn (8)
dū́cō, dū́cere, dū́xī, dúctum - to lead; consider, regard; prolong (8)
gérō, gérere, géssī, géstum - to carry; carry on, manage, conduct, wage, accomplish, perform (8)
intéllegō, intellégere, intellḗxī, intellḗctum - to understand (11)
iúngō, iúngere, iū́nxī, iū́nctum - to join (13)
míttō, míttere, mī́sī, míssum - to send, let go (11)
scrī́bō, scrī́bere, scrī́psī, scrī́ptum to write, compose (8)
tráhō, tráhere, trā́xī, tráctum - to draw, drag; derive, acquire (8)
víncō, víncere, vī́cī, víctum - to conquer, overcome (8)
vī́vō, vī́vere, vī́xī, vī́ctum - to live (10)

3rd Conjugation -iō

cápiō, cápere, cḗpī, cáptum - to take, capture, seize, get (10)
fáciō, fácere, fḗcī, fáctum - to make, do, accomplish (10)
fúgiō, fúgere, fū́gī, fugitū́rum - to flee, hurry away; escape; go into exile; avoid, shun (10)

4th Conjugation

aúdiō, audī́re, audī́vī, audī́tum - to hear, listen to (10)
invéniō, invenī́re, invḗnī, invéntum - to come upon, find (10)
séntiō, sentī́re, sḗnsī, sḗnsum - to feel, perceive, think, experience (11)
véniō, venī́re, vḗnī, véntum - to come (10)

Irregular

póssum, pósse, pótuī - to be able, can, could, have power (6)
sum, ésse, fúī, futū́rum - to be, exist (4)

Adverbs

ánte (+acc.) - before, previously (13)
béne - well, satisfactorily, quite (11)
crās - tomorrow (5)
díū - long, for a long time (12)
étiam - even, also (11)
héri - yesterday (5)
hódiē - today (3)
íbi - there (6)
nímis, nímium - too, too much, excessively; *(in a positive sense, esp. with adjectives and adverbs)* exceedingly, very (9)
nōn - not (1)
númquam - never (8)
nunc - now, at present (6)
nū́per - recently (12)
ṓlim - once (upon a time), long ago, formerly; some day, in the future (13)
quándō - when (5)

quā́rē - because of which thing *(lit.)*; therefore, wherefore, why (6)
saépe - often (1)
sátis - enough, sufficiently (5)
sémper - always (3)
támen - nevertheless, still (8)
tum - then, at that time; thereupon, in the next place (5)
úbi - where, when (6)

Conjunctions

aútem - however; moreover (11)
dum - while, as long as, at the same time that; *or* until *(+subjunctive)* (8)
énim - for, in fact, truly (9)
et - and; even (2)
et . . . et - both . . . and (2)
ígitur - therefore, consequently (5)
nam - for (13)
néque, nec - and not, nor (11)
néque . . . néque, nec . . . nec - neither . . . nor (11)
quod - because (11)
quóniam - since, inasmuch as (10)
sed - but (2)
sī - if (1)

Prepositions

ab, ā (+abl.) - away from, from; by (14)
ad (+acc.) - to, up to, near to (8)
ánte (+acc.) - before *(in place or time)*, in front of (13)
cum (+abl.) - with (10)
dē (+abl.) - down from, from; concerning, about (3)
ex, ē (abl.+) - out of, from, from within; by reason of, on account of ; of *(after cardinal numerals)* (8)
in (+acc.) - into, toward; against (9)
in (+abl.) - in, on (3)
per (+acc.) - through; by *(with reflexive pronoun)* (13)
post (+acc.) - after, behind (7)
prō (+abl.) - in front of, before, on behalf of, for the sake of, in return for, instead of, for, as (12)
própter (+acc.) - on account of, because of (5)
síne (+abl.) - without (2)
sub (+abl. w/ verbs of rest *or* +acc. w/ verbs of motion) - under, up under, close to, down to/into, to/at the foot of (7)
trāns (+acc.) - across (14)

Interjection

ō - O!, Oh! (2)

Idioms

amā́bō tē - please (1)
grā́tiās ágere (+dat.) - to thank someone; to give thanks to (8)
nōn sṓlum . . . sed étiam - not only . . . but also (9)
poénās dáre - to pay the penalty (2)
sī quándō - if ever (5)

Suffixes

-ne – interrogative suffix attached to the first word of a sentence, typically the verb or another word on which the question hinges, to introduce a question whose answer is uncertain (5)
-que - and *(enclitic conjunction; appended to the second of two words to be joined)* (6)

Chapter 15

Nouns

1st Declension

adulēscéntia, adulēscéntiae (f) - youth, young manhood; youthfulness (5)
agrícola, agrícolae (m) - farmer (3)
amíca, amícae (f) - friend (female) (3)
amīcítia, amīcítiae (f) - friendship (10)
áqua, áquae (f) - water (14)
Ásia, Ásiae (f) - Asia (12)
cṓpia, cṓpiae (f) - abundance, supply (8)
cṓpiae, cōpiā́rum (f) - supplies, troops, forces (8)
cúlpa, cúlpae (f) - fault, blame (5)
cū́ra, cū́rae (f) - care, attention, caution, anxiety (4)
déa, déae (f) - goddess (6)
discípula, discípulae (f) - learner, pupil, student (female) (6)
dīvítiae, dīvitiā́rum (f. pl.) - riches, wealth (13)
fā́ma, fā́mae (f) - rumor, report; fame, reputation (2)
fḗmina, fḗminae (f) - woman (3)
fī́lia, fī́liae (f) - daughter (3)
fṓrma, fṓrmae (f) - form, shape; beauty (2)
fortū́na, fortū́nae (f) - fortune, luck (2)
glṓria, glṓriae (f) - glory, fame (5)
hṓra, hṓrae (f) - hour, time (10)
īnsídiae, īnsidiā́rum (f) - ambush, plot, treachery (6)
ī́ra, ī́rae (f) - ire, anger (2)
Itália, Itáliae (f) - Italy (15)
líttera, lítterae (f) - a letter of the alphabet (7)
lítterae, litterā́rum (f) - a letter (epistle), literature (7)
magístra, magístrae (f) - schoolmistress, teacher, mistress (4)
médica, médicae (f) - doctor, physician (female) (12)
memória, memóriae (f) - memory, recollection (15)
móra, mórae (f) - delay (4)
nātū́ra, nātū́rae (f) - nature (10)
naúta, naútae (m) - sailor (2)
patiéntia, patiéntiae (f) - suffering; patience, endurance (12)
pátria, pátriae (f) - fatherland, native land, (one's) country (2)
pecū́nia, pecū́niae (f) - money (2)
philosóphia, philosóphiae (f) - philosophy (2)
poéna, poénae (f) - penalty, punishment (2)
poḗta, poḗtae (m) - poet (2)
pórta, pórtae (f) - gate, entrance (2)
puélla, puéllae (f) - girl (2)
rēgī́na, rēgī́nae (f) - queen (7)
Rṓma, Rṓmae (f) - Rome (14)
rósa, rósae (f) - rose (2)
sapiéntia, sapiéntiae (f) - wisdom (3)
senténtia, senténtiae (f) - feeling, thought, opinion, vote, sentence (2)
térra, térrae (f) - earth, ground, land, country (7)
túrba, túrbae (f) - uproar, disturbance; mob, crowd, multitude (14)
vía, víae (f) - way, road, street (10)
victṓria, victṓriae (f) - victory (8)
vī́ta, vī́tae (f) - life; mode of life (2)

2nd Declension

áger, ágrī (m) - field, farm (3)
amī́cus, amī́cī (m) - friend (male) (3)
ánimī, animṓrum (m) - high spirits, pride, courage (5)
ánimus, ánimī (m) - soul, spirit, mind (5)
ánnus, ánnī (m) - year (12)
bā́sium, bā́siī (n) - kiss (4)
béllum, béllī (n) - war (4)
caélum, caélī (n) - sky, heaven (5)
cōnsílium, cōnsíliī (n) - plan, purpose, counsel, advice, judgment, wisdom (4)
déus, déī (m) - god (6)
discípulus, discípulī (m) - learner, pupil, student (male) (6)
dṓnum, dṓnī (n) - gift, present (4)
exítium, exítiī (n) - destruction, ruin (4)
fáctum, fáctī (n) - deed, act, achievement (13)
fī́lius, fī́liī (m) - son (3)
Graécus, Graécī (m) - a Greek (6)
líber, líbrī (m) - book (6)
lóca, locṓrum (n) - places, region (9)
lócī, locṓrum (m) - passages in literature (9)
lócus, lócī (m) - place; passage in literature (9)
magíster, magístrī (m) - schoolmaster, teacher, master (4)
médicus, médicī (m) - doctor, physician (male) (12)
mórbus, mórbī (m) - disease, sickness (9)
númerus, númerī (m) - number (3)
óculus, óculī (m) - eye (4)
offícium, offíciī (n) - duty, service (4)

ṓtium, ṓtiī (n) - leisure, peace (4)
perī́culum, perī́culī (n) - danger, risk (4)
pópulus, pópulī (m) - the people, a people, a nation (3)
prīncípium, prīncípiī (n) - beginning (12)
púer, púerī (m) - boy; boys, children *(pl.)* (3)
remédium, remédiī (n) - cure, remedy (4)
sígnum, sígnī (n) - sign, signal, indication; seal (13)
stúdium, stúdiī (n) - eagerness, zeal, pursuit, study (9)
stúltus, stúltī (m) - a fool (4)
tyránnus, tyránnī (m) - absolute ruler, tyrant (6)
vérbum, vérbī (n)- word (5)
vir, vírī (m) - man, hero (3)
vítium, vítiī (n) - fault, crime, vice (6)

3rd Declension
adulḗscēns, adulēscéntis (m *or* f) - young man *or* woman (12)
ámor, amṓris (m) - love (7)
Caésar, Caésaris (m) - Caesar (12)
cáput, cápitis (n) - head; leader; beginning; life; heading; chapter (11)
cármen, cárminis (n) - song, poem (7)
Cícerō, Cicerṓnis (m) - (Marcus Tullius) Cicero (8)
cī́vitās, cīvitā́tis (f) - state, citizenship (7)
cṓnsul, cṓnsulis (m) - consul (11)
córpus, córporis (n) - body (7)
cupíditās, cupiditā́tis (f) - desire, longing, passion; cupidity, avarice (10)
frā́ter, frā́tris (m) - brother (8)
hómō, hóminis (m) - human being, man (7)
iūs, iū́ris (n) - right, justice, law (14)
lábor, labṓris (m)- labor, work, toil; a work, production (7)
laus, laúdis (f) - praise, glory, fame (8)
lībértās, lībertā́tis (f) - liberty (8)
mā́ter, mā́tris (f) - mother (12)
mṓrēs, mṓrum (m) - habits, morals, character (7)
mōs, mṓris (m) - habit, custom, manner (7)
nḗmō, nūllī́us, nḗminī, nḗminem, nū́llō, nū́llā (m *or* f) - no one, nobody (11)
nṓmen, nṓminis (n) - name (7)
ōs, ṓris (n) - mouth, face (14)
páter, pátris (m) - father (12)
pāx, pā́cis (f) - peace (7)
rátiō, ratiṓnis (f) - reckoning, account; reason, judgment, consideration; system; manner, method (8)
rēx, rḗgis (m) - king (7)
scrī́ptor, scrīptṓris (m) - writer, author (8)
senéctūs, senectū́tis (f) - old age (10)
sóror, sorṓris (f) - sister (8)
tempéstās, tempestā́tis (f) - period of time, season; weather, storm (15)
témpus, témporis (n) - time; occasion, opportunity (7)
tímor, timṓris (m) - fear (10)
úxor, uxṓris (f) - wife (7)
vḗritās, vēritā́tis (f) - truth (10)
vírgō, vírginis (f) - maiden, virgin (7)
vírtūs, virtū́tis (f) - manliness, courage; excellence, character, worth, virtue (7)
volúptās, voluptā́tis (f) - pleasure (10)

3rd Declension I-Stem
ánimal, animā́lis (n) - a living creature, animal (14)
ars, ártis (f) - art, skill (14)
aúris, aúris (f) - ear (14)
cī́vis, cī́vis (m *or* f) - citizen (14)
máre, máris (n) - sea (14)
mors, mórtis (f) - death (14)
nū́bēs, nū́bis (f) - cloud (14)
pars, pártis (f) - part, share; direction (14)
urbs, úrbis (f) - city (14)
vī́rēs, vī́rium (f. pl.) - strength (14)
vīs, vīs (f) - force, power, violence (14)

Indeclinable
níhil - nothing (1)
sátis - enough (5)

Pronouns

égo, méī - I (11)
hic, haec, hoc - this; the latter; he, she, it, they (9)
ídem, éadem, ídem - the same (11)
ílle, ílla, íllud - that; the former; the famous; he, she, it, they (9)
ípse, ípsa, ípsum - myself, yourself, himself, herself, itself, *etc.,* the very, the actual (13)
is, éa, id - this, that; he, she, it (11)
íste, ísta, ístud - that of yours, that; such (as you have, as you speak of); *sometimes with contemptuous force, e.g.,* that despicable, that wretched (9)
quid - what (1)
quísque, quídque, cuiúsque, cuíque - each one, each person , each thing (13)
súī - himself, herself, itself, themselves (13)
tū, túī - you *(sing.)* (11)

Adjectives

acérbus, acérba, acérbum - harsh, bitter, grievous (12)
áliī . . . áliī - some . . . others (9)
álius, ália, áliud - other, another (9)
álter, áltera, álterum - the other (of two), second (9)
amī́cus, amī́ca, amī́cum - friendly (11)
antī́quus, antī́qua, antī́quum - ancient, old-time (2)
avā́rus, avā́ra, avā́rum - greedy, avaricious (3)
beā́tus, beā́ta, beā́tum - happy, fortunate, blessed (10)
béllus, bélla, béllum - pretty, handsome, charming (4)
bónus, bóna, bónum - good, kind (4)
cā́rus, cā́ra, cā́rum - dear (11)
dóctus, dócta, dóctum - taught, learned, skilled (13)
fortūnā́tus, fortūnā́ta, fortūnā́tum - lucky, fortunate, happy (13)
Graécus, Graéca, Graécum - Greek (6)
hūmā́nus, hūmā́na, hūmā́num - pertaining to man, human; humane, kind; refined, cultivated (4)
lī́ber, lī́bera, lī́berum - free (5)
mágnus, mágna, mágnum - large, great; important (2)
málus, mála, málum - bad, wicked, evil (4)
méus, méa, méum - my (2)
míser, mísera, míserum - wretched, miserable, unfortunate (15)
múltus, múlta, múltum - much, many (2)
neúter, neútra, neútrum - not either, neither (9)
nóster, nóstra, nóstrum - our, ours (5)
nóvus, nóva, nóvum - new; strange (7)
nū́llus, nū́lla, nū́llum - not any, no, none (9)
párvus, párva, párvum - small, little (4)
paúcī, paúcae, paúca - few, a few (3)
perpétuus, perpétua, perpétuum perpetual, lasting, uninterrupted, continuous (6)
plḗnus, plḗna, plḗnum - full, abundant, generous (6)
púlcher, púlchra, púlchrum - beautiful, handsome; fine (5)
Rōmā́nus, Rōmā́na, Rōmā́num - Roman (3)
sálvus, sálva, sálvum - safe, sound (6)
sā́nus, sā́na, sā́num - sound, healthy, sane (5)
secúndus, secúnda, secúndum - second; favorable (6)
sṓlus, sṓla, sṓlum - alone, only, the only (9)
stúltus, stúlta, stúltum - foolish (4)
súus, súa, súum - his own, her own, its own, their own (13)
tṓtus, tṓta, tṓtum - whole, entire (9)
túus, túa, túum - your *(sing.)* (2)
ū́llus, ū́lla, ū́llum - any (9)
ū́nus, ū́na, ū́num - one, single, alone (9)
úter, útra, útrum - either, which (of two) (9)
vḗrus, vḗra, vḗrum - true, real, proper (4)
véster, véstra, véstrum - your *(pl.)* (6)

Indeclinable

sátis - enough, sufficient (5)

Verbs

1st Conjugation

ádiuvō, adiuvā́re, adiū́vī, adiū́tum - to help, aid, assist; to please (4)
ámō, amā́re, amā́vī, amā́tum - to love, like (1)
appéllō, appellā́re, appellā́vī, appellā́tum - to speak to, address (as), call, name (14)
cḗnō, cēnā́re, cēnā́vī, cēnā́tum - to dine (5)
cṓgitō, cōgitā́re, cōgitā́vī, cōgitā́tum - to think, ponder, consider, plan (1)
cōnsérvō, cōnservā́re, cōnservā́vī, cōnservā́tum - to preserve, conserve, maintain (1)
créō, creā́re, creā́vī, creā́tum - to create (12)
cúlpō, culpā́re, culpā́vī, culpā́tum - to blame, censure (5)
dēmṓnstrō, dēmōnstrā́re, dēmōnstrā́vī, dēmōnstrā́tum to point out, show, demonstrate (8)
dō, dáre, dédī, dátum - to give, offer (1)
érrō, errā́re, errā́vī, errā́tum - to wander; err, go astray, make a mistake, be mistaken (1)
exspéctō, exspectā́re, exspectā́vī, exspectā́tum - to look for, expect, await (15)
iúvō, iuvā́re, iū́vī, iū́tum - to help, aid, assist; to please (4)
laúdō, laudā́re, laudā́vī, laudā́tum - to praise (1)
mū́tō, mūtā́re, mūtā́vī, mūtā́tum to change, alter; exchange (14)
nécō, necā́re, necā́vī, necā́tum - to murder, kill (7)

sátiō, satiā́re, satiā́vī, satiā́tum - to satisfy, sate (3)

sérvō, servā́re, servā́vī, servā́tum - to preserve, save, keep, guard (1)

stō, stā́re, stétī, stā́tum - to stand, stand still *or* firm (13)

súperō, superā́re, superā́vī, superā́tum - to be above, have the upper hand, surpass; overcome, conquer (5)

tólerō, tolerā́re, tolerā́vī, tolerā́tum - to bear, endure (6)

vī́tō, vītā́re, vītā́vī, vītā́tum - to avoid, shun (14)

vócō, vocā́re, vocā́vī, vocā́tum - to call, summon (1)

2nd Conjugation

aúdeō, audḗre, aúsus sum - to dare (7)

dḗbeō, dēbḗre, dḗbuī, dḗbitum - to owe; ought, must, should (1)

dóceō, docḗre, dócuī, dóctum - to teach (8)

hábeō, habḗre, hábuī, hábitum - to have, hold, possess; consider, regard (3)

máneō, manḗre, mā́nsī, mā́nsum - to remain, stay, stay behind, abide, continue (5)

móneō, monḗre, mónuī, mónitum - to remind, advise, warn (1)

remáneō, remanḗre, remā́nsī, remā́nsum - to remain, stay, stay behind, abide, continue (5)

sálvē, salvḗte - hello, greetings (1)

sálveō, salvḗre - to be well, be in good health (1)

téneō, tenḗre, ténuī, téntum - to hold, keep, possess; restrain (14)

térreō, terrḗre, térruī, térritum - to frighten, terrify (1)

tímeō, timḗre, tímuī - to fear, be afraid (of) (15)

válē, valḗte - good-bye, farewell (1)

váleō, valḗre, váluī, valitū́rum - to be strong, have power; be well (1)

vídeō, vidḗre, vī́dī, vī́sum - to see; observe, understand (1)

3rd Conjugation

ágō, ágere, ḗgī, ā́ctum - to drive, lead, do, act; pass, spend *(life or time)* (8)

álō, álere, áluī, áltum - to nourish, support, sustain, increase; cherish (13)

āmíttō, āmíttere, āmī́sī, āmíssum - to send away; lose, let go (12)

cádō, cádere, cécidī, cāsū́rum - to fall (12)

commíttō, commíttere, commī́sī, commíssum - to entrust, commit (15)

cúrrō, cúrrere, cucúrrī, cúrsum - to run, rush, move quickly (14)

dī́cō, dī́cere, dī́xī, díctum - to say, tell, speak; name, call (10)

dī́ligō, dīlígere, dīlḗxī, dīlḗctum - to esteem, love (13)

dīscō, dīscere, dídicī - to learn (8)

dū́cō, dū́cere, dū́xī, dúctum - to lead; consider, regard; prolong (8)

gérō, gérere, géssī, géstum - to carry; carry on, manage, conduct, wage, accomplish, perform (8)

intéllegō, intellégere, intellḗxī, intellḗctum - to understand (11)

iúngō, iúngere, iū́nxī, iū́nctum - to join (13)

míttō, míttere, mī́sī, míssum - to send, let go (11)

scrī́bō, scrī́bere, scrī́psī, scrī́ptum to write, compose (8)

tráhō, tráhere, trā́xī, tráctum - to draw, drag; derive, acquire (8)

víncō, víncere, vī́cī, víctum - to conquer, overcome (8)

vī́vō, vī́vere, vī́xī, vī́ctum - to live (10)

3rd Conjugation -iō

cápiō, cápere, cḗpī, cáptum - to take, capture, seize, get (10)

fáciō, fácere, fḗcī, fáctum - to make, do, accomplish (10)

fúgiō, fúgere, fū́gī, fugitū́rum - to flee, hurry away; escape; go into exile; avoid, shun (10)

iáciō, iácere, iḗcī, iáctum - to throw, hurl (15)

4th Conjugation

aúdiō, audī́re, audī́vī, audī́tum - to hear, listen to (10)

invéniō, invenī́re, invḗnī, invéntum - to come upon, find (10)

séntiō, sentī́re, sḗnsī, sḗnsum - to feel, perceive, think, experience (11)

véniō, venī́re, vḗnī, véntum - to come (10)

Irregular

póssum, pósse, pótuī - to be able, can, could, have power (6)

sum, ésse, fúī, futū́rum - to be, exist (4)

Adverbs

ánte (+acc.) - before, previously (13)
béne - well, satisfactorily, quite (11)
crās - tomorrow (5)
díū - long, for a long time (12)
étiam - even, also (11)
héri - yesterday (5)
hódiē - today (3)
íbi - there (6)
ítaque - and so, therefore (15)
nímis, nímium - too, too much, excessively; *(in a positive sense, esp. with adjectives and adverbs)* exceedingly, very (9)
nōn - not (1)
númquam - never (8)
nunc - now, at present (6)
nū́per - recently (12)
ṓlim - once (upon a time), long ago, formerly; some day, in the future (13)
quándō - when (5)
quā́rē - because of which thing *(lit.);* therefore, wherefore, why (6)
saépe - often (1)
sátis - enough, sufficiently (5)
sémper - always (3)
támen - nevertheless, still (8)
tum - then, at that time; thereupon, in the next place (5)
úbi - where, when (6)

Conjunctions

aútem - however; moreover (11)
dum - while, as long as, at the same time that; *or* until *(+subjunctive)* (8)
énim - for, in fact, truly (9)
et - and; even (2)
et . . . et - both . . . and (2)
ígitur - therefore, consequently (5)
nam - for (13)
néque, nec - and not, nor (11)
néque . . . néque, nec . . . nec - neither . . . nor (11)
quod - because (11)
quóniam - since, inasmuch as (10)
sed - but (2)
sī - if (1)

Prepositions

ab, ā (+abl.) - away from, from; by (14)
ad (+acc.) - to, up to, near to (8)
ánte (+acc.) - before *(in place or time),* in front of (13)
cum (+abl.) - with (10)
dē (+abl.) - down from, from; concerning, about (3)
ex, ē (abl.+) - out of, from, from within; by reason of, on account of ; of *(after cardinal numerals)* (8)
in (+acc.) - into, toward; against (9)
in (+abl.) - in, on (3)
ínter (+acc.) - between, among (15)
per (+acc.) - through; by *(with reflexive pronoun)* (13)
post (+acc.) - after, behind (7)
prō (+abl.) - in front of, before, on behalf of, for the sake of, in return for, instead of, for, as (12)
própter (+acc.) - on account of, because of (5)
síne (+abl.) - without (2)
sub (+abl. w/ verbs of rest *or* **+acc. w/ verbs of motion)** - under, up under, close to, down to/into, to/at the foot of (7)
trāns (+acc.) - across (14)

Interjection

ō - O!, Oh! (2)

Idioms

amā́bō tē - please (1)
grā́tiās ágere (+dat.) - to thank someone; to give thanks to (8)
nōn sṓlum . . . sed étiam - not only . . . but also (9)
poénās dáre - to pay the penalty (2)
sī quándō - if ever (5)

Suffixes

-ne – interrogative suffix attached to the first word of a sentence, typically the verb or another word on which the question hinges, to introduce a question whose answer is uncertain (5)
-que - and *(enclitic conjunction; appended to the second of two words to be joined)* (6)

Numerals

Cardinal - ū́nus *to* vīgíntī quī́nque (15)
Ordinal - prī́mus *to* duodécimus (15)

----

céntum - a hundred (15)
mī́lia, mī́lium (n. pl.) - thousands (15)
mī́lle - thousand (15)

Chapter 16

Nouns

1st Declension

adulēscéntia, adulēscéntiae (f) - youth, young manhood; youthfulness (5)

agrícola, agrícolae (m) - farmer (3)

amī́ca, amī́cae (f) - friend (female) (3)

amīcítia, amīcítiae (f) - friendship (10)

áqua, áquae (f) - water (14)

Ásia, Ásiae (f) - Asia (12)

clēméntia, clēméntiae (f) - mildness, gentleness, mercy (16)

cṓpia, cṓpiae (f) - abundance, supply (8)

cṓpiae, cōpiā́rum (f) - supplies, troops, forces (8)

cúlpa, cúlpae (f) - fault, blame (5)

cū́ra, cū́rae (f) - care, attention, caution, anxiety (4)

déa, déae (f) - goddess (6)

discípula, discípulae (f) - learner, pupil, student (female) (6)

dīvítiae, dīvitiā́rum (f. pl.) - riches, wealth (13)

fā́ma, fā́mae (f) - rumor, report; fame, reputation (2)

fḗmina, fḗminae (f) - woman (3)

fī́lia, fī́liae (f) - daughter (3)

fṓrma, fṓrmae (f) - form, shape; beauty (2)

fortū́na, fortū́nae (f) - fortune, luck (2)

glṓria, glṓriae (f) - glory, fame (5)

hṓra, hṓrae (f) - hour, time (10)

īnsídiae, īnsidiā́rum (f) - ambush, plot, treachery (6)

ī́ra, ī́rae (f) - ire, anger (2)

Itália, Itáliae (f) - Italy (15)

líttera, lítterae (f) - a letter of the alphabet (7)

lítterae, litterā́rum (f) - a letter (epistle), literature (7)

magístra, magístrae (f) - schoolmistress, teacher, mistress (4)

médica, médicae (f) - doctor, physician (female) (12)

memória, memóriae (f) - memory, recollection (15)

móra, mórae (f) - delay (4)

nātū́ra, nātū́rae (f) - nature (10)

naúta, naútae (m) - sailor (2)

patiéntia, patiéntiae (f) - suffering; patience, endurance (12)

pátria, pátriae (f) - fatherland, native land, (one's) country (2)

pecū́nia, pecū́niae (f) - money (2)

philosóphia, philosóphiae (f) - philosophy (2)

poéna, poénae (f) - penalty, punishment (2)

poḗta, poḗtae (m) - poet (2)

pórta, pórtae (f) - gate, entrance (2)

puélla, puéllae (f) - girl (2)

rēgī́na, rēgī́nae (f) - queen (7)

Rṓma, Rṓmae (f) - Rome (14)

rósa, rósae (f) - rose (2)

sapiéntia, sapiéntiae (f) - wisdom (3)

sátura, sáturae (f) - satire (16)

senténtia, senténtiae (f) - feeling, thought, opinion, vote, sentence (2)

térra, térrae (f) - earth, ground, land, country (7)

túrba, túrbae (f) - uproar, disturbance; mob, crowd, multitude (14)

vía, víae (f) - way, road, street (10)

victṓria, victṓriae (f) - victory (8)

vī́ta, vī́tae (f) - life; mode of life (2)

2nd Declension

áger, ágrī (m) - field, farm (3)

amī́cus, amī́cī (m) - friend (male) (3)

ánimī, animṓrum (m) - high spirits, pride, courage (5)

ánimus, ánimī (m) - soul, spirit, mind (5)

ánnus, ánnī (m) - year (12)

bā́sium, bā́siī (n) - kiss (4)

béllum, béllī (n) - war (4)

caélum, caélī (n) - sky, heaven (5)

cōnsílium, cōnsíliī (n) - plan, purpose, counsel, advice, judgment, wisdom (4)

déus, déī (m) - god (6)

discípulus, discípulī (m) - learner, pupil, student (male) (6)

dṓnum, dṓnī (n) - gift, present (4)

exítium, exítiī (n) - destruction, ruin (4)

fáctum, fáctī (n) - deed, act, achievement (13)

fī́lius, fī́liī (m) - son (3)

Graécus, Graécī (m) - a Greek (6)

líber, líbrī (m) - book (6)

lóca, locṓrum (n) - places, region (9)

lócī, locṓrum (m) - passages in literature (9)

lócus, lócī (m) - place; passage in literature (9)

magíster, magístrī (m) - schoolmaster, teacher, master (4)

médicus, médicī (m) - doctor, physician (male) (12)

mórbus, mórbī (m) - disease, sickness (9)

númerus, númerī (m) - number (3)

óculus, óculī (m) - eye (4)

offícium, offíciī (n) - duty, service (4)

ṓtium, ṓtiī (n) - leisure, peace (4)
perī́culum, perī́culī (n) - danger, risk (4)
pópulus, pópulī (m) - the people, a people, a nation (3)
prīncípium, prīncípiī (n) - beginning (12)
púer, púerī (m) - boy; boys, children *(pl.)* (3)
remédium, remédiī (n) - cure, remedy (4)
sígnum, sígnī (n) - sign, signal, indication; seal (13)
stúdium, stúdiī (n) - eagerness, zeal, pursuit, study (9)
stúltus, stúltī (m) - a fool (4)
tyránnus, tyránnī (m) - absolute ruler, tyrant (6)
vérbum, vérbī (n)- word (5)
vir, vírī (m) - man, hero (3)
vítium, vítiī (n) - fault, crime, vice (6)

3rd Declension

adulḗscēns, adulēscéntis (m *or* f) - young man *or* woman (12)
aétās, aetā́tis (f) - period of life, life, age, an age, time (16)
ámor, amṓris (m) - love (7)
audī́tor, audītṓris (m) - hearer, listener, member of an audience (16)
Caésar, Caésaris (m) - Caesar (12)
cáput, cápitis (n) - head; leader; beginning; life; heading; chapter (11)
cármen, cárminis (n) - song, poem (7)
Cícerō, Cicerṓnis (m) - (Marcus Tullius) Cicero (8)
cī́vitās, cīvitā́tis (f) - state, citizenship (7)
cṓnsul, cṓnsulis (m) - consul (11)
córpus, córporis (n) - body (7)
cupíditās, cupiditā́tis (f) - desire, longing, passion; cupidity, avarice (10)
frā́ter, frā́tris (m) - brother (8)
hómō, hóminis (m) - human being, man (7)
iūs, iū́ris (n) - right, justice, law (14)
lábor, labṓris (m)- labor, work, toil; a work, production (7)
laus, laúdis (f) - praise, glory, fame (8)
lībértās, lībertā́tis (f) - liberty (8)
mā́ter, mā́tris (f) - mother (12)
mṓrēs, mṓrum (m) - habits, morals, character (7)
mōs, mṓris (m) - habit, custom, manner (7)
nḗmō, nūllī́us, nḗminī, nḗminem, nū́llō, nū́llā (m *or* f) - no one, nobody (11)
nṓmen, nṓminis (n) - name (7)
ōs, ṓris (n) - mouth, face (14)
páter, pátris (m) - father (12)
pāx, pā́cis (f) - peace (7)
rátiō, ratiṓnis (f) - reckoning, account; reason, judgment, consideration; system; manner, method (8)
rēx, rḗgis (m) - king (7)
scrī́ptor, scrīptṓris (m) - writer, author (8)
senéctūs, senectū́tis (f) - old age (10)
sénex, sénis (m) - old man (16)
sóror, sorṓris (f) - sister (8)
tempéstās, tempestā́tis (f) - period of time, season; weather, storm (15)
témpus, témporis (n) - time; occasion, opportunity (7)
tímor, timṓris (m) - fear (10)
úxor, uxṓris (f) - wife (7)
vḗritās, vēritā́tis (f) - truth (10)
vírgō, vírginis (f) - maiden, virgin (7)
vírtūs, virtū́tis (f) - manliness, courage; excellence, character, worth, virtue (7)
volúptās, voluptā́tis (f) - pleasure (10)

3rd Declension I-Stem

ánimal, animā́lis (n) - a living creature, animal (14)
ars, ártis (f) - art, skill (14)
aúris, aúris (f) - ear (14)
cī́vis, cī́vis (m *or* f) - citizen (14)
máre, máris (n) - sea (14)
mēns, méntis (f) - mind, thought, intention (16)
mors, mórtis (f) - death (14)
nū́bēs, nū́bis (f) - cloud (14)
pars, pártis (f) - part, share; direction (14)
urbs, úrbis (f) - city (14)
vī́rēs, vī́rium (f. pl.) - strength (14)
vīs, vīs (f) - force, power, violence (14)

Indeclinable

níhil - nothing (1)
sátis - enough (5)

Pronouns

égo, méī - I (11)
hic, haec, hoc - this; the latter; he, she, it, they (9)
ī́dem, éadem, ī́dem - the same (11)
ílle, ílla, íllud - that; the former; the famous; he, she, it, they (9)
ípse, ípsa, ípsum - myself, yourself, himself, herself, itself, *etc.,* the very, the actual (13)
is, éa, id - this, that; he, she, it (11)
íste, ísta, ístud - that of yours, that; such (as you have, as you speak of); *sometimes with contemptuous force, e.g.,* that despicable, that wretched (9)
quid - what (1)

quísque, quídque, cuiúsque, cuíque - each one, each person, each thing (13)
súī - himself, herself, itself, themselves (13)
tū, túī - you *(sing.)* (11)

Adjectives

1st & 2nd Declension

acérbus, acérba, acérbum - harsh, bitter, grievous (12)
álīī . . . álīī - some . . . others (9)
álius, ália, áliud - other, another (9)
álter, áltera, álterum - the other (of two), second (9)
amī́cus, amī́ca, amī́cum - friendly (11)
antī́quus, antī́qua, antī́quum - ancient, old-time (2)
avā́rus, avā́ra, avā́rum - greedy, avaricious (3)
beā́tus, beā́ta, beā́tum - happy, fortunate, blessed (10)
béllus, bélla, béllum - pretty, handsome, charming (4)
bónus, bóna, bónum - good, kind (4)
cā́rus, cā́ra, cā́rum - dear (11)
dóctus, dócta, dóctum - taught, learned, skilled (13)
fortūnā́tus, fortūnā́ta, fortūnā́tum - lucky, fortunate, happy (13)
Graécus, Graéca, Graécum - Greek (6)
hūmā́nus, hūmā́na, hūmā́num - pertaining to man, human; humane, kind; refined, cultivated (4)
iūcúndus, iūcúnda, iūcúndum - pleasant, delightful, agreeable, pleasing (16)
lī́ber, lī́bera, lī́berum - free (5)
lóngus, lónga, lóngum - long (16)
mágnus, mágna, mágnum - large, great; important (2)
málus, mála, málum - bad, wicked, evil (4)
méus, méa, méum - my (2)
míser, mísera, míserum - wretched, miserable, unfortunate (15)
múltus, múlta, múltum - much, many (2)
neúter, neútra, neútrum - not either, neither (9)
nóster, nóstra, nóstrum - our, ours (5)
nóvus, nóva, nóvum - new; strange (7)
nū́llus, nū́lla, nū́llum - not any, no, none (9)
párvus, párva, párvum - small, little (4)
paúcī, paúcae, paúca - few, a few (3)
perpétuus, perpétua, perpétuum perpetual, lasting, uninterrupted, continuous (6)
plḗnus, plḗna, plḗnum - full, abundant, generous (6)
púlcher, púlchra, púlchrum - beautiful, handsome; fine (5)
Rōmā́nus, Rōmā́na, Rōmā́num - Roman (3)
sálvus, sálva, sálvum - safe, sound (6)
sā́nus, sā́na, sā́num - sound, healthy, sane (5)
secúndus, secúnda, secúndum - second; favorable (6)
sṓlus, sṓla, sṓlum - alone, only, the only (9)
stúltus, stúlta, stúltum - foolish (4)
súus, súa, súum - his own, her own, its own, their own (13)
tṓtus, tṓta, tṓtum - whole, entire (9)
túus, túa, túum - your *(sing.)* (2)
ū́llus, ū́lla, ū́llum - any (9)
ū́nus, ū́na, ū́num - one, single, alone (9)
úter, útra, útrum - either, which (of two) (9)
vḗrus, vḗra, vḗrum - true, real, proper (4)
véster, véstra, véstrum - your *(pl.)* (6)

3rd Declension

ā́cer, ā́cris, ā́cre - sharp, keen, eager; severe, fierce (16)
brévis, bréve - short, small, brief (16)
céler, céleris, célere - swift, quick, rapid (16)
diffícilis, diffícile - hard, difficult, troublesome (16)
dúlcis, dúlce - sweet; pleasant, agreeable (16)
fácilis, fácile - easy; agreeable (16)
fórtis, fórte - strong, brave (16)
íngēns, *gen.* **ingéntis** - huge (16)
ómnis, ómne - every, all (16)
pótēns, *gen.* **poténtis** - able, powerful, mighty, strong (16)
sénex, *gen.* **sénis** - old, aged (16)

Indeclinable

sátis - enough, sufficient (5)

Verbs

1st Conjugation

ádiuvō, adiuvā́re, adiū́vī, adiū́tum - to help, aid, assist; to please (4)
ámō, amā́re, amā́vī, amā́tum - to love, like (1)
appéllō, appellā́re, appellā́vī, appellā́tum - to speak to, address (as), call, name (14)
cḗnō, cēnā́re, cēnā́vī, cēnā́tum - to dine (5)

cógitō, cōgitáre, cōgitávī, cōgitátum- to think, ponder, consider, plan (1)
cōnsérvō, cōnserváre, cōnservávī, cōnservátum - to preserve, conserve, maintain (1)
créō, creáre, creávī, creátum - to create (12)
cúlpō, culpáre, culpávī, culpátum - to blame, censure (5)
dēmṓnstrō, dēmōnstráre, dēmōnstrávī, dēmōnstrátum to point out, show, demonstrate (8)
dō, dáre, dédī, dátum - to give, offer (1)
érrō, erráre, errávī, errátum - to wander; err, go astray, make a mistake, be mistaken (1)
exspéctō, exspectáre, exspectávī, exspectátum - to look for, expect, await (15)
iúvō, iuváre, iū́vī, iū́tum - to help, aid, assist; to please (4)
laúdō, laudáre, laudávī, laudátum - to praise (1)
mū́tō, mūtáre, mūtávī, mūtátum to change, alter; exchange (14)
nécō, necáre, necávī, necátum - to murder, kill (7)
sátiō, satiáre, satiávī, satiátum - to satisfy, sate (3)
sérvō, serváre, servávī, servátum - to preserve, save, keep, guard (1)
stō, stáre, stétī, státum - to stand, stand still *or* firm (13)
súperō, superáre, superávī, superátum - to be above, have the upper hand, surpass; overcome, conquer (5)
tólerō, toleráre, tolerávī, tolerátum - to bear, endure (6)
vī́tō, vītáre, vītávī, vītátum - to avoid, shun (14)
vócō, vocáre, vocávī, vocátum - to call, summon (1)

2nd Conjugation

aúdeō, audḗre, aúsus sum - to dare (7)
dḗbeō, dēbḗre, dḗbuī, dḗbitum - to owe; ought, must, should (1)
dóceō, docḗre, dócuī, dóctum - to teach (8)
hábeō, habḗre, hábuī, hábitum - to have, hold, possess; consider, regard (3)
máneō, manḗre, mánsī, mánsum - to remain, stay, stay behind, abide, continue (5)
móneō, monḗre, mónuī, mónitum - to remind, advise, warn (1)
remáneō, remanḗre, remánsī, remánsum - to remain, stay, stay behind, abide, continue (5)
sálvē, salvḗte - hello, greetings (1)
sálveō, salvḗre - to be well, be in good health (1)
téneō, tenḗre, ténuī, téntum - to hold, keep, possess; restrain (14)
térreō, terrḗre, térruī, térritum - to frighten, terrify (1)
tímeō, timḗre, tímuī - to fear, be afraid (of) (15)
válē, valḗte - good-bye, farewell (1)
váleō, valḗre, váluī, valitū́rum - to be strong, have power; be well (1)
vídeō, vidḗre, vī́dī, vī́sum - to see; observe, understand (1)

3rd Conjugation

ágō, ágere, ḗgī, ā́ctum - to drive, lead, do, act; pass, spend *(life or time)* (8)
álō, álere, áluī, áltum - to nourish, support, sustain, increase; cherish (13)
āmíttō, āmíttere, āmī́sī, āmíssum - to send away; lose, let go (12)
cádō, cádere, cécidī, cāsū́rum - to fall (12)
commíttō, commíttere, commī́sī, commíssum - to entrust, commit (15)
cúrrō, cúrrere, cucúrrī, cúrsum - to run, rush, move quickly (14)
dī́cō, dī́cere, dī́xī, díctum - to say, tell, speak; name, call (10)
dī́ligō, dīlígere, dīléxī, dīléctum - to esteem, love (13)
díscō, díscere, dídicī - to learn (8)
dū́cō, dū́cere, dū́xī, dúctum - to lead; consider, regard; prolong (8)
gérō, gérere, géssī, géstum - to carry; carry on, manage, conduct, wage, accomplish, perform (8)
intéllegō, intellégere, intelléxī, intelléctum - to understand (11)
iúngō, iúngere, iū́nxī, iū́nctum - to join (13)
míttō, míttere, mī́sī, míssum - to send, let go (11)
régō, régere, rḗxī, rḗctum - to rule, guide, direct (16)
scrī́bō, scrī́bere, scrī́psī, scrī́ptum to write, compose (8)
tráhō, tráhere, trā́xī, tráctum - to draw, drag; derive, acquire (8)
víncō, víncere, vī́cī, víctum - to conquer, overcome (8)

vī́vō, vī́vere, vī́xī, vī́ctum - to live (10)

3rd Conjugation -iō

cápiō, cápere, cḗpī, cáptum - to take, capture, seize, get (10)

fáciō, fácere, fḗcī, fáctum - to make, do, accomplish (10)

fúgiō, fúgere, fū́gī, fugitū́rum - to flee, hurry away; escape; go into exile; avoid, shun (10)

iáciō, iácere, iḗcī, iáctum - to throw, hurl (15)

4th Conjugation

aúdiō, audī́re, audī́vī, audī́tum - to hear, listen to (10)

invéniō, invenī́re, invḗnī, invéntum - to come upon, find (10)

séntiō, sentī́re, sḗnsī, sḗnsum - to feel, perceive, think, experience (11)

véniō, venī́re, vḗnī, véntum - to come (10)

Irregular

póssum, pósse, pótuī - to be able, can, could, have power (6)

sum, ésse, fúī, futū́rum - to be, exist (4)

Adverbs

ánte (+acc.) - before, previously (13)

béne - well, satisfactorily, quite (11)

crās - tomorrow (5)

díū - long, for a long time (12)

étiam - even, also (11)

héri - yesterday (5)

hódiē - today (3)

íbi - there (6)

ítaque - and so, therefore (15)

nímis, nímium - too, too much, excessively; *(in a positive sense, esp. with adjectives and adverbs)* exceedingly, very (9)

nōn - not (1)

númquam - never (8)

nunc - now, at present (6)

nū́per - recently (12)

ṓlim - once (upon a time), long ago, formerly; some day, in the future (13)

quam - how (16)

quándō - when (5)

quā́rē - because of which thing *(lit.)*; therefore, wherefore, why (6)

saépe - often (1)

sátis - enough, sufficiently (5)

sémper - always (3)

támen - nevertheless, still (8)

tum - then, at that time; thereupon, in the next place (5)

úbi - where, when (6)

Conjunctions

aútem - however; moreover (11)

dum - while, as long as, at the same time that; *or* until *(+subjunctive)* (8)

énim - for, in fact, truly (9)

et - and; even (2)

et . . . et - both . . . and (2)

ígitur - therefore, consequently (5)

nam - for (13)

néque, nec - and not, nor (11)

néque . . . néque, nec . . . nec - neither . . . nor (11)

quod - because (11)

quóniam - since, inasmuch as (10)

sed - but (2)

sī - if (1)

Prepositions

ab, ā (+abl.) - away from, from; by (14)

ad (+acc.) - to, up to, near to (8)

ánte (+acc.) - before *(in place or time)*, in front of (13)

cum (+abl.) - with (10)

dē (+abl.) - down from, from; concerning, about (3)

ex, ē (abl.+) - out of, from, from within; by reason of, on account of; of *(after cardinal numerals)* (8)

in (+acc.) - into, toward; against (9)

in (+abl.) - in, on (3)

ínter (+acc.) - between, among (15)

per (+acc.) - through; by *(with reflexive pronoun)* (13)

post (+acc.) - after, behind (7)

prō (+abl.) - in front of, before, on behalf of, for the sake of, in return for, instead of, for, as (12)

própter (+acc.) - on account of, because of (5)

síne (+abl.) - without (2)

sub (+abl. w/ verbs of rest *or* **+acc. w/ verbs of motion)** - under, up under, close to, down to/into, to/at the foot of (7)

trāns (+acc.) - across (14)

Interjection

ō - O!, Oh! (2)

Idioms

amā́bō tē - please (1)

grā́tiās ágere (+dat.) - to thank someone; to give thanks to (8)

nōn sṓlum . . . sed étiam - not only . . . but also (9)

poénās dáre - to pay the penalty (2)

sī quándō - if ever (5)

Suffixes

-ne – interrogative suffix attached to the first word of a sentence, typically the verb or another word on which the question hinges, to introduce a question whose answer is uncertain (5)

-que - and *(enclitic conjunction; appended to the second of two words to be joined)* (6)

Numerals

Cardinal - ū́nus *to* vīgíntī quī́nque (15)

Ordinal - prī́mus *to* duodécimus (15)

----

céntum - a hundred (15)

mī́lia, mī́lium (n. pl.) - thousands (15)

mī́lle - thousand (15)

Chapter 17

Nouns

1st Declension

adulēscéntia, adulēscéntiae (f) - youth, young manhood; youthfulness (5)

agrícola, agrícolae (m) - farmer (3)

amī́ca, amī́cae (f) - friend (female) (3)

amīcítia, amīcítiae (f) - friendship (10)

áqua, áquae (f) - water (14)

Ásia, Ásiae (f) - Asia (12)

clēméntia, clēméntiae (f) - mildness, gentleness, mercy (16)

cṓpia, cṓpiae (f) - abundance, supply (8)

cṓpiae, cōpiā́rum (f) - supplies, troops, forces (8)

cúlpa, cúlpae (f) - fault, blame (5)

cū́ra, cū́rae (f) - care, attention, caution, anxiety (4)

déa, déae (f) - goddess (6)

discípula, discípulae (f) - learner, pupil, student (female) (6)

dīvítiae, dīvitiā́rum (f. pl.) - riches, wealth (13)

fā́ma, fā́mae (f) - rumor, report; fame, reputation (2)

fḗmina, fḗminae (f) - woman (3)

fī́lia, fī́liae (f) - daughter (3)

fṓrma, fṓrmae (f) - form, shape; beauty (2)

fortū́na, fortū́nae (f) - fortune, luck (2)

glṓria, glṓriae (f) - glory, fame (5)

hṓra, hṓrae (f) - hour, time (10)

īnsídiae, īnsidiā́rum (f) - ambush, plot, treachery (6)

ī́ra, ī́rae (f) - ire, anger (2)

Itália, Itáliae (f) - Italy (15)

líttera, lítterae (f) - a letter of the alphabet (7)

lítterae, litterā́rum (f) - a letter (epistle), literature (7)

magístra, magístrae (f) - schoolmistress, teacher, mistress (4)

médica, médicae (f) - doctor, physician (female) (12)

memória, memóriae (f) - memory, recollection (15)

móra, mórae (f) - delay (4)

nātū́ra, nātū́rae (f) - nature (10)

naúta, naútae (m) - sailor (2)

patiéntia, patiéntiae (f) - suffering; patience, endurance (12)

pátria, pátriae (f) - fatherland, native land, (one's) country (2)

pecū́nia, pecū́niae (f) - money (2)

philosóphia, philosóphiae (f) - philosophy (2)

poéna, poénae (f) - penalty, punishment (2)

poḗta, poḗtae (m) - poet (2)

pórta, pórtae (f) - gate, entrance (2)

puélla, puéllae (f) - girl (2)

rēgī́na, rēgī́nae (f) - queen (7)

Rṓma, Rṓmae (f) - Rome (14)

rósa, rósae (f) - rose (2)

sapiéntia, sapiéntiae (f) - wisdom (3)

sátura, sáturae (f) - satire (16)

senténtia, senténtiae (f) - feeling, thought, opinion, vote, sentence (2)

térra, térrae (f) - earth, ground, land, country (7)

túrba, túrbae (f) - uproar, disturbance; mob, crowd, multitude (14)

vía, víae (f) - way, road, street (10)

victṓria, victṓriae (f) - victory (8)

vī́ta, vī́tae (f) - life; mode of life (2)

2nd Declension

áger, ágrī (m) - field, farm (3)

amī́cus, amī́cī (m) - friend (male) (3)

ánimī, animṓrum (m) - high spirits, pride, courage (5)

ánimus, ánimī (m) - soul, spirit, mind (5)

ánnus, ánnī (m) - year (12)

bā́sium, bā́siī (n) - kiss (4)

béllum, béllī (n) - war (4)

caélum, caélī (n) - sky, heaven (5)

cōnsílium, cōnsíliī (n) - plan, purpose, counsel, advice, judgment, wisdom (4)

déus, déī (m) - god (6)

discípulus, discípulī (m) - learner, pupil, student (male) (6)

dṓnum, dṓnī (n) - gift, present (4)

exítium, exítiī (n) - destruction, ruin (4)

fáctum, fáctī (n) - deed, act, achievement (13)

fī́lius, fī́liī (m) - son (3)

Graécus, Graécī (m) - a Greek (6)

libéllus, libéllī (m) - little book (17)

líber, líbrī (m) - book (6)

lóca, locṓrum (n) - places, region (9)

lócī, locṓrum (m) - passages in literature (9)

lócus, lócī (m) - place; passage in literature (9)

magíster, magístrī (m) - schoolmaster, teacher, master (4)

médicus, médicī (m) - doctor, physician (male) (12)

mórbus, mórbī (m) - disease, sickness (9)

númerus, númerī (m) - number (3)

óculus, óculī (m) - eye (4)

offícium, offíciī (n) - duty, service (4)
ṓtium, ṓtiī (n) - leisure, peace (4)
perículum, perículī (n) - danger, risk (4)
pópulus, pópulī (m) - the people, a people, a nation (3)
prīncípium, prīncípiī (n) - beginning (12)
púer, púerī (m) - boy; boys, children *(pl.)* (3)
remédium, remédiī (n) - cure, remedy (4)
sígnum, sígnī (n) - sign, signal, indication; seal (13)
stúdium, stúdiī (n) - eagerness, zeal, pursuit, study (9)
stúltus, stúltī (m) - a fool (4)
tyránnus, tyránnī (m) - absolute ruler, tyrant (6)
vérbum, vérbī (n)- word (5)
vir, vírī (m) - man, hero (3)
vítium, vítiī (n) - fault, crime, vice (6)

3rd Declension
adulḗscēns, adulēscéntis (m *or* f) - young man *or* woman (12)
aétās, aetā́tis (f) - period of life, life, age, an age, time (16)
ámor, amṓris (m) - love (7)
audī́tor, audītṓris (m) - hearer, listener, member of an audience (16)
Caésar, Caésaris (m) - Caesar (12)
cáput, cápitis (n) - head; leader; beginning; life; heading; chapter (11)
cármen, cárminis (n) - song, poem (7)
Cícerō, Cicerṓnis (m) - (Marcus Tullius) Cicero (8)
cī́vitās, cīvitā́tis (f) - state, citizenship (7)
cṓnsul, cṓnsulis (m) - consul (11)
córpus, córporis (n) - body (7)
cupíditās, cupiditā́tis (f) - desire, longing, passion; cupidity, avarice (10)
frā́ter, frā́tris (m) - brother (8)
hómō, hóminis (m) - human being, man (7)
iūs, iū́ris (n) - right, justice, law (14)
lábor, labṓris (m)- labor, work, toil; a work, production (7)
laus, laúdis (f) - praise, glory, fame (8)
lībértās, lībertā́tis (f) - liberty (8)
mā́ter, mā́tris (f) - mother (12)
mṓrēs, mṓrum (m) - habits, morals, character (7)
mōs, mṓris (m) - habit, custom, manner (7)
nḗmō, nūllī́us, nḗminī, nḗminem, nū́llō, nū́llā (m *or* f) - no one, nobody (11)
nṓmen, nṓminis (n) - name (7)
ōs, ṓris (n) - mouth, face (14)
páter, pátris (m) - father (12)
pāx, pā́cis (f) - peace (7)
rátiō, ratiṓnis (f) - reckoning, account; reason, judgment, consideration; system; manner, method (8)
rēx, rḗgis (m) - king (7)
scrī́ptor, scrīptṓris (m) - writer, author (8)
senéctūs, senectū́tis (f) - old age (10)
sénex, sénis (m) - old man (16)
sóror, sorṓris (f) - sister (8)
tempéstās, tempestā́tis (f) - period of time, season; weather, storm (15)
témpus, témporis (n) - time; occasion, opportunity (7)
tímor, timṓris (m) - fear (10)
úxor, uxṓris (f) - wife (7)
vḗritās, vēritā́tis (f) - truth (10)
vírgō, vírginis (f) - maiden, virgin (7)
vírtūs, virtū́tis (f) - manliness, courage; excellence, character, worth, virtue (7)
volúptās, voluptā́tis (f) - pleasure (10)

3rd Declension I-Stem
ánimal, animā́lis (n) - a living creature, animal (14)
ars, ártis (f) - art, skill (14)
aúris, aúris (f) - ear (14)
cī́vis, cī́vis (m *or* f) - citizen (14)
máre, máris (n) - sea (14)
mēns, méntis (f) - mind, thought, intention (16)
mors, mórtis (f) - death (14)
nū́bēs, nū́bis (f) - cloud (14)
pars, pártis (f) - part, share; direction (14)
urbs, úrbis (f) - city (14)
vī́rēs, vī́rium (f. pl.) - strength (14)
vīs, vīs (f) - force, power, violence (14)

Indeclinable
níhil - nothing (1)
sátis - enough (5)

Pronouns

égo, méī - I (11)
hic, haec, hoc - this; the latter; he, she, it, they (9)
ī́dem, éadem, ídem - the same (11)
ílle, ílla, íllud - that; the former; the famous; he, she, it, they (9)
ípse, ípsa, ípsum - myself, yourself, himself, herself, itself, *etc.*, the very, the actual (13)
is, éa, id - this, that; he, she, it (11)

íste, ísta, ístud - that of yours, that; such (as you have, as you speak of); *sometimes with contemptuous force, e.g.,* that despicable, that wretched (9)

quī, quae, quod - who, which, what, that (17)

quid - what (1)

quísque, quídque, cuiúsque, cuíque - each one, each person, each thing (13)

súī - himself, herself, itself, themselves (13)

tū, túī - you *(sing.)* (11)

Adjectives

1st & 2nd Declension

acérbus, acérba, acérbum - harsh, bitter, grievous (12)

áliī . . . áliī - some . . . others (9)

álius, ália, áliud - other, another (9)

álter, áltera, álterum - the other (of two), second (9)

amī́cus, amī́ca, amī́cum - friendly (11)

antī́quus, antī́qua, antī́quum - ancient, old-time (2)

avā́rus, avā́ra, avā́rum - greedy, avaricious (3)

beā́tus, beā́ta, beā́tum - happy, fortunate, blessed (10)

béllus, bélla, béllum - pretty, handsome, charming (4)

bónus, bóna, bónum - good, kind (4)

caécus, caéca, caécum - blind (17)

cā́rus, cā́ra, cā́rum - dear (11)

dóctus, dócta, dóctum - taught, learned, skilled (13)

fortūnā́tus, fortūnā́ta, fortūnā́tum - lucky, fortunate, happy (13)

Graécus, Graéca, Graécum - Greek (6)

hūmā́nus, hūmā́na, hūmā́num - pertaining to man, human; humane, kind; refined, cultivated (4)

iūcúndus, iūcúnda, iūcúndum - pleasant, delightful, agreeable, pleasing (16)

lī́ber, lī́bera, lī́berum - free (5)

lóngus, lónga, lóngum - long (16)

mágnus, mágna, mágnum - large, great; important (2)

málus, mála, málum - bad, wicked, evil (4)

méus, méa, méum - my (2)

míser, mísera, míserum - wretched, miserable, unfortunate (15)

múltus, múlta, múltum - much, many (2)

neúter, neútra, neútrum - not either, neither (9)

nóster, nóstra, nóstrum - our, ours (5)

nóvus, nóva, nóvum - new; strange (7)

nū́llus, nū́lla, nū́llum - not any, no, none (9)

párvus, párva, párvum - small, little (4)

paúcī, paúcae, paúca - few, a few (3)

perpétuus, perpétua, perpétuum perpetual, lasting, uninterrupted, continuous (6)

plḗnus, plḗna, plḗnum - full, abundant, generous (6)

púlcher, púlchra, púlchrum - beautiful, handsome; fine (5)

Rōmā́nus, Rōmā́na, Rōmā́num - Roman (3)

sálvus, sálva, sálvum - safe, sound (6)

sā́nus, sā́na, sā́num - sound, healthy, sane (5)

secúndus, secúnda, secúndum - second; favorable (6)

sṓlus, sṓla, sṓlum - alone, only, the only (9)

stúltus, stúlta, stúltum - foolish (4)

súus, súa, súum - his own, her own, its own, their own (13)

tṓtus, tṓta, tṓtum - whole, entire (9)

túus, túa, túum - your *(sing.)* (2)

ū́llus, ū́lla, ū́llum - any (9)

ū́nus, ū́na, ū́num - one, single, alone (9)

úter, útra, útrum - either, which (of two) (9)

vḗrus, vḗra, vḗrum - true, real, proper (4)

véster, véstra, véstrum - your *(pl.)* (6)

3rd Declension

ā́cer, ā́cris, ā́cre - sharp, keen, eager; severe, fierce (16)

brévis, bréve - short, small, brief (16)

céler, céleris, célere - swift, quick, rapid (16)

diffícilis, diffícile - hard, difficult, troublesome (16)

dúlcis, dúlce - sweet; pleasant, agreeable (16)

fácilis, fácile - easy; agreeable (16)

fórtis, fórte - strong, brave (16)

íngēns, *gen.* ingéntis - huge (16)

lévis, léve - light; easy; slight, trivial (17)

ómnis, ómne - every, all (16)

pótēns, *gen.* poténtis - able, powerful, mighty, strong (16)

sénex, *gen.* sénis - old, aged (16)

Indeclinable

sátis - enough, sufficient (5)

Verbs

1st Conjugation

ádiuvō, adiuvā́re, adiū́vī, adiū́tum - to help, aid, assist; to please (4)

ámō, amā́re, amā́vī, amā́tum - to love, like (1)

appéllō, appellā́re, appellā́vī, appellā́tum - to speak to, address (as), call, name (14)

cḗnō, cēnā́re, cēnā́vī, cēnā́tum - to dine (5)

cṓgitō, cōgitā́re, cōgitā́vī, cōgitā́tum- to think, ponder, consider, plan (1)

cōnsérvō, cōnservā́re, cōnservā́vī, cōnservā́tum - to preserve, conserve, maintain (1)

créō, creā́re, creā́vī, creā́tum - to create (12)

cúlpō, culpā́re, culpā́vī, culpā́tum - to blame, censure (5)

dēmṓnstrō, dēmōnstrā́re, dēmōnstrā́vī, dēmōnstrā́tum to point out, show, demonstrate (8)

dēsī́derō, dēsīderā́re, dēsīderā́vī, dēsīderā́tum - to desire, long for, miss (17)

dō, dáre, dédī, dátum - to give, offer (1)

érrō, errā́re, errā́vī, errā́tum - to wander; err, go astray, make a mistake, be mistaken (1)

exspéctō, exspectā́re, exspectā́vī, exspectā́tum - to look for, expect, await (15)

iúvō, iuvā́re, iū́vī, iū́tum - to help, aid, assist; to please (4)

laúdō, laudā́re, laudā́vī, laudā́tum - to praise (1)

mū́tō, mūtā́re, mūtā́vī, mūtā́tum to change, alter; exchange (14)

nā́vigō, nāvigā́re, nāvigā́vī, nāvigā́tum - to sail, navigate (17)

nécō, necā́re, necā́vī, necā́tum - to murder, kill (7)

récitō, recitā́re, recitā́vī, recitā́tum - to read aloud, recite (17)

sátiō, satiā́re, satiā́vī, satiā́tum - to satisfy, sate (3)

sérvō, servā́re, servā́vī, servā́tum - to preserve, save, keep, guard (1)

stō, stā́re, stétī, státum - to stand, stand still *or* firm (13)

súperō, superā́re, superā́vī, superā́tum - to be above, have the upper hand, surpass; overcome, conquer (5)

tólerō, tolerā́re, tolerā́vī, tolerā́tum - to bear, endure (6)

vī́tō, vītā́re, vītā́vī, vītā́tum - to avoid, shun (14)

vócō, vocā́re, vocā́vī, vocā́tum - to call, summon (1)

2nd Conjugation

aúdeō, audḗre, aúsus sum - to dare (7)

dḗbeō, dēbḗre, dḗbuī, dḗbitum - to owe; ought, must, should (1)

dḗleō, dēlḗre, dēlḗvī, dēlḗtum - to destroy, wipe out, erase (17)

dóceō, docḗre, dócuī, dóctum - to teach (8)

hábeō, habḗre, hábuī, hábitum - to have, hold, possess; consider, regard (3)

máneō, manḗre, mā́nsī, mā́nsum - to remain, stay, stay behind, abide, continue (5)

móneō, monḗre, mónuī, mónitum - to remind, advise, warn (1)

remáneō, remanḗre, remā́nsī, remā́nsum - to remain, stay, stay behind, abide, continue (5)

sálvē, salvḗte - hello, greetings (1)

sálveō, salvḗre - to be well, be in good health (1)

téneō, tenḗre, ténuī, téntum - to hold, keep, possess; restrain (14)

térreō, terrḗre, térruī, térritum - to frighten, terrify (1)

tímeō, timḗre, tímuī - to fear, be afraid (of) (15)

válē, valḗte - good-bye, farewell (1)

váleō, valḗre, váluī, valitū́rum - to be strong, have power; be well (1)

vídeō, vidḗre, vī́dī, vī́sum - to see; observe, understand (1)

3rd Conjugation

admíttō, admíttere, admī́sī, admíssum - to admit, receive, let in (17)

ágō, ágere, ḗgī, ā́ctum - to drive, lead, do, act; pass, spend *(life or time)* (8)

álō, álere, áluī, áltum - to nourish, support, sustain, increase; cherish (13)

āmíttō, āmíttere, āmī́sī, āmíssum - to send away; lose, let go (12)

cádō, cádere, cécidī, cāsū́rum - to fall (12)

commíttō, commíttere, commī́sī, commíssum - to entrust, commit (15)

cúrrō, cúrrere, cucúrrī, cúrsum - to run, rush, move quickly (14)

dī́cō, dī́cere, dī́xī, díctum - to say, tell, speak; name, call (10)
dī́ligō, dīlígere, dīlḗxī, dīlḗctum - to esteem, love (13)
dī́scō, dī́scere, dídicī - to learn (8)
dū́cō, dū́cere, dū́xī, dúctum - to lead; consider, regard; prolong (8)
gérō, gérere, géssī, géstum - to carry; carry on, manage, conduct, wage, accomplish, perform (8)
intéllegō, intellégere, intellḗxī, intellḗctum - to understand (11)
iúngō, iúngere, iū́nxī, iū́nctum - to join (13)
míttō, míttere, mī́sī, míssum - to send, let go (11)
néglegō, neglégere, neglḗxī, neglḗctum - to neglect, disregard (17)
régō, régere, rḗxī, rḗctum - to rule, guide, direct (16)
scrī́bō, scrī́bere, scrī́psī, scrī́ptum to write, compose (8)
tráhō, tráhere, trā́xī, tráctum - to draw, drag; derive, acquire (8)
víncō, víncere, vī́cī, víctum - to conquer, overcome (8)
vī́vō, vī́vere, vī́xī, vī́ctum - to live (10)

3rd Conjugation -iō

cápiō, cápere, cḗpī, cáptum - to take, capture, seize, get (10)
cúpiō, cúpere, cupī́vī, cupī́tum - to desire, wish, long for (17)
fáciō, fácere, fḗcī, fáctum - to make, do, accomplish (10)
fúgiō, fúgere, fū́gī, fugitū́rum - to flee, hurry away; escape; go into exile; avoid, shun (10)
iáciō, iácere, iḗcī, iáctum - to throw, hurl (15)
incípiō, incípere, incḗpī, incéptum - to begin (17)

4th Conjugation

aúdiō, audī́re, audī́vī, audī́tum - to hear, listen to (10)
invéniō, invenī́re, invḗnī, invéntum - to come upon, find (10)
séntiō, sentī́re, sḗnsī, sḗnsum - to feel, perceive, think, experience (11)
véniō, venī́re, vḗnī, véntum - to come (10)

Irregular

póssum, pósse, pótuī - to be able, can, could, have power (6)
sum, ésse, fúī, futū́rum - to be, exist (4)

Defective

coépī, coepísse, coéptum - began (17)

Adverbs

ánte (+acc.) - before, previously (13)
béne - well, satisfactorily, quite (11)
cíto - quickly (17)
crās - tomorrow (5)
díū - long, for a long time (12)
étiam - even, also (11)
héri - yesterday (5)
hódiē - today (3)
íbi - there (6)
ítaque - and so, therefore (15)
nímis, nímium - too, too much, excessively; *(in a positive sense, esp. with adjectives and adverbs)* exceedingly, very (9)
nōn - not (1)
númquam - never (8)
nunc - now, at present (6)
nū́per - recently (12)
ṓlim - once (upon a time), long ago, formerly; some day, in the future (13)
quam - how (16)
quándō - when (5)
quā́rē - because of which thing *(lit.)*; therefore, wherefore, why (6)
quóque - also, too (17)
saépe - often (1)
sátis - enough, sufficiently (5)
sémper - always (3)
támen - nevertheless, still (8)
tum - then, at that time; thereupon, in the next place (5)
úbi - where, when (6)

Conjunctions

aut - or (17)
aut . . . aut - either . . . or (17)
aútem - however; moreover (11)
dum - while, as long as, at the same time that; *or* until *(+subjunctive)* (8)
énim - for, in fact, truly (9)
et - and; even (2)
et . . . et - both . . . and (2)
ígitur - therefore, consequently (5)
nam - for (13)
néque , nec - and not, nor (11)
néque . . . néque, nec . . . nec - neither . . . nor (11)
quod - because (11)
quóniam - since, inasmuch as (10)
sed - but (2)
sī - if (1)

Prepositions

ab, ā (+abl.) - away from, from; by (14)
ad (+acc.) - to, up to, near to (8)
ánte (+acc.) - before *(in place or time)*, in front of (13)
cum (+abl.) - with (10)

dē (+abl.) - down from, from; concerning, about (3)
ex, ē (abl.+) - out of, from, from within; by reason of, on account of ; of *(after cardinal numerals)* (8)
in (+acc.) - into, toward; against (9)
in (+abl.) - in, on (3)
ínter (+acc.) - between, among (15)
per (+acc.) - through; by *(with reflexive pronoun)* (13)
post (+acc.) - after, behind (7)
prō (+abl.) - in front of, before, on behalf of, for the sake of, in return for, instead of, for, as (12)
própter (+acc.) - on account of, because of (5)
síne (+abl.) - without (2)
sub (+abl. w/ verbs of rest *or* **+acc. w/ verbs of motion)** - under, up under, close to, down to/into, to/at the foot of (7)
trāns (+acc.) - across (14)

Interjection

ō - O!, Oh! (2)

Idioms

amā́bō tē - please (1)
grā́tiās ágere (+dat.) - to thank someone; to give thanks to (8)
nōn sṓlum . . . sed étiam - not only . . . but also (9)
poénās dáre - to pay the penalty (2)
sī quándō - if ever (5)

Suffixes

-ne – interrogative suffix attached to the first word of a sentence, typically the verb or another word on which the question hinges, to introduce a question whose answer is uncertain (5)
-que - and *(enclitic conjunction; appended to the second of two words to be joined)* (6)

Numerals

Cardinal - ū́nus *to* vīgíntī quī́nque (15)
Ordinal - prī́mus *to* duodécimus (15)

----

céntum - a hundred (15)
mī́lia, mī́lium (n. pl.) - thousands (15)
mī́lle - thousand (15)

Chapter 18

Nouns

1st Declension

adulēscéntia, adulēscéntiae (f) - youth, young manhood; youthfulness (5)
agrícola, agrícolae (m) - farmer (3)
amíca, amícae (f) - friend (female) (3)
amīcítia, amīcítiae (f) - friendship (10)
áqua, áquae (f) - water (14)
Ásia, Ásiae (f) - Asia (12)
clēméntia, clēméntiae (f) - mildness, gentleness, mercy (16)
cṓpia, cṓpiae (f) - abundance, supply (8)
cṓpiae, cōpiā́rum (f) - supplies, troops, forces (8)
cúlpa, cúlpae (f) - fault, blame (5)
cū́ra, cū́rae (f) - care, attention, caution, anxiety (4)
déa, déae (f) - goddess (6)
discípula, discípulae (f) - learner, pupil, student (female) (6)
dīvítiae, dīvitiā́rum (f. pl.) - riches, wealth (13)
fā́ma, fā́mae (f) - rumor, report; fame, reputation (2)
fḗmina, fḗminae (f) - woman (3)
fī́lia, fī́liae (f) - daughter (3)
fṓrma, fṓrmae (f) - form, shape; beauty (2)
fortū́na, fortū́nae (f) - fortune, luck (2)
glṓria, glṓriae (f) - glory, fame (5)
hṓra, hṓrae (f) - hour, time (10)
īnsídiae, īnsidiā́rum (f) - ambush, plot, treachery (6)
ī́ra, ī́rae (f) - ire, anger (2)
Itália, Itáliae (f) - Italy (15)
líttera, lítterae (f) - a letter of the alphabet (7)
lítterae, litterā́rum (f) - a letter (epistle), literature (7)
magístra, magístrae (f) - schoolmistress, teacher, mistress (4)
médica, médicae (f) - doctor, physician (female) (12)
memória, memóriae (f) - memory, recollection (15)
móra, mórae (f) - delay (4)
nātū́ra, nātū́rae (f) - nature (10)
naúta, naútae (m) - sailor (2)
patiéntia, patiéntiae (f) - suffering; patience, endurance (12)
pátria, pátriae (f) - fatherland, native land, (one's) country (2)
pecū́nia, pecū́niae (f) - money (2)
philosóphia, philosóphiae (f) - philosophy (2)
poéna, poénae (f) - penalty, punishment (2)
poḗta, poḗtae (m) - poet (2)
pórta, pórtae (f) - gate, entrance (2)
puélla, puéllae (f) - girl (2)
rēgī́na, rēgī́nae (f) - queen (7)
Rṓma, Rṓmae (f) - Rome (14)
rósa, rósae (f) - rose (2)
sapiéntia, sapiéntiae (f) - wisdom (3)
sátura, sáturae (f) - satire (16)
sciéntia, sciéntiae (f) - knowledge (18)
senténtia, senténtiae (f) - feeling, thought, opinion, vote, sentence (2)
térra, térrae (f) - earth, ground, land, country (7)
túrba, túrbae (f) - uproar, disturbance; mob, crowd, multitude (14)
vía, víae (f) - way, road, street (10)
victṓria, victṓriae (f) - victory (8)
vī́ta, vī́tae (f) - life; mode of life (2)

2nd Declension

áger, ágrī (m) - field, farm (3)
amī́cus, amī́cī (m) - friend (male) (3)
ánimī, animṓrum (m) - high spirits, pride, courage (5)
ánimus, ánimī (m) - soul, spirit, mind (5)
ánnus, ánnī (m) - year (12)
bā́sium, bā́siī (n) - kiss (4)
béllum, béllī (n) - war (4)
caélum, caélī (n) - sky, heaven (5)
cōnsílium, cōnsíliī (n) - plan, purpose, counsel, advice, judgment, wisdom (4)
déus, déī (m) - god (6)
discípulus, discípulī (m) - learner, pupil, student (male) (6)
dṓnum, dṓnī (n) - gift, present (4)
exítium, exítiī (n) - destruction, ruin (4)
fáctum, fáctī (n) - deed, act, achievement (13)
fī́lius, fī́liī (m) - son (3)
Graécus, Graécī (m) - a Greek (6)
libéllus, libéllī (m) - little book (17)
líber, líbrī (m) - book (6)
lóca, locṓrum (n) - places, region (9)
lócī, locṓrum (m) - passages in literature (9)
lócus, lócī (m) - place; passage in literature (9)
lū́dus, lū́dī (m) - game, sport; school (18)
magíster, magístrī (m) - schoolmaster, teacher, master (4)
médicus, médicī (m) - doctor, physician (male) (12)

mórbus, mórbī (m) - disease, sickness (9)
númerus, númerī (m) - number (3)
óculus, óculī (m) - eye (4)
offícium, offíciī (n) - duty, service (4)
ṓtium, ṓtiī (n) - leisure, peace (4)
perīculum, perīculī (n) - danger, risk (4)
pópulus, pópulī (m) - the people, a people, a nation (3)
prīncípium, prīncípiī (n) - beginning (12)
púer, púerī (m) - boy; boys, children *(pl.)* (3)
remédium, remédiī (n) - cure, remedy (4)
sígnum, sígnī (n) - sign, signal, indication; seal (13)
stúdium, stúdiī (n) - eagerness, zeal, pursuit, study (9)
stúltus, stúltī (m) - a fool (4)
tyránnus, tyránnī (m) - absolute ruler, tyrant (6)
vérbum, vérbī (n)- word (5)
vir, vírī (m) - man, hero (3)
vítium, vítiī (n) - fault, crime, vice (6)

3rd Declension
adulḗscēns, adulēscéntis (m ***or*** **f)** - young man *or* woman (12)
aétās, aetā́tis (f) - period of life, life, age, an age, time (16)
ámor, amṓris (m) - love (7)
audī́tor, audītṓris (m) - hearer, listener, member of an audience (16)
Caésar, Caésaris (m) - Caesar (12)
cáput, cápitis (n) - head; leader; beginning; life; heading; chapter (11)
cármen, cárminis (n) - song, poem (7)
Cícerō, Cicerṓnis (m) - (Marcus Tullius) Cicero (8)
cī́vitās, cīvitā́tis (f) - state, citizenship (7)
cṓnsul, cṓnsulis (m) - consul (11)
córpus, córporis (n) - body (7)
cupíditās, cupiditā́tis (f) - desire, longing, passion; cupidity, avarice (10)
flū́men, flū́minis (n) - river (18)
frā́ter, frā́tris (m) - brother (8)
génus, géneris (n) - origin; kind, type, sort, class (18)
hómō, hóminis (m) - human being, man (7)
iūs, iū́ris (n) - right, justice, law (14)
lábor, labṓris (m)- labor, work, toil; a work, production (7)
laus, laúdis (f) - praise, glory, fame (8)
lībértās, lībertā́tis (f) - liberty (8)
mā́ter, mā́tris (f) - mother (12)
mṓrēs, mṓrum (m) - habits, morals, character (7)
mōs, mṓris (m) - habit, custom, manner (7)
nḗmō, nūllī́us, nḗminī, nḗminem, nū́llō, nū́llā (m ***or*** **f)** - no one, nobody (11)
nṓmen, nṓminis (n) - name (7)
ōs, ṓris (n) - mouth, face (14)
páter, pátris (m) - father (12)
pāx, pā́cis (f) - peace (7)
próbitās, probitā́tis (f) - uprightness, honesty (18)
rátiō, ratiṓnis (f) - reckoning, account; reason, judgment, consideration; system; manner, method (8)
rēx, rḗgis (m) - king (7)
scrī́ptor, scrīptṓris (m) - writer, author (8)
senéctūs, senectū́tis (f) - old age (10)
sénex, sénis (m) - old man (16)
sóror, sorṓris (f) - sister (8)
tempéstās, tempestā́tis (f) - period of time, season; weather, storm (15)
témpus, témporis (n) - time; occasion, opportunity (7)
tímor, timṓris (m) - fear (10)
úxor, uxṓris (f) - wife (7)
vḗritās, vēritā́tis (f) - truth (10)
vírgō, vírginis (f) - maiden, virgin (7)
vírtūs, virtū́tis (f) - manliness, courage; excellence, character, worth, virtue (7)
volúptās, voluptā́tis (f) - pleasure (10)

3rd Declension I-Stem
ánimal, animā́lis (n) - a living creature, animal (14)
ars, ártis (f) - art, skill (14)
aúris, aúris (f) - ear (14)
cī́vis, cī́vis (m ***or*** **f)** - citizen (14)
hóstēs, hóstium (m) - the enemy (18)
hóstis, hóstis (m) - an enemy *(of the state)* (18)
máre, máris (n) - sea (14)
mēns, méntis (f) - mind, thought, intention (16)
mors, mórtis (f) - death (14)
nū́bēs, nū́bis (f) - cloud (14)
pars, pártis (f) - part, share; direction (14)
urbs, úrbis (f) - city (14)
vī́rēs, vī́rium (f. pl.) - strength (14)
vīs, vīs (f) - force, power, violence (14)

Indeclinable
níhil - nothing (1)
sátis - enough (5)

Pronouns
égo, méī - I (11)
hic, haec, hoc - this; the latter; he, she, it, they (9)
ī́dem, éadem, ídem - the same (11)

ílle, ílla, íllud - that; the former; the famous; he, she, it, they (9)
ípse, ípsa, ípsum - myself, yourself, himself, herself, itself, *etc.,* the very, the actual (13)
is, éa, id - this, that; he, she, it (11)
íste, ísta, ístud - that of yours, that; such (as you have, as you speak of); *sometimes with contemptuous force, e.g.,* that despicable, that wretched (9)
quī, quae, quod - who, which, what, that (17)
quid - what (1)
quísque, quídque, cuiúsque, cuíque - each one, each person, each thing (13)
súī - himself, herself, itself, themselves (13)
tū, túī - you *(sing.)* (11)

Adjectives

1st & 2nd Declension

acérbus, acérba, acérbum - harsh, bitter, grievous (12)
áliī . . . áliī - some . . . others (9)
álius, ália, áliud - other, another (9)
álter, áltera, álterum - the other (of two), second (9)
amī́cus, amī́ca, amī́cum - friendly (11)
antī́quus, antī́qua, antī́quum - ancient, old-time (2)
avā́rus, avā́ra, avā́rum - greedy, avaricious (3)
beā́tus, beā́ta, beā́tum - happy, fortunate, blessed (10)
béllus, bélla, béllum - pretty, handsome, charming (4)
bónus, bóna, bónum - good, kind (4)
caécus, caéca, caécum - blind (17)
cā́rus, cā́ra, cā́rum - dear (11)
clā́rus, clā́ra, clā́rum - clear, bright; renowned, famous, illustrious (18)
dóctus, dócta, dóctum - taught, learned, skilled (13)
fortūnā́tus, fortūnā́ta, fortūnā́tum - lucky, fortunate, happy (13)
Graécus, Graéca, Graécum - Greek (6)
hūmā́nus, hūmā́na, hūmā́num - pertaining to man, human; humane, kind; refined, cultivated (4)
iūcúndus, iūcúnda, iūcúndum - pleasant, delightful, agreeable, pleasing (16)
lī́ber, lī́bera, lī́berum - free (5)
lóngus, lónga, lóngum - long (16)
mágnus, mágna, mágnum - large, great; important (2)
málus, mála, málum - bad, wicked, evil (4)
méus, méa, méum - my (2)
míser, mísera, míserum - wretched, miserable, unfortunate (15)
múltus, múlta, múltum - much, many (2)
neúter, neútra, neútrum - not either, neither (9)
nóster, nóstra, nóstrum - our, ours (5)
nóvus, nóva, nóvum - new; strange (7)
nū́llus, nū́lla, nū́llum - not any, no, none (9)
párvus, párva, párvum - small, little (4)
paúcī, paúcae, paúca - few, a few (3)
perpétuus, perpétua, perpétuum perpetual, lasting, uninterrupted, continuous (6)
plḗnus, plḗna, plḗnum - full, abundant, generous (6)
púlcher, púlchra, púlchrum - beautiful, handsome; fine (5)
Rōmā́nus, Rōmā́na, Rōmā́num - Roman (3)
sálvus, sálva, sálvum - safe, sound (6)
sā́nus, sā́na, sā́num - sound, healthy, sane (5)
secúndus, secúnda, secúndum - second; favorable (6)
sṓlus, sṓla, sṓlum - alone, only, the only (9)
stúltus, stúlta, stúltum - foolish (4)
súus, súa, súum - his own, her own, its own, their own (13)
tṓtus, tṓta, tṓtum - whole, entire (9)
túus, túa, túum - your *(sing.)* (2)
ū́llus, ū́lla, ū́llum - any (9)
ū́nus, ū́na, ū́num - one, single, alone (9)
úter, útra, útrum - either, which (of two) (9)
vḗrus, vḗra, vḗrum - true, real, proper (4)
véster, véstra, véstrum - your *(pl.)* (6)

3rd Declension

ā́cer, ā́cris, ā́cre - sharp, keen, eager; severe, fierce (16)
brévis, bréve - short, small, brief (16)
céler, céleris, célere - swift, quick, rapid (16)
diffícilis, diffícile - hard, difficult, troublesome (16)
dúlcis, dúlce - sweet; pleasant, agreeable (16)
fácilis, fácile - easy; agreeable (16)
fórtis, fórte - strong, brave (16)
íngēns, *gen.* **ingéntis** - huge (16)

lévis, léve - light; easy; slight, trivial (17)
mortā́lis, mortā́le - mortal (18)
ómnis, ómne - every, all (16)
pótēns, ***gen.*** **poténtis** - able, powerful, mighty, strong (16)
sénex, ***gen.*** **sénis** - old, aged (16)

Indeclinable
sátis - enough, sufficient (5)

Verbs

1st Conjugation
ádiuvō, adiuvā́re, adiū́vī, adiū́tum - to help, aid, assist; to please (4)
ámō, amā́re, amā́vī, amā́tum - to love, like (1)
appéllō, appellā́re, appellā́vī, appellā́tum - to speak to, address (as), call, name (14)
cḗnō, cēnā́re, cēnā́vī, cēnā́tum - to dine (5)
cṓgitō, cōgitā́re, cōgitā́vī, cōgitā́tum- to think, ponder, consider, plan (1)
cōnsérvō, cōnservā́re, cōnservā́vī, cōnservā́tum - to preserve, conserve, maintain (1)
créō, creā́re, creā́vī, creā́tum - to create (12)
cúlpō, culpā́re, culpā́vī, culpā́tum - to blame, censure (5)
dēmṓnstrō, dēmōnstrā́re, dēmōnstrā́vī, dēmōnstrā́tum to point out, show, demonstrate (8)
dēsī́derō, dēsīderā́re, dēsīderā́vī, dēsīderā́tum - to desire, long for, miss (17)
dō, dáre, dédī, dátum - to give, offer (1)
érrō, errā́re, errā́vī, errā́tum - to wander; err, go astray, make a mistake, be mistaken (1)
exspéctō, exspectā́re, exspectā́vī, exspectā́tum - to look for, expect, await (15)
iúvō, iuvā́re, iū́vī, iū́tum - to help, aid, assist; to please (4)
laúdō, laudā́re, laudā́vī, laudā́tum - to praise (1)
mū́tō, mūtā́re, mūtā́vī, mūtā́tum to change, alter; exchange (14)
nā́vigō, nāvigā́re, nāvigā́vī, nāvigā́tum - to sail, navigate (17)
nécō, necā́re, necā́vī, necā́tum - to murder, kill (7)
récitō, recitā́re, recitā́vī, recitā́tum - to read aloud, recite (17)
sátiō, satiā́re, satiā́vī, satiā́tum - to satisfy, sate (3)
sérvō, servā́re, servā́vī, servā́tum - to preserve, save, keep, guard (1)
stō, stā́re, stétī, státum - to stand, stand still *or* firm (13)
súperō, superā́re, superā́vī, superā́tum - to be above, have the upper hand, surpass; overcome, conquer (5)
tólerō, tolerā́re, tolerā́vī, tolerā́tum - to bear, endure (6)
vī́tō, vītā́re, vītā́vī, vītā́tum - to avoid, shun (14)
vócō, vocā́re, vocā́vī, vocā́tum - to call, summon (1)

2nd Conjugation
aúdeō, audḗre, aúsus sum - to dare (7)
dḗbeō, dēbḗre, dḗbuī, dḗbitum - to owe; ought, must, should (1)
dḗleō, dēlḗre, dēlḗvī, dēlḗtum - to destroy, wipe out, erase (17)
dóceō, docḗre, dócuī, dóctum - to teach (8)
hábeō, habḗre, hábuī, hábitum - to have, hold, possess; consider, regard (3)
máneō, manḗre, mā́nsī, mā́nsum - to remain, stay, stay behind, abide, continue (5)
mísceō, miscḗre, míscuī, míxtum to mix, stir up, disturb (18)
móneō, monḗre, mónuī, mónitum - to remind, advise, warn (1)
móveō, movḗre, mṓvī, mṓtum - to move; arouse, affect (18)
remáneō, remanḗre, remā́nsī, remā́nsum - to remain, stay, stay behind, abide, continue (5)
sálvē, salvḗte - hello, greetings (1)
sálveō, salvḗre - to be well, be in good health (1)
téneō, tenḗre, ténuī, téntum - to hold, keep, possess; restrain (14)
térreō, terrḗre, térruī, térritum - to frighten, terrify (1)
tímeō, timḗre, tímuī - to fear, be afraid (of) (15)
válē, valḗte - good-bye, farewell (1)
váleō, valḗre, váluī, valitū́rum - to be strong, have power; be well (1)
vídeō, vidḗre, vī́dī, vī́sum - to see; observe, understand (1)
vídeor, vidḗrī, vī́sus sum - to be seen, seem, appear (18)

3rd Conjugation

admíttō, admíttere, admī́sī, admíssum - to admit, receive, let in (17)
ágō, ágere, ḗgī, ā́ctum - to drive, lead, do, act; pass, spend *(life or time)* (8)
álō, álere, áluī, áltum - to nourish, support, sustain, increase; cherish (13)
āmíttō, āmíttere, āmī́sī, āmíssum - to send away; lose, let go (12)
cádō, cádere, cécidī, cāsū́rum - to fall (12)
commíttō, commíttere, commī́sī, commíssum - to entrust, commit (15)
cúrrō, cúrrere, cucúrrī, cúrsum - to run, rush, move quickly (14)
dī́cō, dī́cere, dī́xī, díctum - to say, tell, speak; name, call (10)
dī́ligō, dīlígere, dīlḗxī, dīlḗctum - to esteem, love (13)
dískō, dískere, dídicī - to learn (8)
dū́cō, dū́cere, dū́xī, dúctum - to lead; consider, regard; prolong (8)
flúō, flúere, flū́xī, flū́xum - to flow (18)
gérō, gérere, géssī, géstum - to carry; carry on, manage, conduct, wage, accomplish, perform (8)
intéllegō, intellégere, intellḗxī, intellḗctum - to understand (11)
iúngō, iúngere, iū́nxī, iū́nctum - to join (13)
légō, légere, lḗgī, lḗctum - to pick out, choose; read (18)
míttō, míttere, mī́sī, míssum - to send, let go (11)
néglegō, neglégere, neglḗxī, neglḗctum - to neglect, disregard (17)
régō, régere, rḗxī, rḗctum - to rule, guide, direct (16)
scrī́bō, scrī́bere, scrī́psī, scrī́ptum to write, compose (8)
tráhō, tráhere, trā́xī, tráctum - to draw, drag; derive, acquire (8)
víncō, víncere, vī́cī, víctum - to conquer, overcome (8)
vī́vō, vī́vere, vī́xī, vī́ctum - to live (10)

3rd Conjugation -iō

cápiō, cápere, cḗpī, cáptum - to take, capture, seize, get (10)
cúpiō, cúpere, cupī́vī, cupī́tum - to desire, wish, long for (17)
fáciō, fácere, fḗcī, fáctum - to make, do, accomplish (10)
fúgiō, fúgere, fū́gī, fugitū́rum - to flee, hurry away; escape; go into exile; avoid, shun (10)
iáciō, iácere, iḗcī, iáctum - to throw, hurl (15)
incípiō, incípere, incḗpī, incéptum - to begin (17)

4th Conjugation

aúdiō, audī́re, audī́vī, audī́tum - to hear, listen to (10)
invéniō, invenī́re, invḗnī, invéntum - to come upon, find (10)
séntiō, sentī́re, sḗnsī, sḗnsum - to feel, perceive, think, experience (11)
véniō, venī́re, vḗnī, véntum - to come (10)

Irregular

póssum, pósse, pótuī - to be able, can, could, have power (6)
sum, ésse, fúī, futū́rum - to be, exist (4)

Defective Verb

coépī, coepísse, coéptum - began (17)

Adverbs

ánte (+acc.) - before, previously (13)
béne - well, satisfactorily, quite (11)
cíto - quickly (17)
crās - tomorrow (5)
cūr - why (18)
deínde - thereupon, next, then (18)
díū - long, for a long time (12)
étiam - even, also (11)
héri - yesterday (5)
hódiē - today (3)
íbi - there (6)
ítaque - and so, therefore (15)
nímis, nímium - too, too much, excessively; *(in a positive sense, esp. with adjectives and adverbs)* exceedingly, very (9)
nōn - not (1)
númquam - never (8)
nunc - now, at present (6)
nū́per - recently (12)
ṓlim - once (upon a time), long ago, formerly; some day, in the future (13)
quam - how (16)
quándō - when (5)
quā́rē - because of which thing *(lit.);* therefore, wherefore, why (6)
quóque - also, too (17)
saépe - often (1)
sátis - enough, sufficiently (5)
sémper - always (3)
támen - nevertheless, still (8)
tum - then, at that time; thereupon, in the next place (5)
úbi - where, when (6)

Conjunctions

aut - or (17)
aut . . . aut - either . . . or (17)
aútem - however; moreover (11)
dum - while, as long as, at the same time that; *or* until *(+subjunctive)* (8)
énim - for, in fact, truly (9)
et - and; even (2)
et . . . et - both . . . and (2)
ígitur - therefore, consequently (5)
nam - for (13)
néque, nec - and not, nor (11)
néque . . . néque, nec . . . nec - neither . . . nor (11)
quod - because (11)
quóniam - since, inasmuch as (10)
sed - but (2)
sī - if (1)

Prepositions

ab, ā (+abl.) - away from, from; by (14)
ad (+acc.) - to, up to, near to (8)
ánte (+acc.) - before *(in place or time)*, in front of (13)
cum (+abl.) - with (10)
dē (+abl.) - down from, from; concerning, about (3)
ex, ē (abl.+) - out of, from, from within; by reason of, on account of ; of *(after cardinal numerals)* (8)
in (+acc.) - into, toward; against (9)
in (+abl.) - in, on (3)
ínter (+acc.) - between, among (15)
per (+acc.) - through; by *(with reflexive pronoun)* (13)
post (+acc.) - after, behind (7)
prō (+abl.) - in front of, before, on behalf of, for the sake of, in return for, instead of, for, as (12)
própter (+acc.) - on account of, because of (5)
síne (+abl.) - without (2)
sub (+abl. w/ verbs of rest ***or*** **+acc. w/ verbs of motion)** - under, up under, close to, down to/into, to/at the foot of (7)
trāns (+acc.) - across (14)

Interjection

ō - O!, Oh! (2)

Idioms

amā́bō tē - please (1)
grā́tiās ágere (+dat.) - to thank someone; to give thanks to (8)
nōn sṓlum . . . sed étiam - not only . . . but also (9)
poénās dáre - to pay the penalty (2)
sī quándō - if ever (5)

Suffixes

-ne – interrogative suffix attached to the first word of a sentence, typically the verb or another word on which the question hinges, to introduce a question whose answer is uncertain (5)
-que - and *(enclitic conjunction; appended to the second of two words to be joined)* (6)

Numerals

Cardinal - ū́nus *to* vīgíntī quī́nque (15)
Ordinal - prī́mus *to* duodécimus (15)

----

céntum - a hundred (15)
mī́lia, mī́lium (n. pl.) - thousands (15)
mī́lle - thousand (15)

Chapter 19

Nouns

1st Declension

adulēscéntia, adulēscéntiae (f) - youth, young manhood; youthfulness (5)
agrícola, agrícolae (m) - farmer (3)
amíca, amícae (f) - friend (female) (3)
amīcítia, amīcítiae (f) - friendship (10)
áqua, áquae (f) - water (14)
Ásia, Ásiae (f) - Asia (12)
clēméntia, clēméntiae (f) - mildness, gentleness, mercy (16)
cṓpia, cṓpiae (f) - abundance, supply (8)
cṓpiae, cōpiā́rum (f) - supplies, troops, forces (8)
cúlpa, cúlpae (f) - fault, blame (5)
cū́ra, cū́rae (f) - care, attention, caution, anxiety (4)
déa, déae (f) - goddess (6)
discípula, discípulae (f) - learner, pupil, student (female) (6)
dīvítiae, dīvitiā́rum (f. pl.) - riches, wealth (13)
fā́ma, fā́mae (f) - rumor, report; fame, reputation (2)
família, famíliae (f) - household, family (19)
fḗmina, fḗminae (f) - woman (3)
fī́lia, fī́liae (f) - daughter (3)
fṓrma, fṓrmae (f) - form, shape; beauty (2)
fortū́na, fortū́nae (f) - fortune, luck (2)
glṓria, glṓriae (f) - glory, fame (5)
Graécia, Graéciae (f) - Greece (19)
hṓra, hṓrae (f) - hour, time (10)
īnsídiae, īnsidiā́rum (f) - ambush, plot, treachery (6)
ī́ra, ī́rae (f) - ire, anger (2)
Itália, Itáliae (f) - Italy (15)
líttera, lítterae (f) - a letter of the alphabet (7)
lítterae, litterā́rum (f) - a letter (epistle), literature (7)
magístra, magístrae (f) - schoolmistress, teacher, mistress (4)
médica, médicae (f) - doctor, physician (female) (12)
memória, memóriae (f) - memory, recollection (15)
móra, mórae (f) - delay (4)
nātū́ra, nātū́rae (f) - nature (10)
naúta, naútae (m) - sailor (2)
patiéntia, patiéntiae (f) - suffering; patience, endurance (12)
pátria, pátriae (f) - fatherland, native land, (one's) country (2)
pecū́nia, pecū́niae (f) - money (2)
philosóphia, philosóphiae (f) - philosophy (2)
poéna, poénae (f) - penalty, punishment (2)
poḗta, poḗtae (m) - poet (2)
pórta, pórtae (f) - gate, entrance (2)
puélla, puéllae (f) - girl (2)
rēgī́na, rēgī́nae (f) - queen (7)
Rṓma, Rṓmae (f) - Rome (14)
rósa, rósae (f) - rose (2)
sapiéntia, sapiéntiae (f) - wisdom (3)
sátura, sáturae (f) - satire (16)
sciéntia, sciéntiae (f) - knowledge (18)
senténtia, senténtiae (f) - feeling, thought, opinion, vote, sentence (2)
térra, térrae (f) - earth, ground, land, country (7)
túrba, túrbae (f) - uproar, disturbance; mob, crowd, multitude (14)
vía, víae (f) - way, road, street (10)
victṓria, victṓriae (f) - victory (8)
vī́ta, vī́tae (f) - life; mode of life (2)

2nd Declension

áger, ágrī (m) - field, farm (3)
amī́cus, amī́cī (m) - friend (male) (3)
ánimī, animṓrum (m) - high spirits, pride, courage (5)
ánimus, ánimī (m) - soul, spirit, mind (5)
ánnus, ánnī (m) - year (12)
argūméntum, argūméntī (n) - proof, evidence, argument (19)
bā́sium, bā́siī (n) - kiss (4)
béllum, béllī (n) - war (4)
benefícium, benefíciī (n) - benefit, kindness; favor (19)
caélum, caélī (n) - sky, heaven (5)
cōnsílium, cōnsíliī (n) - plan, purpose, counsel, advice, judgment, wisdom (4)
déus, déī (m) - god (6)
discípulus, discípulī (m) - learner, pupil, student (male) (6)
dṓnum, dṓnī (n) - gift, present (4)
exítium, exítiī (n) - destruction, ruin (4)
fáctum, fáctī (n) - deed, act, achievement (13)
fī́lius, fī́liī (m) - son (3)
Graécus, Graécī (m) - a Greek (6)
iūdícium, iūdíciī (n) - judgment, decision, opinion; trial (19)
libéllus, libéllī (m) - little book (17)
líber, líbrī (m) - book (6)
lóca, locṓrum (n) - places, region (9)

lócī, locṓrum (m) - passages in literature (9)
lócus, lócī (m) - place; passage in literature (9)
lū́dus, lū́dī (m) - game, sport; school (18)
magíster, magístrī (m) - schoolmaster, teacher, master (4)
médicus, médicī (m) - doctor, physician (male) (12)
mórbus, mórbī (m) - disease, sickness (9)
númerus, númerī (m) - number (3)
óculus, óculī (m) - eye (4)
offícium, offíciī (n) - duty, service (4)
ṓtium, ṓtiī (n) - leisure, peace (4)
perī́culum, perī́culī (n) - danger, risk (4)
pópulus, pópulī (m) - the people, a people, a nation (3)
prīncípium, prīncípiī (n) - beginning (12)
púer, púerī (m) - boy; boys, children *(pl.)* (3)
remédium, remédiī (n) - cure, remedy (4)
sígnum, sígnī (n) - sign, signal, indication; seal (13)
stúdium, stúdiī (n) - eagerness, zeal, pursuit, study (9)
stúltus, stúltī (m) - a fool (4)
tyránnus, tyránnī (m) - absolute ruler, tyrant (6)
vérbum, vérbī (n)- word (5)
vir, vírī (m) - man, hero (3)
vítium, vítiī (n) - fault, crime, vice (6)

3rd Declension

adulḗscēns, adulēscéntis (m *or* f) - young man *or* woman (12)
aétās, aetā́tis (f) - period of life, life, age, an age, time (16)
ámor, amṓris (m) - love (7)
aúctor, auctṓris (m) - increaser; author, originator (19)
audī́tor, audītṓris (m) - hearer, listener, member of an audience (16)
Caésar, Caésaris (m) - Caesar (12)
cáput, cápitis (n) - head; leader; beginning; life; heading; chapter (11)
cármen, cárminis (n) - song, poem (7)
Cī́cero, Cicerṓnis (m) - (Marcus Tullius) Cicero (8)
cī́vitās, cīvitā́tis (f) - state, citizenship (7)
cṓnsul, cṓnsulis (m) - consul (11)
córpus, córporis (n) - body (7)
cupíditās, cupiditā́tis (f) - desire, longing, passion; cupidity, avarice (10)
flū́men, flū́minis (n) - river (18)
frā́ter, frā́tris (m) - brother (8)
génus, géneris (n) - origin; kind, type, sort, class (18)
hómō, hóminis (m) - human being, man (7)
iū́dex, iū́dicis (m) - judge, juror (19)
iūs, iū́ris (n) - right, justice, law (14)
lábor, labṓris (m)- labor, work, toil; a work, production (7)
laus, laúdis (f) - praise, glory, fame (8)
lībértās, lībertā́tis (f) - liberty (8)
mā́ter, mā́tris (f) - mother (12)
mṓrēs, mṓrum (m) - habits, morals, character (7)
mōs, mṓris (m) - habit, custom, manner (7)
nḗmō, nūllī́us, nḗminī, nḗminem, nū́llō, nū́llā (m *or* f) - no one, nobody (11)
nṓmen, nṓminis (n) - name (7)
ōs, ṓris (n) - mouth, face (14)
páter, pátris (m) - father (12)
pāx, pā́cis (f) - peace (7)
próbitās, probitā́tis (f) - uprightness, honesty (18)
rátiō, ratiṓnis (f) - reckoning, account; reason, judgment, consideration; system; manner, method (8)
rēx, rḗgis (m) - king (7)
scélus, scéleris (n) - evil deed, crime, sin, wickedness (19)
scrī́ptor, scrīptṓris (m) - writer, author (8)
senéctūs, senectū́tis (f) - old age (10)
sénex, sénis (m) - old man (16)
sóror, sorṓris (f) - sister (8)
tempéstās, tempestā́tis (f) - period of time, season; weather, storm (15)
témpus, témporis (n) - time; occasion, opportunity (7)
tímor, timṓris (m) - fear (10)
úxor, uxṓris (f) - wife (7)
vḗritās, vēritā́tis (f) - truth (10)
vírgō, vírginis (f) - maiden, virgin (7)
vírtūs, virtū́tis (f) - manliness, courage; excellence, character, worth, virtue (7)
volúptās, voluptā́tis (f) - pleasure (10)

3rd Declension I-Stem

ánimal, animā́lis (n) - a living creature, animal (14)
ars, ártis (f) - art, skill (14)
aúris, aúris (f) - ear (14)
cī́vis, cī́vis (m *or* f) - citizen (14)
hóstēs, hóstium (m) - the enemy (18)
hóstis, hóstis (m) - an enemy *(of the state)* (18)
máre, máris (n) - sea (14)
mēns, méntis (f) - mind, thought, intention (16)
mors, mórtis (f) - death (14)
nū́bēs, nū́bis (f) - cloud (14)
pars, pártis (f) - part, share; direction (14)
urbs, úrbis (f) - city (14)

vī́rēs, vī́rium (f. pl.) - strength (14)
vīs, vīs (f) - force, power, violence (14)

Indeclinable
níhil - nothing (1)
sátis - enough (5)

Pronouns

égo, méī - I (11)
hic, haec, hoc - this; the latter; he, she, it, they (9)
ī́dem, éadem, ídem - the same (11)
ílle, ílla, íllud - that; the former; the famous; he, she, it, they (9)
ípse, ípsa, ípsum - myself, yourself, himself, herself, itself, *etc.*, the very, the actual (13)
is, éa, id - this, that; he, she, it (11)
íste, ísta, ístud - that of yours, that; such (as you have, as you speak of); *sometimes with contemptuous force, e.g.,* that despicable, that wretched (9)
quī, quae, quod - who, which, what, that (17)
quid - what (1)
quis? quid? - who? whose? whom? what? which? (19)
quísque, quídque, cuiúsque, cuíque - each one, each person, each thing (13)
súī - himself, herself, itself, themselves (13)
tū, túī - you *(sing.)* (11)

Adjectives

1st & 2nd Declension
acérbus, acérba, acérbum - harsh, bitter, grievous (12)
áliī . . . áliī - some . . . others (9)
álius, ália, áliud - other, another (9)
álter, áltera, álterum - the other (of two), second (9)
amī́cus, amī́ca, amī́cum - friendly (11)
antī́quus, antī́qua, antī́quum - ancient, old-time (2)
avā́rus, avā́ra, avā́rum - greedy, avaricious (3)
beā́tus, beā́ta, beā́tum - happy, fortunate, blessed (10)
béllus, bélla, béllum - pretty, handsome, charming (4)
bónus, bóna, bónum - good, kind (4)
caécus, caéca, caécum - blind (17)
cā́rus, cā́ra, cā́rum - dear (11)
cértus, cérta, cértum - definite, sure, certain, reliable (19)
clā́rus, clā́ra, clā́rum - clear, bright; renowned, famous, illustrious (18)
dóctus, dócta, dóctum - taught, learned, skilled (13)
fortūnā́tus, fortūnā́ta, fortūnā́tum - lucky, fortunate, happy (13)
Graécus, Graéca, Graécum - Greek (6)
hūmā́nus, hūmā́na, hūmā́num - pertaining to man, human; humane, kind; refined, cultivated (4)
iūcúndus, iūcúnda, iūcúndum - pleasant, delightful, agreeable, pleasing (16)
lī́ber, lī́bera, lī́berum - free (5)
lóngus, lónga, lóngum - long (16)
mágnus, mágna, mágnum - large, great; important (2)
málus, mála, málum - bad, wicked, evil (4)
méus, méa, méum - my (2)
míser, mísera, míserum - wretched, miserable, unfortunate (15)
múltus, múlta, múltum - much, many (2)
neúter, neútra, neútrum - not either, neither (9)
nóster, nóstra, nóstrum - our, ours (5)
nóvus, nóva, nóvum - new; strange (7)
nū́llus, nū́lla, nū́llum - not any, no, none (9)
párvus, párva, párvum - small, little (4)
paúcī, paúcae, paúca - few, a few (3)
perpétuus, perpétua, perpétuum perpetual, lasting, uninterrupted, continuous (6)
plḗnus, plḗna, plḗnum - full, abundant, generous (6)
púlcher, púlchra, púlchrum - beautiful, handsome; fine (5)
Rōmā́nus, Rōmā́na, Rōmā́num - Roman (3)
sálvus, sálva, sálvum - safe, sound (6)
sā́nus, sā́na, sā́num - sound, healthy, sane (5)
secúndus, secúnda, secúndum - second; favorable (6)
sṓlus, sṓla, sṓlum - alone, only, the only (9)
stúltus, stúlta, stúltum - foolish (4)
súus, súa, súum - his own, her own, its own, their own (13)
tṓtus, tṓta, tṓtum - whole, entire (9)
túus, túa, túum - your *(sing.)* (2)
ū́llus, ū́lla, ū́llum - any (9)
ū́nus, ū́na, ū́num - one, single, alone (9)
úter, útra, útrum - either, which (of two) (9)

vḗrus, vḗra, vḗrum - true, real, proper (4)
véster, véstra, véstrum - your *(pl.)* (6)

3rd Declension
ā́cer, ā́cris, ā́cre - sharp, keen, eager; severe, fierce (16)
brévis, bréve - short, small, brief (16)
céler, céleris, célere - swift, quick, rapid (16)
diffícilis, diffícile - hard, difficult, troublesome (16)
dúlcis, dúlce - sweet; pleasant, agreeable (16)
fácilis, fácile - easy; agreeable (16)
fórtis, fórte - strong, brave (16)
grávis, gráve - heavy, weighty; serious, important; severe, grievous (19)
immortā́lis, immortā́le - not subject to death, immortal (19)
íngēns, ***gen.*** **ingéntis** - huge (16)
lévis, léve - light; easy; slight, trivial (17)
mortā́lis, mortā́le - mortal (18)
ómnis, ómne - every, all (16)
pótēns, ***gen.*** **poténtis** - able, powerful, mighty, strong (16)
sénex, ***gen.*** **sénis** - old, aged (16)

Indeclinable
sátis - enough, sufficient (5)

Interrogative Adjective
quī?, quae?, quod? - what? which? what kind of?; *(sometimes with exclamatory force)* what (a)! what sort of! (19)

Verbs

1st Conjugation
ádiuvō, adiuvā́re, adiū́vī, adiū́tum - to help, aid, assist; to please (4)
ámō, amā́re, amā́vī, amā́tum - to love, like (1)
appéllō, appellā́re, appellā́vī, appellā́tum - to speak to, address (as), call, name (14)
cḗnō, cēnā́re, cēnā́vī, cēnā́tum - to dine (5)
cṓgitō, cōgitā́re, cōgitā́vī, cōgitā́tum- to think, ponder, consider, plan (1)
cōnsérvō, cōnservā́re, cōnservā́vī, cōnservā́tum - to preserve, conserve, maintain (1)
créō, creā́re, creā́vī, creā́tum - to create (12)
cúlpō, culpā́re, culpā́vī, culpā́tum - to blame, censure (5)
dēléctō, dēlectā́re, dēlectā́vī, dēlectā́tum - to delight, charm, please (19)
dēmṓnstrō, dēmōnstrā́re, dēmōnstrā́vī, dēmōnstrā́tum to point out, show, demonstrate (8)
dēsī́derō, dēsīderā́re, dēsīderā́vī, dēsīderā́tum - to desire, long for, miss (17)
dō, dáre, dédī, dátum - to give, offer (1)
érrō, errā́re, errā́vī, errā́tum - to wander; err, go astray, make a mistake, be mistaken (1)
exspéctō, exspectā́re, exspectā́vī, exspectā́tum - to look for, expect, await (15)
iúvō, iuvā́re, iū́vī, iū́tum - to help, aid, assist; to please (4)
laúdō, laudā́re, laudā́vī, laudā́tum - to praise (1)
lī́berō, līberā́re, līberā́vī, līberā́tum - to free, liberate (19)
mū́tō, mūtā́re, mūtā́vī, mūtā́tum to change, alter; exchange (14)
nā́vigō, nāvigā́re, nāvigā́vī, nāvigā́tum - to sail, navigate (17)
nécō, necā́re, necā́vī, necā́tum - to murder, kill (7)
párō, parā́re, parā́vī, parā́tum - to prepare, provide; get, obtain (19)
récitō, recitā́re, recitā́vī, recitā́tum - to read aloud, recite (17)
sátiō, satiā́re, satiā́vī, satiā́tum - to satisfy, sate (3)
sérvō, servā́re, servā́vī, servā́tum - to preserve, save, keep, guard (1)
stō, stā́re, stétī, státum - to stand, stand still *or* firm (13)
súperō, superā́re, superā́vī, superā́tum - to be above, have the upper hand, surpass; overcome, conquer (5)
tólerō, tolerā́re, tolerā́vī, tolerā́tum - to bear, endure (6)
vī́tō, vītā́re, vītā́vī, vītā́tum - to avoid, shun (14)
vócō, vocā́re, vocā́vī, vocā́tum - to call, summon (1)

2nd Conjugation
aúdeō, audḗre, aúsus sum - to dare (7)
dḗbeō, dēbḗre, dḗbuī, dḗbitum - to owe; ought, must, should (1)
dḗleō, dēlḗre, dēlḗvī, dēlḗtum - to destroy, wipe out, erase (17)

dóceō, docḗre, dócuī, dóctum - to teach (8)
hábeō, habḗre, hábuī, hábitum - to have, hold, possess; consider, regard (3)
máneō, manḗre, mā́nsī, mā́nsum - to remain, stay, stay behind, abide, continue (5)
mísceō, miscḗre, míscuī, míxtum to mix, stir up, disturb (18)
móneō, monḗre, mónuī, mónitum - to remind, advise, warn (1)
móveō, movḗre, mṓvī, mṓtum - to move; arouse, affect (18)
remáneō, remanḗre, remā́nsī, remā́nsum - to remain, stay, stay behind, abide, continue (5)
sálvē, salvḗte - hello, greetings (1)
sálveō, salvḗre - to be well, be in good health (1)
téneō, tenḗre, ténuī, téntum - to hold, keep, possess; restrain (14)
térreō, terrḗre, térruī, térritum - to frighten, terrify (1)
tímeō, timḗre, tímuī - to fear, be afraid (of) (15)
válē, valḗte - good-bye, farewell (1)
váleō, valḗre, váluī, valitū́rum - to be strong, have power; be well (1)
vídeō, vidḗre, vī́dī, vī́sum - to see; observe, understand (1)
vídeor, vidḗrī, vī́sus sum - to be seen, seem, appear (18)

3rd Conjugation

admíttō, admíttere, admī́sī, admíssum - to admit, receive, let in (17)
ágō, ágere, ḗgī, ā́ctum - to drive, lead, do, act; pass, spend *(life or time)* (8)
álō, álere, áluī, áltum - to nourish, support, sustain, increase; cherish (13)
āmíttō, āmíttere, āmī́sī, āmíssum - to send away; lose, let go (12)
cádō, cádere, cécidī, cāsū́rum - to fall (12)
commíttō, commíttere, commī́sī, commíssum - to entrust, commit (15)
cúrrō, cúrrere, cucúrrī, cúrsum - to run, rush, move quickly (14)
dī́cō, dī́cere, dī́xī, díctum - to say, tell, speak; name, call (10)
dī́ligō, dīlígere, dīlḗxī, dīlḗctum - to esteem, love (13)
díscō, díscere, dídicī - to learn (8)
dū́cō, dū́cere, dū́xī, dúctum - to lead; consider, regard; prolong (8)
flúō, flúere, flū́xī, flū́xum - to flow (18)
gérō, gérere, géssī, géstum - to carry; carry on, manage, conduct, wage, accomplish, perform (8)
intéllegō, intellégere, intellḗxī, intellḗctum - to understand (11)
iúngō, iúngere, iū́nxī, iū́nctum - to join (13)
légō, légere, lḗgī, lḗctum - to pick out, choose; read (18)
míttō, míttere, mī́sī, míssum - to send, let go (11)
néglegō, neglégere, neglḗxī, neglḗctum - to neglect, disregard (17)
régō, régere, rḗxī, rḗctum - to rule, guide, direct (16)
scrī́bō, scrī́bere, scrī́psī, scrī́ptum to write, compose (8)
tráhō, tráhere, trā́xī, tráctum - to draw, drag; derive, acquire (8)
víncō, víncere, vī́cī, víctum - to conquer, overcome (8)
vī́vō, vī́vere, vī́xī, vī́ctum - to live (10)

3rd Conjugation -iō

cápiō, cápere, cḗpī, cáptum - to take, capture, seize, get (10)
cúpiō, cúpere, cupī́vī, cupī́tum - to desire, wish, long for (17)
fáciō, fácere, fḗcī, fáctum - to make, do, accomplish (10)
fúgiō, fúgere, fū́gī, fugitū́rum - to flee, hurry away; escape; go into exile; avoid, shun (10)
iáciō, iácere, iḗcī, iáctum - to throw, hurl (15)
incípiō, incípere, incḗpī, incéptum - to begin (17)

4th Conjugation

aúdiō, audī́re, audī́vī, audī́tum - to hear, listen to (10)
invéniō, invenī́re, invḗnī, invéntum - to come upon, find (10)
séntiō, sentī́re, sḗnsī, sḗnsum - to feel, perceive, think, experience (11)
véniō, venī́re, vḗnī, véntum - to come (10)

Irregular

póssum, pósse, pótuī - to be able, can, could, have power (6)
sum, ésse, fúī, futū́rum - to be, exist (4)

Defective Verb
coépī, coepísse, coéptum - began (17)

Adverbs

ánte (+acc.) - before, previously (13)
béne - well, satisfactorily, quite (11)
cíto - quickly (17)
crās - tomorrow (5)
cūr - why (18)
deínde - thereupon, next, then (18)
díū - long, for a long time (12)
étiam - even, also (11)
héri - yesterday (5)
hódiē - today (3)
iam - now, already, soon (19)
íbi - there (6)
ítaque - and so, therefore (15)
nímis, nímium - too, too much, excessively; *(in a positive sense, esp. with adjectives and adverbs)* exceedingly, very (9)
nōn - not (1)
númquam - never (8)
nunc - now, at present (6)
nū́per - recently (12)
ṓlim - once (upon a time), long ago, formerly; some day, in the future (13)
quam - how (16)
quándō - when (5)
quā́rē - because of which thing *(lit.)*; therefore, wherefore, why (6)
quóque - also, too (17)
saépe - often (1)
sátis - enough, sufficiently (5)
sémper - always (3)
támen - nevertheless, still (8)
tum - then, at that time; thereupon, in the next place (5)
úbi - where, when (6)

Conjunctions

at - but; but, mind you; but, you say (19)
aut - or (17)
aut . . . aut - either . . . or (17)
aútem - however; moreover (11)
dum - while, as long as, at the same time that; *or* until *(+subjunctive)* (8)
énim - for, in fact, truly (9)
et - and; even (2)
et . . . et - both . . . and (2)
ígitur - therefore, consequently (5)
nam - for (13)
néque, nec - and not, nor (11)
néque . . . néque, nec . . . nec - neither . . . nor (11)
nísi - if . . . not, unless; except (19)
quod - because (11)
quóniam - since, inasmuch as (10)
sed - but (2)
sī - if (1)

Prepositions

ab, ā (+abl.) - away from, from; by (14)
ad (+acc.) - to, up to, near to (8)
ánte (+acc.) - before *(in place or time)*, in front of (13)
cóntrā (+acc.) - against (19)
cum (+abl.) - with (10)
dē (+abl.) - down from, from; concerning, about (3)
ex, ē (abl.+) - out of, from, from within; by reason of, on account of; of *(after cardinal numerals)* (8)
in (+acc.) - into, toward; against (9)
in (+abl.) - in, on (3)
ínter (+acc.) - between, among (15)
per (+acc.) - through; by *(with reflexive pronoun)* (13)
post (+acc.) - after, behind (7)
prō (+abl.) - in front of, before, on behalf of, for the sake of, in return for, instead of, for, as (12)
própter (+acc.) - on account of, because of (5)
síne (+abl.) - without (2)
sub (+abl. w/ verbs of rest *or* +acc. w/ verbs of motion) - under, up under, close to, down to/into, to/at the foot of (7)
trāns (+acc.) - across (14)

Interjection

ō - O!, Oh! (2)

Idioms

amā́bō tē - please (1)
grā́tiās ágere (+dat.) - to thank someone; to give thanks to (8)
nōn sṓlum . . . sed étiam - not only . . . but also (9)
poénās dáre - to pay the penalty (2)
sī quándō - if ever (5)

Suffixes

-ne – interrogative suffix attached to the first word of a sentence, typically the verb or another word on which the question hinges, to introduce a question whose answer is uncertain (5)
-que - and *(enclitic conjunction; appended to the second of two words to be joined)* (6)

Numerals

Cardinal - ū́nus *to*
vīgíntī quī́nque (15)
Ordinal - prī́mus *to*
duodécimus (15)

----

céntum - a hundred (15)
mī́lia, mī́lium (n. pl.) -
thousands (15)
mī́lle - thousand (15)

Chapter 20

Nouns

1st Declension

adulēscéntia, adulēscéntiae (f) - youth, young manhood; youthfulness (5)
agrícola, agrícolae (m) - farmer (3)
amíca, amícae (f) - friend (female) (3)
amīcítia, amīcítiae (f) - friendship (10)
áqua, áquae (f) - water (14)
Ásia, Ásiae (f) - Asia (12)
clēméntia, clēméntiae (f) - mildness, gentleness, mercy (16)
cṓpia, cṓpiae (f) - abundance, supply (8)
cṓpiae, cōpiā́rum (f) - supplies, troops, forces (8)
cúlpa, cúlpae (f) - fault, blame (5)
cū́ra, cū́rae (f) - care, attention, caution, anxiety (4)
déa, déae (f) - goddess (6)
discípula, discípulae (f) - learner, pupil, student (female) (6)
dīvítiae, dīvitiā́rum (f. pl.) - riches, wealth (13)
fā́ma, fā́mae (f) - rumor, report; fame, reputation (2)
família, famíliae (f) - household, family (19)
fḗmina, fḗminae (f) - woman (3)
fī́lia, fī́liae (f) - daughter (3)
fṓrma, fṓrmae (f) - form, shape; beauty (2)
fortū́na, fortū́nae (f) - fortune, luck (2)
glṓria, glṓriae (f) - glory, fame (5)
Graécia, Graéciae (f) - Greece (19)
hṓra, hṓrae (f) - hour, time (10)
īnsídiae, īnsidiā́rum (f) - ambush, plot, treachery (6)
ī́ra, ī́rae (f) - ire, anger (2)
Itália, Itáliae (f) - Italy (15)
líttera, lítterae (f) - a letter of the alphabet (7)
lítterae, litterā́rum (f) - a letter (epistle), literature (7)
magístra, magístrae (f) - schoolmistress, teacher, mistress (4)
médica, médicae (f) - doctor, physician (female) (12)
memória, memóriae (f) - memory, recollection (15)
móra, mórae (f) - delay (4)
nātū́ra, nātū́rae (f) - nature (10)
naúta, naútae (m) - sailor (2)
patiéntia, patiéntiae (f) - suffering; patience, endurance (12)
pátria, pátriae (f) - fatherland, native land, (one's) country (2)
pecū́nia, pecū́niae (f) - money (2)
philosóphia, philosóphiae (f) - philosophy (2)
poéna, poénae (f) - penalty, punishment (2)
poḗta, poḗtae (m) - poet (2)
pórta, pórtae (f) - gate, entrance (2)
puélla, puéllae (f) - girl (2)
rēgī́na, rēgī́nae (f) - queen (7)
Rṓma, Rṓmae (f) - Rome (14)
rósa, rósae (f) - rose (2)
sapiéntia, sapiéntiae (f) - wisdom (3)
sátura, sáturae (f) - satire (16)
sciéntia, sciéntiae (f) - knowledge (18)
senténtia, senténtiae (f) - feeling, thought, opinion, vote, sentence (2)
térra, térrae (f) - earth, ground, land, country (7)
túrba, túrbae (f) - uproar, disturbance; mob, crowd, multitude (14)
vía, víae (f) - way, road, street (10)
victṓria, victṓriae (f) - victory (8)
vī́ta, vī́tae (f) - life; mode of life (2)

2nd Declension

áger, ágrī (m) - field, farm (3)
amī́cus, amī́cī (m) - friend (male) (3)
ánimī, animṓrum (m) - high spirits, pride, courage (5)
ánimus, ánimī (m) - soul, spirit, mind (5)
ánnus, ánnī (m) - year (12)
argūméntum, argūméntī (n) - proof, evidence, argument (19)
bā́sium, bā́siī (n) - kiss (4)
béllum, béllī (n) - war (4)
benefícium, benefíciī (n) - benefit, kindness; favor (19)
caélum, caélī (n) - sky, heaven (5)
coniūrā́tī, coniūrātṓrum (m. pl.) - conspirators (20)
cōnsílium, cōnsíliī (n) - plan, purpose, counsel, advice, judgment, wisdom (4)
déus, déī (m) - god (6)
discípulus, discípulī (m) - learner, pupil, student (male) (6)
dṓnum, dṓnī (n) - gift, present (4)
exítium, exítiī (n) - destruction, ruin (4)
fáctum, fáctī (n) - deed, act, achievement (13)
fī́lius, fī́liī (m) - son (3)
Graécus, Graécī (m) - a Greek (6)
iūdícium, iūdíciī (n) - judgment, decision, opinion; trial (19)
libéllus, libéllī (m) - little book (17)
líber, líbrī (m) - book (6)

lóca, locṓrum (n) - places, region (9)
lócī, locṓrum (m) - passages in literature (9)
lócus, lócī (m) - place; passage in literature (9)
lū́dus, lū́dī (m) - game, sport; school (18)
magíster, magístrī (m) - schoolmaster, teacher, master (4)
médicus, médicī (m) - doctor, physician (male) (12)
mórbus, mórbī (m) - disease, sickness (9)
númerus, númerī (m) - number (3)
óculus, óculī (m) - eye (4)
offícium, offíciī (n) - duty, service (4)
ṓtium, ṓtiī (n) - leisure, peace (4)
perī́culum, perī́culī (n) - danger, risk (4)
pópulus, pópulī (m) - the people, a people, a nation (3)
prīncípium, prīncípiī (n) - beginning (12)
púer, púerī (m) - boy; boys, children *(pl.)* (3)
remédium, remédiī (n) - cure, remedy (4)
sígnum, sígnī (n) - sign, signal, indication; seal (13)
stúdium, stúdiī (n) - eagerness, zeal, pursuit, study (9)
stúltus, stúltī (m) - a fool (4)
tyránnus, tyránnī (m) - absolute ruler, tyrant (6)
vérbum, vérbī (n)- word (5)
vir, vírī (m) - man, hero (3)
vítium, vítiī (n) - fault, crime, vice (6)

3rd Declension

adulḗscēns, adulēscéntis (m *or* f) - young man *or* woman (12)
aétās, aetā́tis (f) - period of life, life, age, an age, time (16)
ámor, amṓris (m) - love (7)
aúctor, auctṓris (m) - increaser; author, originator (19)
audī́tor, audītṓris (m) - hearer, listener, member of an audience (16)
Caésar, Caésaris (m) - Caesar (12)
cáput, cápitis (n) - head; leader; beginning; life; heading; chapter (11)
cármen, cárminis (n) - song, poem (7)
Cícerō, Ciceṓnis (m) - (Marcus Tullius) Cicero (8)
cī́vitās, cīvitā́tis (f) - state, citizenship (7)
cṓnsul, cṓnsulis (m) - consul (11)
córpus, córporis (n) - body (7)
cupíditās, cupiditā́tis (f) - desire, longing, passion; cupidity, avarice (10)
flū́men, flū́minis (n) - river (18)
frā́ter, frā́tris (m) - brother (8)
génus, géneris (n) - origin; kind, type, sort, class (18)
hómō, hóminis (m) - human being, man (7)
iū́dex, iū́dicis (m) - judge, juror (19)
iūs, iū́ris (n) - right, justice, law (14)
lábor, labṓris (m)- labor, work, toil; a work, production (7)
laus, laúdis (f) - praise, glory, fame (8)
lībértās, lībertā́tis (f) - liberty (8)
mā́ter, mā́tris (f) - mother (12)
mṓrēs, mṓrum (m) - habits, morals, character (7)
mōs, mṓris (m) - habit, custom, manner (7)
nḗmō, nūllī́us, nḗminī, nḗminem, nū́llō, nū́llā (m *or* f) - no one, nobody (11)
nṓmen, nṓminis (n) - name (7)
ōs, ṓris (n) - mouth, face (14)
páter, pátris (m) - father (12)
pāx, pā́cis (f) - peace (7)
próbitās, probitā́tis (f) - uprightness, honesty (18)
rátiō, ratiṓnis (f) - reckoning, account; reason, judgment, consideration; system; manner, method (8)
rēx, rḗgis (m) - king (7)
scélus, scéleris (n) - evil deed, crime, sin, wickedness (19)
scrī́ptor, scrīptṓris (m) - writer, author (8)
senéctūs, senectū́tis (f) - old age (10)
sénex, sénis (m) - old man (16)
sérvitūs, servitū́tis (f) - servitude, slavery (20)
sóror, sorṓris (f) - sister (8)
tempéstās, tempestā́tis (f) - period of time, season; weather, storm (15)
témpus, témporis (n) - time; occasion, opportunity (7)
tímor, timṓris (m) - fear (10)
úxor, uxṓris (f) - wife (7)
vḗritās, vēritā́tis (f) - truth (10)
vírgō, vírginis (f) - maiden, virgin (7)
vírtūs, virtū́tis (f) - manliness, courage; excellence, character, worth, virtue (7)
volúptās, voluptā́tis (f) - pleasure (10)

3rd Declension I-Stem

ánimal, animā́lis (n) - a living creature, animal (14)
ars, ártis (f) - art, skill (14)
aúris, aúris (f) - ear (14)
cī́vis, cī́vis (m *or* f) - citizen (14)
hóstēs, hóstium (m) - the enemy (18)
hóstis, hóstis (m) - an enemy *(of the state)* (18)
máre, máris (n) - sea (14)
mēns, méntis (f) - mind, thought, intention (16)

mōns, móntis (m) - mountain (20)
mors, mórtis (f) - death (14)
nū́bēs, nū́bis (f) - cloud (14)
pars, pártis (f) - part, share; direction (14)
urbs, úrbis (f) - city (14)
vī́rēs, vī́rium (f. pl.) - strength (14)
vīs, vīs (f) - force, power, violence (14)

4th Declension
córnū, córnūs (n) - horn (20)
frū́ctus, frū́ctūs (m) - fruit; profit, benefit, enjoyment (20)
génū, génūs (n) - knee (20)
mánus, mánūs (f) - hand; handwriting; band (20)
métus, métūs (m) - fear, dread, anxiety (20)
senā́tus, senā́tūs (m) - senate (20)
sḗnsus, sḗnsūs (m) - feeling, sense (20)
spī́ritus, spī́ritūs (m) - breath, breathing; spirit, soul (20)
vérsus, vérsūs (m) - line of verse (20)

Indeclinable
níhil - nothing (1)
sátis - enough (5)

Pronouns

égo, méī - I (11)
hic, haec, hoc - this; the latter; he, she, it, they (9)
ī́dem, éadem, ídem - the same (11)
ílle, ílla, íllud - that; the former; the famous; he, she, it, they (9)
ípse, ípsa, ípsum - myself, yourself, himself, herself, itself, *etc.,* the very, the actual (13)
is, éa, id - this, that; he, she, it (11)
íste, ísta, ístud - that of yours, that; such (as you have, as you speak of); *sometimes with contemptuous force, e.g.,* that despicable, that wretched (9)
quī, quae, quod - who, which, what, that (17)
quid - what (1)
quis? quid? - who? whose? whom? what? which? (19)
quísque, quídque, cuiúsque, cuíque - each one, each person, each thing (13)
súī - himself, herself, itself, themselves (13)
tū, túī - you *(sing.)* (11)

Adjectives

1st & 2nd Declension
acérbus, acérba, acérbum - harsh, bitter, grievous (12)
áliī . . . áliī - some . . . others (9)
álius, ália, áliud - other, another (9)
álter, áltera, álterum - the other (of two), second (9)
amī́cus, amī́ca, amī́cum - friendly (11)
antī́quus, antī́qua, antī́quum - ancient, old-time (2)
avā́rus, avā́ra, avā́rum - greedy, avaricious (3)
beā́tus, beā́ta, beā́tum - happy, fortunate, blessed (10)
béllus, bélla, béllum - pretty, handsome, charming (4)
bónus, bóna, bónum - good, kind (4)
caécus, caéca, caécum - blind (17)
cā́rus, cā́ra, cā́rum - dear (11)
cértus, cérta, cértum - definite, sure, certain, reliable (19)
clā́rus, clā́ra, clā́rum - clear, bright; renowned, famous, illustrious (18)
déxter, déxtra, déxtrum - right, right-hand (20)
dóctus, dócta, dóctum - taught, learned, skilled (13)
fortūnā́tus, fortūnā́ta, fortūnā́tum - lucky, fortunate, happy (13)
Graécus, Graéca, Graécum - Greek (6)
hūmā́nus, hūmā́na, hūmā́num - pertaining to man, human; humane, kind; refined, cultivated (4)
iūcúndus, iūcúnda, iūcúndum - pleasant, delightful, agreeable, pleasing (16)
lī́ber, lī́bera, lī́berum - free (5)
lóngus, lónga, lóngum - long (16)
mágnus, mágna, mágnum - large, great; important (2)
málus, mála, málum - bad, wicked, evil (4)
méus, méa, méum - my (2)
míser, mísera, míserum - wretched, miserable, unfortunate (15)
múltus, múlta, múltum - much, many (2)
neúter, neútra, neútrum - not either, neither (9)
nóster, nóstra, nóstrum - our, ours (5)
nóvus, nóva, nóvum - new; strange (7)
nū́llus, nū́lla, nū́llum - not any, no, none (9)
párvus, párva, párvum - small, little (4)
paúcī, paúcae, paúca - few, a few (3)
perpétuus, perpétua, perpétuum perpetual, lasting, uninterrupted, continuous (6)

plḗnus, plḗna, plḗnum - full, abundant, generous (6)
púlcher, púlchra, púlchrum - beautiful, handsome; fine (5)
Rōmā́nus, Rōmā́na, Rōmā́num - Roman (3)
sálvus, sálva, sálvum - safe, sound (6)
sā́nus, sā́na, sā́num - sound, healthy, sane (5)
secúndus, secúnda, secúndum - second; favorable (6)
siníster, sinístra, sinístrum - left, left-hand; harmful, ill-omened (20)
sṓlus, sṓla, sṓlum - alone, only, the only (9)
stúltus, stúlta, stúltum - foolish (4)
súus, súa, súum - his own, her own, its own, their own (13)
tṓtus, tṓta, tṓtum - whole, entire (9)
túus, túa, túum - your *(sing.)* (2)
ū́llus, ū́lla, ū́llum - any (9)
ū́nus, ū́na, ū́num - one, single, alone (9)
úter, útra, útrum - either, which (of two) (9)
vḗrus, vḗra, vḗrum - true, real, proper (4)
véster, véstra, véstrum - your *(pl.)* (6)

3rd Declension
ā́cer, ā́cris, ā́cre - sharp, keen, eager; severe, fierce (16)
brévis, bréve - short, small, brief (16)
céler, céleris, célere - swift, quick, rapid (16)
commū́nis, commū́ne - common, general, of / for the community (20)
diffícilis, diffícile - hard, difficult, troublesome (16)
dúlcis, dúlce - sweet; pleasant, agreeable (16)
fácilis, fácile - easy; agreeable (16)
fórtis, fórte - strong, brave (16)
grávis, gráve - heavy, weighty; serious, important; severe, grievous (19)
immortā́lis, immortā́le - not subject to death, immortal (19)
íngēns, *gen.* **ingéntis** - huge (16)
lévis, léve - light; easy; slight, trivial (17)
mortā́lis, mortā́le - mortal (18)
ómnis, ómne - every, all (16)
pótēns, *gen.* **poténtis** - able, powerful, mighty, strong (16)
sénex, *gen.* **sénis** - old, aged (16)

Indeclinable
sátis - enough, sufficient (5)

Interrogative Adjective
quī?, quae?, quod? - what? which? what kind of?; *(sometimes with exclamatory force)* what (a)! what sort of! (19)

Verbs

1st Conjugation
ádiuvō, adiuvā́re, adiū́vī, adiū́tum - to help, aid, assist; to please (4)
ámō, amā́re, amā́vī, amā́tum - to love, like (1)
appéllō, appellā́re, appellā́vī, appellā́tum - to speak to, address (as), call, name (14)
cḗnō, cēnā́re, cēnā́vī, cēnā́tum - to dine (5)
cṓgitō, cōgitā́re, cōgitā́vī, cōgitā́tum - to think, ponder, consider, plan (1)
cōnsérvō, cōnservā́re, cōnservā́vī, cōnservā́tum - to preserve, conserve, maintain (1)
créō, creā́re, creā́vī, creā́tum - to create (12)
cúlpō, culpā́re, culpā́vī, culpā́tum - to blame, censure (5)
dēléctō, dēlectā́re, dēlectā́vī, dēlectā́tum - to delight, charm, please (19)
dēmṓnstrō, dēmōnstrā́re, dēmōnstrā́vī, dēmōnstrā́tum to point out, show, demonstrate (8)
dēsíderō, dēsīderā́re, dēsīderā́vī, dēsīderā́tum - to desire, long for, miss (17)
dō, dáre, dédī, dátum - to give, offer (1)
érrō, errā́re, errā́vī, errā́tum - to wander; err, go astray, make a mistake, be mistaken (1)
exspéctō, exspectā́re, exspectā́vī, exspectā́tum - to look for, expect, await (15)
iúvō, iuvā́re, iū́vī, iū́tum - to help, aid, assist; to please (4)
laúdō, laudā́re, laudā́vī, laudā́tum - to praise (1)
lī́berō, līberā́re, līberā́vī, līberā́tum - to free, liberate (19)
mū́tō, mūtā́re, mūtā́vī, mūtā́tum to change, alter; exchange (14)
nā́vigō, nāvigā́re, nāvigā́vī, nāvigā́tum - to sail, navigate (17)
nécō, necā́re, necā́vī, necā́tum - to murder, kill (7)
párō, parā́re, parā́vī, parā́tum - to prepare, provide; get, obtain (19)

prōnū́ntiō, prōnūntiā́re, prōnūntiā́vī, prōnūntiā́tum - to proclaim, announce; declaim; pronounce (20)
récitō, recitā́re, recitā́vī, recitā́tum - to read aloud, recite (17)
sátiō, satiā́re, satiā́vī, satiā́tum - to satisfy, sate (3)
sérvō, servā́re, servā́vī, servā́tum - to preserve, save, keep, guard (1)
stō, stā́re, stétī, státum - to stand, stand still *or* firm (13)
súperō, superā́re, superā́vī, superā́tum - to be above, have the upper hand, surpass; overcome, conquer (5)
tólerō, tolerā́re, tolerā́vī, tolerā́tum - to bear, endure (6)
vī́tō, vītā́re, vītā́vī, vītā́tum - to avoid, shun (14)
vócō, vocā́re, vocā́vī, vocā́tum - to call, summon (1)

2nd Conjugation

aúdeō, audḗre, aúsus sum - to dare (7)
cáreō, carḗre, cáruī, caritū́rum (+abl.) - to be without, be deprived of, want, lack; be free from (20)
dḗbeō, dēbḗre, dḗbuī, dḗbitum - to owe; ought, must, should (1)
déleō, dēlḗre, dēlḗvī, dēlḗtum - to destroy, wipe out, erase (17)
dóceō, docḗre, dócuī, dóctum - to teach (8)
hábeō, habḗre, hábuī, hábitum - to have, hold, possess; consider, regard (3)
máneō, manḗre, mā́nsī, mā́nsum - to remain, stay, stay behind, abide, continue (5)
mísceō, miscḗre, míscuī, míxtum to mix, stir up, disturb (18)
móneō, monḗre, mónuī, mónitum - to remind, advise, warn (1)
móveō, movḗre, mṓvī, mṓtum - to move; arouse, affect (18)
prohíbeō, prohibḗre, prohíbuī, prohíbitum - to keep (back), prevent, hinder, restrain, prohibit (20)
remáneō, remanḗre, remā́nsī, remā́nsum - to remain, stay, stay behind, abide, continue (5)
sálvē, salvḗte - hello, greetings (1)
sálveō, salvḗre - to be well, be in good health (1)
téneō, tenḗre, ténuī, téntum - to hold, keep, possess; restrain (14)
térreō, terrḗre, térruī, térritum - to frighten, terrify (1)
tímeō, timḗre, tímuī - to fear, be afraid (of) (15)
válē, valḗte - good-bye, farewell (1)
váleō, valḗre, váluī, valitū́rum - to be strong, have power; be well (1)
vídeō, vidḗre, vī́dī, vī́sum - to see; observe, understand (1)
vídeor, vidḗrī, vī́sus sum - to be seen, seem, appear (18)

3rd Conjugation

admíttō, admíttere, admī́sī, admíssum - to admit, receive, let in (17)
ágō, ágere, ḗgī, ā́ctum - to drive, lead, do, act; pass, spend *(life or time)* (8)
álō, álere, áluī, áltum - to nourish, support, sustain, increase; cherish (13)
āmíttō, āmíttere, āmī́sī, āmíssum - to send away; lose, let go (12)
cádō, cádere, cécidī, cāsū́rum - to fall (12)
commíttō, commíttere, commī́sī, commíssum - to entrust, commit (15)
cúrrō, cúrrere, cucúrrī, cúrsum - to run, rush, move quickly (14)
dēféndō, dēféndere, dēféndī, dēfḗnsum - to ward off; defend, protect (20)
dī́cō, dī́cere, dī́xī, díctum - to say, tell, speak; name, call (10)
dī́ligō, dīlígere, dīlḗxī, dīlḗctum - to esteem, love (13)
discḗdō, discḗdere, discéssī, discéssum - to go away, depart (20)
díscō, díscere, dídicī - to learn (8)
dū́cō, dū́cere, dū́xī, dúctum - to lead; consider, regard; prolong (8)
flúō, flúere, flū́xī, flū́xum - to flow (18)
gérō, gérere, géssī, géstum - to carry; carry on, manage, conduct, wage, accomplish, perform (8)
intéllegō, intellégere, intellḗxī, intellḗctum - to understand (11)
iúngō, iúngere, iū́nxī, iū́nctum - to join (13)
légō, légere, lḗgī, lḗctum - to pick out, choose; read (18)
míttō, míttere, mī́sī, míssum - to send, let go (11)
néglegō, neglégere, neglḗxī, neglḗctum - to neglect, disregard (17)

régō, régere, rḗxī, rḗctum - to rule, guide, direct (16)
scrī́bō, scrī́bere, scrī́psī, scrī́ptum to write, compose (8)
tráhō, tráhere, trā́xī, tráctum - to draw, drag; derive, acquire (8)
víncō, víncere, vī́cī, víctum - to conquer, overcome (8)
vī́vō, vī́vere, vī́xī, vī́ctum - to live (10)

3rd Conjugation -iō

cápiō, cápere, cḗpī, cáptum - to take, capture, seize, get (10)
cúpiō, cúpere, cupī́vī, cupī́tum - to desire, wish, long for (17)
fáciō, fácere, fḗcī, fáctum - to make, do, accomplish (10)
fúgiō, fúgere, fū́gī, fugitū́rum - to flee, hurry away; escape; go into exile; avoid, shun (10)
iáciō, iácere, iḗcī, iáctum - to throw, hurl (15)
incípiō, incípere, incḗpī, incéptum - to begin (17)

4th Conjugation

aúdiō, audī́re, audī́vī, audī́tum - to hear, listen to (10)
invéniō, invenī́re, invḗnī, invéntum - to come upon, find (10)
séntiō, sentī́re, sḗnsī, sḗnsum - to feel, perceive, think, experience (11)
véniō, venī́re, vḗnī, véntum - to come (10)

Irregular

póssum, pósse, pótuī - to be able, can, could, have power (6)
sum, ésse, fúī, futū́rum - to be, exist (4)

Defective

coépī, coepísse, coéptum - began (17)
ṓdī, ōdísse, ōsū́rum - to hate (20)

Adverbs

ánte (+acc.) - before, previously (13)
béne - well, satisfactorily, quite (11)
cíto - quickly (17)
crās - tomorrow (5)
cūr - why (18)
deínde - thereupon, next, then (18)
díū - long, for a long time (12)
étiam - even, also (11)
héri - yesterday (5)
hódiē - today (3)
iam - now, already, soon (19)
íbi - there (6)
ítaque - and so, therefore (15)
nímis, nímium - too, too much, excessively; *(in a positive sense, esp. with adjectives and adverbs)* exceedingly, very (9)
nōn - not (1)
númquam - never (8)
nunc - now, at present (6)
nū́per - recently (12)
ṓlim - once (upon a time), long ago, formerly; some day, in the future (13)
quam - how (16)
quándō - when (5)
quā́rē - because of which thing *(lit.)*; therefore, wherefore, why (6)
quóque - also, too (17)
saépe - often (1)
sátis - enough, sufficiently (5)
sémper - always (3)
támen - nevertheless, still (8)
tum - then, at that time; thereupon, in the next place (5)
úbi - where, when (6)

Conjunctions

at - but; but, mind you; but, you say (19)
aut - or (17)
aut . . . aut - either . . . or (17)
aútem - however; moreover (11)
dum - while, as long as, at the same time that; *or* until *(+subjunctive)* (8)
énim - for, in fact, truly (9)
et - and; even (2)
et . . . et - both . . . and (2)
ígitur - therefore, consequently (5)
nam - for (13)
néque, nec - and not, nor (11)
néque . . . néque, nec . . . nec - neither . . . nor (11)
nísi - if . . . not, unless; except (19)
quod - because (11)
quóniam - since, inasmuch as (10)
sed - but (2)
sī - if (1)

Prepositions

ab, ā (+abl.) - away from, from; by (14)
ad (+acc.) - to, up to, near to (8)
ánte (+acc.) - before *(in place or time)*, in front of (13)
cóntrā (+acc.) - against (19)
cum (+abl.) - with (10)
dē (+abl.) - down from, from; concerning, about (3)
ex, ē (abl.+) - out of, from, from within; by reason of, on account of ; of *(after cardinal numerals)* (8)
in (+acc.) - into, toward; against (9)
in (+abl.) - in, on (3)
ínter (+acc.) - between, among (15)
per (+acc.) - through; by *(with reflexive pronoun)* (13)
post (+acc.) - after, behind (7)

prō (+abl.) - in front of, before, on behalf of, for the sake of, in return for, instead of, for, as (12)
própter (+acc.) - on account of, because of (5)
síne (+abl.) - without (2)
sub (+abl. w/ verbs of rest *or* **+acc. w/ verbs of motion)** - under, up under, close to, down to/into, to/at the foot of (7)
trāns (+acc.) - across (14)

Interjection

ō - O!, Oh! (2)

Idioms

amā́bō tē - please (1)
grā́tiās ágere (+dat.) - to thank someone; to give thanks to (8)
nōn sṓlum . . . sed étiam - not only . . . but also (9)
poénās dáre - to pay the penalty (2)
sī quándō - if ever (5)

Suffixes

-ne – interrogative suffix attached to the first word of a sentence, typically the verb or another word on which the question hinges, to introduce a question whose answer is uncertain (5)
-que - and *(enclitic conjunction; appended to the second of two words to be joined)* (6)

Numerals

Cardinal - ū́nus *to* vīgíntī quī́nque (15)
Ordinal - prī́mus *to* duodécimus (15)

----

céntum - a hundred (15)
mī́lia, mī́lium (n. pl.) - thousands (15)
mī́lle - thousand (15)

Chapter 21

Nouns

1st Declension

adulēscéntia, adulēscéntiae (f) - youth, young manhood; youthfulness (5)
agrícola, agrícolae (m) - farmer (3)
amíca, amícae (f) - friend (female) (3)
amīcítia, amīcítiae (f) - friendship (10)
áqua, áquae (f) - water (14)
Ásia, Ásiae (f) - Asia (12)
cása, cásae (f) - house, cottage, hut (21)
caúsa, caúsae (f) - cause, reason; case, situation (21)
caúsā (abl. + preceding gen.) - for the sake of, on account of (21)
clēméntia, clēméntiae (f) - mildness, gentleness, mercy (16)
cṓpia, cṓpiae (f) - abundance, supply (8)
cṓpiae, cōpiā́rum (f) - supplies, troops, forces (8)
cúlpa, cúlpae (f) - fault, blame (5)
cū́ra, cū́rae (f) - care, attention, caution, anxiety (4)
déa, déae (f) - goddess (6)
discípula, discípulae (f) - learner, pupil, student (female) (6)
dīvítiae, dīvitiā́rum (f. pl.) - riches, wealth (13)
fā́ma, fā́mae (f) - rumor, report; fame, reputation (2)
família, famíliae (f) - household, family (19)
fḗmina, fḗminae (f) - woman (3)
fenéstra, fenéstrae (f) - window (21)
fī́lia, fī́liae (f) - daughter (3)
fṓrma, fṓrmae (f) - form, shape; beauty (2)
fortū́na, fortū́nae (f) - fortune, luck (2)
glṓria, glṓriae (f) - glory, fame (5)
Graécia, Graéciae (f) - Greece (19)
hṓra, hṓrae (f) - hour, time (10)
īnsídiae, īnsidiā́rum (f) - ambush, plot, treachery (6)
ī́ra, ī́rae (f) - ire, anger (2)
Itália, Itáliae (f) - Italy (15)
líttera, lítterae (f) - a letter of the alphabet (7)
lítterae, litterā́rum (f) - a letter (epistle), literature (7)
magístra, magístrae (f) - schoolmistress, teacher, mistress (4)
médica, médicae (f) - doctor, physician (female) (12)
memória, memóriae (f) - memory, recollection (15)
móra, mórae (f) - delay (4)
nātū́ra, nātū́rae (f) - nature (10)
naúta, naútae (m) - sailor (2)
patiéntia, patiéntiae (f) - suffering; patience, endurance (12)
pátria, pátriae (f) - fatherland, native land, (one's) country (2)
pecū́nia, pecū́niae (f) - money (2)
philosóphia, philosóphiae (f) - philosophy (2)
poéna, poénae (f) - penalty, punishment (2)
poḗta, poḗtae (m) - poet (2)
pórta, pórtae (f) - gate, entrance (2)
puélla, puéllae (f) - girl (2)
rēgī́na, rēgī́nae (f) - queen (7)
Rṓma, Rṓmae (f) - Rome (14)
rósa, rósae (f) - rose (2)
sapiéntia, sapiéntiae (f) - wisdom (3)
sátura, sáturae (f) - satire (16)
sciéntia, sciéntiae (f) - knowledge (18)
sententia, senténtiae (f) - feeling, thought, opinion, vote, sentence (2)
térra, térrae (f) - earth, ground, land, country (7)
Trṓia, Trṓiae (f) - Troy (21)
túrba, túrbae (f) - uproar, disturbance; mob, crowd, multitude (14)
vía, víae (f) - way, road, street (10)
vīcī́na, vīcī́nae (f) - neighbor (female) (21)
victṓria, victṓriae (f) - victory (8)
vī́ta, vī́tae (f) - life; mode of life (2)

2nd Declension

áger, ágrī (m) - field, farm (3)
amī́cus, amī́cī (m) - friend (male) (3)
ánimī, animṓrum (m) - high spirits, pride, courage (5)
ánimus, ánimī (m) - soul, spirit, mind (5)
ánnus, ánnī (m) - year (12)
argūméntum, argūméntī (n) - proof, evidence, argument (19)
bā́sium, bā́siī (n) - kiss (4)
béllum, béllī (n) - war (4)
benefícium, benefíciī (n) - benefit, kindness; favor (19)
caélum, caélī (n) - sky, heaven (5)
coniūrā́tī, coniūrātṓrum (m. pl.) - conspirators (20)
cōnsílium, cōnsíliī (n) - plan, purpose, counsel, advice, judgment, wisdom (4)
déus, déī (m) - god (6)
discípulus, discípulī (m) - learner, pupil, student (male) (6)
dṓnum, dṓnī (n) - gift, present (4)

exítium, exítiī (n) - destruction, ruin (4)
fáctum, fáctī (n) - deed, act, achievement (13)
fī́lius, fī́liī (m) - son (3)
Graécus, Graécī (m) - a Greek (6)
iūdícium, iūdíciī (n) - judgment, decision, opinion; trial (19)
libéllus, libéllī (m) - little book (17)
líber, líbrī (m) - book (6)
lóca, locṓrum (n) - places, region (9)
lócī, locṓrum (m) - passages in literature (9)
lócus, lócī (m) - place; passage in literature (9)
lū́dus, lū́dī (m) - game, sport; school (18)
magíster, magístrī (m) - schoolmaster, teacher, master (4)
médicus, médicī (m) - doctor, physician (male) (12)
mórbus, mórbī (m) - disease, sickness (9)
múndus, múndī (m) - world, universe (21)
númerus, númerī (m) - number (3)
óculus, óculī (m) - eye (4)
offícium, offíciī (n) - duty, service (4)
ṓtium, ṓtiī (n) - leisure, peace (4)
perī́culum, perī́culī (n) - danger, risk (4)
pópulus, pópulī (m) - the people, a people, a nation (3)
prīncípium, prīncípiī (n) - beginning (12)
púer, púerī (m) - boy; boys, children *(pl.)* (3)
remédium, remédiī (n) - cure, remedy (4)
sígnum, sígnī (n) - sign, signal, indication; seal (13)
stúdium, stúdiī (n) - eagerness, zeal, pursuit, study (9)
stúltus, stúltī (m) - a fool (4)
tyránnus, tyránnī (m) - absolute ruler, tyrant (6)
vérbum, vérbī (n)- word (5)
vīcī́nus, vīcī́nī (m) - neighbor (male) (21)
vir, vírī (m) - man, hero (3)
vítium, vítiī (n) - fault, crime, vice (6)
vúlgus, vúlgī (n) - the common people, mob, rabble (21)

3rd Declension

aduléscēns, adulēscéntis (m *or* f) - young man *or* woman (12)
aétās, aetā́tis (f) - period of life, life, age, an age, time (16)
ámor, amṓris (m) - love (7)
aúctor, auctṓris (m) - increaser; author, originator (19)
audī́tor, audītṓris (m) - hearer, listener, member of an audience (16)
Caésar, Caésaris (m) - Caesar (12)
cáput, cápitis (n) - head; leader; beginning; life; heading; chapter (11)
cármen, cárminis (n) - song, poem (7)
Cícerō, Cicerṓnis (m) - (Marcus Tullius) Cicero (8)
cī́vitās, cīvitā́tis (f) - state, citizenship (7)
cṓnsul, cṓnsulis (m) - consul (11)
córpus, córporis (n) - body (7)
cupíditās, cupiditā́tis (f) - desire, longing, passion; cupidity, avarice (10)
flū́men, flū́minis (n) - river (18)
frā́ter, frā́tris (m) - brother (8)
génus, géneris (n) - origin; kind, type, sort, class (18)
hómō, hóminis (m) - human being, man (7)
iū́dex, iū́dicis (m) - judge, juror (19)
iūs, iū́ris (n) - right, justice, law (14)
lábor, labṓris (m)- labor, work, toil; a work, production (7)
laus, laúdis (f) - praise, glory, fame (8)
lībértās, lībertā́tis (f) - liberty (8)
mā́ter, mā́tris (f) - mother (12)
mṓrēs, mṓrum (m) - habits, morals, character (7)
mōs, mṓris (m) - habit, custom, manner (7)
nḗmō, nūllī́us, nḗminī, nḗminem, nū́llō, nū́llā (m *or* f) - no one, nobody (11)
nṓmen, nṓminis (n) - name (7)
ōs, ṓris (n) - mouth, face (14)
páter, pátris (m) - father (12)
pāx, pā́cis (f) - peace (7)
próbitās, probitā́tis (f) - uprightness, honesty (18)
rátiō, ratiṓnis (f) - reckoning, account; reason, judgment, consideration; system; manner, method (8)
rēx, rḗgis (m) - king (7)
sálūs, salū́tis (f) - health, safety; greeting (21)
scélus, scéleris (n) - evil deed, crime, sin, wickedness (19)
scrī́ptor, scrīptṓris (m) - writer, author (8)
senéctūs, senectū́tis (f) - old age (10)
sénex, sénis (m) - old man (16)
sérvitūs, servitū́tis (f) - servitude, slavery (20)
sóror, sorṓris (f) - sister (8)
tempéstās, tempestā́tis (f) - period of time, season; weather, storm (15)
témpus, témporis (n) - time; occasion, opportunity (7)
tímor, timṓris (m) - fear (10)
úxor, uxṓris (f) - wife (7)
vḗritās, vēritā́tis (f) - truth (10)

vírgō, vírginis (f) - maiden, virgin (7)
vírtūs, virtū́tis (f) - manliness, courage; excellence, character, worth, virtue (7)
volúptās, voluptā́tis (f) - pleasure (10)

3rd Declension I-Stem
ánimal, animā́lis (n) - a living creature, animal (14)
ars, ártis (f) - art, skill (14)
aúris, aúris (f) - ear (14)
cī́vis, cī́vis (m *or* f) - citizen (14)
fī́nēs, fī́nium (m) - boundaries, territory (21)
fī́nis, fī́nis (m) - end, limit, boundary; purpose (21)
gēns, géntis (f) - clan, race, nation, people (21)
hóstēs, hóstium (m) - the enemy (18)
hóstis, hóstis (m) - an enemy *(of the state)* (18)
máre, máris (n) - sea (14)
mēns, méntis (f) - mind, thought, intention (16)
mōns, móntis (m) - mountain (20)
mors, mórtis (f) - death (14)
nā́vis, nā́vis (f) - ship, boat (21)
nū́bēs, nū́bis (f) - cloud (14)
pars, pártis (f) - part, share; direction (14)
urbs, úrbis (f) - city (14)
vī́rēs, vī́rium (f. pl.) - strength (14)
vīs, vīs (f) - force, power, violence (14)

4th Declension
córnū, córnūs (n) - horn (20)
frū́ctus, frū́ctūs (m) - fruit; profit, benefit, enjoyment (20)
génū, génūs (n) - knee (20)
mánus, mánūs (f) - hand; handwriting; band (20)
métus, métūs (m) - fear, dread, anxiety (20)
senā́tus, senā́tūs (m) - senate (20)
sḗnsus, sḗnsūs (m) - feeling, sense (20)
spī́ritus, spī́ritūs (m) - breath, breathing; spirit, soul (20)
vérsus, vérsūs (m) - line of verse (20)

Indeclinable
níhil - nothing (1)
sátis - enough (5)

Pronouns

égo, méī - I (11)
hic, haec, hoc - this; the latter; he, she, it, they (9)
ī́dem, éadem, ídem - the same (11)
ílle, ílla, íllud - that; the former; the famous; he, she, it, they (9)
ípse, ípsa, ípsum - myself, yourself, himself, herself, itself, *etc.,* the very, the actual (13)
is, éa, id - this, that; he, she, it (11)
íste, ísta, ístud - that of yours, that; such (as you have, as you speak of); *sometimes with contemptuous force, e.g.,* that despicable, that wretched (9)
quī, quae, quod - who, which, what, that (17)
quid - what (1)
quis? quid? - who? whose? whom? what? which? (19)
quísque, quídque, cuiúsque, cuíque - each one, each person, each thing (13)
súī - himself, herself, itself, themselves (13)
tū, túī - you *(sing.)* (11)

Adjectives

1st & 2nd Declension
acérbus, acérba, acérbum - harsh, bitter, grievous (12)
áliī . . . áliī - some . . . others (9)
álius, ália, áliud - other, another (9)
álter, áltera, álterum - the other (of two), second (9)
amī́cus, amī́ca, amī́cum - friendly (11)
antī́quus, antī́qua, antī́quum - ancient, old-time (2)
ásper, áspera, ásperum - rough, harsh (21)
avā́rus, avā́ra, avā́rum - greedy, avaricious (3)
beā́tus, beā́ta, beā́tum - happy, fortunate, blessed (10)
béllus, bélla, béllum - pretty, handsome, charming (4)
bónus, bóna, bónum - good, kind (4)
caécus, caéca, caécum - blind (17)
cā́rus, cā́ra, cā́rum - dear (11)
cértus, cérta, cértum - definite, sure, certain, reliable (19)
clā́rus, clā́ra, clā́rum - clear, bright; renowned, famous, illustrious (18)
déxter, déxtra, déxtrum - right, right-hand (20)
dóctus, dócta, dóctum - taught, learned, skilled (13)
fortūnā́tus, fortūnā́ta, fortūnā́tum - lucky, fortunate, happy (13)
Graécus, Graéca, Graécum - Greek (6)
hūmā́nus, hūmā́na, hūmā́num - pertaining to man, human; humane, kind; refined, cultivated (4)
iūcúndus, iūcúnda, iūcúndum - pleasant, delightful, agreeable, pleasing (16)
lī́ber, lī́bera, lī́berum - free (5)

lóngus, lónga, lóngum - long (16)
mágnus, mágna, mágnum - large, great; important (2)
málus, mála, málum - bad, wicked, evil (4)
méus, méa, méum - my (2)
míser, mísera, míserum - wretched, miserable, unfortunate (15)
múltus, múlta, múltum - much, many (2)
neúter, neútra, neútrum - not either, neither (9)
nóster, nóstra, nóstrum - our, ours (5)
nóvus, nóva, nóvum - new; strange (7)
nū́llus, nū́lla, nū́llum - not any, no, none (9)
párvus, párva, párvum - small, little (4)
paúcī, paúcae, paúca - few, a few (3)
perpétuus, perpétua, perpétuum perpetual, lasting, uninterrupted, continuous (6)
plḗnus, plḗna, plḗnum - full, abundant, generous (6)
púlcher, púlchra, púlchrum - beautiful, handsome; fine (5)
Rōmā́nus, Rōmā́na, Rōmā́num - Roman (3)
sálvus, sálva, sálvum - safe, sound (6)
sā́nus, sā́na, sā́num - sound, healthy, sane (5)
secúndus, secúnda, secúndum - second; favorable (6)
siníster, sinístra, sinístrum - left, left-hand; harmful, ill-omened (20)
sṓlus, sṓla, sṓlum - alone, only, the only (9)
stúltus, stúlta, stúltum - foolish (4)
súus, súa, súum - his own, her own, its own, their own (13)
tṓtus, tṓta, tṓtum - whole, entire (9)
túus, túa, túum - your *(sing.)* (2)
ū́llus, ū́lla, ū́llum - any (9)
ū́nus, ū́na, ū́num - one, single, alone (9)
úter, útra, útrum - either, which (of two) (9)
vḗrus, vḗra, vḗrum - true, real, proper (4)
véster, véstra, véstrum - your *(pl.)* (6)

3rd Declension

ā́cer, ā́cris, ā́cre - sharp, keen, eager; severe, fierce (16)
brévis, bréve - short, small, brief (16)
céler, céleris, célere - swift, quick, rapid (16)
commū́nis, commū́ne - common, general, of / for the community (20)
diffícilis, diffícile - hard, difficult, troublesome (16)
dúlcis, dúlce - sweet; pleasant, agreeable (16)
fácilis, fácile - easy; agreeable (16)
fórtis, fórte - strong, brave (16)
grávis, gráve - heavy, weighty; serious, important; severe, grievous (19)
immortā́lis, immortā́le - not subject to death, immortal (19)
íngēns, ***gen.*** **ingéntis** - huge (16)
lévis, léve - light; easy; slight, trivial (17)
mortā́lis, mortā́le - mortal (18)
ómnis, ómne - every, all (16)
pótēns, ***gen.*** **poténtis** - able, powerful, mighty, strong (16)
sénex, ***gen.*** **sénis** - old, aged (16)

Indeclinable

sátis - enough, sufficient (5)

Interrogative Adjective

quī?, quae?, quod? - what? which? what kind of?; *(sometimes with exclamatory force)* what (a)! what sort of! (19)

Verbs

1st Conjugation

ádiuvō, adiuvā́re, adiū́vī, adiū́tum - to help, aid, assist; to please (4)
ámō, amā́re, amā́vī, amā́tum - to love, like (1)
appéllō, appellā́re, appellā́vī, appellā́tum - to speak to, address (as), call, name (14)
cḗnō, cēnā́re, cēnā́vī, cēnā́tum - to dine (5)
cṓgitō, cōgitā́re, cōgitā́vī, cōgitā́tum- to think, ponder, consider, plan (1)
cōnsérvō, cōnservā́re, cōnservā́vī, cōnservā́tum - to preserve, conserve, maintain (1)
créō, creā́re, creā́vī, creā́tum - to create (12)
cúlpō, culpā́re, culpā́vī, culpā́tum - to blame, censure (5)
dēléctō, dēlectā́re, dēlectā́vī, dēlectā́tum - to delight, charm, please (19)
dēmṓnstrō, dēmōnstrā́re, dēmōnstrā́vī, dēmōnstrā́tum to point out, show, demonstrate (8)
dēsī́derō, dēsīderā́re, dēsīderā́vī, dēsīderā́tum - to desire, long for, miss (17)

dō, dáre, dédī, dátum - to give, offer (1)
érrō, erráre, errávī, errátum - to wander; err, go astray, make a mistake, be mistaken (1)
exspéctō, exspectáre, exspectávī, exspectátum - to look for, expect, await (15)
iúvō, iuváre, iū́vī, iū́tum - to help, aid, assist; to please (4)
labṓrō, labōráre, labōrávī, labōrátum - to labor; be in distress (21)
laúdō, laudáre, laudávī, laudátum - to praise (1)
lī́berō, līberáre, līberávī, līberátum - to free, liberate (19)
mū́tō, mūtáre, mūtávī, mūtátum to change, alter; exchange (14)
nā́vigō, nāvigáre, nāvigávī, nāvigátum - to sail, navigate (17)
nécō, necáre, necávī, necátum - to murder, kill (7)
párō, paráre, parávī, parátum - to prepare, provide; get, obtain (19)
prōnū́ntiō, prōnūntiáre, prōnūntiávī, prōnūntiátum - to proclaim, announce; declaim; pronounce (20)
récitō, recitáre, recitávī, recitátum - to read aloud, recite (17)
sátiō, satiáre, satiávī, satiátum - to satisfy, sate (3)
sérvō, serváre, servávī, servátum - to preserve, save, keep, guard (1)
stō, stáre, stétī, státum - to stand, stand still *or* firm (13)
súperō, superáre, superávī, superátum - to be above, have the upper hand, surpass; overcome, conquer (5)
tólerō, toleráre, tolerávī, tolerátum - to bear, endure (6)
vī́tō, vītáre, vītávī, vītátum - to avoid, shun (14)
vócō, vocáre, vocávī, vocátum - to call, summon (1)

2nd Conjugation

aúdeō, audḗre, aúsus sum - to dare (7)
cáreō, carḗre, cáruī, caritū́rum (+abl.) - to be without, be deprived of, want, lack; be free from (20)
contíneō, continḗre, contínuī, conténtum - to hold together, contain, keep, enclose, restrain (21)
dḗbeō, dēbḗre, dḗbuī, dḗbitum - to owe; ought, must, should (1)
dḗleō, dēlḗre, dēlḗvī, dēlḗtum - to destroy, wipe out, erase (17)
dóceō, docḗre, dócuī, dóctum - to teach (8)
hábeō, habḗre, hábuī, hábitum - to have, hold, possess; consider, regard (3)
iúbeō, iubḗre, iússī, iússum - to bid, order, command (21)
máneō, manḗre, mā́nsī, mā́nsum - to remain, stay, stay behind, abide, continue (5)
mísceō, miscḗre, míscuī, míxtum to mix, stir up, disturb (18)
móneō, monḗre, mónuī, mónitum - to remind, advise, warn (1)
móveō, movḗre, mṓvī, mṓtum - to move; arouse, affect (18)
prohíbeō, prohibḗre, prohíbuī, prohíbitum - to keep (back), prevent, hinder, restrain, prohibit (20)
remáneō, remanḗre, remā́nsī, remā́nsum - to remain, stay, stay behind, abide, continue (5)
sálvē, salvḗte - hello, greetings (1)
sálveō, salvḗre - to be well, be in good health (1)
téneō, tenḗre, ténuī, téntum - to hold, keep, possess; restrain (14)
térreō, terrḗre, térruī, térritum - to frighten, terrify (1)
tímeō, timḗre, tímuī - to fear, be afraid (of) (15)
válē, valḗte - good-bye, farewell (1)
váleō, valḗre, váluī, valitū́rum - to be strong, have power; be well (1)
vídeō, vidḗre, vī́dī, vī́sum - to see; observe, understand (1)
vídeor, vidḗrī, vī́sus sum - to be seen, seem, appear (18)

3rd Conjugation

admíttō, admíttere, admī́sī, admíssum - to admit, receive, let in (17)
ágō, ágere, ḗgī, ā́ctum - to drive, lead, do, act; pass, spend *(life or time)* (8)
álō, álere, áluī, áltum - to nourish, support, sustain, increase; cherish (13)
āmíttō, āmíttere, āmī́sī, āmíssum - to send away; lose, let go (12)
cádō, cádere, cécidī, cāsū́rum - to fall (12)
commíttō, commíttere, commī́sī, commíssum - to entrust, commit (15)

cúrrō, cúrrere, cucúrrī, cúrsum - to run, rush, move quickly (14)
dēféndō, dēféndere, dēféndī, dēfḗnsum - to ward off; defend, protect (20)
dī́cō, dī́cere, dī́xī, díctum - to say, tell, speak; name, call (10)
dī́ligō, dīlígere, dīlḗxī, dīlḗctum - to esteem, love (13)
discḗdō, discḗdere, discéssī, discéssum - to go away, depart (20)
díscō, díscere, dídicī - to learn (8)
dū́cō, dū́cere, dū́xī, dúctum - to lead; consider, regard; prolong (8)
flúō, flúere, flū́xī, flū́xum - to flow (18)
gérō, gérere, géssī, géstum - to carry; carry on, manage, conduct, wage, accomplish, perform (8)
intéllegō, intellégere, intellḗxī, intellḗctum - to understand (11)
iúngō, iúngere, iū́nxī, iū́nctum - to join (13)
légō, légere, lḗgī, lḗctum - to pick out, choose; read (18)
míttō, míttere, mī́sī, míssum - to send, let go (11)
néglegō, neglégere, neglḗxī, neglḗctum - to neglect, disregard (17)
régō, régere, rḗxī, rḗctum - to rule, guide, direct (16)
relínquō, relínquere, relī́quī, relíctum - to leave behind, leave, abandon, desert (21)
scrī́bō, scrī́bere, scrī́psī, scrī́ptum to write, compose (8)
tángō, tángere, tétigī, tā́ctum - to touch (21)
tráhō, tráhere, trā́xī, tráctum - to draw, drag; derive, acquire (8)
víncō, víncere, vī́cī, víctum - to conquer, overcome (8)
vī́vō, vī́vere, vī́xī, vī́ctum - to live (10)

3rd Conjugation -iō
cápiō, cápere, cḗpī, cáptum - to take, capture, seize, get (10)
cúpiō, cúpere, cupī́vī, cupī́tum - to desire, wish, long for (17)
fáciō, fácere, fḗcī, fáctum - to make, do, accomplish (10)
fúgiō, fúgere, fū́gī, fugitū́rum - to flee, hurry away; escape; go into exile; avoid, shun (10)
iáciō, iácere, iḗcī, iáctum - to throw, hurl (15)
incípiō, incípere, incḗpī, incéptum - to begin (17)
rápiō, rápere, rápuī, ráptum - to seize, snatch, carry away (21)

4th Conjugation
aúdiō, audī́re, audī́vī, audī́tum - to hear, listen to (10)
invéniō, invenī́re, invḗnī, invéntum - to come upon, find (10)
scíō, scī́re, scī́vī, scī́tum - to know (21)
séntiō, sentī́re, sḗnsī, sḗnsum - to feel, perceive, think, experience (11)
véniō, venī́re, vḗnī, véntum - to come (10)

Irregular
póssum, pósse, pótuī - to be able, can, could, have power (6)
sum, ésse, fúī, futū́rum - to be, exist (4)

Defective
coépī, coepísse, coéptum - began (17)
ṓdī, ōdísse, ōsū́rum - to hate (20)

Adverbs
ánte (+acc.) - before, previously (13)
béne - well, satisfactorily, quite (11)
cíto - quickly (17)
crās - tomorrow (5)
cūr - why (18)
deínde - thereupon, next, then (18)
díū - long, for a long time (12)
étiam - even, also (11)
héri - yesterday (5)
hódiē - today (3)
iam - now, already, soon (19)
íbi - there (6)
ítaque - and so, therefore (15)
íterum - again, a second time (21)
nímis, nímium - too, too much, excessively; *(in a positive sense, esp. with adjectives and adverbs)* exceedingly, very (9)
nōn - not (1)
númquam - never (8)
nunc - now, at present (6)
nū́per - recently (12)
ṓlim - once (upon a time), long ago, formerly; some day, in the future (13)
quam - how (16)
quándō - when (5)
quā́rē - because of which thing *(lit.);* therefore, wherefore, why (6)
quóque - also, too (17)
saépe - often (1)
sátis - enough, sufficiently (5)
sémper - always (3)
támen - nevertheless, still (8)

tum - then, at that time; thereupon, in the next place (5)
úbi - where, when (6)

Conjunctions

at - but; but, mind you; but, you say (19)
átque, ac - and also, and even, and in fact (21)
aut - or (17)
aut . . . aut - either . . . or (17)
aútem - however; moreover (11)
dum - while, as long as, at the same time that; *or* until *(+subjunctive)* (8)
énim - for, in fact, truly (9)
et - and; even (2)
et . . . et - both . . . and (2)
ígitur - therefore, consequently (5)
nam - for (13)
néque, nec - and not, nor (11)
néque . . . néque, nec . . . nec - neither . . . nor (11)
nísi - if . . . not, unless; except (19)
quod - because (11)
quóniam - since, inasmuch as (10)
sed - but (2)
sī - if (1)

Prepositions

ab, ā (+abl.) - away from, from; by (14)
ad (+acc.) - to, up to, near to (8)
ánte (+acc.) - before *(in place or time)*, in front of (13)
cóntrā (+acc.) - against (19)
cum (+abl.) - with (10)
dē (+abl.) - down from, from; concerning, about (3)
ex, ē (abl.+) - out of, from, from within; by reason of, on account of ; of *(after cardinal numerals)* (8)
in (+acc.) - into, toward; against (9)
in (+abl.) - in, on (3)
ínter (+acc.) - between, among (15)
per (+acc.) - through; by *(with reflexive pronoun)* (13)
post (+acc.) - after, behind (7)
prō (+abl.) - in front of, before, on behalf of, for the sake of, in return for, instead of, for, as (12)
própter (+acc.) - on account of, because of (5)
síne (+abl.) - without (2)
sub (+abl. w/ verbs of rest *or* +acc. w/ verbs of motion) - under, up under, close to, down to/into, to/at the foot of (7)
trāns (+acc.) - across (14)

Interjection

ō - O!, Oh! (2)

Idioms

amā́bō tē - please (1)
grā́tiās ágere (+dat.) - to thank someone; to give thanks to (8)
nōn sṓlum . . . sed étiam - not only . . . but also (9)
poénās dáre - to pay the penalty (2)
sī quándō - if ever (5)

Suffixes

-ne – interrogative suffix attached to the first word of a sentence, typically the verb or another word on which the question hinges, to introduce a question whose answer is uncertain (5)
-que - and *(enclitic conjunction; appended to the second of two words to be joined)* (6)

Numerals

Cardinal - ū́nus *to* vīgíntī quī́nque (15)
Ordinal - prī́mus *to* duodécimus (15)

----

céntum - a hundred (15)
mī́lia, mī́lium (n. pl.) - thousands (15)
mī́lle - thousand (15)

Chapter 22

Nouns

1st Declension

adulēscéntia, adulēscéntiae (f) - youth, young manhood; youthfulness (5)
agrícola, agrícolae (m) - farmer (3)
amíca, amícae (f) - friend (female) (3)
amīcítia, amīcítiae (f) - friendship (10)
áqua, áquae (f) - water (14)
Ásia, Ásiae (f) - Asia (12)
cása, cásae (f) - house, cottage, hut (21)
caúsa, caúsae (f) - cause, reason; case, situation (21)
caúsā (abl. + preceding gen.) - for the sake of, on account of (21)
clēméntia, clēméntiae (f) - mildness, gentleness, mercy (16)
cṓpia, cṓpiae (f) - abundance, supply (8)
cṓpiae, cōpiā́rum (f) - supplies, troops, forces (8)
cúlpa, cúlpae (f) - fault, blame (5)
cū́ra, cū́rae (f) - care, attention, caution, anxiety (4)
déa, déae (f) - goddess (6)
discípula, discípulae (f) - learner, pupil, student (female) (6)
dīvítiae, dīvitiā́rum (f. pl.) - riches, wealth (13)
fā́ma, fā́mae (f) - rumor, report; fame, reputation (2)
família, famíliae (f) - household, family (19)
fḗmina, fḗminae (f) - woman (3)
fenéstra, fenéstrae (f) - window (21)
fī́lia, fī́liae (f) - daughter (3)
fṓrma, fṓrmae (f) - form, shape; beauty (2)
fortū́na, fortū́nae (f) - fortune, luck (2)
glṓria, glṓriae (f) - glory, fame (5)
Graécia, Graéciae (f) - Greece (19)
hṓra, hṓrae (f) - hour, time (10)
īnsídiae, īnsidiā́rum (f) - ambush, plot, treachery (6)
ī́ra, ī́rae (f) - ire, anger (2)
Itália, Itáliae (f) - Italy (15)
líttera, lítterae (f) - a letter of the alphabet (7)
lítterae, litterā́rum (f) - a letter (epistle), literature (7)
magístra, magístrae (f) - schoolmistress, teacher, mistress (4)
médica, médicae (f) - doctor, physician (female) (12)
memória, memóriae (f) - memory, recollection (15)
móra, mórae (f) - delay (4)
nātū́ra, nātū́rae (f) - nature (10)
naúta, naútae (m) - sailor (2)
patiéntia, patiéntiae (f) - suffering; patience, endurance (12)
pátria, pátriae (f) - fatherland, native land, (one's) country (2)
pecū́nia, pecū́niae (f) - money (2)
philosóphia, philosóphiae (f) - philosophy (2)
poéna, poénae (f) - penalty, punishment (2)
poḗta, poḗtae (m) - poet (2)
pórta, pórtae (f) - gate, entrance (2)
puélla, puéllae (f) - girl (2)
rēgī́na, rēgī́nae (f) - queen (7)
Rṓma, Rṓmae (f) - Rome (14)
rósa, rósae (f) - rose (2)
sapiéntia, sapiéntiae (f) - wisdom (3)
sátura, sáturae (f) - satire (16)
sciéntia, sciéntiae (f) - knowledge (18)
senténtia, senténtiae (f) - feeling, thought, opinion, vote, sentence (2)
térra, térrae (f) - earth, ground, land, country (7)
Trṓia, Trṓiae (f) - Troy (21)
túrba, túrbae (f) - uproar, disturbance; mob, crowd, multitude (14)
vía, víae (f) - way, road, street (10)
vīcī́na, vīcī́nae (f) - neighbor (female) (21)
victṓria, victṓriae (f) - victory (8)
vī́ta, vī́tae (f) - life; mode of life (2)

2nd Declension

áger, ágrī (m) - field, farm (3)
amī́cus, amī́cī (m) - friend (male) (3)
ánimī, animṓrum (m) - high spirits, pride, courage (5)
ánimus, ánimī (m) - soul, spirit, mind (5)
ánnus, ánnī (m) - year (12)
argūméntum, argūméntī (n) - proof, evidence, argument (19)
bā́sium, bā́siī (n) - kiss (4)
béllum, béllī (n) - war (4)
benefícium, benefíciī (n) - benefit, kindness; favor (19)
caélum, caélī (n) - sky, heaven (5)
coniūrā́tī, coniūrātṓrum (m. pl.) - conspirators (20)
cōnsílium, cōnsíliī (n) - plan, purpose, counsel, advice, judgment, wisdom (4)
déus, déī (m) - god (6)
discípulus, discípulī (m) - learner, pupil, student (male) (6)
dṓnum, dṓnī (n) - gift, present (4)

exítium, exítiī (n) - destruction, ruin (4)
fáctum, fáctī (n) - deed, act, achievement (13)
férrum, férrī (n) - iron; sword (22)
fīlius, fīliī (m) - son (3)
Graécus, Graécī (m) - a Greek (6)
iūdícium, iūdíciī (n) - judgment, decision, opinion; trial (19)
libéllus, libéllī (m) - little book (17)
líber, líbrī (m) - book (6)
lóca, locṓrum (n) - places, region (9)
lócī, locṓrum (m) - passages in literature (9)
lócus, lócī (m) - place; passage in literature (9)
lū́dus, lū́dī (m) - game, sport; school (18)
magíster, magístrī (m) - schoolmaster, teacher, master (4)
médicus, médicī (m) - doctor, physician (male) (12)
módus, módī (m) - measure, bound, limit; manner, method, mode, way (22)
mórbus, mórbī (m) - disease, sickness (9)
múndus, múndī (m) - world, universe (21)
númerus, númerī (m) - number (3)
óculus, óculī (m) - eye (4)
offícium, offíciī (n) - duty, service (4)
ṓtium, ṓtiī (n) - leisure, peace (4)
perī́culum, perī́culī (n) - danger, risk (4)
pópulus, pópulī (m) - the people, a people, a nation (3)
prīncípium, prīncípiī (n) - beginning (12)
púer, púerī (m) - boy; boys, children *(pl.)* (3)
remédium, remédiī (n) - cure, remedy (4)
sígnum, sígnī (n) - sign, signal, indication; seal (13)
stúdium, stúdiī (n) - eagerness, zeal, pursuit, study (9)
stúltus, stúltī (m) - a fool (4)
tyránnus, tyránnī (m) - absolute ruler, tyrant (6)
vérbum, vérbī (n)- word (5)
vīcī́nus, vīcī́nī (m) - neighbor (male) (21)
vir, vírī (m) - man, hero (3)
vítium, vítiī (n) - fault, crime, vice (6)
vúlgus, vúlgī (n) - the common people, mob, rabble (21)

3rd Declension

adulḗscēns, adulēscéntis (m *or* f) - young man *or* woman (12)
aétās, aetā́tis (f) - period of life, life, age, an age, time (16)
ámor, amṓris (m) - love (7)
aúctor, auctṓris (m) - increaser; author, originator (19)
audī́tor, audītṓris (m) - hearer, listener, member of an audience (16)
Caésar, Caésaris (m) - Caesar (12)
cáput, cápitis (n) - head; leader; beginning; life; heading; chapter (11)
cármen, cárminis (n) - song, poem (7)
Cícerō, Cicerṓnis (m) - (Marcus Tullius) Cicero (8)
cī́vitās, cīvitā́tis (f) - state, citizenship (7)
cṓnsul, cṓnsulis (m) - consul (11)
córpus, córporis (n) - body (7)
cupíditās, cupiditā́tis (f) - desire, longing, passion; cupidity, avarice (10)
flū́men, flū́minis (n) - river (18)
frā́ter, frā́tris (m) - brother (8)
génus, géneris (n) - origin; kind, type, sort, class (18)
hómō, hóminis (m) - human being, man (7)
iū́dex, iū́dicis (m) - judge, juror (19)
iūs, iū́ris (n) - right, justice, law (14)
lábor, labṓris (m)- labor, work, toil; a work, production (7)
laus, laúdis (f) - praise, glory, fame (8)
lībértās, lībertā́tis (f) - liberty (8)
mā́ter, mā́tris (f) - mother (12)
mṓrēs, mṓrum (m) - habits, morals, character (7)
mōs, mṓris (m) - habit, custom, manner (7)
nḗmō, nūllī́us, nḗminī, nḗminem, nū́llō, nū́llā (m *or* f) - no one, nobody (11)
nṓmen, nṓminis (n) - name (7)
ōs, ṓris (n) - mouth, face (14)
páter, pátris (m) - father (12)
pāx, pā́cis (f) - peace (7)
próbitās, probitā́tis (f) - uprightness, honesty (18)
rátiō, ratiṓnis (f) - reckoning, account; reason, judgment, consideration; system; manner, method (8)
rēx, rḗgis (m) - king (7)
sálūs, salū́tis (f) - health, safety; greeting (21)
scélus, scéleris (n) - evil deed, crime, sin, wickedness (19)
scrī́ptor, scrīptṓris (m) - writer, author (8)
senéctūs, senectū́tis (f) - old age (10)
sénex, sénis (m) - old man (16)
sérvitūs, servitū́tis (f) - servitude, slavery (20)
sóror, sorṓris (f) - sister (8)
tempéstās, tempestā́tis (f) - period of time, season; weather, storm (15)
témpus, témporis (n) - time; occasion, opportunity (7)

tímor, timṓris (m) - fear (10)
úxor, uxṓris (f) - wife (7)
vḗritās, vēritā́tis (f) - truth (10)
vírgō, vírginis (f) - maiden, virgin (7)
vírtūs, virtū́tis (f) - manliness, courage; excellence, character, worth, virtue (7)
volúptās, voluptā́tis (f) - pleasure (10)

3rd Declension I-Stem
ánimal, animā́lis (n) - a living creature, animal (14)
ars, ártis (f) - art, skill (14)
aúris, aúris (f) - ear (14)
cī́vis, cī́vis (m *or* f) - citizen (14)
fī́nēs, fī́nium (m) - boundaries, territory (21)
fī́nis, fī́nis (m) - end, limit, boundary; purpose (21)
gēns, géntis (f) - clan, race, nation, people (21)
hóstēs, hóstium (m) - the enemy (18)
hóstis, hóstis (m) - an enemy *(of the state)* (18)
ígnis, ígnis (m) - fire (22)
máre, máris (n) - sea (14)
mēns, méntis (f) - mind, thought, intention (16)
mōns, móntis (m) - mountain (20)
mors, mórtis (f) - death (14)
nā́vis, nā́vis (f) - ship, boat (21)
nū́bēs, nū́bis (f) - cloud (14)
pars, pártis (f) - part, share; direction (14)
urbs, úrbis (f) - city (14)
vī́rēs, vī́rium (f. pl.) - strength (14)
vīs, vīs (f) - force, power, violence (14)

4th Declension
córnū, córnūs (n) - horn (20)
frū́ctus, frū́ctūs (m) - fruit; profit, benefit, enjoyment (20)
génū, génūs (n) - knee (20)
mánus, mánūs (f) - hand; handwriting; band (20)
métus, métūs (m) - fear, dread, anxiety (20)
senā́tus, senā́tūs (m) - senate (20)
sḗnsus, sḗnsūs (m) - feeling, sense (20)
spī́ritus, spī́ritūs (m) - breath, breathing; spirit, soul (20)
vérsus, vérsūs (m) - line of verse (20)

5th Declension
díēs, diḗī (m) - day (22)
fídēs, fídeī (f) - faith, trust, trustworthiness, fidelity, promise, guarantee, protection (22)
rēs, réī (f) - thing, matter, property, business, affair (22)
rēs pū́blica, réī pū́blicae (f) - state, commonwealth, republic (22)
spēs, spéī (f) - hope (22)

Indeclinable
níhil - nothing (1)
sátis - enough (5)

Pronouns
égo, méī - I (11)
hic, haec, hoc - this; the latter; he, she, it, they (9)
ī́dem, éadem, ídem - the same (11)
ílle, ílla, íllud - that; the former; the famous; he, she, it, they (9)
ípse, ípsa, ípsum - myself, yourself, himself, herself, itself, *etc.,* the very, the actual (13)
is, éa, id - this, that; he, she, it (11)
íste, ísta, ístud - that of yours, that; such (as you have, as you speak of); *sometimes with contemptuous force, e.g.,* that despicable, that wretched (9)
quī, quae, quod - who, which, what, that (17)
quid - what (1)
quis? quid? - who? whose? whom? what? which? (19)
quísque, quídque, cuiúsque, cuíque - each one, each person, each thing (13)
súī - himself, herself, itself, themselves (13)
tū, túī - you *(sing.)* (11)

Adjectives
1st & 2nd Declension
acérbus, acérba, acérbum - harsh, bitter, grievous (12)
aéquus, aéqua, aéquum - level, even; calm; equal, just; favorable (22)
áliī . . . áliī - some . . . others (9)
álius, ália, áliud - other, another (9)
álter, áltera, álterum - the other (of two), second (9)
amī́cus, amī́ca, amī́cum - friendly (11)
antī́quus, antī́qua, antī́quum - ancient, old-time (2)
ásper, áspera, ásperum - rough, harsh (21)
avā́rus, avā́ra, avā́rum - greedy, avaricious (3)
beā́tus, beā́ta, beā́tum - happy, fortunate, blessed (10)
béllus, bélla, béllum - pretty, handsome, charming (4)
bónus, bóna, bónum - good, kind (4)
caécus, caéca, caécum - blind (17)
cā́rus, cā́ra, cā́rum - dear (11)

cértus, cérta, cértum - definite, sure, certain, reliable (19)
clā́rus, clā́ra, clā́rum - clear, bright; renowned, famous, illustrious (18)
déxter, déxtra, déxtrum - right, right-hand (20)
dóctus, dócta, dóctum - taught, learned, skilled (13)
fortūnā́tus, fortūnā́ta, fortūnā́tum - lucky, fortunate, happy (13)
Graécus, Graéca, Graécum - Greek (6)
hūmā́nus, hūmā́na, hūmā́num - pertaining to man, human; humane, kind; refined, cultivated (4)
incértus, incérta, incértum - uncertain, unsure, doubtful (22)
iūcúndus, iūcúnda, iūcúndum - pleasant, delightful, agreeable, pleasing (16)
Latī́nus, Latī́na, Latī́num - Latin (22)
lī́ber, lī́bera, lī́berum - free (5)
lóngus, lónga, lóngum - long (16)
mágnus, mágna, mágnum - large, great; important (2)
málus, mála, málum - bad, wicked, evil (4)
médius, média, médium - middle; the middle of (22)
méus, méa, méum - my (2)
míser, mísera, míserum - wretched, miserable, unfortunate (15)
múltus, múlta, múltum - much, many (2)
neúter, neútra, neútrum - not either, neither (9)
nóster, nóstra, nóstrum - our, ours (5)
nóvus, nóva, nóvum - new; strange (7)
nū́llus, nū́lla, nū́llum - not any, no, none (9)
párvus, párva, párvum - small, little (4)
paúcī, paúcae, paúca - few, a few (3)
perpétuus, perpétua, perpétuum perpetual, lasting, uninterrupted, continuous (6)
plḗnus, plḗna, plḗnum - full, abundant, generous (6)
púlcher, púlchra, púlchrum - beautiful, handsome; fine (5)
Rōmā́nus, Rōmā́na, Rōmā́num - Roman (3)
sálvus, sálva, sálvum - safe, sound (6)
sā́nus, sā́na, sā́num - sound, healthy, sane (5)
secúndus, secúnda, secúndum - second; favorable (6)
siníster, sinístra, sinístrum - left, left-hand; harmful, ill-omened (20)
sṓlus, sṓla, sṓlum - alone, only, the only (9)
stúltus, stúlta, stúltum - foolish (4)
súus, súa, súum - his own, her own, its own, their own (13)
tṓtus, tṓta, tṓtum - whole, entire (9)
túus, túa, túum - your *(sing.)* (2)
ū́llus, ū́lla, ū́llum - any (9)
ū́nus, ū́na, ū́num - one, single, alone (9)
úter, útra, útrum - either, which (of two) (9)
vḗrus, vḗra, vḗrum - true, real, proper (4)
véster, véstra, véstrum - your *(pl.)* (6)

3rd Declension
ā́cer, ā́cris, ā́cre - sharp, keen, eager; severe, fierce (16)
brévis, bréve - short, small, brief (16)
céler, céleris, célere - swift, quick, rapid (16)
commū́nis, commū́ne - common, general, of / for the community (20)
diffícilis, diffícile - hard, difficult, troublesome (16)
dúlcis, dúlce - sweet; pleasant, agreeable (16)
fácilis, fácile - easy; agreeable (16)
fḗlīx, *gen.* **fēlī́cis** - lucky, fortunate, happy (22)
fórtis, fórte - strong, brave (16)
grávis, gráve - heavy, weighty; serious, important; severe, grievous (19)
immortā́lis, immortā́le - not subject to death, immortal (19)
íngēns, *gen.* **ingéntis** - huge (16)
lévis, léve - light; easy; slight, trivial (17)
mortā́lis, mortā́le - mortal (18)
ómnis, ómne - every, all (16)
pótēns, *gen.* **poténtis** - able, powerful, mighty, strong (16)
sénex, *gen.* **sénis** - old, aged (16)

Indeclinable
sátis - enough, sufficient (5)

Interrogative Adjective
quī?, quae?, quod? - what? which? what kind of?; *(sometimes with exclamatory force)* what (a)! what sort of! (19)

Verbs
1st Conjugation
ádiuvō, adiuvā́re, adiū́vī, adiū́tum - to help, aid, assist; to please (4)

ámō, amā́re, amā́vī, amā́tum - to love, like (1)
appéllō, appellā́re, appellā́vī, appellā́tum - to speak to, address (as), call, name (14)
cḗnō, cēnā́re, cēnā́vī, cēnā́tum - to dine (5)
cṓgitō, cōgitā́re, cōgitā́vī, cōgitā́tum- to think, ponder, consider, plan (1)
cōnsérvō, cōnservā́re, cōnservā́vī, cōnservā́tum - to preserve, conserve, maintain (1)
créō, creā́re, creā́vī, creā́tum - to create (12)
cúlpō, culpā́re, culpā́vī, culpā́tum - to blame, censure (5)
dēléctō, dēlectā́re, dēlectā́vī, dēlectā́tum - to delight, charm, please (19)
dēmṓnstrō, dēmōnstrā́re, dēmōnstrā́vī, dēmōnstrā́tum to point out, show, demonstrate (8)
dēsī́derō, dēsīderā́re, dēsīderā́vī, dēsīderā́tum - to desire, long for, miss (17)
dō, dáre, dédī, dátum - to give, offer (1)
érrō, errā́re, errā́vī, errā́tum - to wander; err, go astray, make a mistake, be mistaken (1)
exspéctō, exspectā́re, exspectā́vī, exspectā́tum - to look for, expect, await (15)
iúvō, iuvā́re, iū́vī, iū́tum - to help, aid, assist; to please (4)
labṓrō, labōrā́re, labōrā́vī, labōrā́tum - to labor; be in distress (21)
laúdō, laudā́re, laudā́vī, laudā́tum - to praise (1)
lī́berō, līberā́re, līberā́vī, līberā́tum - to free, liberate (19)
mū́tō, mūtā́re, mūtā́vī, mūtā́tum to change, alter; exchange (14)
nā́vigō, nāvigā́re, nāvigā́vī, nāvigā́tum - to sail, navigate (17)
nécō, necā́re, necā́vī, necā́tum - to murder, kill (7)
párō, parā́re, parā́vī, parā́tum - to prepare, provide; get, obtain (19)
prōnū́ntiō, prōnūntiā́re, prōnūntiā́vī, prōnūntiā́tum - to proclaim, announce; declaim; pronounce (20)
récitō, recitā́re, recitā́vī, recitā́tum - to read aloud, recite (17)
sátiō, satiā́re, satiā́vī, satiā́tum - to satisfy, sate (3)
sérvō, servā́re, servā́vī, servā́tum - to preserve, save, keep, guard (1)
stō, stā́re, stétī, stā́tum - to stand, stand still *or* firm (13)
súperō, superā́re, superā́vī, superā́tum - to be above, have the upper hand, surpass; overcome, conquer (5)
tólerō, tolerā́re, tolerā́vī, tolerā́tum - to bear, endure (6)
vī́tō, vītā́re, vītā́vī, vītā́tum - to avoid, shun (14)
vócō, vocā́re, vocā́vī, vocā́tum - to call, summon (1)

2nd Conjugation

aúdeō, audḗre, aúsus sum - to dare (7)
cáreō, carḗre, cáruī, caritū́rum (+abl.) - to be without, be deprived of, want, lack; be free from (20)
contíneō, continḗre, contínuī, conténtum - to hold together, contain, keep, enclose, restrain (21)
dḗbeō, dēbḗre, dḗbuī, dḗbitum - to owe; ought, must, should (1)
déleō, dēlḗre, dēlḗvī, dēlḗtum - to destroy, wipe out, erase (17)
dóceō, docḗre, dócuī, dóctum - to teach (8)
hábeō, habḗre, hábuī, hábitum - to have, hold, possess; consider, regard (3)
iúbeō, iubḗre, iússī, iússum - to bid, order, command (21)
máneō, manḗre, mā́nsī, mā́nsum - to remain, stay, stay behind, abide, continue (5)
mísceō, miscḗre, míscuī, míxtum to mix, stir up, disturb (18)
móneō, monḗre, mónuī, mónitum - to remind, advise, warn (1)
móveō, movḗre, mṓvī, mṓtum - to move; arouse, affect (18)
prohíbeō, prohibḗre, prohíbuī, prohíbitum - to keep (back), prevent, hinder, restrain, prohibit (20)
remáneō, remanḗre, remā́nsī, remā́nsum - to remain, stay, stay behind, abide, continue (5)
sálvē, salvḗte - hello, greetings (1)
sálveō, salvḗre - to be well, be in good health (1)
téneō, tenḗre, ténuī, téntum - to hold, keep, possess; restrain (14)
térreō, terrḗre, térruī, térritum - to frighten, terrify (1)
tímeō, timḗre, tímuī - to fear, be afraid (of) (15)
válē, valḗte - good-bye, farewell (1)

váleō, valḗre, váluī, valitū́rum - to be strong, have power; be well (1)

vídeō, vidḗre, vī́dī, vī́sum - to see; observe, understand (1)

vídeor, vidḗrī, vī́sus sum - to be seen, seem, appear (18)

3rd Conjugation

admíttō, admíttere, admī́sī, admíssum - to admit, receive, let in (17)

ágō, ágere, ḗgī, ā́ctum - to drive, lead, do, act; pass, spend *(life or time)* (8)

álō, álere, áluī, áltum - to nourish, support, sustain, increase; cherish (13)

āmíttō, āmíttere, āmī́sī, āmíssum - to send away; lose, let go (12)

cádō, cádere, cécidī, cāsū́rum - to fall (12)

cérnō, cérnere, crḗvī, crḗtum - to distinguish, discern, perceive (22)

commíttō, commíttere, commī́sī, commíssum - to entrust, commit (15)

cúrrō, cúrrere, cucúrrī, cúrsum - to run, rush, move quickly (14)

dēféndō, dēféndere, dēféndī, dēfḗnsum - to ward off; defend, protect (20)

dī́cō, dī́cere, dī́xī, díctum - to say, tell, speak; name, call (10)

dī́ligō, dīlígere, dīlḗxī, dīléctum - to esteem, love (13)

discḗdō, discḗdere, discéssī, discéssum - to go away, depart (20)

díscō, díscere, dídicī - to learn (8)

dū́cō, dū́cere, dū́xī, dúctum - to lead; consider, regard; prolong (8)

flúō, flúere, flū́xī, flū́xum - to flow (18)

gérō, gérere, géssī, géstum - to carry; carry on, manage, conduct, wage, accomplish, perform (8)

intéllegō, intellégere, intellḗxī, intellḗctum - to understand (11)

iúngō, iúngere, iū́nxī, iū́nctum - to join (13)

légō, légere, lḗgī, lḗctum - to pick out, choose; read (18)

míttō, míttere, mī́sī, míssum - to send, let go (11)

néglegō, neglégere, neglḗxī, neglḗctum - to neglect, disregard (17)

régō, régere, rḗxī, rḗctum - to rule, guide, direct (16)

relínquō, relínquere, relī́quī, relíctum - to leave behind, leave, abandon, desert (21)

scrī́bō, scrī́bere, scrī́psī, scrī́ptum to write, compose (8)

tángō, tángere, tétigī, tā́ctum - to touch (21)

tóllō, tóllere, sústulī, sublā́tum - to raise, lift up; take away, remove, destroy (22)

tráhō, tráhere, trā́xī, tráctum - to draw, drag; derive, acquire (8)

víncō, víncere, vī́cī, víctum - to conquer, overcome (8)

vī́vō, vī́vere, vī́xī, vī́ctum - to live (10)

3rd Conjugation -iō

cápiō, cápere, cḗpī, cáptum - to take, capture, seize, get (10)

cúpiō, cúpere, cupī́vī, cupī́tum - to desire, wish, long for (17)

ērípiō, ērípere, ērípuī, ēréptum - to snatch away, take away; rescue (22)

fáciō, fácere, fḗcī, fáctum - to make, do, accomplish (10)

fúgiō, fúgere, fū́gī, fugitū́rum - to flee, hurry away; escape; go into exile; avoid, shun (10)

iáciō, iácere, iḗcī, iáctum - to throw, hurl (15)

incípiō, incípere, incḗpī, incéptum - to begin (17)

rápiō, rápere, rápuī, ráptum - to seize, snatch, carry away (21)

4th Conjugation

aúdiō, audī́re, audī́vī, audī́tum - to hear, listen to (10)

invéniō, invenī́re, invḗnī, invéntum - to come upon, find (10)

scíō, scī́re, scī́vī, scī́tum - to know (21)

séntiō, sentī́re, sḗnsī, sḗnsum - to feel, perceive, think, experience (11)

véniō, venī́re, vḗnī, véntum - to come (10)

Irregular

póssum, pósse, pótuī - to be able, can, could, have power (6)

sum, ésse, fúī, futū́rum - to be, exist (4)

Defective

coépī, coepísse, coéptum - began (17)

ínquit - he says *or* said (22)

ṓdī, ōdísse, ōsū́rum - to hate (20)

Adverbs

ánte (+acc.) - before, previously (13)
béne - well, satisfactorily, quite (11)
cíto - quickly (17)
crās - tomorrow (5)
cūr - why (18)
deínde - thereupon, next, then (18)
díū - long, for a long time (12)
étiam - even, also (11)
héri - yesterday (5)
hódiē - today (3)
iam - now, already, soon (19)
íbi - there (6)
ítaque - and so, therefore (15)
íterum - again, a second time (21)
nímis, nímium - too, too much, excessively; *(in a positive sense, esp. with adjectives and adverbs)* exceedingly, very (9)
nōn - not (1)
númquam - never (8)
nunc - now, at present (6)
nū́per - recently (12)
ṓlim - once (upon a time), long ago, formerly; some day, in the future (13)
prṓtinus - immediately (22)
quam - how (16)
quándō - when (5)
quā́rē - because of which thing *(lit.)*; therefore, wherefore, why (6)
quóndam - formerly, once (22)
quóque - also, too (17)
saépe - often (1)
sátis - enough, sufficiently (5)
sémper - always (3)
támen - nevertheless, still (8)
tum - then, at that time; thereupon, in the next place (5)
úbi - where, when (6)
últrā - on the other side of, beyond (22)

Conjunctions

at - but; but, mind you; but, you say (19)
átque, ac - and also, and even, and in fact (21)
aut - or (17)
aut . . . aut - either . . . or (17)
aútem - however; moreover (11)
dum - while, as long as, at the same time that; *or* until *(+subjunctive)* (8)
énim - for, in fact, truly (9)
et - and; even (2)
et . . . et - both . . . and (2)
ígitur - therefore, consequently (5)
nam - for (13)
néque, nec - and not, nor (11)
néque . . . néque, nec . . . nec - neither . . . nor (11)
nísi - if . . . not, unless; except (19)
quod - because (11)
quóniam - since, inasmuch as (10)
sed - but (2)
sī - if (1)

Prepositions

ab, ā (+abl.) - away from, from; by (14)
ad (+acc.) - to, up to, near to (8)
ánte (+acc.) - before *(in place or time)*, in front of (13)
cóntrā (+acc.) - against (19)
cum (+abl.) - with (10)
dē (+abl.) - down from, from; concerning, about (3)
ex, ē (abl.+) - out of, from, from within; by reason of, on account of; of *(after cardinal numerals)* (8)
in (+acc.) - into, toward; against (9)
in (+abl.) - in, on (3)
ínter (+acc.) - between, among (15)
per (+acc.) - through; by *(with reflexive pronoun)* (13)
post (+acc.) - after, behind (7)
prō (+abl.) - in front of, before, on behalf of, for the sake of, in return for, instead of, for, as (12)
própter (+acc.) - on account of, because of (5)
síne (+abl.) - without (2)
sub (+abl. w/ verbs of rest *or* **+acc. w/ verbs of motion)** - under, up under, close to, down to/into, to/at the foot of (7)
trāns (+acc.) - across (14)
últrā (adv. and prep. +acc.) - on the other side of, beyond (22)

Interjection

ō - O!, Oh! (2)

Idioms

amā́bō tē - please (1)
grā́tiās ágere (+dat.) - to thank someone; to give thanks to (8)
nōn sṓlum . . . sed étiam - not only . . . but also (9)
poénās dáre - to pay the penalty (2)
sī quándō - if ever (5)

Suffixes

-ne – interrogative suffix attached to the first word of a sentence, typically the verb or another word on which the question hinges, to introduce a question whose answer is uncertain (5)
-que - and *(enclitic conjunction; appended to the second of two words to be joined)* (6)

Numerals

Cardinal - ū́nus *to* vīgíntī quī́nque (15)
Ordinal - prī́mus *to* duodécimus (15)

----

céntum - a hundred (15)
mī́lia, mī́lium (n. pl.) - thousands (15)
mī́lle - thousand (15)

Chapter 23

Nouns

1st Declension

adulēscéntia, adulēscéntiae (f) - youth, young manhood; youthfulness (5)
agrícola, agrícolae (m) - farmer (3)
amíca, amícae (f) - friend (female) (3)
amīcítia, amīcítiae (f) - friendship (10)
áqua, áquae (f) - water (14)
Ásia, Ásiae (f) - Asia (12)
cása, cásae (f) - house, cottage, hut (21)
caúsa, caúsae (f) - cause, reason; case, situation (21)
caúsā (abl. + preceding gen.) - for the sake of, on account of (21)
clēméntia, clēméntiae (f) - mildness, gentleness, mercy (16)
cṓpia, cṓpiae (f) - abundance, supply (8)
cṓpiae, cōpiā́rum (f) - supplies, troops, forces (8)
cúlpa, cúlpae (f) - fault, blame (5)
cū́ra, cū́rae (f) - care, attention, caution, anxiety (4)
déa, déae (f) - goddess (6)
discípula, discípulae (f) - learner, pupil, student (female) (6)
dīvítiae, dīvitiā́rum (f. pl.) - riches, wealth (13)
fā́ma, fā́mae (f) - rumor, report; fame, reputation (2)
família, famíliae (f) - household, family (19)
fḗmina, fḗminae (f) - woman (3)
fenéstra, fenéstrae (f) - window (21)
fī́lia, fī́liae (f) - daughter (3)
fṓrma, fṓrmae (f) - form, shape; beauty (2)
fortū́na, fortū́nae (f) - fortune, luck (2)
glṓria, glṓriae (f) - glory, fame (5)
Graécia, Graéciae (f) - Greece (19)
hásta, hástae (f) - spear (23)
hṓra, hṓrae (f) - hour, time (10)
īnsídiae, īnsidiā́rum (f) - ambush, plot, treachery (6)
ī́nsula, ī́nsulae (f) - island (23)
ī́ra, ī́rae (f) - ire, anger (2)
Itália, Itáliae (f) - Italy (15)
líttera, lítterae (f) - a letter of the alphabet (7)
lítterae, litterā́rum (f) - a letter (epistle), literature (7)
magístra, magístrae (f) - schoolmistress, teacher, mistress (4)
médica, médicae (f) - doctor, physician (female) (12)
memória, memóriae (f) - memory, recollection (15)
móra, mórae (f) - delay (4)
nātū́ra, nātū́rae (f) - nature (10)
naúta, naútae (m) - sailor (2)
patiéntia, patiéntiae (f) - suffering; patience, endurance (12)
pátria, pátriae (f) - fatherland, native land, (one's) country (2)
pecū́nia, pecū́niae (f) - money (2)
philosóphia, philosóphiae (f) - philosophy (2)
poéna, poénae (f) - penalty, punishment (2)
poḗta, poḗtae (m) - poet (2)
pórta, pórtae (f) - gate, entrance (2)
puélla, puéllae (f) - girl (2)
rēgī́na, rēgī́nae (f) - queen (7)
Rṓma, Rṓmae (f) - Rome (14)
rósa, rósae (f) - rose (2)
sapiéntia, sapiéntiae (f) - wisdom (3)
sátura, săturae (f) - satire (16)
sciéntia, sciéntiae (f) - knowledge (18)
senténtia, senténtiae (f) - feeling, thought, opinion, vote, sentence (2)
térra, térrae (f) - earth, ground, land, country (7)
Trṓia, Trṓiae (f) - Troy (21)
túrba, túrbae (f) - uproar, disturbance; mob, crowd, multitude (14)
vía, víae (f) - way, road, street (10)
vīcī́na, vīcī́nae (f) - neighbor (female) (21)
victṓria, victṓriae (f) - victory (8)
vī́ta, vī́tae (f) - life; mode of life (2)

2nd Declension

áger, ágrī (m) - field, farm (3)
amī́cus, amī́cī (m) - friend (male) (3)
ánimī, animṓrum (m) - high spirits, pride, courage (5)
ánimus, ánimī (m) - soul, spirit, mind (5)
ánnus, ánnī (m) - year (12)
argūméntum, argūméntī (n) - proof, evidence, argument (19)
bā́sium, bā́siī (n) - kiss (4)
béllum, béllī (n) - war (4)
benefícium, benefíciī (n) - benefit, kindness; favor (19)
caélum, caélī (n) - sky, heaven (5)
coniūrā́tī, coniūrātṓrum (m. pl.) - conspirators (20)
cōnsílium, cōnsíliī (n) - plan, purpose, counsel, advice, judgment, wisdom (4)
déus, déī (m) - god (6)

discípulus, discípulī (m) - learner, pupil, student (male) (6)
dṓnum, dṓnī (n) - gift, present (4)
équus, équī (m) - horse (23)
exítium, exítiī (n) - destruction, ruin (4)
fáctum, fáctī (n) - deed, act, achievement (13)
férrum, férrī (n) - iron; sword (22)
fī́lius, fī́liī (m) - son (3)
Graécus, Graécī (m) - a Greek (6)
iūdícium, iūdíciī (n) - judgment, decision, opinion; trial (19)
libéllus, libéllī (m) - little book (17)
líber, líbrī (m) - book (6)
lóca, locṓrum (n) - places, region (9)
lócī, locṓrum (m) - passages in literature (9)
lócus, lócī (m) - place; passage in literature (9)
lū́dus, lū́dī (m) - game, sport; school (18)
magíster, magístrī (m) - schoolmaster, teacher, master (4)
médicus, médicī (m) - doctor, physician (male) (12)
módus, módī (m) - measure, bound, limit; manner, method, mode, way (22)
mórbus, mórbī (m) - disease, sickness (9)
múndus, múndī (m) - world, universe (21)
númerus, númerī (m) - number (3)
óculus, óculī (m) - eye (4)
offícium, offíciī (n) - duty, service (4)
ṓtium, ṓtiī (n) - leisure, peace (4)
perī́culum, perī́culī (n) - danger, risk (4)
pópulus, pópulī (m) - the people, a people, a nation (3)
prīncípium, prīncípiī (n) - beginning (12)
púer, púerī (m) - boy; boys, children *(pl.)* (3)
remédium, remédiī (n) - cure, remedy (4)
sígnum, sígnī (n) - sign, signal, indication; seal (13)
stúdium, stúdiī (n) - eagerness, zeal, pursuit, study (9)
stúltus, stúltī (m) - a fool (4)
tyránnus, tyránnī (m) - absolute ruler, tyrant (6)
vérbum, vérbī (n)- word (5)
vīcī́nus, vīcī́nī (m) - neighbor (male) (21)
vir, vírī (m) - man, hero (3)
vítium, vítiī (n) - fault, crime, vice (6)
vúlgus, vúlgī (n) - the common people, mob, rabble (21)

3rd Declension

adulḗscēns, adulēscéntis (m *or* f) - young man *or* woman (12)
aétās, aetā́tis (f) - period of life, life, age, an age, time (16)
ámor, amṓris (m) - love (7)
aúctor, auctṓris (m) - increaser; author, originator (19)
audī́tor, audītṓris (m) - hearer, listener, member of an audience (16)
Caésar, Caésaris (m) - Caesar (12)
cáput, cápitis (n) - head; leader; beginning; life; heading; chapter (11)
cármen, cárminis (n) - song, poem (7)
Cícerō, Cicerṓnis (m) - (Marcus Tullius) Cicero (8)
cī́vitās, cīvitā́tis (f) - state, citizenship (7)
cṓnsul, cṓnsulis (m) - consul (11)
córpus, córporis (n) - body (7)
cupíditās, cupiditā́tis (f) - desire, longing, passion; cupidity, avarice (10)
dux, dúcis (m) - leader, guide; commander, general (23)
flū́men, flū́minis (n) - river (18)
frā́ter, frā́tris (m) - brother (8)
génus, géneris (n) - origin; kind, type, sort, class (18)
hómō, hóminis (m) - human being, man (7)
iū́dex, iū́dicis (m) - judge, juror (19)
iūs, iū́ris (n) - right, justice, law (14)
lábor, labṓris (m)- labor, work, toil; a work, production (7)
laus, laúdis (f) - praise, glory, fame (8)
lībértās, lībertā́tis (f) - liberty (8)
lī́tus, lī́toris (n) - shore, coast (23)
mā́ter, mā́tris (f) - mother (12)
mī́les, mī́litis (m) - soldier (23)
mṓrēs, mṓrum (m) - habits, morals, character (7)
mōs, mṓris (m) - habit, custom, manner (7)
nḗmō, nūllī́us, nḗminī, nḗminem, nū́llō, nū́llā (m *or* f) - no one, nobody (11)
nṓmen, nṓminis (n) - name (7)
ōrā́tor, ōrātṓris (m) - orator, speaker (23)
ōs, ṓris (n) - mouth, face (14)
páter, pátris (m) - father (12)
pāx, pā́cis (f) - peace (7)
próbitās, probitā́tis (f) - uprightness, honesty (18)
rátiō, ratiṓnis (f) - reckoning, account; reason, judgment, consideration; system; manner, method (8)
rēx, rḗgis (m) - king (7)
sacérdōs, sacerdṓtis (m) - priest (23)
sálūs, salū́tis (f) - health, safety; greeting (21)

scélus, scéleris (n) - evil deed, crime, sin, wickedness (19)
scrī́ptor, scrīptṓris (m) - writer, author (8)
senéctūs, senectū́tis (f) - old age (10)
sénex, sénis (m) - old man (16)
sérvitūs, servitū́tis (f) - servitude, slavery (20)
sóror, sorṓris (f) - sister (8)
tempéstās, tempestā́tis (f) - period of time, season; weather, storm (15)
témpus, témporis (n) - time; occasion, opportunity (7)
tímor, timṓris (m) - fear (10)
úxor, uxṓris (f) - wife (7)
vḗritās, vēritā́tis (f) - truth (10)
vírgō, vírginis (f) - maiden, virgin (7)
vírtūs, virtū́tis (f) - manliness, courage; excellence, character, worth, virtue (7)
volúptās, voluptā́tis (f) - pleasure (10)

3rd Declension I-Stem
ánimal, animā́lis (n) - a living creature, animal (14)
ars, ártis (f) - art, skill (14)
arx, árcis (f) - citadel, stronghold (23)
aúris, aúris (f) - ear (14)
cī́vis, cī́vis (m *or* f) - citizen (14)
fī́nēs, fī́nium (m) - boundaries, territory (21)
fī́nis, fī́nis (m) - end, limit, boundary; purpose (21)
gēns, géntis (f) - clan, race, nation, people (21)
hóstēs, hóstium (m) - the enemy (18)
hóstis, hóstis (m) - an enemy *(of the state)* (18)
ígnis, ígnis (m) - fire (22)
máre, máris (n) - sea (14)
mēns, méntis (f) - mind, thought, intention (16)
mōns, móntis (m) - mountain (20)
mors, mórtis (f) - death (14)
nā́vis, nā́vis (f) - ship, boat (21)
nū́bēs, nū́bis (f) - cloud (14)
pars, pártis (f) - part, share; direction (14)
urbs, úrbis (f) - city (14)
vī́rēs, vī́rium (f. pl.) - strength (14)
vīs, vīs (f) - force, power, violence (14)

4th Declension
córnū, córnūs (n) - horn (20)
frū́ctus, frū́ctūs (m) - fruit; profit, benefit, enjoyment (20)
génū, génūs (n) - knee (20)
mánus, mánūs (f) - hand; handwriting; band (20)
métus, métūs (m) - fear, dread, anxiety (20)
senā́tus, senā́tūs (m) - senate (20)
sḗnsus, sḗnsūs (m) - feeling, sense (20)
spī́ritus, spī́ritūs (m) - breath, breathing; spirit, soul (20)
vérsus, vérsūs (m) - line of verse (20)

5th Declension
díēs, diḗī (m) - day (22)
fídēs, fídeī (f) - faith, trust, trustworthiness, fidelity, promise, guarantee, protection (22)
rēs, réī (f) - thing, matter, property, business, affair (22)
rēs pū́blica, réī pū́blicae (f) - state, commonwealth, republic (22)
spēs, spéī (f) - hope (22)

Indeclinable
níhil - nothing (1)
sátis - enough (5)

Pronouns
áliquis, áliquid - someone, somebody, something (23)
égo, méī - I (11)
hic, haec, hoc - this; the latter; he, she, it, they (9)
ī́dem, éadem, ídem - the same (11)
ílle, ílla, íllud - that; the former; the famous; he, she, it, they (9)
ípse, ípsa, ípsum - myself, yourself, himself, herself, itself, *etc.,* the very, the actual (13)
is, éa, id - this, that; he, she, it (11)
íste, ísta, ístud - that of yours, that; such (as you have, as you speak of); *sometimes with contemptuous force, e.g.,* that despicable, that wretched (9)
quī, quae, quod - who, which, what, that (17)
quid - what (1)
quis? quid? - who? whose? whom? what? which? (19)
quísque, quídque, cuiúsque, cuíque - each one, each person, each thing (13)
quísquis, quídquid - whoever, whatever (23)
súī - himself, herself, itself, themselves (13)
tū, túī - you *(sing.)* (11)

Adjectives
1st & 2nd Declension
acérbus, acérba, acérbum - harsh, bitter, grievous (12)
aéquus, aéqua, aéquum - level, even; calm; equal, just; favorable (22)
áliī . . . áliī - some . . . others (9)
álius, ália, áliud - other, another (9)

álter, áltera, álterum - the other (of two), second (9)
amī́cus, amī́ca, amī́cum - friendly (11)
antī́quus, antī́qua, antī́quum - ancient, old-time (2)
ásper, áspera, ásperum - rough, harsh (21)
avā́rus, avā́ra, avā́rum - greedy, avaricious (3)
beā́tus, beā́ta, beā́tum - happy, fortunate, blessed (10)
béllus, bélla, béllum - pretty, handsome, charming (4)
bónus, bóna, bónum - good, kind (4)
caécus, caéca, caécum - blind (17)
cā́rus, cā́ra, cā́rum - dear (11)
cértus, cérta, cértum - definite, sure, certain, reliable (19)
clā́rus, clā́ra, clā́rum - clear, bright; renowned, famous, illustrious (18)
déxter, déxtra, déxtrum - right, right-hand (20)
dóctus, dócta, dóctum - taught, learned, skilled (13)
fortūnā́tus, fortūnā́ta, fortūnā́tum - lucky, fortunate, happy (13)
Graécus, Graéca, Graécum - Greek (6)
hūmā́nus, hūmā́na, hūmā́num - pertaining to man, human; humane, kind; refined, cultivated (4)
incértus, incérta, incértum - uncertain, unsure, doubtful (22)
iūcúndus, iūcúnda, iūcúndum - pleasant, delightful, agreeable, pleasing (16)
Latī́nus, Latī́na, Latī́num - Latin (22)
lī́ber, lī́bera, lī́berum - free (5)
lóngus, lónga, lóngum - long (16)
magnánimus, magnánima, magnánimum - great-hearted, brave, magnanimous (23)
mágnus, mágna, mágnum - large, great; important (2)
málus, mála, málum - bad, wicked, evil (4)
médius, média, médium - middle; the middle of (22)
méus, méa, méum - my (2)
míser, mísera, míserum - wretched, miserable, unfortunate (15)
múltus, múlta, múltum - much, many (2)
neúter, neútra, neútrum - not either, neither (9)
nóster, nóstra, nóstrum - our, ours (5)
nóvus, nóva, nóvum - new; strange (7)
nū́llus, nū́lla, nū́llum - not any, no, none (9)
párvus, párva, párvum - small, little (4)
paúcī, paúcae, paúca - few, a few (3)
perpétuus, perpétua, perpétuum perpetual, lasting, uninterrupted, continuous (6)
plḗnus, plḗna, plḗnum - full, abundant, generous (6)
púlcher, púlchra, púlchrum - beautiful, handsome; fine (5)
Rōmā́nus, Rōmā́na, Rōmā́num - Roman (3)
sálvus, sálva, sálvum - safe, sound (6)
sā́nus, sā́na, sā́num - sound, healthy, sane (5)
secúndus, secúnda, secúndum - second; favorable (6)
siníster, sinístra, sinístrum - left, left-hand; harmful, ill-omened (20)
sṓlus, sṓla, sṓlum - alone, only, the only (9)
stúltus, stúlta, stúltum - foolish (4)
súus, súa, súum - his own, her own, its own, their own (13)
tṓtus, tṓta, tṓtum - whole, entire (9)
túus, túa, túum - your *(sing.)* (2)
ū́llus, ū́lla, ū́llum - any (9)
ū́nus, ū́na, ū́num - one, single, alone (9)
úter, útra, útrum - either, which (of two) (9)
vḗrus, vḗra, vḗrum - true, real, proper (4)
véster, véstra, véstrum - your *(pl.)* (6)

3rd Declension

ā́cer, ā́cris, ā́cre - sharp, keen, eager; severe, fierce (16)
brévis, bréve - short, small, brief (16)
céler, céleris, célere - swift, quick, rapid (16)
commū́nis, commū́ne - common, general, of / for the community (20)
diffícilis, diffícile - hard, difficult, troublesome (16)
dúlcis, dúlce - sweet; pleasant, agreeable (16)
fácilis, fácile - easy; agreeable (16)
fḗlīx, *gen.* **fēlī́cis** - lucky, fortunate, happy (22)
fórtis, fórte - strong, brave (16)
grávis, gráve - heavy, weighty; serious, important; severe, grievous (19)
immortā́lis, immortā́le - not subject to death, immortal (19)
íngēns, *gen.* **ingéntis** - huge (16)

lévis, léve - light; easy; slight, trivial (17)
mortā́lis, mortā́le - mortal (18)
ómnis, ómne - every, all (16)
pótēns, ***gen.*** **poténtis** - able, powerful, mighty, strong (16)
sénex, ***gen.*** **sénis** - old, aged (16)

Indeclinable
sátis - enough, sufficient (5)

Interrogative Adjective
quī?, quae?, quod? - what? which? what kind of?; *(sometimes with exclamatory force)* what (a)! what sort of! (19)

Verbs

1st Conjugation
ádiuvō, adiuvā́re, adiū́vī, adiū́tum - to help, aid, assist; to please (4)
ámō, amā́re, amā́vī, amā́tum - to love, like (1)
appéllō, appellā́re, appellā́vī, appellā́tum - to speak to, address (as), call, name (14)
cḗnō, cēnā́re, cēnā́vī, cēnā́tum - to dine (5)
cṓgitō, cōgitā́re, cōgitā́vī, cōgitā́tum- to think, ponder, consider, plan (1)
cōnsérvō, cōnservā́re, cōnservā́vī, cōnservā́tum - to preserve, conserve, maintain (1)
créō, creā́re, creā́vī, creā́tum - to create (12)
cúlpō, culpā́re, culpā́vī, culpā́tum - to blame, censure (5)
dēléctō, dēlectā́re, dēlectā́vī, dēlectā́tum - to delight, charm, please (19)
dēmṓnstrō, dēmōnstrā́re, dēmōnstrā́vī, dēmōnstrā́tum to point out, show, demonstrate (8)
dēsī́derō, dēsīderā́re, dēsīderā́vī, dēsīderā́tum - to desire, long for, miss (17)
dō, dáre, dédī, dátum - to give, offer (1)
ḗducō, ēducā́re, ēducā́vī, ēducā́tum - to bring up, educate (23)
érrō, errā́re, errā́vī, errā́tum - to wander; err, go astray, make a mistake, be mistaken (1)
exspéctō, exspectā́re, exspectā́vī, exspectā́tum - to look for, expect, await (15)
iúvō, iuvā́re, iū́vī, iū́tum - to help, aid, assist; to please (4)
labṓrō, labōrā́re, labōrā́vī, labōrā́tum - to labor; be in distress (21)
laúdō, laudā́re, laudā́vī, laudā́tum - to praise (1)
lī́berō, līberā́re, līberā́vī, līberā́tum - to free, liberate (19)
mū́tō, mūtā́re, mūtā́vī, mūtā́tum to change, alter; exchange (14)
nā́vigō, nāvigā́re, nāvigā́vī, nāvigā́tum - to sail, navigate (17)
nécō, necā́re, necā́vī, necā́tum - to murder, kill (7)
párō, parā́re, parā́vī, parā́tum - to prepare, provide; get, obtain (19)
prōnū́ntiō, prōnūntiā́re, prōnūntiā́vī, prōnūntiā́tum - to proclaim, announce; declaim; pronounce (20)
récitō, recitā́re, recitā́vī, recitā́tum - to read aloud, recite (17)
sátiō, satiā́re, satiā́vī, satiā́tum - to satisfy, sate (3)
sérvō, servā́re, servā́vī, servā́tum - to preserve, save, keep, guard (1)
stō, stā́re, stétī, státum - to stand, stand still *or* firm (13)
súperō, superā́re, superā́vī, superā́tum - to be above, have the upper hand, surpass; overcome, conquer (5)
tólerō, tolerā́re, tolerā́vī, tolerā́tum - to bear, endure (6)
vī́tō, vītā́re, vītā́vī, vītā́tum - to avoid, shun (14)
vócō, vocā́re, vocā́vī, vocā́tum - to call, summon (1)

2nd Conjugation
aúdeō, audḗre, aúsus sum - to dare (7)
cáreō, carḗre, cáruī, caritū́rum (+abl.) - to be without, be deprived of, want, lack; be free from (20)
contíneō, continḗre, contínuī, conténtum - to hold together, contain, keep, enclose, restrain (21)
dḗbeō, dēbḗre, dḗbuī, dḗbitum - to owe; ought, must, should (1)
déleō, dēlḗre, dēlḗvī, dēlḗtum - to destroy, wipe out, erase (17)
dóceō, docḗre, dócuī, dóctum - to teach (8)
gaúdeō, gaudḗre, gāvī́sus sum - to be glad, rejoice (23)
hábeō, habḗre, hábuī, hábitum - to have, hold, possess; consider, regard (3)
iúbeō, iubḗre, iússī, iússum - to bid, order, command (21)

máneō, manḗre, mā́nsī, mā́nsum - to remain, stay, stay behind, abide, continue (5)
mísceō, miscḗre, míscuī, míxtum to mix, stir up, disturb (18)
móneō, monḗre, mónuī, mónitum - to remind, advise, warn (1)
móveō, movḗre, mṓvī, mṓtum - to move; arouse, affect (18)
prohíbeō, prohibḗre, prohíbuī, prohíbitum - to keep (back), prevent, hinder, restrain, prohibit (20)
remáneō, remanḗre, remā́nsī, remā́nsum - to remain, stay, stay behind, abide, continue (5)
sálvē, salvḗte - hello, greetings (1)
sálveō, salvḗre - to be well, be in good health (1)
téneō, tenḗre, ténuī, téntum - to hold, keep, possess; restrain (14)
térreō, terrḗre, térruī, térritum - to frighten, terrify (1)
tímeō, timḗre, tímuī - to fear, be afraid (of) (15)
válē, valḗte - good-bye, farewell (1)
váleō, valḗre, váluī, valitū́rum - to be strong, have power; be well (1)
vídeō, vidḗre, vī́dī, vī́sum - to see; observe, understand (1)
vídeor, vidḗrī, vī́sus sum - to be seen, seem, appear (18)

3rd Conjugation

admíttō, admíttere, admī́sī, admíssum - to admit, receive, let in (17)
ágō, ágere, ḗgī, ā́ctum - to drive, lead, do, act; pass, spend *(life or time)* (8)
álō, álere, áluī, áltum - to nourish, support, sustain, increase; cherish (13)
āmíttō, āmíttere, āmī́sī, āmíssum - to send away; lose, let go (12)
āvértō, āvértere, āvértī, āvérsum - to turn away, avert (23)
cádō, cádere, cécidī, cāsū́rum - to fall (12)
cérnō, cérnere, crḗvī, crḗtum - to distinguish, discern, perceive (22)
commíttō, commíttere, commī́sī, commíssum - to entrust, commit (15)
cúrrō, cúrrere, cucúrrī, cúrsum - to run, rush, move quickly (14)
dēféndō, dēféndere, dēféndī, dēfḗnsum - to ward off; defend, protect (20)
dī́cō, dī́cere, dī́xī, díctum - to say, tell, speak; name, call (10)
dī́ligō, dīlígere, dīlḗxī, dīlḗctum - to esteem, love (13)
discḗdō, discḗdere, discéssī, discéssum - to go away, depart (20)
dísco, díscere, dídicī - to learn (8)
dū́cō, dū́cere, dū́xī, dúctum - to lead; consider, regard; prolong (8)
flúō, flúere, flū́xī, flū́xum - to flow (18)
gérō, gérere, géssī, géstum - to carry; carry on, manage, conduct, wage, accomplish, perform (8)
intéllegō, intellégere, intellḗxī, intellḗctum - to understand (11)
iúngō, iúngere, iū́nxī, iū́nctum - to join (13)
légō, légere, lḗgī, lḗctum - to pick out, choose; read (18)
míttō, míttere, mī́sī, míssum - to send, let go (11)
néglegō, neglégere, neglḗxī, neglḗctum - to neglect, disregard (17)
ópprimō, opprímere, oppréssī, oppréssum - to suppress, overwhelm, overpower, check (23)
osténdō, osténdere, osténdī, osténtum - to exhibit, show, display (23)
pétō, pétere, petī́vī, petī́tum - to seek, aim at, beg, beseech (23)
prémō, prémere, préssī, préssum - to press; press hard, pursue (23)
régō, régere, rḗxī, rḗctum - to rule, guide, direct (16)
relínquō, relínquere, relī́quī, relíctum - to leave behind, leave, abandon, desert (21)
revértō, revértere, revértī, revérsum - turn back (23)
scrī́bō, scrī́bere, scrī́psī, scrī́ptum to write, compose (8)
tángō, tángere, tétigī, tā́ctum - to touch (21)
tóllō, tóllere, sústulī, sublā́tum - to raise, lift up; take away, remove, destroy (22)
tráhō, tráhere, trā́xī, tráctum - to draw, drag; derive, acquire (8)
vértō, vértere, vértī, vérsum - to turn; change (23)
víncō, víncere, vī́cī, víctum - to conquer, overcome (8)
vī́vō, vī́vere, vī́xī, vī́ctum - to live (10)

3rd Conjugation -iō

cápiō, cápere, cḗpī, cáptum - to take, capture, seize, get (10)

cúpiō, cúpere, cupī́vī, cupī́tum - to desire, wish, long for (17)

ēripiō, ērípere, ērípuī, ēréptum - to snatch away, take away; rescue (22)

fáciō, fácere, fḗcī, fáctum - to make, do, accomplish (10)

fúgiō, fúgere, fū́gī, fugitū́rum - to flee, hurry away; escape; go into exile; avoid, shun (10)

iáciō, iácere, iḗcī, iáctum - to throw, hurl (15)

incípiō, incípere, incḗpī, incéptum - to begin (17)

rápiō, rápere, rápuī, ráptum - to seize, snatch, carry away (21)

4th Conjugation

aúdiō, audī́re, audī́vī, audī́tum - to hear, listen to (10)

invéniō, invenī́re, invḗnī, invéntum - to come upon, find (10)

scíō, scī́re, scī́vī, scī́tum - to know (21)

séntiō, sentī́re, sḗnsī, sḗnsum - to feel, perceive, think, experience (11)

véniō, venī́re, vḗnī, véntum - to come (10)

Irregular

póssum, pósse, pótuī - to be able, can, could, have power (6)

sum, ésse, fúī, futū́rum - to be, exist (4)

Defective

coépī, coepísse, coéptum - began (17)

ínquit - he says *or* said (22)

ṓdī, ōdísse, ōsū́rum - to hate (20)

Adverbs

ánte (+acc.) - before, previously (13)

béne - well, satisfactorily, quite (11)

cíto - quickly (17)

crās - tomorrow (5)

cūr - why (18)

deínde - thereupon, next, then (18)

díū - long, for a long time (12)

étiam - even, also (11)

héri - yesterday (5)

hódiē - today (3)

iam - now, already, soon (19)

íbi - there (6)

ítaque - and so, therefore (15)

íterum - again, a second time (21)

nímis, nímium - too, too much, excessively; *(in a positive sense, esp. with adjectives and adverbs)* exceedingly, very (9)

nōn - not (1)

númquam - never (8)

nunc - now, at present (6)

nū́per - recently (12)

ṓlim - once (upon a time), long ago, formerly; some day, in the future (13)

prṓtinus - immediately (22)

quam - how (16)

quándō - when (5)

quā́rē - because of which thing *(lit.);* therefore, wherefore, why (6)

quóndam - formerly, once (22)

quóque - also, too (17)

saépe - often (1)

sátis - enough, sufficiently (5)

sémper - always (3)

támen - nevertheless, still (8)

tum - then, at that time; thereupon, in the next place (5)

úbi - where, when (6)

últrā - on the other side of, beyond (22)

úmquam - ever, at any time (23)

Conjunctions

at - but; but, mind you; but, you say (19)

átque, ac - and also, and even, and in fact (21)

aut - or (17)

aut . . . aut - either . . . or (17)

aútem - however; moreover (11)

dum - while, as long as, at the same time that; *or* until *(+subjunctive)* (8)

énim - for, in fact, truly (9)

et - and; even (2)

et . . . et - both . . . and (2)

ígitur - therefore, consequently (5)

nam - for (13)

néque, nec - and not, nor (11)

néque . . . néque, nec . . . nec - neither . . . nor (11)

nísi - if . . . not, unless; except (19)

quod - because (11)

quóniam - since, inasmuch as (10)

sed - but (2)

sī - if (1)

Prepositions

ab, ā (+abl.) - away from, from; by (14)

ad (+acc.) - to, up to, near to (8)

ánte (+acc.) - before *(in place or time)*, in front of (13)

cóntrā (+acc.) - against (19)

cum (+abl.) - with (10)

dē (+abl.) - down from, from; concerning, about (3)

ex, ē (abl.+) - out of, from, from within; by reason of, on account of ; of *(after cardinal numerals)* (8)

in (+acc.) - into, toward; against (9)
in (+abl.) - in, on (3)
ínter (+acc.) - between, among (15)
per (+acc.) - through; by *(with reflexive pronoun)* (13)
post (+acc.) - after, behind (7)
prō (+abl.) - in front of, before, on behalf of, for the sake of, in return for, instead of, for, as (12)
própter (+acc.) - on account of, because of (5)
síne (+abl.) - without (2)
sub (+abl. w/ verbs of rest *or* **+acc. w/ verbs of motion)** - under, up under, close to, down to/into, to/at the foot of (7)
trāns (+acc.) - across (14)
últrā (adv. and prep. +acc.) - on the other side of, beyond (22)

Interjection

ō - O!, Oh! (2)

Idioms

amā́bō tē - please (1)
grā́tiās ágere (+dat.) - to thank someone; to give thanks to (8)
nōn sṓlum . . . sed étiam - not only . . . but also (9)
poénās dáre - to pay the penalty (2)
sī quándō - if ever (5)

Suffixes

-ne – interrogative suffix attached to the first word of a sentence, typically the verb or another word on which the question hinges, to introduce a question whose answer is uncertain (5)
-que - and *(enclitic conjunction; appended to the second of two words to be joined)* (6)

Numerals

Cardinal - ū́nus *to* vīgíntī quī́nque (15)
Ordinal - prī́mus *to* duodécimus (15)

----

céntum - a hundred (15)
mī́lia, mī́lium (n. pl.) - thousands (15)
mī́lle - thousand (15)

Chapter 24

Nouns

1st Declension

adulēscéntia, adulēscéntiae (f) - youth, young manhood; youthfulness (5)
agrícola, agrícolae (m) - farmer (3)
amíca, amícae (f) - friend (female) (3)
amīcítia, amīcítiae (f) - friendship (10)
áqua, áquae (f) - water (14)
Ásia, Ásiae (f) - Asia (12)
cása, cásae (f) - house, cottage, hut (21)
caúsa, caúsae (f) - cause, reason; case, situation (21)
caúsā (abl. + preceding gen.) - for the sake of, on account of (21)
clēméntia, clēméntiae (f) - mildness, gentleness, mercy (16)
cṓpia, cṓpiae (f) - abundance, supply (8)
cṓpiae, cōpiā́rum (f) - supplies, troops, forces (8)
cúlpa, cúlpae (f) - fault, blame (5)
cū́ra, cū́rae (f) - care, attention, caution, anxiety (4)
déa, déae (f) - goddess (6)
discípula, discípulae (f) - learner, pupil, student (female) (6)
dīvítiae, dīvitiā́rum (f. pl.) - riches, wealth (13)
fā́bula, fā́bulae (f) - story, tale; play (24)
fā́ma, fā́mae (f) - rumor, report; fame, reputation (2)
família, famíliae (f) - household, family (19)
fḗmina, fḗminae (f) - woman (3)
fenéstra, fenéstrae (f) - window (21)
fília, fíliae (f) - daughter (3)
fṓrma, fṓrmae (f) - form, shape; beauty (2)
fortū́na, fortū́nae (f) - fortune, luck (2)
glṓria, glṓriae (f) - glory, fame (5)
Graécia, Graéciae (f) - Greece (19)
hásta, hástae (f) - spear (23)
hṓra, hṓrae (f) - hour, time (10)
īnsídiae, īnsidiā́rum (f) - ambush, plot, treachery (6)
ínsula, ínsulae (f) - island (23)
íra, írae (f) - ire, anger (2)
Itália, Itáliae (f) - Italy (15)
líttera, lítterae (f) - a letter of the alphabet (7)
lítterae, litterā́rum (f) - a letter (epistle), literature (7)
magístra, magístrae (f) - schoolmistress, teacher, mistress (4)
médica, médicae (f) - doctor, physician (female) (12)
memória, memóriae (f) - memory, recollection (15)
móra, mórae (f) - delay (4)
nātū́ra, nātū́rae (f) - nature (10)
naúta, naútae (m) - sailor (2)
patiéntia, patiéntiae (f) - suffering; patience, endurance (12)
pátria, pátriae (f) - fatherland, native land, (one's) country (2)
pecū́nia, pecū́niae (f) - money (2)
philosóphia, philosóphiae (f) - philosophy (2)
poéna, poénae (f) - penalty, punishment (2)
poḗta, poḗtae (m) - poet (2)
pórta, pórtae (f) - gate, entrance (2)
puélla, puéllae (f) - girl (2)
rēgína, rēgínae (f) - queen (7)
Rṓma, Rṓmae (f) - Rome (14)
rósa, rósae (f) - rose (2)
sapiéntia, sapiéntiae (f) - wisdom (3)
sátura, sáturae (f) - satire (16)
sciéntia, sciéntiae (f) - knowledge (18)
senténtia, senténtiae (f) - feeling, thought, opinion, vote, sentence (2)
sérva, sérvae (f) - slave (female) (24)
térra, térrae (f) - earth, ground, land, country (7)
Trṓia, Trṓiae (f) - Troy (21)
túrba, túrbae (f) - uproar, disturbance; mob, crowd, multitude (14)
vía, víae (f) - way, road, street (10)
vīcína, vīcínae (f) - neighbor (female) (21)
victṓria, victṓriae (f) - victory (8)
víta, vítae (f) - life; mode of life (2)

2nd Declension

áger, ágrī (m) - field, farm (3)
amícus, amícī (m) - friend (male) (3)
ánimī, animṓrum (m) - high spirits, pride, courage (5)
ánimus, ánimī (m) - soul, spirit, mind (5)
ánnus, ánnī (m) - year (12)
argūméntum, argūméntī (n) - proof, evidence, argument (19)
bā́sium, bā́siī (n) - kiss (4)
béllum, béllī (n) - war (4)
benefícium, benefíciī (n) - benefit, kindness; favor (19)
caélum, caélī (n) - sky, heaven (5)
coniūrā́tī, coniūrātṓrum (m. pl.) - conspirators (20)

cōnsílium, cōnsíliī (n) - plan, purpose, counsel, advice, judgment, wisdom (4)
déus, déī (m) - god (6)
discípulus, discípulī (m) - learner, pupil, student (male) (6)
dṓnum, dṓnī (n) - gift, present (4)
équus, équī (m) - horse (23)
exítium, exítiī (n) - destruction, ruin (4)
fáctum, fáctī (n) - deed, act, achievement (13)
férrum, férrī (n) - iron; sword (22)
fī́lius, fī́liī (m) - son (3)
Graécus, Graécī (m) - a Greek (6)
impérium, impériī (n) - power to command, supreme power, authority, command, control (24)
iūdícium, iūdíciī (n) - judgment, decision, opinion; trial (19)
libéllus, libéllī (m) - little book (17)
líber, líbrī (m) - book (6)
lóca, locṓrum (n) - places, region (9)
lócī, locṓrum (m) - passages in literature (9)
lócus, lócī (m) - place; passage in literature (9)
lū́dus, lū́dī (m) - game, sport; school (18)
magíster, magístrī (m) - schoolmaster, teacher, master (4)
médicus, médicī (m) - doctor, physician (male) (12)
módus, módī (m) - measure, bound, limit; manner, method, mode, way (22)
mórbus, mórbī (m) - disease, sickness (9)
múndus, múndī (m) - world, universe (21)
númerus, númerī (m) - number (3)
óculus, óculī (m) - eye (4)
offícium, offíciī (n) - duty, service (4)
ṓtium, ṓtiī (n) - leisure, peace (4)
perfúgium, perfúgiī (n) - refuge, shelter (24)
perī́culum, perī́culī (n) - danger, risk (4)
pópulus, pópulī (m) - the people, a people, a nation (3)
prīncípium, prīncípiī (n) - beginning (12)
púer, púerī (m) - boy; boys, children *(pl.)* (3)
remédium, remédiī (n) - cure, remedy (4)
sérvus, sérvī (m) - slave (male) (24)
sígnum, sígnī (n) - sign, signal, indication; seal (13)
sōlā́cium, sōlā́ciī (n) - comfort, relief (24)
stúdium, stúdiī (n) - eagerness, zeal, pursuit, study (9)
stúltus, stúltī (m) - a fool (4)
tyránnus, tyránnī (m) - absolute ruler, tyrant (6)
vérbum, vérbī (n)- word (5)
vīcī́nus, vīcī́nī (m) - neighbor (male) (21)
vir, vírī (m) - man, hero (3)
vítium, vítiī (n) - fault, crime, vice (6)
vúlgus, vúlgī (n) - the common people, mob, rabble (21)

3rd Declension

adulḗscēns, adulēscéntis (m *or* f) - young man *or* woman (12)
aétās, aetā́tis (f) - period of life, life, age, an age, time (16)
ámor, amṓris (m) - love (7)
aúctor, auctṓris (m) - increaser; author, originator (19)
audī́tor, audītṓris (m) - hearer, listener, member of an audience (16)
Caésar, Caésaris (m) - Caesar (12)
cáput, cápitis (n) - head; leader; beginning; life; heading; chapter (11)
cármen, cárminis (n) - song, poem (7)
Carthā́gō, Carthā́ginis (f) - Carthage (24)
Cícerō, Cicerṓnis (m) - (Marcus Tullius) Cicero (8)
cī́vitās, cīvitā́tis (f) - state, citizenship (7)
cṓnsul, cṓnsulis (m) - consul (11)
córpus, córporis (n) - body (7)
cupíditās, cupiditā́tis (f) - desire, longing, passion; cupidity, avarice (10)
dux, dúcis (m) - leader, guide; commander, general (23)
flū́men, flū́minis (n) - river (18)
frā́ter, frā́tris (m) - brother (8)
génus, géneris (n) - origin; kind, type, sort, class (18)
hómō, hóminis (m) - human being, man (7)
imperā́tor, imperātṓris (m) - general, commander-in-chief, emperor (24)
iū́dex, iū́dicis (m) - judge, juror (19)
iūs, iū́ris (n) - right, justice, law (14)
lábor, labṓris (m)- labor, work, toil; a work, production (7)
laus, laúdis (f) - praise, glory, fame (8)
lībértās, lībertā́tis (f) - liberty (8)
lī́tus, lī́toris (n) - shore, coast (23)
mā́ter, mā́tris (f) - mother (12)
mī́les, mī́litis (m) - soldier (23)
mṓrēs, mṓrum (m) - habits, morals, character (7)
mōs, mṓris (m) - habit, custom, manner (7)

némō, nūllíus, néminī, néminem, núllō, núllā (m *or* f) - no one, nobody (11)
nṓmen, nṓminis (n) - name (7)
ōrā́tor, ōrātṓris (m) - orator, speaker (23)
ōs, ṓris (n) - mouth, face (14)
páter, pátris (m) - father (12)
pāx, pā́cis (f) - peace (7)
próbitās, probitā́tis (f) - uprightness, honesty (18)
rátiō, ratiṓnis (f) - reckoning, account; reason, judgment, consideration; system; manner, method (8)
rēx, rḗgis (m) - king (7)
sacérdōs, sacerdṓtis (m) - priest (23)
sálūs, salū́tis (f) - health, safety; greeting (21)
scélus, scéleris (n) - evil deed, crime, sin, wickedness (19)
scrī́ptor, scrīptṓris (m) - writer, author (8)
senéctūs, senectū́tis (f) - old age (10)
sénex, sénis (m) - old man (16)
sérvitūs, servitū́tis (f) - servitude, slavery (20)
sóror, sorṓris (f) - sister (8)
tempéstās, tempestā́tis (f) - period of time, season; weather, storm (15)
témpus, témporis (n) - time; occasion, opportunity (7)
tímor, timṓris (m) - fear (10)
úxor, uxṓris (f) - wife (7)
vḗritās, vēritā́tis (f) - truth (10)
vírgō, vírginis (f) - maiden, virgin (7)
vírtūs, virtū́tis (f) - manliness, courage; excellence, character, worth, virtue (7)
volúptās, voluptā́tis (f) - pleasure (10)
vúlnus, vúlneris (n) - wound (24)

3rd Declension I-Stem

ánimal, animā́lis (n) - a living creature, animal (14)
ars, ártis (f) - art, skill (14)
arx, árcis (f) - citadel, stronghold (23)
aúris, aúris (f) - ear (14)
cī́vis, cī́vis (m *or* f) - citizen (14)
fī́nēs, fī́nium (m) - boundaries, territory (21)
fī́nis, fī́nis (m) - end, limit, boundary; purpose (21)
gēns, géntis (f) - clan, race, nation, people (21)
hóstēs, hóstium (m) - the enemy (18)
hóstis, hóstis (m) - an enemy *(of the state)* (18)
ígnis, ígnis (m) - fire (22)
máre, máris (n) - sea (14)
mēns, méntis (f) - mind, thought, intention (16)
mōns, móntis (m) - mountain (20)
mors, mórtis (f) - death (14)
nā́vis, nā́vis (f) - ship, boat (21)
nū́bēs, nū́bis (f) - cloud (14)
pars, pártis (f) - part, share; direction (14)
urbs, úrbis (f) - city (14)
vī́rēs, vī́rium (f. pl.) - strength (14)
vīs, vīs (f) - force, power, violence (14)

4th Declension

córnū, córnūs (n) - horn (20)
frū́ctus, frū́ctūs (m) - fruit; profit, benefit, enjoyment (20)
génū, génūs (n) - knee (20)
mánus, mánūs (f) - hand; handwriting; band (20)
métus, métūs (m) - fear, dread, anxiety (20)
senā́tus, senā́tūs (m) - senate (20)
sḗnsus, sḗnsūs (m) - feeling, sense (20)
spī́ritus, spī́ritūs (m) - breath, breathing; spirit, soul (20)
vérsus, vérsūs (m) - line of verse (20)

5th Declension

díēs, diḗī (m) - day (22)
fídēs, fídeī (f) - faith, trust, trustworthiness, fidelity, promise, guarantee, protection (22)
rēs, réī (f) - thing, matter, property, business, affair (22)
rēs pū́blica, réī pū́blicae (f) - state, commonwealth, republic (22)
spēs, spéī (f) - hope (22)

Indeclinable

níhil - nothing (1)
sátis - enough (5)

Pronouns

áliquis, áliquid - someone, somebody, something (23)
égo, méī - I (11)
hic, haec, hoc - this; the latter; he, she, it, they (9)
ī́dem, éadem, ídem - the same (11)
ílle, ílla, íllud - that; the former; the famous; he, she, it, they (9)
ípse, ípsa, ípsum - myself, yourself, himself, herself, itself, *etc.,* the very, the actual (13)
is, éa, id - this, that; he, she, it (11)
íste, ísta, ístud - that of yours, that; such (as you have, as you speak of); *sometimes with contemptuous force, e.g.,* that despicable, that wretched (9)
quī, quae, quod - who, which, what, that (17)
quid - what (1)

quis? quid? - who? whose? whom? what? which? (19)
quísque, quídque, cuiúsque, cuíque - each one, each person, each thing (13)
quísquis, quídquid - whoever, whatever (23)
súī - himself, herself, itself, themselves (13)
tū, túī - you *(sing.)* (11)

Adjectives

1st & 2nd Declension

acérbus, acérba, acérbum - harsh, bitter, grievous (12)
aéquus, aéqua, aéquum - level, even; calm; equal, just; favorable (22)
áliī . . . áliī - some . . . others (9)
álius, ália, áliud - other, another (9)
álter, áltera, álterum - the other (of two), second (9)
amī́cus, amī́ca, amī́cum - friendly (11)
antī́quus, antī́qua, antī́quum - ancient, old-time (2)
ásper, áspera, ásperum - rough, harsh (21)
avā́rus, avā́ra, avā́rum - greedy, avaricious (3)
beā́tus, beā́ta, beā́tum - happy, fortunate, blessed (10)
béllus, béllla, béllum - pretty, handsome, charming (4)
bónus, bóna, bónum - good, kind (4)
caécus, caéca, caécum - blind (17)
cā́rus, cā́ra, cā́rum - dear (11)
cértus, cérta, cértum - definite, sure, certain, reliable (19)
clā́rus, clā́ra, clā́rum - clear, bright; renowned, famous, illustrious (18)
déxter, déxtra, déxtrum - right, right-hand (20)
dóctus, dócta, dóctum - taught, learned, skilled (13)
fortūnā́tus, fortūnā́ta, fortūnā́tum - lucky, fortunate, happy (13)
Graécus, Graéca, Graécum - Greek (6)
hūmā́nus, hūmā́na, hūmā́num - pertaining to man, human; humane, kind; refined, cultivated (4)
incértus, incérta, incértum - uncertain, unsure, doubtful (22)
iūcúndus, iūcúnda, iūcúndum - pleasant, delightful, agreeable, pleasing (16)
Latī́nus, Latī́na, Latī́num - Latin (22)
lī́ber, lī́bera, lī́berum - free (5)
lóngus, lónga, lóngum - long (16)
magnánimus, magnánima, magnánimum - great-hearted, brave, magnanimous (23)
mágnus, mágna, mágnum - large, great; important (2)
málus, mála, málum - bad, wicked, evil (4)
médius, média, médium - middle; the middle of (22)
méus, méa, méum - my (2)
míser, mísera, míserum - wretched, miserable, unfortunate (15)
múltus, múlta, múltum - much, many (2)
neúter, neútra, neútrum - not either, neither (9)
nóster, nóstra, nóstrum - our, ours (5)
nóvus, nóva, nóvum - new; strange (7)
nū́llus, nū́lla, nū́llum - not any, no, none (9)
párvus, párva, párvum - small, little (4)
paúcī, paúcae, paúca - few, a few (3)
perpétuus, perpétua, perpétuum perpetual, lasting, uninterrupted, continuous (6)
plḗnus, plḗna, plḗnum - full, abundant, generous (6)
púlcher, púlchra, púlchrum - beautiful, handsome; fine (5)
Rōmā́nus, Rōmā́na, Rōmā́num - Roman (3)
sálvus, sálva, sálvum - safe, sound (6)
sā́nus, sā́na, sā́num - sound, healthy, sane (5)
secúndus, secúnda, secúndum - second; favorable (6)
siníster, sinístra, sinístrum - left, left-hand; harmful, ill-omened (20)
sṓlus, sṓla, sṓlum - alone, only, the only (9)
stúltus, stúlta, stúltum - foolish (4)
súus, súa, súum - his own, her own, its own, their own (13)
tṓtus, tṓta, tṓtum - whole, entire (9)
túus, túa, túum - your *(sing.)* (2)
ū́llus, ū́lla, ū́llum - any (9)
ū́nus, ū́na, ū́num - one, single, alone (9)
úter, útra, útrum - either, which (of two) (9)
vḗrus, vḗra, vḗrum - true, real, proper (4)
véster, véstra, véstrum - your *(pl.)* (6)

3rd Declension

ā́cer, ā́cris, ā́cre - sharp, keen, eager; severe, fierce (16)
brévis, bréve - short, small, brief (16)

céler, céleris, célere - swift, quick, rapid (16)
commū́nis, commū́ne - common, general, of / for the community (20)
diffícilis, diffícile - hard, difficult, troublesome (16)
dúlcis, dúlce - sweet; pleasant, agreeable (16)
fácilis, fácile - easy; agreeable (16)
fḗlīx, ***gen.*** **fēlī́cis** - lucky, fortunate, happy (22)
fórtis, fórte - strong, brave (16)
grávis, gráve - heavy, weighty; serious, important; severe, grievous (19)
immortā́lis, immortā́le - not subject to death, immortal (19)
íngēns, ***gen.*** **ingéntis** - huge (16)
lévis, léve - light; easy; slight, trivial (17)
mortā́lis, mortā́le - mortal (18)
ómnis, ómne - every, all (16)
pótēns, ***gen.*** **poténtis** - able, powerful, mighty, strong (16)
sénex, ***gen.*** **sénis** - old, aged (16)

Indeclinable
sátis - enough, sufficient (5)

Interrogative Adjective
quī?, quae?, quod? - what? which? what kind of?; *(sometimes with exclamatory force)* what (a)! what sort of! (19)

Verbs
1st Conjugation
ádiuvō, adiuvā́re, adiū́vī, adiū́tum - to help, aid, assist; to please (4)
ámō, amā́re, amā́vī, amā́tum - to love, like (1)
appéllō, appellā́re, appellā́vī, appellā́tum - to speak to, address (as), call, name (14)
cḗnō, cēnā́re, cēnā́vī, cēnā́tum - to dine (5)
cṓgitō, cōgitā́re, cōgitā́vī, cōgitā́tum- to think, ponder, consider, plan (1)
cōnsérvō, cōnservā́re, cōnservā́vī, cōnservā́tum - to preserve, conserve, maintain (1)
créō, creā́re, creā́vī, creā́tum - to create (12)
cúlpō, culpā́re, culpā́vī, culpā́tum - to blame, censure (5)
dēléctō, dēlectā́re, dēlectā́vī, dēlectā́tum - to delight, charm, please (19)
dēmṓnstrō, dēmōnstrā́re, dēmōnstrā́vī, dēmōnstrā́tum to point out, show, demonstrate (8)
dēsī́derō, dēsīderā́re, dēsīderā́vī, dēsīderā́tum - to desire, long for, miss (17)
dō, dáre, dédī, dátum - to give, offer (1)
ḗducō, ēducā́re, ēducā́vī, ēducā́tum - to bring up, educate (23)
érrō, errā́re, errā́vī, errā́tum - to wander; err, go astray, make a mistake, be mistaken (1)
exspéctō, exspectā́re, exspectā́vī, exspectā́tum - to look for, expect, await (15)
iúvō, iuvā́re, iū́vī, iū́tum - to help, aid, assist; to please (4)
labṓrō, labōrā́re, labōrā́vī, labōrā́tum - to labor; be in distress (21)
laúdō, laudā́re, laudā́vī, laudā́tum - to praise (1)
lī́berō, līberā́re, līberā́vī, līberā́tum - to free, liberate (19)
mū́tō, mūtā́re, mūtā́vī, mūtā́tum to change, alter; exchange (14)
nárrō, nārrā́re, nārrā́vī, nārrā́tum - to tell, report, narrate (24)
nā́vigō, nāvigā́re, nāvigā́vī, nāvigā́tum - to sail, navigate (17)
nécō, necā́re, necā́vī, necā́tum - to murder, kill (7)
párō, parā́re, parā́vī, parā́tum - to prepare, provide; get, obtain (19)
prōnū́ntiō, prōnūntiā́re, prōnūntiā́vī, prōnūntiā́tum - to proclaim, announce; declaim; pronounce (20)
récitō, recitā́re, recitā́vī, recitā́tum - to read aloud, recite (17)
sátiō, satiā́re, satiā́vī, satiā́tum - to satisfy, sate (3)
sérvō, servā́re, servā́vī, servā́tum - to preserve, save, keep, guard (1)
stō, stā́re, stétī, stā́tum - to stand, stand still *or* firm (13)
súperō, superā́re, superā́vī, superā́tum - to be above, have the upper hand, surpass; overcome, conquer (5)
tólerō, tolerā́re, tolerā́vī, tolerā́tum - to bear, endure (6)
vī́tō, vītā́re, vītā́vī, vītā́tum - to avoid, shun (14)
vócō, vocā́re, vocā́vī, vocā́tum - to call, summon (1)

2nd Conjugation
aúdeō, audḗre, aúsus sum - to dare (7)

cáreō, carḗre, cáruī, caritū́rum (+abl.) - to be without, be deprived of, want, lack; be free from (20)

contíneō, continḗre, contínuī, conténtum - to hold together, contain, keep, enclose, restrain (21)

dḗbeō, dēbḗre, dḗbuī, dḗbitum - to owe; ought, must, should (1)

dḗleō, dēlḗre, dēlḗvī, dēlḗtum - to destroy, wipe out, erase (17)

dóceō, docḗre, dócuī, dóctum - to teach (8)

gaúdeō, gaudḗre, gāvī́sus sum - to be glad, rejoice (23)

hábeō, habḗre, hábuī, hábitum - to have, hold, possess; consider, regard (3)

iúbeō, iubḗre, iússī, iússum - to bid, order, command (21)

máneō, manḗre, mā́nsī, mā́nsum - to remain, stay, stay behind, abide, continue (5)

mísceō, miscḗre, míscuī, míxtum to mix, stir up, disturb (18)

móneō, monḗre, mónuī, mónitum - to remind, advise, warn (1)

móveō, movḗre, mṓvī, mṓtum - to move; arouse, affect (18)

prohíbeō, prohibḗre, prohíbuī, prohíbitum - to keep (back), prevent, hinder, restrain, prohibit (20)

remáneō, remanḗre, remā́nsī, remā́nsum - to remain, stay, stay behind, abide, continue (5)

rī́deō, rīdḗre, rī́sī, rī́sum - to laugh, laugh at (24)

sálvē, salvḗte - hello, greetings (1)

sálveō, salvḗre - to be well, be in good health (1)

téneō, tenḗre, ténuī, téntum - to hold, keep, possess; restrain (14)

térreō, terrḗre, térruī, térritum - to frighten, terrify (1)

tímeō, timḗre, tímuī - to fear, be afraid (of) (15)

válē, valḗte - good-bye, farewell (1)

váleō, valḗre, váluī, valitū́rum - to be strong, have power; be well (1)

vídeō, vidḗre, vī́dī, vī́sum - to see; observe, understand (1)

vídeor, vidḗrī, vī́sus sum - to be seen, seem, appear (18)

3rd Conjugation

admíttō, admíttere, admī́sī, admíssum - to admit, receive, let in (17)

ágō, ágere, ḗgī, ā́ctum - to drive, lead, do, act; pass, spend *(life or time)* (8)

álō, álere, áluī, áltum - to nourish, support, sustain, increase; cherish (13)

āmíttō, āmíttere, āmī́sī, āmíssum - to send away; lose, let go (12)

āvértō, āvértere, āvértī, āvérsum - to turn away, avert (23)

cádō, cádere, cécidī, cāsū́rum - to fall (12)

cérnō, cérnere, crḗvī, crḗtum - to distinguish, discern, perceive (22)

commíttō, commíttere, commī́sī, commíssum - to entrust, commit (15)

cúrrō, cúrrere, cucúrrī, cúrsum - to run, rush, move quickly (14)

dēféndō, dēféndere, dēféndī, dēfḗnsum - to ward off; defend, protect (20)

dī́cō, dī́cere, dī́xī, díctum - to say, tell, speak; name, call (10)

dī́ligō, dīlígere, dīlḗxī, dīlḗctum - to esteem, love (13)

discḗdō, discḗdere, discéssī, discéssum - to go away, depart (20)

díscō, díscere, dídicī - to learn (8)

dū́cō, dū́cere, dū́xī, dúctum - to lead; consider, regard; prolong (8)

expéllō, expéllere, éxpulī, expúlsum - to drive out, expel, banish (24)

flúō, flúere, flū́xī, flū́xum - to flow (18)

gérō, gérere, géssī, géstum - to carry; carry on, manage, conduct, wage, accomplish, perform (8)

intéllegō, intellégere, intellḗxī, intellḗctum - to understand (11)

iúngō, iúngere, iū́nxī, iū́nctum - to join (13)

légō, légere, lḗgī, lḗctum - to pick out, choose; read (18)

míttō, míttere, mī́sī, míssum - to send, let go (11)

néglegō, neglégere, neglḗxī, neglḗctum - to neglect, disregard (17)

ópprimō, opprímere, oppréssī, oppréssum - to suppress, overwhelm, overpower, check (23)

osténdō, osténdere, osténdī, osténtum - to exhibit, show, display (23)

péllō, péllere, pépulī, púlsum - to strike, push; drive out, banish (24)

pétō, pétere, petī́vī, petī́tum - to seek, aim at, beg, beseech (23)

prémō, prémere, préssī, préssum - to press; press hard, pursue (23)
quaérō, quaérere, quaesī́vī, quaesī́tum - to seek, look for, strive for; ask, inquire, inquire into (24)
régō, régere, rḗxī, rḗctum - to rule, guide, direct (16)
relínquō, relínquere, relī́quī, relíctum - to leave behind, leave, abandon, desert (21)
revértō, revértere, revértī, revérsum - turn back (23)
scrī́bō, scrī́bere, scrī́psī, scrī́ptum to write, compose (8)
tángō, tángere, tétigī, tā́ctum - to touch (21)
tóllō, tóllere, sústulī, sublā́tum - to raise, lift up; take away, remove, destroy (22)
tráhō, tráhere, trā́xī, tráctum - to draw, drag; derive, acquire (8)
vértō, vértere, vértī, vérsum - to turn; change (23)
víncō, víncere, vī́cī, víctum - to conquer, overcome (8)
vī́vō, vī́vere, vī́xī, vī́ctum - to live (10)

3rd Conjugation -iō

accípiō, accípere, accḗpī, accéptum - to take *(to one's self)*, receive, accept (24)
cápiō, cápere, cḗpī, cáptum - to take, capture, seize, get (10)
cúpiō, cúpere, cupī́vī, cupī́tum - to desire, wish, long for (17)
ērípiō, ērípere, ērípuī, ēréptum - to snatch away, take away; rescue (22)
excípiō, excípere, excḗpī, excéptum - to take out, except; take, receive, capture (24)
fáciō, fácere, fḗcī, fáctum - to make, do, accomplish (10)
fúgiō, fúgere, fū́gī, fugitū́rum - to flee, hurry away; escape; go into exile; avoid, shun (10)
iáciō, iácere, iḗcī, iáctum - to throw, hurl (15)
incípiō, incípere, incḗpī, incéptum - to begin (17)
rápiō, rápere, rápuī, ráptum - to seize, snatch, carry away (21)
recípiō, recípere, recḗpī, recéptum - to take back, regain; admit, receive (24)

4th Conjugation

aúdiō, audī́re, audī́vī, audī́tum - to hear, listen to (10)
invéniō, invenī́re, invḗnī, invéntum - to come upon, find (10)
scíō, scī́re, scī́vī, scī́tum - to know (21)
séntiō, sentī́re, sḗnsī, sḗnsum - to feel, perceive, think, experience (11)
véniō, venī́re, vḗnī, véntum - to come (10)

Irregular

póssum, pósse, pótuī - to be able, can, could, have power (6)
sum, ésse, fúī, futū́rum - to be, exist (4)

Defective

coépī, coepísse, coéptum - began (17)
ínquit - he says *or* said (22)
ṓdī, ōdísse, ōsū́rum - to hate (20)

Adverbs

ánte (+acc.) - before, previously (13)
béne - well, satisfactorily, quite (11)
cíto - quickly (17)
crās - tomorrow (5)
cūr - why (18)
deínde - thereupon, next, then (18)
díū - long, for a long time (12)
étiam - even, also (11)
héri - yesterday (5)
hódiē - today (3)
iam - now, already, soon (19)
íbi - there (6)
ítaque - and so, therefore (15)
íterum - again, a second time (21)
nímis, nímium - too, too much, excessively; *(in a positive sense, esp. with adjectives and adverbs)* exceedingly, very (9)
nōn - not (1)
númquam - never (8)
nunc - now, at present (6)
nū́per - recently (12)
ṓlim - once (upon a time), long ago, formerly; some day, in the future (13)
pósteā - afterwards (24)
prṓtinus - immediately (22)
quam - how (16)
quándō - when (5)
quā́rē - because of which thing *(lit.)*; therefore, wherefore, why (6)
quóndam - formerly, once (22)
quóque - also, too (17)
saépe - often (1)
sátis - enough, sufficiently (5)
sémper - always (3)
támen - nevertheless, still (8)
tum - then, at that time; thereupon, in the next place (5)
úbi - where, when (6)
últrā - on the other side of, beyond (22)
úmquam - ever, at any time (23)

Conjunctions

at - but; but, mind you; but, you say (19)
átque, ac - and also, and even, and in fact (21)
aut - or (17)
aut . . . aut - either . . . or (17)
aútem - however; moreover (11)
dum - while, as long as, at the same time that; *or* until *(+subjunctive)* (8)
énim - for, in fact, truly (9)
et - and; even (2)
et . . . et - both . . . and (2)
ígitur - therefore, consequently (5)
nam - for (13)
néque, nec - and not, nor (11)
néque . . . néque, nec . . . nec - neither . . . nor (11)
nísi - if . . . not, unless; except (19)
quod - because (11)
quóniam - since, inasmuch as (10)
sed - but (2)
sī - if (1)
ut - as, just as, when (24)

Prepositions

ab, ā (+abl.) - away from, from; by (14)
ad (+acc.) - to, up to, near to (8)
ánte (+acc.) - before *(in place or time)*, in front of (13)
cóntrā (+acc.) - against (19)
cum (+abl.) - with (10)
dē (+abl.) - down from, from; concerning, about (3)
ex, ē (abl.+) - out of, from, from within; by reason of, on account of; of *(after cardinal numerals)* (8)
in (+acc.) - into, toward; against (9)
in (+abl.) - in, on (3)
ínter (+acc.) - between, among (15)
per (+acc.) - through; by *(with reflexive pronoun)* (13)
post (+acc.) - after, behind (7)
prō (+abl.) - in front of, before, on behalf of, for the sake of, in return for, instead of, for, as (12)
própter (+acc.) - on account of, because of (5)
síne (+abl.) - without (2)
sub (+abl. w/ verbs of rest *or* +acc. w/ verbs of motion) - under, up under, close to, down to/into, to/at the foot of (7)
trāns (+acc.) - across (14)
últrā (adv. and prep. +acc.) - on the other side of, beyond (22)

Interjection

ō - O!, Oh! (2)

Idioms

amā́bō tē - please (1)
grā́tiās ágere (+dat.) - to thank someone; to give thanks to (8)
nōn sṓlum . . . sed étiam - not only . . . but also (9)
poénās dáre - to pay the penalty (2)
sī quándō - if ever (5)

Prefix

re-, red- - again, back (24)

Suffixes

-ne – interrogative suffix attached to the first word of a sentence, typically the verb or another word on which the question hinges, to introduce a question whose answer is uncertain (5)
-que - and *(enclitic conjunction; appended to the second of two words to be joined)* (6)

Numerals

Cardinal - ū́nus *to* vīgíntī quī́nque (15)
Ordinal - prī́mus *to* duodécimus (15)

----

céntum - a hundred (15)
mī́lia, mī́lium (n. pl.) - thousands (15)
mī́lle - thousand (15)

Chapter 25

Nouns

1st Declension

adulēscéntia, adulēscéntiae (f) - youth, young manhood; youthfulness (5)
agrícola, agrícolae (m) - farmer (3)
amíca, amícae (f) - friend (female) (3)
amīcítia, amīcítiae (f) - friendship (10)
áqua, áquae (f) - water (14)
Ásia, Ásiae (f) - Asia (12)
cása, cásae (f) - house, cottage, hut (21)
caúsa, caúsae (f) - cause, reason; case, situation (21)
caúsā (abl. + preceding gen.) - for the sake of, on account of (21)
clēméntia, clēméntiae (f) - mildness, gentleness, mercy (16)
cṓpia, cṓpiae (f) - abundance, supply (8)
cṓpiae, cōpiā́rum (f) - supplies, troops, forces (8)
cúlpa, cúlpae (f) - fault, blame (5)
cū́ra, cū́rae (f) - care, attention, caution, anxiety (4)
déa, déae (f) - goddess (6)
discípula, discípulae (f) - learner, pupil, student (female) (6)
dīvítiae, dīvitiā́rum (f. pl.) - riches, wealth (13)
fā́bula, fā́bulae (f) - story, tale; play (24)
fā́ma, fā́mae (f) - rumor, report; fame, reputation (2)
família, famíliae (f) - household, family (19)
fḗmina, fḗminae (f) - woman (3)
fenéstra, fenéstrae (f) - window (21)
fī́lia, fī́liae (f) - daughter (3)
fṓrma, fṓrmae (f) - form, shape; beauty (2)
fortū́na, fortū́nae (f) - fortune, luck (2)
glṓria, glṓriae (f) - glory, fame (5)
Graécia, Graéciae (f) - Greece (19)
hásta, hástae (f) - spear (23)
hṓra, hṓrae (f) - hour, time (10)
īnsídiae, īnsidiā́rum (f) - ambush, plot, treachery (6)
ī́nsula, ī́nsulae (f) - island (23)
ī́ra, ī́rae (f) - ire, anger (2)
Itália, Itáliae (f) - Italy (15)
língua, línguae (f) - tongue; language (25)
líttera, lítterae (f) - a letter of the alphabet (7)
lítterae, litterā́rum (f) - a letter (epistle), literature (7)
magístra, magístrae (f) - schoolmistress, teacher, mistress (4)
médica, médicae (f) - doctor, physician (female) (12)
memória, memóriae (f) - memory, recollection (15)
móra, mórae (f) - delay (4)
nātū́ra, nātū́rae (f) - nature (10)
naúta, naútae (m) - sailor (2)
patiéntia, patiéntiae (f) - suffering; patience, endurance (12)
pátria, pátriae (f) - fatherland, native land, (one's) country (2)
pecū́nia, pecū́niae (f) - money (2)
philosóphia, philosóphiae (f) - philosophy (2)
poéna, poénae (f) - penalty, punishment (2)
poḗta, poḗtae (m) - poet (2)
pórta, pórtae (f) - gate, entrance (2)
puélla, puéllae (f) - girl (2)
rēgī́na, rēgī́nae (f) - queen (7)
Rṓma, Rṓmae (f) - Rome (14)
rósa, rósae (f) - rose (2)
sapiéntia, sapiéntiae (f) - wisdom (3)
sátura, sáturae (f) - satire (16)
sciéntia, sciéntiae (f) - knowledge (18)
senténtia, senténtiae (f) - feeling, thought, opinion, vote, sentence (2)
sérva, sérvae (f) - slave (female) (24)
térra, térrae (f) - earth, ground, land, country (7)
Trṓia, Trṓiae (f) - Troy (21)
túrba, túrbae (f) - uproar, disturbance; mob, crowd, multitude (14)
vía, víae (f) - way, road, street (10)
vīcī́na, vīcī́nae (f) - neighbor (female) (21)
victṓria, victṓriae (f) - victory (8)
vī́ta, vī́tae (f) - life; mode of life (2)

2nd Declension

áger, ágrī (m) - field, farm (3)
amī́cus, amī́cī (m) - friend (male) (3)
ánimī, animṓrum (m) - high spirits, pride, courage (5)
ánimus, ánimī (m) - soul, spirit, mind (5)
ánnus, ánnī (m) - year (12)
argūméntum, argūméntī (n) - proof, evidence, argument (19)
bā́sium, bā́siī (n) - kiss (4)
béllum, béllī (n) - war (4)
benefícium, benefíciī (n) - benefit, kindness; favor (19)
caélum, caélī (n) - sky, heaven (5)
coniūrā́tī, coniūrātṓrum (m. pl.) - conspirators (20)

cōnsílium, cōnsíliī (n) - plan, purpose, counsel, advice, judgment, wisdom (4)
déus, déī (m) - god (6)
discípulus, discípulī (m) - learner, pupil, student (male) (6)
dṓnum, dṓnī (n) - gift, present (4)
équus, équī (m) - horse (23)
exítium, exítiī (n) - destruction, ruin (4)
fáctum, fáctī (n) - deed, act, achievement (13)
férrum, férrī (n) - iron; sword (22)
fīlius, fīliī (m) - son (3)
Graécus, Graécī (m) - a Greek (6)
impérium, impériī (n) - power to command, supreme power, authority, command, control (24)
iūdícium, iūdíciī (n) - judgment, decision, opinion; trial (19)
libéllus, libéllī (m) - little book (17)
líber, líbrī (m) - book (6)
lóca, locṓrum (n) - places, region (9)
lócī, locṓrum (m) - passages in literature (9)
lócus, lócī (m) - place; passage in literature (9)
lū́dus, lū́dī (m) - game, sport; school (18)
magíster, magístrī (m) - schoolmaster, teacher, master (4)
médicus, médicī (m) - doctor, physician (male) (12)
módus, módī (m) - measure, bound, limit; manner, method, mode, way (22)
mórbus, mórbī (m) - disease, sickness (9)
múndus, múndī (m) - world, universe (21)
númerus, númerī (m) - number (3)
óculus, óculī (m) - eye (4)
offícium, offíciī (n) - duty, service (4)
ṓtium, ṓtiī (n) - leisure, peace (4)
perfúgium, perfúgiī (n) - refuge, shelter (24)
perīculum, perīculī (n) - danger, risk (4)
pópulus, pópulī (m) - the people, a people, a nation (3)
prīncípium, prīncípiī (n) - beginning (12)
púer, púerī (m) - boy; boys, children *(pl.)* (3)
remédium, remédiī (n) - cure, remedy (4)
sérvus, sérvī (m) - slave (male) (24)
sígnum, sígnī (n) - sign, signal, indication; seal (13)
sōlā́cium, sōlā́ciī (n) - comfort, relief (24)
stúdium, stúdiī (n) - eagerness, zeal, pursuit, study (9)
stúltus, stúltī (m) - a fool (4)
tyránnus, tyránnī (m) - absolute ruler, tyrant (6)
vérbum, vérbī (n) - word (5)
vīcīnus, vīcīnī (m) - neighbor (male) (21)
vir, vírī (m) - man, hero (3)
vítium, vítiī (n) - fault, crime, vice (6)
vúlgus, vúlgī (n) - the common people, mob, rabble (21)

3rd Declension

aduléscēns, adulēscéntis (m *or* f) - young man *or* woman (12)
aétās, aetā́tis (f) - period of life, life, age, an age, time (16)
ámor, amṓris (m) - love (7)
aúctor, auctṓris (m) - increaser; author, originator (19)
audītor, audītṓris (m) - hearer, listener, member of an audience (16)
Caésar, Caésaris (m) - Caesar (12)
cáput, cápitis (n) - head; leader; beginning; life; heading; chapter (11)
cármen, cárminis (n) - song, poem (7)
Carthā́gō, Carthā́ginis (f) - Carthage (24)
Cícerō, Cicerṓnis (m) - (Marcus Tullius) Cicero (8)
cīvitās, cīvitā́tis (f) - state, citizenship (7)
cṓnsul, cṓnsulis (m) - consul (11)
córpus, córporis (n) - body (7)
cupíditās, cupiditā́tis (f) - desire, longing, passion; cupidity, avarice (10)
dux, dúcis (m) - leader, guide; commander, general (23)
flū́men, flū́minis (n) - river (18)
frā́ter, frā́tris (m) - brother (8)
génus, géneris (n) - origin; kind, type, sort, class (18)
hómō, hóminis (m) - human being, man (7)
imperā́tor, imperātṓris (m) - general, commander-in-chief, emperor (24)
iū́dex, iū́dicis (m) - judge, juror (19)
iūs, iū́ris (n) - right, justice, law (14)
lábor, labṓris (m)- labor, work, toil; a work, production (7)
laus, laúdis (f) - praise, glory, fame (8)
lībértās, lībertā́tis (f) - liberty (8)
lītus, lītoris (n) - shore, coast (23)
mā́ter, mā́tris (f) - mother (12)
mīles, mīlitis (m) - soldier (23)
mṓrēs, mṓrum (m) - habits, morals, character (7)
mōs, mṓris (m) - habit, custom, manner (7)

némō, nūllíus, némini, néminem, núllō, núllā (m *or* f) - no one, nobody (11)
nṓmen, nṓminis (n) - name (7)
ōrā́tor, ōrātṓris (m) - orator, speaker (23)
ōs, ṓris (n) - mouth, face (14)
páter, pátris (m) - father (12)
pāx, pā́cis (f) - peace (7)
próbitās, probitā́tis (f) - uprightness, honesty (18)
rátiō, ratiṓnis (f) - reckoning, account; reason, judgment, consideration; system; manner, method (8)
rēx, rḗgis (m) - king (7)
sacérdōs, sacerdṓtis (m) - priest (23)
sálūs, salū́tis (f) - health, safety; greeting (21)
sápiēns, sapiéntis (m/f) - a wise man/woman, philosopher (25)
scélus, scéleris (n) - evil deed, crime, sin, wickedness (19)
scrī́ptor, scrīptṓris (m) - writer, author (8)
senéctūs, senectū́tis (f) - old age (10)
sénex, sénis (m) - old man (16)
sérvitūs, servitū́tis (f) - servitude, slavery (20)
sóror, sorṓris (f) - sister (8)
tempéstās, tempestā́tis (f) - period of time, season; weather, storm (15)
témpus, témporis (n) - time; occasion, opportunity (7)
tímor, timṓris (m) - fear (10)
úxor, uxṓris (f) - wife (7)
vḗritās, vēritā́tis (f) - truth (10)
vírgō, vírginis (f) - maiden, virgin (7)
vírtūs, virtū́tis (f) - manliness, courage; excellence, character, worth, virtue (7)
volúptās, voluptā́tis (f) - pleasure (10)
vúlnus, vúlneris (n) - wound (24)

3rd Declension I-Stem

ánimal, animā́lis (n) - a living creature, animal (14)
ars, ártis (f) - art, skill (14)
arx, árcis (f) - citadel, stronghold (23)
aúris, aúris (f) - ear (14)
cī́vis, cī́vis (m *or* f) - citizen (14)
fī́nēs, fī́nium (m) - boundaries, territory (21)
fī́nis, fī́nis (m) - end, limit, boundary; purpose (21)
gēns, géntis (f) - clan, race, nation, people (21)
hóstēs, hóstium (m) - the enemy (18)
hóstis, hóstis (m) - an enemy *(of the state)* (18)
ígnis, ígnis (m) - fire (22)
máre, máris (n) - sea (14)
mēns, méntis (f) - mind, thought, intention (16)
mōns, móntis (m) - mountain (20)
mors, mórtis (f) - death (14)
nā́vis, nā́vis (f) - ship, boat (21)
nū́bēs, nū́bis (f) - cloud (14)
pars, pártis (f) - part, share; direction (14)
urbs, úrbis (f) - city (14)
vī́rēs, vī́rium (f. pl.) - strength (14)
vīs, vīs (f) - force, power, violence (14)

4th Declension

córnū, córnūs (n) - horn (20)
frū́ctus, frū́ctūs (m) - fruit; profit, benefit, enjoyment (20)
génū, génūs (n) - knee (20)
mánus, mánūs (f) - hand; handwriting; band (20)
métus, métūs (m) - fear, dread, anxiety (20)
senā́tus, senā́tūs (m) - senate (20)
sḗnsus, sḗnsūs (m) - feeling, sense (20)
spī́ritus, spī́ritūs (m) - breath, breathing; spirit, soul (20)
vérsus, vérsūs (m) - line of verse (20)

5th Declension

díēs, diḗī (m) - day (22)
fídēs, fídeī (f) - faith, trust, trustworthiness, fidelity, promise, guarantee, protection (22)
rēs, réī (f) - thing, matter, property, business, affair (22)
rēs pū́blica, réī pū́blicae (f) - state, commonwealth, republic (22)
spēs, spéī (f) - hope (22)

Indeclinable

níhil - nothing (1)
sátis - enough (5)

Pronouns

áliquis, áliquid - someone, somebody, something (23)
égo, méī - I (11)
hic, haec, hoc - this; the latter; he, she, it, they (9)
ī́dem, éadem, ídem - the same (11)
ílle, ílla, íllud - that; the former; the famous; he, she, it, they (9)
ípse, ípsa, ípsum - myself, yourself, himself, herself, itself, *etc.*, the very, the actual (13)
is, éa, id - this, that; he, she, it (11)

íste, ísta, ístud - that of yours, that; such (as you have, as you speak of); *sometimes with contemptuous force, e.g.,* that despicable, that wretched (9)
quī, quae, quod - who, which, what, that (17)
quid - what (1)
quis? quid? - who? whose? whom? what? which? (19)
quísque, quídque, cuiúsque, cuíque - each one, each person, each thing (13)
quísquis, quídquid - whoever, whatever (23)
súī - himself, herself, itself, themselves (13)
tū, túī - you *(sing.)* (11)

Adjectives

1st & 2nd Declension

acérbus, acérba, acérbum - harsh, bitter, grievous (12)
aéquus, aéqua, aéquum - level, even; calm; equal, just; favorable (22)
áliī . . . áliī - some . . . others (9)
álius, ália, áliud - other, another (9)
álter, áltera, álterum - the other (of two), second (9)
amī́cus, amī́ca, amī́cum - friendly (11)
antī́quus, antī́qua, antī́quum - ancient, old-time (2)
ásper, áspera, ásperum - rough, harsh (21)
avā́rus, avā́ra, avā́rum - greedy, avaricious (3)
beā́tus, beā́ta, beā́tum - happy, fortunate, blessed (10)
béllus, bélla, béllum - pretty, handsome, charming (4)
bónus, bóna, bónum - good, kind (4)
caécus, caéca, caécum - blind (17)
cā́rus, cā́ra, cā́rum - dear (11)
cértus, cérta, cértum - definite, sure, certain, reliable (19)
clā́rus, clā́ra, clā́rum - clear, bright; renowned, famous, illustrious (18)
déxter, déxtra, déxtrum - right, right-hand (20)
dóctus, dócta, dóctum - taught, learned, skilled (13)
fortūnā́tus, fortūnā́ta, fortūnā́tum - lucky, fortunate, happy (13)
géminus, gémina, géminum - twin (25)
Graécus, Graéca, Graécum - Greek (6)
hūmā́nus, hūmā́na, hūmā́num - pertaining to man, human; humane, kind; refined, cultivated (4)
incértus, incérta, incértum - uncertain, unsure, doubtful (22)
iūcúndus, iūcúnda, iūcúndum - pleasant, delightful, agreeable, pleasing (16)
Latī́nus, Latī́na, Latī́num - Latin (22)
lī́ber, lī́bera, lī́berum - free (5)
lóngus, lónga, lóngum - long (16)
magnánimus, magnánima, magnánimum - great-hearted, brave, magnanimous (23)
mágnus, mágna, mágnum - large, great; important (2)
málus, mála, málum - bad, wicked, evil (4)
médius, média, médium - middle; the middle of (22)
méus, méa, méum - my (2)
míser, mísera, míserum - wretched, miserable, unfortunate (15)
múltus, múlta, múltum - much, many (2)
neúter, neútra, neútrum - not either, neither (9)
nóster, nóstra, nóstrum - our, ours (5)
nóvus, nóva, nóvum - new; strange (7)
nū́llus, nū́lla, nū́llum - not any, no, none (9)
párvus, párva, párvum - small, little (4)
paúcī, paúcae, paúca - few, a few (3)
perpétuus, perpétua, perpétuum perpetual, lasting, uninterrupted, continuous (6)
plḗnus, plḗna, plḗnum - full, abundant, generous (6)
púlcher, púlchra, púlchrum - beautiful, handsome; fine (5)
Rōmā́nus, Rōmā́na, Rōmā́num - Roman (3)
sálvus, sálva, sálvum - safe, sound (6)
sā́nus, sā́na, sā́num - sound, healthy, sane (5)
secúndus, secúnda, secúndum - second; favorable (6)
siníster, sinístra, sinístrum - left, left-hand; harmful, ill-omened (20)
sṓlus, sṓla, sṓlum - alone, only, the only (9)
stúltus, stúlta, stúltum - foolish (4)
súus, súa, súum - his own, her own, its own, their own (13)
tṓtus, tṓta, tṓtum - whole, entire (9)
túus, túa, túum - your *(sing.)* (2)
ū́llus, ū́lla, ū́llum - any (9)
últimus, última, últimum - farthest, extreme; last, final (25)
ū́nus, ū́na, ū́num - one, single, alone (9)

úter, útra, útrum - either, which (of two) (9)
vḗrus, vḗra, vḗrum - true, real, proper (4)
véster, véstra, véstrum - your *(pl.)* (6)

3rd Declension
ā́cer, ā́cris, ā́cre - sharp, keen, eager; severe, fierce (16)
brévis, bréve - short, small, brief (16)
céler, céleris, célere - swift, quick, rapid (16)
commū́nis, commū́ne - common, general, of / for the community (20)
diffícilis, diffícile - hard, difficult, troublesome (16)
dúlcis, dúlce - sweet; pleasant, agreeable (16)
fácilis, fácile - easy; agreeable (16)
fḗlīx, ***gen.*** **fēlī́cis** - lucky, fortunate, happy (22)
férōx, ***gen.*** **ferṓcis** - fierce, savage (25)
fidḗlis, fidḗle - faithful, loyal (25)
fórtis, fórte - strong, brave (16)
grávis, gráve - heavy, weighty; serious, important; severe, grievous (19)
immortā́lis, immortā́le - not subject to death, immortal (19)
íngēns, ***gen.*** **ingéntis** - huge (16)
lévis, léve - light; easy; slight, trivial (17)
mortā́lis, mortā́le - mortal (18)
ómnis, ómne - every, all (16)
pótēns, ***gen.*** **poténtis** - able, powerful, mighty, strong (16)
sápiēns, ***gen.*** **sapiéntis** - wise, judicious (25)
sénex, ***gen.*** **sénis** - old, aged (16)

Indeclinable
sátis - enough, sufficient (5)

Interrogative Adjective
quī?, quae?, quod? - what? which? what kind of?; *(sometimes with exclamatory force)* what (a)! what sort of! (19)

Verbs

1st Conjugation
ádiuvō, adiuvā́re, adiū́vī, adiū́tum - to help, aid, assist; to please (4)
ámō, amā́re, amā́vī, amā́tum - to love, like (1)
appéllō, appellā́re, appellā́vī, appellā́tum - to speak to, address (as), call, name (14)
cḗnō, cēnā́re, cēnā́vī, cēnā́tum - to dine (5)
cṓgitō, cōgitā́re, cōgitā́vī, cōgitā́tum- to think, ponder, consider, plan (1)
cōnsérvō, cōnservā́re, cōnservā́vī, cōnservā́tum - to preserve, conserve, maintain (1)
créō, creā́re, creā́vī, creā́tum - to create (12)
cúlpō, culpā́re, culpā́vī, culpā́tum - to blame, censure (5)
dēléctō, dēlectā́re, dēlectā́vī, dēlectā́tum - to delight, charm, please (19)
dēmṓnstrō, dēmōnstrā́re, dēmōnstrā́vī, dēmōnstrā́tum to point out, show, demonstrate (8)
dēsī́derō, dēsīderā́re, dēsīderā́vī, dēsīderā́tum - to desire, long for, miss (17)
dō, dáre, dédī, dátum - to give, offer (1)
ḗducō, ēducā́re, ēducā́vī, ēducā́tum - to bring up, educate (23)
érrō, errā́re, errā́vī, errā́tum - to wander; err, go astray, make a mistake, be mistaken (1)
exspéctō, exspectā́re, exspectā́vī, exspectā́tum - to look for, expect, await (15)
iúvō, iuvā́re, iū́vī, iū́tum - to help, aid, assist; to please (4)
labṓrō, labōrā́re, labōrā́vī, labōrā́tum - to labor; be in distress (21)
laúdō, laudā́re, laudā́vī, laudā́tum - to praise (1)
lī́berō, līberā́re, līberā́vī, līberā́tum - to free, liberate (19)
mū́tō, mūtā́re, mūtā́vī, mūtā́tum to change, alter; exchange (14)
nárrō, nārrā́re, nārrā́vī, nārrā́tum - to tell, report, narrate (24)
nā́vigō, nāvigā́re, nāvigā́vī, nāvigā́tum - to sail, navigate (17)
nécō, necā́re, necā́vī, necā́tum - to murder, kill (7)
négō, negā́re, negā́vī, negā́tum to deny, say that . . . not (25)
nū́ntiō, nūntiā́re, nūntiā́vī, nūntiā́tum - to announce, report, relate (25)
párō, parā́re, parā́vī, parā́tum - to prepare, provide; get, obtain (19)
prōnū́ntiō, prōnūntiā́re, prōnūntiā́vī, prōnūntiā́tum - to proclaim, announce; declaim; pronounce (20)
pútō, putā́re, putā́vī, putā́tum - to reckon, suppose, judge, think, imagine (25)

récitō, recitā́re, recitā́vī, recitā́tum - to read aloud, recite (17)

sátiō, satiā́re, satiā́vī, satiā́tum - to satisfy, sate (3)

sérvō, servā́re, servā́vī, servā́tum - to preserve, save, keep, guard (1)

spḗrō, spērā́re, spērā́vī, spērā́tum - to hope for, hope (25)

stō, stā́re, stétī, státum - to stand, stand still *or* firm (13)

súperō, superā́re, superā́vī, superā́tum - to be above, have the upper hand, surpass; overcome, conquer (5)

tólerō, tolerā́re, tolerā́vī, tolerā́tum - to bear, endure (6)

vī́tō, vītā́re, vītā́vī, vītā́tum - to avoid, shun (14)

vócō, vocā́re, vocā́vī, vocā́tum - to call, summon (1)

2nd Conjugation

aúdeō, audḗre, aúsus sum - to dare (7)

cáreō, carḗre, cáruī, caritū́rum (+abl.) - to be without, be deprived of, want, lack; be free from (20)

contíneō, continḗre, contínuī, conténtum - to hold together, contain, keep, enclose, restrain (21)

dḗbeō, dēbḗre, dḗbuī, dḗbitum - to owe; ought, must, should (1)

dḗleō, dēlḗre, dēlḗvī, dēlḗtum - to destroy, wipe out, erase (17)

dóceō, docḗre, dócuī, dóctum - to teach (8)

gaúdeō, gaudḗre, gāvī́sus sum - to be glad, rejoice (23)

hábeō, habḗre, hábuī, hábitum - to have, hold, possess; consider, regard (3)

iáceō, iacḗre, iácuī - to lie; lie prostrate; lie dead (25)

iúbeō, iubḗre, iússī, iússum - to bid, order, command (21)

máneō, manḗre, mā́nsī, mā́nsum - to remain, stay, stay behind, abide, continue (5)

mísceō, miscḗre, míscuī, míxtum to mix, stir up, disturb (18)

móneō, monḗre, mónuī, mónitum - to remind, advise, warn (1)

móveō, movḗre, mṓvī, mṓtum - to move; arouse, affect (18)

prohíbeō, prohibḗre, prohíbuī, prohíbitum - to keep (back), prevent, hinder, restrain, prohibit (20)

remáneō, remanḗre, remā́nsī, remā́nsum - to remain, stay, stay behind, abide, continue (5)

rī́deō, rīdḗre, rī́sī, rī́sum - to laugh, laugh at (24)

sálvē, salvḗte - hello, greetings (1)

sálveō, salvḗre - to be well, be in good health (1)

téneō, tenḗre, ténuī, téntum - to hold, keep, possess; restrain (14)

térreō, terrḗre, térruī, térritum - to frighten, terrify (1)

tímeō, timḗre, tímuī - to fear, be afraid (of) (15)

válē, valḗte - good-bye, farewell (1)

váleō, valḗre, váluī, valitū́rum - to be strong, have power; be well (1)

vídeō, vidḗre, vī́dī, vī́sum - to see; observe, understand (1)

vídeor, vidḗrī, vī́sus sum - to be seen, seem, appear (18)

3rd Conjugation

admíttō, admíttere, admī́sī, admíssum - to admit, receive, let in (17)

ágō, ágere, ḗgī, ā́ctum - to drive, lead, do, act; pass, spend *(life or time)* (8)

álō, álere, áluī, áltum - to nourish, support, sustain, increase; cherish (13)

āmíttō, āmíttere, āmī́sī, āmíssum - to send away; lose, let go (12)

āvértō, āvértere, āvértī, āvérsum - to turn away, avert (23)

cádō, cádere, cécidī, cāsū́rum - to fall (12)

cérnō, cérnere, crḗvī, crḗtum - to distinguish, discern, perceive (22)

commíttō, commíttere, commī́sī, commíssum - to entrust, commit (15)

crḗdō, crḗdere, crḗdidī, crḗditum to believe, trust (25)

cúrrō, cúrrere, cucúrrī, cúrsum - to run, rush, move quickly (14)

dēféndō, dēféndere, dēféndī, dēfḗnsum - to ward off; defend, protect (20)

dī́cō, dī́cere, dī́xī, díctum - to say, tell, speak; name, call (10)

dī́ligō, dīlígere, dīlḗxī, dīlḗctum - to esteem, love (13)

discḗdō, discḗdere, discéssī, discéssum - to go away, depart (20)

díscō, díscere, dídicī - to learn (8)

dū́cō, dū́cere, dū́xī, dúctum - to lead; consider, regard; prolong (8)

expéllō, expéllere, éxpulī, expúlsum - to drive out, expel, banish (24)
flúō, flúere, flū́xī, flū́xum - to flow (18)
gérō, gérere, géssī, géstum - to carry; carry on, manage, conduct, wage, accomplish, perform (8)
intéllegō, intellégere, intellḗxī, intellḗctum - to understand (11)
iúngō, iúngere, iū́nxī, iū́nctum - to join (13)
légō, légere, lḗgī, lḗctum - to pick out, choose; read (18)
míttō, míttere, mī́sī, míssum - to send, let go (11)
néglegō, neglégere, neglḗxī, neglḗctum - to neglect, disregard (17)
ópprimō, opprímere, oppréssī, oppréssum - to suppress, overwhelm, overpower, check (23)
osténdō, osténdere, osténdī, osténtum - to exhibit, show, display (23)
péllō, péllere, pépulī, púlsum - to strike, push; drive out, banish (24)
pétō, pétere, petī́vī, petī́tum - to seek, aim at, beg, beseech (23)
prémō, prémere, préssī, préssum - to press; press hard, pursue (23)
quaérō, quaérere, quaesī́vī, quaesī́tum - to seek, look for, strive for; ask, inquire, inquire into (24)
régō, régere, rḗxī, rḗctum - to rule, guide, direct (16)
relínquō, relínquere, relī́quī, relíctum - to leave behind, leave, abandon, desert (21)
revértō, revértere, revértī, revérsum - turn back (23)
scrī́bō, scrī́bere, scrī́psī, scrī́ptum to write, compose (8)
tángō, tángere, tétigī, tā́ctum - to touch (21)
tóllō, tóllere, sústulī, sublā́tum - to raise, lift up; take away, remove, destroy (22)
tráhō, tráhere, trā́xī, tráctum - to draw, drag; derive, acquire (8)
vértō, vértere, vértī, vérsum - to turn; change (23)
víncō, víncere, vī́cī, víctum - to conquer, overcome (8)
vī́vō, vī́vere, vī́xī, vī́ctum - to live (10)

3rd Conjugation -iō

accípiō, accípere, accḗpī, accéptum - to take *(to one's self)*, receive, accept (24)
cápiō, cápere, cḗpī, cáptum - to take, capture, seize, get (10)
cúpiō, cúpere, cupī́vī, cupī́tum - to desire, wish, long for (17)
ērípiō, ērípere, ērípuī, ēréptum - to snatch away, take away; rescue (22)
excípiō, excípere, excḗpī, excéptum - to take out, except; take, receive, capture (24)
fáciō, fácere, fḗcī, fáctum - to make, do, accomplish (10)
fúgiō, fúgere, fū́gī, fugitū́rum - to flee, hurry away; escape; go into exile; avoid, shun (10)
iáciō, iácere, iḗcī, iáctum - to throw, hurl (15)
incípiō, incípere, incḗpī, incéptum - to begin (17)
patefáciō, patefácere, patefḗcī, patefáctum - to make open, open; disclose, expose (25)
rápiō, rápere, rápuī, ráptum - to seize, snatch, carry away (21)
recípiō, recípere, recḗpī, recéptum - to take back, regain; admit, receive (24)
suscípiō, suscípere, suscḗpī, suscéptum - to undertake (25)

4th Conjugation

aúdiō, audī́re, audī́vī, audī́tum - to hear, listen to (10)
invéniō, invenī́re, invḗnī, invéntum - to come upon, find (10)
nésciō, nescī́re, nescī́vī, nescī́tum - to not know, be ignorant (25)
scíō, scī́re, scī́vī, scī́tum - to know (21)
séntiō, sentī́re, sḗnsī, sḗnsum - to feel, perceive, think, experience (11)
véniō, venī́re, vḗnī, véntum - to come (10)

Irregular

póssum, pósse, pótuī - to be able, can, could, have power (6)
sum, ésse, fúī, futū́rum - to be, exist (4)

Defective

ā́it, ā́iunt - he says, they say, assert (25)
coépī, coepísse, coéptum - began (17)
ínquit - he says *or* said (22)
ṓdī, ōdísse, ōsū́rum - to hate (20)

Adverbs

ánte (+acc.) - before, previously (13)
béne - well, satisfactorily, quite (11)
cíto - quickly (17)

crās - tomorrow (5)
cūr - why (18)
déhinc - then, next (25)
deínde - thereupon, next, then (18)
díū - long, for a long time (12)
étiam - even, also (11)
héri - yesterday (5)
hīc - here (25)
hódiē - today (3)
iam - now, already, soon (19)
íbi - there (6)
ítaque - and so, therefore (15)
íterum - again, a second time (21)
nímis, nímium - too, too much, excessively; *(in a positive sense, esp. with adjectives and adverbs)* exceedingly, very (9)
nōn - not (1)
númquam - never (8)
nunc - now, at present (6)
nū́per - recently (12)
ṓlim - once (upon a time), long ago, formerly; some day, in the future (13)
pósteā - afterwards (24)
prṓtinus - immediately (22)
quam - how (16)
quándō - when (5)
quā́rē - because of which thing *(lit.);* therefore, wherefore, why (6)
quóndam - formerly, once (22)
quóque - also, too (17)
saépe - often (1)
sátis - enough, sufficiently (5)
sémper - always (3)
támen - nevertheless, still (8)
tum - then, at that time; thereupon, in the next place (5)
úbi - where, when (6)
últrā - on the other side of, beyond (22)
úmquam - ever, at any time (23)

Conjunctions

at - but; but, mind you; but, you say (19)
átque, ac - and also, and even, and in fact (21)
aut - or (17)
aut . . . aut - either . . . or (17)
aútem - however; moreover (11)
dum - while, as long as, at the same time that; *or* until *(+subjunctive)* (8)
énim - for, in fact, truly (9)
et - and; even (2)
et . . . et - both . . . and (2)
ígitur - therefore, consequently (5)
nam - for (13)
néque, nec - and not, nor (11)
néque . . . néque, nec . . . nec - neither . . . nor (11)
nísi - if . . . not, unless; except (19)
quod - because (11)
quóniam - since, inasmuch as (10)
sed - but (2)
sī - if (1)
ut - as, just as, when (24)

Prepositions

ab, ā (+abl.) - away from, from; by (14)
ad (+acc.) - to, up to, near to (8)
ánte (+acc.) - before *(in place or time),* in front of (13)
cóntrā (+acc.) - against (19)
cum (+abl.) - with (10)
dē (+abl.) - down from, from; concerning, about (3)
ex, ē (abl.+) - out of, from, from within; by reason of, on account of ; of *(after cardinal numerals)* (8)
in (+acc.) - into, toward; against (9)
in (+abl.) - in, on (3)
ínter (+acc.) - between, among (15)
per (+acc.) - through; by *(with reflexive pronoun)* (13)
post (+acc.) - after, behind (7)
prō (+abl.) - in front of, before, on behalf of, for the sake of, in return for, instead of, for, as (12)
própter (+acc.) - on account of, because of (5)
síne (+abl.) - without (2)
sub (+abl. w/ verbs of rest *or* +acc. w/ verbs of motion) - under, up under, close to, down to/into, to/at the foot of (7)
trāns (+acc.) - across (14)
últrā (adv. and prep. +acc.) - on the other side of, beyond (22)

Interjection

ō - O!, Oh! (2)

Idioms

amā́bō tē - please (1)
grā́tiās ágere (+dat.) - to thank someone; to give thanks to (8)
nōn sṓlum . . . sed étiam - not only . . . but also (9)
poénās dáre - to pay the penalty (2)
sī quándō - if ever (5)

Prefix

re-, red- - again, back (24)

Suffixes

-ne – interrogative suffix attached to the first word of a sentence, typically the verb or another word on which the question hinges, to introduce a question whose answer is uncertain (5)

-que - and *(enclitic conjunction; appended to the second of two words to be joined)* (6)

Numerals

Cardinal - ū́nus *to* vīgíntī quī́nque (15)

Ordinal - prī́mus *to* duodécimus (15)

----

céntum - a hundred (15)

mī́lia, mī́lium (n. pl.) - thousands (15)

mī́lle - thousand (15)

Chapter 26

Nouns

1st Declension

adulēscéntia, adulēscéntiae (f) - youth, young manhood; youthfulness (5)
agrícola, agrícolae (m) - farmer (3)
amíca, amícae (f) - friend (female) (3)
amīcítia, amīcítiae (f) - friendship (10)
áqua, áquae (f) - water (14)
Ásia, Ásiae (f) - Asia (12)
cása, cásae (f) - house, cottage, hut (21)
caúsa, caúsae (f) - cause, reason; case, situation (21)
caúsā (abl. + preceding gen.) - for the sake of, on account of (21)
cḗna, cḗnae (f) - dinner (26)
clēméntia, clēméntiae (f) - mildness, gentleness, mercy (16)
cṓpia, cṓpiae (f) - abundance, supply (8)
cṓpiae, cōpiā́rum (f) - supplies, troops, forces (8)
cúlpa, cúlpae (f) - fault, blame (5)
cū́ra, cū́rae (f) - care, attention, caution, anxiety (4)
déa, déae (f) - goddess (6)
discípula, discípulae (f) - learner, pupil, student (female) (6)
dīvítiae, dīvitiā́rum (f. pl.) - riches, wealth (13)
fā́bula, fā́bulae (f) - story, tale; play (24)
fā́ma, fā́mae (f) - rumor, report; fame, reputation (2)
família, famíliae (f) - household, family (19)
fḗmina, fḗminae (f) - woman (3)
fenéstra, fenéstrae (f) - window (21)
fī́lia, fī́liae (f) - daughter (3)
fṓrma, fṓrmae (f) - form, shape; beauty (2)
fortū́na, fortū́nae (f) - fortune, luck (2)
glṓria, glṓriae (f) - glory, fame (5)
Graécia, Graéciae (f) - Greece (19)
hásta, hástae (f) - spear (23)
hṓra, hṓrae (f) - hour, time (10)
īnsídiae, īnsidiā́rum (f) - ambush, plot, treachery (6)
ī́nsula, ī́nsulae (f) - island (23)
ī́ra, ī́rae (f) - ire, anger (2)
Itália, Itáliae (f) - Italy (15)
língua, línguae (f) - tongue; language (25)
líttera, lítterae (f) - a letter of the alphabet (7)
lítterae, litterā́rum (f) - a letter (epistle), literature (7)
magístra, magístrae (f) - schoolmistress, teacher, mistress (4)
médica, médicae (f) - doctor, physician (female) (12)
memória, memóriae (f) - memory, recollection (15)
mḗnsa, mḗnsae (f) - table; dining; dish, course (26)
móra, mórae (f) - delay (4)
nātū́ra, nātū́rae (f) - nature (10)
naúta, naútae (m) - sailor (2)
patiéntia, patiéntiae (f) - suffering; patience, endurance (12)
pátria, pátriae (f) - fatherland, native land, (one's) country (2)
pecū́nia, pecū́niae (f) - money (2)
philosóphia, philosóphiae (f) - philosophy (2)
poéna, poénae (f) - penalty, punishment (2)
poḗta, poḗtae (m) - poet (2)
pórta, pórtae (f) - gate, entrance (2)
puélla, puéllae (f) - girl (2)
rēgī́na, rēgī́nae (f) - queen (7)
Rṓma, Rṓmae (f) - Rome (14)
rósa, rósae (f) - rose (2)
sapiéntia, sapiéntiae (f) - wisdom (3)
sátura, sáturae (f) - satire (16)
sciéntia, sciéntiae (f) - knowledge (18)
senténtia, senténtiae (f) - feeling, thought, opinion, vote, sentence (2)
sérva, sérvae (f) - slave (female) (24)
térra, térrae (f) - earth, ground, land, country (7)
Trṓia, Trṓiae (f) - Troy (21)
túrba, túrbae (f) - uproar, disturbance; mob, crowd, multitude (14)
vía, víae (f) - way, road, street (10)
vīcī́na, vīcī́nae (f) - neighbor (female) (21)
victṓria, victṓriae (f) - victory (8)
vī́ta, vī́tae (f) - life; mode of life (2)

2nd Declension

áger, ágrī (m) - field, farm (3)
amī́cus, amī́cī (m) - friend (male) (3)
ánimī, animṓrum (m) - high spirits, pride, courage (5)
ánimus, ánimī (m) - soul, spirit, mind (5)
ánnus, ánnī (m) - year (12)
argūméntum, argūméntī (n) - proof, evidence, argument (19)
bā́sium, bā́siī (n) - kiss (4)
béllum, béllī (n) - war (4)
benefícium, benefíciī (n) - benefit, kindness; favor (19)

caélum, caélī (n) - sky, heaven (5)
coniūrā́tī, coniūrātṓrum (m. pl.) - conspirators (20)
cōnsílium, cōnsíliī (n) - plan, purpose, counsel, advice, judgment, wisdom (4)
déus, déī (m) - god (6)
discípulus, discípulī (m) - learner, pupil, student (male) (6)
dṓnum, dṓnī (n) - gift, present (4)
équus, équī (m) - horse (23)
exítium, exítiī (n) - destruction, ruin (4)
fáctum, fáctī (n) - deed, act, achievement (13)
férrum, férrī (n) - iron; sword (22)
fī́lius, fī́liī (m) - son (3)
fórum, fórī (n) - marketplace, forum (26)
Graécus, Graécī (m) - a Greek (6)
impérium, impériī (n) - power to command, supreme power, authority, command, control (24)
iūdícium, iūdíciī (n) - judgment, decision, opinion; trial (19)
libéllus, libéllī (m) - little book (17)
líber, líbrī (m) - book (6)
lóca, locṓrum (n) - places, region (9)
lócī, locṓrum (m) - passages in literature (9)
lócus, lócī (m) - place; passage in literature (9)
lū́dus, lū́dī (m) - game, sport; school (18)
magíster, magístrī (m) - schoolmaster, teacher, master (4)
médicus, médicī (m) - doctor, physician (male) (12)
módus, módī (m) - measure, bound, limit; manner, method, mode, way (22)
mórbus, mórbī (m) - disease, sickness (9)
múndus, múndī (m) - world, universe (21)
númerus, númerī (m) - number (3)
óculus, óculī (m) - eye (4)
offícium, offíciī (n) - duty, service (4)
ṓtium, ṓtiī (n) - leisure, peace (4)
perfúgium, perfúgiī (n) - refuge, shelter (24)
perī́culum, perī́culī (n) - danger, risk (4)
pópulus, pópulī (m) - the people, a people, a nation (3)
prīncípium, prīncípiī (n) - beginning (12)
púer, púerī (m) - boy; boys, children *(pl.)* (3)
remédium, remédiī (n) - cure, remedy (4)
sérvus, sérvī (m) - slave (male) (24)
sígnum, sígnī (n) - sign, signal, indication; seal (13)
sōlā́cium, sōlā́ciī (n) - comfort, relief (24)
sómnus, sómnī (m) - sleep (26)
stúdium, stúdiī (n) - eagerness, zeal, pursuit, study (9)
stúltus, stúltī (m) - a fool (4)
tyránnus, tyránnī (m) - absolute ruler, tyrant (6)
vérbum, vérbī (n)- word (5)
vīcī́nus, vīcī́nī (m) - neighbor (male) (21)
vir, vírī (m) - man, hero (3)
vítium, vítiī (n) - fault, crime, vice (6)
vúlgus, vúlgī (n) - the common people, mob, rabble (21)

3rd Declension

adulēscēns, adulēscéntis (m *or* f) - young man *or* woman (12)
aétās, aetā́tis (f) - period of life, life, age, an age, time (16)
ámor, amṓris (m) - love (7)
aúctor, auctṓris (m) - increaser; author, originator (19)
audī́tor, audītṓris (m) - hearer, listener, member of an audience (16)
Caésar, Caésaris (m) - Caesar (12)
cáput, cápitis (n) - head; leader; beginning; life; heading; chapter (11)
cármen, cárminis (n) - song, poem (7)
Carthā́gō, Carthā́ginis (f) - Carthage (24)
Cícerō, Cicerṓnis (m) - (Marcus Tullius) Cicero (8)
cī́vitās, cīvitā́tis (f) - state, citizenship (7)
cṓnsul, cṓnsulis (m) - consul (11)
córpus, córporis (n) - body (7)
cupíditās, cupiditā́tis (f) - desire, longing, passion; cupidity, avarice (10)
dux, dúcis (m) - leader, guide; commander, general (23)
flū́men, flū́minis (n) - river (18)
frā́ter, frā́tris (m) - brother (8)
génus, géneris (n) - origin; kind, type, sort, class (18)
hómō, hóminis (m) - human being, man (7)
imperā́tor, imperātṓris (m) - general, commander-in-chief, emperor (24)
iū́dex, iū́dicis (m) - judge, juror (19)
iūs, iū́ris (n) - right, justice, law (14)
lábor, labṓris (m)- labor, work, toil; a work, production (7)
laus, laúdis (f) - praise, glory, fame (8)
lēx, lḗgis (f) - law, statute (26)
lībértās, lībertā́tis (f) - liberty (8)

lī́men, lī́minis (n) - threshold (26)
lī́tus, lī́toris (n) - shore, coast (23)
lūx, lū́cis (f) - light (26)
mā́ter, mā́tris (f) - mother (12)
mī́les, mī́litis (m) - soldier (23)
mṓrēs, mṓrum (m) - habits, morals, character (7)
mōs, mṓris (m) - habit, custom, manner (7)
nḗmō, nūllī́us, nḗminī, nḗminem, nū́llō, nū́llā (m *or* f) - no one, nobody (11)
nṓmen, nṓminis (n) - name (7)
ōrā́tor, ōrātṓris (m) - orator, speaker (23)
ōs, ṓris (n) - mouth, face (14)
páter, pátris (m) - father (12)
pāx, pā́cis (f) - peace (7)
próbitās, probitā́tis (f) - uprightness, honesty (18)
rátiō, ratiṓnis (f) - reckoning, account; reason, judgment, consideration; system; manner, method (8)
rēx, rḗgis (m) - king (7)
sacérdōs, sacerdṓtis (m) - priest (23)
sálūs, salū́tis (f) - health, safety; greeting (21)
sápiēns, sapiéntis (m/f) - a wise man/woman, philosopher (25)
scélus, scéleris (n) - evil deed, crime, sin, wickedness (19)
scrī́ptor, scrīptṓris (m) - writer, author (8)
senéctūs, senectū́tis (f) - old age (10)
sénex, sénis (m) - old man (16)
sérvitūs, servitū́tis (f) - servitude, slavery (20)
sóror, sorṓris (f) - sister (8)
tempéstās, tempestā́tis (f) - period of time, season; weather, storm (15)
témpus, témporis (n) - time; occasion, opportunity (7)
tímor, timṓris (m) - fear (10)
úxor, uxṓris (f) - wife (7)
vḗritās, vēritā́tis (f) - truth (10)
vírgō, vírginis (f) - maiden, virgin (7)
vírtūs, virtū́tis (f) - manliness, courage; excellence, character, worth, virtue (7)
volúptās, voluptā́tis (f) - pleasure (10)
vúlnus, vúlneris (n) - wound (24)

3rd Declension I-Stem

ánimal, animā́lis (n) - a living creature, animal (14)
ars, ártis (f) - art, skill (14)
arx, árcis (f) - citadel, stronghold (23)
aúris, aúris (f) - ear (14)
cī́vis, cī́vis (m *or* f) - citizen (14)
fī́nēs, fī́nium (m) - boundaries, territory (21)
fī́nis, fī́nis (m) - end, limit, boundary; purpose (21)
gēns, géntis (f) - clan, race, nation, people (21)
hóstēs, hóstium (m) - the enemy (18)
hóstis, hóstis (m) - an enemy *(of the state)* (18)
ígnis, ígnis (m) - fire (22)
máre, máris (n) - sea (14)
mēns, méntis (f) - mind, thought, intention (16)
mōns, móntis (m) - mountain (20)
mors, mórtis (f) - death (14)
nā́vis, nā́vis (f) - ship, boat (21)
nox, nóctis (f) - night (26)
nū́bēs, nū́bis (f) - cloud (14)
pars, pártis (f) - part, share; direction (14)
urbs, úrbis (f) - city (14)
vī́rēs, vī́rium (f. pl.) - strength (14)
vīs, vīs (f) - force, power, violence (14)

4th Declension

córnū, córnūs (n) - horn (20)
frū́ctus, frū́ctūs (m) - fruit; profit, benefit, enjoyment (20)
génū, génūs (n) - knee (20)
mánus, mánūs (f) - hand; handwriting; band (20)
métus, métūs (m) - fear, dread, anxiety (20)
senā́tus, senā́tūs (m) - senate (20)
sḗnsus, sḗnsūs (m) - feeling, sense (20)
spī́ritus, spī́ritūs (m) - breath, breathing; spirit, soul (20)
vérsus, vérsūs (m) - line of verse (20)

5th Declension

díēs, diḗī (m) - day (22)
fídēs, fídeī (f) - faith, trust, trustworthiness, fidelity, promise, guarantee, protection (22)
rēs, réī (f) - thing, matter, property, business, affair (22)
rēs pū́blica, réī pū́blicae (f) - state, commonwealth, republic (22)
spēs, spéī (f) - hope (22)

Indeclinable

níhil - nothing (1)
sátis - enough (5)

Pronouns

áliquis, áliquid - someone, somebody, something (23)
égo, méī - I (11)
hic, haec, hoc - this; the latter; he, she, it, they (9)
ī́dem, éadem, ídem - the same (11)
ílle, ílla, íllud - that; the former; the famous; he, she, it, they (9)

ípse, ípsa, ípsum - myself, yourself, himself, herself, itself, *etc.,* the very, the actual (13)
is, éa, id - this, that; he, she, it (11)
íste, ísta, ístud - that of yours, that; such (as you have, as you speak of); *sometimes with contemptuous force, e.g.,* that despicable, that wretched (9)
quī, quae, quod - who, which, what, that (17)
quid - what (1)
quídam, quaédam, quíddam - a certain one or thing, someone, something (26)
quis? quid? - who? whose? whom? what? which? (19)
quísque, quídque, cuiúsque, cuíque - each one, each person, each thing (13)
quísquis, quídquid - whoever, whatever (23)
súī - himself, herself, itself, themselves (13)
tū, túī - you *(sing.)* (11)

Adjectives

1st & 2nd Declension

acérbus, acérba, acérbum - harsh, bitter, grievous (12)
aéquus, aéqua, aéquum - level, even; calm; equal, just; favorable (22)
áliī . . . áliī - some . . . others (9)
álius, ália, áliud - other, another (9)
álter, áltera, álterum - the other (of two), second (9)
amīcus, amīca, amīcum - friendly (11)
antīquus, antīqua, antīquum - ancient, old-time (2)
ásper, áspera, ásperum - rough, harsh (21)
avārus, avāra, avārum - greedy, avaricious (3)
beātus, beāta, beātum - happy, fortunate, blessed (10)
béllus, bélla, béllum - pretty, handsome, charming (4)
bónus, bóna, bónum - good, kind (4)
caécus, caéca, caécum - blind (17)
cārus, cāra, cārum - dear (11)
cértus, cérta, cértum - definite, sure, certain, reliable (19)
clārus, clāra, clārum - clear, bright; renowned, famous, illustrious (18)
déxter, déxtra, déxtrum - right, right-hand (20)
dóctus, dócta, dóctum - taught, learned, skilled (13)
fortūnātus, fortūnāta, fortūnātum - lucky, fortunate, happy (13)
géminus, gémina, géminum - twin (25)
Graécus, Graéca, Graécum - Greek (6)
hūmānus, hūmāna, hūmānum - pertaining to man, human; humane, kind; refined, cultivated (4)
incértus, incérta, incértum - uncertain, unsure, doubtful (22)
iūcúndus, iūcúnda, iūcúndum - pleasant, delightful, agreeable, pleasing (16)
Latīnus, Latīna, Latīnum - Latin (22)
līber, lībera, līberum - free (5)
lóngus, lónga, lóngum - long (16)
magnánimus, magnánima, magnánimum - great-hearted, brave, magnanimous (23)
mágnus, mágna, mágnum - large, great; important (2)
málus, mála, málum - bad, wicked, evil (4)
médius, média, médium - middle; the middle of (22)
méus, méa, méum - my (2)
míser, mísera, míserum - wretched, miserable, unfortunate (15)
múltus, múlta, múltum - much, many (2)
neúter, neútra, neútrum - not either, neither (9)
nóster, nóstra, nóstrum - our, ours (5)
nóvus, nóva, nóvum - new; strange (7)
nūllus, nūlla, nūllum - not any, no, none (9)
párvus, párva, párvum - small, little (4)
paúcī, paúcae, paúca - few, a few (3)
perpétuus, perpétua, perpétuum perpetual, lasting, uninterrupted, continuous (6)
plēnus, plēna, plēnum - full, abundant, generous (6)
pudīcus, pudīca, pudīcum - modest, chaste (26)
púlcher, púlchra, púlchrum - beautiful, handsome; fine (5)
Rōmānus, Rōmāna, Rōmānum - Roman (3)
sálvus, sálva, sálvum - safe, sound (6)
sānus, sāna, sānum - sound, healthy, sane (5)
secúndus, secúnda, secúndum - second; favorable (6)
siníster, sinístra, sinístrum - left, left-hand; harmful, ill-omened (20)
sōlus, sōla, sōlum - alone, only, the only (9)
stúltus, stúlta, stúltum - foolish (4)

supérbus, supérba, supérbum - arrogant, overbearing, haughty, proud (26)
súus, súa, súum - his own, her own, its own, their own (13)
tṓtus, tṓta, tṓtum - whole, entire (9)
túus, túa, túum - your *(sing.)* (2)
ū́llus, ū́lla, ū́llum - any (9)
últimus, última, últimum - farthest, extreme; last, final (25)
ū́nus, ū́na, ū́num - one, single, alone (9)
urbā́nus, urbā́na, urbā́num - of the city, urban; urbane, elegant (26)
úter, útra, útrum - either, which (of two) (9)
vḗrus, vḗra, vḗrum - true, real, proper (4)
véster, véstra, véstrum - your *(pl.)* (6)

3rd Declension
ā́cer, ā́cris, ā́cre - sharp, keen, eager; severe, fierce (16)
brévis, bréve - short, small, brief (16)
céler, céleris, célere - swift, quick, rapid (16)
commū́nis, commū́ne - common, general, of / for the community (20)
diffícilis, diffícile - hard, difficult, troublesome (16)
dúlcis, dúlce - sweet; pleasant, agreeable (16)
fácilis, fácile - easy; agreeable (16)
fḗlīx, ***gen.*** **fēlī́cis** - lucky, fortunate, happy (22)
férōx, ***gen.*** **ferṓcis** - fierce, savage (25)
fidḗlis, fidḗle - faithful, loyal (25)
fórtis, fórte - strong, brave (16)
grávis, gráve - heavy, weighty; serious, important; severe, grievous (19)
immortā́lis, immortā́le - not subject to death, immortal (19)
íngēns, ***gen.*** **ingéntis** - huge (16)
lévis, léve - light; easy; slight, trivial (17)
mortā́lis, mortā́le - mortal (18)
ómnis, ómne - every, all (16)
pótēns, ***gen.*** **poténtis** - able, powerful, mighty, strong (16)
sápiēns, ***gen.*** **sapiéntis** - wise, judicious (25)
sénex, ***gen.*** **sénis** - old, aged (16)
trístis, tríste - sad, sorrowful; joyless, grim, severe (26)
túrpis, túrpe - ugly; shameful, base, disgraceful (26)

Indeclinable
sátis - enough, sufficient (5)

Indefinite Adjective
quídam, quaédam, quóddam - a certain, some (26)

Interrogative Adjective
quī?, quae?, quod? - what? which? what kind of?; *(sometimes with exclamatory force)* what (a)! what sort of! (19)

Verbs

1st Conjugation
ádiuvō, adiuvā́re, adiū́vī, adiū́tum - to help, aid, assist; to please (4)
ámō, amā́re, amā́vī, amā́tum - to love, like (1)
appéllō, appellā́re, appellā́vī, appellā́tum - to speak to, address (as), call, name (14)
cḗnō, cēnā́re, cēnā́vī, cēnā́tum - to dine (5)
cṓgitō, cōgitā́re, cōgitā́vī, cōgitā́tum - to think, ponder, consider, plan (1)
cōnsérvō, cōnservā́re, cōnservā́vī, cōnservā́tum - to preserve, conserve, maintain (1)
créō, creā́re, creā́vī, creā́tum - to create (12)
cúlpō, culpā́re, culpā́vī, culpā́tum - to blame, censure (5)
dēléctō, dēlectā́re, dēlectā́vī, dēlectā́tum - to delight, charm, please (19)
dēmṓnstrō, dēmōnstrā́re, dēmōnstrā́vī, dēmōnstrā́tum to point out, show, demonstrate (8)
dēsī́derō, dēsīderā́re, dēsīderā́vī, dēsīderā́tum - to desire, long for, miss (17)
dō, dáre, dédī, dátum - to give, offer (1)
ḗducō, ēducā́re, ēducā́vī, ēducā́tum - to bring up, educate (23)
érrō, errā́re, errā́vī, errā́tum - to wander; err, go astray, make a mistake, be mistaken (1)
exspéctō, exspectā́re, exspectā́vī, exspectā́tum - to look for, expect, await (15)
invī́tō, invītā́re, invītā́vī, invītā́tum - to entertain, invite, summon (26)
iúvō, iuvā́re, iū́vī, iū́tum - to help, aid, assist; to please (4)
labṓrō, labōrā́re, labōrā́vī, labōrā́tum - to labor; be in distress (21)
laúdō, laudā́re, laudā́vī, laudā́tum - to praise (1)

líberō, līberāre, līberāvī, līberātum - to free, liberate (19)
mū́tō, mūtāre, mūtāvī, mūtātum to change, alter; exchange (14)
nā́rrō, nārrāre, nārrāvī, nārrātum - to tell, report, narrate (24)
nā́vigō, nāvigāre, nāvigāvī, nāvigātum - to sail, navigate (17)
nécō, necāre, necāvī, necātum - to murder, kill (7)
négō, negāre, negāvī, negātum to deny, say that . . . not (25)
nū́ntiō, nūntiāre, nūntiāvī, nūntiātum - to announce, report, relate (25)
párō, parāre, parāvī, parātum - to prepare, provide; get, obtain (19)
prōnū́ntiō, prōnūntiāre, prōnūntiāvī, prōnūntiātum - to proclaim, announce; declaim; pronounce (20)
pútō, putāre, putāvī, putātum - to reckon, suppose, judge, think, imagine (25)
récitō, recitāre, recitāvī, recitātum - to read aloud, recite (17)
sátiō, satiāre, satiāvī, satiātum - to satisfy, sate (3)
sérvō, servāre, servāvī, servātum - to preserve, save, keep, guard (1)
spḗrō, spērāre, spērāvī, spērātum - to hope for, hope (25)
stō, stāre, stétī, státum - to stand, stand still *or* firm (13)
súperō, superāre, superāvī, superātum - to be above, have the upper hand, surpass; overcome, conquer (5)
tólerō, tolerāre, tolerāvī, tolerātum - to bear, endure (6)
vítō, vītāre, vītāvī, vītātum - to avoid, shun (14)
vócō, vocāre, vocāvī, vocātum - to call, summon (1)

2nd Conjugation

aúdeō, audḗre, aúsus sum - to dare (7)
cáreō, carḗre, cáruī, caritū́rum (+abl.) - to be without, be deprived of, want, lack; be free from (20)
contíneō, continḗre, contínuī, conténtum - to hold together, contain, keep, enclose, restrain (21)
dḗbeō, dēbḗre, dḗbuī, dḗbitum - to owe; ought, must, should (1)
dḗleō, dēlḗre, dēlḗvī, dēlḗtum - to destroy, wipe out, erase (17)
dóceō, docḗre, dócuī, dóctum - to teach (8)
gaúdeō, gaudḗre, gāvī́sus sum - to be glad, rejoice (23)
hábeō, habḗre, hábuī, hábitum - to have, hold, possess; consider, regard (3)
iáceō, iacḗre, iácuī - to lie; lie prostrate; lie dead (25)
iúbeō, iubḗre, iússī, iússum - to bid, order, command (21)
máneō, manḗre, mā́nsī, mā́nsum - to remain, stay, stay behind, abide, continue (5)
mísceō, miscḗre, míscuī, míxtum to mix, stir up, disturb (18)
móneō, monḗre, mónuī, mónitum - to remind, advise, warn (1)
móveō, movḗre, mṓvī, mṓtum - to move; arouse, affect (18)
prohíbeō, prohibḗre, prohíbuī, prohíbitum - to keep (back), prevent, hinder, restrain, prohibit (20)
remáneō, remanḗre, remā́nsī, remā́nsum - to remain, stay, stay behind, abide, continue (5)
rī́deō, rīdḗre, rī́sī, rī́sum - to laugh, laugh at (24)
sálvē, salvḗte - hello, greetings (1)
sálveō, salvḗre - to be well, be in good health (1)
téneō, tenḗre, ténuī, téntum - to hold, keep, possess; restrain (14)
térreō, terrḗre, térruī, térritum - to frighten, terrify (1)
tímeō, timḗre, tímuī - to fear, be afraid (of) (15)
válē, valḗte - good-bye, farewell (1)
váleō, valḗre, váluī, valitū́rum - to be strong, have power; be well (1)
vídeō, vidḗre, vī́dī, vī́sum - to see; observe, understand (1)
vídeor, vidḗrī, vī́sus sum - to be seen, seem, appear (18)

3rd Conjugation

admíttō, admíttere, admī́sī, admíssum - to admit, receive, let in (17)
ágō, ágere, ḗgī, ā́ctum - to drive, lead, do, act; pass, spend *(life or time)* (8)
álō, álere, áluī, áltum - to nourish, support, sustain, increase; cherish (13)
āmíttō, āmíttere, āmī́sī, āmíssum - to send away; lose, let go (12)
āvértō, āvértere, āvértī, āvérsum - to turn away, avert (23)

cádō, cádere, cécidī, cāsū́rum - to fall (12)

cérnō, cérnere, crḗvī, crḗtum - to distinguish, discern, perceive (22)

commíttō, commíttere, commī́sī, commíssum - to entrust, commit (15)

crḗdō, crḗdere, crḗdidī, crḗditum to believe, trust (25)

cúrrō, cúrrere, cucúrrī, cúrsum - to run, rush, move quickly (14)

dēféndō, dēféndere, dēféndī, dēfḗnsum - to ward off; defend, protect (20)

dī́cō, dī́cere, dī́xī, díctum - to say, tell, speak; name, call (10)

dī́ligō, dīlígere, dīlḗxī, dīléctum - to esteem, love (13)

discḗdō, discḗdere, discéssī, discéssum - to go away, depart (20)

díscō, díscere, dídicī - to learn (8)

dū́cō, dū́cere, dū́xī, dúctum - to lead; consider, regard; prolong (8)

expéllō, expéllere, éxpulī, expúlsum - to drive out, expel, banish (24)

flúō, flúere, flū́xī, flū́xum - to flow (18)

gérō, gérere, géssī, géstum - to carry; carry on, manage, conduct, wage, accomplish, perform (8)

intéllegō, intellégere, intellḗxī, intellḗctum - to understand (11)

iúngō, iúngere, iū́nxī, iū́nctum - to join (13)

légō, légere, lḗgī, léctum - to pick out, choose; read (18)

míttō, míttere, mī́sī, míssum - to send, let go (11)

néglegō, neglégere, neglḗxī, neglḗctum - to neglect, disregard (17)

ópprimō, opprímere, oppréssī, oppréssum - to suppress, overwhelm, overpower, check (23)

osténdō, osténdere, osténdī, osténtum - to exhibit, show, display (23)

péllō, péllere, pépulī, púlsum - to strike, push; drive out, banish (24)

pétō, pétere, petī́vī, petī́tum - to seek, aim at, beg, beseech (23)

prémō, prémere, préssī, préssum - to press; press hard, pursue (23)

quaérō, quaérere, quaesī́vī, quaesī́tum - to seek, look for, strive for; ask, inquire, inquire into (24)

régō, régere, rḗxī, rḗctum - to rule, guide, direct (16)

relínquō, relínquere, relī́quī, relíctum - to leave behind, leave, abandon, desert (21)

revértō, revértere, revértī, revérsum - turn back (23)

scrī́bō, scrī́bere, scrī́psī, scrī́ptum to write, compose (8)

tángō, tángere, tétigī, tā́ctum - to touch (21)

tóllō, tóllere, sústulī, sublā́tum - to raise, lift up; take away, remove, destroy (22)

tráhō, tráhere, trā́xī, tráctum - to draw, drag; derive, acquire (8)

vértō, vértere, vértī, vérsum - to turn; change (23)

víncō, víncere, vī́cī, víctum - to conquer, overcome (8)

vī́vō, vī́vere, vī́xī, víctum - to live (10)

3rd Conjugation -iō

accípiō, accípere, accḗpī, accéptum - to take *(to one's self)*, receive, accept (24)

cápiō, cápere, cḗpī, cáptum - to take, capture, seize, get (10)

cúpiō, cúpere, cupī́vī, cupī́tum - to desire, wish, long for (17)

ērípiō, ērípere, ērípuī, ēréptum - to snatch away, take away; rescue (22)

excípiō, excípere, excḗpī, excéptum - to take out, except; take, receive, capture (24)

fáciō, fácere, fḗcī, fáctum - to make, do, accomplish (10)

fúgiō, fúgere, fū́gī, fugitū́rum - to flee, hurry away; escape; go into exile; avoid, shun (10)

iáciō, iácere, iḗcī, iáctum - to throw, hurl (15)

incípiō, incípere, incḗpī, incéptum - to begin (17)

patefáciō, patefácere, patefḗcī, patefáctum - to make open, open; disclose, expose (25)

rápiō, rápere, rápuī, ráptum - to seize, snatch, carry away (21)

recípiō, recípere, recḗpī, recéptum - to take back, regain; admit, receive (24)

suscípiō, suscípere, suscḗpī, suscéptum - to undertake (25)

4th Conjugation

aúdiō, audī́re, audī́vī, audī́tum - to hear, listen to (10)

invéniō, invenī́re, invḗnī, invéntum - to come upon, find (10)

nésciō, nescī́re, nescī́vī, nescī́tum - to not know, be ignorant (25)

scíō, scī́re, scī́vī, scī́tum - to know (21)
séntiō, sentī́re, sḗnsī, sḗnsum - to feel, perceive, think, experience (11)
véniō, venī́re, vḗnī, véntum - to come (10)

Irregular
póssum, pósse, pótuī - to be able, can, could, have power (6)
sum, ésse, fúī, futū́rum - to be, exist (4)

Defective
ā́it, ā́iunt - he says, they say, assert (25)
coépī, coepísse, coéptum - began (17)
ínquit - he says *or* said (22)
ṓdī, ōdísse, ōsū́rum - to hate (20)

Adverbs

ánte (+acc.) - before, previously (13)
béne - well, satisfactorily, quite (11)
cíto - quickly (17)
crās - tomorrow (5)
cūr - why (18)
déhinc - then, next (25)
deínde - thereupon, next, then (18)
díū - long, for a long time (12)
étiam - even, also (11)
héri - yesterday (5)
hīc - here (25)
hódiē - today (3)
iam - now, already, soon (19)
íbi - there (6)
ítaque - and so, therefore (15)
íterum - again, a second time (21)
nímis, nímium - too, too much, excessively; *(in a positive sense, esp. with adjectives and adverbs)* exceedingly, very (9)
nōn - not (1)
númquam - never (8)
nunc - now, at present (6)
nū́per - recently (12)
ṓlim - once (upon a time), long ago, formerly; some day, in the future (13)
pósteā - afterwards (24)
prṓtinus - immediately (22)
quam - how (16)
quam - than *(after comparatives)*; as . . . as possible *(with superlatives)* (26)
quándō - when (5)
quā́rē - because of which thing *(lit.)*; therefore, wherefore, why (6)
quóndam - formerly, once (22)
quóque - also, too (17)
saépe - often (1)
sátis - enough, sufficiently(5)
sémper - always (3)
támen - nevertheless, still (8)
tántum - only (26)
tum - then, at that time; thereupon, in the next place (5)
úbi - where, when (6)
últrā - on the other side of, beyond (22)
úmquam - ever, at any time (23)

Conjunctions

at - but; but, mind you; but, you say (19)
átque, ac - and also, and even, and in fact (21)
aut - or (17)
aut . . . aut - either . . . or (17)
aútem - however; moreover (11)
dum - while, as long as, at the same time that; *or* until *(+subjunctive)* (8)
énim - for, in fact, truly (9)
et - and; even (2)
et . . . et - both . . . and (2)
ígitur - therefore, consequently (5)
nam - for (13)
néque, nec - and not, nor (11)
néque . . . néque, nec . . . nec - neither . . . nor (11)
nísi - if . . . not, unless; except (19)
quod - because (11)
quóniam - since, inasmuch as (10)
sed - but (2)
sī - if (1)
ut - as, just as, when (24)

Prepositions

ab, ā (+abl.) - away from, from; by (14)
ad (+acc.) - to, up to, near to (8)
ánte (+acc.) - before *(in place or time)*, in front of (13)
cóntrā (+acc.) - against (19)
cum (+abl.) - with (10)
dē (+abl.) - down from, from; concerning, about (3)
ex, ē (abl.+) - out of, from, from within; by reason of, on account of ; of *(after cardinal numerals)* (8)
in (+acc.) - into, toward; against (9)
in (+abl.) - in, on (3)

ínter (+acc.) - between, among (15)
per (+acc.) - through; by *(with reflexive pronoun)* (13)
post (+acc.) - after, behind (7)
prae (+abl.) - in front of, before (26)

prō (+abl.) - in front of, before, on behalf of, for the sake of, in return for, instead of, for, as (12)
própter (+acc.) - on account of, because of (5)
síne (+abl.) - without (2)
sub (+abl. w/ verbs of rest *or* **+acc. w/ verbs of motion)** - under, up under, close to, down to/into, to/at the foot of (7)
trāns (+acc.) - across (14)
últrā (adv. and prep. +acc.) - on the other side of, beyond (22)

Interjection

ō - O!, Oh! (2)

Idioms

amā́bō tē - please (1)
grā́tiās ágere (+dat.) - to thank someone; to give thanks to (8)
mḗnsa secúnda (f) - dessert (26)
nōn sṓlum . . . sed étiam - not only . . . but also (9)
poénās dáre - to pay the penalty (2)
sī quándō - if ever (5)

Prefix

re-, red- - again, back (24)

Suffixes

-ne – interrogative suffix attached to the first word of a sentence, typically the verb or another word on which the question hinges, to introduce a question whose answer is uncertain (5)
-que - and *(enclitic conjunction; appended to the second of two words to be joined)* (6)

Numerals

Cardinal - ū́nus *to* vīgíntī quī́nque (15)
Ordinal - prī́mus *to* duodécimus (15)

----

céntum - a hundred (15)
mī́lia, mī́lium (n. pl.) - thousands (15)
mī́lle - thousand (15)

Chapter 27

Nouns

1st Declension

adulēscéntia, adulēscéntiae (f) - youth, young manhood; youthfulness (5)
agrícola, agrícolae (m) - farmer (3)
amī́ca, amī́cae (f) - friend (female) (3)
amīcítia, amīcítiae (f) - friendship (10)
áqua, áquae (f) - water (14)
Ásia, Ásiae (f) - Asia (12)
cása, cásae (f) - house, cottage, hut (21)
caúsa, caúsae (f) - cause, reason; case, situation (21)
caúsā (abl. + preceding gen.) - for the sake of, on account of (21)
cḗna, cḗnae (f) - dinner (26)
clēméntia, clēméntiae (f) - mildness, gentleness, mercy (16)
cṓpia, cṓpiae (f) - abundance, supply (8)
cṓpiae, cōpiā́rum (f) - supplies, troops, forces (8)
cúlpa, cúlpae (f) - fault, blame (5)
cū́ra, cū́rae (f) - care, attention, caution, anxiety (4)
déa, déae (f) - goddess (6)
discípula, discípulae (f) - learner, pupil, student (female) (6)
dīvítiae, dīvitiā́rum (f. pl.) - riches, wealth (13)
fā́bula, fā́bulae (f) - story, tale; play (24)
fā́ma, fā́mae (f) - rumor, report; fame, reputation (2)
família, famíliae (f) - household, family (19)
fḗmina, fḗminae (f) - woman (3)
fenéstra, fenéstrae (f) - window (21)
fī́lia, fī́liae (f) - daughter (3)
fṓrma, fṓrmae (f) - form, shape; beauty (2)
fortū́na, fortū́nae (f) - fortune, luck (2)
glṓria, glṓriae (f) - glory, fame (5)
Graécia, Graéciae (f) - Greece (19)
hásta, hástae (f) - spear (23)
hṓra, hṓrae (f) - hour, time (10)
īnsídiae, īnsidiā́rum (f) - ambush, plot, treachery (6)
ī́nsula, ī́nsulae (f) - island (23)
ī́ra, ī́rae (f) - ire, anger (2)
Itália, Itáliae (f) - Italy (15)
língua, línguae (f) - tongue; language (25)
líttera, lítterae (f) - a letter of the alphabet (7)
lítterae, litterā́rum (f) - a letter (epistle), literature (7)
magístra, magístrae (f) - schoolmistress, teacher, mistress (4)
médica, médicae (f) - doctor, physician (female) (12)
memória, memóriae (f) - memory, recollection (15)
mḗnsa, mḗnsae (f) - table; dining; dish, course (26)
móra, mórae (f) - delay (4)
nātū́ra, nātū́rae (f) - nature (10)
naúta, naútae (m) - sailor (2)
patiéntia, patiéntiae (f) - suffering; patience, endurance (12)
pátria, pátriae (f) - fatherland, native land, (one's) country (2)
pecū́nia, pecū́niae (f) - money (2)
philosóphia, philosóphiae (f) - philosophy (2)
poéna, poénae (f) - penalty, punishment (2)
poḗta, poḗtae (m) - poet (2)
pórta, pórtae (f) - gate, entrance (2)
puélla, puéllae (f) - girl (2)
rēgī́na, rēgī́nae (f) - queen (7)
Rṓma, Rṓmae (f) - Rome (14)
rósa, rósae (f) - rose (2)
sapiéntia, sapiéntiae (f) - wisdom (3)
sátura, sáturae (f) - satire (16)
sciéntia, sciéntiae (f) - knowledge (18)
senténtia, senténtiae (f) - feeling, thought, opinion, vote, sentence (2)
sérva, sérvae (f) - slave (female) (24)
térra, térrae (f) - earth, ground, land, country (7)
Trṓia, Trṓiae (f) - Troy (21)
túrba, túrbae (f) - uproar, disturbance; mob, crowd, multitude (14)
vía, víae (f) - way, road, street (10)
vīcī́na, vīcī́nae (f) - neighbor (female) (21)
victṓria, victṓriae (f) - victory (8)
vī́ta, vī́tae (f) - life; mode of life (2)

2nd Declension

áger, ágrī (m) - field, farm (3)
amī́cus, amī́cī (m) - friend (male) (3)
ánimī, animṓrum (m) - high spirits, pride, courage (5)
ánimus, ánimī (m) - soul, spirit, mind (5)
ánnus, ánnī (m) - year (12)
argūméntum, argūméntī (n) - proof, evidence, argument (19)
bā́sium, bā́siī (n) - kiss (4)
béllum, béllī (n) - war (4)
benefícium, benefíciī (n) - benefit, kindness; favor (19)

caélum, caélī (n) - sky, heaven (5)
coniūrā́tī, coniūrātṓrum (m. pl.) - conspirators (20)
cōnsílium, cōnsíliī (n) - plan, purpose, counsel, advice, judgment, wisdom (4)
déus, déī (m) - god (6)
discípulus, discípulī (m) - learner, pupil, student (male) (6)
dṓnum, dṓnī (n) - gift, present (4)
équus, équī (m) - horse (23)
exítium, exítiī (n) - destruction, ruin (4)
fáctum, fáctī (n) - deed, act, achievement (13)
férrum, férrī (n) - iron; sword (22)
fī́lius, fī́liī (m) - son (3)
fórum, fórī (n) - marketplace, forum (26)
Graécus, Graécī (m) - a Greek (6)
impérium, impériī (n) - power to command, supreme power, authority, command, control (24)
iūdícium, iūdíciī (n) - judgment, decision, opinion; trial (19)
libéllus, libéllī (m) - little book (17)
líber, líbrī (m) - book (6)
lóca, locṓrum (n) - places, region (9)
lócī, locṓrum (m) - passages in literature (9)
lócus, lócī (m) - place; passage in literature (9)
lū́dus, lū́dī (m) - game, sport; school (18)
magíster, magístrī (m) - schoolmaster, teacher, master (4)
médicus, médicī (m) - doctor, physician (male) (12)
módus, módī (m) - measure, bound, limit; manner, method, mode, way (22)
mórbus, mórbī (m) - disease, sickness (9)
múndus, múndī (m) - world, universe (21)
númerus, númerī (m) - number (3)
óculus, óculī (m) - eye (4)
offícium, offíciī (n) - duty, service (4)
ṓtium, ṓtiī (n) - leisure, peace (4)
perfúgium, perfúgiī (n) - refuge, shelter (24)
perī́culum, perī́culī (n) - danger, risk (4)
pópulus, pópulī (m) - the people, a people, a nation (3)
prīncípium, prīncípiī (n) - beginning (12)
púer, púerī (m) - boy; boys, children *(pl.)* (3)
remédium, remédiī (n) - cure, remedy (4)
sérvus, sérvī (m) - slave (male) (24)
sígnum, sígnī (n) - sign, signal, indication; seal (13)
sōlā́cium, sōlā́ciī (n) - comfort, relief (24)
sómnus, sómnī (m) - sleep (26)
stúdium, stúdiī (n) - eagerness, zeal, pursuit, study (9)
stúltus, stúltī (m) - a fool (4)
súperī, superṓrum (m. pl.) - the gods (27)
tyránnus, tyránnī (m) - absolute ruler, tyrant (6)
vérbum, vérbī (n) - word (5)
vīcī́nus, vīcī́nī (m) - neighbor (male) (21)
vir, vírī (m) - man, hero (3)
vítium, vítiī (n) - fault, crime, vice (6)
vúlgus, vúlgī (n) - the common people, mob, rabble (21)

3rd Declension

adulḗscēns, adulēscéntis (m *or* f) - young man *or* woman (12)
aétās, aetā́tis (f) - period of life, life, age, an age, time (16)
ámor, amṓris (m) - love (7)
aúctor, auctṓris (m) - increaser; author, originator (19)
audī́tor, audītṓris (m) - hearer, listener, member of an audience (16)
Caésar, Caésaris (m) - Caesar (12)
cáput, cápitis (n) - head; leader; beginning; life; heading; chapter (11)
cármen, cárminis (n) - song, poem (7)
Karthā́gō, Karthā́ginis (f) - Carthage (24)
Cícerō, Cicerṓnis (m) - (Marcus Tullius) Cicero (8)
cī́vitās, cīvitā́tis (f) - state, citizenship (7)
cṓnsul, cṓnsulis (m) - consul (11)
córpus, córporis (n) - body (7)
cupíditās, cupiditā́tis (f) - desire, longing, passion; cupidity, avarice (10)
dēlectā́tiō, dēlectātiṓnis (f) - delight, pleasure, enjoyment (27)
dux, dúcis (m) - leader, guide; commander, general (23)
flū́men, flū́minis (n) - river (18)
frā́ter, frā́tris (m) - brother (8)
génus, géneris (n) - origin; kind, type, sort, class (18)
hómō, hóminis (m) - human being, man (7)
imperā́tor, imperātṓris (m) - general, commander-in-chief, emperor (24)
iū́dex, iū́dicis (m) - judge, juror (19)
iūs, iū́ris (n) - right, justice, law (14)

lábor, labṓris (m)- labor, work, toil; a work, production (7)
laus, laúdis (f) - praise, glory, fame (8)
lēx, lḗgis (f) - law, statute (26)
lībértās, lībertā́tis (f) - liberty (8)
lī́men, lī́minis (n) - threshold (26)
lī́tus, lī́toris (n) - shore, coast (23)
lūx, lū́cis (f) - light (26)
maiṓrēs, maiṓrum (m. pl.) - ancestors (27)
mā́ter, mā́tris (f) - mother (12)
mī́les, mī́litis (m) - soldier (23)
mṓrēs, mṓrum (m) - habits, morals, character (7)
mōs, mṓris (m) - habit, custom, manner (7)
nḗmō, nūllī́us, nḗminī, nḗminem, nū́llō, nū́llā (m *or* f) - no one, nobody (11)
népōs, nepṓtis (m) - grandson, descendant (27)
nṓmen, nṓminis (n) - name (7)
ōrā́tor, ōrātṓris (m) - orator, speaker (23)
ōs, ṓris (n) - mouth, face (14)
páter, pátris (m) - father (12)
pāx, pā́cis (f) - peace (7)
próbitās, probitā́tis (f) - uprightness, honesty (18)
rátiō, ratiṓnis (f) - reckoning, account; reason, judgment, consideration; system; manner, method (8)
rēx, rḗgis (m) - king (7)
sacérdōs, sacerdṓtis (m) - priest (23)
sálūs, salū́tis (f) - health, safety; greeting (21)
sápiēns, sapiéntis (m/f) - a wise man/woman, philosopher (25)
scélus, scéleris (n) - evil deed, crime, sin, wickedness (19)
scrī́ptor, scrīptṓris (m) - writer, author (8)
senéctūs, senectū́tis (f) - old age (10)
sénex, sénis (m) - old man (16)
sérvitūs, servitū́tis (f) - servitude, slavery (20)
sōl, sṓlis (m) - sun (27)
sóror, sorṓris (f) - sister (8)
tempéstās, tempestā́tis (f) - period of time, season; weather, storm (15)
témpus, témporis (n) - time; occasion, opportunity (7)
tímor, timṓris (m) - fear (10)
úxor, uxṓris (f) - wife (7)
vḗritās, vēritā́tis (f) - truth (10)
vírgō, vírginis (f) - maiden, virgin (7)
vírtūs, virtū́tis (f) - manliness, courage; excellence, character, worth, virtue (7)
volúptās, voluptā́tis (f) - pleasure (10)
vúlnus, vúlneris (n) - wound (24)

3rd Declension I-Stem

ánimal, animā́lis (n) - a living creature, animal (14)
ars, ártis (f) - art, skill (14)
arx, árcis (f) - citadel, stronghold (23)
aúris, aúris (f) - ear (14)
cī́vis, cī́vis (m *or* f) - citizen (14)
fī́nēs, fī́nium (m) - boundaries, territory (21)
fī́nis, fī́nis (m) - end, limit, boundary; purpose (21)
gēns, géntis (f) - clan, race, nation, people (21)
hóstēs, hóstium (m) - the enemy (18)
hóstis, hóstis (m) - an enemy *(of the state)* (18)
ígnis, ígnis (m) - fire (22)
máre, máris (n) - sea (14)
mēns, méntis (f) - mind, thought, intention (16)
mōns, móntis (m) - mountain (20)
mors, mórtis (f) - death (14)
nā́vis, nā́vis (f) - ship, boat (21)
nox, nóctis (f) - night (26)
nū́bēs, nū́bis (f) - cloud (14)
pars, pártis (f) - part, share; direction (14)
urbs, úrbis (f) - city (14)
vī́rēs, vī́rium (f. pl.) - strength (14)
vīs, vīs (f) - force, power, violence (14)

4th Declension

córnū, córnūs (n) - horn (20)
frū́ctus, frū́ctūs (m) - fruit; profit, benefit, enjoyment (20)
génū, génūs (n) - knee (20)
mánus, mánūs (f) - hand; handwriting; band (20)
métus, métūs (m) - fear, dread, anxiety (20)
senā́tus, senā́tūs (m) - senate (20)
sḗnsus, sḗnsūs (m) - feeling, sense (20)
spī́ritus, spī́ritūs (m) - breath, breathing; spirit, soul (20)
vérsus, vérsūs (m) - line of verse (20)

5th Declension

díēs, diḗī (m) - day (22)
fídēs, fídeī (f) - faith, trust, trustworthiness, fidelity, promise, guarantee, protection (22)
rēs, réī (f) - thing, matter, property, business, affair (22)
rēs pū́blica, réī pū́blicae (f) - state, commonwealth, republic (22)
spēs, spéī (f) - hope (22)

Indeclinable

níhil - nothing (1)
sátis - enough (5)

Pronouns

áliquis, áliquid - someone, somebody, something (23)
égo, méī - I (11)
hic, haec, hoc - this; the latter; he, she, it, they (9)
ídem, éadem, ídem - the same (11)
ílle, ílla, íllud - that; the former; the famous; he, she, it, they (9)
ípse, ípsa, ípsum - myself, yourself, himself, herself, itself, *etc.,* the very, the actual (13)
is, éa, id - this, that; he, she, it (11)
íste, ísta, ístud - that of yours, that; such (as you have, as you speak of); *sometimes with contemptuous force, e.g.,* that despicable, that wretched (9)
quī, quae, quod - who, which, what, that (17)
quid - what (1)
quídam, quaédam, quíddam - a certain one or thing, someone, something (26)
quis? quid? - who? whose? whom? what? which? (19)
quísque, quídque, cuiúsque, cuíque - each one, each person, each thing (13)
quísquis, quídquid - whoever, whatever (23)
súī - himself, herself, itself, themselves (13)
tū, túī - you *(sing.)* (11)

Adjectives

1st & 2nd Declension

acérbus, acérba, acérbum - harsh, bitter, grievous (12)
aéquus, aéqua, aéquum - level, even; calm; equal, just; favorable (22)
áliī . . . áliī - some . . . others (9)
álius, ália, áliud - other, another (9)
álter, áltera, álterum - the other (of two), second (9)
amīcus, amīca, amīcum - friendly (11)
antīquus, antīqua, antīquum - ancient, old-time (2)
ásper, áspera, ásperum - rough, harsh (21)
avārus, avāra, avārum - greedy, avaricious (3)
beātus, beāta, beātum - happy, fortunate, blessed (10)
béllus, bélla, béllum - pretty, handsome, charming (4)
bónus, bóna, bónum - good, kind (4)
caécus, caéca, caécum - blind (17)
cārus, cāra, cārum - dear (11)
cértus, cérta, cértum - definite, sure, certain, reliable (19)
clārus, clāra, clārum - clear, bright; renowned, famous, illustrious (18)
déxter, déxtra, déxtrum - right, right-hand (20)
dóctus, dócta, dóctum - taught, learned, skilled (13)
fortūnātus, fortūnāta, fortūnātum - lucky, fortunate, happy (13)
géminus, gémina, géminum - twin (25)
Graécus, Graéca, Graécum - Greek (6)
hūmānus, hūmāna, hūmānum - pertaining to man, human; humane, kind; refined, cultivated (4)
incértus, incérta, incértum - uncertain, unsure, doubtful (22)
iūcúndus, iūcúnda, iūcúndum - pleasant, delightful, agreeable, pleasing (16)
Latīnus, Latīna, Latīnum - Latin (22)
līber, lībera, līberum - free (5)
lóngus, lónga, lóngum - long (16)
magnánimus, magnánima, magnánimum - great-hearted, brave, magnanimous (23)
mágnus, mágna, mágnum - large, great; important (2)
málus, mála, málum - bad, wicked, evil (4)
médius, média, médium - middle; the middle of (22)
méus, méa, méum - my (2)
míser, mísera, míserum - wretched, miserable, unfortunate (15)
múltus, múlta, múltum - much, many (2)
neúter, neútra, neútrum - not either, neither (9)
nóster, nóstra, nóstrum - our, ours (5)
nóvus, nóva, nóvum - new; strange (7)
nūllus, nūlla, nūllum - not any, no, none (9)
párvus, párva, párvum - small, little (4)
paúcī, paúcae, paúca - few, a few (3)
perpétuus, perpétua, perpétuum perpetual, lasting, uninterrupted, continuous (6)
plēnus, plēna, plēnum - full, abundant, generous (6)
prīmus, prīma, prīmum - first, foremost, chief, principal (27)
pudīcus, pudīca, pudīcum - modest, chaste (26)
púlcher, púlchra, púlchrum - beautiful, handsome; fine (5)
Rōmānus, Rōmāna, Rōmānum - Roman (3)

sálvus, sálva, sálvum - safe, sound (6)
sā́nus, sā́na, sā́num - sound, healthy, sane (5)
secúndus, secúnda, secúndum - second; favorable (6)
siníster, sinístra, sinístrum - left, left-hand; harmful, ill-omened (20)
sṓlus, sṓla, sṓlum - alone, only, the only (9)
stúltus, stúlta, stúltum - foolish (4)
supérbus, supérba, supérbum - arrogant, overbearing, haughty, proud (26)
súperus, súpera, súperum - above, upper (27)
súus, súa, súum - his own, her own, its own, their own (13)
tṓtus, tṓta, tṓtum - whole, entire (9)
túus, túa, túum - your *(sing.)* (2)
ū́llus, ū́lla, ū́llum - any (9)
últimus, última, últimum - farthest, extreme; last, final (25)
ū́nus, ū́na, ū́num - one, single, alone (9)
urbā́nus, urbā́na, urbā́num - of the city, urban; urbane, elegant (26)
úter, útra, útrum - either, which (of two) (9)
vḗrus, vḗra, vḗrum - true, real, proper (4)
véster, véstra, véstrum - your *(pl.)* (6)

3rd Declension
ā́cer, ā́cris, ā́cre - sharp, keen, eager; severe, fierce (16)
brévis, bréve - short, small, brief (16)
céler, céleris, célere - swift, quick, rapid (16)
commū́nis, commū́ne - common, general, of / for the community (20)
diffícilis, diffícile - hard, difficult, troublesome (16)
dī́ligēns, *gen.* **dīligéntis** - diligent, careful (27)
dissímilis, dissímile - unlike, different (27)
dúlcis, dúlce - sweet; pleasant, agreeable (16)
fácilis, fácile - easy; agreeable (16)
fḗlīx, *gen.* **fēlī́cis** - lucky, fortunate, happy (22)
férōx, *gen.* **ferṓcis** - fierce, savage (25)
fidḗlis, fidḗle - faithful, loyal (25)
fórtis, fórte - strong, brave (16)
grácilis, grácile - slender, thin (27)
grávis, gráve - heavy, weighty; serious, important; severe, grievous (19)
húmilis, húmile - lowly, humble (27)
immortā́lis, immortā́le - not subject to death, immortal (19)
íngēns, *gen.* **ingéntis** - huge (16)
lévis, léve - light; easy; slight, trivial (17)
máior, máius - greater; older (27)
mortā́lis, mortā́le - mortal (18)
ómnis, ómne - every, all (16)
pótēns, *gen.* **poténtis** - able, powerful, mighty, strong (16)
sápiēns, *gen.* **sapiéntis** - wise, judicious (25)
sénex, *gen.* **sénis** - old, aged (16)
símilis, símile (+gen. or dat.) - similar (to), like, resembling (27)
trī́stis, trī́ste - sad, sorrowful; joyless, grim, severe (26)
túrpis, túrpe - ugly; shameful, base, disgraceful (26)
ū́tilis, ū́tile - useful, advantageous (27)

Indeclinable Adjectives
quot - how many, as many as (27)
sátis - enough, sufficient (5)

Indefinite Adjective
quī́dam, quaédam, quóddam - a certain, some (26)

Interrogative Adjective
quī?, quae?, quod? - what? which? what kind of?; *(sometimes with exclamatory force)* what (a)! what sort of! (19)

Verbs
1st Conjugation
ádiuvō, adiuvā́re, adiū́vī, adiū́tum - to help, aid, assist; to please (4)
ámō, amā́re, amā́vī, amā́tum - to love, like (1)
appéllō, appellā́re, appellā́vī, appellā́tum - to speak to, address (as), call, name (14)
cḗnō, cēnā́re, cēnā́vī, cēnā́tum - to dine (5)
cṓgitō, cōgitā́re, cōgitā́vī, cōgitā́tum - to think, ponder, consider, plan (1)
cōnsérvō, cōnservā́re, cōnservā́vī, cōnservā́tum - to preserve, conserve, maintain (1)
créō, creā́re, creā́vī, creā́tum - to create (12)
cúlpō, culpā́re, culpā́vī, culpā́tum - to blame, censure (5)

dēléctō, dēlectáre, dēlectávī, dēlectátum - to delight, charm, please (19)
dēmṓnstrō, dēmōnstráre, dēmōnstrávī, dēmōnstrátum to point out, show, demonstrate (8)
dēsíderō, dēsīderáre, dēsīderávī, dēsīderátum - to desire, long for, miss (17)
dō, dáre, dédī, dátum - to give, offer (1)
ḗducō, ēducáre, ēducávī, ēducátum - to bring up, educate (23)
érrō, erráre, errávī, errátum - to wander; err, go astray, make a mistake, be mistaken (1)
exspéctō, exspectáre, exspectávī, exspectátum - to look for, expect, await (15)
invítō, invītáre, invītávī, invītátum - to entertain, invite, summon (26)
iúvō, iuváre, iū́vī, iū́tum - to help, aid, assist; to please (4)
labṓrō, labōráre, labōrávī, labōrátum - to labor; be in distress (21)
laúdō, laudáre, laudávī, laudátum - to praise (1)
lī́berō, līberáre, līberávī, līberátum - to free, liberate (19)
mū́tō, mūtáre, mūtávī, mūtátum to change, alter; exchange (14)
nā́rrō, nārráre, nārrávī, nārrátum - to tell, report, narrate (24)
nā́vigō, nāvigáre, nāvigávī, nāvigátum - to sail, navigate (17)
nécō, necáre, necávī, necátum - to murder, kill (7)
négō, negáre, negávī, negátum to deny, say that . . . not (25)
nū́ntiō, nūntiáre, nūntiávī, nūntiátum - to announce, report, relate (25)
párō, paráre, parávī, parátum - to prepare, provide; get, obtain (19)
próbō, probáre, probávī, probátum - to approve, recommend; test (27)
prōnū́ntiō, prōnūntiáre, prōnūntiávī, prōnūntiátum - to proclaim, announce; declaim; pronounce (20)
pútō, putáre, putávī, putátum - to reckon, suppose, judge, think, imagine (25)
récitō, recitáre, recitávī, recitátum - to read aloud, recite (17)
sátiō, satiáre, satiávī, satiátum - to satisfy, sate (3)
sérvō, serváre, servávī, servátum - to preserve, save, keep, guard (1)
spḗrō, spēráre, spērávī, spērátum - to hope for, hope (25)
stō, stáre, stétī, státum - to stand, stand still *or* firm (13)
súperō, superáre, superávī, superátum - to be above, have the upper hand, surpass; overcome, conquer (5)
tólerō, toleráre, tolerávī, tolerátum - to bear, endure (6)
vítō, vītáre, vītávī, vītátum - to avoid, shun (14)
vócō, vocáre, vocávī, vocátum - to call, summon (1)

2nd Conjugation

aúdeō, audḗre, aúsus sum - to dare (7)
cáreō, carḗre, cáruī, caritū́rum (+abl.) - to be without, be deprived of, want, lack; be free from (20)
contíneō, continḗre, contínuī, conténtum - to hold together, contain, keep, enclose, restrain (21)
dḗbeō, dēbḗre, dḗbuī, dḗbitum - to owe; ought, must, should (1)
dḗleō, dēlḗre, dēlḗvī, dēlḗtum - to destroy, wipe out, erase (17)
dóceō, docḗre, dócuī, dóctum - to teach (8)
gaúdeō, gaudḗre, gāvī́sus sum - to be glad, rejoice (23)
hábeō, habḗre, hábuī, hábitum - to have, hold, possess; consider, regard (3)
iáceō, iacḗre, iácuī - to lie; lie prostrate; lie dead (25)
iúbeō, iubḗre, iússī, iússum - to bid, order, command (21)
máneō, manḗre, mā́nsī, mā́nsum - to remain, stay, stay behind, abide, continue (5)
mísceō, miscḗre, míscuī, míxtum to mix, stir up, disturb (18)
móneō, monḗre, mónuī, mónitum - to remind, advise, warn (1)
móveō, movḗre, mṓvī, mṓtum - to move; arouse, affect (18)
prohíbeō, prohibḗre, prohíbuī, prohíbitum - to keep (back), prevent, hinder, restrain, prohibit (20)
remáneō, remanḗre, remā́nsī, remā́nsum - to remain, stay, stay behind, abide, continue (5)
rī́deō, rīdḗre, rī́sī, rī́sum - to laugh, laugh at (24)
sálvē, salvḗte - hello, greetings (1)

sálveō, salvḗre - to be well, be in good health (1)
téneō, tenḗre, ténuī, téntum - to hold, keep, possess; restrain (14)
térreō, terrḗre, térruī, térritum - to frighten, terrify (1)
tímeō, timḗre, tímuī - to fear, be afraid (of) (15)
válē, valḗte - good-bye, farewell (1)
váleō, valḗre, váluī, valitū́rum - to be strong, have power; be well (1)
vídeō, vidḗre, vī́dī, vī́sum - to see; observe, understand (1)
vídeor, vidḗrī, vī́sus sum - to be seen, seem, appear (18)

3rd Conjugation
admíttō, admíttere, admī́sī, admíssum - to admit, receive, let in (17)
ágō, ágere, ḗgī, ā́ctum - to drive, lead, do, act; pass, spend *(life or time)* (8)
álō, álere, áluī, áltum - to nourish, support, sustain, increase; cherish (13)
āmíttō, āmíttere, āmī́sī, āmíssum - to send away; lose, let go (12)
āvértō, āvértere, āvértī, āvérsum - to turn away, avert (23)
cádō, cádere, cécidī, cāsū́rum - to fall (12)
cérnō, cérnere, crḗvī, crḗtum - to distinguish, discern, perceive (22)
commíttō, commíttere, commī́sī, commíssum - to entrust, commit (15)
crḗdō, crḗdere, crḗdidī, crḗditum to believe, trust (25)
cúrrō, cúrrere, cucúrrī, cúrsum - to run, rush, move quickly (14)
dēféndō, dēféndere, dēféndī, dēfḗnsum - to ward off; defend, protect (20)
dī́cō, dī́cere, dī́xī, díctum - to say, tell, speak; name, call (10)
dī́ligō, dīlígere, dīlḗxī, dīlḗctum - to esteem, love (13)
discḗdō, discḗdere, discéssī, discéssum - to go away, depart (20)
díscō, díscere, dídicī - to learn (8)
dū́cō, dū́cere, dū́xī, dúctum - to lead; consider, regard; prolong (8)
expéllō, expéllere, éxpulī, expúlsum - to drive out, expel, banish (24)
flúō, flúere, flū́xī, flū́xum - to flow (18)
gérō, gérere, géssī, géstum - to carry; carry on, manage, conduct, wage, accomplish, perform (8)
intéllegō, intellégere, intellḗxī, intellḗctum - to understand (11)
iúngō, iúngere, iū́nxī, iū́nctum - to join (13)
légō, légere, lḗgī, lḗctum - to pick out, choose; read (18)
míttō, míttere, mī́sī, míssum - to send, let go (11)
néglegō, neglégere, neglḗxī, neglḗctum - to neglect, disregard (17)
ópprimō, opprímere, oppréssī, oppréssum - to suppress, overwhelm, overpower, check (23)
osténdō, osténdere, osténdī, osténtum - to exhibit, show, display (23)
péllō, péllere, pépulī, púlsum - to strike, push; drive out, banish (24)
pétō, pétere, petī́vī, petī́tum - to seek, aim at, beg, beseech (23)
pṓnō, pṓnere, pósuī, pósitum - to put, place, set (27)
prémō, prémere, préssī, préssum - to press; press hard, pursue (23)
quaérō, quaérere, quaesī́vī, quaesī́tum - to seek, look for, strive for; ask, inquire, inquire into (24)
régō, régere, rḗxī, rḗctum - to rule, guide, direct (16)
relínquō, relínquere, relī́quī, relíctum - to leave behind, leave, abandon, desert (21)
revértō, revértere, revértī, revérsum - turn back (23)
scrī́bō, scrī́bere, scrī́psī, scrī́ptum to write, compose (8)
tángō, tángere, tétigī, tā́ctum - to touch (21)
tóllō, tóllere, sústulī, sublā́tum - to raise, lift up; take away, remove, destroy (22)
tráhō, tráhere, trā́xī, tráctum - to draw, drag; derive, acquire (8)
vértō, vértere, vértī, vérsum - to turn; change (23)
víncō, víncere, vī́cī, víctum - to conquer, overcome (8)
vī́vō, vī́vere, vī́xī, vī́ctum - to live (10)

3rd Conjugation -iō
accípiō, accípere, accḗpī, accéptum - to take *(to one's self)*, receive, accept (24)
cápiō, cápere, cḗpī, cáptum - to take, capture, seize, get (10)
cúpiō, cúpere, cupī́vī, cupī́tum - to desire, wish, long for (17)

ērípiō, ērípere, ērípuī, ēréptum - to snatch away, take away; rescue (22)
excípiō, excípere, excḗpī, excéptum - to take out, except; take, receive, capture (24)
fáciō, fácere, fḗcī, fáctum - to make, do, accomplish (10)
fúgiō, fúgere, fū́gī, fugitū́rum - to flee, hurry away; escape; go into exile; avoid, shun (10)
iáciō, iácere, iḗcī, iáctum - to throw, hurl (15)
incípiō, incípere, incḗpī, incéptum - to begin (17)
patefáciō, patefácere, patefḗcī, patefáctum - to make open, open; disclose, expose (25)
rápiō, rápere, rápuī, ráptum - to seize, snatch, carry away (21)
recípiō, recípere, recḗpī, recéptum - to take back, regain; admit, receive (24)
suscípiō, suscípere, suscḗpī, suscéptum - to undertake (25)

4th Conjugation
aúdiō, audī́re, audī́vī, audī́tum - to hear, listen to (10)
invéniō, invenī́re, invḗnī, invéntum - to come upon, find (10)
nésciō, nescī́re, nescī́vī, nescī́tum - to not know, be ignorant (25)
scíō, scī́re, scī́vī, scī́tum - to know (21)
séntiō, sentī́re, sḗnsī, sḗnsum - to feel, perceive, think, experience (11)
véniō, venī́re, vḗnī, véntum - to come (10)

Irregular
póssum, pósse, pótuī - to be able, can, could, have power (6)
sum, ésse, fúī, futū́rum - to be, exist (4)

Defective
ā́it, ā́iunt - he says, they say, assert (25)
coépī, coepísse, coéptum - began (17)
ínquit - he says *or* said (22)
ṓdī, ōdísse, ōsū́rum - to hate (20)

Adverbs

ánte (+acc.) - before, previously (13)
béne - well, satisfactorily, quite (11)
cíto - quickly (17)
crās - tomorrow (5)
cūr - why (18)
déhinc - then, next (25)
deínde - thereupon, next, then (18)
díū - long, for a long time (12)
étiam - even, also (11)
héri - yesterday (5)
hīc - here (25)
hódiē - today (3)
iam - now, already, soon (19)
íbi - there (6)
ítaque - and so, therefore (15)
íterum - again, a second time (21)
nímis, nímium - too, too much, excessively; *(in a positive sense, esp. with adjectives and adverbs)* exceedingly, very (9)
nōn - not (1)
númquam - never (8)
nunc - now, at present (6)
nū́per - recently (12)
ṓlim - once (upon a time), long ago, formerly; some day, in the future (13)
pósteā - afterwards (24)
prṓtinus - immediately (22)
quam - how (16)
quam - than *(after comparatives);* as . . . as possible *(with superlatives)* (26)
quándō - when (5)
quā́rē - because of which thing *(lit.);* therefore, wherefore, why (6)
quóndam - formerly, once (22)
quóque - also, too (17)
saépe - often (1)
sátis - enough, sufficiently (5)
sémper - always (3)
támen - nevertheless, still (8)
tántum - only (26)
tum - then, at that time; thereupon, in the next place (5)
úbi - where, when (6)
últrā - on the other side of, beyond (22)
úmquam - ever, at any time (23)

Conjunctions

at - but; but, mind you; but, you say (19)
átque, ac - and also, and even, and in fact (21)
aut - or (17)
aut . . . aut - either . . . or (17)
aútem - however; moreover (11)
dum - while, as long as, at the same time that; *or* until *(+subjunctive)* (8)
énim - for, in fact, truly (9)
et - and; even (2)
et . . . et - both . . . and (2)
ígitur - therefore, consequently (5)
nam - for (13)
néque, nec - and not, nor (11)
néque . . . néque, nec . . . nec - neither . . . nor (11)
nísi - if . . . not, unless; except (19)

quod - because (11)
quóniam - since, inasmuch as (10)
sed - but (2)
sī - if (1)
ut - as, just as, when (24)

Prepositions

ab, ā (+abl.) - away from, from; by (14)
ad (+acc.) - to, up to, near to (8)
ánte (+acc.) - before *(in place or time)*, in front of (13)
cóntrā (+acc.) - against (19)
cum (+abl.) - with (10)
dē (+abl.) - down from, from; concerning, about (3)
ex, ē (abl.+) - out of, from, from within; by reason of, on account of ; of *(after cardinal numerals)* (8)
in (+acc.) - into, toward; against (9)
in (+abl.) - in, on (3)
ínter (+acc.) - between, among (15)
per (+acc.) - through; by *(with reflexive pronoun)* (13)
post (+acc.) - after, behind (7)
prae (+abl.) - in front of, before (26)
prō (+abl.) - in front of, before, on behalf of, for the sake of, in return for, instead of, for, as (12)
própter (+acc.) - on account of, because of (5)
síne (+abl.) - without (2)
sub (+abl. w/ verbs of rest *or* +acc. w/ verbs of motion) - under, up under, close to, down to/into, to/at the foot of (7)
trāns (+acc.) - across (14)
últrā (adv. and prep. +acc.) - on the other side of, beyond (22)

Interjection

ō - O!, Oh! (2)

Idioms

amā́bō tē - please (1)
grā́tiās ágere (+dat.) - to thank someone; to give thanks to (8)
mḗnsa secúnda (f) - dessert (26)
nōn sṓlum . . . sed étiam - not only . . . but also (9)
poénās dáre - to pay the penalty (2)
sī quándō - if ever (5)

Prefix

re-, red- - again, back (24)

Suffixes

-ne – interrogative suffix attached to the first word of a sentence, typically the verb or another word on which the question hinges, to introduce a question whose answer is uncertain (5)
-que - and *(enclitic conjunction; appended to the second of two words to be joined)* (6)

Numerals

Cardinal - ū́nus *to* vīgíntī quī́nque (15)
Ordinal - prī́mus *to* duodécimus (15)

----

céntum - a hundred (15)
mī́lia, mī́lium (n. pl.) - thousands (15)
mī́lle - thousand (15)

Chapter 28

Nouns

1st Declension

adulēscéntia, adulēscéntiae (f) - youth, young manhood; youthfulness (5)
agrícola, agrícolae (m) - farmer (3)
amíca, amícae (f) - friend (female) (3)
amīcítia, amīcítiae (f) - friendship (10)
áqua, áquae (f) - water (14)
Ásia, Ásiae (f) - Asia (12)
cása, cásae (f) - house, cottage, hut (21)
caúsa, caúsae (f) - cause, reason; case, situation (21)
caúsā (abl. + preceding gen.) - for the sake of, on account of (21)
cḗna, cḗnae (f) - dinner (26)
clēméntia, clēméntiae (f) - mildness, gentleness, mercy (16)
cṓpia, cṓpiae (f) - abundance, supply (8)
cṓpiae, cōpiā́rum (f) - supplies, troops, forces (8)
cúlpa, cúlpae (f) - fault, blame (5)
cū́ra, cū́rae (f) - care, attention, caution, anxiety (4)
déa, déae (f) - goddess (6)
discípula, discípulae (f) - learner, pupil, student (female) (6)
dīvítiae, dīvitiā́rum (f. pl.) - riches, wealth (13)
fā́bula, fā́bulae (f) - story, tale; play (24)
fā́ma, fā́mae (f) - rumor, report; fame, reputation (2)
família, famíliae (f) - household, family (19)
fḗmina, fḗminae (f) - woman (3)
fenéstra, fenéstrae (f) - window (21)
fī́lia, fī́liae (f) - daughter (3)
fṓrma, fṓrmae (f) - form, shape; beauty (2)
fortū́na, fortū́nae (f) - fortune, luck (2)
glṓria, glṓriae (f) - glory, fame (5)
Graécia, Graéciae (f) - Greece (19)
hásta, hástae (f) - spear (23)
hṓra, hṓrae (f) - hour, time (10)
īnsídiae, īnsidiā́rum (f) - ambush, plot, treachery (6)
ī́nsula, ī́nsulae (f) - island (23)
ī́ra, ī́rae (f) - ire, anger (2)
Itália, Itáliae (f) - Italy (15)
língua, línguae (f) - tongue; language (25)
líttera, lítterae (f) - a letter of the alphabet (7)
lítterae, litterā́rum (f) - a letter (epistle), literature (7)
lū́na, lū́nae (f) - moon (28)
magístra, magístrae (f) - schoolmistress, teacher, mistress (4)
médica, médicae (f) - doctor, physician (female) (12)
memória, memóriae (f) - memory, recollection (15)
mḗnsa, mḗnsae (f) - table; dining; dish, course (26)
móra, mórae (f) - delay (4)
nātū́ra, nātū́rae (f) - nature (10)
naúta, naútae (m) - sailor (2)
patiéntia, patiéntiae (f) - suffering; patience, endurance (12)
pátria, pátriae (f) - fatherland, native land, (one's) country (2)
pecū́nia, pecū́niae (f) - money (2)
philosóphia, philosóphiae (f) - philosophy (2)
poéna, poénae (f) - penalty, punishment (2)
poḗta, poḗtae (m) - poet (2)
pórta, pórtae (f) - gate, entrance (2)
puélla, puéllae (f) - girl (2)
rēgī́na, rēgī́nae (f) - queen (7)
Rṓma, Rṓmae (f) - Rome (14)
rósa, rósae (f) - rose (2)
sapiéntia, sapiéntiae (f) - wisdom (3)
sátura, sáturae (f) - satire (16)
sciéntia, sciéntiae (f) - knowledge (18)
senténtia, senténtiae (f) - feeling, thought, opinion, vote, sentence (2)
sérva, sérvae (f) - slave (female) (24)
stḗlla, stḗllae (f) - star, planet (28)
térra, térrae (f) - earth, ground, land, country (7)
Trṓia, Trṓiae (f) - Troy (21)
túrba, túrbae (f) - uproar, disturbance; mob, crowd, multitude (14)
vía, víae (f) - way, road, street (10)
vīcī́na, vīcī́nae (f) - neighbor (female) (21)
victṓria, victṓriae (f) - victory (8)
vī́ta, vī́tae (f) - life; mode of life (2)

2nd Declension

áger, ágrī (m) - field, farm (3)
amī́cus, amī́cī (m) - friend (male) (3)
ánimī, animṓrum (m) - high spirits, pride, courage (5)
ánimus, ánimī (m) - soul, spirit, mind (5)
ánnus, ánnī (m) - year (12)
argūméntum, argūméntī (n) - proof, evidence, argument (19)
árma, armṓrum (n. pl.) - arms, weapons (28)
bā́sium, bā́siī (n) - kiss (4)

béllum, béllī (n) - war (4)
beneficium, beneficiī (n) - benefit, kindness; favor (19)
caélum, caélī (n) - sky, heaven (5)
coniūrā́tī, coniūrātṓrum (m. pl.) - conspirators (20)
cōnsílium, cōnsíliī (n) - plan, purpose, counsel, advice, judgment, wisdom (4)
déus, déī (m) - god (6)
discípulus, discípulī (m) - learner, pupil, student (male) (6)
dṓnum, dṓnī (n) - gift, present (4)
équus, équī (m) - horse (23)
exítium, exítiī (n) - destruction, ruin (4)
fáctum, fáctī (n) - deed, act, achievement (13)
férrum, férrī (n) - iron; sword (22)
fī́lius, fī́liī (m) - son (3)
fórum, fórī (n) - marketplace, forum (26)
Graécus, Graécī (m) - a Greek (6)
impérium, impériī (n) - power to command, supreme power, authority, command, control (24)
iūdícium, iūdíciī (n) - judgment, decision, opinion; trial (19)
libéllus, libéllī (m) - little book (17)
líber, líbrī (m) - book (6)
lóca, locṓrum (n) - places, region (9)
lócī, locṓrum (m) - passages in literature (9)
lócus, lócī (m) - place; passage in literature (9)
lū́dus, lū́dī (m) - game, sport; school (18)
magíster, magístrī (m) - schoolmaster, teacher, master (4)
médicus, médicī (m) - doctor, physician (male) (12)
módus, módī (m) - measure, bound, limit; manner, method, mode, way (22)
mórbus, mórbī (m) - disease, sickness (9)
múndus, múndī (m) - world, universe (21)
númerus, númerī (m) - number (3)
óculus, óculī (m) - eye (4)
offícium, offíciī (n) - duty, service (4)
ṓtium, ṓtiī (n) - leisure, peace (4)
perfúgium, perfúgiī (n) - refuge, shelter (24)
perī́culum, perī́culī (n) - danger, risk (4)
pópulus, pópulī (m) - the people, a people, a nation (3)
prīncípium, prīncípiī (n) - beginning (12)
púer, púerī (m) - boy; boys, children *(pl.)* (3)
remédium, remédiī (n) - cure, remedy (4)
sérvus, sérvī (m) - slave (male) (24)
sígnum, sígnī (n) - sign, signal, indication; seal (13)
sōlā́cium, sōlā́ciī (n) - comfort, relief (24)
sómnus, sómnī (m) - sleep (26)
stúdium, stúdiī (n) - eagerness, zeal, pursuit, study (9)
stúltus, stúltī (m) - a fool (4)
súperī, superṓrum (m. pl.) - the gods (27)
tyránnus, tyránnī (m) - absolute ruler, tyrant (6)
vérbum, vérbī (n) - word (5)
vīcī́nus, vīcī́nī (m) - neighbor (male) (21)
vir, vírī (m) - man, hero (3)
vítium, vítiī (n) - fault, crime, vice (6)
vúlgus, vúlgī (n) - the common people, mob, rabble (21)

3rd Declension

adulḗscēns, adulēscéntis (m *or* f) - young man *or* woman (12)
aétās, aetā́tis (f) - period of life, life, age, an age, time (16)
ámor, amṓris (m) - love (7)
aúctor, auctṓris (m) - increaser; author, originator (19)
audī́tor, audītṓris (m) - hearer, listener, member of an audience (16)
Caésar, Caésaris (m) - Caesar (12)
cáput, cápitis (n) - head; leader; beginning; life; heading; chapter (11)
cármen, cárminis (n) - song, poem (7)
Carthā́gō, Carthā́ginis (f) - Carthage (24)
Cícerō, Cicerṓnis (m) - (Marcus Tullius) Cicero (8)
cī́vitās, cīvitā́tis (f) - state, citizenship (7)
cṓnsul, cṓnsulis (m) - consul (11)
córpus, córporis (n) - body (7)
cupíditās, cupiditā́tis (f) - desire, longing, passion; cupidity, avarice (10)
dēlectā́tiō, dēlectātiṓnis (f) - delight, pleasure, enjoyment (27)
dux, dúcis (m) - leader, guide; commander, general (23)
flū́men, flū́minis (n) - river (18)
frā́ter, frā́tris (m) - brother (8)
génus, géneris (n) - origin; kind, type, sort, class (18)
hómō, hóminis (m) - human being, man (7)
imperā́tor, imperātṓris (m) - general, commander-in-chief, emperor (24)
iū́dex, iū́dicis (m) - judge, juror (19)
iūs, iū́ris (n) - right, justice, law (14)

lábor, labṓris (m)- labor, work, toil; a work, production (7)
laus, laúdis (f) - praise, glory, fame (8)
lēx, lḗgis (f) - law, statute (26)
lībértās, lībertā́tis (f) - liberty (8)
lī́men, lī́minis (n) - threshold (26)
lī́tus, lī́toris (n) - shore, coast (23)
lūx, lū́cis (f) - light (26)
maiṓrēs, maiṓrum (m. pl.) - ancestors (27)
mā́ter, mā́tris (f) - mother (12)
mī́les, mī́litis (m) - soldier (23)
mṓrēs, mṓrum (m) - habits, morals, character (7)
mōs, mṓris (m) - habit, custom, manner (7)
nḗmō, nūllī́us, nḗminī, nḗminem, nū́llō, nū́llā (m *or* f) - no one, nobody (11)
népōs, nepṓtis (m) - grandson, descendant (27)
nṓmen, nṓminis (n) - name (7)
occā́siō, occāsiṓnis (f) - occasion, opportunity (28)
ōrā́tor, ōrātṓris (m) - orator, speaker (23)
ōs, ṓris (n) - mouth, face (14)
párēns, paréntis (m *or* f) - parent (28)
páter, pátris (m) - father (12)
pāx, pā́cis (f) - peace (7)
prī́nceps, prī́ncipis (m *or* f) - leader, emperor (28)
próbitās, probitā́tis (f) - uprightness, honesty (18)
rátiō, ratiṓnis (f) - reckoning, account; reason, judgment, consideration; system; manner, method (8)
rēx, rḗgis (m) - king (7)
sacérdōs, sacerdṓtis (m) - priest (23)
sálūs, salū́tis (f) - health, safety; greeting (21)
sápiēns, sapiéntis (m/f) - a wise man/woman, philosopher (25)
scélus, scéleris (n) - evil deed, crime, sin, wickedness (19)
scrī́ptor, scrīptṓris (m) - writer, author (8)
senéctūs, senectū́tis (f) - old age (10)
sénex, sénis (m) - old man (16)
sérvitūs, servitū́tis (f) - servitude, slavery (20)
sōl, sṓlis (m) - sun (27)
sóror, sorṓris (f) - sister (8)
tempéstās, tempestā́tis (f) - period of time, season; weather, storm (15)
témpus, témporis (n) - time; occasion, opportunity (7)
tímor, timṓris (m) - fear (10)
úxor, uxṓris (f) - wife (7)
vḗritās, vēritā́tis (f) - truth (10)
vésper, vésperis *or* vésperī (m) - evening; evening star (28)
vírgō, vírginis (f) - maiden, virgin (7)
vírtūs, virtū́tis (f) - manliness, courage; excellence, character, worth, virtue (7)
volúptās, voluptā́tis (f) - pleasure (10)
vúlnus, vúlneris (n) - wound (24)

3rd Declension I-Stem

ánimal, animā́lis (n) - a living creature, animal (14)
ars, ártis (f) - art, skill (14)
arx, árcis (f) - citadel, stronghold (23)
aúris, aúris (f) - ear (14)
cī́vis, cī́vis (m *or* f) - citizen (14)
fī́nēs, fī́nium (m) - boundaries, territory (21)
fī́nis, fī́nis (m) - end, limit, boundary; purpose (21)
gēns, géntis (f) - clan, race, nation, people (21)
hóstēs, hóstium (m) - the enemy (18)
hóstis, hóstis (m) - an enemy *(of the state)* (18)
ígnis, ígnis (m) - fire (22)
máre, máris (n) - sea (14)
mēns, méntis (f) - mind, thought, intention (16)
mōns, móntis (m) - mountain (20)
mors, mórtis (f) - death (14)
nā́vis, nā́vis (f) - ship, boat (21)
nox, nóctis (f) - night (26)
nū́bēs, nū́bis (f) - cloud (14)
pars, pártis (f) - part, share; direction (14)
urbs, úrbis (f) - city (14)
vī́rēs, vī́rium (f. pl.) - strength (14)
vīs, vīs (f) - force, power, violence (14)

4th Declension

córnū, córnūs (n) - horn (20)
cúrsus, cúrsūs (m) - running, race; course (28)
frū́ctus, frū́ctūs (m) - fruit; profit, benefit, enjoyment (20)
génū, génūs (n) - knee (20)
mánus, mánūs (f) - hand; handwriting; band (20)
métus, métūs (m) - fear, dread, anxiety (20)
senā́tus, senā́tūs (m) - senate (20)
sḗnsus, sḗnsūs (m) - feeling, sense (20)
spī́ritus, spī́ritūs (m) - breath, breathing; spirit, soul (20)
vérsus, vérsūs (m) - line of verse (20)

5th Declension

díēs, diḗī (m) - day (22)
fídēs, fídeī (f) - faith, trust, trustworthiness, fidelity, promise, guarantee, protection (22)

rēs, réī (f) - thing, matter, property, business, affair (22)
rēs pública, réī públicae (f) - state, commonwealth, republic (22)
spēs, spéī (f) - hope (22)

Indeclinable
níhil - nothing (1)
sátis - enough (5)

Pronouns

áliquis, áliquid - someone, somebody, something (23)
égo, méī - I (11)
hic, haec, hoc - this; the latter; he, she, it, they (9)
ídem, éadem, ídem - the same (11)
ílle, ílla, íllud - that; the former; the famous; he, she, it, they (9)
ípse, ípsa, ípsum - myself, yourself, himself, herself, itself, *etc.,* the very, the actual (13)
is, éa, id - this, that; he, she, it (11)
íste, ísta, ístud - that of yours, that; such (as you have, as you speak of); *sometimes with contemptuous force, e.g.,* that despicable, that wretched (9)
quī, quae, quod - who, which, what, that (17)
quid - what (1)
quídam, quaédam, quíddam - a certain one or thing, someone, something (26)
quis? quid? - who? whose? whom? what? which? (19)
quísque, quídque, cuiúsque, cuíque - each one, each person, each thing (13)
quísquis, quídquid - whoever, whatever (23)
súī - himself, herself, itself, themselves (13)
tū, túī - you *(sing.)* (11)

Adjectives

1st & 2nd Declension
acérbus, acérba, acérbum - harsh, bitter, grievous (12)
aéquus, aéqua, aéquum - level, even; calm; equal, just; favorable (22)
áliī . . . áliī - some . . . others (9)
álius, ália, áliud - other, another (9)
álter, áltera, álterum - the other (of two), second (9)
amícus, amíca, amícum - friendly (11)
antíquus, antíqua, antíquum - ancient, old-time (2)
ásper, áspera, ásperum - rough, harsh (21)
avā́rus, avā́ra, avā́rum - greedy, avaricious (3)
beā́tus, beā́ta, beā́tum - happy, fortunate, blessed (10)
béllus, bélla, béllum - pretty, handsome, charming (4)
bónus, bóna, bónum - good, kind (4)
caécus, caéca, caécum - blind (17)
cā́rus, cā́ra, cā́rum - dear (11)
cértus, cérta, cértum - definite, sure, certain, reliable (19)
clā́rus, clā́ra, clā́rum - clear, bright; renowned, famous, illustrious (18)
déxter, déxtra, déxtrum - right, right-hand (20)
dóctus, dócta, dóctum - taught, learned, skilled (13)
fortūnā́tus, fortūnā́ta, fortūnā́tum - lucky, fortunate, happy (13)
géminus, gémina, géminum - twin (25)
Graécus, Graéca, Graécum - Greek (6)
hūmā́nus, hūmā́na, hūmā́num - pertaining to man, human; humane, kind; refined, cultivated (4)
incértus, incérta, incértum - uncertain, unsure, doubtful (22)
iūcúndus, iūcúnda, iūcúndum - pleasant, delightful, agreeable, pleasing (16)
Latī́nus, Latī́na, Latī́num - Latin (22)
lī́ber, lī́bera, lī́berum - free (5)
lóngus, lónga, lóngum - long (16)
magnánimus, magnánima, magnánimum - great-hearted, brave, magnanimous (23)
mágnus, mágna, mágnum - large, great; important (2)
málus, mála, málum - bad, wicked, evil (4)
médius, média, médium - middle; the middle of (22)
méus, méa, méum - my (2)
míser, mísera, míserum - wretched, miserable, unfortunate (15)
mórtuus, mórtua, mórtuum - dead (28)
múltus, múlta, múltum - much, many (2)
neúter, neútra, neútrum - not either, neither (9)
nóster, nóstra, nóstrum - our, ours (5)
nóvus, nóva, nóvum - new; strange (7)
nū́llus, nū́lla, nū́llum - not any, no, none (9)
párvus, párva, párvum - small, little (4)
paúcī, paúcae, paúca - few, a few (3)

perpétuus, perpétua, perpétuum perpetual, lasting, uninterrupted, continuous (6)
plḗnus, plḗna, plḗnum - full, abundant, generous (6)
prī́mus, prī́ma, prī́mum - first, foremost, chief, principal (27)
pudī́cus, pudī́ca, pudī́cum - modest, chaste (26)
púlcher, púlchra, púlchrum - beautiful, handsome; fine (5)
Rōmā́nus, Rōmā́na, Rōmā́num - Roman (3)
sálvus, sálva, sálvum - safe, sound (6)
sā́nus, sā́na, sā́num - sound, healthy, sane (5)
secúndus, secúnda, secúndum - second; favorable (6)
siníster, sinístra, sinístrum - left, left-hand; harmful, ill-omened (20)
sṓlus, sṓla, sṓlum - alone, only, the only (9)
stúltus, stúlta, stúltum - foolish (4)
supérbus, supérba, supérbum - arrogant, overbearing, haughty, proud (26)
súperus, súpera, súperum - above, upper (27)
súus, súa, súum - his own, her own, its own, their own (13)
tṓtus, tṓta, tṓtum - whole, entire (9)
túus, túa, túum - your *(sing.)* (2)
ū́llus, ū́lla, ū́llum - any (9)
últimus, última, últimum - farthest, extreme; last, final (25)
ū́nus, ū́na, ū́num - one, single, alone (9)
urbā́nus, urbā́na, urbā́num - of the city, urban; urbane, elegant (26)
úter, útra, útrum - either, which (of two) (9)
vḗrus, vḗra, vḗrum - true, real, proper (4)
véster, véstra, véstrum - your *(pl.)* (6)

3rd Declension
ā́cer, ā́cris, ā́cre - sharp, keen, eager; severe, fierce (16)
brévis, bréve - short, small, brief (16)
céler, céleris, célere - swift, quick, rapid (16)
commū́nis, commū́ne - common, general, of / for the community (20)
diffícilis, diffícile - hard, difficult, troublesome (16)
dī́ligēns, ***gen.*** **dīligéntis** - diligent, careful (27)
dissímilis, dissímile - unlike, different (27)
dúlcis, dúlce - sweet; pleasant, agreeable (16)
fácilis, fácile - easy; agreeable (16)
fḗlīx, ***gen.*** **fēlī́cis** - lucky, fortunate, happy (22)
férōx, ***gen.*** **ferṓcis** - fierce, savage (25)
fidḗlis, fidḗle - faithful, loyal (25)
fórtis, fórte - strong, brave (16)
grácilis, grácile - slender, thin (27)
grávis, gráve - heavy, weighty; serious, important; severe, grievous (19)
húmilis, húmile - lowly, humble (27)
immortā́lis, immortā́le - not subject to death, immortal (19)
íngēns, ***gen.*** **ingéntis** - huge (16)
lévis, léve - light; easy; slight, trivial (17)
máior, máius - greater; older (27)
mortā́lis, mortā́le - mortal (18)
ómnis, ómne - every, all (16)
pótēns, ***gen.*** **poténtis** - able, powerful, mighty, strong (16)
prī́nceps, ***gen.*** **prī́ncipis** - chief, foremost (28)
sápiēns, ***gen.*** **sapiéntis** - wise, judicious (25)
sénex, ***gen.*** **sénis** - old, aged (16)
símilis, símile (+gen. or dat.) - similar (to), like, resembling (27)
trī́stis, trī́ste - sad, sorrowful; joyless, grim, severe (26)
túrpis, túrpe - ugly; shameful, base, disgraceful (26)
ū́tilis, ū́tile - useful, advantageous (27)

Indeclinable Adjectives
quot - how many, as many as (27)
sátis - enough, sufficient (5)

Indefinite Adjective
quī́dam, quaédam, quóddam - a certain, some (26)

Interrogative Adjective
quī?, quae?, quod? - what? which? what kind of?; *(sometimes with exclamatory force)* what (a)! what sort of! (19)

Verbs
1st Conjugation
ádiuvō, adiuvā́re, adiū́vī, adiū́tum - to help, aid, assist; to please (4)

ámō, amā́re, amā́vī, amā́tum - to love, like (1)
appéllō, appellā́re, appellā́vī, appellā́tum - to speak to, address (as), call, name (14)
cḗnō, cēnā́re, cēnā́vī, cēnā́tum - to dine (5)
cṓgitō, cōgitā́re, cōgitā́vī, cōgitā́tum- to think, ponder, consider, plan (1)
cōnsérvō, cōnservā́re, cōnservā́vī, cōnservā́tum - to preserve, conserve, maintain (1)
créō, creā́re, creā́vī, creā́tum - to create (12)
cúlpō, culpā́re, culpā́vī, culpā́tum - to blame, censure (5)
dḗdicō, dēdicā́re, dēdicā́vī, dēdicā́tum - to dedicate (28)
dēléctō, dēlectā́re, dēlectā́vī, dēlectā́tum - to delight, charm, please (19)
dēmṓnstrō, dēmōnstrā́re, dēmōnstrā́vī, dēmōnstrā́tum to point out, show, demonstrate (8)
dēsī́derō, dēsīderā́re, dēsīderā́vī, dēsīderā́tum - to desire, long for, miss (17)
dō, dáre, dédī, dátum - to give, offer (1)
ḗducō, ēducā́re, ēducā́vī, ēducā́tum - to bring up, educate (23)
érrō, errā́re, errā́vī, errā́tum - to wander; err, go astray, make a mistake, be mistaken (1)
exspéctō, exspectā́re, exspectā́vī, exspectā́tum - to look for, expect, await (15)
invī́tō, invītā́re, invītā́vī, invītā́tum - to entertain, invite, summon (26)
iúvō, iuvā́re, iū́vī, iū́tum - to help, aid, assist; to please (4)
labṓrō, labōrā́re, labōrā́vī, labōrā́tum - to labor; be in distress (21)
laúdō, laudā́re, laudā́vī, laudā́tum - to praise (1)
lī́berō, līberā́re, līberā́vī, līberā́tum - to free, liberate (19)
mū́tō, mūtā́re, mūtā́vī, mūtā́tum to change, alter; exchange (14)
nā́rrō, nārrā́re, nārrā́vī, nārrā́tum - to tell, report, narrate (24)
nā́vigō, nāvigā́re, nāvigā́vī, nāvigā́tum - to sail, navigate (17)
nécō, necā́re, necā́vī, necā́tum - to murder, kill (7)
négō, negā́re, negā́vī, negā́tum to deny, say that . . . not (25)
nū́ntiō, nūntiā́re, nūntiā́vī, nūntiā́tum - to announce, report, relate (25)
párō, parā́re, parā́vī, parā́tum - to prepare, provide; get, obtain (19)
praéstō, praestā́re, praéstitī, praéstitum - to excel; exhibit, show, offer, supply, furnish (28)
próbō, probā́re, probā́vī, probā́tum - to approve, recommend; test (27)
prōnū́ntiō, prōnūntiā́re, prōnūntiā́vī, prōnūntiā́tum - to proclaim, announce; declaim; pronounce (20)
pútō, putā́re, putā́vī, putā́tum - to reckon, suppose, judge, think, imagine (25)
récitō, recitā́re, recitā́vī, recitā́tum - to read aloud, recite (17)
sátiō, satiā́re, satiā́vī, satiā́tum - to satisfy, sate (3)
sérvō, servā́re, servā́vī, servā́tum - to preserve, save, keep, guard (1)
spḗrō, spērā́re, spērā́vī, spērā́tum - to hope for, hope (25)
stō, stā́re, stétī, státum - to stand, stand still *or* firm (13)
súperō, superā́re, superā́vī, superā́tum - to be above, have the upper hand, surpass; overcome, conquer (5)
tólerō, tolerā́re, tolerā́vī, tolerā́tum - to bear, endure (6)
vī́tō, vītā́re, vītā́vī, vītā́tum - to avoid, shun (14)
vócō, vocā́re, vocā́vī, vocā́tum - to call, summon (1)

2nd Conjugation

aúdeō, audḗre, aúsus sum - to dare (7)
cáreō, carḗre, cáruī, caritū́rum (+abl.) - to be without, be deprived of, want, lack; be free from (20)
contíneō, continḗre, contínuī, conténtum - to hold together, contain, keep, enclose, restrain (21)
dḗbeō, dēbḗre, dḗbuī, dḗbitum - to owe; ought, must, should (1)
dḗleō, dēlḗre, dēlḗvī, dēlḗtum - to destroy, wipe out, erase (17)
dóceō, docḗre, dócuī, dóctum - to teach (8)
égeō, egḗre, éguī (+ abl. or gen.) - to need, lack, want (28)
éxpleō, explḗre, explḗvī, explḗtum - to fill, fill up, complete (28)
gaúdeō, gaudḗre, gāvī́sus sum - to be glad, rejoice (23)

hábeō, habḗre, hábuī, hábitum - to have, hold, possess; consider, regard (3)
iáceō, iacḗre, iácuī - to lie; lie prostrate; lie dead (25)
iúbeō, iubḗre, iússī, iússum - to bid, order, command (21)
máneō, manḗre, mánsī, mánsum - to remain, stay, stay behind, abide, continue (5)
mísceō, miscḗre, míscuī, míxtum to mix, stir up, disturb (18)
móneō, monḗre, mónuī, mónitum - to remind, advise, warn (1)
móveō, movḗre, mṓvī, mṓtum - to move; arouse, affect (18)
prohíbeō, prohibḗre, prohíbuī, prohíbitum - to keep (back), prevent, hinder, restrain, prohibit (20)
remáneō, remanḗre, remánsī, remánsum - to remain, stay, stay behind, abide, continue (5)
rī́deō, rīdḗre, rī́sī, rī́sum - to laugh, laugh at (24)
sálvē, salvḗte - hello, greetings (1)
sálveō, salvḗre - to be well, be in good health (1)
táceō, tacḗre, tácuī, tácitum - to be silent, leave unmentioned (28)
téneō, tenḗre, ténuī, téntum - to hold, keep, possess; restrain (14)
térreō, terrḗre, térruī, térritum - to frighten, terrify (1)
tímeō, timḗre, tímuī - to fear, be afraid (of) (15)
válē, valḗte - good-bye, farewell (1)
váleō, valḗre, váluī, valitū́rum - to be strong, have power; be well (1)
vídeō, vidḗre, vī́dī, vī́sum - to see; observe, understand (1)
vídeor, vidḗrī, vī́sus sum - to be seen, seem, appear (18)

3rd Conjugation

admíttō, admíttere, admī́sī, admíssum - to admit, receive, let in (17)
ágō, ágere, ḗgī, ā́ctum - to drive, lead, do, act; pass, spend *(life or time)* (8)
álō, álere, áluī, áltum - to nourish, support, sustain, increase; cherish (13)
āmíttō, āmíttere, āmī́sī, āmíssum - to send away; lose, let go (12)
āvértō, āvértere, āvértī, āvérsum - to turn away, avert (23)
cádō, cádere, cécidī, cāsū́rum - to fall (12)
cḗdō, cḗdere, céssī, céssum - to go, withdraw; yield to, grant, submit (28)
cérnō, cérnere, crḗvī, crḗtum - to distinguish, discern, perceive (22)
commíttō, commíttere, commī́sī, commíssum - to entrust, commit (15)
crḗdō, crḗdere, crḗdidī, crḗditum to believe, trust (25)
cúrrō, cúrrere, cucúrrī, cúrsum - to run, rush, move quickly (14)
dēféndō, dēféndere, dēféndī, dēfḗnsum - to ward off; defend, protect (20)
dī́cō, dī́cere, dī́xī, díctum - to say, tell, speak; name, call (10)
dī́ligō, dīlígere, dīlḗxī, dīlḗctum - to esteem, love (13)
discḗdō, discḗdere, discéssī, discéssum - to go away, depart (20)
díscō, díscere, dídicī - to learn (8)
dū́cō, dū́cere, dū́xī, dúctum - to lead; consider, regard; prolong (8)
expéllō, expéllere, éxpulī, expúlsum - to drive out, expel, banish (24)
flúō, flúere, flū́xī, flū́xum - to flow (18)
gérō, gérere, géssī, géstum - to carry; carry on, manage, conduct, wage, accomplish, perform (8)
intéllegō, intellégere, intellḗxī, intellḗctum - to understand (11)
iúngō, iúngere, iū́nxī, iū́nctum - to join (13)
légō, légere, lḗgī, lḗctum - to pick out, choose; read (18)
míttō, míttere, mī́sī, míssum - to send, let go (11)
néglegō, neglégere, neglḗxī, neglḗctum - to neglect, disregard (17)
ópprimō, opprímere, oppréssī, oppréssum - to suppress, overwhelm, overpower, check (23)
osténdō, osténdere, osténdī, osténtum - to exhibit, show, display (23)
péllō, péllere, pépulī, púlsum - to strike, push; drive out, banish (24)
pétō, pétere, petī́vī, petī́tum - to seek, aim at, beg, beseech (23)
pṓnō, pṓnere, pósuī, pósitum - to put, place, set (27)
prémō, prémere, préssī, préssum - to press; press hard, pursue (23)

quaérō, quaérere, quaesī́vī, quaesī́tum - to seek, look for, strive for; ask, inquire, inquire into (24)
régō, régere, rḗxī, rḗctum - to rule, guide, direct (16)
relínquō, relínquere, relī́quī, relíctum - to leave behind, leave, abandon, desert (21)
revértō, revértere, revértī, revérsum - turn back (23)
scrī́bō, scrī́bere, scrī́psī, scrī́ptum to write, compose (8)
tángō, tángere, tétigī, tā́ctum - to touch (21)
tóllō, tóllere, sústulī, sublā́tum - to raise, lift up; take away, remove, destroy (22)
tráhō, tráhere, trā́xī, tráctum - to draw, drag; derive, acquire (8)
vértō, vértere, vértī, vérsum - to turn; change (23)
víncō, víncere, vī́cī, víctum - to conquer, overcome (8)
vī́vō, vī́vere, vī́xī, vī́ctum - to live (10)

3rd Conjugation -iō

accípiō, accípere, accḗpī, accéptum - to take *(to one's self)*, receive, accept (24)
cápiō, cápere, cḗpī, cáptum - to take, capture, seize, get (10)
cúpiō, cúpere, cupī́vī, cupī́tum - to desire, wish, long for (17)
ērípiō, ērípere, ērípuī, ēréptum - to snatch away, take away; rescue (22)
excípiō, excípere, excḗpī, excéptum - to take out, except; take, receive, capture (24)
fáciō, fácere, fḗcī, fáctum - to make, do, accomplish (10)
fúgiō, fúgere, fū́gī, fugitū́rum - to flee, hurry away; escape; go into exile; avoid, shun (10)
iáciō, iácere, iḗcī, iáctum - to throw, hurl (15)
incípiō, incípere, incḗpī, incéptum - to begin (17)
patefáciō, patefácere, patefḗcī, patefáctum - to make open, open; disclose, expose (25)
rápiō, rápere, rápuī, ráptum - to seize, snatch, carry away (21)
recípiō, recípere, recḗpī, recéptum - to take back, regain; admit, receive (24)
suscípiō, suscípere, suscḗpī, suscéptum - to undertake (25)

4th Conjugation

aúdiō, audī́re, audī́vī, audī́tum - to hear, listen to (10)
invéniō, invenī́re, invḗnī, invéntum - to come upon, find (10)
nésciō, nescī́re, nescī́vī, nescī́tum - to not know, be ignorant (25)
scíō, scī́re, scī́vī, scī́tum - to know (21)
séntiō, sentī́re, sḗnsī, sḗnsum - to feel, perceive, think, experience (11)
véniō, venī́re, vḗnī, véntum - to come (10)

Irregular

póssum, pósse, pótuī - to be able, can, could, have power (6)
sum, ésse, fúī, futū́rum - to be, exist (4)

Defective

ā́it, ā́iunt - he says, they say, assert (25)
coépī, coepísse, coéptum - began (17)
ínquit - he says *or* said (22)
ṓdī, ōdísse, ōsū́rum - to hate (20)

Adverbs

ánte (+acc.) - before, previously (13)
béne - well, satisfactorily, quite (11)
cíto - quickly (17)
crās - tomorrow (5)
cūr - why (18)
déhinc - then, next (25)
deínde - thereupon, next, then (18)
díū - long, for a long time (12)
étiam - even, also (11)
héri - yesterday (5)
hīc - here (25)
hódiē - today (3)
iam - now, already, soon (19)
íbi - there (6)
ítaque - and so, therefore (15)
íterum - again, a second time (21)
nímis, nímium - too, too much, excessively; *(in a positive sense, esp. with adjectives and adverbs)* exceedingly, very (9)
nōn - not (1)
númquam - never (8)
nunc - now, at present (6)
nū́per - recently (12)
ṓlim - once (upon a time), long ago, formerly; some day, in the future (13)
pósteā - afterwards (24)
prṓtinus - immediately (22)
quam - how (16)
quam - than *(after comparatives)*; as . . . as possible *(with superlatives)* (26)
quándō - when (5)

quā́rē - because of which thing *(lit.);* therefore, wherefore, why (6)
quóndam - formerly, once (22)
quóque - also, too (17)
saépe - often (1)
sátis - enough, sufficiently (5)
sémper - always (3)
támen - nevertheless, still (8)
tántum - only (26)
tum - then, at that time; thereupon, in the next place (5)
úbi - where, when (6)
últrā - on the other side of, beyond (22)
úmquam - ever, at any time (23)

Conjunctions

at - but; but, mind you; but, you say (19)
átque, ac - and also, and even, and in fact (21)
aut - or (17)
aut . . . aut - either . . . or (17)
aútem - however; moreover (11)
dum - while, as long as, at the same time that; *or* until *(+subjunctive)* (8)
énim - for, in fact, truly (9)
et - and; even (2)
et . . . et - both . . . and (2)
ígitur - therefore, consequently (5)
nam - for (13)
nē - not; in order that . . . not, that . . . not, in order not to (28)
néque, nec - and not, nor (11)
néque . . . néque, nec . . . nec - neither . . . nor (11)
nísi - if . . . not, unless; except (19)
quod - because (11)
quóniam - since, inasmuch as (10)
sed - but (2)
sī - if (1)
ut (+indic.) - as, just as, when (24)
ut (+ subj.) - in order that, so that, that, in order to, so as to, to (28)

Prepositions

ab, ā (+abl.) - away from, from; by (14)
ad (+acc.) - to, up to, near to (8)
ánte (+acc.) - before *(in place or time),* in front of (13)
cóntrā (+acc.) - against (19)
cum (+abl.) - with (10)
dē (+abl.) - down from, from; concerning, about (3)
ex, ē (abl.+) - out of, from, from within; by reason of, on account of ; of *(after cardinal numerals)* (8)
in (+acc.) - into, toward; against (9)
in (+abl.) - in, on (3)
ínter (+acc.) - between, among (15)
per (+acc.) - through; by *(with reflexive pronoun)* (13)
post (+acc.) - after, behind (7)
prae (+abl.) - in front of, before (26)
prō (+abl.) - in front of, before, on behalf of, for the sake of, in return for, instead of, for, as (12)
própter (+acc.) - on account of, because of (5)
síne (+abl.) - without (2)
sub (+abl. w/ verbs of rest *or* **+acc. w/ verbs of motion)** - under, up under, close to, down to/into, to/at the foot of (7)
trāns (+acc.) - across (14)
últrā (adv. and prep. +acc.) - on the other side of, beyond (22)

Interjection

ō - O!, Oh! (2)

Idioms

amā́bō tē - please (1)
grā́tiās ágere (+dat.) - to thank someone; to give thanks to (8)
mḗnsa secúnda (f) - dessert (26)
nōn sṓlum . . . sed étiam - not only . . . but also (9)
poénās dáre - to pay the penalty (2)
sī quándō - if ever (5)

Prefix

re-, red- - again, back (24)

Suffixes

-ne – interrogative suffix attached to the first word of a sentence, typically the verb or another word on which the question hinges, to introduce a question whose answer is uncertain (5)
-que - and *(enclitic conjunction; appended to the second of two words to be joined)* (6)

Numerals

Cardinal - ū́nus *to* vīgíntī quī́nque (15)
Ordinal - prī́mus *to* duodécimus (15)

----

céntum - a hundred (15)
mī́lia, mī́lium (n. pl.) - thousands (15)
mī́lle - thousand (15)

Chapter 29

Nouns

1st Declension

adulēscéntia, adulēscéntiae (f) - youth, young manhood; youthfulness (5)
agrícola, agrícolae (m) - farmer (3)
amíca, amícae (f) - friend (female) (3)
amīcítia, amīcítiae (f) - friendship (10)
áqua, áquae (f) - water (14)
Ásia, Ásiae (f) - Asia (12)
cása, cásae (f) - house, cottage, hut (21)
caúsa, caúsae (f) - cause, reason; case, situation (21)
caúsā (abl. + preceding gen.) - for the sake of, on account of (21)
cḗna, cḗnae (f) - dinner (26)
clēméntia, clēméntiae (f) - mildness, gentleness, mercy (16)
cṓpia, cṓpiae (f) - abundance, supply (8)
cṓpiae, cōpiā́rum (f) - supplies, troops, forces (8)
cúlpa, cúlpae (f) - fault, blame (5)
cū́ra, cū́rae (f) - care, attention, caution, anxiety (4)
déa, déae (f) - goddess (6)
discípula, discípulae (f) - learner, pupil, student (female) (6)
dīvítiae, dīvitiā́rum (f. pl.) - riches, wealth (13)
fā́bula, fā́bulae (f) - story, tale; play (24)
fā́ma, fā́mae (f) - rumor, report; fame, reputation (2)
família, famíliae (f) - household, family (19)
fḗmina, fḗminae (f) - woman (3)
fenéstra, fenéstrae (f) - window (21)
fī́lia, fī́liae (f) - daughter (3)
fṓrma, fṓrmae (f) - form, shape; beauty (2)
fortū́na, fortū́nae (f) - fortune, luck (2)
glṓria, glṓriae (f) - glory, fame (5)
Graécia, Graéciae (f) - Greece (19)
hásta, hástae (f) - spear (23)
hṓra, hṓrae (f) - hour, time (10)
īnsídiae, īnsidiā́rum (f) - ambush, plot, treachery (6)
ī́nsula, ī́nsulae (f) - island (23)
ī́ra, ī́rae (f) - ire, anger (2)
Itália, Itáliae (f) - Italy (15)
língua, línguae (f) - tongue; language (25)
líttera, lítterae (f) - a letter of the alphabet (7)
lítterae, litterā́rum (f) - a letter (epistle), literature (7)
lū́na, lū́nae (f) - moon (28)
magístra, magístrae (f) - schoolmistress, teacher, mistress (4)
médica, médicae (f) - doctor, physician (female) (12)
memória, memóriae (f) - memory, recollection (15)
mḗnsa, mḗnsae (f) - table; dining; dish, course (26)
móra, mórae (f) - delay (4)
nā́ta, nā́tae (f) - daughter (29)
nātū́ra, nātū́rae (f) - nature (10)
naúta, naútae (m) - sailor (2)
patiéntia, patiéntiae (f) - suffering; patience, endurance (12)
pátria, pátriae (f) - fatherland, native land, (one's) country (2)
pecū́nia, pecū́niae (f) - money (2)
philosóphia, philosóphiae (f) - philosophy (2)
poéna, poénae (f) - penalty, punishment (2)
poḗta, poḗtae (m) - poet (2)
pórta, pórtae (f) - gate, entrance (2)
puélla, puéllae (f) - girl (2)
rēgī́na, rēgī́nae (f) - queen (7)
Rṓma, Rṓmae (f) - Rome (14)
rósa, rósae (f) - rose (2)
sapiéntia, sapiéntiae (f) - wisdom (3)
sátura, sáturae (f) - satire (16)
sciéntia, sciéntiae (f) - knowledge (18)
senténtia, senténtiae (f) - feeling, thought, opinion, vote, sentence (2)
sérva, sérvae (f) - slave (female) (24)
stḗlla, stḗllae (f) - star, planet (28)
térra, térrae (f) - earth, ground, land, country (7)
Trṓia, Trṓiae (f) - Troy (21)
túrba, túrbae (f) - uproar, disturbance; mob, crowd, multitude (14)
vía, víae (f) - way, road, street (10)
vīcī́na, vīcī́nae (f) - neighbor (female) (21)
victṓria, victṓriae (f) - victory (8)
vī́ta, vī́tae (f) - life; mode of life (2)

2nd Declension

áger, ágrī (m) - field, farm (3)
amī́cus, amī́cī (m) - friend (male) (3)
ánimī, animṓrum (m) - high spirits, pride, courage (5)
ánimus, ánimī (m) - soul, spirit, mind (5)
ánnus, ánnī (m) - year (12)
argūméntum, argūméntī (n) - proof, evidence, argument (19)
árma, armṓrum (n. pl.) - arms, weapons (28)

bā́sium, bā́siī (n) - kiss (4)
béllum, béllī (n) - war (4)
benefícium, benefíciī (n) - benefit, kindness; favor (19)
caélum, caélī (n) - sky, heaven (5)
coniūrā́tī, coniūrātṓrum (m. pl.) - conspirators (20)
cōnsílium, cōnsíliī (n) - plan, purpose, counsel, advice, judgment, wisdom (4)
déus, déī (m) - god (6)
discípulus, discípulī (m) - learner, pupil, student (male) (6)
dṓnum, dṓnī (n) - gift, present (4)
équus, équī (m) - horse (23)
exítium, exítiī (n) - destruction, ruin (4)
fáctum, fáctī (n) - deed, act, achievement (13)
fā́tum, fā́tī (n) - fate; death (29)
férrum, férrī (n) - iron; sword (22)
fī́lius, fī́liī (m) - son (3)
fórum, fórī (n) - marketplace, forum (26)
Graécus, Graécī (m) - a Greek (6)
impérium, impériī (n) - power to command, supreme power, authority, command, control (24)
ingénium, ingéniī (n) - nature, innate talent (29)
iūdícium, iūdíciī (n) - judgment, decision, opinion; trial (19)
libéllus, libéllī (m) - little book (17)
líber, líbrī (m) - book (6)
lóca, locṓrum (n) - places, region (9)
lócī, locṓrum (m) - passages in literature (9)
lócus, lócī (m) - place; passage in literature (9)
lū́dus, lū́dī (m) - game, sport; school (18)
magíster, magístrī (m) - schoolmaster, teacher, master (4)
médicus, médicī (m) - doctor, physician (male) (12)
módus, módī (m) - measure, bound, limit; manner, method, mode, way (22)
mórbus, mórbī (m) - disease, sickness (9)
múndus, múndī (m) - world, universe (21)
númerus, númerī (m) - number (3)
óculus, óculī (m) - eye (4)
offícium, offíciī (n) - duty, service (4)
ṓsculum, ṓsculī (n) - kiss (29)
ṓtium, ṓtiī (n) - leisure, peace (4)
perfúgium, perfúgiī (n) - refuge, shelter (24)
perī́culum, perī́culī (n) - danger, risk (4)
pópulus, pópulī (m) - the people, a people, a nation (3)
prīncípium, prīncípiī (n) - beginning (12)
púer, púerī (m) - boy; boys, children *(pl.)* (3)
remédium, remédiī (n) - cure, remedy (4)
sérvus, sérvī (m) - slave (male) (24)
sígnum, sígnī (n) - sign, signal, indication; seal (13)
sōlā́cium, sōlā́ciī (n) - comfort, relief (24)
sómnus, sómnī (m) - sleep (26)
stúdium, stúdiī (n) - eagerness, zeal, pursuit, study (9)
stúltus, stúltī (m) - a fool (4)
súperī, superṓrum (m. pl.) - the gods (27)
tyránnus, tyránnī (m) - absolute ruler, tyrant (6)
vérbum, vérbī (n)- word (5)
vīcī́nus, vīcī́nī (m) - neighbor (male) (21)
vir, vírī (m) - man, hero (3)
vítium, vítiī (n) - fault, crime, vice (6)
vúlgus, vúlgī (n) - the common people, mob, rabble (21)

3rd Declension

adulḗscēns, adulēscéntis (m *or* f) - young man *or* woman (12)
aétās, aetā́tis (f) - period of life, life, age, an age, time (16)
ámor, amṓris (m) - love (7)
aúctor, auctṓris (m) - increaser; author, originator (19)
audī́tor, audītṓris (m) - hearer, listener, member of an audience (16)
Caésar, Caésaris (m) - Caesar (12)
cáput, cápitis (n) - head; leader; beginning; life; heading; chapter (11)
cármen, cárminis (n) - song, poem (7)
Carthā́gō, Carthā́ginis (f) - Carthage (24)
Cícerō, Cicerṓnis (m) - (Marcus Tullius) Cicero (8)
cī́vitās, cīvitā́tis (f) - state, citizenship (7)
cṓnsul, cṓnsulis (m) - consul (11)
córpus, córporis (n) - body (7)
cupíditās, cupiditā́tis (f) - desire, longing, passion; cupidity, avarice (10)
dēlectā́tiō, dēlectātiṓnis (f) - delight, pleasure, enjoyment (27)
dux, dúcis (m) - leader, guide; commander, general (23)
flū́men, flū́minis (n) - river (18)
frā́ter, frā́tris (m) - brother (8)
génus, géneris (n) - origin; kind, type, sort, class (18)
hómō, hóminis (m) - human being, man (7)

imperátor, imperātóris (m) - general, commander-in-chief, emperor (24)
iúdex, iúdicis (m) - judge, juror (19)
iūs, iúris (n) - right, justice, law (14)
lábor, labóris (m)- labor, work, toil; a work, production (7)
laus, laúdis (f) - praise, glory, fame (8)
lēx, lḗgis (f) - law, statute (26)
lībértās, lībertā́tis (f) - liberty (8)
límen, líminis (n) - threshold (26)
lítus, lítoris (n) - shore, coast (23)
lūx, lúcis (f) - light (26)
maiṓrēs, maiṓrum (m. pl.) - ancestors (27)
mā́ter, mā́tris (f) - mother (12)
míles, mílitis (m) - soldier (23)
mṓrēs, mṓrum (m) - habits, morals, character (7)
mōs, mṓris (m) - habit, custom, manner (7)
nḗmō, nūllíus, nḗminī, nḗminem, núllō, núllā (m *or* f) - no one, nobody (11)
népōs, nepṓtis (m) - grandson, descendant (27)
nṓmen, nṓminis (n) - name (7)
occā́siō, occāsiṓnis (f) - occasion, opportunity (28)
ōrā́tor, ōrātṓris (m) - orator, speaker (23)
ōs, ṓris (n) - mouth, face (14)
párēns, paréntis (m *or* f) - parent (28)
páter, pátris (m) - father (12)
pāx, pā́cis (f) - peace (7)
prínceps, príncipis (m *or* f) - leader, emperor (28)
próbitās, probitā́tis (f) - uprightness, honesty (18)
rátiō, ratiṓnis (f) - reckoning, account; reason, judgment, consideration; system; manner, method (8)
rēx, rḗgis (m) - king (7)
sacérdōs, sacerdṓtis (m) - priest (23)
sálūs, salū́tis (f) - health, safety; greeting (21)
sápiēns, sapiéntis (m/f) - a wise man/woman, philosopher (25)
scélus, scéleris (n) - evil deed, crime, sin, wickedness (19)
scríptor, scrīptṓris (m) - writer, author (8)
senéctūs, senectū́tis (f) - old age (10)
sénex, sénis (m) - old man (16)
sérvitūs, servitū́tis (f) - servitude, slavery (20)
sídus, síderis (n) - constellation, star (29)
sōl, sṓlis (m) - sun (27)
sóror, sorṓris (f) - sister (8)
tempéstās, tempestā́tis (f) - period of time, season; weather, storm (15)
témpus, témporis (n) - time; occasion, opportunity (7)
tímor, timṓris (m) - fear (10)
úxor, uxṓris (f) - wife (7)
vḗritās, vēritā́tis (f) - truth (10)
vésper, vésperis *or* vésperī (m) - evening; evening star (28)
vírgō, vírginis (f) - maiden, virgin (7)
vírtūs, virtū́tis (f) - manliness, courage; excellence, character, worth, virtue (7)
volúptās, voluptā́tis (f) - pleasure (10)
vúlnus, vúlneris (n) - wound (24)

3rd Declension I-Stem

ánimal, animā́lis (n) - a living creature, animal (14)
ars, ártis (f) - art, skill (14)
arx, árcis (f) - citadel, stronghold (23)
aúris, aúris (f) - ear (14)
cī́vis, cī́vis (m *or* f) - citizen (14)
fī́nēs, fī́nium (m) - boundaries, territory (21)
fī́nis, fī́nis (m) - end, limit, boundary; purpose (21)
gēns, géntis (f) - clan, race, nation, people (21)
hóstēs, hóstium (m) - the enemy (18)
hóstis, hóstis (m) - an enemy *(of the state)* (18)
ígnis, ígnis (m) - fire (22)
máre, máris (n) - sea (14)
mēns, méntis (f) - mind, thought, intention (16)
moénia, moénium (n. pl.) - walls of a city (29)
mōns, móntis (m) - mountain (20)
mors, mórtis (f) - death (14)
nā́vis, nā́vis (f) - ship, boat (21)
nox, nóctis (f) - night (26)
nū́bēs, nū́bis (f) - cloud (14)
pars, pártis (f) - part, share; direction (14)
urbs, úrbis (f) - city (14)
vī́rēs, vī́rium (f. pl.) - strength (14)
vīs, vīs (f) - force, power, violence (14)

4th Declension

córnū, córnūs (n) - horn (20)
cúrsus, cúrsūs (m) - running, race; course (28)
frū́ctus, frū́ctūs (m) - fruit; profit, benefit, enjoyment (20)
génū, génūs (n) - knee (20)
mánus, mánūs (f) - hand; handwriting; band (20)
métus, métūs (m) - fear, dread, anxiety (20)
senā́tus, senā́tūs (m) - senate (20)
sḗnsus, sḗnsūs (m) - feeling, sense (20)
spī́ritus, spī́ritūs (m) - breath, breathing; spirit, soul (20)

vérsus, vérsūs (m) - line of verse (20)

5th Declension

díēs, diḗī (m) - day (22)

fídēs, fídeī (f) - faith, trust, trustworthiness, fidelity, promise, guarantee, protection (22)

rēs, réī (f) - thing, matter, property, business, affair (22)

rēs pū́blica, réī pū́blicae (f) - state, commonwealth, republic (22)

spēs, spéī (f) - hope (22)

Indeclinable

níhil - nothing (1)

sátis - enough (5)

Pronouns

áliquis, áliquid - someone, somebody, something (23)

égo, méī - I (11)

hic, haec, hoc - this; the latter; he, she, it, they (9)

ídem, éadem, ídem - the same (11)

ílle, ílla, íllud - that; the former; the famous; he, she, it, they (9)

ípse, ípsa, ípsum - myself, yourself, himself, herself, itself, *etc.,* the very, the actual (13)

is, éa, id - this, that; he, she, it (11)

íste, ísta, ístud - that of yours, that; such (as you have, as you speak of); *sometimes with contemptuous force, e.g.,* that despicable, that wretched (9)

quī, quae, quod - who, which, what, that (17)

quid - what (1)

quídam, quaédam, quíddam - a certain one or thing, someone, something (26)

quis? quid? - who? whose? whom? what? which? (19)

quísque, quídque, cuiúsque, cuíque - each one, each person, each thing (13)

quísquis, quídquid - whoever, whatever (23)

súī - himself, herself, itself, themselves (13)

tū, túī - you *(sing.)* (11)

Adjectives

1st & 2nd Declension

acérbus, acérba, acérbum - harsh, bitter, grievous (12)

aéquus, aéqua, aéquum - level, even; calm; equal, just; favorable (22)

áliī . . . áliī - some . . . others (9)

álius, ália, áliud - other, another (9)

álter, áltera, álterum - the other (of two), second (9)

amícus, amíca, amícum - friendly (11)

antíquus, antíqua, antíquum - ancient, old-time (2)

ásper, áspera, ásperum - rough, harsh (21)

avā́rus, avā́ra, avā́rum - greedy, avaricious (3)

beā́tus, beā́ta, beā́tum - happy, fortunate, blessed (10)

béllus, bélla, béllum - pretty, handsome, charming (4)

bónus, bóna, bónum - good, kind (4)

caécus, caéca, caécum - blind (17)

cā́rus, cā́ra, cā́rum - dear (11)

cértus, cérta, cértum - definite, sure, certain, reliable (19)

clā́rus, clā́ra, clā́rum - clear, bright; renowned, famous, illustrious (18)

déxter, déxtra, déxtrum - right, right-hand (20)

dígnus, dígna, dígnum (+abl.) - worthy, worthy of (29)

dóctus, dócta, dóctum - taught, learned, skilled (13)

dū́rus, dū́ra, dū́rum - hard, harsh, rough, stern, unfeeling, hardy, difficult (29)

fortūnā́tus, fortūnā́ta, fortūnā́tum - lucky, fortunate, happy (13)

géminus, gémina, géminum - twin (25)

Graécus, Graéca, Graécum - Greek (6)

hūmā́nus, hūmā́na, hūmā́num - pertaining to man, human; humane, kind; refined, cultivated (4)

incértus, incérta, incértum - uncertain, unsure, doubtful (22)

iūcúndus, iūcúnda, iūcúndum - pleasant, delightful, agreeable, pleasing (16)

Latī́nus, Latī́na, Latī́num - Latin (22)

lī́ber, lī́bera, lī́berum - free (5)

lóngus, lónga, lóngum - long (16)

magnánimus, magnánima, magnánimum - great-hearted, brave, magnanimous (23)

mágnus, mágna, mágnum - large, great; important (2)

málus, mála, málum - bad, wicked, evil (4)

médius, média, médium - middle; the middle of (22)

méus, méa, méum - my (2)

míser, mísera, míserum - wretched, miserable, unfortunate (15)

mórtuus, mórtua, mórtuum - dead (28)

múltus, múlta, múltum - much, many (2)
neúter, neútra, neútrum - not either, neither (9)
nóster, nóstra, nóstrum - our, ours (5)
nóvus, nóva, nóvum - new; strange (7)
nū́llus, nū́lla, nū́llum - not any, no, none (9)
párvus, párva, párvum - small, little (4)
paúcī, paúcae, paúca - few, a few (3)
perpétuus, perpétua, perpétuum perpetual, lasting, uninterrupted, continuous (6)
plḗnus, plḗna, plḗnum - full, abundant, generous (6)
prī́mus, prī́ma, prī́mum - first, foremost, chief, principal (27)
pudī́cus, pudī́ca, pudī́cum - modest, chaste (26)
púlcher, púlchra, púlchrum - beautiful, handsome; fine (5)
Rōmā́nus, Rōmā́na, Rōmā́num - Roman (3)
sálvus, sálva, sálvum - safe, sound (6)
sā́nus, sā́na, sā́num - sound, healthy, sane (5)
secúndus, secúnda, secúndum - second; favorable (6)
siníster, sinístra, sinístrum - left, left-hand; harmful, ill-omened (20)
sṓlus, sṓla, sṓlum - alone, only, the only (9)
stúltus, stúlta, stúltum - foolish (4)
supérbus, supérba, supérbum - arrogant, overbearing, haughty, proud (26)
súperus, súpera, súperum - above, upper (27)
súus, súa, súum - his own, her own, its own, their own (13)
tántus, tánta, tántum - so large, so great, of such a size (29)
tṓtus, tṓta, tṓtum - whole, entire (9)
túus, túa, túum - your *(sing.)* (2)
ū́llus, ū́lla, ū́llum - any (9)
últimus, última, últimum - farthest, extreme; last, final (25)
ū́nus, ū́na, ū́num - one, single, alone (9)
urbā́nus, urbā́na, urbā́num - of the city, urban; urbane, elegant (26)
úter, útra, útrum - either, which (of two) (9)
vḗrus, vḗra, vḗrum - true, real, proper (4)
véster, véstra, véstrum - your *(pl.)* (6)

3rd Declension

ā́cer, ā́cris, ā́cre - sharp, keen, eager; severe, fierce (16)
brévis, bréve - short, small, brief (16)
céler, céleris, célere - swift, quick, rapid (16)
commū́nis, commū́ne - common, general, of / for the community (20)
diffícilis, diffícile - hard, difficult, troublesome (16)
dī́ligēns, *gen.* dīligéntis - diligent, careful (27)
dissímilis, dissímile - unlike, different (27)
dúlcis, dúlce - sweet; pleasant, agreeable (16)
fácilis, fácile - easy; agreeable (16)
fḗlīx, *gen.* fēlī́cis - lucky, fortunate, happy (22)
férōx, *gen.* ferṓcis - fierce, savage (25)
fidḗlis, fidḗle - faithful, loyal (25)
fórtis, fórte - strong, brave (16)
grácilis, grácile - slender, thin (27)
grávis, gráve - heavy, weighty; serious, important; severe, grievous (19)
húmilis, húmile - lowly, humble (27)
immortā́lis, immortā́le - not subject to death, immortal (19)
íngēns, *gen.* ingéntis - huge (16)
lévis, léve - light; easy; slight, trivial (17)
máior, máius - greater; older (27)
mortā́lis, mortā́le - mortal (18)
ómnis, ómne - every, all (16)
pótēns, *gen.* poténtis - able, powerful, mighty, strong (16)
prī́nceps, *gen.* prī́ncipis - chief, foremost (28)
sápiēns, *gen.* sapiéntis - wise, judicious (25)
sénex, *gen.* sénis - old, aged (16)
símilis, símile (+gen. or dat.) - similar (to), like, resembling (27)
trī́stis, trī́ste - sad, sorrowful; joyless, grim, severe (26)
túrpis, túrpe - ugly; shameful, base, disgraceful (26)
ū́tilis, ū́tile - useful, advantageous (27)

Indeclinable Adjective

quot - how many, as many as (27)
sátis - enough, sufficient (5)

Indefinite Adjective

quī́dam, quaédam, quóddam - a certain, some (26)

Interrogative Adjective

quī?, quae?, quod? - what? which? what kind of?; *(sometimes with exclamatory force)* what (a)! what sort of! (19)

Verbs

1st Conjugation

ádiuvō, adiuvā́re, adiū́vī, adiū́tum - to help, aid, assist; to please (4)

ámō, amā́re, amā́vī, amā́tum - to love, like (1)

appéllō, appellā́re, appellā́vī, appellā́tum - to speak to, address (as), call, name (14)

cḗnō, cēnā́re, cēnā́vī, cēnā́tum - to dine (5)

cṓgitō, cōgitā́re, cōgitā́vī, cōgitā́tum- to think, ponder, consider, plan (1)

cōnsérvō, cōnservā́re, cōnservā́vī, cōnservā́tum - to preserve, conserve, maintain (1)

créō, creā́re, creā́vī, creā́tum - to create (12)

cúlpō, culpā́re, culpā́vī, culpā́tum - to blame, censure (5)

dḗdicō, dēdicā́re, dēdicā́vī, dēdicā́tum - to dedicate (28)

dēléctō, dēlectā́re, dēlectā́vī, dēlectā́tum - to delight, charm, please (19)

dēmṓnstrō, dēmōnstrā́re, dēmōnstrā́vī, dēmōnstrā́tum to point out, show, demonstrate (8)

dēsī́derō, dēsīderā́re, dēsīderā́vī, dēsīderā́tum - to desire, long for, miss (17)

dō, dáre, dédī, dátum - to give, offer (1)

ḗducō, ēducā́re, ēducā́vī, ēducā́tum - to bring up, educate (23)

érrō, errā́re, errā́vī, errā́tum - to wander; err, go astray, make a mistake, be mistaken (1)

exspéctō, exspectā́re, exspectā́vī, exspectā́tum - to look for, expect, await (15)

invī́tō, invītā́re, invītā́vī, invītā́tum - to entertain, invite, summon (26)

iúvō, iuvā́re, iū́vī, iū́tum - to help, aid, assist; to please (4)

labṓrō, labōrā́re, labōrā́vī, labōrā́tum - to labor; be in distress (21)

laúdō, laudā́re, laudā́vī, laudā́tum - to praise (1)

lī́berō, līberā́re, līberā́vī, līberā́tum - to free, liberate (19)

mū́tō, mūtā́re, mūtā́vī, mūtā́tum to change, alter; exchange (14)

nā́rrō, nārrā́re, nārrā́vī, nārrā́tum - to tell, report, narrate (24)

nā́vigō, nāvigā́re, nāvigā́vī, nāvigā́tum - to sail, navigate (17)

nécō, necā́re, necā́vī, necā́tum - to murder, kill (7)

négō, negā́re, negā́vī, negā́tum to deny, say that . . . not (25)

nū́ntiō, nūntiā́re, nūntiā́vī, nūntiā́tum - to announce, report, relate (25)

párō, parā́re, parā́vī, parā́tum - to prepare, provide; get, obtain (19)

praéstō, praestā́re, praéstitī, praéstitum - to excel; exhibit, show, offer, supply, furnish (28)

próbō, probā́re, probā́vī, probā́tum - to approve, recommend; test (27)

prōnū́ntiō, prōnūntiā́re, prōnūntiā́vī, prōnūntiā́tum - to proclaim, announce; declaim; pronounce (20)

púgnō, pugnā́re, pugnā́vī, pugnā́tum - to fight (29)

pútō, putā́re, putā́vī, putā́tum - to reckon, suppose, judge, think, imagine (25)

récitō, recitā́re, recitā́vī, recitā́tum - to read aloud, recite (17)

sátiō, satiā́re, satiā́vī, satiā́tum - to satisfy, sate (3)

sérvō, servā́re, servā́vī, servā́tum - to preserve, save, keep, guard (1)

spḗrō, spērā́re, spērā́vī, spērā́tum - to hope for, hope (25)

stō, stā́re, stétī, státum - to stand, stand still *or* firm (13)

súperō, superā́re, superā́vī, superā́tum - to be above, have the upper hand, surpass; overcome, conquer (5)

tólerō, tolerā́re, tolerā́vī, tolerā́tum - to bear, endure (6)

vī́tō, vītā́re, vītā́vī, vītā́tum - to avoid, shun (14)

vócō, vocā́re, vocā́vī, vocā́tum - to call, summon (1)

2nd Conjugation

aúdeō, audḗre, aúsus sum - to dare (7)

cáreō, carḗre, cáruī, caritū́rum (+abl.) - to be without, be deprived of, want, lack; be free from (20)

contíneō, continḗre, contínuī, conténtum - to hold together, contain, keep, enclose, restrain (21)

débeō, dēbḗre, dḗbuī, dḗbitum - to owe; ought, must, should (1)
déleō, dēlḗre, dēlḗvī, dēlḗtum - to destroy, wipe out, erase (17)
dóceō, docḗre, dócuī, dóctum - to teach (8)
égeō, egḗre, éguī (+ abl. or gen.) - to need, lack, want (28)
éxpleō, explḗre, explḗvī, explḗtum - to fill, fill up, complete (28)
gaúdeō, gaudḗre, gāvī́sus sum - to be glad, rejoice (23)
hábeō, habḗre, hábuī, hábitum - to have, hold, possess; consider, regard (3)
iáceō, iacḗre, iácuī - to lie; lie prostrate; lie dead (25)
iúbeō, iubḗre, iússī, iússum - to bid, order, command (21)
máneō, manḗre, mā́nsī, mā́nsum - to remain, stay, stay behind, abide, continue (5)
mísceō, miscḗre, míscuī, míxtum to mix, stir up, disturb (18)
móneō, monḗre, mónuī, mónitum - to remind, advise, warn (1)
móveō, movḗre, mṓvī, mṓtum - to move; arouse, affect (18)
prohíbeō, prohibḗre, prohíbuī, prohíbitum - to keep (back), prevent, hinder, restrain, prohibit (20)
remáneō, remanḗre, remā́nsī, remā́nsum - to remain, stay, stay behind, abide, continue (5)
respóndeō, respondḗre, respóndī, respṓnsum - to answer (29)
rī́deō, rīdḗre, rī́sī, rī́sum - to laugh, laugh at (24)
sálvē, salvḗte - hello, greetings (1)
sálveō, salvḗre - to be well, be in good health (1)
táceō, tacḗre, tácuī, tácitum - to be silent, leave unmentioned (28)
téneō, tenḗre, ténuī, téntum - to hold, keep, possess; restrain (14)
térreō, terrḗre, térruī, térritum - to frighten, terrify (1)
tímeō, timḗre, tímuī - to fear, be afraid (of) (15)
válē, valḗte - good-bye, farewell (1)
váleō, valḗre, váluī, valitū́rum - to be strong, have power; be well (1)
vídeō, vidḗre, vī́dī, vī́sum - to see; observe, understand (1)
vídeor, vidḗrī, vī́sus sum - to be seen, seem, appear (18)

3rd Conjugation

admíttō, admíttere, admī́sī, admíssum - to admit, receive, let in (17)
ágō, ágere, ḗgī, ā́ctum - to drive, lead, do, act; pass, spend *(life or time)* (8)
álō, álere, áluī, áltum - to nourish, support, sustain, increase; cherish (13)
āmíttō, āmíttere, āmī́sī, āmíssum - to send away; lose, let go (12)
āvértō, āvértere, āvértī, āvérsum - to turn away, avert (23)
cádō, cádere, cécidī, cāsū́rum - to fall (12)
cḗdō, cḗdere, céssī, céssum - to go, withdraw; yield to, grant, submit (28)
cérnō, cérnere, crḗvī, crḗtum - to distinguish, discern, perceive (22)
commíttō, commíttere, commī́sī, commíssum - to entrust, commit (15)
cóndō, cóndere, cóndidī, cónditum - to put together *or* into, store; found, establish (29)
conténdō, conténdere, conténdī, conténtum - to strive, struggle, contend; hasten (29)
crḗdō, crḗdere, crḗdidī, crḗditum to believe, trust (25)
cúrrō, cúrrere, cucúrrī, cúrsum - to run, rush, move quickly (14)
dēféndō, dēféndere, dēféndī, dēfḗnsum - to ward off; defend, protect (20)
dī́cō, dī́cere, dī́xī, díctum - to say, tell, speak; name, call (10)
dī́ligō, dīlígere, dīlḗxī, dīléctum - to esteem, love (13)
discḗdō, discḗdere, discéssī, discéssum - to go away, depart (20)
díscō, díscere, dídicī - to learn (8)
dū́cō, dū́cere, dū́xī, dúctum - to lead; consider, regard; prolong (8)
expéllō, expéllere, éxpulī, expúlsum - to drive out, expel, banish (24)
flúō, flúere, flū́xī, flū́xum - to flow (18)
gérō, gérere, géssī, géstum - to carry; carry on, manage, conduct, wage, accomplish, perform (8)
intéllegō, intellégere, intellḗxī, intellḗctum - to understand (11)
iúngō, iúngere, iū́nxī, iū́nctum - to join (13)
légō, légere, lḗgī, lḗctum - to pick out, choose; read (18)

míttō, míttere, mísī, míssum - to send, let go (11)
néglegō, neglégere, negléxī, negléctum - to neglect, disregard (17)
ópprimō, opprímere, oppréssī, oppréssum - to suppress, overwhelm, overpower, check (23)
osténdō, osténdere, osténdī, osténtum - to exhibit, show, display (23)
péllō, péllere, pépulī, púlsum - to strike, push; drive out, banish (24)
pétō, pétere, petívī, petítum - to seek, aim at, beg, beseech (23)
pṓnō, pṓnere, pósuī, pósitum - to put, place, set (27)
prémō, prémere, préssī, préssum - to press; press hard, pursue (23)
quaérō, quaérere, quaesívī, quaesítum - to seek, look for, strive for; ask, inquire, inquire into (24)
régō, régere, réxī, réctum - to rule, guide, direct (16)
relínquō, relínquere, relíquī, relíctum - to leave behind, leave, abandon, desert (21)
revértō, revértere, revértī, revérsum - turn back (23)
scríbō, scríbere, scrípsī, scríptum to write, compose (8)
súrgō, súrgere, surréxī, surréctum - to get up, arise (29)
tángō, tángere, tétigī, táctum - to touch (21)
tóllō, tóllere, sústulī, sublátum - to raise, lift up; take away, remove, destroy (22)
tráhō, tráhere, tráxī, tráctum - to draw, drag; derive, acquire (8)
vértō, vértere, vértī, vérsum - to turn; change (23)
víncō, víncere, vícī, víctum - to conquer, overcome (8)
vívō, vívere, víxī, víctum - to live (10)

3rd Conjugation -iō

accípiō, accípere, accḗpī, accéptum - to take *(to one's self)*, receive, accept (24)
cápiō, cápere, cḗpī, cáptum - to take, capture, seize, get (10)
cúpiō, cúpere, cupívī, cupítum - to desire, wish, long for (17)
ērípiō, ērípere, ērípuī, ēréptum - to snatch away, take away; rescue (22)
excípiō, excípere, excḗpī, excéptum - to take out, except; take, receive, capture (24)
fáciō, fácere, fḗcī, fáctum - to make, do, accomplish (10)
fúgiō, fúgere, fū́gī, fugitū́rum - to flee, hurry away; escape; go into exile; avoid, shun (10)
iáciō, iácere, iḗcī, iáctum - to throw, hurl (15)
incípiō, incípere, incḗpī, incéptum - to begin (17)
patefáciō, patefácere, patefḗcī, patefáctum - to make open, open; disclose, expose (25)
rápiō, rápere, rápuī, ráptum - to seize, snatch, carry away (21)
recípiō, recípere, recḗpī, recéptum - to take back, regain; admit, receive (24)
suscípiō, suscípere, suscḗpī, suscéptum - to undertake (25)

4th Conjugation

aúdiō, audíre, audívī, audítum - to hear, listen to (10)
invéniō, inveníre, invḗnī, invéntum - to come upon, find (10)
mólliō, mollíre, mollívī, mollítum to soften; make calm *or* less hostile (29)
nésciō, nescíre, nescívī, nescítum - to not know, be ignorant (25)
scíō, scíre, scívī, scítum - to know (21)
séntiō, sentíre, sḗnsī, sḗnsum - to feel, perceive, think, experience (11)
véniō, veníre, vḗnī, véntum - to come (10)

Irregular

póssum, pósse, pótuī - to be able, can, could, have power (6)
sum, ésse, fúī, futū́rum - to be, exist (4)

Defective

áit, áiunt - he says, they say, assert (25)
coépī, coepísse, coéptum - began (17)
ínquit - he says *or* said (22)
ṓdī, ōdísse, ōsū́rum - to hate (20)

Adverbs

ánte (+acc.) - before, previously (13)
béne - well, satisfactorily, quite (11)
cíto - quickly (17)
crās - tomorrow (5)
cūr - why (18)
déhinc - then, next (25)
deínde - thereupon, next, then (18)
dḗnique - at last, finally, lastly (29)
diū - long, for a long time (12)
étiam - even, also (11)
héri - yesterday (5)

hīc - here (25)
hódiē - today (3)
iam - now, already, soon (19)
íbi - there (6)
íta - so, thus (29)
ítaque - and so, therefore (15)
íterum - again, a second time (21)
nē . . . quídem - not . . . even (29)
nímis, nímium - too, too much, excessively; *(in a positive sense, esp. with adjectives and adverbs)* exceedingly, very (9)
nōn - not (1)
númquam - never (8)
nunc - now, at present (6)
nū́per - recently (12)
ṓlim - once (upon a time), long ago, formerly; some day, in the future (13)
pósteā - afterwards (24)
prṓtinus - immediately (22)
quam - how (16)
quam - than *(after comparatives);* as . . . as possible *(with superlatives)* (26)
quándō - when (5)
quā́rē - because of which thing *(lit.);* therefore, wherefore, why (6)
quídem - indeed, certainly, at least, even (29)
quóndam - formerly, once (22)
quóque - also, too (17)
saépe - often (1)
sátis - enough, sufficiently (5)
sémper - always (3)
sīc - so, thus (29)
tam - so, to such a degree (29)
tam . . . quam - so . . . as (29)
támen - nevertheless, still (8)
tamquam - as it were, as if, so to speak (29)
tántum - only (26)
tum - then, at that time; thereupon, in the next place (5)
úbi - where, when (6)
últrā - on the other side of, beyond (22)
úmquam - ever, at any time (23)
vḗrō - in truth, indeed, to be sure, however (29)

Conjunctions

at - but; but, mind you; but, you say (19)
átque, ac - and also, and even, and in fact (21)
aut - or (17)
aut . . . aut - either . . . or (17)
aútem - however; moreover (11)
dum - while, as long as, at the same time that; *or* until *(+subjunctive)* (8)
énim - for, in fact, truly (9)
et - and; even (2)
et . . . et - both . . . and (2)
ígitur - therefore, consequently (5)
nam - for (13)
nē - not; in order that . . . not, that . . . not, in order not to (28)
néque, nec - and not, nor (11)
néque . . . néque, nec . . . nec - neither . . . nor (11)
nísi - if . . . not, unless; except (19)
quod - because (11)
quóniam - since, inasmuch as (10)
sed - but (2)
sī - if (1)
ut (+indic.) - as, just as, when (24)
ut (+ subj.) - in order that, so that, that, in order to, so as to, to (28)

Prepositions

ab, ā (+abl.) - away from, from; by (14)
ad (+acc.) - to, up to, near to (8)
ánte (+acc.) - before *(in place or time),* in front of (13)
cóntrā (+acc.) - against (19)
cum (+abl.) - with (10)
dē (+abl.) - down from, from; concerning, about (3)
ex, ē (abl.+) - out of, from, from within; by reason of, on account of ; of *(after cardinal numerals)* (8)
in (+acc.) - into, toward; against (9)
in (+abl.) - in, on (3)
ínter (+acc.) - between, among (15)
per (+acc.) - through; by *(with reflexive pronoun)* (13)
post (+acc.) - after, behind (7)
prae (+abl.) - in front of, before (26)
prō (+abl.) - in front of, before, on behalf of, for the sake of, in return for, instead of, for, as (12)
própter (+acc.) - on account of, because of (5)
síne (+abl.) - without (2)
sub (+abl. w/ verbs of rest *or* +acc. w/ verbs of motion) - under, up under, close to, down to/into, to/at the foot of (7)
trāns (+acc.) - across (14)
últrā (adv. and prep. +acc.) - on the other side of, beyond (22)

Interjection

ō - O!, Oh! (2)

Idioms

amā́bō tē - please (1)
grā́tiās ágere (+dat.) - to thank someone; to give thanks to (8)
mḗnsa secúnda (f) - dessert (26)
nōn sṓlum . . . sed étiam - not only . . . but also (9)

poénās dáre - to pay the penalty (2)
sī quándō - if ever (5)

Prefix

re-, red- - again, back (24)

Suffixes

-ne – interrogative suffix attached to the first word of a sentence, typically the verb or another word on which the question hinges, to introduce a question whose answer is uncertain (5)
-que - and *(enclitic conjunction; appended to the second of two words to be joined)* (6)

Numerals

Cardinal - ū́nus *to* vīgíntī quī́nque (15)
Ordinal - prī́mus *to* duodécimus (15)

----

céntum - a hundred (15)
mī́lia, mī́lium (n. pl.) - thousands (15)
mī́lle - thousand (15)

Chapter 30

Nouns

1st Declension

adulēscéntia, adulēscéntiae (f) - youth, young manhood; youthfulness (5)
agrícola, agrícolae (m) - farmer (3)
amíca, amícae (f) - friend (female) (3)
amīcítia, amīcítiae (f) - friendship (10)
áqua, áquae (f) - water (14)
Ásia, Ásiae (f) - Asia (12)
cása, cásae (f) - house, cottage, hut (21)
caúsa, caúsae (f) - cause, reason; case, situation (21)
caúsā (abl. + preceding gen.) - for the sake of, on account of (21)
cḗna, cḗnae (f) - dinner (26)
clēméntia, clēméntiae (f) - mildness, gentleness, mercy (16)
cṓpia, cṓpiae (f) - abundance, supply (8)
cṓpiae, cōpiā́rum (f) - supplies, troops, forces (8)
cúlpa, cúlpae (f) - fault, blame (5)
cū́ra, cū́rae (f) - care, attention, caution, anxiety (4)
déa, déae (f) - goddess (6)
discípula, discípulae (f) - learner, pupil, student (female) (6)
dīvítiae, dīvitiā́rum (f. pl.) - riches, wealth (13)
fā́bula, fā́bulae (f) - story, tale; play (24)
fā́ma, fā́mae (f) - rumor, report; fame, reputation (2)
família, famíliae (f) - household, family (19)
fḗmina, fḗminae (f) - woman (3)
fenéstra, fenéstrae (f) - window (21)
fī́lia, fī́liae (f) - daughter (3)
fṓrma, fṓrmae (f) - form, shape; beauty (2)
fortū́na, fortū́nae (f) - fortune, luck (2)
glṓria, glṓriae (f) - glory, fame (5)
Graécia, Graéciae (f) - Greece (19)
hásta, hástae (f) - spear (23)
hṓra, hṓrae (f) - hour, time (10)
īnsídiae, īnsidiā́rum (f) - ambush, plot, treachery (6)
ī́nsula, ī́nsulae (f) - island (23)
ī́ra, ī́rae (f) - ire, anger (2)
Itália, Itáliae (f) - Italy (15)
língua, línguae (f) - tongue; language (25)
líttera, lítterae (f) - a letter of the alphabet (7)
lítterae, litterā́rum (f) - a letter (epistle), literature (7)
lū́na, lū́nae (f) - moon (28)
magístra, magístrae (f) - schoolmistress, teacher, mistress (4)
médica, médicae (f) - doctor, physician (female) (12)
memória, memóriae (f) - memory, recollection (15)
mḗnsa, mḗnsae (f) - table; dining; dish, course (26)
móra, mórae (f) - delay (4)
nā́ta, nā́tae (f) - daughter (29)
nātū́ra, nātū́rae (f) - nature (10)
naúta, naútae (m) - sailor (2)
patiéntia, patiéntiae (f) - suffering; patience, endurance (12)
pátria, pátriae (f) - fatherland, native land, (one's) country (2)
pecū́nia, pecū́niae (f) - money (2)
philosóphia, philosóphiae (f) - philosophy (2)
poéna, poénae (f) - penalty, punishment (2)
poḗta, poḗtae (m) - poet (2)
pórta, pórtae (f) - gate, entrance (2)
puélla, puéllae (f) - girl (2)
rēgī́na, rēgī́nae (f) - queen (7)
Rṓma, Rṓmae (f) - Rome (14)
rósa, rósae (f) - rose (2)
sapiéntia, sapiéntiae (f) - wisdom (3)
sátura, sáturae (f) - satire (16)
sciéntia, sciéntiae (f) - knowledge (18)
senténtia, senténtiae (f) - feeling, thought, opinion, vote, sentence (2)
sérva, sérvae (f) - slave (female) (24)
stḗlla, stḗllae (f) - star, planet (28)
térra, térrae (f) - earth, ground, land, country (7)
Trṓia, Trṓiae (f) - Troy (21)
túrba, túrbae (f) - uproar, disturbance; mob, crowd, multitude (14)
vía, víae (f) - way, road, street (10)
vīcī́na, vīcī́nae (f) - neighbor (female) (21)
victṓria, victṓriae (f) - victory (8)
vī́ta, vī́tae (f) - life; mode of life (2)

2nd Declension

áger, ágrī (m) - field, farm (3)
amī́cus, amī́cī (m) - friend (male) (3)
ánimī, animṓrum (m) - high spirits, pride, courage (5)
ánimus, ánimī (m) - soul, spirit, mind (5)
ánnus, ánnī (m) - year (12)
argūméntum, argūméntī (n) - proof, evidence, argument (19)
árma, armṓrum (n. pl.) - arms, weapons (28)

bā́sium, bā́siī (n) - kiss (4)
béllum, béllī (n) - war (4)
benefícium, benefíciī (n) - benefit, kindness; favor (19)
caélum, caélī (n) - sky, heaven (5)
coniūrā́tī, coniūrātṓrum (m. pl.) - conspirators (20)
cōnsílium, cōnsíliī (n) - plan, purpose, counsel, advice, judgment, wisdom (4)
déus, déī (m) - god (6)
discípulus, discípulī (m) - learner, pupil, student (male) (6)
dṓnum, dṓnī (n) - gift, present (4)
équus, équī (m) - horse (23)
exítium, exítiī (n) - destruction, ruin (4)
fáctum, fáctī (n) - deed, act, achievement (13)
fā́tum, fā́tī (n) - fate; death (29)
férrum, férrī (n) - iron; sword (22)
fī́lius, fī́liī (m) - son (3)
fórum, fórī (n) - marketplace, forum (26)
Graécus, Graécī (m) - a Greek (6)
impérium, impériī (n) - power to command, supreme power, authority, command, control (24)
ingénium, ingéniī (n) - nature, innate talent (29)
iūdícium, iūdíciī (n) - judgment, decision, opinion; trial (19)
libéllus, libéllī (m) - little book (17)
líber, líbrī (m) - book (6)
lóca, locṓrum (n) - places, region (9)
lócī, locṓrum (m) - passages in literature (9)
lócus, lócī (m) - place; passage in literature (9)
lū́dus, lū́dī (m) - game, sport; school (18)
magíster, magístrī (m) - schoolmaster, teacher, master (4)
médicus, médicī (m) - doctor, physician (male) (12)
módus, módī (m) - measure, bound, limit; manner, method, mode, way (22)
mórbus, mórbī (m) - disease, sickness (9)
múndus, múndī (m) - world, universe (21)
númerus, númerī (m) - number (3)
óculus, óculī (m) - eye (4)
offícium, offíciī (n) - duty, service (4)
ṓsculum, ṓsculī (n) - kiss (29)
ṓtium, ṓtiī (n) - leisure, peace (4)
perfúgium, perfúgiī (n) - refuge, shelter (24)
perī́culum, perī́culī (n) - danger, risk (4)
pópulus, pópulī (m) - the people, a people, a nation (3)
prīncípium, prīncípiī (n) - beginning (12)
púer, púerī (m) - boy; boys, children *(pl.)* (3)
remédium, remédiī (n) - cure, remedy (4)
sérvus, sérvī (m) - slave (male) (24)
sígnum, sígnī (n) - sign, signal, indication; seal (13)
sōlā́cium, sōlā́ciī (n) - comfort, relief (24)
sómnus, sómnī (m) - sleep (26)
stúdium, stúdiī (n) - eagerness, zeal, pursuit, study (9)
stúltus, stúltī (m) - a fool (4)
súperī, superṓrum (m. pl.) - the gods (27)
tyránnus, tyránnī (m) - absolute ruler, tyrant (6)
vérbum, vérbī (n)- word (5)
vīcī́nus, vīcī́nī (m) - neighbor (male) (21)
vir, vírī (m) - man, hero (3)
vítium, vítiī (n) - fault, crime, vice (6)
vúlgus, vúlgī (n) - the common people, mob, rabble (21)

3rd Declension

adulḗscēns, adulēscéntis (m *or* f) - young man *or* woman (12)
aétās, aetā́tis (f) - period of life, life, age, an age, time (16)
ámor, amṓris (m) - love (7)
aúctor, auctṓris (m) - increaser; author, originator (19)
audī́tor, audītṓris (m) - hearer, listener, member of an audience (16)
Caésar, Caésaris (m) - Caesar (12)
cáput, cápitis (n) - head; leader; beginning; life; heading; chapter (11)
cármen, cárminis (n) - song, poem (7)
Carthā́gō, Carthā́ginis (f) - Carthage (24)
Cícerō, Cicerṓnis (m) - (Marcus Tullius) Cicero (8)
cī́vitās, cīvitā́tis (f) - state, citizenship (7)
cṓnsul, cṓnsulis (m) - consul (11)
córpus, córporis (n) - body (7)
cupíditās, cupiditā́tis (f) - desire, longing, passion; cupidity, avarice (10)
dēlectā́tiō, dēlectātiṓnis (f) - delight, pleasure, enjoyment (27)
dux, dúcis (m) - leader, guide; commander, general (23)
flū́men, flū́minis (n) - river (18)
frā́ter, frā́tris (m) - brother (8)
génus, géneris (n) - origin; kind, type, sort, class (18)
hómō, hóminis (m) - human being, man (7)

hónor, honṓris (m) - honor, esteem; public office (30)
imperā́tor, imperātṓris (m) - general, commander-in-chief, emperor (24)
iū́dex, iū́dicis (m) - judge, juror (19)
iūs, iū́ris (n) - right, justice, law (14)
lábor, labṓris (m)- labor, work, toil; a work, production (7)
laus, laúdis (f) - praise, glory, fame (8)
lēx, lḗgis (f) - law, statute (26)
lībértās, lībertā́tis (f) - liberty (8)
lī́men, lī́minis (n) - threshold (26)
lī́tus, lī́toris (n) - shore, coast (23)
lūx, lū́cis (f) - light (26)
maiṓrēs, maiṓrum (m. pl.) - ancestors (27)
mā́ter, mā́tris (f) - mother (12)
mī́les, mī́litis (m) - soldier (23)
mṓrēs, mṓrum (m) - habits, morals, character (7)
mōs, mṓris (m) - habit, custom, manner (7)
nḗmō, nūllī́us, nḗminī, nḗminem, nū́llō, nū́llā (m *or* f) - no one, nobody (11)
népōs, nepṓtis (m) - grandson, descendant (27)
nṓmen, nṓminis (n) - name (7)
occā́siō, occāsiṓnis (f) - occasion, opportunity (28)
ōrā́tor, ōrātṓris (m) - orator, speaker (23)
ōs, ṓris (n) - mouth, face (14)
párēns, paréntis (m *or* f) - parent (28)
páter, pátris (m) - father (12)
pāx, pā́cis (f) - peace (7)
prī́nceps, prī́ncipis (m *or* f) - leader, emperor (28)
próbitās, probitā́tis (f) - uprightness, honesty (18)
rátiō, ratiṓnis (f) - reckoning, account; reason, judgment, consideration; system; manner, method (8)
rēx, rḗgis (m) - king (7)
sacérdōs, sacerdṓtis (m) - priest (23)
sálūs, salū́tis (f) - health, safety; greeting (21)
sápiēns, sapiéntis (m/f) - a wise man/woman, philosopher (25)
scélus, scéleris (n) - evil deed, crime, sin, wickedness (19)
scrī́ptor, scrīptṓris (m) - writer, author (8)
senéctūs, senectū́tis (f) - old age (10)
sénex, sénis (m) - old man (16)
sérvitūs, servitū́tis (f) - servitude, slavery (20)
sī́dus, sī́deris (n) - constellation, star (29)
sōl, sṓlis (m) - sun (27)
sóror, sorṓris (f) - sister (8)
tempéstās, tempestā́tis (f) - period of time, season; weather, storm (15)
témpus, témporis (n) - time; occasion, opportunity (7)
tímor, timṓris (m) - fear (10)
úxor, uxṓris (f) - wife (7)
vḗritās, vēritā́tis (f) - truth (10)
vésper, vésperis *or* vésperī (m) - evening; evening star (28)
vírgō, vírginis (f) - maiden, virgin (7)
vírtūs, virtū́tis (f) - manliness, courage; excellence, character, worth, virtue (7)
volúptās, voluptā́tis (f) - pleasure (10)
vúlnus, vúlneris (n) - wound (24)

3rd Declension I-Stem

ánimal, animā́lis (n) - a living creature, animal (14)
ars, ártis (f) - art, skill (14)
arx, árcis (f) - citadel, stronghold (23)
aúris, aúris (f) - ear (14)
cī́vis, cī́vis (m *or* f) - citizen (14)
fī́nēs, fī́nium (m) - boundaries, territory (21)
fī́nis, fī́nis (m) - end, limit, boundary; purpose (21)
gēns, géntis (f) - clan, race, nation, people (21)
hóstēs, hóstium (m) - the enemy (18)
hóstis, hóstis (m) - an enemy *(of the state)* (18)
ígnis, ígnis (m) - fire (22)
máre, máris (n) - sea (14)
mēns, méntis (f) - mind, thought, intention (16)
moénia, moénium (n. pl.) - walls of a city (29)
mōns, móntis (m) - mountain (20)
mors, mórtis (f) - death (14)
nā́vis, nā́vis (f) - ship, boat (21)
nox, nóctis (f) - night (26)
nū́bēs, nū́bis (f) - cloud (14)
pars, pártis (f) - part, share; direction (14)
urbs, úrbis (f) - city (14)
vī́rēs, vī́rium (f. pl.) - strength (14)
vīs, vīs (f) - force, power, violence (14)

4th Declension

córnū, córnūs (n) - horn (20)
cúrsus, cúrsūs (m) - running, race; course (28)
frū́ctus, frū́ctūs (m) - fruit; profit, benefit, enjoyment (20)
génū, génūs (n) - knee (20)
mánus, mánūs (f) - hand; handwriting; band (20)
métus, métūs (m) - fear, dread, anxiety (20)
senā́tus, senā́tūs (m) - senate (20)

sḗnsus, sḗnsūs (m) - feeling, sense (20)
spī́ritus, spī́ritūs (m) - breath, breathing; spirit, soul (20)
vérsus, vérsūs (m) - line of verse (20)

5th Declension
díēs, diḗī (m) - day (22)
fídēs, fídeī (f) - faith, trust, trustworthiness, fidelity, promise, guarantee, protection (22)
rēs, réī (f) - thing, matter, property, business, affair (22)
rēs pū́blica, réī pū́blicae (f) - state, commonwealth, republic (22)
spēs, spéī (f) - hope (22)

Indeclinable
níhil - nothing (1)
sátis - enough (5)

Pronouns
áliquis, áliquid - someone, somebody, something (23)
égo, méī - I (11)
hic, haec, hoc - this; the latter; he, she, it, they (9)
ī́dem, éadem, ídem - the same (11)
ílle, ílla, íllud - that; the former; the famous; he, she, it, they (9)
ípse, ípsa, ípsum - myself, yourself, himself, herself, itself, *etc.*, the very, the actual (13)
is, éa, id - this, that; he, she, it (11)
íste, ísta, ístud - that of yours, that; such (as you have, as you speak of); *sometimes with contemptuous force, e.g.,* that despicable, that wretched (9)
quī, quae, quod - who, which, what, that (17)
quid - what (1)
quī́dam, quaédam, quíddam - a certain one or thing, someone, something (26)
quis? quid? - who? whose? whom? what? which? (19)
quísque, quídque, cuiúsque, cuíque - each one, each person, each thing (13)
quísquis, quídquid - whoever, whatever (23)
súī - himself, herself, itself, themselves (13)
tū, túī - you *(sing.)* (11)

Adjectives
1st & 2nd Declension
acérbus, acérba, acérbum - harsh, bitter, grievous (12)
aéquus, aéqua, aéquum - level, even; calm; equal, just; favorable (22)
áliī . . . áliī - some . . . others (9)
álius, ália, áliud - other, another (9)
álter, áltera, álterum - the other (of two), second (9)
amī́cus, amī́ca, amī́cum - friendly (11)
antī́quus, antī́qua, antī́quum - ancient, old-time (2)
ásper, áspera, ásperum - rough, harsh (21)
avā́rus, avā́ra, avā́rum - greedy, avaricious (3)
beā́tus, beā́ta, beā́tum - happy, fortunate, blessed (10)
béllus, bélla, béllum - pretty, handsome, charming (4)
bónus, bóna, bónum - good, kind (4)
caécus, caéca, caécum - blind (17)
cā́rus, cā́ra, cā́rum - dear (11)
cértus, cérta, cértum - definite, sure, certain, reliable (19)
cḗterī, cḗterae, cḗtera - the remaining, the rest, the other, all the others (30)
clā́rus, clā́ra, clā́rum - clear, bright; renowned, famous, illustrious (18)
déxter, déxtra, déxtrum - right, right-hand (20)
dígnus, dígna, dígnum (+abl.) - worthy, worthy of (29)
dóctus, dócta, dóctum - taught, learned, skilled (13)
dū́rus, dū́ra, dū́rum - hard, harsh, rough, stern, unfeeling, hardy, difficult (29)
fortūnā́tus, fortūnā́ta, fortūnā́tum - lucky, fortunate, happy (13)
géminus, gémina, géminum - twin (25)
Graécus, Graéca, Graécum - Greek (6)
hūmā́nus, hūmā́na, hūmā́num - pertaining to man, human; humane, kind; refined, cultivated (4)
incértus, incérta, incértum - uncertain, unsure, doubtful (22)
iūcúndus, iūcúnda, iūcúndum - pleasant, delightful, agreeable, pleasing (16)
Latī́nus, Latī́na, Latī́num - Latin (22)
lī́ber, lī́bera, lī́berum - free (5)
lóngus, lónga, lóngum - long (16)
magnánimus, magnánima, magnánimum - great-hearted, brave, magnanimous (23)
mágnus, mágna, mágnum - large, great; important (2)
málus, mála, málum - bad, wicked, evil (4)
médius, média, médium - middle; the middle of (22)
méus, méa, méum - my (2)

míser, mísera, míserum - wretched, miserable, unfortunate (15)
mórtuus, mórtua, mórtuum - dead (28)
múltus, múlta, múltum - much, many (2)
neúter, neútra, neútrum - not either, neither (9)
nóster, nóstra, nóstrum - our, ours (5)
nóvus, nóva, nóvum - new; strange (7)
nū́llus, nū́lla, nū́llum - not any, no, none (9)
párvus, párva, párvum - small, little (4)
paúcī, paúcae, paúca - few, a few (3)
perpétuus, perpétua, perpétuum perpetual, lasting, uninterrupted, continuous (6)
plḗnus, plḗna, plḗnum - full, abundant, generous (6)
prī́mus, prī́ma, prī́mum - first, foremost, chief, principal (27)
pudī́cus, pudī́ca, pudī́cum - modest, chaste (26)
púlcher, púlchra, púlchrum - beautiful, handsome; fine (5)
quántus, quánta, quántum - how large, how great, how much (30)
rīdículus, rīdícula, rīdículum - laughable, ridiculous (30)
Rōmā́nus, Rōmā́na, Rōmā́num - Roman (3)
sálvus, sálva, sálvum - safe, sound (6)
sā́nus, sā́na, sā́num - sound, healthy, sane (5)
secúndus, secúnda, secúndum - second; favorable (6)
siníster, sinístra, sinístrum - left, left-hand; harmful, ill-omened (20)

sṓlus, sṓla, sṓlum - alone, only, the only (9)
stúltus, stúlta, stúltum - foolish (4)
supérbus, supérba, supérbum - arrogant, overbearing, haughty, proud (26)
súperus, súpera, súperum - above, upper (27)
súus, súa, súum - his own, her own, its own, their own (13)
tántus, tánta, tántum - so large, so great, of such a size (29)
tántus . . . quántus - just as much (many) . . . as (30)
tṓtus, tṓta, tṓtum - whole, entire (9)
túus, túa, túum - your *(sing.)* (2)
ū́llus, ū́lla, ū́llum - any (9)
últimus, última, últimum - farthest, extreme; last, final (25)
ū́nus, ū́na, ū́num - one, single, alone (9)
urbā́nus, urbā́na, urbā́num - of the city, urban; urbane, elegant (26)
úter, útra, útrum - either, which (of two) (9)
vḗrus, vḗra, vḗrum - true, real, proper (4)
véster, véstra, véstrum - your *(pl.)* (6)
vī́vus, vī́va, vī́vum - alive, living (30)

3rd Declension

ā́cer, ā́cris, ā́cre - sharp, keen, eager; severe, fierce (16)
brévis, bréve - short, small, brief (16)
céler, céleris, célere - swift, quick, rapid (16)
commū́nis, commū́ne - common, general, of / for the community (20)

diffícilis, diffícile - hard, difficult, troublesome (16)
dī́ligēns, ***gen.*** **dīligéntis** - diligent, careful (27)
dissímilis, dissímile - unlike, different (27)
dúlcis, dúlce - sweet; pleasant, agreeable (16)
fácilis, fácile - easy; agreeable (16)
fḗlīx, ***gen.*** **fēlī́cis** - lucky, fortunate, happy (22)
férōx, ***gen.*** **ferṓcis** - fierce, savage (25)
fidḗlis, fidḗle - faithful, loyal (25)
fórtis, fórte - strong, brave (16)
grácilis, grácile - slender, thin (27)
grávis, gráve - heavy, weighty; serious, important; severe, grievous (19)
húmilis, húmile - lowly, humble (27)
immortā́lis, immortā́le - not subject to death, immortal (19)
íngēns, ***gen.*** **ingéntis** - huge (16)
lévis, léve - light; easy; slight, trivial (17)
máior, máius - greater; older (27)
mortā́lis, mortā́le - mortal (18)
ómnis, ómne - every, all (16)
pótēns, ***gen.*** **poténtis** - able, powerful, mighty, strong (16)
prī́nceps, ***gen.*** **prī́ncipis** - chief, foremost (28)
sápiēns, ***gen.*** **sapiéntis** - wise, judicious (25)
sénex, ***gen.*** **sénis** - old, aged (16)
símilis, símile (+gen. or dat.) - similar (to), like, resembling (27)
trī́stis, trī́ste - sad, sorrowful; joyless, grim, severe (26)

túrpis, túrpe - ugly; shameful, base, disgraceful (26)
ū́tilis, ū́tile - useful, advantageous (27)

Indeclinable Adjectives
quot - how many, as many as (27)
sátis - enough, sufficient (5)

Indefinite Adjective
quídam, quaédam, quóddam - a certain, some (26)

Interrogative Adjective
quī?, quae?, quod? - what? which? what kind of?; *(sometimes with exclamatory force)* what (a)! what sort of! (19)

Verbs

1st Conjugation
ádiuvō, adiuvā́re, adiū́vī, adiū́tum - to help, aid, assist; to please (4)
ámō, amā́re, amā́vī, amā́tum - to love, like (1)
appéllō, appellā́re, appellā́vī, appellā́tum - to speak to, address (as), call, name (14)
cḗnō, cēnā́re, cēnā́vī, cēnā́tum - to dine (5)
cṓgitō, cōgitā́re, cōgitā́vī, cōgitā́tum- to think, ponder, consider, plan (1)
cōnsérvō, cōnservā́re, cōnservā́vī, cōnservā́tum - to preserve, conserve, maintain (1)
créō, creā́re, creā́vī, creā́tum - to create (12)
cúlpō, culpā́re, culpā́vī, culpā́tum - to blame, censure (5)
dḗdicō, dēdicā́re, dēdicā́vī, dēdicā́tum - to dedicate (28)
dēléctō, dēlectā́re, dēlectā́vī, dēlectā́tum - to delight, charm, please (19)
dēmṓnstrō, dēmōnstrā́re, dēmōnstrā́vī, dēmōnstrā́tum to point out, show, demonstrate (8)
dēsī́derō, dēsīderā́re, dēsīderā́vī, dēsīderā́tum - to desire, long for, miss (17)
dō, dáre, dédī, dátum - to give, offer (1)
dúbitō, dubitā́re, dubitā́vī, dubitā́tum - to doubt, hesitate (30)
ḗducō, ēducā́re, ēducā́vī, ēducā́tum - to bring up, educate (23)
érrō, errā́re, errā́vī, errā́tum - to wander; err, go astray, make a mistake, be mistaken (1)
exspéctō, exspectā́re, exspectā́vī, exspectā́tum - to look for, expect, await (15)
invī́tō, invītā́re, invītā́vī, invītā́tum - to entertain, invite, summon (26)
iúvō, iuvā́re, iū́vī, iū́tum - to help, aid, assist; to please (4)
labṓrō, labōrā́re, labōrā́vī, labōrā́tum - to labor; be in distress (21)
laúdō, laudā́re, laudā́vī, laudā́tum - to praise (1)
lī́berō, līberā́re, līberā́vī, līberā́tum - to free, liberate (19)
mū́tō, mūtā́re, mūtā́vī, mūtā́tum to change, alter; exchange (14)
nā́rrō, nārrā́re, nārrā́vī, nārrā́tum - to tell, report, narrate (24)
nā́vigō, nāvigā́re, nāvigā́vī, nāvigā́tum - to sail, navigate (17)
nécō, necā́re, necā́vī, necā́tum - to murder, kill (7)
négō, negā́re, negā́vī, negā́tum to deny, say that . . . not (25)
nū́ntiō, nūntiā́re, nūntiā́vī, nūntiā́tum - to announce, report, relate (25)
párō, parā́re, parā́vī, parā́tum - to prepare, provide; get, obtain (19)
praéstō, praestā́re, praéstitī, praéstitum - to excel; exhibit, show, offer, supply, furnish (28)
próbō, probā́re, probā́vī, probā́tum - to approve, recommend; test (27)
prōnū́ntiō, prōnūntiā́re, prōnūntiā́vī, prōnūntiā́tum - to proclaim, announce; declaim; pronounce (20)
púgnō, pugnā́re, pugnā́vī, pugnā́tum - to fight (29)
pútō, putā́re, putā́vī, putā́tum - to reckon, suppose, judge, think, imagine (25)
récitō, recitā́re, recitā́vī, recitā́tum - to read aloud, recite (17)
rógō, rogā́re, rogā́vī, rogā́tum - to ask (30)
sátiō, satiā́re, satiā́vī, satiā́tum - to satisfy, sate (3)
sérvō, servā́re, servā́vī, servā́tum - to preserve, save, keep, guard (1)
spḗrō, spērā́re, spērā́vī, spērā́tum - to hope for, hope (25)
stō, stā́re, stétī, státum - to stand, stand still *or* firm (13)
súperō, superā́re, superā́vī, superā́tum - to be above, have the upper hand, surpass; overcome, conquer (5)

tólerō, tolerā́re, tolerā́vī, tolerā́tum - to bear, endure (6)
vī́tō, vītā́re, vītā́vī, vītā́tum - to avoid, shun (14)
vócō, vocā́re, vocā́vī, vocā́tum - to call, summon (1)

2nd Conjugation

aúdeō, audḗre, aúsus sum - to dare (7)
cáreō, carḗre, cáruī, caritū́rum (+abl.) - to be without, be deprived of, want, lack; be free from (20)
contíneō, continḗre, contínuī, conténtum - to hold together, contain, keep, enclose, restrain (21)
dḗbeō, dēbḗre, dḗbuī, dḗbitum - to owe; ought, must, should (1)
dḗleō, dēlḗre, dēlḗvī, dēlḗtum - to destroy, wipe out, erase (17)
dóceō, docḗre, dócuī, dóctum - to teach (8)
égeō, egḗre, éguī (+ abl. or gen.) - to need, lack, want (28)
éxpleō, explḗre, explḗvī, explḗtum - to fill, fill up, complete (28)
gaúdeō, gaudḗre, gāvī́sus sum - to be glad, rejoice (23)
hábeō, habḗre, hábuī, hábitum - to have, hold, possess; consider, regard (3)
iáceō, iacḗre, iácuī - to lie; lie prostrate; lie dead (25)
iúbeō, iubḗre, iússī, iússum - to bid, order, command (21)
máneō, manḗre, mā́nsī, mā́nsum - to remain, stay, stay behind, abide, continue (5)
mísceō, miscḗre, míscuī, míxtum to mix, stir up, disturb (18)
móneō, monḗre, mónuī, mónitum - to remind, advise, warn (1)
móveō, movḗre, mṓvī, mṓtum - to move; arouse, affect (18)
prohíbeō, prohibḗre, prohíbuī, prohíbitum - to keep (back), prevent, hinder, restrain, prohibit (20)
remáneō, remanḗre, remā́nsī, remā́nsum - to remain, stay, stay behind, abide, continue (5)
respóndeō, respondḗre, respóndī, respṓnsum - to answer (29)
rī́deō, rīdḗre, rī́sī, rī́sum - to laugh, laugh at (24)
sálvē, salvḗte - hello, greetings (1)
sálveō, salvḗre - to be well, be in good health (1)
táceō, tacḗre, tácuī, tácitum - to be silent, leave unmentioned (28)
téneō, tenḗre, ténuī, téntum - to hold, keep, possess; restrain (14)
térreō, terrḗre, térruī, térritum - to frighten, terrify (1)
tímeō, timḗre, tímuī - to fear, be afraid (of) (15)
válē, valḗte - good-bye, farewell (1)
váleō, valḗre, váluī, valitū́rum - to be strong, have power; be well (1)
vídeō, vidḗre, vī́dī, vī́sum - to see; observe, understand (1)
vídeor, vidḗrī, vī́sus sum - to be seen, seem, appear (18)

3rd Conjugation

admíttō, admíttere, admī́sī, admíssum - to admit, receive, let in (17)
ágō, ágere, ḗgī, ā́ctum - to drive, lead, do, act; pass, spend *(life or time)* (8)
álō, álere, áluī, áltum - to nourish, support, sustain, increase; cherish (13)
āmíttō, āmíttere, āmī́sī, āmíssum - to send away; lose, let go (12)
āvértō, āvértere, āvértī, āvérsum - to turn away, avert (23)
bíbō, bíbere, bíbī - to drink (30)
cádō, cádere, cécidī, cāsū́rum - to fall (12)
cḗdō, cḗdere, céssī, céssum - to go, withdraw; yield to, grant, submit (28)
cérnō, cérnere, crḗvī, crḗtum - to distinguish, discern, perceive (22)
cognṓscō, cognṓscere, cognṓvī, cógnitum - to become acquainted with, learn, recognize; know *(in perfect tenses)* (30)
commíttō, commíttere, commī́sī, commíssum - to entrust, commit (15)
comprehéndō, comprehéndere, comprehéndī, comprehḗnsum - to grasp, seize, arrest; comprehend, understand (30)
cóndō, cóndere, cóndidī, cónditum - to put together *or* into, store; found, establish (29)
cōnsū́mō, cōnsū́mere, cōnsū́mpsī, cōnsū́mptum - to consume, use up (30)
conténdō, conténdere, conténdī, conténtum - to strive, struggle, contend; hasten (29)
crḗdō, crḗdere, crḗdidī, crḗditum to believe, trust (25)

cúrrō, cúrrere, cucúrrī, cúrsum - to run, rush, move quickly (14)
dēféndō, dēféndere, dēféndī, dēfénsum - to ward off; defend, protect (20)
dícō, dícere, díxī, díctum - to say, tell, speak; name, call (10)
díligō, dīlígere, dīléxī, dīléctum - to esteem, love (13)
discédō, discédere, discéssī, discéssum - to go away, depart (20)
díscō, díscere, dídicī - to learn (8)
dúcō, dúcere, dúxī, dúctum - to lead; consider, regard; prolong (8)
expéllō, expéllere, éxpulī, expúlsum - to drive out, expel, banish (24)
expṓnō, expṓnere, expósuī, expósitum - to set forth, explain, expose (30)
flúō, flúere, flúxī, flúxum - to flow (18)
gérō, gérere, géssī, géstum - to carry; carry on, manage, conduct, wage, accomplish, perform (8)
intéllegō, intellégere, intelléxī, intelléctum - to understand (11)
iúngō, iúngere, iúnxī, iúnctum - to join (13)
légō, légere, légī, léctum - to pick out, choose; read (18)
mínuō, minúere, mínuī, minútum - to lessen, diminish (30)
míttō, míttere, mísī, míssum - to send, let go (11)
néglegō, neglégere, negléxī, negléctum - to neglect, disregard (17)
nṓscō, nṓscere, nṓvī, nṓtum - to become acquainted with, learn, recognize; know *(in perfect tenses)* (30)
ópprimō, opprímere, oppréssī, oppréssum - to suppress, overwhelm, overpower, check (23)
osténdō, osténdere, osténdī, osténtum - to exhibit, show, display (23)
péllō, péllere, pépulī, púlsum - to strike, push; drive out, banish (24)
pétō, pétere, petívī, petítum - to seek, aim at, beg, beseech (23)
pṓnō, pṓnere, pósuī, pósitum - to put, place, set (27)
prémō, prémere, préssī, préssum - to press; press hard, pursue (23)
quaérō, quaérere, quaesívī, quaesítum - to seek, look for, strive for; ask, inquire, inquire into (24)
régō, régere, réxī, réctum - to rule, guide, direct (16)
relínquō, relínquere, relíquī, relíctum - to leave behind, leave, abandon, desert (21)
revértō, revértere, revértī, revérsum - turn back (23)
scríbō, scríbere, scrípsī, scríptum to write, compose (8)
súrgō, súrgere, surréxī, surréctum - to get up, arise (29)
tángō, tángere, tétigī, táctum - to touch (21)
tóllō, tóllere, sústulī, sublátum - to raise, lift up; take away, remove, destroy (22)
tráhō, tráhere, tráxī, tráctum - to draw, drag; derive, acquire (8)
vértō, vértere, vértī, vérsum - to turn; change (23)
víncō, víncere, vícī, víctum - to conquer, overcome (8)
vívō, vívere, víxī, víctum - to live (10)

3rd Conjugation -iō

accípiō, accípere, accépī, accéptum - to take *(to one's self)*, receive, accept (24)
cápiō, cápere, cépī, cáptum - to take, capture, seize, get (10)
cúpiō, cúpere, cupívī, cupítum - to desire, wish, long for (17)
ērípiō, ērípere, ērípuī, ēréptum - to snatch away, take away; rescue (22)
excípiō, excípere, excépī, excéptum - to take out, except; take, receive, capture (24)
fáciō, fácere, fécī, fáctum - to make, do, accomplish (10)
fúgiō, fúgere, fúgī, fugitúrum - to flee, hurry away; escape; go into exile; avoid, shun (10)
iáciō, iácere, iécī, iáctum - to throw, hurl (15)
incípiō, incípere, incépī, incéptum - to begin (17)
patefáciō, patefácere, patefécī, patefáctum - to make open, open; disclose, expose (25)
rápiō, rápere, rápuī, ráptum - to seize, snatch, carry away (21)
recípiō, recípere, recépī, recéptum - to take back, regain; admit, receive (24)
suscípiō, suscípere, suscépī, suscéptum - to undertake (25)

4th Conjugation

aúdiō, audíre, audívī, audítum - to hear, listen to (10)

invéniō, invenī́re, invḗnī, invéntum - to come upon, find (10)
mólliō, mollī́re, mollī́vī, mollī́tum to soften; make calm *or* less hostile (29)
nésciō, nescī́re, nescī́vī, nescī́tum - to not know, be ignorant (25)
scíō, scī́re, scī́vī, scī́tum - to know (21)
séntiō, sentī́re, sḗnsī, sḗnsum - to feel, perceive, think, experience (11)
véniō, venī́re, vḗnī, véntum - to come (10)

Irregular
póssum, pósse, pótuī - to be able, can, could, have power (6)
sum, ésse, fúī, futū́rum - to be, exist (4)

Defective
ā́it, ā́iunt - he says, they say, assert (25)
coépī, coepísse, coéptum - began (17)
ínquit - he says *or* said (22)
ṓdī, ōdísse, ōsū́rum - to hate (20)

Adverbs

ánte (+acc.) - before, previously (13)
béne - well, satisfactorily, quite (11)
cíto - quickly (17)
crās - tomorrow (5)
cūr - why (18)
déhinc - then, next (25)
deínde - thereupon, next, then (18)
dḗnique - at last, finally, lastly (29)
díū - long, for a long time (12)
étiam - even, also (11)
fū́rtim - stealthily, secretly (30)
héri - yesterday (5)
hīc - here (25)
hódiē - today (3)
iam - now, already, soon (19)
íbi - there (6)
íta - so, thus (29)
ítaque - and so, therefore (15)
íterum - again, a second time (21)
mox - soon (30)
nē . . . quídem - not . . . even (29)
nímis, nímium - too, too much, excessively; *(in a positive sense, esp. with adjectives and adverbs)* exceedingly, very (9)
nōn - not (1)
númquam - never (8)
nunc - now, at present (6)
nū́per - recently (12)
ṓlim - once (upon a time), long ago, formerly; some day, in the future (13)
póstea - afterwards (24)
prī́mō - at first, at the beginning (30)
prṓtinus - immediately (22)
quam - how (16)
quam - than *(after comparatives);* as . . . as possible *(with superlatives)* (26)
quándō - when (5)
quā́rē - because of which thing *(lit.);* therefore, wherefore, why (6)
quídem - indeed, certainly, at least, even (29)
quóndam - formerly, once (22)
quóque - also, too (17)
repénte - suddenly (30)
saépe - often (1)
sátis - enough, sufficiently (5)
sémper - always (3)
sīc - so, thus (29)
tam - so, to such a degree (29)
tam . . . quam - so . . . as (29)
támen - nevertheless, still (8)
tamquam - as it were, as if, so to speak (29)
tántum - only (26)
tum - then, at that time; thereupon, in the next place (5)
úbi - where, when (6)
últrā - on the other side of, beyond (22)
úmquam - ever, at any time (23)
únde - whence, from what *or* which place, from which, from whom (30)
vḗrō - in truth, indeed, to be sure, however (29)

Conjunctions

at - but; but, mind you; but, you say (19)
átque, ac - and also, and even, and in fact (21)
aut - or (17)
aut . . . aut - either . . . or (17)
aútem - however; moreover (11)
dum - while, as long as, at the same time that; *or* until *(+subjunctive)* (8)
énim - for, in fact, truly (9)
et - and; even (2)
et . . . et - both . . . and (2)
ígitur - therefore, consequently (5)
nam - for (13)
nē - not; in order that . . . not, that . . . not, in order not to (28)
néque , nec - and not, nor (11)
néque . . . néque, nec . . . nec - neither . . . nor (11)
nísi - if . . . not, unless; except (19)
quod - because (11)
quóniam - since, inasmuch as (10)
sed - but (2)
sī - if (1)
ut (+indic.) - as, just as, when (24)

ut (+ subj.) - in order that, so that, that, in order to, so as to, to (28)
útrum . . . an - whether . . . or (30)

Prepositions

ab, ā (+abl.) - away from, from; by (14)
ad (+acc.) - to, up to, near to (8)
ánte (+acc.) - before *(in place or time)*, in front of (13)
cóntrā (+acc.) - against (19)
cum (+abl.) - with (10)
dē (+abl.) - down from, from; concerning, about (3)
ex , ē (abl.+) - out of, from, from within; by reason of, on account of ; of *(after cardinal numerals)* (8)
in (+acc.) - into, toward; against (9)
in (+abl.) - in, on (3)
ínter (+acc.) - between, among (15)
per (+acc.) - through; by *(with reflexive pronoun)* (13)
post (+acc.) - after, behind (7)
prae (+abl.) - in front of, before (26)
prō (+abl.) - in front of, before, on behalf of, for the sake of, in return for, instead of, for, as (12)
própter (+acc.) - on account of, because of (5)
síne (+abl.) - without (2)
sub (+abl. w/ verbs of rest *or* **+acc. w/ verbs of motion)** - under, up under, close to, down to/into, to/at the foot of (7)
trāns (+acc.) - across (14)
últrā (adv. and prep. +acc.) - on the other side of, beyond (22)

Interjection

ō - O!, Oh! (2)

Idioms

amā́bō tē - please (1)
grā́tiās ágere (+dat.) - to thank someone; to give thanks to (8)
mḗnsa secúnda (f) - dessert (26)
nōn sṓlum . . . sed étiam - not only . . . but also (9)
poénās dáre - to pay the penalty (2)
sī quándō - if ever (5)

Prefix

re- , red- - again, back (24)

Suffixes

-ne – interrogative suffix attached to the first word of a sentence, typically the verb or another word on which the question hinges, to introduce a question whose answer is uncertain (5)
-que - and *(enclitic conjunction; appended to the second of two words to be joined)* (6)

Numerals

Cardinal - ū́nus *to* vīgíntī quī́nque (15)
Ordinal - prī́mus *to* duodécimus (15)

----

céntum - a hundred (15)
mī́lia, mī́lium (n. pl.) - thousands (15)
mī́lle - thousand (15)

Chapter 31

Nouns

1st Declension

adulēscéntia, adulēscéntiae (f) - youth, young manhood; youthfulness (5)
agrícola, agrícolae (m) - farmer (3)
amíca, amícae (f) - friend (female) (3)
amīcítia, amīcítiae (f) - friendship (10)
áqua, áquae (f) - water (14)
Ásia, Ásiae (f) - Asia (12)
cása, cásae (f) - house, cottage, hut (21)
caúsa, caúsae (f) - cause, reason; case, situation (21)
caúsā (abl. + preceding gen.) - for the sake of, on account of (21)
cḗna, cḗnae (f) - dinner (26)
clēméntia, clēméntiae (f) - mildness, gentleness, mercy (16)
cṓpia, cṓpiae (f) - abundance, supply (8)
cṓpiae, cōpiā́rum (f) - supplies, troops, forces (8)
cúlpa, cúlpae (f) - fault, blame (5)
cū́ra, cū́rae (f) - care, attention, caution, anxiety (4)
déa, déae (f) - goddess (6)
discípula, discípulae (f) - learner, pupil, student (female) (6)
dīvítiae, dīvitiā́rum (f. pl.) - riches, wealth (13)
fā́bula, fā́bulae (f) - story, tale; play (24)
fā́ma, fā́mae (f) - rumor, report; fame, reputation (2)
família, famíliae (f) - household, family (19)
fḗmina, fḗminae (f) - woman (3)
fenéstra, fenéstrae (f) - window (21)
fī́lia, fī́liae (f) - daughter (3)
fṓrma, fṓrmae (f) - form, shape; beauty (2)
fortū́na, fortū́nae (f) - fortune, luck (2)
glṓria, glṓriae (f) - glory, fame (5)
Graécia, Graéciae (f) - Greece (19)
hásta, hástae (f) - spear (23)
hṓra, hṓrae (f) - hour, time (10)
īnsídiae, īnsidiā́rum (f) - ambush, plot, treachery (6)
ī́nsula, ī́nsulae (f) - island (23)
invídia, invídiae (f) - envy, jealousy, hatred (31)
ī́ra, ī́rae (f) - ire, anger (2)
Itália, Itáliae (f) - Italy (15)
língua, línguae (f) - tongue; language (25)
líttera, lítterae (f) - a letter of the alphabet (7)
lítterae, litterā́rum (f) - a letter (epistle), literature (7)
lū́na, lū́nae (f) - moon (28)
magístra, magístrae (f) - schoolmistress, teacher, mistress (4)
médica, médicae (f) - doctor, physician (female) (12)
memória, memóriae (f) - memory, recollection (15)
mḗnsa, mḗnsae (f) - table; dining; dish, course (26)
móra, mórae (f) - delay (4)
nā́ta, nā́tae (f) - daughter (29)
nātū́ra, nātū́rae (f) - nature (10)
naúta, naútae (m) - sailor (2)
patiéntia, patiéntiae (f) - suffering; patience, endurance (12)
pátria, pátriae (f) - fatherland, native land, (one's) country (2)
pecū́nia, pecū́niae (f) - money (2)
philosóphia, philosóphiae (f) - philosophy (2)
poéna, poénae (f) - penalty, punishment (2)
poḗta, poḗtae (m) - poet (2)
pórta, pórtae (f) - gate, entrance (2)
puélla, puéllae (f) - girl (2)
rēgī́na, rēgī́nae (f) - queen (7)
Rṓma, Rṓmae (f) - Rome (14)
rósa, rósae (f) - rose (2)
sapiéntia, sapiéntiae (f) - wisdom (3)
sátura, sáturae (f) - satire (16)
sciéntia, sciéntiae (f) - knowledge (18)
senténtia, senténtiae (f) - feeling, thought, opinion, vote, sentence (2)
sérva, sérvae (f) - slave (female) (24)
stḗlla, stḗllae (f) - star, planet (28)
térra, térrae (f) - earth, ground, land, country (7)
Trṓia, Trṓiae (f) - Troy (21)
túrba, túrbae (f) - uproar, disturbance; mob, crowd, multitude (14)
vía, víae (f) - way, road, street (10)
vīcī́na, vīcī́nae (f) - neighbor (female) (21)
victṓria, victṓriae (f) - victory (8)
vī́ta, vī́tae (f) - life; mode of life (2)

2nd Declension

áger, ágrī (m) - field, farm (3)
amī́cus, amī́cī (m) - friend (male) (3)
ánimī, animṓrum (m) - high spirits, pride, courage (5)
ánimus, ánimī (m) - soul, spirit, mind (5)
ánnus, ánnī (m) - year (12)
argūméntum, argūméntī (n) - proof, evidence, argument (19)

árma, armṓrum (n. pl.) - arms, weapons (28)
auxílium, auxíliī (n) - aid, help (31)
bā́sium, bā́siī (n) - kiss (4)
béllum, béllī (n) - war (4)
benefícium, benefíciī (n) - benefit, kindness; favor (19)
caélum, caélī (n) - sky, heaven (5)
coniūrā́tī, coniūrātṓrum (m. pl.) - conspirators (20)
cōnsílium, cōnsíliī (n) - plan, purpose, counsel, advice, judgment, wisdom (4)
déus, déī (m) - god (6)
dígitus, dígitī (m) - finger, toe (31)
discípulus, discípulī (m) - learner, pupil, student (male) (6)
dṓnum, dṓnī (n) - gift, present (4)
elephántus, elephántī (m and f) - elephant (31)
équus, équī (m) - horse (23)
exítium, exítiī (n) - destruction, ruin (4)
exsílium, exsíliī (n) - exile, banishment (31)
fáctum, fáctī (n) - deed, act, achievement (13)
fā́tum, fā́tī (n) - fate; death (29)
férrum, férrī (n) - iron; sword (22)
fī́lius, fī́liī (m) - son (3)
fórum, fórī (n) - marketplace, forum (26)
Graécus, Graécī (m) - a Greek (6)
impérium, impériī (n) - power to command, supreme power, authority, command, control (24)
ingénium, ingéniī (n) - nature, innate talent (29)
iūdícium, iūdíciī (n) - judgment, decision, opinion; trial (19)
libéllus, libéllī (m) - little book (17)
líber, líbrī (m) - book (6)
lóca, locṓrum (n) - places, region (9)
lócī, locṓrum (m) - passages in literature (9)
lócus, lócī (m) - place; passage in literature (9)
lū́dus, lū́dī (m) - game, sport; school (18)
magíster, magístrī (m) - schoolmaster, teacher, master (4)
médicus, médicī (m) - doctor, physician (male) (12)
módus, módī (m) - measure, bound, limit; manner, method, mode, way (22)
mórbus, mórbī (m) - disease, sickness (9)
múndus, múndī (m) - world, universe (21)
númerus, númerī (m) - number (3)
óculus, óculī (m) - eye (4)
offícium, offíciī (n) - duty, service (4)
ṓsculum, ṓsculī (n) - kiss (29)
ṓtium, ṓtiī (n) - leisure, peace (4)
perfúgium, perfúgiī (n) - refuge, shelter (24)
perī́culum, perī́culī (n) - danger, risk (4)
pópulus, pópulī (m) - the people, a people, a nation (3)
prīncípium, prīncípiī (n) - beginning (12)
púer, púerī (m) - boy; boys, children *(pl.)* (3)
remédium, remédiī (n) - cure, remedy (4)
sérvus, sérvī (m) - slave (male) (24)
sígnum, sígnī (n) - sign, signal, indication; seal (13)
sōlā́cium, sōlā́ciī (n) - comfort, relief (24)
sómnus, sómnī (m) - sleep (26)
stúdium, stúdiī (n) - eagerness, zeal, pursuit, study (9)
stúltus, stúltī (m) - a fool (4)
súperī, superṓrum (m. pl.) - the gods (27)
tyránnus, tyránnī (m) - absolute ruler, tyrant (6)
vérbum, vérbī (n) - word (5)
vīcī́nus, vīcī́nī (m) - neighbor (male) (21)
vī́num, vī́nī (n) - wine (31)
vir, vírī (m) - man, hero (3)
vítium, vítiī (n) - fault, crime, vice (6)
vúlgus, vúlgī (n) - the common people, mob, rabble (21)

3rd Declension

adulḗscēns, adulēscéntis (m *or* f) - young man *or* woman (12)
aétās, aetā́tis (f) - period of life, life, age, an age, time (16)
ámor, amṓris (m) - love (7)
aúctor, auctṓris (m) - increaser; author, originator (19)
audī́tor, audītṓris (m) - hearer, listener, member of an audience (16)
Caésar, Caésaris (m) - Caesar (12)
cáput, cápitis (n) - head; leader; beginning; life; heading; chapter (11)
cármen, cárminis (n) - song, poem (7)
Carthā́gō, Carthā́ginis (f) - Carthage (24)
Cícerō, Cicerṓnis (m) - (Marcus Tullius) Cicero (8)
cī́vitās, cīvitā́tis (f) - state, citizenship (7)
cṓnsul, cṓnsulis (m) - consul (11)
córpus, córporis (n) - body (7)
cupíditās, cupiditā́tis (f) - desire, longing, passion; cupidity, avarice (10)

dēlectā́tiō, dēlectātiṓnis (f) - delight, pleasure, enjoyment (27)
dux, dúcis (m) - leader, guide; commander, general (23)
flū́men, flū́minis (n) - river (18)
frā́ter, frā́tris (m) - brother (8)
génus, géneris (n) - origin; kind, type, sort, class (18)
hómō, hóminis (m) - human being, man (7)
hónor, honṓris (m) - honor, esteem; public office (30)
imperā́tor, imperātṓris (m) - general, commander-in-chief, emperor (24)
iū́dex, iū́dicis (m) - judge, juror (19)
iūs, iū́ris (n) - right, justice, law (14)
lábor, labṓris (m)- labor, work, toil; a work, production (7)
laus, laúdis (f) - praise, glory, fame (8)
lēx, lḗgis (f) - law, statute (26)
lībértās, lībertā́tis (f) - liberty (8)
lī́men, lī́minis (n) - threshold (26)
lī́tus, lī́toris (n) - shore, coast (23)
lūx, lū́cis (f) - light (26)
maiṓrēs, maiṓrum (m. pl.) - ancestors (27)
mā́ter, mā́tris (f) - mother (12)
mī́les, mī́litis (m) - soldier (23)
mṓrēs, mṓrum (m) - habits, morals, character (7)
mōs, mṓris (m) - habit, custom, manner (7)
nḗmō, nūllī́us, nḗminī, nḗminem, nū́llō, nū́llā (m *or* f) - no one, nobody (11)
népōs, nepṓtis (m) - grandson, descendant (27)
nṓmen, nṓminis (n) - name (7)
occā́siō, occāsiṓnis (f) - occasion, opportunity (28)
ōrā́tor, ōrātṓris (m) - orator, speaker (23)
ōs, ṓris (n) - mouth, face (14)
párēns, paréntis (m *or* f) - parent (28)
páter, pátris (m) - father (12)
pāx, pā́cis (f) - peace (7)
prī́nceps, prī́ncipis (m *or* f) - leader, emperor (28)
próbitās, probitā́tis (f) - uprightness, honesty (18)
rátiō, ratiṓnis (f) - reckoning, account; reason, judgment, consideration; system; manner, method (8)
rēx, rḗgis (m) - king (7)
rū́mor, rūmṓris (m) - rumor, gossip (31)
sacérdōs, sacerdṓtis (m) - priest (23)
sálūs, salū́tis (f) - health, safety; greeting (21)
sápiēns, sapiéntis (m/f) - a wise man/woman, philosopher (25)
scélus, scéleris (n) - evil deed, crime, sin, wickedness (19)
scrī́ptor, scrīptṓris (m) - writer, author (8)
senéctūs, senectū́tis (f) - old age (10)
sénex, sénis (m) - old man (16)
sérvitūs, servitū́tis (f) - servitude, slavery (20)
sī́dus, sī́deris (n) - constellation, star (29)
sōl, sṓlis (m) - sun (27)
sóror, sorṓris (f) - sister (8)
tempéstās, tempestā́tis (f) - period of time, season; weather, storm (15)
témpus, témporis (n) - time; occasion, opportunity (7)
tímor, timṓris (m) - fear (10)
úxor, uxṓris (f) - wife (7)
vḗritās, vēritā́tis (f) - truth (10)
vésper, vésperis *or* vésperī (m) - evening; evening star (28)
vírgō, vírginis (f) - maiden, virgin (7)
vírtūs, virtū́tis (f) - manliness, courage; excellence, character, worth, virtue (7)
volúptās, voluptā́tis (f) - pleasure (10)
vúlnus, vúlneris (n) - wound (24)

3rd Declension I-Stem

ánimal, animā́lis (n) - a living creature, animal (14)
ars, ártis (f) - art, skill (14)
arx, árcis (f) - citadel, stronghold (23)
as, ássis (m) - an as *(a small copper coin)* (31)
aúris, aúris (f) - ear (14)
cī́vis, cī́vis (m *or* f) - citizen (14)
fī́nēs, fī́nium (m) - boundaries, territory (21)
fī́nis, fī́nis (m) - end, limit, boundary; purpose (21)
gēns, géntis (f) - clan, race, nation, people (21)
hóstēs, hóstium (m) - the enemy (18)
hóstis, hóstis (m) - an enemy *(of the state)* (18)
ígnis, ígnis (m) - fire (22)
máre, máris (n) - sea (14)
mēns, méntis (f) - mind, thought, intention (16)
moénia, moénium (n. pl.) - walls of a city (29)
mōns, móntis (m) - mountain (20)
mors, mórtis (f) - death (14)
nā́vis, nā́vis (f) - ship, boat (21)
nox, nóctis (f) - night (26)
nū́bēs, nū́bis (f) - cloud (14)
pars, pártis (f) - part, share; direction (14)
urbs, úrbis (f) - city (14)
vī́rēs, vī́rium (f. pl.) - strength (14)
vīs, vīs (f) - force, power, violence (14)

4th Declension

córnū, córnūs (n) - horn (20)
cúrsus, cúrsūs (m) - running, race; course (28)
frúctus, frúctūs (m) - fruit; profit, benefit, enjoyment (20)
génū, génūs (n) - knee (20)
mánus, mánūs (f) - hand; handwriting; band (20)
métus, métūs (m) - fear, dread, anxiety (20)
senátus, senátūs (m) - senate (20)
sénsus, sénsūs (m) - feeling, sense (20)
spíritus, spíritūs (m) - breath, breathing; spirit, soul (20)
vérsus, vérsūs (m) - line of verse (20)

5th Declension

díēs, diéī (m) - day (22)
fídēs, fídeī (f) - faith, trust, trustworthiness, fidelity, promise, guarantee, protection (22)
rēs, réī (f) - thing, matter, property, business, affair (22)
rēs pública, réī públicae (f) - state, commonwealth, republic (22)
spēs, spéī (f) - hope (22)

Indeclinable

níhil - nothing (1)
sátis - enough (5)

Pronouns

áliquis, áliquid - someone, somebody, something (23)
égo, méī - I (11)
hic, haec, hoc - this; the latter; he, she, it, they (9)
ídem, éadem, ídem - the same (11)
ílle, ílla, íllud - that; the former; the famous; he, she, it, they (9)
ípse, ípsa, ípsum - myself, yourself, himself, herself, itself, *etc.,* the very, the actual (13)
is, éa, id - this, that; he, she, it (11)
íste, ísta, ístud - that of yours, that; such (as you have, as you speak of); *sometimes with contemptuous force, e.g.,* that despicable, that wretched (9)
quī, quae, quod - who, which, what, that (17)
quid - what (1)
quídam, quaédam, quíddam - a certain one or thing, someone, something (26)
quis? quid? - who? whose? whom? what? which? (19)
quísque, quídque, cuiúsque, cuíque - each one, each person, each thing (13)
quísquis, quídquid - whoever, whatever (23)
súī - himself, herself, itself, themselves (13)
tū, túī - you *(sing.)* (11)

Adjectives

1st & 2nd Declension

acérbus, acérba, acérbum - harsh, bitter, grievous (12)
aéquus, aéqua, aéquum - level, even; calm; equal, just; favorable (22)
áliī . . . áliī - some . . . others (9)
álius, ália, áliud - other, another (9)
álter, áltera, álterum - the other (of two), second (9)
amícus, amíca, amícum - friendly (11)
antíquus, antíqua, antíquum - ancient, old-time (2)
ásper, áspera, ásperum - rough, harsh (21)
avárus, avára, avárum - greedy, avaricious (3)
beátus, beáta, beátum - happy, fortunate, blessed (10)
béllus, bélla, béllum - pretty, handsome, charming (4)
bónus, bóna, bónum - good, kind (4)
caécus, caéca, caécum - blind (17)
cárus, cára, cárum - dear (11)
cértus, cérta, cértum - definite, sure, certain, reliable (19)
céterī, céterae, cétera - the remaining, the rest, the other, all the others (30)
clárus, clára, clárum - clear, bright; renowned, famous, illustrious (18)
déxter, déxtra, déxtrum - right, right-hand (20)
dígnus, dígna, dígnum (+abl.) - worthy, worthy of (29)
dóctus, dócta, dóctum - taught, learned, skilled (13)
dúrus, dúra, dúrum - hard, harsh, rough, stern, unfeeling, hardy, difficult (29)
fortūnátus, fortūnáta, fortūnátum - lucky, fortunate, happy (13)
géminus, gémina, géminum - twin (25)
Graécus, Graéca, Graécum - Greek (6)
hūmánus, hūmána, hūmánum - pertaining to man, human; humane, kind; refined, cultivated (4)
incértus, incérta, incértum - uncertain, unsure, doubtful (22)
iūcúndus, iūcúnda, iūcúndum - pleasant, delightful, agreeable, pleasing (16)

Latínus, Latína, Latínum - Latin (22)
líber, líbera, líberum - free (5)
lóngus, lónga, lóngum - long (16)
magnánimus, magnánima, magnánimum - great-hearted, brave, magnanimous (23)
mágnus, mágna, mágnum - large, great; important (2)
málus, mála, málum - bad, wicked, evil (4)
médius, média, médium - middle; the middle of (22)
méus, méa, méum - my (2)
míser, mísera, míserum - wretched, miserable, unfortunate (15)
mórtuus, mórtua, mórtuum - dead (28)
múltus, múlta, múltum - much, many (2)
neúter, neútra, neútrum - not either, neither (9)
nóster, nóstra, nóstrum - our, ours (5)
nóvus, nóva, nóvum - new; strange (7)
núllus, núlla, núllum - not any, no, none (9)
párvus, párva, párvum - small, little (4)
paúcī, paúcae, paúca - few, a few (3)
perpétuus, perpétua, perpétuum perpetual, lasting, uninterrupted, continuous (6)
plénus, pléna, plénum - full, abundant, generous (6)
prímus, príma, prímum - first, foremost, chief, principal (27)
pudícus, pudíca, pudícum - modest, chaste (26)
púlcher, púlchra, púlchrum - beautiful, handsome; fine (5)
quántus, quánta, quántum - how large, how great, how much (30)
rīdículus, rīdícula, rīdículum - laughable, ridiculous (30)
Rōmánus, Rōmána, Rōmánum - Roman (3)
sálvus, sálva, sálvum - safe, sound (6)
sánus, sána, sánum - sound, healthy, sane (5)
secúndus, secúnda, secúndum - second; favorable (6)
sinístex, sinístra, sinístrum - left, left-hand; harmful, ill-omened (20)
sólus, sóla, sólum - alone, only, the only (9)
stúltus, stúlta, stúltum - foolish (4)
supérbus, supérba, supérbum - arrogant, overbearing, haughty, proud (26)
súperus, súpera, súperum - above, upper (27)
súus, súa, súum - his own, her own, its own, their own (13)
tántus, tánta, tántum - so large, so great, of such a size (29)
tántus . . . quántus - just as much (many) . . . as (30)
tótus, tóta, tótum - whole, entire (9)
túus, túa, túum - your *(sing.)* (2)
úllus, úlla, úllum - any (9)
últimus, última, últimum - farthest, extreme; last, final (25)
únus, úna, únum - one, single, alone (9)
urbánus, urbána, urbánum - of the city, urban; urbane, elegant (26)
úter, útra, útrum - either, which (of two) (9)
vérus, véra, vérum - true, real, proper (4)
véster, véstra, véstrum - your *(pl.)* (6)
vívus, víva, vívum - alive, living (30)

3rd Declension

ácer, ácris, ácre - sharp, keen, eager; severe, fierce (16)
brévis, bréve - short, small, brief (16)
céler, céleris, célere - swift, quick, rapid (16)
commúnis, commúne - common, general, of / for the community (20)
diffícilis, diffícile - hard, difficult, troublesome (16)
díligēns, ***gen.*** **dīligéntis** - diligent, careful (27)
dissímilis, dissímile - unlike, different (27)
dúlcis, dúlce - sweet; pleasant, agreeable (16)
fácilis, fácile - easy; agreeable (16)
félīx, ***gen.*** **fēlícis** - lucky, fortunate, happy (22)
férōx, ***gen.*** **ferócis** - fierce, savage (25)
fidélis, fidéle - faithful, loyal (25)
fórtis, fórte - strong, brave (16)
grácilis, grácile - slender, thin (27)
grávis, gráve - heavy, weighty; serious, important; severe, grievous (19)
húmilis, húmile - lowly, humble (27)
immortális, immortále - not subject to death, immortal (19)
íngēns, ***gen.*** **ingéntis** - huge (16)
lévis, léve - light; easy; slight, trivial (17)
máior, máius - greater; older (27)

medíocris, medíocre - ordinary, moderate, mediocre (31)
mortā́lis, mortā́le - mortal (18)
ómnis, ómne - every, all (16)
pótēns, ***gen.*** **poténtis** - able, powerful, mighty, strong (16)
prī́nceps, ***gen.*** **prī́ncipis** - chief, foremost (28)
sápiēns, ***gen.*** **sapiéntis** - wise, judicious (25)
sénex, ***gen.*** **sénis** - old, aged (16)
símilis, símile (+gen. or dat.) - similar (to), like, resembling (27)
trī́stis, trī́ste - sad, sorrowful; joyless, grim, severe (26)
túrpis, túrpe - ugly; shameful, base, disgraceful (26)
ū́tilis, ū́tile - useful, advantageous (27)

Indeclinable Adjective
quot - how many, as many as (27)
sátis - enough, sufficient (5)

Indefinite Adjective
quī́dam, quaédam, quóddam - a certain, some (26)

Interrogative Adjective
quī?, quae?, quod? - what? which? what kind of?; *(sometimes with exclamatory force)* what (a)! what sort of! (19)

Verbs
1st Conjugation
ádiuvō, adiuvā́re, adiū́vī, adiū́tum - to help, aid, assist; to please (4)
ámō, amā́re, amā́vī, amā́tum - to love, like (1)
appéllō, appellā́re, appellā́vī, appellā́tum - to speak to, address (as), call, name (14)
cḗnō, cēnā́re, cēnā́vī, cēnā́tum - to dine (5)
cṓgitō, cōgitā́re, cōgitā́vī, cōgitā́tum- to think, ponder, consider, plan (1)
cōnsérvō, cōnservā́re, cōnservā́vī, cōnservā́tum - to preserve, conserve, maintain (1)
créō, creā́re, creā́vī, creā́tum - to create (12)
cúlpō, culpā́re, culpā́vī, culpā́tum - to blame, censure (5)
dḗdicō, dēdicā́re, dēdicā́vī, dēdicā́tum - to dedicate (28)
dēléctō, dēlectā́re, dēlectā́vī, dēlectā́tum - to delight, charm, please (19)
dēmṓnstrō, dēmōnstrā́re, dēmōnstrā́vī, dēmōnstrā́tum to point out, show, demonstrate (8)
dēsī́derō, dēsīderā́re, dēsīderā́vī, dēsīderā́tum - to desire, long for, miss (17)
dō, dáre, dédī, dátum - to give, offer (1)
dúbitō, dubitā́re, dubitā́vī, dubitā́tum - to doubt, hesitate (30)
ḗducō, ēducā́re, ēducā́vī, ēducā́tum - to bring up, educate (23)
érrō, errā́re, errā́vī, errā́tum - to wander; err, go astray, make a mistake, be mistaken (1)
exspéctō, exspectā́re, exspectā́vī, exspectā́tum - to look for, expect, await (15)
invī́tō, invītā́re, invītā́vī, invītā́tum - to entertain, invite, summon (26)
iúvō, iuvā́re, iū́vī, iū́tum - to help, aid, assist; to please (4)
labṓrō, labōrā́re, labōrā́vī, labōrā́tum - to labor; be in distress (21)
laúdō, laudā́re, laudā́vī, laudā́tum - to praise (1)
lī́berō, līberā́re, līberā́vī, līberā́tum - to free, liberate (19)
mū́tō, mūtā́re, mūtā́vī, mūtā́tum to change, alter; exchange (14)
nā́rrō, nārrā́re, nārrā́vī, nārrā́tum - to tell, report, narrate (24)
nā́vigō, nāvigā́re, nāvigā́vī, nāvigā́tum - to sail, navigate (17)
nécō, necā́re, necā́vī, necā́tum - to murder, kill (7)
négō, negā́re, negā́vī, negā́tum to deny, say that . . . not (25)
nū́ntiō, nūntiā́re, nūntiā́vī, nūntiā́tum - to announce, report, relate (25)
párō, parā́re, parā́vī, parā́tum - to prepare, provide; get, obtain (19)
praéstō, praestā́re, praéstitī, praéstitum - to excel; exhibit, show, offer, supply, furnish (28)
próbō, probā́re, probā́vī, probā́tum - to approve, recommend; test (27)
prōnū́ntiō, prōnūntiā́re, prōnūntiā́vī, prōnūntiā́tum - to proclaim, announce; declaim; pronounce (20)
púgnō, pugnā́re, pugnā́vī, pugnā́tum - to fight (29)
pútō, putā́re, putā́vī, putā́tum - to reckon, suppose, judge, think, imagine (25)
récitō, recitā́re, recitā́vī, recitā́tum - to read aloud, recite (17)

rógō, rogā́re, rogā́vī, rogā́tum - to ask (30)
sátiō, satiā́re, satiā́vī, satiā́tum - to satisfy, sate (3)
sérvō, servā́re, servā́vī, servā́tum - to preserve, save, keep, guard (1)
spḗrō, spērā́re, spērā́vī, spērā́tum - to hope for, hope (25)
stō, stā́re, stétī, stā́tum - to stand, stand still *or* firm (13)
súperō, superā́re, superā́vī, superā́tum - to be above, have the upper hand, surpass; overcome, conquer (5)
tólerō, tolerā́re, tolerā́vī, tolerā́tum - to bear, endure (6)
vī́tō, vītā́re, vītā́vī, vītā́tum - to avoid, shun (14)
vócō, vocā́re, vocā́vī, vocā́tum - to call, summon (1)

2nd Conjugation

aúdeō, audḗre, aúsus sum - to dare (7)
cáreō, carḗre, cáruī, caritū́rum (+abl.) - to be without, be deprived of, want, lack; be free from (20)
contíneō, continḗre, contínuī, conténtum - to hold together, contain, keep, enclose, restrain (21)
dḗbeō, dēbḗre, dḗbuī, dḗbitum - to owe; ought, must, should (1)
dḗleō, dēlḗre, dēlḗvī, dēlḗtum - to destroy, wipe out, erase (17)
dóceō, docḗre, dócuī, dóctum - to teach (8)
dóleō, dolḗre, dóluī, dolitū́rum - to grieve, suffer; hurt, give pain (31)
égeō, egḗre, éguī (+ abl. or gen.) - to need, lack, want (28)
éxpleō, explḗre, explḗvī, explḗtum - to fill, fill up, complete (28)
gaúdeō, gaudḗre, gāvī́sus sum - to be glad, rejoice (23)
hábeō, habḗre, hábuī, hábitum - to have, hold, possess; consider, regard (3)
iáceō, iacḗre, iácuī - to lie; lie prostrate; lie dead (25)
invídeō, invidḗre, invī́dī, invī́sum to be envious; to look at with envy, envy, be jealous of (+dat.) (31)
iúbeō, iubḗre, iússī, iússum - to bid, order, command (21)
máneō, manḗre, mā́nsī, mā́nsum - to remain, stay, stay behind, abide, continue (5)
mísceō, miscḗre, míscuī, míxtum to mix, stir up, disturb (18)
móneō, monḗre, mónuī, mónitum - to remind, advise, warn (1)
móveō, movḗre, mṓvī, mṓtum - to move; arouse, affect (18)
prohíbeō, prohibḗre, prohíbuī, prohíbitum - to keep (back), prevent, hinder, restrain, prohibit (20)
remáneō, remanḗre, remā́nsī, remā́nsum - to remain, stay, stay behind, abide, continue (5)
respóndeō, respondḗre, respóndī, respṓnsum - to answer (29)
rī́deō, rīdḗre, rī́sī, rī́sum - to laugh, laugh at (24)
sálvē, salvḗte - hello, greetings (1)
sálveō, salvḗre - to be well, be in good health (1)
táceō, tacḗre, tácuī, tácitum - to be silent, leave unmentioned (28)
téneō, tenḗre, ténuī, téntum - to hold, keep, possess; restrain (14)
térreō, terrḗre, térruī, térritum - to frighten, terrify (1)
tímeō, timḗre, tímuī - to fear, be afraid (of) (15)
válē, valḗte - good-bye, farewell (1)
váleō, valḗre, váluī, valitū́rum - to be strong, have power; be well (1)
vídeō, vidḗre, vī́dī, vī́sum - to see; observe, understand (1)
vídeor, vidḗrī, vī́sus sum - to be seen, seem, appear (18)

3rd Conjugation

admíttō, admíttere, admī́sī, admíssum - to admit, receive, let in (17)
ágō, ágere, ḗgī, ā́ctum - to drive, lead, do, act; pass, spend *(life or time)* (8)
álō, álere, áluī, áltum - to nourish, support, sustain, increase; cherish (13)
āmíttō, āmíttere, āmī́sī, āmíssum - to send away; lose, let go (12)
āvértō, āvértere, āvértī, āvérsum - to turn away, avert (23)
bíbō, bíbere, bíbī - to drink (30)
cádō, cádere, cécidī, cāsū́rum - to fall (12)
cḗdō, cḗdere, céssī, céssum - to go, withdraw; yield to, grant, submit (28)
cérnō, cérnere, crḗvī, crḗtum - to distinguish, discern, perceive (22)

cognṓscō, cognṓscere, cognṓvī, cógnitum - to become acquainted with, learn, recognize; know *(in perfect tenses)* (30)
commíttō, commíttere, commī́sī, commíssum - to entrust, commit (15)
comprehéndō, comprehéndere, comprehéndī, comprehḗnsum - to grasp, seize, arrest; comprehend, understand (30)
cóndō, cóndere, cóndidī, cónditum - to put together *or* into, store; found, establish (29)
cōnsū́mō, cōnsū́mere, cōnsū́mpsī, cōnsū́mptum - to consume, use up (30)
conténdō, conténdere, conténdī, conténtum - to strive, struggle, contend; hasten (29)
crḗdō, crḗdere, crḗdidī, crḗditum to believe, trust (25)
cúrrō, cúrrere, cucúrrī, cúrsum - to run, rush, move quickly (14)
dēféndō, dēféndere, dēféndī, dēfḗnsum - to ward off; defend, protect (20)
dī́cō, dī́cere, dī́xī, díctum - to say, tell, speak; name, call (10)
dī́ligō, dīlígere, dīlḗxī, dīlḗctum - to esteem, love (13)
discḗdō, discḗdere, discéssī, discéssum - to go away, depart (20)
díscō, díscere, dídicī - to learn (8)
dū́cō, dū́cere, dū́xī, dúctum - to lead; consider, regard; prolong (8)
expéllō, expéllere, éxpulī, expúlsum - to drive out, expel, banish (24)
expṓnō, expṓnere, expósuī, expósitum - to set forth, explain, expose (30)
flúō, flúere, flū́xī, flū́xum - to flow (18)
gérō, gérere, géssī, géstum - to carry; carry on, manage, conduct, wage, accomplish, perform (8)
intéllegō, intellégere, intellḗxī, intellḗctum - to understand (11)
iúngō, iúngere, iū́nxī, iū́nctum - to join (13)
légō, légere, lḗgī, lḗctum - to pick out, choose; read (18)
mínuō, minúere, mínuī, minū́tum - to lessen, diminish (30)
míttō, míttere, mī́sī, míssum - to send, let go (11)
néglegō, neglégere, neglḗxī, neglḗctum - to neglect, disregard (17)
nṓscō, nṓscere, nṓvī, nṓtum - to become acquainted with, learn, recognize; know *(in perfect tenses)* (30)
óccidō, occídere, óccidī, occā́sum - to fall down; die; set (31)
ópprimō, opprímere, oppréssī, oppréssum - to suppress, overwhelm, overpower, check (23)
osténdō, osténdere, osténdī, osténtum - to exhibit, show, display (23)
péllō, péllere, pépulī, púlsum - to strike, push; drive out, banish (24)
pétō, pétere, petī́vī, petī́tum - to seek, aim at, beg, beseech (23)
pṓnō, pṓnere, pósuī, pósitum - to put, place, set (27)
prémō, prémere, préssī, préssum - to press; press hard, pursue (23)
quaérō, quaérere, quaesī́vī, quaesī́tum - to seek, look for, strive for; ask, inquire, inquire into (24)
régō, régere, rḗxī, rḗctum - to rule, guide, direct (16)
relínquō, relínquere, relī́quī, relíctum - to leave behind, leave, abandon, desert (21)
revértō, revértere, revértī, revérsum - turn back (23)
scrī́bō, scrī́bere, scrī́psī, scrī́ptum to write, compose (8)
súrgō, súrgere, surrḗxī, surrḗctum - to get up, arise (29)
tángō, tángere, tétigī, tā́ctum - to touch (21)
tóllō, tóllere, sústulī, sublā́tum - to raise, lift up; take away, remove, destroy (22)
tráhō, tráhere, trā́xī, tráctum - to draw, drag; derive, acquire (8)
vértō, vértere, vértī, vérsum - to turn; change (23)
víncō, víncere, vī́cī, víctum - to conquer, overcome (8)
vī́vō, vī́vere, vī́xī, vī́ctum - to live (10)

3rd Conjugation -iō

accípiō, accípere, accḗpī, accéptum - to take *(to one's self)*, receive, accept (24)
cápiō, cápere, cḗpī, cáptum - to take, capture, seize, get (10)
cúpiō, cúpere, cupī́vī, cupī́tum - to desire, wish, long for (17)
ērípiō, ērípere, ērípuī, ēréptum - to snatch away, take away; rescue (22)

excípiō, excípere, excḗpī, excéptum - to take out, except; take, receive, capture (24)
fáciō, fácere, fḗcī, fáctum - to make, do, accomplish (10)
fúgiō, fúgere, fū́gī, fugitū́rum - to flee, hurry away; escape; go into exile; avoid, shun (10)
iáciō, iácere, iḗcī, iáctum - to throw, hurl (15)
incípiō, incípere, incḗpī, incéptum - to begin (17)
patefáciō, patefácere, patefḗcī, patefáctum - to make open, open; disclose, expose (25)
rápiō, rápere, rápuī, ráptum - to seize, snatch, carry away (21)
recípiō, recípere, recḗpī, recéptum - to take back, regain; admit, receive (24)
suscípiō, suscípere, suscḗpī, suscéptum - to undertake (25)

4th Conjugation
aúdiō, audī́re, audī́vī, audī́tum - to hear, listen to (10)
dórmiō, dormī́re, dormī́vī, dormī́tum - to sleep (31)
invéniō, invenī́re, invḗnī, invéntum - to come upon, find (10)
mólliō, mollī́re, mollī́vī, mollī́tum to soften; make calm *or* less hostile (29)
nésciō, nescī́re, nescī́vī, nescī́tum - to not know, be ignorant (25)
scíō, scī́re, scī́vī, scī́tum - to know (21)
séntiō, sentī́re, sḗnsī, sḗnsum - to feel, perceive, think, experience (11)
véniō, venī́re, vḗnī, véntum - to come (10)

Irregular
ádferō, adférre, áttulī, allā́tum - to bring to (31)
cṓnferō, cōnférre, cóntulī, collā́tum - to bring together, compare; confer, bestow (31)
férō, férre, túlī, lā́tum - to bear, carry, bring; suffer, endure, tolerate; say, report (31)
ófferō, offérre, óbtulī, oblā́tum - to offer (31)
póssum, pósse, pótuī - to be able, can, could, have power (6)
réferō, reférre, réttulī, relā́tum - to carry back, bring back; repeat, answer, report (31)
sum, ésse, fúī, futū́rum - to be, exist (4)

Defective
ā́it, ā́iunt - he says, they say, assert (25)
coépī, coepísse, coéptum - began (17)
ínquit - he says *or* said (22)
ṓdī, ōdísse, ōsū́rum - to hate (20)

Adverbs

ánte (+acc.) - before, previously (13)
béne - well, satisfactorily, quite (11)
cíto - quickly (17)
crās - tomorrow (5)
cūr - why (18)
déhinc - then, next (25)
deínde - thereupon, next, then (18)
dḗnique - at last, finally, lastly (29)
díū - long, for a long time (12)
étiam - even, also (11)
fū́rtim - stealthily, secretly (30)
héri - yesterday (5)
hīc - here (25)
hódiē - today (3)
iam - now, already, soon (19)
íbi - there (6)
íta - so, thus (29)
ítaque - and so, therefore (15)
íterum - again, a second time (21)
mox - soon (30)
nē . . . quídem - not . . . even (29)
nímis, nímium - too, too much, excessively; *(in a positive sense, esp. with adjectives and adverbs)* exceedingly, very (9)
nōn - not (1)
númquam - never (8)
nunc - now, at present (6)
nū́per - recently (12)
ṓlim - once (upon a time), long ago, formerly; some day, in the future (13)
pósteā - afterwards (24)
prī́mō - at first, at the beginning (30)
prṓtinus - immediately (22)
quam - how (16)
quam - than *(after comparatives)*; as . . . as possible *(with superlatives)* (26)
quándō - when (5)
quā́rē - because of which thing *(lit.)*; therefore, wherefore, why (6)
quídem - indeed, certainly, at least, even (29)
quóndam - formerly, once (22)
quóque - also, too (17)
repénte - suddenly (30)
saépe - often (1)
sátis - enough, sufficient (5)
sémel - a single time, once, once and for all, simultaneously (31)
sémper - always (3)
sīc - so, thus (29)
tam - so, to such a degree (29)
tam . . . quam - so . . . as (29)
támen - nevertheless, still (8)

tamquam - as it were, as if, so to speak (29)
tántum - only (26)
tum - then, at that time; thereupon, in the next place (5)
úbi - where, when (6)
últrā - on the other side of, beyond (22)
úmquam - ever, at any time (23)
únde - whence, from what *or* which place, from which, from whom (30)
úsque - all the way, up (to), even (to), continuously, always (31)
vḗrō - in truth, indeed, to be sure, however (29)

Conjunctions

at - but; but, mind you; but, you say (19)
átque, ac - and also, and even, and in fact (21)
aut - or (17)
aut . . . aut - either . . . or (17)
aútem - however; moreover (11)
cum (+indic.) - when (31)
cum (+subj.) - when, since, although (31)
dum - while, as long as, at the same time that; *or* until *(+subjunctive)* (8)
énim - for, in fact, truly (9)
et - and; even (2)
et . . . et - both . . . and (2)
ígitur - therefore, consequently (5)
nam - for (13)
nē - not; in order that . . . not, that . . . not, in order not to (28)
néque, nec - and not, nor (11)
néque . . . néque, nec . . . nec - neither . . . nor (11)
nísi - if . . . not, unless; except (19)
quod - because (11)
quóniam - since, inasmuch as (10)
sed - but (2)
sī - if (1)
ut (+indic.) - as, just as, when (24)
ut (+ subj.) - in order that, so that, that, in order to, so as to, to (28)
útrum . . . an - whether . . . or (30)

Prepositions

ab, ā (+abl.) - away from, from; by (14)
ad (+acc.) - to, up to, near to (8)
ánte (+acc.) - before *(in place or time)*, in front of (13)
ápud (+acc.) - among, in the presence of, at the house of (31)
cóntrā (+acc.) - against (19)
cum (+abl.) - with (10)
dē (+abl.) - down from, from; concerning, about (3)
ex, ē (abl.+) - out of, from, from within; by reason of, on account of ; of *(after cardinal numerals)* (8)
in (+acc.) - into, toward; against (9)
in (+abl.) - in, on (3)
ínter (+acc.) - between, among (15)
per (+acc.) - through; by *(with reflexive pronoun)* (13)
post (+acc.) - after, behind (7)
prae (+abl.) - in front of, before (26)
prō (+abl.) - in front of, before, on behalf of, for the sake of, in return for, instead of, for, as (12)
própter (+acc.) - on account of, because of (5)
síne (+abl.) - without (2)
sub (+abl. w/ verbs of rest *or* **+acc. w/ verbs of motion)** - under, up under, close to, down to/into, to/at the foot of (7)
trāns (+acc.) - across (14)
últrā (adv. and prep. +acc.) - on the other side of, beyond (22)

Interjection

ō - O!, Oh! (2)

Idioms

amā́bō tē - please (1)
grā́tiās ágere (+dat.) - to thank someone; to give thanks to (8)
mḗnsa secúnda (f) - dessert (26)
nōn sṓlum . . . sed étiam - not only . . . but also (9)
poénās dáre - to pay the penalty (2)
sē cōnférre - to go (31)
sī quándō - if ever (5)

Prefix

re-, red- - again, back (24)

Suffixes

-ne – interrogative suffix attached to the first word of a sentence, typically the verb or another word on which the question hinges, to introduce a question whose answer is uncertain (5)
-que - and *(enclitic conjunction; appended to the second of two words to be joined)* (6)

Numerals

Cardinal - ū́nus *to*
vīgíntī quī́nque (15)
Ordinal - prī́mus *to*
duodécimus (15)

----

céntum - a hundred (15)
mī́lia, mī́lium (n. pl.) -
thousands (15)
mī́lle - thousand (15)

Chapter 32

Nouns

1st Declension

adulēscéntia, adulēscéntiae (f) - youth, young manhood; youthfulness (5)
agrícola, agrícolae (m) - farmer (3)
amī́ca, amī́cae (f) - friend (female) (3)
amīcítia, amīcítiae (f) - friendship (10)
áqua, áquae (f) - water (14)
Ásia, Ásiae (f) - Asia (12)
cása, cásae (f) - house, cottage, hut (21)
caúsa, caúsae (f) - cause, reason; case, situation (21)
caúsā (abl. + preceding gen.) - for the sake of, on account of (21)
cḗna, cḗnae (f) - dinner (26)
clēméntia, clēméntiae (f) - mildness, gentleness, mercy (16)
cṓpia, cṓpiae (f) - abundance, supply (8)
cṓpiae, cōpiā́rum (f) - supplies, troops, forces (8)
cúlpa, cúlpae (f) - fault, blame (5)
cū́ra, cū́rae (f) - care, attention, caution, anxiety (4)
custṓdia, custṓdiae (f) - protection, custody; guards *(pl.)* (32)
déa, déae (f) - goddess (6)
discípula, discípulae (f) - learner, pupil, student (female) (6)
dīvítiae, dīvitiā́rum (f. pl.) - riches, wealth (13)
fā́bula, fā́bulae (f) - story, tale; play (24)
fā́ma, fā́mae (f) - rumor, report; fame, reputation (2)
família, famíliae (f) - household, family (19)
fḗmina, fḗminae (f) - woman (3)
fenéstra, fenéstrae (f) - window (21)
fī́lia, fī́liae (f) - daughter (3)
fṓrma, fṓrmae (f) - form, shape; beauty (2)
fortū́na, fortū́nae (f) - fortune, luck (2)
glṓria, glṓriae (f) - glory, fame (5)
Graécia, Graéciae (f) - Greece (19)
hásta, hástae (f) - spear (23)
hṓra, hṓrae (f) - hour, time (10)
īnsídiae, īnsidiā́rum (f) - ambush, plot, treachery (6)
ī́nsula, ī́nsulae (f) - island (23)
invídia, invídiae (f) - envy, jealousy, hatred (31)
ī́ra, ī́rae (f) - ire, anger (2)
Itália, Itáliae (f) - Italy (15)
língua, línguae (f) - tongue; language (25)
líttera, lítterae (f) - a letter of the alphabet (7)
lítterae, litterā́rum (f) - a letter (epistle), literature (7)
lū́na, lū́nae (f) - moon (28)
magístra, magístrae (f) - schoolmistress, teacher, mistress (4)
médica, médicae (f) - doctor, physician (female) (12)
memória, memóriae (f) - memory, recollection (15)
mḗnsa, mḗnsae (f) - table; dining; dish, course (26)
móra, mórae (f) - delay (4)
nā́ta, nā́tae (f) - daughter (29)
nātū́ra, nātū́rae (f) - nature (10)
naúta, naútae (m) - sailor (2)
patiéntia, patiéntiae (f) - suffering; patience, endurance (12)
pátria, pátriae (f) - fatherland, native land, (one's) country (2)
pecū́nia, pecū́niae (f) - money (2)
philosóphia, philosóphiae (f) - philosophy (2)
poéna, poénae (f) - penalty, punishment (2)
poḗta, poḗtae (m) - poet (2)
pórta, pórtae (f) - gate, entrance (2)
puélla, puéllae (f) - girl (2)
rēgī́na, rēgī́nae (f) - queen (7)
Rṓma, Rṓmae (f) - Rome (14)
rósa, rósae (f) - rose (2)
sapiéntia, sapiéntiae (f) - wisdom (3)
sátura, sáturae (f) - satire (16)
sciéntia, sciéntiae (f) - knowledge (18)
senténtia, senténtiae (f) - feeling, thought, opinion, vote, sentence (2)
sérva, sérvae (f) - slave (female) (24)
stḗlla, stḗllae (f) - star, planet (28)
térra, térrae (f) - earth, ground, land, country (7)
Trṓia, Trṓiae (f) - Troy (21)
túrba, túrbae (f) - uproar, disturbance; mob, crowd, multitude (14)
vía, víae (f) - way, road, street (10)
vīcī́na, vīcī́nae (f) - neighbor (female) (21)
victṓria, victṓriae (f) - victory (8)
vī́ta, vī́tae (f) - life; mode of life (2)

2nd Declension

áger, ágrī (m) - field, farm (3)
amī́cus, amī́cī (m) - friend (male) (3)
ánimī, animṓrum (m) - high spirits, pride, courage (5)
ánimus, ánimī (m) - soul, spirit, mind (5)

ánnus, ánnī (m) - year (12)
argūméntum, argūméntī (n) - proof, evidence, argument (19)
árma, armṓrum (n. pl.) - arms, weapons (28)
auxílium, auxíliī (n) - aid, help (31)
bā́sium, bā́siī (n) - kiss (4)
béllum, béllī (n) - war (4)
benefícium, benefíciī (n) - benefit, kindness; favor (19)
caélum, caélī (n) - sky, heaven (5)
coniūrā́tī, coniūrātṓrum (m. pl.) - conspirators (20)
cōnsílium, cōnsíliī (n) - plan, purpose, counsel, advice, judgment, wisdom (4)
déus, déī (m) - god (6)
dígitus, dígitī (m) - finger, toe (31)
discípulus, discípulī (m) - learner, pupil, student (male) (6)
dṓnum, dṓnī (n) - gift, present (4)
elephántus, elephántī (m and f) - elephant (31)
équus, équī (m) - horse (23)
exítium, exítiī (n) - destruction, ruin (4)
exsílium, exsíliī (n) - exile, banishment (31)
fáctum, fáctī (n) - deed, act, achievement (13)
fā́tum, fā́tī (n) - fate; death (29)
férrum, férrī (n) - iron; sword (22)
fī́lius, fī́liī (m) - son (3)
fórum, fórī (n) - marketplace, forum (26)
Graécus, Graécī (m) - a Greek (6)
impérium, impériī (n) - power to command, supreme power, authority, command, control (24)
ingénium, ingéniī (n) - nature, innate talent (29)
iūdícium, iūdíciī (n) - judgment, decision, opinion; trial (19)
libéllus, libéllī (m) - little book (17)
líber, líbrī (m) - book (6)
lóca, locṓrum (n) - places, region (9)
lócī, locṓrum (m) - passages in literature (9)
lócus, lócī (m) - place; passage in literature (9)
lū́dus, lū́dī (m) - game, sport; school (18)
magíster, magístrī (m) - schoolmaster, teacher, master (4)
médicus, médicī (m) - doctor, physician (male) (12)
módus, módī (m) - measure, bound, limit; manner, method, mode, way (22)
mórbus, mórbī (m) - disease, sickness (9)
múndus, múndī (m) - world, universe (21)
númerus, númerī (m) - number (3)
óculus, óculī (m) - eye (4)
offícium, offíciī (n) - duty, service (4)
ṓsculum, ṓsculī (n) - kiss (29)
ṓtium, ṓtiī (n) - leisure, peace (4)
perfúgium, perfúgiī (n) - refuge, shelter (24)
perī́culum, perī́culī (n) - danger, risk (4)
pópulus, pópulī (m) - the people, a people, a nation (3)
prīncípium, prīncípiī (n) - beginning (12)
púer, púerī (m) - boy; boys, children *(pl.)* (3)
remédium, remédiī (n) - cure, remedy (4)
sérvus, sérvī (m) - slave (male) (24)
sígnum, sígnī (n) - sign, signal, indication; seal (13)
sōlā́cium, sōlā́ciī (n) - comfort, relief (24)
sómnus, sómnī (m) - sleep (26)
stúdium, stúdiī (n) - eagerness, zeal, pursuit, study (9)
stúltus, stúltī (m) - a fool (4)
súperī, superṓrum (m. pl.) - the gods (27)
tyránnus, tyránnī (m) - absolute ruler, tyrant (6)
vérbum, vérbī (n)- word (5)
vīcī́nus, vīcī́nī (m) - neighbor (male) (21)
vī́num, vī́nī (n) - wine (31)
vir, vírī (m) - man, hero (3)
vítium, vítiī (n) - fault, crime, vice (6)
vúlgus, vúlgī (n) - the common people, mob, rabble (21)

3rd Declension

adulḗscēns, adulēscéntis (m *or* f) - young man *or* woman (12)
aétās, aetā́tis (f) - period of life, life, age, an age, time (16)
ámor, amṓris (m) - love (7)
aúctor, auctṓris (m) - increaser; author, originator (19)
audī́tor, audītṓris (m) - hearer, listener, member of an audience (16)
Caésar, Caésaris (m) - Caesar (12)
cáput, cápitis (n) - head; leader; beginning; life; heading; chapter (11)
cármen, cárminis (n) - song, poem (7)
Carthā́gō, Carthā́ginis (f) - Carthage (24)
Cícerō, Cicerṓnis (m) - (Marcus Tullius) Cicero (8)
cī́vitās, cīvitā́tis (f) - state, citizenship (7)
cṓnsul, cṓnsulis (m) - consul (11)
córpus, córporis (n) - body (7)

cupíditās, cupiditā́tis (f) - desire, longing, passion; cupidity, avarice (10)
dēlectā́tiō, dēlectātiṓnis (f) - delight, pleasure, enjoyment (27)
dux, dúcis (m) - leader, guide; commander, general (23)
flū́men, flū́minis (n) - river (18)
frā́ter, frā́tris (m) - brother (8)
génus, géneris (n) - origin; kind, type, sort, class (18)
hómō, hóminis (m) - human being, man (7)
hónor, honṓris (m) - honor, esteem; public office (30)
imperā́tor, imperātṓris (m) - general, commander-in-chief, emperor (24)
iū́dex, iū́dicis (m) - judge, juror (19)
iūs, iū́ris (n) - right, justice, law (14)
lábor, labṓris (m)- labor, work, toil; a work, production (7)
laus, laúdis (f) - praise, glory, fame (8)
lēx, lḗgis (f) - law, statute (26)
lībértās, lībertā́tis (f) - liberty (8)
lī́men, lī́minis (n) - threshold (26)
lī́tus, lī́toris (n) - shore, coast (23)
lūx, lū́cis (f) - light (26)
maiṓrēs, maiṓrum (m. pl.) - ancestors (27)
mā́ter, mā́tris (f) - mother (12)
mī́les, mī́litis (m) - soldier (23)
mṓrēs, mṓrum (m) - habits, morals, character (7)
mōs, mṓris (m) - habit, custom, manner (7)
nḗmō, nūllī́us, nḗminī, nḗminem, nū́llō, nū́llā (m *or* f) - no one, nobody (11)
népōs, nepṓtis (m) - grandson, descendant (27)
nṓmen, nṓminis (n) - name (7)
occā́siō, occāsiṓnis (f) - occasion, opportunity (28)
ōrā́tor, ōrātṓris (m) - orator, speaker (23)
ōs, ṓris (n) - mouth, face (14)
párēns, paréntis (m *or* f) - parent (28)
páter, pátris (m) - father (12)
paupértās, paupertā́tis (f) - poverty, humble circumstances (32)
pāx, pā́cis (f) - peace (7)
prī́nceps, prī́ncipis (m *or* f) - leader, emperor (28)
próbitās, probitā́tis (f) - uprightness, honesty (18)
rátiō, ratiṓnis (f) - reckoning, account; reason, judgment, consideration; system; manner, method (8)
rēx, rḗgis (m) - king (7)
rū́mor, rūmṓris (m) - rumor, gossip (31)
sacérdōs, sacerdṓtis (m) - priest (23)
sálūs, salū́tis (f) - health, safety; greeting (21)
sápiēns, sapiéntis (m/f) - a wise man/woman, philosopher (25)
scélus, scéleris (n) - evil deed, crime, sin, wickedness (19)
scrī́ptor, scrīptṓris (m) - writer, author (8)
senéctūs, senectū́tis (f) - old age (10)
sénex, sénis (m) - old man (16)
sérvitūs, servitū́tis (f) - servitude, slavery (20)
sī́dus, sī́deris (n) - constellation, star (29)
sōl, sṓlis (m) - sun (27)
sóror, sorṓris (f) - sister (8)
tempéstās, tempestā́tis (f) - period of time, season; weather, storm (15)
témpus, témporis (n) - time; occasion, opportunity (7)
tímor, timṓris (m) - fear (10)
úxor, uxṓris (f) - wife (7)
vḗritās, vēritā́tis (f) - truth (10)
vésper, vésperis *or* vésperī (m) - evening; evening star (28)
vírgō, vírginis (f) - maiden, virgin (7)
vírtūs, virtū́tis (f) - manliness, courage; excellence, character, worth, virtue (7)
volúptās, voluptā́tis (f) - pleasure (10)
vúlnus, vúlneris (n) - wound (24)

3rd Declension I-Stem

ánimal, animā́lis (n) - a living creature, animal (14)
ars, ártis (f) - art, skill (14)
arx, árcis (f) - citadel, stronghold (23)
as, ássis (m) - an as *(a small copper coin)* (31)
aúris, aúris (f) - ear (14)
cī́vis, cī́vis (m *or* f) - citizen (14)
fī́nēs, fī́nium (m) - boundaries, territory (21)
fī́nis, fī́nis (m) - end, limit, boundary; purpose (21)
gēns, géntis (f) - clan, race, nation, people (21)
hóstēs, hóstium (m) - the enemy (18)
hóstis, hóstis (m) - an enemy *(of the state)* (18)
ígnis, ígnis (m) - fire (22)
máre, máris (n) - sea (14)
mēns, méntis (f) - mind, thought, intention (16)
moénia, moénium (n. pl.) - walls of a city (29)
mōns, móntis (m) - mountain (20)
mors, mórtis (f) - death (14)
nā́vis, nā́vis (f) - ship, boat (21)
nox, nóctis (f) - night (26)
nū́bēs, nū́bis (f) - cloud (14)
pars, pártis (f) - part, share; direction (14)
urbs, úrbis (f) - city (14)

vī́rēs, vī́rium (f. pl.) - strength (14)
vīs, vīs (f) - force, power, violence (14)

4th Declension
córnū, córnūs (n) - horn (20)
cúrsus, cúrsūs (m) - running, race; course (28)
exércitus, exércitūs (m) - army (32)
frū́ctus, frū́ctūs (m) - fruit; profit, benefit, enjoyment (20)
génū, génūs (n) - knee (20)
mánus, mánūs (f) - hand; handwriting; band (20)
métus, métūs (m) - fear, dread, anxiety (20)
senā́tus, senā́tūs (m) - senate (20)
sḗnsus, sḗnsūs (m) - feeling, sense (20)
spī́ritus, spī́ritūs (m) - breath, breathing; spirit, soul (20)
vérsus, vérsūs (m) - line of verse (20)

5th Declension
díēs, diḗī (m) - day (22)
fídēs, fídeī (f) - faith, trust, trustworthiness, fidelity, promise, guarantee, protection (22)
rēs, réī (f) - thing, matter, property, business, affair (22)
rēs pū́blica, réī pū́blicae (f) - state, commonwealth, republic (22)
spēs, spéī (f) - hope (22)

Indeclinable
níhil - nothing (1)
sátis - enough (5)

Pronouns

áliquis, áliquid - someone, somebody, something (23)
égo, méī - I (11)
hic, haec, hoc - this; the latter; he, she, it, they (9)
ī́dem, éadem, ídem - the same (11)
ílle, ílla, íllud - that; the former; the famous; he, she, it, they (9)
ípse, ípsa, ípsum - myself, yourself, himself, herself, itself, *etc.*, the very, the actual (13)
is, éa, id - this, that; he, she, it (11)
íste, ísta, ístud - that of yours, that; such (as you have, as you speak of); *sometimes with contemptuous force, e.g.,* that despicable, that wretched (9)
quī, quae, quod - who, which, what, that (17)
quid - what (1)
quī́dam, quaédam, quíddam - a certain one or thing, someone, something (26)
quis? quid? - who? whose? whom? what? which? (19)
quísque, quídque, cuiúsque, cuíque - each one, each person, each thing (13)
quísquis, quídquid - whoever, whatever (23)
súī - himself, herself, itself, themselves (13)
tū, túī - you *(sing.)* (11)

Adjectives

1st & 2nd Declension
acérbus, acérba, acérbum - harsh, bitter, grievous (12)
aéquus, aéqua, aéquum - level, even; calm; equal, just; favorable (22)
áliī . . . áliī - some . . . others (9)
álius, ália, áliud - other, another (9)
álter, áltera, álterum - the other (of two), second (9)
amī́cus, amī́ca, amī́cum - friendly (11)
antī́quus, antī́qua, antī́quum - ancient, old-time (2)
ásper, áspera, ásperum - rough, harsh (21)
avā́rus, avā́ra, avā́rum - greedy, avaricious (3)
beā́tus, beā́ta, beā́tum - happy, fortunate, blessed (10)
béllus, bélla, béllum - pretty, handsome, charming (4)
bónus, bóna, bónum - good, kind (4)
caécus, caéca, caécum - blind (17)
cā́rus, cā́ra, cā́rum - dear (11)
cértus, cérta, cértum - definite, sure, certain, reliable (19)
cḗterī, cḗterae, cḗtera - the remaining, the rest, the other, all the others (30)
clā́rus, clā́ra, clā́rum - clear, bright; renowned, famous, illustrious (18)
déxter, déxtra, déxtrum - right, right-hand (20)
dígnus, dígna, dígnum (+abl.) - worthy, worthy of (29)
dóctus, dócta, dóctum - taught, learned, skilled (13)
dū́rus, dū́ra, dū́rum - hard, harsh, rough, stern, unfeeling, hardy, difficult (29)
fortūnā́tus, fortūnā́ta, fortūnā́tum - lucky, fortunate, happy (13)
géminus, gémina, géminum - twin (25)
Graécus, Graéca, Graécum - Greek (6)

hūmā́nus, hūmā́na, hūmā́num - pertaining to man, human; humane, kind; refined, cultivated (4)
incértus, incérta, incértum - uncertain, unsure, doubtful (22)
iūcúndus, iūcúnda, iūcúndum - pleasant, delightful, agreeable, pleasing (16)
Latī́nus, Latī́na, Latī́num - Latin (22)
lī́ber, lī́bera, lī́berum - free (5)
lóngus, lónga, lóngum - long (16)
magnánimus, magnánima, magnánimum - great-hearted, brave, magnanimous (23)
mágnus, mágna, mágnum - large, great; important (2)
málus, mála, málum - bad, wicked, evil (4)
médius, média, médium - middle; the middle of (22)
méus, méa, méum - my (2)
míser, mísera, míserum - wretched, miserable, unfortunate (15)
mórtuus, mórtua, mórtuum - dead (28)
múltus, múlta, múltum - much, many (2)
neúter, neútra, neútrum - not either, neither (9)
nóster, nóstra, nóstrum - our, ours (5)
nóvus, nóva, nóvum - new; strange (7)
nū́llus, nū́lla, nū́llum - not any, no, none (9)
párvus, párva, párvum - small, little (4)
paúcī, paúcae, paúca - few, a few (3)
perpétuus, perpétua, perpétuum perpetual, lasting, uninterrupted, continuous (6)
plḗnus, plḗna, plḗnum - full, abundant, generous (6)
prī́mus, prī́ma, prī́mum - first, foremost, chief, principal (27)
pudī́cus, pudī́ca, pudī́cum - modest, chaste (26)
púlcher, púlchra, púlchrum - beautiful, handsome; fine (5)
quántus, quánta, quántum - how large, how great, how much (30)
rīdículus, rīdícula, rīdículum - laughable, ridiculous (30)
Rōmā́nus, Rōmā́na, Rōmā́num - Roman (3)
sálvus, sálva, sálvum - safe, sound (6)
sā́nus, sā́na, sā́num - sound, healthy, sane (5)
secúndus, secúnda, secúndum - second; favorable (6)
siníster, sinístra, sinístrum - left, left-hand; harmful, ill-omened (20)
sṓlus, sṓla, sṓlum - alone, only, the only (9)
stúltus, stúlta, stúltum - foolish (4)
supérbus, supérba, supérbum - arrogant, overbearing, haughty, proud (26)
súperus, súpera, súperum - above, upper (27)
súus, súa, súum - his own, her own, its own, their own (13)
tántus, tánta, tántum - so large, so great, of such a size (29)
tántus . . . quántus - just as much (many) . . . as (30)
tṓtus, tṓta, tṓtum - whole, entire (9)
túus, túa, túum - your *(sing.)* (2)
ū́llus, ū́lla, ū́llum - any (9)
últimus, última, últimum - farthest, extreme; last, final (25)
ū́nus, ū́na, ū́num - one, single, alone (9)
urbā́nus, urbā́na, urbā́num - of the city, urban; urbane, elegant (26)
úter, útra, útrum - either, which (of two) (9)
vḗrus, vḗra, vḗrum - true, real, proper (4)
véster, véstra, véstrum - your *(pl.)* (6)
vī́vus, vī́va, vī́vum - alive, living (30)

3rd Declension

ā́cer, ā́cris, ā́cre - sharp, keen, eager; severe, fierce (16)
brévis, bréve - short, small, brief (16)
céler, céleris, célere - swift, quick, rapid (16)
commū́nis, commū́ne - common, general, of / for the community (20)
diffícilis, diffícile - hard, difficult, troublesome (16)
dī́ligēns, ***gen.*** **dīligéntis** - diligent, careful (27)
dissímilis, dissímile - unlike, different (27)
dī́ves, ***gen.*** **dī́vitis** ***or*** **dī́tis** - rich, wealthy (32)
dúlcis, dúlce - sweet; pleasant, agreeable (16)
fácilis, fácile - easy; agreeable (16)
fḗlīx, ***gen.*** **fēlī́cis** - lucky, fortunate, happy (22)
férōx, ***gen.*** **ferṓcis** - fierce, savage (25)
fidḗlis, fidḗle - faithful, loyal (25)
fórtis, fórte - strong, brave (16)
grácilis, grácile - slender, thin (27)

grávis, gráve - heavy, weighty; serious, important; severe, grievous (19)
húmilis, húmile - lowly, humble (27)
immortális, immortále - not subject to death, immortal (19)
íngēns, ***gen.*** **ingéntis** - huge (16)
lévis, léve - light; easy; slight, trivial (17)
máior, máius - greater; older (27)
medíocris, medíocre - ordinary, moderate, mediocre (31)
mortális, mortále - mortal (18)
ómnis, ómne - every, all (16)
pār, ***gen.*** **páris (+dat.)** - equal, like (32)
paúper, ***gen.*** **paúperis** - of small means, poor (32)
pótēns, ***gen.*** **poténtis** - able, powerful, mighty, strong (16)
prínceps, ***gen.*** **príncipis** - chief, foremost (28)
sápiēns, ***gen.*** **sapiéntis** - wise, judicious (25)
sénex, ***gen.*** **sénis** - old, aged (16)
símilis, símile (+gen. or dat.) - similar (to), like, resembling (27)
trístis, tríste - sad, sorrowful; joyless, grim, severe (26)
túrpis, túrpe - ugly; shameful, base, disgraceful (26)
ū́tilis, ū́tile - useful, advantageous (27)

Indeclinable Adjectives
quot - how many, as many as (27)
sátis - enough, sufficient (5)

Indefinite Adjective
quídam, quaédam, quóddam - a certain, some (26)

Interrogative Adjective
quī?, quae?, quod? - what? which? what kind of?; *(sometimes with exclamatory force)* what (a)! what sort of! (19)

Verbs

1st Conjugation
ádiuvō, adiuváre, adiū́vī, adiū́tum - to help, aid, assist; to please (4)
ámō, amáre, amávī, amátum - to love, like (1)
appéllō, appelláre, appellávī, appellátum - to speak to, address (as), call, name (14)
cḗnō, cēnáre, cēnávī, cēnátum - to dine (5)
cṓgitō, cōgitáre, cōgitávī, cōgitátum- to think, ponder, consider, plan (1)
cōnsérvō, cōnserváre, cōnservávī, cōnservátum - to preserve, conserve, maintain (1)
créō, creáre, creávī, creátum - to create (12)
cúlpō, culpáre, culpávī, culpátum - to blame, censure (5)
dédicō, dēdicáre, dēdicávī, dēdicátum - to dedicate (28)
dēléctō, dēlectáre, dēlectávī, dēlectátum - to delight, charm, please (19)
dēmṓnstrō, dēmōnstráre, dēmōnstrávī, dēmōnstrátum to point out, show, demonstrate (8)
dēsíderō, dēsīderáre, dēsīderávī, dēsīderátum - to desire, long for, miss (17)
dō, dáre, dédī, dátum - to give, offer (1)
dúbitō, dubitáre, dubitávī, dubitátum - to doubt, hesitate (30)
ḗducō, ēducáre, ēducávī, ēducátum - to bring up, educate (23)
érrō, erráre, errávī, errátum - to wander; err, go astray, make a mistake, be mistaken (1)
exspéctō, exspectáre, exspectávī, exspectátum - to look for, expect, await (15)
invī́tō, invītáre, invītávī, invītátum - to entertain, invite, summon (26)
iúvō, iuváre, iū́vī, iū́tum - to help, aid, assist; to please (4)
labṓrō, labōráre, labōrávī, labōrátum - to labor; be in distress (21)
laúdō, laudáre, laudávī, laudátum - to praise (1)
lī́berō, līberáre, līberávī, līberátum - to free, liberate (19)
mū́tō, mūtáre, mūtávī, mūtátum to change, alter; exchange (14)
nárrō, nārráre, nārrávī, nārrátum - to tell, report, narrate (24)
návigō, nāvigáre, nāvigávī, nāvigátum - to sail, navigate (17)
nécō, necáre, necávī, necátum - to murder, kill (7)
négō, negáre, negávī, negátum to deny, say that . . . not (25)
nū́ntiō, nūntiáre, nūntiávī, nūntiátum - to announce, report, relate (25)
párō, paráre, parávī, parátum - to prepare, provide; get, obtain (19)
praéstō, praestáre, praéstitī, praéstitum - to excel; exhibit, show, offer, supply, furnish (28)

próbō, probáre, probávī, probátum - to approve, recommend; test (27)
prōnúntiō, prōnūntiáre, prōnūntiávī, prōnūntiátum - to proclaim, announce; declaim; pronounce (20)
púgnō, pugnáre, pugnávī, pugnátum - to fight (29)
pútō, putáre, putávī, putátum - to reckon, suppose, judge, think, imagine (25)
récitō, recitáre, recitávī, recitátum - to read aloud, recite (17)
rógō, rogáre, rogávī, rogátum - to ask (30)
sátiō, satiáre, satiávī, satiátum - to satisfy, sate (3)
sérvō, serváre, servávī, servátum - to preserve, save, keep, guard (1)
spérō, spēráre, spērávī, spērátum - to hope for, hope (25)
stō, stáre, stétī, státum - to stand, stand still *or* firm (13)
súperō, superáre, superávī, superátum - to be above, have the upper hand, surpass; overcome, conquer (5)
tólerō, toleráre, tolerávī, tolerátum - to bear, endure (6)
vítō, vītáre, vītávī, vītátum - to avoid, shun (14)
vócō, vocáre, vocávī, vocátum - to call, summon (1)

2nd Conjugation

aúdeō, audére, aúsus sum - to dare (7)
cáreō, carére, cáruī, caritúrum (+abl.) - to be without, be deprived of, want, lack; be free from (20)
contíneō, continére, contínuī, conténtum - to hold together, contain, keep, enclose, restrain (21)
débeō, dēbére, débuī, débitum - to owe; ought, must, should (1)
déleō, dēlére, dēlévī, dēlétum - to destroy, wipe out, erase (17)
dóceō, docére, dócuī, dóctum - to teach (8)
dóleō, dolére, dóluī, dolitúrum - to grieve, suffer; hurt, give pain (31)
égeō, egére, éguī (+ abl. or gen.) - to need, lack, want (28)
éxpleō, explére, explévī, explétum - to fill, fill up, complete (28)
gaúdeō, gaudére, gāvísus sum - to be glad, rejoice (23)
hábeō, habére, hábuī, hábitum - to have, hold, possess; consider, regard (3)
iáceō, iacére, iácuī - to lie; lie prostrate; lie dead (25)
invídeō, invidére, invídī, invísum to be envious; to look at with envy, envy, be jealous of (+dat.) (31)
iúbeō, iubére, iússī, iússum - to bid, order, command (21)
máneō, manére, mánsī, mánsum - to remain, stay, stay behind, abide, continue (5)
mísceō, miscére, míscuī, míxtum to mix, stir up, disturb (18)
móneō, monére, mónuī, mónitum - to remind, advise, warn (1)
móveō, movére, móvī, mótum - to move; arouse, affect (18)
páteō, patére, pátuī - to be open, lie open; be accessible; be evident (32)
praébeō, praebére, praébuī, praébitum - to offer, provide (32)
prohíbeō, prohibére, prohíbuī, prohíbitum - to keep (back), prevent, hinder, restrain, prohibit (20)
remáneō, remanére, remánsī, remánsum - to remain, stay, stay behind, abide, continue (5)
respóndeō, respondére, respóndī, respónsum - to answer (29)
rídeō, rīdére, rísī, rísum - to laugh, laugh at (24)
sálvē, salvéte - hello, greetings (1)
sálveō, salvére - to be well, be in good health (1)
táceō, tacére, tácuī, tácitum - to be silent, leave unmentioned (28)
téneō, tenére, ténuī, téntum - to hold, keep, possess; restrain (14)
térreō, terrére, térruī, térritum - to frighten, terrify (1)
tímeō, timére, tímuī - to fear, be afraid (of) (15)
válē, valéte - good-bye, farewell (1)
váleō, valére, váluī, valitúrum - to be strong, have power; be well (1)
vídeō, vidére, vídī, vísum - to see; observe, understand (1)
vídeor, vidérī, vísus sum - to be seen, seem, appear (18)

3rd Conjugation

admíttō, admíttere, admísī, admíssum - to admit, receive, let in (17)
ágō, ágere, égī, áctum - to drive, lead, do, act; pass, spend *(life or time)* (8)

álō, álere, áluī, áltum - to nourish, support, sustain, increase; cherish (13)
āmíttō, āmíttere, āmī́sī, āmíssum - to send away; lose, let go (12)
āvértō, āvértere, āvértī, āvérsum - to turn away, avert (23)
bíbō, bíbere, bíbī - to drink (30)
cádō, cádere, cécidī, cāsū́rum - to fall (12)
cḗdō, cḗdere, céssī, céssum - to go, withdraw; yield to, grant, submit (28)
cérnō, cérnere, crḗvī, crḗtum - to distinguish, discern, perceive (22)
cognṓscō, cognṓscere, cognṓvī, cógnitum - to become acquainted with, learn, recognize; know *(in perfect tenses)* (30)
commíttō, commíttere, commī́sī, commíssum - to entrust, commit (15)
comprehéndō, comprehéndere, comprehéndī, comprehḗnsum - to grasp, seize, arrest; comprehend, understand (30)
cóndō, cóndere, cóndidī, cónditum - to put together *or* into, store; found, establish (29)
cōnsū́mō, cōnsū́mere, cōnsū́mpsī, cōnsū́mptum - to consume, use up (30)
conténdō, conténdere, conténdī, conténtum - to strive, struggle, contend; hasten (29)
crḗdō, crḗdere, crḗdidī, crḗditum to believe, trust (25)
cúrrō, cúrrere, cucúrrī, cúrsum - to run, rush, move quickly (14)
dēféndō, dēféndere, dēféndī, dēfḗnsum - to ward off; defend, protect (20)
dī́cō, dī́cere, dī́xī, díctum - to say, tell, speak; name, call (10)
dī́ligō, dīlígere, dīlḗxī, dīlḗctum - to esteem, love (13)
discḗdō, discḗdere, discéssī, discéssum - to go away, depart (20)
díscō, díscere, dídicī - to learn (8)
dū́cō, dū́cere, dū́xī, dúctum - to lead; consider, regard; prolong (8)
expéllō, expéllere, éxpulī, expúlsum - to drive out, expel, banish (24)
expṓnō, expṓnere, expósuī, expósitum - to set forth, explain, expose (30)
flúō, flúere, flū́xī, flū́xum - to flow (18)
gérō, gérere, géssī, géstum - to carry; carry on, manage, conduct, wage, accomplish, perform (8)
intéllegō, intellégere, intellḗxī, intellḗctum - to understand (11)
iúngō, iúngere, iū́nxī, iū́nctum - to join (13)
légō, légere, lḗgī, lḗctum - to pick out, choose; read (18)
mínuō, minúere, mínuī, minū́tum - to lessen, diminish (30)
míttō, míttere, mī́sī, míssum - to send, let go (11)
néglegō, neglégere, neglḗxī, neglḗctum - to neglect, disregard (17)
nṓscō, nṓscere, nṓvī, nṓtum - to become acquainted with, learn, recognize; know *(in perfect tenses)* (30)
óccidō, occídere, óccidī, occā́sum - to fall down; die; set (31)
ópprimō, opprímere, oppréssī, oppréssum - to suppress, overwhelm, overpower, check (23)
osténdō, osténdere, osténdī, osténtum - to exhibit, show, display (23)
péllō, péllere, pépulī, púlsum - to strike, push; drive out, banish (24)
pétō, pétere, petī́vī, petī́tum - to seek, aim at, beg, beseech (23)
pṓnō, pṓnere, pósuī, pósitum - to put, place, set (27)
prémō, prémere, préssī, préssum - to press; press hard, pursue (23)
prōmíttō, prōmíttere, prōmī́sī, prōmíssum - to send forth; promise (32)
quaérō, quaérere, quaesī́vī, quaesī́tum - to seek, look for, strive for; ask, inquire, inquire into (24)
régō, régere, rḗxī, rḗctum - to rule, guide, direct (16)
relínquō, relínquere, relī́quī, relíctum - to leave behind, leave, abandon, desert (21)
revértō, revértere, revértī, revérsum - turn back (23)
scrī́bō, scrī́bere, scrī́psī, scrī́ptum to write, compose (8)
súrgō, súrgere, surrḗxī, surrḗctum - to get up, arise (29)
tángō, tángere, tétigī, tā́ctum - to touch (21)
tóllō, tóllere, sústulī, sublā́tum - to raise, lift up; take away, remove, destroy (22)
tráhō, tráhere, trā́xī, tráctum - to draw, drag; derive, acquire (8)

vértō, vértere, vértī, vérsum - to turn; change (23)
víncō, víncere, vī́cī, víctum - to conquer, overcome (8)
vī́vō, vī́vere, vī́xī, vī́ctum - to live (10)

3rd Conjugation -iō
accípiō, accípere, accḗpī, accéptum - to take *(to one's self)*, receive, accept (24)
cápiō, cápere, cḗpī, cáptum - to take, capture, seize, get (10)
cúpiō, cúpere, cupī́vī, cupī́tum - to desire, wish, long for (17)
ēripiō, ērípere, ērípuī, ēréptum - to snatch away, take away; rescue (22)
excípiō, excípere, excḗpī, excéptum - to take out, except; take, receive, capture (24)
fáciō, fácere, fḗcī, fáctum - to make, do, accomplish (10)
fúgiō, fúgere, fū́gī, fugitū́rum - to flee, hurry away; escape; go into exile; avoid, shun (10)
iáciō, iácere, iḗcī, iáctum - to throw, hurl (15)
incípiō, incípere, incḗpī, incéptum - to begin (17)
patefáciō, patefácere, patefḗcī, patefáctum - to make open, open; disclose, expose (25)
rápiō, rápere, rápuī, ráptum - to seize, snatch, carry away (21)
recípiō, recípere, recḗpī, recéptum - to take back, regain; admit, receive (24)
suscípiō, suscípere, suscḗpī, suscéptum - to undertake (25)

4th Conjugation
aúdiō, audī́re, audī́vī, audī́tum - to hear, listen to (10)
dórmiō, dormī́re, dormī́vī, dormī́tum - to sleep (31)
invéniō, invenī́re, invḗnī, invéntum - to come upon, find (10)
mólliō, mollī́re, mollī́vī, mollī́tum to soften; make calm *or* less hostile (29)
nésciō, nescī́re, nescī́vī, nescī́tum - to not know, be ignorant (25)
scíō, scī́re, scī́vī, scī́tum - to know (21)
séntiō, sentī́re, sḗnsī, sḗnsum - to feel, perceive, think, experience (11)
véniō, venī́re, vḗnī, véntum - to come (10)

Irregular
ádferō, adférre, áttulī, allā́tum - to bring to (31)
cṓnferō, cōnférre, cóntulī, collā́tum - to bring together, compare; confer, bestow (31)
férō, férre, túlī, lā́tum - to bear, carry, bring; suffer, endure, tolerate; say, report (31)
mā́lō, mā́lle, mā́luī - to want (something) more, instead; prefer (32)
nṓlō, nṓlle, nṓluī - to not . . . wish, be unwilling (32)
ófferō, offérre, óbtulī, oblā́tum - to offer (31)
póssum, pósse, pótuī - to be able, can, could, have power (6)
réferō, reférre, réttulī, relā́tum - to carry back, bring back; repeat, answer, report (31)
sum, ésse, fúī, futū́rum - to be, exist (4)
vólō, vélle, vóluī - to wish, want, be willing, will (32)

Defective
ā́it, ā́iunt - he says, they say, assert (25)
coépī, coepísse, coéptum - began (17)
ínquit - he says *or* said (22)
ṓdī, ōdísse, ōsū́rum - to hate (20)

Adverbs

ánte (+acc.) - before, previously (13)
béne - well, satisfactorily, quite (11)
cíto - quickly (17)
crās - tomorrow (5)
cūr - why (18)
déhinc - then, next (25)
deínde - thereupon, next, then (18)
dḗnique - at last, finally, lastly (29)
díū - long, for a long time (12)
étiam - even, also (11)
fū́rtim - stealthily, secretly (30)
héri - yesterday (5)
hīc - here (25)
hódiē - today (3)
iam - now, already, soon (19)
íbi - there (6)
íta - so, thus (29)
ítaque - and so, therefore (15)
íterum - again, a second time (21)
mox - soon (30)
nē . . . quídem - not . . . even (29)
nímis, nímium - too, too much, excessively; *(in a positive sense, esp. with adjectives and adverbs)* exceedingly, very (9)
nōn - not (1)
númquam - never (8)
nunc - now, at present (6)
nū́per - recently (12)

ṓlim - once (upon a time), long ago, formerly; some day, in the future (13)
pósteā - afterwards (24)
prī́mō - at first, at the beginning (30)
prṓtinus - immediately (22)
quam - how (16)
quam - than *(after comparatives);* as . . . as possible *(with superlatives)* (26)
quándō - when (5)
quā́rē - because of which thing *(lit.);* therefore, wherefore, why (6)
quídem - indeed, certainly, at least, even (29)
quóndam - formerly, once (22)
quóque - also, too (17)
repénte - suddenly (30)
saépe - often (1)
sátis - enough, sufficiently (5)
sémel - a single time, once, once and for all, simultaneously (31)
sémper - always (3)
sīc - so, thus (29)
tam - so, to such a degree (29)
tam . . . quam - so . . . as (29)
támen - nevertheless, still (8)
tamquam - as it were, as if, so to speak (29)
tántum - only (26)
tum - then, at that time; thereupon, in the next place (5)
úbi - where, when (6)
últrā - on the other side of, beyond (22)
úmquam - ever, at any time (23)
únde - whence, from what *or* which place, from which, from whom (30)
úsque - all the way, up (to), even (to), continuously, always (31)
vḗrō - in truth, indeed, to be sure, however (29)

Conjunctions

at - but; but, mind you; but, you say (19)
átque, ac - and also, and even, and in fact (21)
aut - or (17)
aut . . . aut - either . . . or (17)
aútem - however; moreover (11)
cum (+indic.) - when (31)
cum (+subj.) - when, since, although (31)
dum - while, as long as, at the same time that; *or* until *(+subjunctive)* (8)
dúmmodo (+subj.) - provided that, so long as (32)
énim - for, in fact, truly (9)
et - and; even (2)
et . . . et - both . . . and (2)
ígitur - therefore, consequently (5)
nam - for (13)
nē - not; in order that . . . not, that . . . not, in order not to (28)
néque, nec - and not, nor (11)
néque . . . néque, nec . . . nec - neither . . . nor (11)
nísi - if . . . not, unless; except (19)
quod - because (11)
quóniam - since, inasmuch as (10)
sed - but (2)
sī - if (1)
ut (+indic.) - as, just as, when (24)
ut (+ subj.) - in order that, so that, that, in order to, so as to, to (28)
útrum . . . an - whether . . . or (30)

Prepositions

ab, ā (+abl.) - away from, from; by (14)
ad (+acc.) - to, up to, near to (8)
ánte (+acc.) - before *(in place or time),* in front of (13)
ápud (+acc.) - among, in the presence of, at the house of (31)
cóntrā (+acc.) - against (19)
cum (+abl.) - with (10)
dē (+abl.) - down from, from; concerning, about (3)
ex, ē (abl.+) - out of, from, from within; by reason of, on account of ; of *(after cardinal numerals)* (8)
in (+acc.) - into, toward; against (9)
in (+abl.) - in, on (3)
ínter (+acc.) - between, among (15)
per (+acc.) - through; by *(with reflexive pronoun)* (13)
post (+acc.) - after, behind (7)
prae (+abl.) - in front of, before (26)
prō (+abl.) - in front of, before, on behalf of, for the sake of, in return for, instead of, for, as (12)
própter (+acc.) - on account of, because of (5)
síne (+abl.) - without (2)
sub (+abl. w/ verbs of rest *or* +acc. w/ verbs of motion) - under, up under, close to, down to/into, to/at the foot of (7)
trāns (+acc.) - across (14)
últrā (adv. and prep. +acc.) - on the other side of, beyond (22)

Interjection
ō - O!, Oh! (2)

Idioms
amā́bō tē - please (1)
grā́tiās ágere (+dat.) - to thank someone; to give thanks to (8)
mḗnsa secúnda (f) - dessert (26)
nōn sṓlum . . . sed étiam - not only . . . but also (9)
poénās dáre - to pay the penalty (2)
sē cōnférre - to go (31)
sī quándō - if ever (5)

Prefix
re-, red- - again, back (24)

Suffixes
-ne – interrogative suffix attached to the first word of a sentence, typically the verb or another word on which the question hinges, to introduce a question whose answer is uncertain (5)
-que - and *(enclitic conjunction; appended to the second of two words to be joined)* (6)

Numerals
Cardinal - ū́nus *to* vīgíntī quī́nque (15)
Ordinal - prī́mus *to* duodécimus (15)

----

céntum - a hundred (15)
mī́lia, mī́lium (n. pl.) - thousands (15)
mī́lle - thousand (15)

Chapter 33

Nouns

1st Declension

adulēscéntia, adulēscéntiae (f) - youth, young manhood; youthfulness (5)
agrícola, agrícolae (m) - farmer (3)
amíca, amícae (f) - friend (female) (3)
amīcítia, amīcítiae (f) - friendship (10)
áqua, áquae (f) - water (14)
Ásia, Ásiae (f) - Asia (12)
cása, cásae (f) - house, cottage, hut (21)
caúsa, caúsae (f) - cause, reason; case, situation (21)
caúsā (abl. + preceding gen.) - for the sake of, on account of (21)
cḗna, cḗnae (f) - dinner (26)
clēméntia, clēméntiae (f) - mildness, gentleness, mercy (16)
cṓpia, cṓpiae (f) - abundance, supply (8)
cṓpiae, cōpiā́rum (f) - supplies, troops, forces (8)
cúlpa, cúlpae (f) - fault, blame (5)
cū́ra, cū́rae (f) - care, attention, caution, anxiety (4)
custṓdia, custṓdiae (f) - protection, custody; guards *(pl.)* (32)
déa, déae (f) - goddess (6)
discípula, discípulae (f) - learner, pupil, student (female) (6)
dīvítiae, dīvitiā́rum (f. pl.) - riches, wealth (13)
fā́bula, fā́bulae (f) - story, tale; play (24)
fā́ma, fā́mae (f) - rumor, report; fame, reputation (2)
família, famíliae (f) - household, family (19)
fḗmina, fḗminae (f) - woman (3)
fenéstra, fenéstrae (f) - window (21)
fī́lia, fī́liae (f) - daughter (3)
fṓrma, fṓrmae (f) - form, shape; beauty (2)
fortū́na, fortū́nae (f) - fortune, luck (2)
glṓria, glṓriae (f) - glory, fame (5)
Graécia, Graéciae (f) - Greece (19)
hásta, hástae (f) - spear (23)
hṓra, hṓrae (f) - hour, time (10)
īnsídiae, īnsidiā́rum (f) - ambush, plot, treachery (6)
ī́nsula, ī́nsulae (f) - island (23)
invídia, invídiae (f) - envy, jealousy, hatred (31)
ī́ra, ī́rae (f) - ire, anger (2)
Itália, Itáliae (f) - Italy (15)
língua, línguae (f) - tongue; language (25)
líttera, lítterae (f) - a letter of the alphabet (7)
lítterae, litterā́rum (f) - a letter (epistle), literature (7)
lū́na, lū́nae (f) - moon (28)
magístra, magístrae (f) - schoolmistress, teacher, mistress (4)
médica, médicae (f) - doctor, physician (female) (12)
memória, memóriae (f) - memory, recollection (15)
mḗnsa, mḗnsae (f) - table; dining; dish, course (26)
móra, mórae (f) - delay (4)
nā́ta, nā́tae (f) - daughter (29)
nātū́ra, nātū́rae (f) - nature (10)
naúta, naútae (m) - sailor (2)
patiéntia, patiéntiae (f) - suffering; patience, endurance (12)
pátria, pátriae (f) - fatherland, native land, (one's) country (2)
pecū́nia, pecū́niae (f) - money (2)
philósopha, philósophae (f) - philosopher (female) (33)
philosóphia, philosóphiae (f) - philosophy (2)
poéna, poénae (f) - penalty, punishment (2)
poḗta, poḗtae (m) - poet (2)
pórta, pórtae (f) - gate, entrance (2)
puélla, puéllae (f) - girl (2)
rēgī́na, rēgī́nae (f) - queen (7)
Rṓma, Rṓmae (f) - Rome (14)
rósa, rósae (f) - rose (2)
sapiéntia, sapiéntiae (f) - wisdom (3)
sátura, sáturae (f) - satire (16)
sciéntia, sciéntiae (f) - knowledge (18)
senténtia, senténtiae (f) - feeling, thought, opinion, vote, sentence (2)
sérva, sérvae (f) - slave (female) (24)
stḗlla, stḗllae (f) - star, planet (28)
térra, térrae (f) - earth, ground, land, country (7)
Trṓia, Trṓiae (f) - Troy (21)
túrba, túrbae (f) - uproar, disturbance; mob, crowd, multitude (14)
vía, víae (f) - way, road, street (10)
vīcī́na, vīcī́nae (f) - neighbor (female) (21)
victṓria, victṓriae (f) - victory (8)
vī́ta, vī́tae (f) - life; mode of life (2)

2nd Declension

áger, ágrī (m) - field, farm (3)
amī́cus, amī́cī (m) - friend (male) (3)
ánimī, animṓrum (m) - high spirits, pride, courage (5)

ánimus, ánimī (m) - soul, spirit, mind (5)
ánnus, ánnī (m) - year (12)
argūméntum, argūméntī (n) - proof, evidence, argument (19)
árma, armṓrum (n. pl.) - arms, weapons (28)
auxílium, auxíliī (n) - aid, help (31)
bā́sium, bā́siī (n) - kiss (4)
béllum, béllī (n) - war (4)
benefícium, benefíciī (n) - benefit, kindness; favor (19)
caélum, caélī (n) - sky, heaven (5)
coniūrā́tī, coniūrātṓrum (m. pl.) - conspirators (20)
cōnsílium, cōnsíliī (n) - plan, purpose, counsel, advice, judgment, wisdom (4)
déus, déī (m) - god (6)
dígitus, dígitī (m) - finger, toe (31)
discípulus, discípulī (m) - learner, pupil, student (male) (6)
dṓnum, dṓnī (n) - gift, present (4)
elephántus, elephántī (m and f) - elephant (31)
équus, équī (m) - horse (23)
exítium, exítiī (n) - destruction, ruin (4)
exsílium, exsíliī (n) - exile, banishment (31)
fáctum, fáctī (n) - deed, act, achievement (13)
fā́tum, fā́tī (n) - fate; death (29)
férrum, férrī (n) - iron; sword (22)
fī́lius, fī́liī (m) - son (3)
fórum, fórī (n) - marketplace, forum (26)
Graécus, Graécī (m) - a Greek (6)
impérium, impériī (n) - power to command, supreme power, authority, command, control (24)
ingénium, ingéniī (n) - nature, innate talent (29)
inítium, inítiī (n) - beginning, commencement (33)
iūdícium, iūdíciī (n) - judgment, decision, opinion; trial (19)
libéllus, libéllī (m) - little book (17)
líber, líbrī (m) - book (6)
lóca, locṓrum (n) - places, region (9)
lócī, locṓrum (m) - passages in literature (9)
lócus, lócī (m) - place; passage in literature (9)
lū́dus, lū́dī (m) - game, sport; school (18)
magíster, magístrī (m) - schoolmaster, teacher, master (4)
médicus, médicī (m) - doctor, physician (male) (12)
módus, módī (m) - measure, bound, limit; manner, method, mode, way (22)
mórbus, mórbī (m) - disease, sickness (9)
múndus, múndī (m) - world, universe (21)
númerus, númerī (m) - number (3)
óculus, óculī (m) - eye (4)
offícium, offíciī (n) - duty, service (4)
ṓsculum, ṓsculī (n) - kiss (29)
ṓtium, ṓtiī (n) - leisure, peace (4)
perfúgium, perfúgiī (n) - refuge, shelter (24)
perī́culum, perī́culī (n) - danger, risk (4)
philósophus, philósophī (m) - philosopher (male) (33)
pópulus, pópulī (m) - the people, a people, a nation (3)
prīncípium, prīncípiī (n) - beginning (12)
púer, púerī (m) - boy; boys, children *(pl.)* (3)
remédium, remédiī (n) - cure, remedy (4)
sérvus, sérvī (m) - slave (male) (24)
sígnum, sígnī (n) - sign, signal, indication; seal (13)
sōlā́cium, sōlā́ciī (n) - comfort, relief (24)
sómnus, sómnī (m) - sleep (26)
spéculum, spéculī (n) - mirror (33)
stúdium, stúdiī (n) - eagerness, zeal, pursuit, study (9)
stúltus, stúltī (m) - a fool (4)
súperī, superṓrum (m. pl.) - the gods (27)
tyránnus, tyránnī (m) - absolute ruler, tyrant (6)
vérbum, vérbī (n)- word (5)
vīcī́nus, vīcī́nī (m) - neighbor (male) (21)
vī́num, vī́nī (n) - wine (31)
vir, vírī (m) - man, hero (3)
vítium, vítiī (n) - fault, crime, vice (6)
vúlgus, vúlgī (n) - the common people, mob, rabble (21)

3rd Declension

adulḗscēns, adulēscéntis (m *or* f) - young man *or* woman (12)
aétās, aetā́tis (f) - period of life, life, age, an age, time (16)
ámor, amṓris (m) - love (7)
aúctor, auctṓris (m) - increaser; author, originator (19)
audī́tor, audītṓris (m) - hearer, listener, member of an audience (16)
Caésar, Caésaris (m) - Caesar (12)
cáput, cápitis (n) - head; leader; beginning; life; heading; chapter (11)
cármen, cárminis (n) - song, poem (7)
Carthā́gō, Carthā́ginis (f) - Carthage (24)

Cícerō, Cicerṓnis (m) - (Marcus Tullius) Cicero (8)
cī́vitās, cīvitā́tis (f) - state, citizenship (7)
cṓnsul, cṓnsulis (m) - consul (11)
córpus, córporis (n) - body (7)
cupíditās, cupiditā́tis (f) - desire, longing, passion; cupidity, avarice (10)
dēlectā́tiō, dēlectātiṓnis (f) - delight, pleasure, enjoyment (27)
dux, dúcis (m) - leader, guide; commander, general (23)
flū́men, flū́minis (n) - river (18)
frā́ter, frā́tris (m) - brother (8)
génus, géneris (n) - origin; kind, type, sort, class (18)
hómō, hóminis (m) - human being, man (7)
hónor, honṓris (m) - honor, esteem; public office (30)
imperā́tor, imperātṓris (m) - general, commander-in-chief, emperor (24)
iū́dex, iū́dicis (m) - judge, juror (19)
iūs, iū́ris (n) - right, justice, law (14)
lábor, labṓris (m)- labor, work, toil; a work, production (7)
laus, laúdis (f) - praise, glory, fame (8)
lēx, lḗgis (f) - law, statute (26)
lībértās, lībertā́tis (f) - liberty (8)
lī́men, lī́minis (n) - threshold (26)
lī́tus, lī́toris (n) - shore, coast (23)
lūx, lū́cis (f) - light (26)
maiṓrēs, maiṓrum (m. pl.) - ancestors (27)
mā́ter, mā́tris (f) - mother (12)
mī́les, mī́litis (m) - soldier (23)
mṓrēs, mṓrum (m) - habits, morals, character (7)
mōs, mṓris (m) - habit, custom, manner (7)
nḗmō, nūllī́us, nḗminī, nḗminem, nū́llō, nū́llā (m *or* f) - no one, nobody (11)
népōs, nepṓtis (m) - grandson, descendant (27)
nṓmen, nṓminis (n) - name (7)
occā́siō, occāsiṓnis (f) - occasion, opportunity (28)
ópēs, ópum (f. pl.) - power, resources, wealth (33)
ops, ópis (f) - help, aid (33)
ōrā́tor, ōrātṓris (m) - orator, speaker (23)
ōs, ṓris (n) - mouth, face (14)
párēns, paréntis (m *or* f) - parent (28)
páter, pátris (m) - father (12)
paupértās, paupertā́tis (f) - poverty, humble circumstances (32)
pāx, pā́cis (f) - peace (7)
plēbs, plḗbis (f) - the common people, populace, plebeians (33)
prī́nceps, prī́ncipis (m *or* f) - leader, emperor (28)
próbitās, probitā́tis (f) - uprightness, honesty (18)
rátiō, ratiṓnis (f) - reckoning, account; reason, judgment, consideration; system; manner, method (8)
rēx, rḗgis (m) - king (7)
rū́mor, rūmṓris (m) - rumor, gossip (31)
sacérdōs, sacerdṓtis (m) - priest (23)
sāl, sális (m) - salt; wit (33)
sálūs, salū́tis (f) - health, safety; greeting (21)
sápiēns, sapiéntis (m/f) - a wise man/woman, philosopher (25)
scélus, scéleris (n) - evil deed, crime, sin, wickedness (19)
scrī́ptor, scrīptṓris (m) - writer, author (8)
senéctūs, senectū́tis (f) - old age (10)
sénex, sénis (m) - old man (16)
sérvitūs, servitū́tis (f) - servitude, slavery (20)
sī́dus, sī́deris (n) - constellation, star (29)
sōl, sṓlis (m) - sun (27)
sóror, sorṓris (f) - sister (8)
tempéstās, tempestā́tis (f) - period of time, season; weather, storm (15)
témpus, témporis (n) - time; occasion, opportunity (7)
tímor, timṓris (m) - fear (10)
úxor, uxṓris (f) - wife (7)
vḗritās, vēritā́tis (f) - truth (10)
vésper, vésperis *or* vésperī (m) - evening; evening star (28)
vírgō, vírginis (f) - maiden, virgin (7)
vírtūs, virtū́tis (f) - manliness, courage; excellence, character, worth, virtue (7)
volúptās, voluptā́tis (f) - pleasure (10)
vúlnus, vúlneris (n) - wound (24)

3rd Declension I-Stem

ánimal, animā́lis (n) - a living creature, animal (14)
ars, ártis (f) - art, skill (14)
arx, árcis (f) - citadel, stronghold (23)
as, ássis (m) - an as *(a small copper coin)* (31)
aúris, aúris (f) - ear (14)
cī́vis, cī́vis (m *or* f) - citizen (14)
fī́nēs, fī́nium (m) - boundaries, territory (21)
fī́nis, fī́nis (m) - end, limit, boundary; purpose (21)
gēns, géntis (f) - clan, race, nation, people (21)
hóstēs, hóstium (m) - the enemy (18)
hóstis, hóstis (m) - an enemy *(of the state)* (18)
ígnis, ígnis (m) - fire (22)
máre, máris (n) - sea (14)

mēns, méntis (f) - mind, thought, intention (16)
moénia, moénium (n. pl.) - walls of a city (29)
mōns, móntis (m) - mountain (20)
mors, mórtis (f) - death (14)
nā́vis, nā́vis (f) - ship, boat (21)
nox, nóctis (f) - night (26)
nū́bēs, nū́bis (f) - cloud (14)
pars, pártis (f) - part, share; direction (14)
urbs, úrbis (f) - city (14)
vī́rēs, vī́rium (f. pl.) - strength (14)
vīs, vīs (f) - force, power, violence (14)

4th Declension

córnū, córnūs (n) - horn (20)
cúrsus, cúrsūs (m) - running, race; course (28)
exércitus, exércitūs (m) - army (32)
frū́ctus, frū́ctūs (m) - fruit; profit, benefit, enjoyment (20)
génū, génūs (n) - knee (20)
mánus, mánūs (f) - hand; handwriting; band (20)
métus, métūs (m) - fear, dread, anxiety (20)
senā́tus, senā́tūs (m) - senate (20)
sḗnsus, sḗnsūs (m) - feeling, sense (20)
spī́ritus, spī́ritūs (m) - breath, breathing; spirit, soul (20)
vérsus, vérsūs (m) - line of verse (20)

5th Declension

díēs, diḗī (m) - day (22)
fídēs, fídeī (f) - faith, trust, trustworthiness, fidelity, promise, guarantee, protection (22)
rēs, réī (f) - thing, matter, property, business, affair (22)
rēs pū́blica, réī pū́blicae (f) - state, commonwealth, republic (22)
spēs, spéī (f) - hope (22)

Indeclinable

níhil - nothing (1)
sátis - enough (5)

Pronouns

áliquis, áliquid - someone, somebody, something (23)
égo, méī - I (11)
hic, haec, hoc - this; the latter; he, she, it, they (9)
ī́dem, éadem, ídem - the same (11)
ílle, ílla, íllud - that; the former; the famous; he, she, it, they (9)
ípse, ípsa, ípsum - myself, yourself, himself, herself, itself, *etc.,* the very, the actual (13)
is, éa, id - this, that; he, she, it (11)
íste, ísta, ístud - that of yours, that; such (as you have, as you speak of); *sometimes with contemptuous force, e.g.,* that despicable, that wretched (9)
quī, quae, quod - who, which, what, that (17)
quid - what (1)
quī́dam, quaédam, quíddam - a certain one or thing, someone, something (26)
quis, quid (*after* sī, nisi, nē, num) - anyone, anything, someone, something (33)
quis? quid? - who? whose? whom? what? which? (19)
quísque, quídque, cuiúsque, cuíque - each one, each person, each thing (13)
quísquis, quídquid - whoever, whatever (23)
súī - himself, herself, itself, themselves (13)
tū, túī - you *(sing.)* (11)

Adjectives

1st & 2nd Declension

acérbus, acérba, acérbum - harsh, bitter, grievous (12)
aéquus, aéqua, aéquum - level, even; calm; equal, just; favorable (22)
álīī . . . álīī - some . . . others (9)
álius, ália, áliud - other, another (9)
álter, áltera, álterum - the other (of two), second (9)
amī́cus, amī́ca, amī́cum - friendly (11)
antī́quus, antī́qua, antī́quum - ancient, old-time (2)
ásper, áspera, ásperum - rough, harsh (21)
avā́rus, avā́ra, avā́rum - greedy, avaricious (3)
beā́tus, beā́ta, beā́tum - happy, fortunate, blessed (10)
béllus, bélla, béllum - pretty, handsome, charming (4)
bónus, bóna, bónum - good, kind (4)
caécus, caéca, caécum - blind (17)
cándidus, cándida, cándidum - shining, bright, white; beautiful (33)
cā́rus, cā́ra, cā́rum - dear (11)
cértus, cérta, cértum - definite, sure, certain, reliable (19)
cḗterī, cḗterae, cḗtera - the remaining, the rest, the other, all the others (30)
clā́rus, clā́ra, clā́rum - clear, bright; renowned, famous, illustrious (18)

déxter, déxtra, déxtrum - right, right-hand (20)
dígnus, dígna, dígnum (+abl.) - worthy, worthy of (29)
dóctus, dócta, dóctum - taught, learned, skilled (13)
dū́rus, dū́ra, dū́rum - hard, harsh, rough, stern, unfeeling, hardy, difficult (29)
fortūnā́tus, fortūnā́ta, fortūnā́tum - lucky, fortunate, happy (13)
géminus, gémina, géminum - twin (25)
Graécus, Graéca, Graécum - Greek (6)
hūmā́nus, hūmā́na, hūmā́num - pertaining to man, human; humane, kind; refined, cultivated (4)
incértus, incérta, incértum - uncertain, unsure, doubtful (22)
iūcúndus, iūcúnda, iūcúndum - pleasant, delightful, agreeable, pleasing (16)
Latī́nus, Latī́na, Latī́num - Latin (22)
lī́ber, lī́bera, lī́berum - free (5)
lóngus, lónga, lóngum - long (16)
magnánimus, magnánima, magnánimum - great-hearted, brave, magnanimous (23)
mágnus, mágna, mágnum - large, great; important (2)
málus, mála, málum - bad, wicked, evil (4)
médius, média, médium - middle; the middle of (22)
mérus, méra, mérum - pure, undiluted (33)
méus, méa, méum - my (2)
míser, mísera, míserum - wretched, miserable, unfortunate (15)
mórtuus, mórtua, mórtuum - dead (28)
múltus, múlta, múltum - much, many (2)
neúter, neútra, neútrum - not either, neither (9)
nóster, nóstra, nóstrum - our, ours (5)
nóvus, nóva, nóvum - new; strange (7)
nū́llus, nū́lla, nū́llum - not any, no, none (9)
párvus, párva, párvum - small, little (4)
paúcī, paúcae, paúca - few, a few (3)
perpétuus, perpétua, perpétuum perpetual, lasting, uninterrupted, continuous (6)
plḗnus, plḗna, plḗnum - full, abundant, generous (6)
prī́mus, prī́ma, prī́mum - first, foremost, chief, principal (27)
pudī́cus, pudī́ca, pudī́cum - modest, chaste (26)
púlcher, púlchra, púlchrum - beautiful, handsome; fine (5)
quántus, quánta, quántum - how large, how great, how much (30)
rīdículus, rīdícula, rīdículum - laughable, ridiculous (30)
Rōmā́nus, Rōmā́na, Rōmā́num - Roman (3)
sálvus, sálva, sálvum - safe, sound (6)
sā́nus, sā́na, sā́num - sound, healthy, sane (5)
secúndus, secúnda, secúndum - second; favorable (6)
siníster, sinístra, sinístrum - left, left-hand; harmful, ill-omened (20)
sṓlus, sṓla, sṓlum - alone, only, the only (9)
stúltus, stúlta, stúltum - foolish (4)
supérbus, supérba, supérbum - arrogant, overbearing, haughty, proud (26)
súperus, súpera, súperum - above, upper (27)
súus, súa, súum - his own, her own, its own, their own (13)
tántus, tánta, tántum - so large, so great, of such a size (29)
tántus . . . quántus - just as much (many) . . . as (30)
tṓtus, tṓta, tṓtum - whole, entire (9)
túus, túa, túum - your *(sing.)* (2)
ū́llus, ū́lla, ū́llum - any (9)
últimus, última, últimum - farthest, extreme; last, final (25)
ū́nus, ū́na, ū́num - one, single, alone (9)
urbā́nus, urbā́na, urbā́num - of the city, urban; urbane, elegant (26)
úter, útra, útrum - either, which (of two) (9)
vḗrus, vḗra, vḗrum - true, real, proper (4)
véster, véstra, véstrum - your *(pl.)* (6)
vī́vus, vī́va, vī́vum - alive, living (30)

3rd Declension

ā́cer, ā́cris, ā́cre - sharp, keen, eager; severe, fierce (16)
brévis, bréve - short, small, brief (16)
céler, céleris, célere - swift, quick, rapid (16)
commū́nis, commū́ne - common, general, of / for the community (20)
diffícilis, diffícile - hard, difficult, troublesome (16)

dī́ligēns, ***gen.*** **dīligéntis** - diligent, careful (27)
dissímilis, dissímile - unlike, different (27)
dī́ves, ***gen.*** **dī́vitis** ***or*** **dī́tis** - rich, wealthy (32)
dúlcis, dúlce - sweet; pleasant, agreeable (16)
fácilis, fácile - easy; agreeable (16)
fḗlīx, ***gen.*** **fēlī́cis** - lucky, fortunate, happy (22)
férōx, ***gen.*** **ferṓcis** - fierce, savage (25)
fidḗlis, fidḗle - faithful, loyal (25)
fórtis, fórte - strong, brave (16)
grácilis, grácile - slender, thin (27)
grávis, gráve - heavy, weighty; serious, important; severe, grievous (19)
húmilis, húmile - lowly, humble (27)
immortā́lis, immortā́le - not subject to death, immortal (19)
íngēns, ***gen.*** **ingéntis** - huge (16)
lévis, léve - light; easy; slight, trivial (17)
máior, máius - greater; older (27)
medíocris, medíocre - ordinary, moderate, mediocre (31)
mortā́lis, mortā́le - mortal (18)
ómnis, ómne - every, all (16)
pār, ***gen.*** **páris (+dat.)** - equal, like (32)
paúper, ***gen.*** **paúperis** - of small means, poor (32)
pótēns, ***gen.*** **poténtis** - able, powerful, mighty, strong (16)
prī́nceps, ***gen.*** **prī́ncipis** - chief, foremost (28)
sápiēns, ***gen.*** **sapiéntis** - wise, judicious (25)
sénex, ***gen.*** **sénis** - old, aged (16)
símilis, símile (+gen. or dat.) - similar (to), like, resembling (27)
suā́vis, suā́ve - sweet (33)
trī́stis, trī́ste - sad, sorrowful; joyless, grim, severe (26)
túrpis, túrpe - ugly; shameful, base, disgraceful (26)
ū́tilis, ū́tile - useful, advantageous (27)

Indeclinable Adjectives
quot - how many, as many as (27)
sátis - enough, sufficient (5)

Indefinite Adjective
quī́dam, quaédam, quóddam - a certain, some (26)

Interrogative Adjective
quī?, quae?, quod? - what? which? what kind of?; *(sometimes with exclamatory force)* what (a)! what sort of! (19)

Verbs
1st Conjugation
ádiuvō, adiuvā́re, adiū́vī, adiū́tum - to help, aid, assist; to please (4)
ámō, amā́re, amā́vī, amā́tum - to love, like (1)
appéllō, appellā́re, appellā́vī, appellā́tum - to speak to, address (as), call, name (14)
cḗnō, cēnā́re, cēnā́vī, cēnā́tum - to dine (5)
cṓgitō, cōgitā́re, cōgitā́vī, cōgitā́tum- to think, ponder, consider, plan (1)
cōnsérvō, cōnservā́re, cōnservā́vī, cōnservā́tum - to preserve, conserve, maintain (1)
créō, creā́re, creā́vī, creā́tum - to create (12)
cúlpō, culpā́re, culpā́vī, culpā́tum - to blame, censure (5)
dédicō, dēdicā́re, dēdicā́vī, dēdicā́tum - to dedicate (28)
dēléctō, dēlectā́re, dēlectā́vī, dēlectā́tum - to delight, charm, please (19)
dēmṓnstrō, dēmōnstrā́re, dēmōnstrā́vī, dēmōnstrā́tum to point out, show, demonstrate (8)
dēsī́derō, dēsīderā́re, dēsīderā́vī, dēsīderā́tum - to desire, long for, miss (17)
dō, dáre, dédī, dátum - to give, offer (1)
dúbitō, dubitā́re, dubitā́vī, dubitā́tum - to doubt, hesitate (30)
ḗducō, ēducā́re, ēducā́vī, ēducā́tum - to bring up, educate (23)
érrō, errā́re, errā́vī, errā́tum - to wander; err, go astray, make a mistake, be mistaken (1)
exspéctō, exspectā́re, exspectā́vī, exspectā́tum - to look for, expect, await (15)
invī́tō, invītā́re, invītā́vī, invītā́tum - to entertain, invite, summon (26)
iúvō, iuvā́re, iū́vī, iū́tum - to help, aid, assist; to please (4)
labṓrō, labōrā́re, labōrā́vī, labōrā́tum - to labor; be in distress (21)
laúdō, laudā́re, laudā́vī, laudā́tum - to praise (1)
lī́berō, līberā́re, līberā́vī, līberā́tum - to free, liberate (19)
mū́tō, mūtā́re, mūtā́vī, mūtā́tum to change, alter; exchange (14)

nā́rrō, nārrā́re, nārrā́vī, nārrā́tum - to tell, report, narrate (24)

nā́vigō, nāvigā́re, nāvigā́vī, nāvigā́tum - to sail, navigate (17)

nécō, necā́re, necā́vī, necā́tum - to murder, kill (7)

négō, negā́re, negā́vī, negā́tum to deny, say that . . . not (25)

nū́ntiō, nūntiā́re, nūntiā́vī, nūntiā́tum - to announce, report, relate (25)

párō, parā́re, parā́vī, parā́tum - to prepare, provide; get, obtain (19)

praéstō, praestā́re, praéstitī, praéstitum - to excel; exhibit, show, offer, supply, furnish (28)

próbō, probā́re, probā́vī, probā́tum - to approve, recommend; test (27)

prōnū́ntiō, prōnūntiā́re, prōnūntiā́vī, prōnūntiā́tum - to proclaim, announce; declaim; pronounce (20)

púgnō, pugnā́re, pugnā́vī, pugnā́tum - to fight (29)

pútō, putā́re, putā́vī, putā́tum - to reckon, suppose, judge, think, imagine (25)

récitō, recitā́re, recitā́vī, recitā́tum - to read aloud, recite (17)

recū́sō, recūsā́re, recūsā́vī, recūsā́tum - to refuse (33)

rógō, rogā́re, rogā́vī, rogā́tum - to ask (30)

sátiō, satiā́re, satiā́vī, satiā́tum - to satisfy, sate (3)

sérvō, servā́re, servā́vī, servā́tum - to preserve, save, keep, guard (1)

spḗrō, spērā́re, spērā́vī, spērā́tum - to hope for, hope (25)

stō, stā́re, stétī, státum - to stand, stand still *or* firm (13)

súperō, superā́re, superā́vī, superā́tum - to be above, have the upper hand, surpass; overcome, conquer (5)

tólerō, tolerā́re, tolerā́vī, tolerā́tum - to bear, endure (6)

vī́tō, vītā́re, vītā́vī, vītā́tum - to avoid, shun (14)

vócō, vocā́re, vocā́vī, vocā́tum - to call, summon (1)

2nd Conjugation

aúdeō, audḗre, aúsus sum - to dare (7)

cáreō, carḗre, cáruī, caritū́rum (+abl.) - to be without, be deprived of, want, lack; be free from (20)

contíneō, continḗre, contínuī, conténtum - to hold together, contain, keep, enclose, restrain (21)

dḗbeō, dēbḗre, dḗbuī, dḗbitum - to owe; ought, must, should (1)

dḗleō, dēlḗre, dēlḗvī, dēlḗtum - to destroy, wipe out, erase (17)

dóceō, docḗre, dócuī, dóctum - to teach (8)

dóleō, dolḗre, dóluī, dolitū́rum - to grieve, suffer; hurt, give pain (31)

égeō, egḗre, éguī (+ abl. or gen.) - to need, lack, want (28)

éxpleō, explḗre, explḗvī, explḗtum - to fill, fill up, complete (28)

gaúdeō, gaudḗre, gāvī́sus sum - to be glad, rejoice (23)

hábeō, habḗre, hábuī, hábitum - to have, hold, possess; consider, regard (3)

iáceō, iacḗre, iácuī - to lie; lie prostrate; lie dead (25)

invídeō, invidḗre, invī́dī, invī́sum to be envious; to look at with envy, envy, be jealous of (+dat.) (31)

iúbeō, iubḗre, iússī, iússum - to bid, order, command (21)

máneō, manḗre, mā́nsī, mā́nsum - to remain, stay, stay behind, abide, continue (5)

mísceō, miscḗre, míscuī, míxtum to mix, stir up, disturb (18)

móneō, monḗre, mónuī, mónitum - to remind, advise, warn (1)

móveō, movḗre, mṓvī, mṓtum - to move; arouse, affect (18)

páteō, patḗre, pátuī - to be open, lie open; be accessible; be evident (32)

praébeō, praebḗre, praébuī, praébitum - to offer, provide (32)

prohíbeō, prohibḗre, prohíbuī, prohíbitum - to keep (back), prevent, hinder, restrain, prohibit (20)

remáneō, remanḗre, remā́nsī, remā́nsum - to remain, stay, stay behind, abide, continue (5)

respóndeō, respondḗre, respóndī, respṓnsum - to answer (29)

rī́deō, rīdḗre, rī́sī, rī́sum - to laugh, laugh at (24)

sálvē, salvḗte - hello, greetings (1)

sálveō, salvḗre - to be well, be in good health (1)

táceō, tacḗre, tácuī, tácitum - to be silent, leave unmentioned (28)

téneō, tenḗre, ténuī, téntum - to hold, keep, possess; restrain (14)

térreō, terrḗre, térruī, térritum - to frighten, terrify (1)

tímeō, timḗre, tímuī - to fear, be afraid (of) (15)

válē, valḗte - good-bye, farewell (1)

váleō, valḗre, váluī, valitū́rum - to be strong, have power; be well (1)

vídeō, vidḗre, vī́dī, vī́sum - to see; observe, understand (1)

vídeor, vidḗrī, vī́sus sum - to be seen, seem, appear (18)

3rd Conjugation

admíttō, admíttere, admī́sī, admíssum - to admit, receive, let in (17)

ágō, ágere, ḗgī, ā́ctum - to drive, lead, do, act; pass, spend *(life or time)* (8)

álō, álere, áluī, áltum - to nourish, support, sustain, increase; cherish (13)

āmíttō, āmíttere, āmī́sī, āmíssum - to send away; lose, let go (12)

āvértō, āvértere, āvértī, āvérsum - to turn away, avert (23)

bíbō, bíbere, bíbī - to drink (30)

cádō, cádere, cécidī, cāsū́rum - to fall (12)

cḗdō, cḗdere, céssī, céssum - to go, withdraw; yield to, grant, submit (28)

cérnō, cérnere, crḗvī, crḗtum - to distinguish, discern, perceive (22)

cognṓscō, cognṓscere, cognṓvī, cógnitum - to become acquainted with, learn, recognize; know *(in perfect tenses)* (30)

commíttō, commíttere, commī́sī, commíssum - to entrust, commit (15)

comprehéndō, comprehéndere, comprehéndī, comprehḗnsum - to grasp, seize, arrest; comprehend, understand (30)

cóndō, cóndere, cóndidī, cónditum - to put together *or* into, store; found, establish (29)

cōnsū́mō, cōnsū́mere, cōnsū́mpsī, cōnsū́mptum - to consume, use up (30)

conténdō, conténdere, conténdī, conténtum - to strive, struggle, contend; hasten (29)

crḗdō, crḗdere, crḗdidī, crḗditum to believe, trust (25)

cúrrō, cúrrere, cucúrrī, cúrsum - to run, rush, move quickly (14)

dēféndō, dēféndere, dēféndī, dēfḗnsum - to ward off; defend, protect (20)

dī́cō, dī́cere, dī́xī, díctum - to say, tell, speak; name, call (10)

dī́ligō, dīlígere, dīlḗxī, dīlḗctum - to esteem, love (13)

discḗdō, discḗdere, discéssī, discéssum - to go away, depart (20)

díscō, díscere, dídicī - to learn (8)

dū́cō, dū́cere, dū́xī, dúctum - to lead; consider, regard; prolong (8)

expéllō, expéllere, éxpulī, expúlsum - to drive out, expel, banish (24)

expṓnō, expṓnere, expósuī, expósitum - to set forth, explain, expose (30)

flúō, flúere, flū́xī, flū́xum - to flow (18)

gérō, gérere, géssī, géstum - to carry; carry on, manage, conduct, wage, accomplish, perform (8)

intéllegō, intellégere, intellḗxī, intellḗctum - to understand (11)

iúngō, iúngere, iū́nxī, iū́nctum - to join (13)

légō, légere, lḗgī, lḗctum - to pick out, choose; read (18)

mínuō, minúere, mínuī, minū́tum - to lessen, diminish (30)

míttō, míttere, mī́sī, míssum - to send, let go (11)

néglegō, neglégere, neglḗxī, neglḗctum - to neglect, disregard (17)

nṓscō, nṓscere, nṓvī, nṓtum - to become acquainted with, learn, recognize; know *(in perfect tenses)* (30)

óccidō, occídere, óccidī, occā́sum - to fall down; die; set (31)

óprimō, opprímere, oppréssī, oppréssum - to suppress, overwhelm, overpower, check (23)

osténdō, osténdere, osténdī, osténtum - to exhibit, show, display (23)

péllō, péllere, pépulī, púlsum - to strike, push; drive out, banish (24)

pétō, pétere, petī́vī, petī́tum - to seek, aim at, beg, beseech (23)

pṓnō, pṓnere, pósuī, pósitum - to put, place, set (27)

prémō, prémere, préssī, préssum - to press; press hard, pursue (23)

prōmíttō, prōmíttere, prōmī́sī, prōmíssum - to send forth; promise (32)

quaérō, quaérere, quaesī́vī, quaesī́tum - to seek, look for, strive for; ask, inquire, inquire into (24)

régō, régere, rḗxī, rḗctum - to rule, guide, direct (16)
relínquō, relínquere, relī́quī, relíctum - to leave behind, leave, abandon, desert (21)
revértō, revértere, revértī, revérsum - turn back (23)
scrī́bō, scrī́bere, scrī́psī, scrī́ptum to write, compose (8)
súrgō, súrgere, surrḗxī, surrḗctum - to get up, arise (29)
tángō, tángere, tétigī, tā́ctum - to touch (21)
tóllō, tóllere, sústulī, sublā́tum - to raise, lift up; take away, remove, destroy (22)
trā́dō, trā́dere, trā́didī, trā́ditum to give over, surrender; hand down, transmit, teach (33)
tráhō, tráhere, trā́xī, tráctum - to draw, drag; derive, acquire (8)
vértō, vértere, vértī, vérsum - to turn; change (23)
víncō, víncere, vī́cī, víctum - to conquer, overcome (8)
vī́vō, vī́vere, vī́xī, vī́ctum - to live (10)

3rd Conjugation -iō

accípiō, accípere, accḗpī, accéptum - to take *(to one's self)*, receive, accept (24)
cápiō, cápere, cḗpī, cáptum - to take, capture, seize, get (10)
cúpiō, cúpere, cupī́vī, cupī́tum - to desire, wish, long for (17)
ērípiō, ērípere, ērípuī, ēréptum - to snatch away, take away; rescue (22)
excípiō, excípere, excḗpī, excéptum - to take out, except; take, receive, capture (24)
fáciō, fácere, fḗcī, fáctum - to make, do, accomplish (10)
fúgiō, fúgere, fū́gī, fugitū́rum - to flee, hurry away; escape; go into exile; avoid, shun (10)
iáciō, iácere, iḗcī, iáctum - to throw, hurl (15)
incípiō, incípere, incḗpī, incéptum - to begin (17)
patefáciō, patefácere, patefḗcī, patefáctum - to make open, open; disclose, expose (25)
rápiō, rápere, rápuī, ráptum - to seize, snatch, carry away (21)
recípiō, recípere, recḗpī, recéptum - to take back, regain; admit, receive (24)
suscípiō, suscípere, suscḗpī, suscéptum - to undertake (25)

4th Conjugation

aúdiō, audī́re, audī́vī, audī́tum - to hear, listen to (10)
dórmiō, dormī́re, dormī́vī, dormī́tum - to sleep (31)
invéniō, invenī́re, invḗnī, invéntum - to come upon, find (10)
móllio, mollī́re, mollī́vī, mollī́tum to soften; make calm *or* less hostile (29)
nésciō, nescī́re, nescī́vī, nescī́tum - to not know, be ignorant (25)
scíō, scī́re, scī́vī, scī́tum - to know (21)
séntiō, sentī́re, sḗnsī, sḗnsum - to feel, perceive, think, experience (11)
véniō, venī́re, vḗnī, véntum - to come (10)

Irregular

ádferō, adférre, áttulī, allā́tum - to bring to (31)
cṓnferō, cōnférre, cóntulī, collā́tum - to bring together, compare; confer, bestow (31)
férō, férre, túlī, lā́tum - to bear, carry, bring; suffer, endure, tolerate; say, report (31)
mā́lō, mā́lle, mā́luī - to want (something) more, instead; prefer (32)
nṓlō, nṓlle, nṓluī - to not . . . wish, be unwilling (32)
ófferō, offérre, óbtulī, oblā́tum - to offer (31)
póssum, pósse, pótuī - to be able, can, could, have power (6)
réferō, reférre, réttulī, relā́tum - to carry back, bring back; repeat, answer, report (31)
sum, ésse, fúī, futū́rum - to be, exist (4)
vólō, vélle, vóluī - to wish, want, be willing, will (32)

Defective

ā́it, ā́iunt - he says, they say, assert (25)
coépī, coepísse, coéptum - began (17)
ínquit - he says *or* said (22)
ṓdī, ōdísse, ōsū́rum - to hate (20)

Adverbs

ánte (+acc.) - before, previously (13)
béne - well, satisfactorily, quite (11)
cíto - quickly (17)
crās - tomorrow (5)
cūr - why (18)
déhinc - then, next (25)

deínde - thereupon, next, then (18)
dḗnique - at last, finally, lastly (29)
díū - long, for a long time (12)
étiam - even, also (11)
fū́rtim - stealthily, secretly (30)
héri - yesterday (5)
hīc - here (25)
hódiē - today (3)
iam - now, already, soon (19)
íbi - there (6)
íta - so, thus (29)
ítaque - and so, therefore (15)
íterum - again, a second time (21)
mox - soon (30)
nē . . . quídem - not . . . even (29)
nímis, nímium - too, too much, excessively; *(in a positive sense, esp. with adjectives and adverbs)* exceedingly, very (9)
nōn - not (1)
númquam - never (8)
nunc - now, at present (6)
nū́per - recently (12)
ṓlim - once (upon a time), long ago, formerly; some day, in the future (13)
pósteā - afterwards (24)
prī́mō - at first, at the beginning (30)
prṓtinus - immediately (22)
quam - how (16)
quam - than *(after comparatives);* as . . . as possible *(with superlatives)* (26)
quándō - when (5)
quā́rē - because of which thing *(lit.);* therefore, wherefore, why (6)
quídem - indeed, certainly, at least, even (29)
quóndam - formerly, once (22)
quóque - also, too (17)
repénte - suddenly (30)
saépe - often (1)
sátis - enough, sufficiently (5)
sémel - a single time, once, once and for all, simultaneously (31)
sémper - always (3)
sīc - so, thus (29)
súbitō - suddenly (33)
tam - so, to such a degree (29)
tam . . . quam - so . . . as (29)
támen - nevertheless, still (8)
tamquam - as it were, as if, so to speak (29)
tántum - only (26)
tum - then, at that time; thereupon, in the next place (5)
úbi - where, when (6)
últrā - on the other side of, beyond (22)
úmquam - ever, at any time (23)
únde - whence, from what *or* which place, from which, from whom (30)
úsque - all the way, up (to), even (to), continuously, always (31)
vḗrō - in truth, indeed, to be sure, however (29)

Conjunctions

at - but; but, mind you; but, you say (19)
átque, ac - and also, and even, and in fact (21)
aut - or (17)
aut . . . aut - either . . . or (17)
aútem - however; moreover (11)
cum (+indic.) - when (31)
cum (+subj.) - when, since, although (31)
dum - while, as long as, at the same time that; *or* until *(+subjunctive)* (8)
dúmmodo (+subj.) - provided that, so long as (32)
énim - for, in fact, truly (9)
et - and; even (2)
et . . . et - both . . . and (2)
ígitur - therefore, consequently (5)
nam - for (13)
nē - not; in order that . . . not, that . . . not, in order not to (28)
néque, nec - and not, nor (11)
néque . . . néque, nec . . . nec - neither . . . nor (11)
nísi - if . . . not, unless; except (19)
quod - because (11)
quóniam - since, inasmuch as (10)
sed - but (2)
sī - if (1)
ut (+indic.) - as, just as, when (24)
ut (+ subj.) - in order that, so that, that, in order to, so as to, to (28)
útrum . . . an - whether . . . or (30)

Prepositions

ab, ā (+abl.) - away from, from; by (14)
ad (+acc.) - to, up to, near to (8)
ánte (+acc.) - before *(in place or time)*, in front of (13)
ápud (+acc.) - among, in the presence of, at the house of (31)
cóntrā (+acc.) - against (19)
cum (+abl.) - with (10)
dē (+abl.) - down from, from; concerning, about (3)
ex, ē (abl.+) - out of, from, from within; by reason of, on account of; of *(after cardinal numerals)* (8)
in (+acc.) - into, toward; against (9)
in (+abl.) - in, on (3)
ínter (+acc.) - between, among (15)
per (+acc.) - through; by *(with reflexive pronoun)* (13)
post (+acc.) - after, behind (7)

prae (+abl.) - in front of, before (26)
prō (+abl.) - in front of, before, on behalf of, for the sake of, in return for, instead of, for, as (12)
própter (+acc.) - on account of, because of (5)
síne (+abl.) - without (2)
sub (+abl. w/ verbs of rest *or* **+acc. w/ verbs of motion)** - under, up under, close to, down to/into, to/at the foot of (7)
trāns (+acc.) - across (14)
últrā (adv. and prep. +acc.) - on the other side of, beyond (22)

Interjections

heu - ah!, alas! (33)
ō - O!, Oh! (2)

Idioms

amā́bō tē - please (1)
grā́tiās ágere (+dat.) - to thank someone; to give thanks to (8)
mḗnsa secúnda (f) - dessert (26)
nōn sṓlum . . . sed étiam - not only . . . but also (9)
poénās dáre - to pay the penalty (2)
sē cōnférre - to go (31)
sī quándō - if ever (5)

Prefix

re-, red- - again, back (24)

Suffixes

-ne – interrogative suffix attached to the first word of a sentence, typically the verb or another word on which the question hinges, to introduce a question whose answer is uncertain (5)
-que - and *(enclitic conjunction; appended to the second of two words to be joined)* (6)
-ve - or (33)

Numerals

Cardinal - ū́nus *to* vīgíntī quī́nque (15)
Ordinal - prī́mus *to* duodécimus (15)

----

céntum - a hundred (15)
mī́lia, mī́lium (n. pl.) - thousands (15)
mī́lle - thousand (15)

Chapter 34

Nouns

1st Declension

adulēscéntia, adulēscéntiae (f) - youth, young manhood; youthfulness (5)
agrícola, agrícolae (m) - farmer (3)
amī́ca, amī́cae (f) - friend (female) (3)
amīcítia, amīcítiae (f) - friendship (10)
ánima, ánimae (f) - air *(breathed by an animal),* breath; soul, spirit (34)
áqua, áquae (f) - water (14)
Ásia, Ásiae (f) - Asia (12)
cása, cásae (f) - house, cottage, hut (21)
caúsa, caúsae (f) - cause, reason; case, situation (21)
caúsā (abl. + preceding gen.) - for the sake of, on account of (21)
cḗna, cḗnae (f) - dinner (26)
clēméntia, clēméntiae (f) - mildness, gentleness, mercy (16)
cṓpia, cṓpiae (f) - abundance, supply (8)
cṓpiae, cōpiā́rum (f) - supplies, troops, forces (8)
cúlpa, cúlpae (f) - fault, blame (5)
cū́ra, cū́rae (f) - care, attention, caution, anxiety (4)
custṓdia, custṓdiae (f) - protection, custody; guards *(pl.)* (32)
déa, déae (f) - goddess (6)
discípula, discípulae (f) - learner, pupil, student (female) (6)
dīvítiae, dīvitiā́rum (f. pl.) - riches, wealth (13)
fā́bula, fā́bulae (f) - story, tale; play (24)
fā́ma, fā́mae (f) - rumor, report; fame, reputation (2)
família, famíliae (f) - household, family (19)
fḗmina, fḗminae (f) - woman (3)
fenéstra, fenéstrae (f) - window (21)
fī́lia, fī́liae (f) - daughter (3)
fṓrma, fṓrmae (f) - form, shape; beauty (2)
fortū́na, fortū́nae (f) - fortune, luck (2)
glṓria, glṓriae (f) - glory, fame (5)
Graécia, Graéciae (f) - Greece (19)
hásta, hástae (f) - spear (23)
hṓra, hṓrae (f) - hour, time (10)
īnsídiae, īnsidiā́rum (f) - ambush, plot, treachery (6)
ī́nsula, ī́nsulae (f) - island (23)
invídia, invídiae (f) - envy, jealousy, hatred (31)
ī́ra, ī́rae (f) - ire, anger (2)
Itália, Itáliae (f) - Italy (15)
língua, línguae (f) - tongue; language (25)
líttera, lítterae (f) - a letter of the alphabet (7)
lítterae, litterā́rum (f) - a letter (epistle), literature (7)
lū́na, lū́nae (f) - moon (28)
magístra, magístrae (f) - schoolmistress, teacher, mistress (4)
médica, médicae (f) - doctor, physician (female) (12)
memória, memóriae (f) - memory, recollection (15)
mḗnsa, mḗnsae (f) - table; dining; dish, course (26)
móra, mórae (f) - delay (4)
nā́ta, nā́tae (f) - daughter (29)
nātū́ra, nātū́rae (f) - nature (10)
naúta, naútae (m) - sailor (2)
patiéntia, patiéntiae (f) - suffering; patience, endurance (12)
pátria, pátriae (f) - fatherland, native land, (one's) country (2)
pecū́nia, pecū́niae (f) - money (2)
philósopha, philósophae (f) - philosopher (female) (33)
philosóphia, philosóphiae (f) - philosophy (2)
poéna, poénae (f) - penalty, punishment (2)
poḗta, poḗtae (m) - poet (2)
pórta, pórtae (f) - gate, entrance (2)
puélla, puéllae (f) - girl (2)
rēgī́na, rēgī́nae (f) - queen (7)
Rṓma, Rṓmae (f) - Rome (14)
rósa, rósae (f) - rose (2)
sapiéntia, sapiéntiae (f) - wisdom (3)
sátura, sáturae (f) - satire (16)
sciéntia, sciéntiae (f) - knowledge (18)
senténtia, senténtiae (f) - feeling, thought, opinion, vote, sentence (2)
sérva, sérvae (f) - slave (female) (24)
stḗlla, stḗllae (f) - star, planet (28)
térra, térrae (f) - earth, ground, land, country (7)
Trṓia, Trṓiae (f) - Troy (21)
túrba, túrbae (f) - uproar, disturbance; mob, crowd, multitude (14)
vía, víae (f) - way, road, street (10)
vīcī́na, vīcī́nae (f) - neighbor (female) (21)
victṓria, victṓriae (f) - victory (8)
vī́ta, vī́tae (f) - life; mode of life (2)

2nd Declension

áger, ágrī (m) - field, farm (3)
amícus, amícī (m) - friend (male) (3)
ánimī, animṓrum (m) - high spirits, pride, courage (5)
ánimus, ánimī (m) - soul, spirit, mind (5)
ánnus, ánnī (m) - year (12)
argūméntum, argūméntī (n) - proof, evidence, argument (19)
árma, armṓrum (n. pl.) - arms, weapons (28)
auxílium, auxíliī (n) - aid, help (31)
bā́sium, bā́siī (n) - kiss (4)
béllum, béllī (n) - war (4)
benefícium, benefíciī (n) - benefit, kindness; favor (19)
caélum, caélī (n) - sky, heaven (5)
coniūrā́tī, coniūrātṓrum (m. pl.) - conspirators (20)
cōnsílium, cōnsíliī (n) - plan, purpose, counsel, advice, judgment, wisdom (4)
déus, déī (m) - god (6)
dígitus, dígitī (m) - finger, toe (31)
discípulus, discípulī (m) - learner, pupil, student (male) (6)
dṓnum, dṓnī (n) - gift, present (4)
elephántus, elephántī (m and f) - elephant (31)
équus, équī (m) - horse (23)
exítium, exítiī (n) - destruction, ruin (4)
exsílium, exsíliī (n) - exile, banishment (31)
fáctum, fáctī (n) - deed, act, achievement (13)
fā́tum, fā́tī (n) - fate; death (29)
férrum, férrī (n) - iron; sword (22)
fílius, fíliī (m) - son (3)
fórum, fórī (n) - marketplace, forum (26)
Graécus, Graécī (m) - a Greek (6)
impérium, impériī (n) - power to command, supreme power, authority, command, control (24)
ingénium, ingéniī (n) - nature, innate talent (29)
inítium, inítiī (n) - beginning, commencement (33)
iūdícium, iūdíciī (n) - judgment, decision, opinion; trial (19)
libéllus, libéllī (m) - little book (17)
líber, líbrī (m) - book (6)
lóca, locṓrum (n) - places, region (9)
lócī, locṓrum (m) - passages in literature (9)
lócus, lócī (m) - place; passage in literature (9)
lū́dus, lū́dī (m) - game, sport; school (18)
magíster, magístrī (m) - schoolmaster, teacher, master (4)
médicus, médicī (m) - doctor, physician (male) (12)
módus, módī (m) - measure, bound, limit; manner, method, mode, way (22)
mórbus, mórbī (m) - disease, sickness (9)
múndus, múndī (m) - world, universe (21)
númerus, númerī (m) - number (3)
óculus, óculī (m) - eye (4)
offícium, offíciī (n) - duty, service (4)
ṓsculum, ṓsculī (n) - kiss (29)
ṓtium, ṓtiī (n) - leisure, peace (4)
perfúgium, perfúgiī (n) - refuge, shelter (24)
perículum, perículī (n) - danger, risk (4)
philósophus, philósophī (m) - philosopher (male) (33)
pópulus, pópulī (m) - the people, a people, a nation (3)
prīncípium, prīncípiī (n) - beginning (12)
púer, púerī (m) - boy; boys, children *(pl.)* (3)
remédium, remédiī (n) - cure, remedy (4)
sérvus, sérvī (m) - slave (male) (24)
sígnum, sígnī (n) - sign, signal, indication; seal (13)
sōlā́cium, sōlā́ciī (n) - comfort, relief (24)
sómnus, sómnī (m) - sleep (26)
spéculum, spéculī (n) - mirror (33)
stúdium, stúdiī (n) - eagerness, zeal, pursuit, study (9)
stúltus, stúltī (m) - a fool (4)
súperī, superṓrum (m. pl.) - the gods (27)
tyránnus, tyránnī (m) - absolute ruler, tyrant (6)
vérbum, vérbī (n)- word (5)
vīcī́nus, vīcī́nī (m) - neighbor (male) (21)
vī́num, vī́nī (n) - wine (31)
vir, vírī (m) - man, hero (3)
vítium, vítiī (n) - fault, crime, vice (6)
vúlgus, vúlgī (n) - the common people, mob, rabble (21)

3rd Declension

adulḗscēns, adulēscéntis (m *or* f) - young man *or* woman (12)
aétās, aetā́tis (f) - period of life, life, age, an age, time (16)
ámor, amṓris (m) - love (7)
aúctor, auctṓris (m) - increaser; author, originator (19)
audī́tor, audītṓris (m) - hearer, listener, member of an audience (16)
Caésar, Caésaris (m) - Caesar (12)

cáput, cápitis (n) - head; leader; beginning; life; heading; chapter (11)
cármen, cárminis (n) - song, poem (7)
Carthā́gō, Carthā́ginis (f) - Carthage (24)
Cícerō, Cicerṓnis (m) - (Marcus Tullius) Cicero (8)
cī́vitās, cīvitā́tis (f) - state, citizenship (7)
cṓnsul, cṓnsulis (m) - consul (11)
córpus, córporis (n) - body (7)
cupíditās, cupiditā́tis (f) - desire, longing, passion; cupidity, avarice (10)
dēlectā́tiō, dēlectātiṓnis (f) - delight, pleasure, enjoyment (27)
dux, dúcis (m) - leader, guide; commander, general (23)
flū́men, flū́minis (n) - river (18)
frā́ter, frā́tris (m) - brother (8)
génus, géneris (n) - origin; kind, type, sort, class (18)
hómō, hóminis (m) - human being, man (7)
hónor, honṓris (m) - honor, esteem; public office (30)
imperā́tor, imperātṓris (m) - general, commander-in-chief, emperor (24)
iū́dex, iū́dicis (m) - judge, juror (19)
iūs, iū́ris (n) - right, justice, law (14)
lábor, labṓris (m)- labor, work, toil; a work, production (7)
laus, laúdis (f) - praise, glory, fame (8)
lēx, lḗgis (f) - law, statute (26)
lībértās, lībertā́tis (f) - liberty (8)
lī́men, lī́minis (n) - threshold (26)
lī́tus, lī́toris (n) - shore, coast (23)
lūx, lū́cis (f) - light (26)
maiṓrēs, maiṓrum (m. pl.) - ancestors (27)
mā́ter, mā́tris (f) - mother (12)
mī́les, mī́litis (m) - soldier (23)
mṓrēs, mṓrum (m) - habits, morals, character (7)
mōs, mṓris (m) - habit, custom, manner (7)
nḗmō, nūllī́us, nḗminī, nḗminem, nū́llō, nū́llā (m *or* f) - no one, nobody (11)
népōs, nepṓtis (m) - grandson, descendant (27)
nṓmen, nṓminis (n) - name (7)
occā́siō, occāsiṓnis (f) - occasion, opportunity (28)
ópēs, ópum (f. pl.) - power, resources, wealth (33)
ops, ópis (f) - help, aid (33)
ōrā́tor, ōrātṓris (m) - orator, speaker (23)
ōs, ṓris (n) - mouth, face (14)
párēns, paréntis (m *or* f) - parent (28)
páter, pátris (m) - father (12)
paupértās, paupertā́tis (f) - poverty, humble circumstances (32)
pāx, pā́cis (f) - peace (7)
plēbs, plḗbis (f) - the common people, populace, plebeians (33)
prī́nceps, prī́ncipis (m *or* f) - leader, emperor (28)
próbitās, probitā́tis (f) - uprightness, honesty (18)
rátiō, ratiṓnis (f) - reckoning, account; reason, judgment, consideration; system; manner, method (8)
remíssiō, remissiṓnis (f) - letting go, release; relaxation (34)
rēx, rḗgis (m) - king (7)
rū́mor, rūmṓris (m) - rumor, gossip (31)
sacérdōs, sacerdṓtis (m) - priest (23)
sāl, sális (m) - salt; wit (33)
sálūs, salū́tis (f) - health, safety; greeting (21)
sápiēns, sapiéntis (m/f) - a wise man/woman, philosopher (25)
scélus, scéleris (n) - evil deed, crime, sin, wickedness (19)
scrī́ptor, scrīptṓris (m) - writer, author (8)
senéctūs, senectū́tis (f) - old age (10)
sénex, sénis (m) - old man (16)
sérvitūs, servitū́tis (f) - servitude, slavery (20)
sī́dus, sī́deris (n) - constellation, star (29)
sōl, sṓlis (m) - sun (27)
sóror, sorṓris (f) - sister (8)
tempéstās, tempestā́tis (f) - period of time, season; weather, storm (15)
témpus, témporis (n) - time; occasion, opportunity (7)
tímor, timṓris (m) - fear (10)
úxor, uxṓris (f) - wife (7)
vḗritās, vēritā́tis (f) - truth (10)
vésper, vésperis *or* vésperī (m) - evening; evening star (28)
vírgō, vírginis (f) - maiden, virgin (7)
vírtūs, virtū́tis (f) - manliness, courage; excellence, character, worth, virtue (7)
volúptās, voluptā́tis (f) - pleasure (10)
vōx, vṓcis (f) - voice, word (34)
vúlnus, vúlneris (n) - wound (24)

3rd Declension I-Stem

ánimal, animā́lis (n) - a living creature, animal (14)
ars, ártis (f) - art, skill (14)
arx, árcis (f) - citadel, stronghold (23)
as, ássis (m) - an as *(a small copper coin)* (31)
aúris, aúris (f) - ear (14)
cī́vis, cī́vis (m *or* f) - citizen (14)

fī́nēs, fī́nium (m) - boundaries, territory (21)
fī́nis, fī́nis (m) - end, limit, boundary; purpose (21)
gēns, géntis (f) - clan, race, nation, people (21)
hóstēs, hóstium (m) - the enemy (18)
hóstis, hóstis (m) - an enemy *(of the state)* (18)
ígnis, ígnis (m) - fire (22)
máre, máris (n) - sea (14)
mēns, méntis (f) - mind, thought, intention (16)
moénia, moénium (n. pl.) - walls of a city (29)
mōns, móntis (m) - mountain (20)
mors, mórtis (f) - death (14)
nā́vis, nā́vis (f) - ship, boat (21)
nox, nóctis (f) - night (26)
nū́bēs, nū́bis (f) - cloud (14)
pars, pártis (f) - part, share; direction (14)
urbs, úrbis (f) - city (14)
vī́rēs, vī́rium (f. pl.) - strength (14)
vīs, vīs (f) - force, power, violence (14)

4th Declension
córnū, córnūs (n) - horn (20)
cúrsus, cúrsūs (m) - running, race; course (28)
exércitus, exércitūs (m) - army (32)
frū́ctus, frū́ctūs (m) - fruit; profit, benefit, enjoyment (20)
génū, génūs (n) - knee (20)
mánus, mánūs (f) - hand; handwriting; band (20)
métus, métūs (m) - fear, dread, anxiety (20)
senā́tus, senā́tūs (m) - senate (20)
sḗnsus, sḗnsūs (m) - feeling, sense (20)
spī́ritus, spī́ritūs (m) - breath, breathing; spirit, soul (20)
vérsus, vérsūs (m) - line of verse (20)

5th Declension
díēs, diḗī (m) - day (22)
fídēs, fídeī (f) - faith, trust, trustworthiness, fidelity, promise, guarantee, protection (22)
rēs, réī (f) - thing, matter, property, business, affair (22)
rēs pū́blica, réī pū́blicae (f) - state, commonwealth, republic (22)
spēs, spéī (f) - hope (22)

Indeclinable
níhil - nothing (1)
sátis - enough (5)

Pronouns
áliquis, áliquid - someone, somebody, something (23)
égo, méī - I (11)
hic, haec, hoc - this; the latter; he, she, it, they (9)
ī́dem, éadem, ídem - the same (11)
ílle, ílla, íllud - that; the former; the famous; he, she, it, they (9)
ípse, ípsa, ípsum - myself, yourself, himself, herself, itself, *etc.*, the very, the actual (13)
is, éa, id - this, that; he, she, it (11)
íste, ísta, ístud - that of yours, that; such (as you have, as you speak of); *sometimes with contemptuous force, e.g.,* that despicable, that wretched (9)
quī, quae, quod - who, which, what, that (17)
quid - what (1)
quídam, quaédam, quíddam - a certain one or thing, someone, something (26)
quis, quid (*after* sī, nisi, nē, num) - anyone, anything, someone, something (33)
quis? quid? - who? whose? whom? what? which? (19)
quísque, quídque, cuiúsque, cuíque - each one, each person, each thing (13)
quísquis, quídquid - whoever, whatever (23)
súī - himself, herself, itself, themselves (13)
tū, túī - you *(sing.)* (11)

Adjectives
1st & 2nd Declension
acérbus, acérba, acérbum - harsh, bitter, grievous (12)
advérsus, advérsa, advérsum - opposite, adverse (34)
aéquus, aéqua, aéquum - level, even; calm; equal, just; favorable (22)
áliī . . . áliī - some . . . others (9)
álius, ália, áliud - other, another (9)
álter, áltera, álterum - the other (of two), second (9)
amī́cus, amī́ca, amī́cum - friendly (11)
antī́quus, antī́qua, antī́quum - ancient, old-time (2)
ásper, áspera, ásperum - rough, harsh (21)
avā́rus, avā́ra, avā́rum - greedy, avaricious (3)
beā́tus, beā́ta, beā́tum - happy, fortunate, blessed (10)
béllus, bélla, béllum - pretty, handsome, charming (4)
bónus, bóna, bónum - good, kind (4)
caécus, caéca, caécum - blind (17)

cándidus, cándida, cándidum - shining, bright, white; beautiful (33)
cā́rus, cā́ra, cā́rum - dear (11)
cértus, cérta, cértum - definite, sure, certain, reliable (19)
cḗterī, cḗterae, cḗtera - the remaining, the rest, the other, all the others (30)
clā́rus, clā́ra, clā́rum - clear, bright; renowned, famous, illustrious (18)
déxter, déxtra, déxtrum - right, right-hand (20)
dígnus, dígna, dígnum (+abl.) - worthy, worthy of (29)
dóctus, dócta, dóctum - taught, learned, skilled (13)
dū́rus, dū́ra, dū́rum - hard, harsh, rough, stern, unfeeling, hardy, difficult (29)
fortūnā́tus, fortūnā́ta, fortūnā́tum - lucky, fortunate, happy (13)
géminus, gémina, géminum - twin (25)
Graécus, Graéca, Graécum - Greek (6)
hūmā́nus, hūmā́na, hūmā́num - pertaining to man, human; humane, kind; refined, cultivated (4)
incértus, incérta, incértum - uncertain, unsure, doubtful (22)
iūcúndus, iūcúnda, iūcúndum - pleasant, delightful, agreeable, pleasing (16)
Latī́nus, Latī́na, Latī́num - Latin (22)
lī́ber, lī́bera, lī́berum - free (5)
lóngus, lónga, lóngum - long (16)
magnánimus, magnánima, magnánimum - great-hearted, brave, magnanimous (23)
mágnus, mágna, mágnum - large, great; important (2)
málus, mála, málum - bad, wicked, evil (4)
médius, média, médium - middle; the middle of (22)
mérus, méra, mérum - pure, undiluted (33)
méus, méa, méum - my (2)
míser, mísera, míserum - wretched, miserable, unfortunate (15)
mórtuus, mórtua, mórtuum - dead (28)
múltus, múlta, múltum - much, many (2)
neúter, neútra, neútrum - not either, neither (9)
nóster, nóstra, nóstrum - our, ours (5)
nóvus, nóva, nóvum - new; strange (7)
nū́llus, nū́lla, nū́llum - not any, no, none (9)
párvus, párva, párvum - small, little (4)
paúcī, paúcae, paúca - few, a few (3)
perpétuus, perpétua, perpétuum perpetual, lasting, uninterrupted, continuous (6)
plḗnus, plḗna, plḗnum - full, abundant, generous (6)
prī́mus, prī́ma, prī́mum - first, foremost, chief, principal (27)
pudī́cus, pudī́ca, pudī́cum - modest, chaste (26)
púlcher, púlchra, púlchrum - beautiful, handsome; fine (5)
quántus, quánta, quántum - how large, how great, how much (30)
rīdículus, rīdícula, rīdículum - laughable, ridiculous (30)
Rōmā́nus, Rōmā́na, Rōmā́num - Roman (3)
sálvus, sálva, sálvum - safe, sound (6)
sā́nus, sā́na, sā́num - sound, healthy, sane (5)
secúndus, secúnda, secúndum - second; favorable (6)
siníster, sinístra, sinístrum - left, left-hand; harmful, ill-omened (20)
sṓlus, sṓla, sṓlum - alone, only, the only (9)
stúltus, stúlta, stúltum - foolish (4)
supérbus, supérba, supérbum - arrogant, overbearing, haughty, proud (26)
súperus, súpera, súperum - above, upper (27)
súus, súa, súum - his own, her own, its own, their own (13)
tántus, tánta, tántum - so large, so great, of such a size (29)
tántus . . . quántus - just as much (many) . . . as (30)
tṓtus, tṓta, tṓtum - whole, entire (9)
túus, túa, túum - your *(sing.)* (2)
ū́llus, ū́lla, ū́llum - any (9)
últimus, última, últimum - farthest, extreme; last, final (25)
ū́nus, ū́na, ū́num - one, single, alone (9)
urbā́nus, urbā́na, urbā́num - of the city, urban; urbane, elegant (26)
úter, útra, útrum - either, which (of two) (9)
vḗrus, vḗra, vḗrum - true, real, proper (4)
véster, véstra, véstrum - your *(pl.)* (6)
vī́vus, vī́va, vī́vum - alive, living (30)

3rd Declension

ā́cer, ā́cris, ā́cre - sharp, keen, eager; severe, fierce (16)
brévis, bréve - short, small, brief (16)
céler, céleris, célere - swift, quick, rapid (16)
commū́nis, commū́ne - common, general, of / for the community (20)
diffícilis, diffícile - hard, difficult, troublesome (16)
dī́ligēns, ***gen.*** **dīligéntis** - diligent, careful (27)
dissímilis, dissímile - unlike, different (27)
dī́ves, ***gen.*** **dī́vitis** ***or*** **dī́tis** - rich, wealthy (32)
dúlcis, dúlce - sweet; pleasant, agreeable (16)
fácilis, fácile - easy; agreeable (16)
fḗlīx, ***gen.*** **fēlī́cis** - lucky, fortunate, happy (22)
férōx, ***gen.*** **ferṓcis** - fierce, savage (25)
fidḗlis, fidḗle - faithful, loyal (25)
fórtis, fórte - strong, brave (16)
grácilis, grácile - slender, thin (27)
grávis, gráve - heavy, weighty; serious, important; severe, grievous (19)
húmilis, húmile - lowly, humble (27)
immortā́lis, immortā́le - not subject to death, immortal (19)
íngēns, ***gen.*** **ingéntis** - huge (16)
lévis, léve - light; easy; slight, trivial (17)
máior, máius - greater; older (27)
medíocris, medíocre - ordinary, moderate, mediocre (31)
mortā́lis, mortā́le - mortal (18)
ómnis, ómne - every, all (16)
pār, ***gen.*** **páris (+dat.)** - equal, like (32)
paúper, ***gen.*** **paúperis** - of small means, poor (32)
pótēns, ***gen.*** **poténtis** - able, powerful, mighty, strong (16)
prī́nceps, ***gen.*** **prī́ncipis** - chief, foremost (28)
sápiēns, ***gen.*** **sapiéntis** - wise, judicious (25)
sénex, ***gen.*** **sénis** - old, aged (16)
símilis, símile (+gen. or dat.) - similar (to), like, resembling (27)
suā́vis, suā́ve - sweet (33)
tā́lis, tā́le - such, of such a sort (34)
trī́stis, trī́ste - sad, sorrowful; joyless, grim, severe (26)
túrpis, túrpe - ugly; shameful, base, disgraceful (26)
ū́tilis, ū́tile - useful, advantageous (27)

Indeclinable Adjectives

quot - how many, as many as (27)
sátis - enough, sufficient (5)

Indefinite Adjective

quī́dam, quaédam, quóddam - a certain, some (26)

Interrogative Adjective

quī?, quae?, quod? - what? which? what kind of?; *(sometimes with exclamatory force)* what (a)! what sort of! (19)

Verbs

1st Conjugation

ádiuvō, adiuvā́re, adiū́vī, adiū́tum - to help, aid, assist; to please (4)
ámō, amā́re, amā́vī, amā́tum - to love, like (1)
appéllō, appellā́re, appellā́vī, appellā́tum - to speak to, address (as), call, name (14)
cḗnō, cēnā́re, cēnā́vī, cēnā́tum - to dine (5)
cṓgitō, cōgitā́re, cōgitā́vī, cōgitā́tum- to think, ponder, consider, plan (1)
cōnsérvō, cōnservā́re, cōnservā́vī, cōnservā́tum - to preserve, conserve, maintain (1)
créō, creā́re, creā́vī, creā́tum - to create (12)
cúlpō, culpā́re, culpā́vī, culpā́tum - to blame, censure (5)
dḗdicō, dēdicā́re, dēdicā́vī, dēdicā́tum - to dedicate (28)
dēléctō, dēlectā́re, dēlectā́vī, dēlectā́tum - to delight, charm, please (19)
dēmṓnstrō, dēmōnstrā́re, dēmōnstrā́vī, dēmōnstrā́tum to point out, show, demonstrate (8)
dēsī́derō, dēsīderā́re, dēsīderā́vī, dēsīderā́tum - to desire, long for, miss (17)
dō, dáre, dédī, dátum - to give, offer (1)
dúbitō, dubitā́re, dubitā́vī, dubitā́tum - to doubt, hesitate (30)
ḗducō, ēducā́re, ēducā́vī, ēducā́tum - to bring up, educate (23)
érrō, errā́re, errā́vī, errā́tum - to wander; err, go astray, make a mistake, be mistaken (1)
exspéctō, exspectā́re, exspectā́vī, exspectā́tum - to look for, expect, await (15)
invī́tō, invītā́re, invītā́vī, invītā́tum - to entertain, invite, summon (26)

iúvō, iuvā́re, iū́vī, iū́tum - to help, aid, assist; to please (4)
labṓrō, labōrā́re, labōrā́vī, labōrā́tum - to labor; be in distress (21)
laúdō, laudā́re, laudā́vī, laudā́tum - to praise (1)
lī́berō, līberā́re, līberā́vī, līberā́tum - to free, liberate (19)
mū́tō, mūtā́re, mūtā́vī, mūtā́tum to change, alter; exchange (14)
nā́rrō, nārrā́re, nārrā́vī, nārrā́tum - to tell, report, narrate (24)
nā́vigō, nāvigā́re, nāvigā́vī, nāvigā́tum - to sail, navigate (17)
nécō, necā́re, necā́vī, necā́tum - to murder, kill (7)
négō, negā́re, negā́vī, negā́tum to deny, say that . . . not (25)
nū́ntiō, nūntiā́re, nūntiā́vī, nūntiā́tum - to announce, report, relate (25)
párō, parā́re, parā́vī, parā́tum - to prepare, provide; get, obtain (19)
praéstō, praestā́re, praéstitī, praéstitum - to excel; exhibit, show, offer, supply, furnish (28)
próbō, probā́re, probā́vī, probā́tum - to approve, recommend; test (27)
prōnū́ntiō, prōnūntiā́re, prōnūntiā́vī, prōnūntiā́tum - to proclaim, announce; declaim; pronounce (20)
púgnō, pugnā́re, pugnā́vī, pugnā́tum - to fight (29)
pútō, putā́re, putā́vī, putā́tum - to reckon, suppose, judge, think, imagine (25)
récitō, recitā́re, recitā́vī, recitā́tum - to read aloud, recite (17)
recū́sō, recūsā́re, recūsā́vī, recūsā́tum - to refuse (33)
rógō, rogā́re, rogā́vī, rogā́tum - to ask (30)
sátiō, satiā́re, satiā́vī, satiā́tum - to satisfy, sate (3)
sérvō, servā́re, servā́vī, servā́tum - to preserve, save, keep, guard (1)
spéctō, spectā́re, spectā́vī, spectā́tum - to look at, see (34)
spḗrō, spērā́re, spērā́vī, spērā́tum - to hope for, hope (25)
stō, stā́re, stétī, státum - to stand, stand still *or* firm (13)
súperō, superā́re, superā́vī, superā́tum - to be above, have the upper hand, surpass; overcome, conquer (5)
tólerō, tolerā́re, tolerā́vī, tolerā́tum - to bear, endure (6)
vī́tō, vītā́re, vītā́vī, vītā́tum - to avoid, shun (14)
vócō, vocā́re, vocā́vī, vocā́tum - to call, summon (1)

2nd Conjugation

aúdeō, audḗre, aúsus sum - to dare (7)
cáreō, carḗre, cáruī, caritū́rum (+abl.) - to be without, be deprived of, want, lack; be free from (20)
contíneō, continḗre, contínuī, conténtum - to hold together, contain, keep, enclose, restrain (21)
dḗbeō, dēbḗre, dḗbuī, dḗbitum - to owe; ought, must, should (1)
dḗleō, dēlḗre, dēlḗvī, dēlḗtum - to destroy, wipe out, erase (17)
dóceō, docḗre, dócuī, dóctum - to teach (8)
dóleō, dolḗre, dóluī, dolitū́rum - to grieve, suffer; hurt, give pain (31)
égeō, egḗre, éguī (+ abl. or gen.) - to need, lack, want (28)
éxpleō, explḗre, explḗvī, explḗtum - to fill, fill up, complete (28)
gaúdeō, gaudḗre, gāvī́sus sum - to be glad, rejoice (23)
hábeō, habḗre, hábuī, hábitum - to have, hold, possess; consider, regard (3)
iáceō, iacḗre, iácuī - to lie; lie prostrate; lie dead (25)
invídeō, invidḗre, invī́dī, invī́sum to be envious; to look at with envy, envy, be jealous of (+dat.) (31)
iúbeō, iubḗre, iússī, iússum - to bid, order, command (21)
máneō, manḗre, mā́nsī, mā́nsum - to remain, stay, stay behind, abide, continue (5)
mísceō, miscḗre, míscuī, míxtum to mix, stir up, disturb (18)
móneō, monḗre, mónuī, mónitum - to remind, advise, warn (1)
móveō, movḗre, mṓvī, mṓtum - to move; arouse, affect (18)
páteō, patḗre, pátuī - to be open, lie open; be accessible; be evident (32)
praébeō, praebḗre, praébuī, praébitum - to offer, provide (32)
prohíbeō, prohibḗre, prohíbuī, prohíbitum - to keep (back), prevent, hinder, restrain, prohibit (20)

remáneō, remanḗre, remā́nsī, remā́nsum - to remain, stay, stay behind, abide, continue (5)
respóndeō, respondḗre, respóndī, respṓnsum - to answer (29)
rī́deō, rīdḗre, rī́sī, rī́sum - to laugh, laugh at (24)
sálvē, salvḗte - hello, greetings (1)
sálveō, salvḗre - to be well, be in good health (1)
sédeō, sedḗre, sḗdī, séssum - to sit (34)
táceō, tacḗre, tácuī, tácitum - to be silent, leave unmentioned (28)
téneō, tenḗre, ténuī, téntum - to hold, keep, possess; restrain (14)
térreō, terrḗre, térruī, térritum - to frighten, terrify (1)
tímeō, timḗre, tímuī - to fear, be afraid (of) (15)
válē, valḗte - good-bye, farewell (1)
váleō, valḗre, váluī, valitū́rum - to be strong, have power; be well (1)
vídeō, vidḗre, vī́dī, vī́sum - to see; observe, understand (1)
vídeor, vidḗrī, vī́sus sum - to be seen, seem, appear (18)

3rd Conjugation

admíttō, admíttere, admī́sī, admíssum - to admit, receive, let in (17)
ágō, ágere, ḗgī, ā́ctum - to drive, lead, do, act; pass, spend *(life or time)* (8)
álō, álere, áluī, áltum - to nourish, support, sustain, increase; cherish (13)
āmíttō, āmíttere, āmī́sī, āmíssum - to send away; lose, let go (12)
āvértō, āvértere, āvértī, āvérsum - to turn away, avert (23)
bíbō, bíbere, bíbī - to drink (30)
cádō, cádere, cécidī, cāsū́rum - to fall (12)
cḗdō, cḗdere, céssī, céssum - to go, withdraw; yield to, grant, submit (28)
cérnō, cérnere, crḗvī, crḗtum - to distinguish, discern, perceive (22)
cognṓscō, cognṓscere, cognṓvī, cógnitum - to become acquainted with, learn, recognize; know *(in perfect tenses)* (30)
commíttō, commíttere, commī́sī, commíssum - to entrust, commit (15)
comprehéndō, comprehéndere, comprehéndī, comprehḗnsum - to grasp, seize, arrest; comprehend, understand (30)
cóndō, cóndere, cóndidī, cónditum - to put together *or* into, store; found, establish (29)
cōnsū́mō, cōnsū́mere, cōnsū́mpsī, cōnsū́mptum - to consume, use up (30)
conténdō, conténdere, conténdī, conténtum - to strive, struggle, contend; hasten (29)
crḗdō, crḗdere, crḗdidī, crḗditum to believe, trust (25)
crḗscō, crḗscere, crḗvī, crḗtum - to increase (34)
cúrrō, cúrrere, cucúrrī, cúrsum - to run, rush, move quickly (14)
dēféndō, dēféndere, dēféndī, dēfḗnsum - to ward off; defend, protect (20)
dī́cō, dī́cere, dī́xī, díctum - to say, tell, speak; name, call (10)
dī́ligō, dīlígere, dīlḗxī, dīlḗctum - to esteem, love (13)
discḗdō, discḗdere, discéssī, discéssum - to go away, depart (20)
dísco, díscere, dídicī - to learn (8)
dū́cō, dū́cere, dū́xī, dúctum - to lead; consider, regard; prolong (8)
expéllō, expéllere, éxpulī, expúlsum - to drive out, expel, banish (24)
expṓnō, expṓnere, expósuī, expósitum - to set forth, explain, expose (30)
flúō, flúere, flū́xī, flū́xum - to flow (18)
gérō, gérere, géssī, géstum - to carry; carry on, manage, conduct, wage, accomplish, perform (8)
intéllegō, intellégere, intellḗxī, intellḗctum - to understand (11)
iúngō, iúngere, iū́nxī, iū́nctum - to join (13)
légō, légere, lḗgī, lḗctum - to pick out, choose; read (18)
mínuō, minúere, mínuī, minū́tum - to lessen, diminish (30)
míttō, míttere, mī́sī, míssum - to send, let go (11)
néglegō, neglégere, neglḗxī, neglḗctum - to neglect, disregard (17)
nṓscō, nṓscere, nṓvī, nṓtum - to become acquainted with, learn, recognize; know *(in perfect tenses)* (30)
óccidō, occídere, óccidī, occā́sum - to fall down; die; set (31)

ópprimō, opprímere, oppréssī, oppréssum - to suppress, overwhelm, overpower, check (23)
osténdō, osténdere, osténdī, osténtum - to exhibit, show, display (23)
péllō, péllere, pépulī, púlsum - to strike, push; drive out, banish (24)
pétō, pétere, petī́vī, petī́tum - to seek, aim at, beg, beseech (23)
pṓnō, pṓnere, pósuī, pósitum - to put, place, set (27)
prémō, prémere, préssī, préssum - to press; press hard, pursue (23)
prōmíttō, prōmíttere, prōmī́sī, prōmíssum - to send forth; promise (32)
quaérō, quaérere, quaesī́vī, quaesī́tum - to seek, look for, strive for; ask, inquire, inquire into (24)
régō, régere, rḗxī, rḗctum - to rule, guide, direct (16)
relínquō, relínquere, relī́quī, relíctum - to leave behind, leave, abandon, desert (21)
revértō, revértere, revértī, revérsum - turn back (23)
scrī́bō, scrī́bere, scrī́psī, scrī́ptum to write, compose (8)
súrgō, súrgere, surrḗxī, surrḗctum - to get up, arise (29)
tángō, tángere, tétigī, tā́ctum - to touch (21)
tóllō, tóllere, sústulī, sublā́tum - to raise, lift up; take away, remove, destroy (22)
trā́dō, trā́dere, trā́didī, trā́ditum to give over, surrender; hand down, transmit, teach (33)
tráhō, tráhere, trā́xī, tráctum - to draw, drag; derive, acquire (8)
vértō, vértere, vértī, vérsum - to turn; change (23)
víncō, víncere, vī́cī, víctum - to conquer, overcome (8)
vī́vō, vī́vere, vī́xī, vī́ctum - to live (10)

3rd Conjugation -iō

accípiō, accípere, accḗpī, accéptum - to take *(to one's self)*, receive, accept (24)
cápiō, cápere, cḗpī, cáptum - to take, capture, seize, get (10)
cúpiō, cúpere, cupī́vī, cupī́tum - to desire, wish, long for (17)
ērípiō, ērípere, ērípuī, ēréptum - to snatch away, take away; rescue (22)
excípiō, excípere, excḗpī, excéptum - to take out, except; take, receive, capture (24)
fáciō, fácere, fḗcī, fáctum - to make, do, accomplish (10)
fúgiō, fúgere, fū́gī, fugitū́rum - to flee, hurry away; escape; go into exile; avoid, shun (10)
iáciō, iácere, iḗcī, iáctum - to throw, hurl (15)
incípiō, incípere, incḗpī, incéptum - to begin (17)
patefáciō, patefácere, patefḗcī, patefáctum - to make open, open; disclose, expose (25)
rápiō, rápere, rápuī, ráptum - to seize, snatch, carry away (21)
recípiō, recípere, recḗpī, recéptum - to take back, regain; admit, receive (24)
suscípiō, suscípere, suscḗpī, suscéptum - to undertake (25)

4th Conjugation

aúdiō, audī́re, audī́vī, audī́tum - to hear, listen to (10)
dórmiō, dormī́re, dormī́vī, dormī́tum - to sleep (31)
invéniō, invenī́re, invḗnī, invéntum - to come upon, find (10)
móllīō, mollī́re, mollī́vī, mollī́tum to soften; make calm *or* less hostile (29)
nésciō, nescī́re, nescī́vī, nescī́tum - to not know, be ignorant (25)
scíō, scī́re, scī́vī, scī́tum - to know (21)
séntiō, sentī́re, sḗnsī, sḗnsum - to feel, perceive, think, experience (11)
véniō, venī́re, vḗnī, véntum - to come (10)

Irregular

ádferō, adférre, áttulī, allā́tum - to bring to (31)
cṓnferō, cōnférre, cóntulī, collā́tum - to bring together, compare; confer, bestow (31)
férō, férre, túlī, lā́tum - to bear, carry, bring; suffer, endure, tolerate; say, report (31)
mā́lō, mā́lle, mā́luī - to want (something) more, instead; prefer (32)
nṓlō, nṓlle, nṓluī - to not . . . wish, be unwilling (32)
ófferō, offérre, óbtulī, oblā́tum - to offer (31)
póssum, pósse, pótuī - to be able, can, could, have power (6)
réferō, reférre, réttulī, relā́tum - to carry back, bring back; repeat, answer, report (31)

sum, ésse, fúī, futū́rum - to be, exist (4)
vólō, vélle, vóluī - to wish, want, be willing, will (32)

Deponent
árbitror, arbitrā́rī, arbitrā́tus sum to judge, think (34)
cṓnor, cōnā́rī, cōnā́tus sum - to try, attempt (34)
ēgrédior, ḗgredī, ēgréssus sum - to go out (34)
fáteor, fatḗrī, fássus sum - to confess, admit (34)
hórtor, hortā́rī, hortā́tus sum - to encourage, urge (34)
lóquor, lóquī, locū́tus sum - to say, speak, tell (34)
mṓlior, mōlī́rī, mōlī́tus sum - to work at, build, undertake, plan (34)
mórior, mórī, mórtuus sum - to die (34)
nā́scor, nā́scī, nā́tus sum - to be born; spring forth, arrive (34)
pátior, pátī, pássus sum - to suffer, endure; permit (34)
proficī́scor, proficī́scī, proféctus sum - to set out, start (34)
rū́sticor, rūsticā́rī, rūsticā́tus sum to live in the country (34)
séquor, séquī, secū́tus sum - to follow (34)
ū́tor, ū́tī, ū́sus sum (+abl.) - to use; enjoy, experience (34)

Defective
ā́it, ā́iunt - he says, they say, assert (25)
coépī, coepísse, coéptum - began (17)
ínquit - he says *or* said (22)
ṓdī, ōdísse, ōsū́rum - to hate (20)

Adverbs

ánte (+acc.) - before, previously (13)
béne - well, satisfactorily, quite (11)
cíto - quickly (17)
crās - tomorrow (5)
cūr - why (18)
déhinc - then, next (25)
deínde - thereupon, next, then (18)
dḗnique - at last, finally, lastly (29)
díū - long, for a long time (12)
étiam - even, also (11)
fū́rtim - stealthily, secretly (30)
héri - yesterday (5)
hīc - here (25)
hódiē - today (3)
iam - now, already, soon (19)
íbi - there (6)
íta - so, thus (29)
ítaque - and so, therefore (15)
íterum - again, a second time (21)
mox - soon (30)
nē . . . quídem - not . . . even (29)
nímis, nímium - too, too much, excessively; *(in a positive sense, esp. with adjectives and adverbs)* exceedingly, very (9)
nōn - not (1)
númquam - never (8)
nunc - now, at present (6)
nū́per - recently (12)
ṓlim - once (upon a time), long ago, formerly; some day, in the future (13)
pósteā - afterwards (24)
prī́mō - at first, at the beginning (30)
prṓtinus - immediately (22)
quam - how (16)
quam - than *(after comparatives);* as . . . as possible *(with superlatives)* (26)
quándō - when (5)
quā́rē - because of which thing *(lit.);* therefore, wherefore, why (6)
quídem - indeed, certainly, at least, even (29)
quóndam - formerly, once (22)
quóque - also, too (17)
repénte - suddenly (30)
saépe - often (1)
sátis - enough, sufficiently (5)
sémel - a single time, once, once and for all, simultaneously (31)
sémper - always (3)
sīc - so, thus (29)
súbitō - suddenly (33)
tam - so, to such a degree (29)
tam . . . quam - so . . . as (29)
támen - nevertheless, still (8)
tamquam - as it were, as if, so to speak (29)
tántum - only (26)
tum - then, at that time; thereupon, in the next place (5)
úbi - where, when (6)
últrā - on the other side of, beyond (22)
úmquam - ever, at any time (23)
únde - whence, from what *or* which place, from which, from whom (30)
úsque - all the way, up (to), even (to), continuously, always (31)
vḗrō - in truth, indeed, to be sure, however (29)

Conjunctions

at - but; but, mind you; but, you say (19)
átque, ac - and also, and even, and in fact (21)
aut - or (17)
aut . . . aut - either . . . or (17)
aútem - however; moreover (11)
cum (+indic.) - when (31)

cum (+subj.) - when, since, although (31)
dum - while, as long as, at the same time that; *or* until *(+subjunctive)* (8)
dúmmodo (+subj.) - provided that, so long as (32)
énim - for, in fact, truly (9)
et - and; even (2)
et . . . et - both . . . and (2)
ígitur - therefore, consequently (5)
nam - for (13)
nē - not; in order that . . . not, that . . . not, in order not to (28)
néque, nec - and not, nor (11)
néque . . . néque, nec . . . nec - neither . . . nor (11)
nísi - if . . . not, unless; except (19)
quod - because (11)
quóniam - since, inasmuch as (10)
sed - but (2)
sī - if (1)
ut (+indic.) - as, just as, when (24)
ut (+ subj.) - in order that, so that, that, in order to, so as to, to (28)
útrum . . . an - whether . . . or (30)

Prepositions

ab, ā (+abl.) - away from, from; by (14)
ad (+acc.) - to, up to, near to (8)
ánte (+acc.) - before *(in place or time)*, in front of (13)
ápud (+acc.) - among, in the presence of, at the house of (31)
cóntrā (+acc.) - against (19)
cum (+abl.) - with (10)
dē (+abl.) - down from, from; concerning, about (3)
ex, ē (abl.+) - out of, from, from within; by reason of, on account of ; of *(after cardinal numerals)* (8)
in (+acc.) - into, toward; against (9)
in (+abl.) - in, on (3)
ínter (+acc.) - between, among (15)
per (+acc.) - through; by *(with reflexive pronoun)* (13)
post (+acc.) - after, behind (7)
prae (+abl.) - in front of, before (26)
prō (+abl.) - in front of, before, on behalf of, for the sake of, in return for, instead of, for, as (12)
própter (+acc.) - on account of, because of (5)
síne (+abl.) - without (2)
sub (+abl. w/ verbs of rest *or* **+acc. w/ verbs of motion)** - under, up under, close to, down to/into, to/at the foot of (7)
trāns (+acc.) - across (14)
últrā (adv. and prep. +acc.) - on the other side of, beyond (22)

Interjections

heu - ah!, alas! (33)
ō - O!, Oh! (2)
vae (often +dat. or acc.) - alas, woe to (34)

Idioms

amā́bō tē - please (1)
grā́tiās ágere (+dat.) - to thank someone; to give thanks to (8)
mḗnsa secúnda (f) - dessert (26)
nōn sṓlum . . . sed étiam - not only . . . but also (9)
poénās dáre - to pay the penalty (2)
sē cōnférre - to go (31)
sī quándō - if ever (5)

Prefix

re-, red- - again, back (24)

Suffixes

-ne – interrogative suffix attached to the first word of a sentence, typically the verb or another word on which the question hinges, to introduce a question whose answer is uncertain (5)
-que - and *(enclitic conjunction; appended to the second of two words to be joined)* (6)
-ve - or (33)

Numerals

Cardinal - ū́nus *to* vīgíntī quī́nque (15)
Ordinal - prī́mus *to* duodécimus (15)

----

céntum - a hundred (15)
mī́lia, mī́lium (n. pl.) - thousands (15)
mī́lle - thousand (15)

Chapter 35

Nouns

1st Declension

adulēscéntia, adulēscéntiae (f) - youth, young manhood; youthfulness (5)

agrícola, agrícolae (m) - farmer (3)

amī́ca, amī́cae (f) - friend (female) (3)

amīcítia, amīcítiae (f) - friendship (10)

ánima, ánimae (f) - air *(breathed by an animal),* breath; soul, spirit (34)

áqua, áquae (f) - water (14)

Ásia, Ásiae (f) - Asia (12)

cása, cásae (f) - house, cottage, hut (21)

caúsa, caúsae (f) - cause, reason; case, situation (21)

caúsā (abl. + preceding gen.) - for the sake of, on account of (21)

cḗna, cḗnae (f) - dinner (26)

clēméntia, clēméntiae (f) - mildness, gentleness, mercy (16)

cṓpia, cṓpiae (f) - abundance, supply (8)

cṓpiae, cōpiā́rum (f) - supplies, troops, forces (8)

cúlpa, cúlpae (f) - fault, blame (5)

cū́ra, cū́rae (f) - care, attention, caution, anxiety (4)

custṓdia, custṓdiae (f) - protection, custody; guards *(pl.)* (32)

déa, déae (f) - goddess (6)

discípula, discípulae (f) - learner, pupil, student (female) (6)

dīvítiae, dīvitiā́rum (f. pl.) - riches, wealth (13)

fā́bula, fā́bulae (f) - story, tale; play (24)

fā́ma, fā́mae (f) - rumor, report; fame, reputation (2)

família, famíliae (f) - household, family (19)

fḗmina, fḗminae (f) - woman (3)

fenéstra, fenéstrae (f) - window (21)

fī́lia, fī́liae (f) - daughter (3)

fṓrma, fṓrmae (f) - form, shape; beauty (2)

fortū́na, fortū́nae (f) - fortune, luck (2)

glṓria, glṓriae (f) - glory, fame (5)

Graécia, Graéciae (f) - Greece (19)

hásta, hástae (f) - spear (23)

hṓra, hṓrae (f) - hour, time (10)

iā́nua, iā́nuae (f) - door (35)

īnsídiae, īnsidiā́rum (f) - ambush, plot, treachery (6)

ī́nsula, ī́nsulae (f) - island (23)

invídia, invídiae (f) - envy, jealousy, hatred (31)

ī́ra, ī́rae (f) - ire, anger (2)

Itália, Itáliae (f) - Italy (15)

língua, línguae (f) - tongue; language (25)

líttera, lítterae (f) - a letter of the alphabet (7)

lítterae, litterā́rum (f) - a letter (epistle), literature (7)

lū́na, lū́nae (f) - moon (28)

magístra, magístrae (f) - schoolmistress, teacher, mistress (4)

médica, médicae (f) - doctor, physician (female) (12)

memória, memóriae (f) - memory, recollection (15)

mḗnsa, mḗnsae (f) - table; dining; dish, course (26)

móra, mórae (f) - delay (4)

nā́ta, nā́tae (f) - daughter (29)

nātū́ra, nātū́rae (f) - nature (10)

naúta, naútae (m) - sailor (2)

patiéntia, patiéntiae (f) - suffering; patience, endurance (12)

pátria, pátriae (f) - fatherland, native land, (one's) country (2)

pecū́nia, pecū́niae (f) - money (2)

philósopha, philósophae (f) - philosopher (female) (33)

philosóphia, philosóphiae (f) - philosophy (2)

poéna, poénae (f) - penalty, punishment (2)

poḗta, poḗtae (m) - poet (2)

pórta, pórtae (f) - gate, entrance (2)

puélla, puéllae (f) - girl (2)

rēgī́na, rēgī́nae (f) - queen (7)

Rṓma, Rṓmae (f) - Rome (14)

rósa, rósae (f) - rose (2)

sapiéntia, sapiéntiae (f) - wisdom (3)

sátura, sáturae (f) - satire (16)

sciéntia, sciéntiae (f) - knowledge (18)

senténtia, senténtiae (f) - feeling, thought, opinion, vote, sentence (2)

sérva, sérvae (f) - slave (female) (24)

stḗlla, stḗllae (f) - star, planet (28)

térra, térrae (f) - earth, ground, land, country (7)

Trṓia, Trṓiae (f) - Troy (21)

túrba, túrbae (f) - uproar, disturbance; mob, crowd, multitude (14)

vía, víae (f) - way, road, street (10)

vīcī́na, vīcī́nae (f) - neighbor (female) (21)

victṓria, victṓriae (f) - victory (8)

vī́ta, vī́tae (f) - life; mode of life (2)

2nd Declension

áger, ágrī (m) - field, farm (3)
amícus, amícī (m) - friend (male) (3)
ánimī, animṓrum (m) - high spirits, pride, courage (5)
ánimus, ánimī (m) - soul, spirit, mind (5)
ánnus, ánnī (m) - year (12)
argūméntum, argūméntī (n) - proof, evidence, argument (19)
árma, armṓrum (n. pl.) - arms, weapons (28)
auxílium, auxíliī (n) - aid, help (31)
bā́sium, bā́siī (n) - kiss (4)
béllum, béllī (n) - war (4)
benefícium, benefíciī (n) - benefit, kindness; favor (19)
caélum, caélī (n) - sky, heaven (5)
coniūrā́tī, coniūrātṓrum (m. pl.) - conspirators (20)
cōnsílium, cōnsíliī (n) - plan, purpose, counsel, advice, judgment, wisdom (4)
déus, déī (m) - god (6)
dígitus, dígitī (m) - finger, toe (31)
discípulus, discípulī (m) - learner, pupil, student (male) (6)
dṓnum, dṓnī (n) - gift, present (4)
elephántus, elephántī (m and f) - elephant (31)
équus, équī (m) - horse (23)
exítium, exítiī (n) - destruction, ruin (4)
exsílium, exsíliī (n) - exile, banishment (31)
fáctum, fáctī (n) - deed, act, achievement (13)
fā́tum, fā́tī (n) - fate; death (29)
férrum, férrī (n) - iron; sword (22)
fī́lius, fī́liī (m) - son (3)
fórum, fórī (n) - marketplace, forum (26)
Graécus, Graécī (m) - a Greek (6)
impérium, impériī (n) - power to command, supreme power, authority, command, control (24)
ingénium, ingéniī (n) - nature, innate talent (29)
inítium, inítiī (n) - beginning, commencement (33)
iūdícium, iūdíciī (n) - judgment, decision, opinion; trial (19)
libéllus, libéllī (m) - little book (17)
líber, líbrī (m) - book (6)
lóca, locṓrum (n) - places, region (9)
lócī, locṓrum (m) - passages in literature (9)
lócus, lócī (m) - place; passage in literature (9)
lū́dus, lū́dī (m) - game, sport; school (18)
magíster, magístrī (m) - schoolmaster, teacher, master (4)
médicus, médicī (m) - doctor, physician (male) (12)
módus, módī (m) - measure, bound, limit; manner, method, mode, way (22)
mórbus, mórbī (m) - disease, sickness (9)
múndus, múndī (m) - world, universe (21)
númerus, númerī (m) - number (3)
óculus, óculī (m) - eye (4)
offícium, offíciī (n) - duty, service (4)
ṓsculum, ṓsculī (n) - kiss (29)
ṓtium, ṓtiī (n) - leisure, peace (4)
perfúgium, perfúgiī (n) - refuge, shelter (24)
perículum, perículī (n) - danger, risk (4)
philósophus, philósophī (m) - philosopher (male) (33)
pópulus, pópulī (m) - the people, a people, a nation (3)
praémium, praémiī (n) - reward, prize (35)
prīncípium, prīncípiī (n) - beginning (12)
púer, púerī (m) - boy; boys, children *(pl.)* (3)
remédium, remédiī (n) - cure, remedy (4)
sérvus, sérvī (m) - slave (male) (24)
sígnum, sígnī (n) - sign, signal, indication; seal (13)
sōlā́cium, sōlā́ciī (n) - comfort, relief (24)
sómnus, sómnī (m) - sleep (26)
spéculum, spéculī (n) - mirror (33)
stúdium, stúdiī (n) - eagerness, zeal, pursuit, study (9)
stúltus, stúltī (m) - a fool (4)
súperī, superṓrum (m. pl.) - the gods (27)
tyránnus, tyránnī (m) - absolute ruler, tyrant (6)
vérbum, vérbī (n)- word (5)
vīcī́nus, vīcī́nī (m) - neighbor (male) (21)
vī́num, vī́nī (n) - wine (31)
vir, vírī (m) - man, hero (3)
vítium, vítiī (n) - fault, crime, vice (6)
vúlgus, vúlgī (n) - the common people, mob, rabble (21)

3rd Declension

adulḗscēns, adulēscéntis (m *or* f) - young man *or* woman (12)
aéstās, aestā́tis (f) - summer (35)
aétās, aetā́tis (f) - period of life, life, age, an age, time (16)
ámor, amṓris (m) - love (7)
aúctor, auctṓris (m) - increaser; author, originator (19)

audítor, audītṓris (m) - hearer, listener, member of an audience (16)

Caésar, Caésaris (m) - Caesar (12)

cáput, cápitis (n) - head; leader; beginning; life; heading; chapter (11)

cármen, cárminis (n) - song, poem (7)

Carthā́gō, Carthā́ginis (f) - Carthage (24)

Cícerō, Cicerṓnis (m) - (Marcus Tullius) Cicero (8)

cī́vitās, cīvitā́tis (f) - state, citizenship (7)

cṓnsul, cṓnsulis (m) - consul (11)

córpus, córporis (n) - body (7)

cupíditās, cupiditā́tis (f) - desire, longing, passion; cupidity, avarice (10)

dēlectā́tiō, dēlectātiṓnis (f) - delight, pleasure, enjoyment (27)

dux, dúcis (m) - leader, guide; commander, general (23)

flū́men, flū́minis (n) - river (18)

frā́ter, frā́tris (m) - brother (8)

génus, géneris (n) - origin; kind, type, sort, class (18)

hómō, hóminis (m) - human being, man (7)

hónor, honṓris (m) - honor, esteem; public office (30)

imperā́tor, imperātṓris (m) - general, commander-in-chief, emperor (24)

iū́dex, iū́dicis (m) - judge, juror (19)

iūs, iū́ris (n) - right, justice, law (14)

lábor, labṓris (m)- labor, work, toil; a work, production (7)

laus, laúdis (f) - praise, glory, fame (8)

lēx, lḗgis (f) - law, statute (26)

lībértās, lībertā́tis (f) - liberty (8)

lī́men, lī́minis (n) - threshold (26)

lī́tus, lī́toris (n) - shore, coast (23)

lūx, lū́cis (f) - light (26)

maiṓrēs, maiṓrum (m. pl.) - ancestors (27)

mā́ter, mā́tris (f) - mother (12)

mī́les, mī́litis (m) - soldier (23)

mṓrēs, mṓrum (m) - habits, morals, character (7)

mōs, mṓris (m) - habit, custom, manner (7)

nḗmō, nūllī́us, nḗminī, nḗminem, nū́llō, nū́llā (m *or* f) - no one, nobody (11)

népōs, nepṓtis (m) - grandson, descendant (27)

nṓmen, nṓminis (n) - name (7)

occā́siō, occāsiṓnis (f) - occasion, opportunity (28)

ópēs, ópum (f. pl.) - power, resources, wealth (33)

ops, ópis (f) - help, aid (33)

ōrā́tor, ōrātṓris (m) - orator, speaker (23)

ōs, ṓris (n) - mouth, face (14)

párēns, paréntis (m *or* f) - parent (28)

páter, pátris (m) - father (12)

paupértās, paupertā́tis (f) - poverty, humble circumstances (32)

pāx, pā́cis (f) - peace (7)

péctus, péctoris (n) - breast, heart (35)

plēbs, plḗbis (f) - the common people, populace, plebeians (33)

prī́nceps, prī́ncipis (m *or* f) - leader, emperor (28)

próbitās, probitā́tis (f) - uprightness, honesty (18)

rátiō, ratiṓnis (f) - reckoning, account; reason, judgment, consideration; system; manner, method (8)

remíssiō, remissiṓnis (f) - letting go, release; relaxation (34)

rēx, rḗgis (m) - king (7)

rū́mor, rūmṓris (m) - rumor, gossip (31)

sacérdōs, sacerdṓtis (m) - priest (23)

sāl, sális (m) - salt; wit (33)

sálūs, salū́tis (f) - health, safety; greeting (21)

sápiēns, sapiéntis (m/f) - a wise man/woman, philosopher (25)

scélus, scéleris (n) - evil deed, crime, sin, wickedness (19)

scrī́ptor, scrīptṓris (m) - writer, author (8)

senéctūs, senectū́tis (f) - old age (10)

sénex, sénis (m) - old man (16)

sérvitūs, servitū́tis (f) - servitude, slavery (20)

sī́dus, sī́deris (n) - constellation, star (29)

sōl, sṓlis (m) - sun (27)

sóror, sorṓris (f) - sister (8)

tempéstās, tempestā́tis (f) - period of time, season; weather, storm (15)

témpus, témporis (n) - time; occasion, opportunity (7)

tímor, timṓris (m) - fear (10)

úxor, uxṓris (f) - wife (7)

vḗritās, vēritā́tis (f) - truth (10)

vésper, vésperis *or* vésperī (m) - evening; evening star (28)

vírgō, vírginis (f) - maiden, virgin (7)

vírtūs, virtū́tis (f) - manliness, courage; excellence, character, worth, virtue (7)

volúptās, voluptā́tis (f) - pleasure (10)

vōx, vṓcis (f) - voice, word (34)

vúlnus, vúlneris (n) - wound (24)

3rd Declension I-Stem
ánimal, animā́lis (n) - a living creature, animal (14)
ars, ártis (f) - art, skill (14)
arx, árcis (f) - citadel, stronghold (23)
as, ássis (m) - an as *(a small copper coin)* (31)
aúris, aúris (f) - ear (14)
cī́vis, cī́vis (m *or* f) - citizen (14)
fī́nēs, fī́nium (m) - boundaries, territory (21)
fī́nis, fī́nis (m) - end, limit, boundary; purpose (21)
gēns, géntis (f) - clan, race, nation, people (21)
hóstēs, hóstium (m) - the enemy (18)
hóstis, hóstis (m) - an enemy *(of the state)* (18)
ígnis, ígnis (m) - fire (22)
máre, máris (n) - sea (14)
mēns, méntis (f) - mind, thought, intention (16)
moénia, moénium (n. pl.) - walls of a city (29)
mōns, móntis (m) - mountain (20)
mors, mórtis (f) - death (14)
nā́vis, nā́vis (f) - ship, boat (21)
nox, nóctis (f) - night (26)
nū́bēs, nū́bis (f) - cloud (14)
pars, pártis (f) - part, share; direction (14)
urbs, úrbis (f) - city (14)
vī́rēs, vī́rium (f. pl.) - strength (14)
vīs, vīs (f) - force, power, violence (14)

4th Declension
córnū, córnūs (n) - horn (20)
cúrsus, cúrsūs (m) - running, race; course (28)
exércitus, exércitūs (m) - army (32)
frū́ctus, frū́ctūs (m) - fruit; profit, benefit, enjoyment (20)
génū, génūs (n) - knee (20)
mánus, mánūs (f) - hand; handwriting; band (20)
métus, métūs (m) - fear, dread, anxiety (20)
senā́tus, senā́tūs (m) - senate (20)
sḗnsus, sḗnsūs (m) - feeling, sense (20)
spī́ritus, spī́ritūs (m) - breath, breathing; spirit, soul (20)
vérsus, vérsūs (m) - line of verse (20)

5th Declension
díēs, diḗī (m) - day (22)
fídēs, fídeī (f) - faith, trust, trustworthiness, fidelity, promise, guarantee, protection (22)
rēs, réī (f) - thing, matter, property, business, affair (22)
rēs pū́blica, réī pū́blicae (f) - state, commonwealth, republic (22)
spēs, spéī (f) - hope (22)

Indeclinable
níhil - nothing (1)
sátis - enough (5)

Pronouns
áliquis, áliquid - someone, somebody, something (23)
égo, méī - I (11)
hic, haec, hoc - this; the latter; he, she, it, they (9)
ī́dem, éadem, ídem - the same (11)
ílle, ílla, íllud - that; the former; the famous; he, she, it, they (9)
ípse, ípsa, ípsum - myself, yourself, himself, herself, itself, *etc.,* the very, the actual (13)
is, éa, id - this, that; he, she, it (11)
íste, ísta, ístud - that of yours, that; such (as you have, as you speak of); *sometimes with contemptuous force, e.g.,* that despicable, that wretched (9)
quī, quae, quod - who, which, what, that (17)
quid - what (1)
quī́dam, quaédam, quíddam - a certain one or thing, someone, something (26)
quis, quid (*after* sī, nisi, nē, num) - anyone, anything, someone, something (33)
quis? quid? - who? whose? whom? what? which? (19)
quísque, quídque, cuiúsque, cuíque - each one, each person, each thing (13)
quísquis, quídquid - whoever, whatever (23)
súī - himself, herself, itself, themselves (13)
tū, túī - you *(sing.)* (11)

Adjectives
1st & 2nd Declension
acérbus, acérba, acérbum - harsh, bitter, grievous (12)
advérsus, advérsa, advérsum - opposite, adverse (34)
aéquus, aéqua, aéquum - level, even; calm; equal, just; favorable (22)
áliī . . . áliī - some . . . others (9)
álius, ália, áliud - other, another (9)
álter, áltera, álterum - the other (of two), second (9)
amī́cus, amī́ca, amī́cum - friendly (11)
antī́quus, antī́qua, antī́quum - ancient, old-time (2)
ásper, áspera, ásperum - rough, harsh (21)
avā́rus, avā́ra, avā́rum - greedy, avaricious (3)

beā́tus, beā́ta, beā́tum - happy, fortunate, blessed (10)
béllus, bélla, béllum - pretty, handsome, charming (4)
bónus, bóna, bónum - good, kind (4)
caécus, caéca, caécum - blind (17)
cándidus, cándida, cándidum - shining, bright, white; beautiful (33)
cā́rus, cā́ra, cā́rum - dear (11)
cértus, cérta, cértum - definite, sure, certain, reliable (19)
cḗterī, cḗterae, cḗtera - the remaining, the rest, the other, all the others (30)
clā́rus, clā́ra, clā́rum - clear, bright; renowned, famous, illustrious (18)
déxter, déxtra, déxtrum - right, right-hand (20)
dígnus, dígna, dígnum (+abl.) - worthy, worthy of (29)
dóctus, dócta, dóctum - taught, learned, skilled (13)
dū́rus, dū́ra, dū́rum - hard, harsh, rough, stern, unfeeling, hardy, difficult (29)
fortūnā́tus, fortūnā́ta, fortūnā́tum - lucky, fortunate, happy (13)
géminus, gémina, géminum - twin (25)
Graécus, Graéca, Graécum - Greek (6)
hūmā́nus, hūmā́na, hūmā́num - pertaining to man, human; humane, kind; refined, cultivated (4)
incértus, incérta, incértum - uncertain, unsure, doubtful (22)
īrā́tus, īrā́ta, īrā́tum - angry (35)
iūcúndus, iūcúnda, iūcúndum - pleasant, delightful, agreeable, pleasing (16)
Latī́nus, Latī́na, Latī́num - Latin (22)
lī́ber, lī́bera, lī́berum - free (5)
lóngus, lónga, lóngum - long (16)
magnánimus, magnánima, magnánimum - great-hearted, brave, magnanimous (23)
mágnus, mágna, mágnum - large, great; important (2)
málus, mála, málum - bad, wicked, evil (4)
médius, média, médium - middle; the middle of (22)
mérus, méra, mérum - pure, undiluted (33)
méus, méa, méum - my (2)
míser, mísera, míserum - wretched, miserable, unfortunate (15)
mórtuus, mórtua, mórtuum - dead (28)
múltus, múlta, múltum - much, many (2)
neúter, neútra, neútrum - not either, neither (9)
nóster, nóstra, nóstrum - our, ours (5)
nóvus, nóva, nóvum - new; strange (7)
nū́llus, nū́lla, nū́llum - not any, no, none (9)
párvus, párva, párvum - small, little (4)
paúcī, paúcae, paúca - few, a few (3)
perpétuus, perpétua, perpétuum perpetual, lasting, uninterrupted, continuous (6)
plḗnus, plḗna, plḗnum - full, abundant, generous (6)
prī́mus, prī́ma, prī́mum - first, foremost, chief, principal (27)
pudī́cus, pudī́ca, pudī́cum - modest, chaste (26)
púlcher, púlchra, púlchrum - beautiful, handsome; fine (5)
quántus, quánta, quántum - how large, how great, how much (30)
rīdículus, rīdícula, rīdículum - laughable, ridiculous (30)
Rōmā́nus, Rōmā́na, Rōmā́num - Roman (3)
sálvus, sálva, sálvum - safe, sound (6)
sā́nus, sā́na, sā́num - sound, healthy, sane (5)
secúndus, secúnda, secúndum - second; favorable (6)
siníster, sinístra, sinístrum - left, left-hand; harmful, ill-omened (20)
sṓlus, sṓla, sṓlum - alone, only, the only (9)
stúltus, stúlta, stúltum - foolish (4)
supérbus, supérba, supérbum - arrogant, overbearing, haughty, proud (26)
súperus, súpera, súperum - above, upper (27)
súus, súa, súum - his own, her own, its own, their own (13)
tántus, tánta, tántum - so large, so great, of such a size (29)
tántus . . . quántus - just as much (many) . . . as (30)
tṓtus, tṓta, tṓtum - whole, entire (9)
túus, túa, túum - your *(sing.)* (2)
ū́llus, ū́lla, ū́llum - any (9)
últimus, última, últimum - farthest, extreme; last, final (25)
ū́nus, ū́na, ū́num - one, single, alone (9)
urbā́nus, urbā́na, urbā́num - of the city, urban; urbane, elegant (26)

úter, útra, útrum - either, which (of two) (9)
vḗrus, vḗra, vḗrum - true, real, proper (4)
véster, véstra, véstrum - your *(pl.)* (6)
vī́vus, vī́va, vī́vum - alive, living (30)

3rd Declension

ā́cer, ā́cris, ā́cre - sharp, keen, eager; severe, fierce (16)
brévis, bréve - short, small, brief (16)
céler, céleris, célere - swift, quick, rapid (16)
commū́nis, commū́ne - common, general, of / for the community (20)
diffícilis, diffícile - hard, difficult, troublesome (16)
dī́ligēns, ***gen.*** **dīligéntis** - diligent, careful (27)
dissímilis, dissímile - unlike, different (27)
dī́ves, ***gen.*** **dī́vitis** ***or*** **dī́tis** - rich, wealthy (32)
dúlcis, dúlce - sweet; pleasant, agreeable (16)
fácilis, fácile - easy; agreeable (16)
fḗlīx, ***gen.*** **fēlī́cis** - lucky, fortunate, happy (22)
férōx, ***gen.*** **ferṓcis** - fierce, savage (25)
fidḗlis, fidḗle - faithful, loyal (25)
fórtis, fórte - strong, brave (16)
grácilis, grácile - slender, thin (27)
grávis, gráve - heavy, weighty; serious, important; severe, grievous (19)
húmilis, húmile - lowly, humble (27)
immortā́lis, immortā́le - not subject to death, immortal (19)
íngēns, ***gen.*** **ingéntis** - huge (16)
lévis, léve - light; easy; slight, trivial (17)
máior, máius - greater; older (27)
medíocris, medíocre - ordinary, moderate, mediocre (31)
mortā́lis, mortā́le - mortal (18)
ómnis, ómne - every, all (16)
pār, ***gen.*** **páris (+dat.)** - equal, like (32)
paúper, ***gen.*** **paúperis** - of small means, poor (32)
pótēns, ***gen.*** **poténtis** - able, powerful, mighty, strong (16)
prī́nceps, ***gen.*** **prī́ncipis** - chief, foremost (28)
sápiēns, ***gen.*** **sapiéntis** - wise, judicious (25)
sénex, ***gen.*** **sénis** - old, aged (16)
símilis, símile (+gen. or dat.) - similar (to), like, resembling (27)
suā́vis, suā́ve - sweet (33)
tā́lis, tā́le - such, of such a sort (34)
trī́stis, trī́ste - sad, sorrowful; joyless, grim, severe (26)
túrpis, túrpe - ugly; shameful, base, disgraceful (26)
ū́tilis, ū́tile - useful, advantageous (27)

Indeclinable Adjectives

quot - how many, as many as (27)
sátis - enough, sufficient (5)

Indefinite Adjective

quī́dam, quaédam, quóddam - a certain, some (26)

Interrogative Adjective

quī?, quae?, quod? - what? which? what kind of?; *(sometimes with exclamatory force)* what (a)! what sort of! (19)

Verbs

1st Conjugation

ádiuvō, adiuvā́re, adiū́vī, adiū́tum - to help, aid, assist; to please (4)
ámō, amā́re, amā́vī, amā́tum - to love, like (1)
appéllō, appellā́re, appellā́vī, appellā́tum - to speak to, address (as), call, name (14)
cḗnō, cēnā́re, cēnā́vī, cēnā́tum - to dine (5)
cṓgitō, cōgitā́re, cōgitā́vī, cōgitā́tum- to think, ponder, consider, plan (1)
cōnsérvō, cōnservā́re, cōnservā́vī, cōnservā́tum - to preserve, conserve, maintain (1)
créō, creā́re, creā́vī, creā́tum - to create (12)
cúlpō, culpā́re, culpā́vī, culpā́tum - to blame, censure (5)
dḗdicō, dēdicā́re, dēdicā́vī, dēdicā́tum - to dedicate (28)
dēléctō, dēlectā́re, dēlectā́vī, dēlectā́tum - to delight, charm, please (19)
dēmṓnstrō, dēmōnstrā́re, dēmōnstrā́vī, dēmōnstrā́tum to point out, show, demonstrate (8)
dēsī́derō, dēsīderā́re, dēsīderā́vī, dēsīderā́tum - to desire, long for, miss (17)
dō, dáre, dédī, dátum - to give, offer (1)
dúbitō, dubitā́re, dubitā́vī, dubitā́tum - to doubt, hesitate (30)

éducō, ēducā́re, ēducā́vī, ēducā́tum - to bring up, educate (23)
érrō, errā́re, errā́vī, errā́tum - to wander; err, go astray, make a mistake, be mistaken (1)
exspéctō, exspectā́re, exspectā́vī, exspectā́tum - to look for, expect, await (15)
ímperō, imperā́re, imperā́vī, imperā́tum (+dat.) - to give orders to, command (35)
invī́tō, invītā́re, invītā́vī, invītā́tum - to entertain, invite, summon (26)
iúvō, iuvā́re, iū́vī, iū́tum - to help, aid, assist; to please (4)
labṓrō, labōrā́re, labōrā́vī, labōrā́tum - to labor; be in distress (21)
laúdō, laudā́re, laudā́vī, laudā́tum - to praise (1)
lī́berō, līberā́re, līberā́vī, līberā́tum - to free, liberate (19)
mū́tō, mūtā́re, mūtā́vī, mūtā́tum to change, alter; exchange (14)
nā́rrō, nārrā́re, nārrā́vī, nārrā́tum - to tell, report, narrate (24)
nā́vigō, nāvigā́re, nāvigā́vī, nāvigā́tum - to sail, navigate (17)
nécō, necā́re, necā́vī, necā́tum - to murder, kill (7)
négō, negā́re, negā́vī, negā́tum to deny, say that . . . not (25)
nū́ntiō, nūntiā́re, nūntiā́vī, nūntiā́tum - to announce, report, relate (25)
párō, parā́re, parā́vī, parā́tum - to prepare, provide; get, obtain (19)
praéstō, praestā́re, praéstitī, praéstitum - to excel; exhibit, show, offer, supply, furnish (28)
próbō, probā́re, probā́vī, probā́tum - to approve, recommend; test (27)
prōnū́ntiō, prōnūntiā́re, prōnūntiā́vī, prōnūntiā́tum - to proclaim, announce; declaim; pronounce (20)
púgnō, pugnā́re, pugnā́vī, pugnā́tum - to fight (29)
pútō, putā́re, putā́vī, putā́tum - to reckon, suppose, judge, think, imagine (25)
récitō, recitā́re, recitā́vī, recitā́tum - to read aloud, recite (17)
recū́sō, recūsā́re, recūsā́vī, recūsā́tum - to refuse (33)
rógō, rogā́re, rogā́vī, rogā́tum - to ask (30)
sátiō, satiā́re, satiā́vī, satiā́tum - to satisfy, sate (3)
sérvō, servā́re, servā́vī, servā́tum - to preserve, save, keep, guard (1)
spéctō, spectā́re, spectā́vī, spectā́tum - to look at, see (34)
spḗrō, spērā́re, spērā́vī, spērā́tum - to hope for, hope (25)
stō, stā́re, stétī, státum - to stand, stand still *or* firm (13)
súperō, superā́re, superā́vī, superā́tum - to be above, have the upper hand, surpass; overcome, conquer (5)
tólerō, tolerā́re, tolerā́vī, tolerā́tum - to bear, endure (6)
vī́tō, vītā́re, vītā́vī, vītā́tum - to avoid, shun (14)
vócō, vocā́re, vocā́vī, vocā́tum - to call, summon (1)

2nd Conjugation

aúdeō, audḗre, aúsus sum - to dare (7)
cáreō, carḗre, cáruī, caritū́rum (+abl.) - to be without, be deprived of, want, lack; be free from (20)
contíneō, continḗre, contínuī, conténtum - to hold together, contain, keep, enclose, restrain (21)
dḗbeō, dēbḗre, dḗbuī, dḗbitum - to owe; ought, must, should (1)
dḗleō, dēlḗre, dēlḗvī, dēlḗtum - to destroy, wipe out, erase (17)
dóceō, docḗre, dócuī, dóctum - to teach (8)
dóleō, dolḗre, dóluī, dolitū́rum - to grieve, suffer; hurt, give pain (31)
égeō, egḗre, éguī (+ abl. or gen.) - to need, lack, want (28)
éxpleō, explḗre, explḗvī, explḗtum - to fill, fill up, complete (28)
fóveō, fovḗre, fṓvī, fṓtum - to comfort, nurture, cherish (35)
gaúdeō, gaudḗre, gāvī́sus sum - to be glad, rejoice (23)
hábeō, habḗre, hábuī, hábitum - to have, hold, possess; consider, regard (3)
iáceō, iacḗre, iácuī - to lie; lie prostrate; lie dead (25)
invídeō, invidḗre, invī́dī, invī́sum to be envious; to look at with envy, envy, be jealous of (+dat.) (31)
iúbeō, iubḗre, iússī, iússum - to bid, order, command (21)
máneō, manḗre, mā́nsī, mā́nsum - to remain, stay, stay behind, abide, continue (5)

mísceō, miscḗre, míscuī, míxtum to mix, stir up, disturb (18)
móneō, monḗre, mónuī, mónitum - to remind, advise, warn (1)
móveō, movḗre, mṓvī, mṓtum - to move; arouse, affect (18)
nóceō, nocḗre, nócuī, nócitum (+dat.) - to do harm to, harm, injure (35)
páreō, pārḗre, páruī (+dat.) - to be obedient to, obey (35)
páteō, patḗre, pátuī - to be open, lie open; be accessible; be evident (32)
persuā́deō, persuādḗre, persuā́sī, persuā́sum (+dat.) to succeed in urging, persuade, convince (35)
pláceō, placḗre, plácuī, plácitum (+dat.) - to be pleasing to, please (35)
praébeō, praebḗre, praébuī, praébitum - to offer, provide (32)
prohíbeō, prohibḗre, prohíbuī, prohíbitum - to keep (back), prevent, hinder, restrain, prohibit (20)
remáneō, remanḗre, remā́nsī, remā́nsum - to remain, stay, stay behind, abide, continue (5)
respóndeō, respondḗre, respóndī, respṓnsum - to answer (29)
rī́deō, rīdḗre, rī́sī, rī́sum - to laugh, laugh at (24)
sálvē, salvḗte - hello, greetings (1)
sálveō, salvḗre - to be well, be in good health (1)
sédeō, sedḗre, sḗdī, séssum - to sit (34)
stúdeō, studḗre, stúduī (+dat.) - to direct one's zeal to, be eager for, study (35)
subrī́deō, subrīdḗre, subrī́sī, subrī́sum - to smile (down) upon (35)
táceō, tacḗre, tácuī, tácitum - to be silent, leave unmentioned (28)
téneō, tenḗre, ténuī, téntum - to hold, keep, possess; restrain (14)
térreō, terrḗre, térruī, térritum - to frighten, terrify (1)
tímeō, timḗre, tímuī - to fear, be afraid (of) (15)
válē, valḗte - good-bye, farewell (1)
váleō, valḗre, váluī, valitū́rum - to be strong, have power; be well (1)
vídeō, vidḗre, vī́dī, vī́sum - to see; observe, understand (1)
vídeor, vidḗrī, vī́sus sum - to be seen, seem, appear (18)

3rd Conjugation

admíttō, admíttere, admī́sī, admíssum - to admit, receive, let in (17)
ágō, ágere, ḗgī, ā́ctum - to drive, lead, do, act; pass, spend *(life or time)* (8)
álō, álere, áluī, áltum - to nourish, support, sustain, increase; cherish (13)
āmíttō, āmíttere, āmī́sī, āmíssum - to send away; lose, let go (12)
antepṓnō, antepṓnere, antepósuī, antepósitum - to put before, prefer (35)
āvértō, āvértere, āvértī, āvérsum - to turn away, avert (23)
bíbō, bíbere, bíbī - to drink (30)
cádō, cádere, cécidī, cāsū́rum - to fall (12)
cḗdō, cḗdere, céssī, céssum - to go, withdraw; yield to, grant, submit (28)
cérnō, cérnere, crḗvī, crḗtum - to distinguish, discern, perceive (22)
cognṓscō, cognṓscere, cognṓvī, cógnitum - to become acquainted with, learn, recognize; know *(in perfect tenses)* (30)
commíttō, commíttere, commī́sī, commíssum - to entrust, commit (15)
comprehéndō, comprehéndere, comprehéndī, comprehḗnsum - to grasp, seize, arrest; comprehend, understand (30)
cóndō, cóndere, cóndidī, cónditum - to put together *or* into, store; found, establish (29)
cōnsū́mō, cōnsū́mere, cōnsū́mpsī, cōnsū́mptum - to consume, use up (30)
conténdō, conténdere, conténdī, conténtum - to strive, struggle, contend; hasten (29)
crḗdō, crḗdere, crḗdidī, crḗditum to believe, trust (25)
crḗscō, crḗscere, crḗvī, crḗtum - to increase (34)
cúrrō, cúrrere, cucúrrī, cúrsum - to run, rush, move quickly (14)
dēféndō, dēféndere, dēféndī, dēfḗnsum - to ward off; defend, protect (20)
dī́cō, dī́cere, dī́xī, díctum - to say, tell, speak; name, call (10)
dī́ligō, dīlígere, dīlḗxī, dīlḗctum - to esteem, love (13)
discḗdō, discḗdere, discḗssī, discéssum - to go away, depart (20)

dísco, díscere, dídicī - to learn (8)
dū́cō, dū́cere, dū́xī, dúctum - to lead; consider, regard; prolong (8)
expéllō, expéllere, éxpulī, expúlsum - to drive out, expel, banish (24)
expṓnō, expṓnere, expósuī, expósitum - to set forth, explain, expose (30)
flúō, flúere, flū́xī, flū́xum - to flow (18)
gérō, gérere, géssī, géstum - to carry; carry on, manage, conduct, wage, accomplish, perform (8)
ignṓscō, ignṓscere, ignṓvī, ignṓtum (+dat.) - to grant pardon to, forgive (35)
intéllegō, intellégere, intellḗxī, intellḗctum - to understand (11)
iúngō, iúngere, iū́nxī, iū́nctum - to join (13)
légō, légere, lḗgī, lḗctum - to pick out, choose; read (18)
mínuō, minúere, mínuī, minū́tum - to lessen, diminish (30)
míttō, míttere, mī́sī, míssum - to send, let go (11)
néglegō, neglégere, neglḗxī, neglḗctum - to neglect, disregard (17)
nṓscō, nṓscere, nṓvī, nṓtum - to become acquainted with, learn, recognize; know *(in perfect tenses)* (30)
nū́bō, nū́bere, nū́psī, nū́ptum (+dat.) - to cover, veil; to be married to, marry (35)
óccidō, occídere, óccidī, occā́sum - to fall down; die; set (31)
ópprimō, opprímere, oppréssī, oppréssum - to suppress, overwhelm, overpower, check (23)
osténdō, osténdere, osténdī, osténtum - to exhibit, show, display (23)
párcō, párcere, pepércī, parsū́rum (+dat.) - to be lenient to, spare (35)
péllō, péllere, pépulī, púlsum - to strike, push; drive out, banish (24)
pétō, pétere, petī́vī, petī́tum - to seek, aim at, beg, beseech (23)
pṓnō, pṓnere, pósuī, pósitum - to put, place, set (27)
prémō, prémere, préssī, préssum - to press; press hard, pursue (23)
prōmíttō, prōmíttere, prōmī́sī, prōmíssum - to send forth; promise (32)
quaérō, quaérere, quaesī́vī, quaesī́tum - to seek, look for, strive for; ask, inquire, inquire into (24)
régō, régere, rḗxī, rḗctum - to rule, guide, direct (16)
relínquō, relínquere, relī́quī, relíctum - to leave behind, leave, abandon, desert (21)
revértō, revértere, revértī, revérsum - turn back (23)
scrī́bō, scrī́bere, scrī́psī, scrī́ptum to write, compose (8)
súrgō, súrgere, surrḗxī, surrḗctum - to get up, arise (29)
tángō, tángere, tétigī, tā́ctum - to touch (21)
tóllō, tóllere, sústulī, sublā́tum - to raise, lift up; take away, remove, destroy (22)
trā́dō, trā́dere, trā́didī, trā́ditum to give over, surrender; hand down, transmit, teach (33)
tráhō, tráhere, trā́xī, tráctum - to draw, drag; derive, acquire (8)
vértō, vértere, vértī, vérsum - to turn; change (23)
víncō, víncere, vī́cī, víctum - to conquer, overcome (8)
vī́vō, vī́vere, vī́xī, vī́ctum - to live (10)

3rd Conjugation -iō

accípiō, accípere, accḗpī, accéptum - to take *(to one's self)*, receive, accept (24)
cápiō, cápere, cḗpī, cáptum - to take, capture, seize, get (10)
cúpiō, cúpere, cupī́vī, cupī́tum - to desire, wish, long for (17)
ērípiō, ērípere, ērípuī, ēréptum - to snatch away, take away; rescue (22)
excípiō, excípere, excḗpī, excéptum - to take out, except; take, receive, capture (24)
fáciō, fácere, fḗcī, fáctum - to make, do, accomplish (10)
fúgiō, fúgere, fū́gī, fugitū́rum - to flee, hurry away; escape; go into exile; avoid, shun (10)
iáciō, iácere, iḗcī, iáctum - to throw, hurl (15)
incípiō, incípere, incḗpī, incéptum - to begin (17)
patefáciō, patefácere, patefḗcī, patefáctum - to make open, open; disclose, expose (25)
rápiō, rápere, rápuī, ráptum - to seize, snatch, carry away (21)
recípiō, recípere, recḗpī, recéptum - to take back, regain; admit, receive (24)
sápiō, sápere, sapī́vī - to have good taste; have good sense, be wise (35)

suscípiō, suscípere, suscḗpī, suscéptum - to undertake (25)

4th Conjugation

aúdiō, audī́re, audī́vī, audī́tum - to hear, listen to (10)
dórmiō, dormī́re, dormī́vī, dormī́tum - to sleep (31)
invéniō, invenī́re, invḗnī, invéntum - to come upon, find (10)
mólliō, mollī́re, mollī́vī, mollī́tum to soften; make calm *or* less hostile (29)
nésciō, nescī́re, nescī́vī, nescī́tum - to not know, be ignorant (25)
scíō, scī́re, scī́vī, scī́tum - to know (21)
séntiō, sentī́re, sḗnsī, sḗnsum - to feel, perceive, think, experience (11)
sérviō, servī́re, servī́vī, servī́tum (+dat.) - to be a slave to, serve (35)
véniō, venī́re, vḗnī, véntum - to come (10)

Irregular

ádferō, adférre, áttulī, allā́tum - to bring to (31)
cṓnferō, cōnférre, cóntulī, collā́tum - to bring together, compare; confer, bestow (31)
férō, férre, túlī, lā́tum - to bear, carry, bring; suffer, endure, tolerate; say, report (31)
mā́lō, mā́lle, mā́luī - to want (something) more, instead; prefer (32)
nṓlō, nṓlle, nṓluī - to not . . . wish, be unwilling (32)
ófferō, offérre, óbtulī, oblā́tum - to offer (31)
póssum, pósse, pótuī - to be able, can, could, have power (6)
réferō, reférre, réttulī, relā́tum - to carry back, bring back; repeat, answer, report (31)
sum, ésse, fúī, futū́rum - to be, exist (4)
vólō, vélle, vóluī - to wish, want, be willing, will (32)

Deponent

árbitror, arbitrā́rī, arbitrā́tus sum to judge, think (34)
cṓnor, cōnā́rī, cōnā́tus sum - to try, attempt (34)
ēgrédior, ḗgredī, ēgréssus sum - to go out (34)
fáteor, fatḗrī, fássus sum - to confess, admit (34)
hórtor, hortā́rī, hortā́tus sum - to encourage, urge (34)
lóquor, lóquī, locū́tus sum - to say, speak, tell (34)
mī́ror, mīrā́rī, mīrā́tus sum - to marvel at, admire, wonder (35)
mṓlior, mōlī́rī, mōlī́tus sum - to work at, build, undertake, plan (34)
mórior, mórī, mórtuus sum - to die (34)
nā́scor, nā́scī, nā́tus sum - to be born; spring forth, arrive (34)
pátior, pátī, pássus sum - to suffer, endure; permit (34)
proficī́scor, proficī́scī, proféctus sum - to set out, start (34)
rū́sticor, rūsticā́rī, rūsticā́tus sum to live in the country (34)
séquor, séquī, secū́tus sum - to follow (34)
ū́tor, ū́tī, ū́sus sum (+abl.) - to use; enjoy, experience (34)

Defective

ā́it, ā́iunt - he says, they say, assert (25)
coépī, coepísse, coéptum - began (17)
ínquit - he says *or* said (22)
ṓdī, ōdísse, ōsū́rum - to hate (20)

Adverbs

ánte (+acc.) - before, previously (13)
béne - well, satisfactorily, quite (11)
cíto - quickly (17)
crās - tomorrow (5)
cūr - why (18)
déhinc - then, next (25)
deínde - thereupon, next, then (18)
dḗnique - at last, finally, lastly (29)
díū - long, for a long time (12)
étiam - even, also (11)
fū́rtim - stealthily, secretly (30)
héri - yesterday (5)
hīc - here (25)
hódiē - today (3)
iam - now, already, soon (19)
íbi - there (6)
íta - so, thus (29)
ítaque - and so, therefore (15)
íterum - again, a second time (21)
mox - soon (30)
nē . . . quídem - not . . . even (29)
nímis, nímium - too, too much, excessively; *(in a positive sense, esp. with adjectives and adverbs)* exceedingly, very (9)
nōn - not (1)
númquam - never (8)
nunc - now, at present (6)
nū́per - recently (12)
ṓlim - once (upon a time), long ago, formerly; some day, in the future (13)
pósteā - afterwards (24)

prī́mō - at first, at the beginning (30)
prṓtinus - immediately (22)
quam - how (16)
quam - than *(after comparatives);* as . . . as possible *(with superlatives)* (26)
quándō - when (5)
quā́rē - because of which thing *(lit.);* therefore, wherefore, why (6)
quídem - indeed, certainly, at least, even (29)
quóndam - formerly, once (22)
quóque - also, too (17)
repénte - suddenly (30)
saépe - often (1)
sátis - enough, sufficiently (5)
sémel - a single time, once, once and for all, simultaneously (31)
sémper - always (3)
sīc - so, thus (29)
súbitō - suddenly (33)
tam - so, to such a degree (29)
tam . . . quam - so . . . as (29)
támen - nevertheless, still (8)
tamquam - as it were, as if, so to speak (29)
tántum - only (26)
tum - then, at that time; thereupon, in the next place (5)
úbi - where, when (6)
últrā - on the other side of, beyond (22)
úmquam - ever, at any time (23)
únde - whence, from what *or* which place, from which, from whom (30)
úsque - all the way, up (to), even (to), continuously, always (31)
vḗrō - in truth, indeed, to be sure, however (29)

Conjunctions

at - but; but, mind you; but, you say (19)
átque, ac - and also, and even, and in fact (21)
aut - or (17)
aut . . . aut - either . . . or (17)
aútem - however; moreover (11)
cum (+indic.) - when (31)
cum (+subj.) - when, since, although (31)
dum - while, as long as, at the same time that; *or* until *(+subjunctive)* (8)
dúmmodo (+subj.) - provided that, so long as (32)
énim - for, in fact, truly (9)
et - and; even (2)
et . . . et - both . . . and (2)
ígitur - therefore, consequently (5)
nam - for (13)
nē - not; in order that . . . not, that . . . not, in order not to (28)
néque, nec - and not, nor (11)
néque . . . néque, nec . . . nec - neither . . . nor (11)
nísi - if . . . not, unless; except (19)
quod - because (11)
quóniam - since, inasmuch as (10)
sed - but (2)
sī - if (1)
ut (+indic.) - as, just as, when (24)
ut (+ subj.) - in order that, so that, that, in order to, so as to, to (28)
útrum . . . an - whether . . . or (30)

Prepositions

ab, ā (+abl.) - away from, from; by (14)
ad (+acc.) - to, up to, near to (8)

ánte (+acc.) - before *(in place or time),* in front of (13)
ápud (+acc.) - among, in the presence of, at the house of (31)
cóntrā (+acc.) - against (19)
cum (+abl.) - with (10)
dē (+abl.) - down from, from; concerning, about (3)
ex, ē (abl.+) - out of, from, from within; by reason of, on account of ; of *(after cardinal numerals)* (8)
in (+acc.) - into, toward; against (9)
in (+abl.) - in, on (3)
ínter (+acc.) - between, among (15)
per (+acc.) - through; by *(with reflexive pronoun)* (13)
post (+acc.) - after, behind (7)
prae (+abl.) - in front of, before (26)
prō (+abl.) - in front of, before, on behalf of, for the sake of, in return for, instead of, for, as (12)
própter (+acc.) - on account of, because of (5)
síne (+abl.) - without (2)
sub (+abl. w/ verbs of rest *or* **+acc. w/ verbs of motion)** - under, up under, close to, down to/into, to/at the foot of (7)
trāns (+acc.) - across (14)
últrā (adv. and prep. +acc.) - on the other side of, beyond (22)

Interjections

heu - ah!, alas! (33)
ō - O!, Oh! (2)
vae (often +dat. or acc.) - alas, woe to (34)

Idioms

amā́bō tē - please (1)
grā́tiās ágere (+dat.) - to thank someone; to give thanks to (8)
mḗnsa secúnda (f) - dessert (26)
nōn sṓlum . . . sed étiam - not only . . . but also (9)
poénās dáre - to pay the penalty (2)
sē cōnférre - to go (31)
sī quándō - if ever (5)

Prefix

re-, red- - again, back (24)

Suffixes

-ne – interrogative suffix attached to the first word of a sentence, typically the verb or another word on which the question hinges, to introduce a question whose answer is uncertain (5)
-que - and *(enclitic conjunction; appended to the second of two words to be joined)* (6)
-ve - or (33)

Numerals

Cardinal - ū́nus *to* vīgíntī quī́nque (15)
Ordinal - prī́mus *to* duodécimus (15)

----

céntum - a hundred (15)
mī́lia, mī́lium (n. pl.) - thousands (15)
mī́lle - thousand (15)

Chapter 36

Nouns

1st Declension

adulēscéntia, adulēscéntiae (f) - youth, young manhood; youthfulness (5)
agrícola, agrícolae (m) - farmer (3)
amī́ca, amī́cae (f) - friend (female) (3)
amīcítia, amīcítiae (f) - friendship (10)
ánima, ánimae (f) - air *(breathed by an animal),* breath; soul, spirit (34)
áqua, áquae (f) - water (14)
Ásia, Ásiae (f) - Asia (12)
cása, cásae (f) - house, cottage, hut (21)
caúsa, caúsae (f) - cause, reason; case, situation (21)
caúsā (abl. + preceding gen.) - for the sake of, on account of (21)
cḗna, cḗnae (f) - dinner (26)
clēméntia, clēméntiae (f) - mildness, gentleness, mercy (16)
cṓpia, cṓpiae (f) - abundance, supply (8)
cṓpiae, cōpiā́rum (f) - supplies, troops, forces (8)
cúlpa, cúlpae (f) - fault, blame (5)
cū́ra, cū́rae (f) - care, attention, caution, anxiety (4)
custṓdia, custṓdiae (f) - protection, custody; guards *(pl.)* (32)
déa, déae (f) - goddess (6)
discípula, discípulae (f) - learner, pupil, student (female) (6)
dīvítiae, dīvitiā́rum (f. pl.) - riches, wealth (13)
fā́bula, fā́bulae (f) - story, tale; play (24)
fā́ma, fā́mae (f) - rumor, report; fame, reputation (2)
família, famíliae (f) - household, family (19)
fḗmina, fḗminae (f) - woman (3)
fenéstra, fenéstrae (f) - window (21)
fī́lia, fī́liae (f) - daughter (3)
fṓrma, fṓrmae (f) - form, shape; beauty (2)
fortū́na, fortū́nae (f) - fortune, luck (2)
glṓria, glṓriae (f) - glory, fame (5)
Graécia, Graéciae (f) - Greece (19)
hásta, hástae (f) - spear (23)
hṓra, hṓrae (f) - hour, time (10)
iā́nua, iā́nuae (f) - door (35)
īnsídiae, īnsidiā́rum (f) - ambush, plot, treachery (6)
ī́nsula, ī́nsulae (f) - island (23)
invídia, invídiae (f) - envy, jealousy, hatred (31)
ī́ra, ī́rae (f) - ire, anger (2)
Itália, Itáliae (f) - Italy (15)
língua, línguae (f) - tongue; language (25)
líttera, lítterae (f) - a letter of the alphabet (7)
lítterae, litterā́rum (f) - a letter (epistle), literature (7)
lū́na, lū́nae (f) - moon (28)
magístra, magístrae (f) - schoolmistress, teacher, mistress (4)
médica, médicae (f) - doctor, physician (female) (12)
memória, memóriae (f) - memory, recollection (15)
mḗnsa, mḗnsae (f) - table; dining; dish, course (26)
móra, mórae (f) - delay (4)
nā́ta, nā́tae (f) - daughter (29)
nātū́ra, nātū́rae (f) - nature (10)
naúta, naútae (m) - sailor (2)
patiéntia, patiéntiae (f) - suffering; patience, endurance (12)
pátria, pátriae (f) - fatherland, native land, (one's) country (2)
pecū́nia, pecū́niae (f) - money (2)
philósopha, philósophae (f) - philosopher (female) (33)
philosóphia, philosóphiae (f) - philosophy (2)
poéna, poénae (f) - penalty, punishment (2)
poḗta, poḗtae (m) - poet (2)
pórta, pórtae (f) - gate, entrance (2)
puélla, puéllae (f) - girl (2)
rēgī́na, rēgī́nae (f) - queen (7)
Rṓma, Rṓmae (f) - Rome (14)
rósa, rósae (f) - rose (2)
sapiéntia, sapiéntiae (f) - wisdom (3)
sátura, sáturae (f) - satire (16)
sciéntia, sciéntiae (f) - knowledge (18)
senténtia, senténtiae (f) - feeling, thought, opinion, vote, sentence (2)
sérva, sérvae (f) - slave (female) (24)
stḗlla, stḗllae (f) - star, planet (28)
térra, térrae (f) - earth, ground, land, country (7)
Trṓia, Trṓiae (f) - Troy (21)
túrba, túrbae (f) - uproar, disturbance; mob, crowd, multitude (14)
vía, víae (f) - way, road, street (10)
vīcī́na, vīcī́nae (f) - neighbor (female) (21)
victṓria, victṓriae (f) - victory (8)
vī́ta, vī́tae (f) - life; mode of life (2)

2nd Declension

áger, ágrī (m) - field, farm (3)
amícus, amícī (m) - friend (male) (3)
ánimī, animṓrum (m) - high spirits, pride, courage (5)
ánimus, ánimī (m) - soul, spirit, mind (5)
ánnus, ánnī (m) - year (12)
argūméntum, argūméntī (n) - proof, evidence, argument (19)
árma, armṓrum (n. pl.) - arms, weapons (28)
auxílium, auxíliī (n) - aid, help (31)
bā́sium, bā́siī (n) - kiss (4)
béllum, béllī (n) - war (4)
benefícium, benefíciī (n) - benefit, kindness; favor (19)
caélum, caélī (n) - sky, heaven (5)
coniūrā́tī, coniūrātṓrum (m. pl.) - conspirators (20)
cōnsílium, cōnsíliī (n) - plan, purpose, counsel, advice, judgment, wisdom (4)
déus, déī (m) - god (6)
dígitus, dígitī (m) - finger, toe (31)
discípulus, discípulī (m) - learner, pupil, student (male) (6)
dṓnum, dṓnī (n) - gift, present (4)
elephántus, elephántī (m and f) - elephant (31)
équus, équī (m) - horse (23)
exítium, exítiī (n) - destruction, ruin (4)
exsílium, exsíliī (n) - exile, banishment (31)
fáctum, fáctī (n) - deed, act, achievement (13)
fā́tum, fā́tī (n) - fate; death (29)
férrum, férrī (n) - iron; sword (22)
fī́lius, fī́liī (m) - son (3)
fórum, fórī (n) - marketplace, forum (26)
Graécus, Graécī (m) - a Greek (6)
impérium, impériī (n) - power to command, supreme power, authority, command, control (24)
ingénium, ingéniī (n) - nature, innate talent (29)
inítium, inítiī (n) - beginning, commencement (33)
iūdícium, iūdíciī (n) - judgment, decision, opinion; trial (19)
libéllus, libéllī (m) - little book (17)
líber, líbrī (m) - book (6)
lóca, locṓrum (n) - places, region (9)
lócī, locṓrum (m) - passages in literature (9)
lócus, lócī (m) - place; passage in literature (9)
lū́dus, lū́dī (m) - game, sport; school (18)
magíster, magístrī (m) - schoolmaster, teacher, master (4)
médicus, médicī (m) - doctor, physician (male) (12)
módus, módī (m) - measure, bound, limit; manner, method, mode, way (22)
mórbus, mórbī (m) - disease, sickness (9)
múndus, múndī (m) - world, universe (21)
númerus, númerī (m) - number (3)
óculus, óculī (m) - eye (4)
offícium, offíciī (n) - duty, service (4)
ṓsculum, ṓsculī (n) - kiss (29)
ṓtium, ṓtiī (n) - leisure, peace (4)
perfúgium, perfúgiī (n) - refuge, shelter (24)
perículum, perículī (n) - danger, risk (4)
philósophus, philósophī (m) - philosopher (male) (33)
pópulus, pópulī (m) - the people, a people, a nation (3)
praémium, praémiī (n) - reward, prize (35)
prīncípium, prīncípiī (n) - beginning (12)
púer, púerī (m) - boy; boys, children *(pl.)* (3)
remédium, remédiī (n) - cure, remedy (4)
sérvus, sérvī (m) - slave (male) (24)
sígnum, sígnī (n) - sign, signal, indication; seal (13)
sōlā́cium, sōlā́ciī (n) - comfort, relief (24)
sómnus, sómnī (m) - sleep (26)
spéculum, spéculī (n) - mirror (33)
stúdium, stúdiī (n) - eagerness, zeal, pursuit, study (9)
stúltus, stúltī (m) - a fool (4)
súperī, superṓrum (m. pl.) - the gods (27)
tyránnus, tyránnī (m) - absolute ruler, tyrant (6)
vérbum, vérbī (n)- word (5)
vīcī́nus, vīcī́nī (m) - neighbor (male) (21)
vínculum, vínculī (n) - bond, chain, fetter (36)
vī́num, vī́nī (n) - wine (31)
vir, vírī (m) - man, hero (3)
vítium, vítiī (n) - fault, crime, vice (6)
vúlgus, vúlgī (n) - the common people, mob, rabble (21)

3rd Declension

adulḗscēns, adulēscéntis (m *or* f) - young man *or* woman (12)
aéstās, aestā́tis (f) - summer (35)
aétās, aetā́tis (f) - period of life, life, age, an age, time (16)
ámor, amṓris (m) - love (7)
aúctor, auctṓris (m) - increaser; author, originator (19)

audī́tor, audītṓris (m) - hearer, listener, member of an audience (16)

Caésar, Caésaris (m) - Caesar (12)

cáput, cápitis (n) - head; leader; beginning; life; heading; chapter (11)

cármen, cárminis (n) - song, poem (7)

Carthā́gō, Carthā́ginis (f) - Carthage (24)

Cícerō, Cicerṓnis (m) - (Marcus Tullius) Cicero (8)

cī́vitās, cīvitā́tis (f) - state, citizenship (7)

cṓnsul, cṓnsulis (m) - consul (11)

córpus, córporis (n) - body (7)

cupíditās, cupiditā́tis (f) - desire, longing, passion; cupidity, avarice (10)

cupī́dō, cupī́dinis (f) - desire, compassion (36)

dēlectā́tiō, dēlectātiṓnis (f) - delight, pleasure, enjoyment (27)

dux, dúcis (m) - leader, guide; commander, general (23)

flū́men, flū́minis (n) - river (18)

frā́ter, frā́tris (m) - brother (8)

génus, géneris (n) - origin; kind, type, sort, class (18)

hómō, hóminis (m) - human being, man (7)

hónor, honṓris (m) - honor, esteem; public office (30)

imperā́tor, imperātṓris (m) - general, commander-in-chief, emperor (24)

iū́dex, iū́dicis (m) - judge, juror (19)

iūs, iū́ris (n) - right, justice, law (14)

lábor, labṓris (m)- labor, work, toil; a work, production (7)

laus, laúdis (f) - praise, glory, fame (8)

lḗctor, lēctṓris (m) - reader (male) (36)

lḗctrīx, lēctrī́cis (f) - reader (female) (36)

lēx, lḗgis (f) - law, statute (26)

lībértās, lībertā́tis (f) - liberty (8)

lī́men, lī́minis (n) - threshold (26)

lī́tus, lī́toris (n) - shore, coast (23)

lūx, lū́cis (f) - light (26)

maiṓrēs, maiṓrum (m. pl.) - ancestors (27)

mā́ter, mā́tris (f) - mother (12)

mī́les, mī́litis (m) - soldier (23)

mṓrēs, mṓrum (m) - habits, morals, character (7)

mōs, mṓris (m) - habit, custom, manner (7)

nḗmō, nūllī́us, nḗminī, nḗminem, nū́llō, nū́llā (m *or* f) - no one, nobody (11)

népōs, nepṓtis (m) - grandson, descendant (27)

nṓmen, nṓminis (n) - name (7)

occā́siō, occāsiṓnis (f) - occasion, opportunity (28)

ópēs, ópum (f. pl.) - power, resources, wealth (33)

ops, ópis (f) - help, aid (33)

ōrā́tor, ōrātṓris (m) - orator, speaker (23)

ōs, ṓris (n) - mouth, face (14)

párēns, paréntis (m *or* f) - parent (28)

páter, pátris (m) - father (12)

paupértās, paupertā́tis (f) - poverty, humble circumstances (32)

pāx, pā́cis (f) - peace (7)

péctus, péctoris (n) - breast, heart (35)

plēbs, plḗbis (f) - the common people, populace, plebeians (33)

prī́nceps, prī́ncipis (m *or* f) - leader, emperor (28)

próbitās, probitā́tis (f) - uprightness, honesty (18)

rátiō, ratiṓnis (f) - reckoning, account; reason, judgment, consideration; system; manner, method (8)

remíssiō, remissiṓnis (f) - letting go, release; relaxation (34)

rēx, rḗgis (m) - king (7)

rū́mor, rūmṓris (m) - rumor, gossip (31)

sacérdōs, sacerdṓtis (m) - priest (23)

sāl, sális (m) - salt; wit (33)

sálūs, salū́tis (f) - health, safety; greeting (21)

sápiēns, sapiéntis (m/f) - a wise man/woman, philosopher (25)

scélus, scéleris (n) - evil deed, crime, sin, wickedness (19)

scrī́ptor, scrīptṓris (m) - writer, author (8)

senéctūs, senectū́tis (f) - old age (10)

sénex, sénis (m) - old man (16)

sérvitūs, servitū́tis (f) - servitude, slavery (20)

sī́dus, sī́deris (n) - constellation, star (29)

sōl, sṓlis (m) - sun (27)

sóror, sorṓris (f) - sister (8)

tempéstās, tempestā́tis (f) - period of time, season; weather, storm (15)

témpus, témporis (n) - time; occasion, opportunity (7)

tímor, timṓris (m) - fear (10)

úxor, uxṓris (f) - wife (7)

vḗritās, vēritā́tis (f) - truth (10)

vésper, vésperis *or* vésperī (m) - evening; evening star (28)

vírgō, vírginis (f) - maiden, virgin (7)

vírtūs, virtū́tis (f) - manliness, courage; excellence, character, worth, virtue (7)

volúptās, voluptā́tis (f) - pleasure (10)

vōx, vṓcis (f) - voice, word (34)
vúlnus, vúlneris (n) - wound (24)

3rd Declension I-Stem

ánimal, animā́lis (n) - a living creature, animal (14)
ars, ártis (f) - art, skill (14)
arx, árcis (f) - citadel, stronghold (23)
as, ássis (m) - an as *(a small copper coin)* (31)
aúris, aúris (f) - ear (14)
cī́vis, cī́vis (m *or* f) - citizen (14)
fī́nēs, fī́nium (m) - boundaries, territory (21)
fī́nis, fī́nis (m) - end, limit, boundary; purpose (21)
gēns, géntis (f) - clan, race, nation, people (21)
hóstēs, hóstium (m) - the enemy (18)
hóstis, hóstis (m) - an enemy *(of the state)* (18)
ígnis, ígnis (m) - fire (22)
máre, máris (n) - sea (14)
mēns, méntis (f) - mind, thought, intention (16)
moénia, moénium (n. pl.) - walls of a city (29)
mōns, móntis (m) - mountain (20)
mors, mórtis (f) - death (14)
nā́vis, nā́vis (f) - ship, boat (21)
nox, nóctis (f) - night (26)
nū́bēs, nū́bis (f) - cloud (14)
pars, pártis (f) - part, share; direction (14)
urbs, úrbis (f) - city (14)
vī́rēs, vī́rium (f. pl.) - strength (14)
vīs, vīs (f) - force, power, violence (14)

4th Declension

córnū, córnūs (n) - horn (20)
cúrsus, cúrsūs (m) - running, race; course (28)
exércitus, exércitūs (m) - army (32)
frū́ctus, frū́ctūs (m) - fruit; profit, benefit, enjoyment (20)
génū, génūs (n) - knee (20)
mánus, mánūs (f) - hand; handwriting; band (20)
métus, métūs (m) - fear, dread, anxiety (20)
senā́tus, senā́tūs (m) - senate (20)
sḗnsus, sḗnsūs (m) - feeling, sense (20)
spī́ritus, spī́ritūs (m) - breath, breathing; spirit, soul (20)
vérsus, vérsūs (m) - line of verse (20)

5th Declension

díēs, diḗī (m) - day (22)
fídēs, fídeī (f) - faith, trust, trustworthiness, fidelity, promise, guarantee, protection (22)
rēs, réī (f) - thing, matter, property, business, affair (22)
rēs pū́blica, réī pū́blicae (f) - state, commonwealth, republic (22)
spēs, spéī (f) - hope (22)

Indeclinable

níhil - nothing (1)
sátis - enough (5)

Pronouns

áliquis, áliquid - someone, somebody, something (23)
égo, méī - I (11)
hic, haec, hoc - this; the latter; he, she, it, they (9)
ī́dem, éadem, ídem - the same (11)
ílle, ílla, íllud - that; the former; the famous; he, she, it, they (9)
ípse, ípsa, ípsum - myself, yourself, himself, herself, itself, *etc.,* the very, the actual (13)
is, éa, id - this, that; he, she, it (11)
íste, ísta, ístud - that of yours, that; such (as you have, as you speak of); *sometimes with contemptuous force, e.g.,* that despicable, that wretched (9)
quī, quae, quod - who, which, what, that (17)
quid - what (1)
quī́dam, quaédam, quíddam - a certain one or thing, someone, something (26)
quis, quid (*after* sī, nisi, nē, num) - anyone, anything, someone, something (33)
quis? quid? - who? whose? whom? what? which? (19)
quísque, quídque, cuiúsque, cuíque - each one, each person, each thing (13)
quísquis, quídquid - whoever, whatever (23)
súī - himself, herself, itself, themselves (13)
tū, túī - you *(sing.)* (11)

Adjectives

1st & 2nd Declension

acérbus, acérba, acérbum - harsh, bitter, grievous (12)
advérsus, advérsa, advérsum - opposite, adverse (34)
aéquus, aéqua, aéquum - level, even; calm; equal, just; favorable (22)
áliī . . . áliī - some . . . others (9)
álius, ália, áliud - other, another (9)
álter, áltera, álterum - the other (of two), second (9)

amī́cus, amī́ca, amī́cum - friendly (11)
antī́quus, antī́qua, antī́quum - ancient, old-time (2)
ásper, áspera, ásperum - rough, harsh (21)
avā́rus, avā́ra, avā́rum - greedy, avaricious (3)
beā́tus, beā́ta, beā́tum - happy, fortunate, blessed (10)
béllus, bélla, béllum - pretty, handsome, charming (4)
bónus, bóna, bónum - good, kind (4)
caécus, caéca, caécum - blind (17)
cándidus, cándida, cándidum - shining, bright, white; beautiful (33)
cā́rus, cā́ra, cā́rum - dear (11)
cértus, cérta, cértum - definite, sure, certain, reliable (19)
cḗterī, cḗterae, cḗtera - the remaining, the rest, the other, all the others (30)
clā́rus, clā́ra, clā́rum - clear, bright; renowned, famous, illustrious (18)
déxter, déxtra, déxtrum - right, right-hand (20)
dígnus, dígna, dígnum (+abl.) - worthy, worthy of (29)
dóctus, dócta, dóctum - taught, learned, skilled (13)
dū́rus, dū́ra, dū́rum - hard, harsh, rough, stern, unfeeling, hardy, difficult (29)
fortūnā́tus, fortūnā́ta, fortūnā́tum - lucky, fortunate, happy (13)
géminus, gémina, géminum - twin (25)
Graécus, Graéca, Graécum - Greek (6)
hūmā́nus, hūmā́na, hūmā́num - pertaining to man, human; humane, kind; refined, cultivated (4)
incértus, incérta, incértum - uncertain, unsure, doubtful (22)
īrā́tus, īrā́ta, īrā́tum - angry (35)
iūcúndus, iūcúnda, iūcúndum - pleasant, delightful, agreeable, pleasing (16)
Latī́nus, Latī́na, Latī́num - Latin (22)
lī́ber, lī́bera, lī́berum - free (5)
lóngus, lónga, lóngum - long (16)
magnánimus, magnánima, magnánimum - great-hearted, brave, magnanimous (23)
mágnus, mágna, mágnum - large, great; important (2)
málus, mála, málum - bad, wicked, evil (4)
médius, média, médium - middle; the middle of (22)
mérus, méra, mérum - pure, undiluted (33)
méus, méa, méum - my (2)
míser, mísera, míserum - wretched, miserable, unfortunate (15)
mórtuus, mórtua, mórtuum - dead (28)
múltus, múlta, múltum - much, many (2)
neúter, neútra, neútrum - not either, neither (9)
nóster, nóstra, nóstrum - our, ours (5)
nóvus, nóva, nóvum - new; strange (7)
nū́llus, nū́lla, nū́llum - not any, no, none (9)
párvus, párva, párvum - small, little (4)
paúcī, paúcae, paúca - few, a few (3)
perpétuus, perpétua, perpétuum perpetual, lasting, uninterrupted, continuous (6)
plḗnus, plḗna, plḗnum - full, abundant, generous (6)
prī́mus, prī́ma, prī́mum - first, foremost, chief, principal (27)
pudī́cus, pudī́ca, pudī́cum - modest, chaste (26)
púlcher, púlchra, púlchrum - beautiful, handsome; fine (5)
quántus, quánta, quántum - how large, how great, how much (30)
rīdículus, rīdícula, rīdículum - laughable, ridiculous (30)
Rōmā́nus, Rōmā́na, Rōmā́num - Roman (3)
sálvus, sálva, sálvum - safe, sound (6)
sā́nus, sā́na, sā́num - sound, healthy, sane (5)
secúndus, secúnda, secúndum - second; favorable (6)
siníster, sinístra, sinístrum - left, left-hand; harmful, ill-omened (20)
sṓlus, sṓla, sṓlum - alone, only, the only (9)
stúltus, stúlta, stúltum - foolish (4)
supérbus, supérba, supérbum - arrogant, overbearing, haughty, proud (26)
súperus, súpera, súperum - above, upper (27)
súus, súa, súum - his own, her own, its own, their own (13)
tántus, tánta, tántum - so large, so great, of such a size (29)
tántus . . . quántus - just as much (many) . . . as (30)
tṓtus, tṓta, tṓtum - whole, entire (9)
túus, túa, túum - your *(sing.)* (2)
ū́llus, ū́lla, ū́llum - any (9)

últimus, última, últimum - farthest, extreme; last, final (25)
ū́nus, ū́na, ū́num - one, single, alone (9)
urbā́nus, urbā́na, urbā́num - of the city, urban; urbane, elegant (26)
úter, útra, útrum - either, which (of two) (9)
vḗrus, vḗra, vḗrum - true, real, proper (4)
véster, véstra, véstrum - your *(pl.)* (6)
vī́vus, vī́va, vī́vum - alive, living (30)

3rd Declension
ā́cer, ā́cris, ā́cre - sharp, keen, eager; severe, fierce (16)
brévis, bréve - short, small, brief (16)
céler, céleris, célere - swift, quick, rapid (16)
commū́nis, commū́ne - common, general, of / for the community (20)
difficilis, difficile - hard, difficult, troublesome (16)
dī́ligēns, ***gen.*** **dīligéntis** - diligent, careful (27)
dissímilis, dissímile - unlike, different (27)
dī́ves, ***gen.*** **dī́vitis** ***or*** **dī́tis** - rich, wealthy (32)
dúlcis, dúlce - sweet; pleasant, agreeable (16)
fácilis, fácile - easy; agreeable (16)
fḗlīx, ***gen.*** **fēlī́cis** - lucky, fortunate, happy (22)
férōx, ***gen.*** **ferṓcis** - fierce, savage (25)
fidḗlis, fidḗle - faithful, loyal (25)
fórtis, fórte - strong, brave (16)
grácilis, grácile - slender, thin (27)
grávis, gráve - heavy, weighty; serious, important; severe, grievous (19)
húmilis, húmile - lowly, humble (27)
immortā́lis, immortā́le - not subject to death, immortal (19)
íngēns, ***gen.*** **ingéntis** - huge (16)
lévis, léve - light; easy; slight, trivial (17)
máior, máius - greater; older (27)
medíocris, medíocre - ordinary, moderate, mediocre (31)
mortā́lis, mortā́le - mortal (18)
ómnis, ómne - every, all (16)
pār, ***gen.*** **páris (+dat.)** - equal, like (32)
paúper, ***gen.*** **paúperis** - of small means, poor (32)
pótēns, ***gen.*** **poténtis** - able, powerful, mighty, strong (16)
prī́nceps, ***gen.*** **prī́ncipis** - chief, foremost (28)
sápiēns, ***gen.*** **sapiéntis** - wise, judicious (25)
sénex, ***gen.*** **sénis** - old, aged (16)
símilis, símile (+gen. or dat.) - similar (to), like, resembling (27)
suā́vis, suā́ve - sweet (33)
tā́lis, tā́le - such, of such a sort (34)
trī́stis, trī́ste - sad, sorrowful; joyless, grim, severe (26)
túrpis, túrpe - ugly; shameful, base, disgraceful (26)
ū́tilis, ū́tile - useful, advantageous (27)

Indeclinable Adjectives
quot - how many, as many as (27)
sátis - enough, sufficient (5)

Indefinite Adjective
quī́dam, quaédam, quóddam - a certain, some (26)

Interrogative Adjective
quī?, quae?, quod? - what? which? what kind of?; *(sometimes with exclamatory force)* what (a)! what sort of! (19)

Verbs
1st Conjugation
ádiuvō, adiuvā́re, adiū́vī, adiū́tum - to help, aid, assist; to please (4)
ámō, amā́re, amā́vī, amā́tum - to love, like (1)
appéllō, appellā́re, appellā́vī, appellā́tum - to speak to, address (as), call, name (14)
cḗnō, cēnā́re, cēnā́vī, cēnā́tum - to dine (5)
cṓgitō, cōgitā́re, cōgitā́vī, cōgitā́tum- to think, ponder, consider, plan (1)
cōnsérvō, cōnservā́re, cōnservā́vī, cōnservā́tum - to preserve, conserve, maintain (1)
créō, creā́re, creā́vī, creā́tum - to create (12)
cúlpō, culpā́re, culpā́vī, culpā́tum - to blame, censure (5)
cū́rō, cūrā́re, cūrā́vī, cūrā́tum - to care for, attend to; heal, cure; take care (36)
dédicō, dēdicā́re, dēdicā́vī, dēdicā́tum - to dedicate (28)
dēléctō, dēlectā́re, dēlectā́vī, dēlectā́tum - to delight, charm, please (19)
dēmṓnstrō, dēmōnstrā́re, dēmōnstrā́vī, dēmōnstrā́tum to point out, show, demonstrate (8)

dēsíderō, dēsīderā́re, dēsīderā́vī, dēsīderā́tum - to desire, long for, miss (17)
dō, dáre, dédī, dátum - to give, offer (1)
dúbitō, dubitā́re, dubitā́vī, dubitā́tum - to doubt, hesitate (30)
ḗducō, ēducā́re, ēducā́vī, ēducā́tum - to bring up, educate (23)
érrō, errā́re, errā́vī, errā́tum - to wander; err, go astray, make a mistake, be mistaken (1)
exspéctō, exspectā́re, exspectā́vī, exspectā́tum - to look for, expect, await (15)
ímperō, imperā́re, imperā́vī, imperā́tum (+dat.) - to give orders to, command (35)
invī́tō, invītā́re, invītā́vī, invītā́tum - to entertain, invite, summon (26)
iúvō, iuvā́re, iū́vī, iū́tum - to help, aid, assist; to please (4)
labṓrō, labōrā́re, labōrā́vī, labōrā́tum - to labor; be in distress (21)
laúdō, laudā́re, laudā́vī, laudā́tum - to praise (1)
lī́berō, līberā́re, līberā́vī, līberā́tum - to free, liberate (19)
mū́tō, mūtā́re, mūtā́vī, mūtā́tum to change, alter; exchange (14)
nā́rrō, nārrā́re, nārrā́vī, nārrā́tum - to tell, report, narrate (24)
nā́vigō, nāvigā́re, nāvigā́vī, nāvigā́tum - to sail, navigate (17)
nécō, necā́re, necā́vī, necā́tum - to murder, kill (7)
négō, negā́re, negā́vī, negā́tum to deny, say that . . . not (25)
nū́ntiō, nūntiā́re, nūntiā́vī, nūntiā́tum - to announce, report, relate (25)
obléctō, oblectā́re, oblectā́vī, oblectā́tum - to please, amuse, delight; pass time pleasantly (36)
ṓrō, ōrā́re, ōrā́vī, ōrā́tum - to speak, plead; beg, beseech, entreat, pray (36)
párō, parā́re, parā́vī, parā́tum - to prepare, provide; get, obtain (19)
praéstō, praestā́re, praéstitī, praéstitum - to excel; exhibit, show, offer, supply, furnish (28)
próbō, probā́re, probā́vī, probā́tum - to approve, recommend; test (27)
prōnū́ntiō, prōnūntiā́re, prōnūntiā́vī, prōnūntiā́tum - to proclaim, announce; declaim; pronounce (20)
púgnō, pugnā́re, pugnā́vī, pugnā́tum - to fight (29)
pútō, putā́re, putā́vī, putā́tum - to reckon, suppose, judge, think, imagine (25)
récitō, recitā́re, recitā́vī, recitā́tum - to read aloud, recite (17)
récreō, recreā́re, recreā́vī, recreā́tum - to restore, revive; refresh, cheer (36)
recū́sō, recūsā́re, recūsā́vī, recūsā́tum - to refuse (33)
rógō, rogā́re, rogā́vī, rogā́tum - to ask (30)
sátiō, satiā́re, satiā́vī, satiā́tum - to satisfy, sate (3)
serḗnō, serēnā́re, serēnā́vī, serēnā́tum - to make clear, brighten; cheer up, soothe (36)
sérvō, servā́re, servā́vī, servā́tum - to preserve, save, keep, guard (1)
spéctō, spectā́re, spectā́vī, spectā́tum - to look at, see (34)
spḗrō, spērā́re, spērā́vī, spērā́tum - to hope for, hope (25)
stō, stā́re, stétī, státum - to stand, stand still *or* firm (13)
súperō, superā́re, superā́vī, superā́tum - to be above, have the upper hand, surpass; overcome, conquer (5)
tólerō, tolerā́re, tolerā́vī, tolerā́tum - to bear, endure (6)
vī́tō, vītā́re, vītā́vī, vītā́tum - to avoid, shun (14)
vócō, vocā́re, vocā́vī, vocā́tum - to call, summon (1)

2nd Conjugation

aúdeō, audḗre, aúsus sum - to dare (7)
cáreō, carḗre, cáruī, caritū́rum (+abl.) - to be without, be deprived of, want, lack; be free from (20)
contíneō, continḗre, contínuī, conténtum - to hold together, contain, keep, enclose, restrain (21)
dḗbeō, dēbḗre, dḗbuī, dḗbitum - to owe; ought, must, should (1)
dḗleō, dēlḗre, dēlḗvī, dēlḗtum - to destroy, wipe out, erase (17)
dóceō, docḗre, dócuī, dóctum - to teach (8)
dóleō, dolḗre, dóluī, dolitū́rum - to grieve, suffer; hurt, give pain (31)
égeō, egḗre, éguī (+ abl. or gen.) - to need, lack, want (28)

éxpleō, explḗre, explḗvī, explḗtum - to fill, fill up, complete (28)
fóveō, fovḗre, fṓvī, fṓtum - to comfort, nurture, cherish (35)
gaúdeō, gaudḗre, gāvī́sus sum - to be glad, rejoice (23)
hábeō, habḗre, hábuī, hábitum - to have, hold, possess; consider, regard (3)
iáceō, iacḗre, iácuī - to lie; lie prostrate; lie dead (25)
invídeō, invidḗre, invī́dī, invī́sum to be envious; to look at with envy, envy, be jealous of (+dat.) (31)
iúbeō, iubḗre, iússī, iússum - to bid, order, command (21)
máneō, manḗre, mā́nsī, mā́nsum - to remain, stay, stay behind, abide, continue (5)
mísceō, miscḗre, míscuī, míxtum to mix, stir up, disturb (18)
móneō, monḗre, mónuī, mónitum - to remind, advise, warn (1)
móveō, movḗre, mṓvī, mṓtum - to move; arouse, affect (18)
nóceō, nocḗre, nócuī, nócitum (+dat.) - to do harm to, harm, injure (35)
pā́reō, pārḗre, pā́ruī (+dat.) - to be obedient to, obey (35)
páteō, patḗre, pátuī - to be open, lie open; be accessible; be evident (32)
persuā́deō, persuādḗre, persuā́sī, persuā́sum (+dat.) to succeed in urging, persuade, convince (35)
pláceō, placḗre, plácuī, plácitum (+dat.) - to be pleasing to, please (35)
praébeō, praebḗre, praébuī, praébitum - to offer, provide (32)
prohíbeō, prohibḗre, prohíbuī, prohíbitum - to keep (back), prevent, hinder, restrain, prohibit (20)
remáneō, remanḗre, remā́nsī, remā́nsum - to remain, stay, stay behind, abide, continue (5)
respóndeō, respondḗre, respóndī, respṓnsum - to answer (29)
rī́deō, rīdḗre, rī́sī, rī́sum - to laugh, laugh at (24)
sálvē, salvḗte - hello, greetings (1)
sálveō, salvḗre - to be well, be in good health (1)
sédeō, sedḗre, sḗdī, séssum - to sit (34)
stúdeō, studḗre, stúduī (+dat.) - to direct one's zeal to, be eager for, study (35)
subrī́deō, subrīdḗre, subrī́sī, subrī́sum - to smile (down) upon (35)
táceō, tacḗre, tácuī, tácitum - to be silent, leave unmentioned (28)
téneō, tenḗre, ténuī, téntum - to hold, keep, possess; restrain (14)
térreō, terrḗre, térruī, térritum - to frighten, terrify (1)
tímeō, timḗre, tímuī - to fear, be afraid (of) (15)
válē, valḗte - good-bye, farewell (1)
váleō, valḗre, váluī, valitū́rum - to be strong, have power; be well (1)
vídeō, vidḗre, vī́dī, vī́sum - to see; observe, understand (1)
vídeor, vidḗrī, vī́sus sum - to be seen, seem, appear (18)

3rd Conjugation

accḗdō, accḗdere, accéssī, accéssum - to come (to), approach (36)
admíttō, admíttere, admī́sī, admíssum - to admit, receive, let in (17)
ágō, ágere, ḗgī, ā́ctum - to drive, lead, do, act; pass, spend *(life or time)* (8)
álō, álere, áluī, áltum - to nourish, support, sustain, increase; cherish (13)
āmíttō, āmíttere, āmī́sī, āmíssum - to send away; lose, let go (12)
antepṓnō, antepṓnere, antepósuī, antepósitum - to put before, prefer (35)
āvértō, āvértere, āvértī, āvérsum - to turn away, avert (23)
bíbō, bíbere, bíbī - to drink (30)
cádō, cádere, cécidī, cāsū́rum - to fall (12)
cárpō, cárpere, cárpsī, cárptum to harvest, pluck; seize (36)
cḗdō, cḗdere, céssī, céssum - to go, withdraw; yield to, grant, submit (28)
cérnō, cérnere, crḗvī, crḗtum - to distinguish, discern, perceive (22)
cognṓscō, cognṓscere, cognṓvī, cógnitum - to become acquainted with, learn, recognize; know *(in perfect tenses)* (30)
cṓgō, cṓgere, coḗgī, coā́ctum - to drive *or* bring together, force, compel (36)
commíttō, commíttere, commī́sī, commíssum - to entrust, commit (15)
comprehéndō, comprehéndere, comprehéndī, comprehḗnsum - to grasp, seize, arrest; comprehend, understand (30)

cóndō, cóndere, cóndidī, cónditum - to put together *or* into, store; found, establish (29)
cōnsū́mō, cōnsū́mere, cōnsū́mpsī, cōnsū́mptum - to consume, use up (30)
contémnō, contémnere, contémpsī, contémptum - to despise, scorn (36)
conténdō, conténdere, conténdī, conténtum - to strive, struggle, contend; hasten (29)
contúndō, contúndere, cóntudī, contū́sum - to beat, crush, bruise, destroy (36)
crḗdō, crḗdere, crḗdidī, crḗditum to believe, trust (25)
crḗscō, crḗscere, crḗvī, crḗtum - to increase (34)
cúrrō, cúrrere, cucúrrī, cúrsum - to run, rush, move quickly (14)
dēcérnō, dēcérnere, dēcrḗvī, dēcrḗtum - to decide, settle, decree (36)
dēféndō, dēféndere, dēféndī, dēfḗnsum - to ward off; defend, protect (20)
dī́cō, dī́cere, dī́xī, díctum - to say, tell, speak; name, call (10)
dī́ligō, dīlígere, dīlḗxī, dīlḗctum - to esteem, love (13)
discḗdō, discḗdere, discéssī, discéssum - to go away, depart (20)
díscō, díscere, dídicī - to learn (8)
dū́cō, dū́cere, dū́xī, dúctum - to lead; consider, regard; prolong (8)
éxigō, exígere, exḗgī, exā́ctum - to drive out, force out, exact; drive through, complete, perfect (36)
expéllō, expéllere, éxpulī, expúlsum - to drive out, expel, banish (24)
expṓnō, expṓnere, expósuī, expósitum - to set forth, explain, expose (30)
flúō, flúere, flū́xī, flū́xum - to flow (18)
gérō, gérere, géssī, géstum - to carry; carry on, manage, conduct, wage, accomplish, perform (8)
ignṓscō, ignṓscere, ignṓvī, ignṓtum (+dat.) - to grant pardon to, forgive (35)
intéllegō, intellégere, intellḗxī, intellḗctum - to understand (11)
iúngō, iúngere, iū́nxī, iū́nctum - to join (13)
légō, légere, lḗgī, lḗctum - to pick out, choose; read (18)
mínuō, minúere, mínuī, minū́tum - to lessen, diminish (30)
míttō, míttere, mī́sī, míssum - to send, let go (11)
néglegō, neglégere, neglḗxī, neglḗctum - to neglect, disregard (17)
nṓscō, nṓscere, nṓvī, nṓtum - to become acquainted with, learn, recognize; know *(in perfect tenses)* (30)
nū́bō, nū́bere, nū́psī, nū́ptum (+dat.) - to cover, veil; to be married to, marry (35)
óccidō, occídere, óccidī, occā́sum - to fall down; die; set (31)
ópprimō, opprímere, oppréssī, oppréssum - to suppress, overwhelm, overpower, check (23)
osténdō, osténdere, osténdī, osténtum - to exhibit, show, display (23)
párcō, párcere, pepércī, parsū́rum (+dat.) - to be lenient to, spare (35)
péllō, péllere, pépulī, púlsum - to strike, push; drive out, banish (24)
pétō, pétere, petī́vī, petī́tum - to seek, aim at, beg, beseech (23)
pṓnō, pṓnere, pósuī, pósitum - to put, place, set (27)
prémō, prémere, préssī, préssum - to press; press hard, pursue (23)
prōmíttō, prōmíttere, prōmī́sī, prōmíssum - to send forth; promise (32)
quaérō, quaérere, quaesī́vī, quaesī́tum - to seek, look for, strive for; ask, inquire, inquire into (24)
régō, régere, rḗxī, rḗctum - to rule, guide, direct (16)
relínquō, relínquere, relī́quī, relíctum - to leave behind, leave, abandon, desert (21)
requī́rō, requī́rere, requīsī́vī, requīsī́tum - to seek, ask for; miss, need, require (36)
revértō, revértere, revértī, revérsum - turn back (23)
scrī́bō, scrī́bere, scrī́psī, scrī́ptum to write, compose (8)
súrgō, súrgere, surrḗxī, surrḗctum - to get up, arise (29)
tángō, tángere, tétigī, tā́ctum - to touch (21)
tóllō, tóllere, sústulī, sublā́tum - to raise, lift up; take away, remove, destroy (22)
trā́dō, trā́dere, trā́didī, trā́ditum to give over, surrender; hand down, transmit, teach (33)
tráhō, tráhere, trā́xī, tráctum - to draw, drag; derive, acquire (8)

vértō, vértere, vértī, vérsum - to turn; change (23)
víncō, víncere, vī́cī, víctum - to conquer, overcome (8)
vī́vō, vī́vere, vī́xī, vī́ctum - to live (10)

3rd Conjugation -iō

accípiō, accípere, accḗpī, accéptum - to take *(to one's self)*, receive, accept (24)
cápiō, cápere, cḗpī, cáptum - to take, capture, seize, get (10)
cúpiō, cúpere, cupī́vī, cupī́tum - to desire, wish, long for (17)
ērípiō, ērípere, ērípuī, ēréptum - to snatch away, take away; rescue (22)
excípiō, excípere, excḗpī, excéptum - to take out, except; take, receive, capture (24)
fáciō, fácere, fḗcī, fáctum - to make, do, accomplish (10)
fúgiō, fúgere, fū́gī, fugitū́rum - to flee, hurry away; escape; go into exile; avoid, shun (10)
iáciō, iácere, iḗcī, iáctum - to throw, hurl (15)
incípiō, incípere, incḗpī, incéptum - to begin (17)
patefáciō, patefácere, patefḗcī, patefáctum - to make open, open; disclose, expose (25)
rápiō, rápere, rápuī, ráptum - to seize, snatch, carry away (21)
recípiō, recípere, recḗpī, recéptum - to take back, regain; admit, receive (24)
sápiō, sápere, sapī́vī - to have good taste; have good sense, be wise (35)
suscípiō, suscípere, suscḗpī, suscéptum - to undertake (25)

4th Conjugation

aúdiō, audī́re, audī́vī, audī́tum - to hear, listen to (10)
dórmiō, dormī́re, dormī́vī, dormī́tum - to sleep (31)
invéniō, invenī́re, invḗnī, invéntum - to come upon, find (10)
mólliō, mollī́re, mollī́vī, mollī́tum to soften; make calm *or* less hostile (29)
nésciō, nescī́re, nescī́vī, nescī́tum - to not know, be ignorant (25)
scíō, scī́re, scī́vī, scī́tum - to know (21)
séntiō, sentī́re, sḗnsī, sḗnsum - to feel, perceive, think, experience (11)
sérviō, servī́re, servī́vī, servī́tum (+dat.) - to be a slave to, serve (35)
véniō, venī́re, vḗnī, véntum - to come (10)

Irregular

ádferō, adférre, áttulī, allā́tum - to bring to (31)
cṓnferō, cōnférre, cóntulī, collā́tum - to bring together, compare; confer, bestow (31)
férō, férre, túlī, lā́tum - to bear, carry, bring; suffer, endure, tolerate; say, report (31)
fī́ō, fíerī, fáctus sum - to occur, happen; become; be made, be done (36)
mā́lō, mā́lle, mā́luī - to want (something) more, instead; prefer (32)
nṓlō, nṓlle, nṓluī - to not . . . wish, be unwilling (32)
ófferō, offérre, óbtulī, oblā́tum - to offer (31)
póssum, pósse, pótuī - to be able, can, could, have power (6)
réferō, reférre, réttulī, relā́tum - to carry back, bring back; repeat, answer, report (31)
sum, ésse, fúī, futū́rum - to be, exist (4)
vólō, vélle, vóluī - to wish, want, be willing, will (32)

Deponent

árbitror, arbitrā́rī, arbitrā́tus sum to judge, think (34)
cṓnor, cōnā́rī, cōnā́tus sum - to try, attempt (34)
ēgrédior, ḗgredī, ēgréssus sum - to go out (34)
fáteor, fatḗrī, fássus sum - to confess, admit (34)
hórtor, hortā́rī, hortā́tus sum - to encourage, urge (34)
lóquor, lóquī, locū́tus sum - to say, speak, tell (34)
mī́ror, mīrā́rī, mīrā́tus sum - to marvel at, admire, wonder (35)
mṓlior, mōlī́rī, mōlī́tus sum - to work at, build, undertake, plan (34)
mórior, mórī, mórtuus sum - to die (34)
nā́scor, nā́scī, nā́tus sum - to be born; spring forth, arrive (34)
pátior, pátī, pássus sum - to suffer, endure; permit (34)
proficī́scor, proficī́scī, proféctus sum - to set out, start (34)
rū́sticor, rūsticā́rī, rūsticā́tus sum to live in the country (34)
séquor, séquī, secū́tus sum - to follow (34)
ū́tor, ū́tī, ū́sus sum (+abl.) - to use; enjoy, experience (34)

Defective

áit, áiunt - he says, they say, assert (25)

coépī, coepísse, coéptum - began (17)

ínquit - he says *or* said (22)

ṓdī, ōdísse, ōsū́rum - to hate (20)

Adverbs

ánte (+acc.) - before, previously (13)

béne - well, satisfactorily, quite (11)

cíto - quickly (17)

cōtī́diē - daily, every day (36)

crās - tomorrow (5)

cūr - why (18)

déhinc - then, next (25)

deínde - thereupon, next, then (18)

dḗnique - at last, finally, lastly (29)

díū - long, for a long time (12)

étiam - even, also (11)

fortásse - perhaps (36)

fū́rtim - stealthily, secretly (30)

héri - yesterday (5)

hīc - here (25)

hódiē - today (3)

iam - now, already, soon (19)

íbi - there (6)

íta - so, thus (29)

ítaque - and so, therefore (15)

íterum - again, a second time (21)

mox - soon (30)

nē . . . quídem - not . . . even (29)

nímis, nímium - too, too much, excessively; *(in a positive sense, esp. with adjectives and adverbs)* exceedingly, very (9)

nōn - not (1)

númquam - never (8)

nunc - now, at present (6)

nū́per - recently (12)

ṓlim - once (upon a time), long ago, formerly; some day, in the future (13)

pósteā - afterwards (24)

prīmō - at first, at the beginning (30)

prṓtinus - immediately (22)

quam - how (16)

quam - than *(after comparatives);* as . . . as possible *(with superlatives)* (26)

quándō - when (5)

quā́rē - because of which thing *(lit.);* therefore, wherefore, why (6)

quídem - indeed, certainly, at least, even (29)

quóndam - formerly, once (22)

quóque - also, too (17)

repénte - suddenly (30)

saépe - often (1)

sátis - enough, sufficiently (5)

sémel - a single time, once, once and for all, simultaneously (31)

sémper - always (3)

sīc - so, thus (29)

súbitō - suddenly (33)

tam - so, to such a degree (29)

tam . . . quam - so . . . as (29)

támen - nevertheless, still (8)

tamquam - as it were, as if, so to speak (29)

tántum - only (26)

tum - then, at that time; thereupon, in the next place (5)

úbi - where, when (6)

últrā - on the other side of, beyond (22)

úmquam - ever, at any time (23)

únde - whence, from what *or* which place, from which, from whom (30)

úsque - all the way, up (to), even (to), continuously, always (31)

vḗrō - in truth, indeed, to be sure, however (29)

Conjunctions

at - but; but, mind you; but, you say (19)

átque, ac - and also, and even, and in fact (21)

aut - or (17)

aut . . . aut - either . . . or (17)

aútem - however; moreover (11)

cum (+indic.) - when (31)

cum (+subj.) - when, since, although (31)

dum - while, as long as, at the same time that; *or* until *(+subjunctive)* (8)

dúmmodo (+subj.) - provided that, so long as (32)

énim - for, in fact, truly (9)

et - and; even (2)

et . . . et - both . . . and (2)

ígitur - therefore, consequently (5)

nam - for (13)

nē - not; in order that . . . not, that . . . not, in order not to (28)

néque , nec - and not, nor (11)

néque . . . néque, nec . . . nec - neither . . . nor (11)

nísi - if . . . not, unless; except (19)

quod - because (11)

quóniam - since, inasmuch as (10)

sed - but (2)

sī - if (1)

ut (+indic.) - as, just as, when (24)

ut (+ subj.) - in order that, so that, that, in order to, so as to, to (28)

útrum . . . an - whether . . . or (30)

Prepositions

ab, ā (+abl.) - away from, from; by (14)
ad (+acc.) - to, up to, near to (8)
ánte (+acc.) - before *(in place or time)*, in front of (13)
ápud (+acc.) - among, in the presence of, at the house of (31)
cóntrā (+acc.) - against (19)
cum (+abl.) - with (10)
dē (+abl.) - down from, from; concerning, about (3)
ex, ē (abl.+) - out of, from, from within; by reason of, on account of ; of *(after cardinal numerals)* (8)
in (+acc.) - into, toward; against (9)
in (+abl.) - in, on (3)
ínter (+acc.) - between, among (15)
per (+acc.) - through; by *(with reflexive pronoun)* (13)
post (+acc.) - after, behind (7)
prae (+abl.) - in front of, before (26)
prō (+abl.) - in front of, before, on behalf of, for the sake of, in return for, instead of, for, as (12)
própter (+acc.) - on account of, because of (5)
síne (+abl.) - without (2)
sub (+abl. w/ verbs of rest *or* +acc. w/ verbs of motion) - under, up under, close to, down to/into, to/at the foot of (7)
trāns (+acc.) - across (14)
últrā (adv. and prep. +acc.) - on the other side of, beyond (22)

Interjections

heu - ah!, alas! (33)
ō - O!, Oh! (2)
vae (often +dat. or acc.) - alas, woe to (34)

Idioms

amā́bō tē - please (1)
grā́tiās ágere (+dat.) - to thank someone; to give thanks to (8)
mḗnsa secúnda (f) - dessert (26)
nōn sṓlum . . . sed étiam - not only . . . but also (9)
poénās dáre - to pay the penalty (2)
sē cōnférre - to go (31)
sī quándō - if ever (5)

Prefix

re-, red- - again, back (24)

Suffixes

-ne – interrogative suffix attached to the first word of a sentence, typically the verb or another word on which the question hinges, to introduce a question whose answer is uncertain (5)
-que - and *(enclitic conjunction; appended to the second of two words to be joined)* (6)
-ve - or (33)

Numerals

Cardinal - ū́nus *to* vīgíntī quī́nque (15)
Ordinal - prī́mus *to* duodécimus (15)

----

céntum - a hundred (15)
mī́lia, mī́lium (n. pl.) - thousands (15)
mī́lle - thousand (15)

Chapter 37

Nouns

1st Declension

adulēscéntia, adulēscéntiae (f) - youth, young manhood; youthfulness (5)

agrícola, agrícolae (m) - farmer (3)

amī́ca, amī́cae (f) - friend (female) (3)

amīcítia, amīcítiae (f) - friendship (10)

ánima, ánimae (f) - air *(breathed by an animal),* breath; soul, spirit (34)

áqua, áquae (f) - water (14)

Ásia, Ásiae (f) - Asia (12)

Athḗnae, Athēnā́rum (f. pl.) - Athens (37)

cása, cásae (f) - house, cottage, hut (21)

caúsa, caúsae (f) - cause, reason; case, situation (21)

caúsā (abl. + preceding gen.) - for the sake of, on account of (21)

cḗna, cḗnae (f) - dinner (26)

clēméntia, clēméntiae (f) - mildness, gentleness, mercy (16)

cṓpia, cṓpiae (f) - abundance, supply (8)

cṓpiae, cōpiā́rum (f) - supplies, troops, forces (8)

cúlpa, cúlpae (f) - fault, blame (5)

cū́ra, cū́rae (f) - care, attention, caution, anxiety (4)

custṓdia, custṓdiae (f) - protection, custody; guards *(pl.)* (32)

déa, déae (f) - goddess (6)

discípula, discípulae (f) - learner, pupil, student (female) (6)

dīvítiae, dīvitiā́rum (f. pl.) - riches, wealth (13)

fā́bula, fā́bulae (f) - story, tale; play (24)

fā́ma, fā́mae (f) - rumor, report; fame, reputation (2)

famÍlia, famíliae (f) - household, family (19)

fḗmina, fḗminae (f) - woman (3)

fenéstra, fenéstrae (f) - window (21)

fī́lia, fī́liae (f) - daughter (3)

fṓrma, fṓrmae (f) - form, shape; beauty (2)

fortū́na, fortū́nae (f) - fortune, luck (2)

glṓria, glṓriae (f) - glory, fame (5)

Graécia, Graéciae (f) - Greece (19)

hásta, hástae (f) - spear (23)

hṓra, hṓrae (f) - hour, time (10)

iā́nua, iā́nuae (f) - door (35)

īnsídiae, īnsidiā́rum (f) - ambush, plot, treachery (6)

ī́nsula, ī́nsulae (f) - island (23)

invídia, invídiae (f) - envy, jealousy, hatred (31)

ī́ra, ī́rae (f) - ire, anger (2)

Itália, Itáliae (f) - Italy (15)

língua, línguae (f) - tongue; language (25)

líttera, lítterae (f) - a letter of the alphabet (7)

lítterae, litterā́rum (f) - a letter (epistle), literature (7)

lū́na, lū́nae (f) - moon (28)

magístra, magístrae (f) - schoolmistress, teacher, mistress (4)

médica, médicae (f) - doctor, physician (female) (12)

memória, memóriae (f) - memory, recollection (15)

mḗnsa, mḗnsae (f) - table; dining; dish, course (26)

móra, mórae (f) - delay (4)

nā́ta, nā́tae (f) - daughter (29)

nātū́ra, nātū́rae (f) - nature (10)

naúta, naútae (m) - sailor (2)

patiéntia, patiéntiae (f) - suffering; patience, endurance (12)

pátria, pátriae (f) - fatherland, native land, (one's) country (2)

pecū́nia, pecū́niae (f) - money (2)

philósopha, philósophae (f) - philosopher (female) (33)

philosóphia, philosóphiae (f) - philosophy (2)

poéna, poénae (f) - penalty, punishment (2)

poḗta, poḗtae (m) - poet (2)

pórta, pórtae (f) - gate, entrance (2)

puélla, puéllae (f) - girl (2)

rēgī́na, rēgī́nae (f) - queen (7)

Rṓma, Rṓmae (f) - Rome (14)

rósa, rósae (f) - rose (2)

sapiéntia, sapiéntiae (f) - wisdom (3)

sátura, sáturae (f) - satire (16)

sciéntia, sciéntiae (f) - knowledge (18)

senténtia, senténtiae (f) - feeling, thought, opinion, vote, sentence (2)

sérva, sérvae (f) - slave (female) (24)

stḗlla, stḗllae (f) - star, planet (28)

Syrācū́sae, Syrācūsā́rum (f. pl.) - Syracuse (37)

térra, térrae (f) - earth, ground, land, country (7)

Trṓia, Trṓiae (f) - Troy (21)

túrba, túrbae (f) - uproar, disturbance; mob, crowd, multitude (14)

vía, víae (f) - way, road, street (10)

vīcī́na, vīcī́nae (f) - neighbor (female) (21)

victṓria, victṓriae (f) - victory (8)

vī́ta, vī́tae (f) - life; mode of life (2)

2nd Declension

áger, ágrī (m) - field, farm (3)
amī́cus, amī́cī (m) - friend (male) (3)
ánimī, animṓrum (m) - high spirits, pride, courage (5)
ánimus, ánimī (m) - soul, spirit, mind (5)
ánnus, ánnī (m) - year (12)
argūméntum, argūméntī (n) - proof, evidence, argument (19)
árma, armṓrum (n. pl.) - arms, weapons (28)
auxílium, auxíliī (n) - aid, help (31)
bā́sium, bā́siī (n) - kiss (4)
béllum, béllī (n) - war (4)
benefícium, benefíciī (n) - benefit, kindness; favor (19)
caélum, caélī (n) - sky, heaven (5)
coniūrā́tī, coniūrātṓrum (m. pl.) - conspirators (20)
cōnsílium, cōnsíliī (n) - plan, purpose, counsel, advice, judgment, wisdom (4)
déus, déī (m) - god (6)
dígitus, dígitī (m) - finger, toe (31)
discípulus, discípulī (m) - learner, pupil, student (male) (6)
dṓnum, dṓnī (n) - gift, present (4)
elephántus, elephántī (m and f) - elephant (31)
équus, équī (m) - horse (23)
exítium, exítiī (n) - destruction, ruin (4)
exsílium, exsíliī (n) - exile, banishment (31)
fáctum, fáctī (n) - deed, act, achievement (13)
fā́tum, fā́tī (n) - fate; death (29)
férrum, férrī (n) - iron; sword (22)
fī́lius, fī́liī (m) - son (3)
fórum, fórī (n) - marketplace, forum (26)
Graécus, Graécī (m) - a Greek (6)
húmus, húmī (f) - ground, earth; soil (37)
impérium, impériī (n) - power to command, supreme power, authority, command, control (24)
ingénium, ingéniī (n) - nature, innate talent (29)
inítium, inítiī (n) - beginning, commencement (33)
iūdícium, iūdíciī (n) - judgment, decision, opinion; trial (19)
libéllus, libéllī (m) - little book (17)
líber, líbrī (m) - book (6)
lóca, locṓrum (n) - places, region (9)
lócī, locṓrum (m) - passages in literature (9)
lócus, lócī (m) - place; passage in literature (9)
lū́dus, lū́dī (m) - game, sport; school (18)
magíster, magístrī (m) - schoolmaster, teacher, master (4)
médicus, médicī (m) - doctor, physician (male) (12)
módus, módī (m) - measure, bound, limit; manner, method, mode, way (22)
mórbus, mórbī (m) - disease, sickness (9)
múndus, múndī (m) - world, universe (21)
númerus, númerī (m) - number (3)
óculus, óculī (m) - eye (4)
offícium, offíciī (n) - duty, service (4)
ṓsculum, ṓsculī (n) - kiss (29)
ṓtium, ṓtiī (n) - leisure, peace (4)
perfúgium, perfúgiī (n) - refuge, shelter (24)
perī́culum, perī́culī (n) - danger, risk (4)
philósophus, philósophī (m) - philosopher (male) (33)
pópulus, pópulī (m) - the people, a people, a nation (3)
praémium, praémiī (n) - reward, prize (35)
prīncípium, prīncípiī (n) - beginning (12)
púer, púerī (m) - boy; boys, children *(pl.)* (3)
remédium, remédiī (n) - cure, remedy (4)
sérvus, sérvī (m) - slave (male) (24)
sígnum, sígnī (n) - sign, signal, indication; seal (13)
sōlā́cium, sōlā́ciī (n) - comfort, relief (24)
sómnus, sómnī (m) - sleep (26)
spéculum, spéculī (n) - mirror (33)
stúdium, stúdiī (n) - eagerness, zeal, pursuit, study (9)
stúltus, stúltī (m) - a fool (4)
súperī, superṓrum (m. pl.) - the gods (27)
tyránnus, tyránnī (m) - absolute ruler, tyrant (6)
vérbum, vérbī (n) - word (5)
vīcī́nus, vīcī́nī (m) - neighbor (male) (21)
vínculum, vínculī (n) - bond, chain, fetter (36)
vī́num, vī́nī (n) - wine (31)
vir, vírī (m) - man, hero (3)
vítium, vítiī (n) - fault, crime, vice (6)
vúlgus, vúlgī (n) - the common people, mob, rabble (21)

3rd Declension

adulḗscēns, adulēscéntis (m *or* f) - young man *or* woman (12)
aéstās, aestā́tis (f) - summer (35)
aétās, aetā́tis (f) - period of life, life, age, an age, time (16)
ámor, amṓris (m) - love (7)
aúctor, auctṓris (m) - increaser; author, originator (19)
audī́tor, audītṓris (m) - hearer, listener, member of an audience (16)
Caésar, Caésaris (m) - Caesar (12)
cáput, cápitis (n) - head; leader; beginning; life; heading; chapter (11)
cármen, cárminis (n) - song, poem (7)
Carthā́gō, Carthā́ginis (f) - Carthage (24)
Cícerō, Cicerṓnis (m) - (Marcus Tullius) Cicero (8)
cī́vitās, cīvitā́tis (f) - state, citizenship (7)
cṓnsul, cṓnsulis (m) - consul (11)
córpus, córporis (n) - body (7)
cupíditās, cupiditā́tis (f) - desire, longing, passion; cupidity, avarice (10)
cupī́dō, cupī́dinis (f) - desire, compassion (36)
dēlectā́tiō, dēlectātiṓnis (f) - delight, pleasure, enjoyment (27)
dux, dúcis (m) - leader, guide; commander, general (23)
flū́men, flū́minis (n) - river (18)
frā́ter, frā́tris (m) - brother (8)
génus, géneris (n) - origin; kind, type, sort, class (18)
hómō, hóminis (m) - human being, man (7)
hónor, honṓris (m) - honor, esteem; public office (30)
imperā́tor, imperātṓris (m) - general, commander-in-chief, emperor (24)
íter, itíneris (n) - journey; route, road (37)
iū́dex, iū́dicis (m) - judge, juror (19)
iūs, iū́ris (n) - right, justice, law (14)
lábor, labṓris (m)- labor, work, toil; a work, production (7)
laus, laúdis (f) - praise, glory, fame (8)
lḗctor, lēctṓris (m) - reader (male) (36)
lḗctrīx, lēctrī́cis (f) - reader (female) (36)
lēx, lḗgis (f) - law, statute (26)
lībértās, lībertā́tis (f) - liberty (8)
lī́men, lī́minis (n) - threshold (26)
lī́tus, lī́toris (n) - shore, coast (23)
lūx, lū́cis (f) - light (26)
maiṓrēs, maiṓrum (m. pl.) - ancestors (27)
mā́ter, mā́tris (f) - mother (12)
mī́les, mī́litis (m) - soldier (23)
mṓrēs, mṓrum (m) - habits, morals, character (7)
mōs, mṓris (m) - habit, custom, manner (7)
nḗmō, nūllī́us, nḗminī, nḗminem, nū́llō, nū́llā (m *or* f) - no one, nobody (11)
népōs, nepṓtis (m) - grandson, descendant (27)
nṓmen, nṓminis (n) - name (7)
occā́siō, occāsiṓnis (f) - occasion, opportunity (28)
ópēs, ópum (f. pl.) - power, resources, wealth (33)
ops, ópis (f) - help, aid (33)
ōrā́tor, ōrātṓris (m) - orator, speaker (23)
ōs, ṓris (n) - mouth, face (14)
párēns, paréntis (m *or* f) - parent (28)
páter, pátris (m) - father (12)
paupértās, paupertā́tis (f) - poverty, humble circumstances (32)
pāx, pā́cis (f) - peace (7)
péctus, péctoris (n) - breast, heart (35)
plēbs, plḗbis (f) - the common people, populace, plebeians (33)
prī́nceps, prī́ncipis (m *or* f) - leader, emperor (28)
próbitās, probitā́tis (f) - uprightness, honesty (18)
rátiō, ratiṓnis (f) - reckoning, account; reason, judgment, consideration; system; manner, method (8)
remíssiō, remissiṓnis (f) - letting go, release; relaxation (34)
rēx, rḗgis (m) - king (7)
rū́mor, rūmṓris (m) - rumor, gossip (31)
rūs, rū́ris (n) - the country, countryside (37)
sacérdōs, sacerdṓtis (m) - priest (23)
sāl, sális (m) - salt; wit (33)
sálūs, salū́tis (f) - health, safety; greeting (21)
sápiēns, sapiéntis (m/f) - a wise man/woman, philosopher (25)
scélus, scéleris (n) - evil deed, crime, sin, wickedness (19)
scrī́ptor, scrīptṓris (m) - writer, author (8)
senéctūs, senectū́tis (f) - old age (10)
sénex, sénis (m) - old man (16)
sérvitūs, servitū́tis (f) - servitude, slavery (20)
sī́dus, sī́deris (n) - constellation, star (29)
sōl, sṓlis (m) - sun (27)
sóror, sorṓris (f) - sister (8)
tempéstās, tempestā́tis (f) - period of time, season; weather, storm (15)

témpus, témporis (n) - time; occasion, opportunity (7)
tímor, timṓris (m) - fear (10)
úxor, uxṓris (f) - wife (7)
vḗritās, vēritā́tis (f) - truth (10)
vésper, vésperis *or* vésperī (m) - evening; evening star (28)
vírgō, vírginis (f) - maiden, virgin (7)
vírtūs, virtū́tis (f) - manliness, courage; excellence, character, worth, virtue (7)
volúptās, voluptā́tis (f) - pleasure (10)
vōx, vṓcis (f) - voice, word (34)
vúlnus, vúlneris (n) - wound (24)

3rd Declension I-Stem

ánimal, animā́lis (n) - a living creature, animal (14)
ars, ártis (f) - art, skill (14)
arx, árcis (f) - citadel, stronghold (23)
as, ássis (m) - an as *(a small copper coin)* (31)
aúris, aúris (f) - ear (14)
cī́vis, cī́vis (m *or* f) - citizen (14)
fī́nēs, fī́nium (m) - boundaries, territory (21)
fī́nis, fī́nis (m) - end, limit, boundary; purpose (21)
gēns, géntis (f) - clan, race, nation, people (21)
hóstēs, hóstium (m) - the enemy (18)
hóstis, hóstis (m) - an enemy *(of the state)* (18)
ígnis, ígnis (m) - fire (22)
máre, máris (n) - sea (14)
mēns, méntis (f) - mind, thought, intention (16)
moénia, moénium (n. pl.) - walls of a city (29)
mōns, móntis (m) - mountain (20)
mors, mórtis (f) - death (14)
nā́vis, nā́vis (f) - ship, boat (21)
nox, nóctis (f) - night (26)
nū́bēs, nū́bis (f) - cloud (14)
pars, pártis (f) - part, share; direction (14)
urbs, úrbis (f) - city (14)
vī́rēs, vī́rium (f. pl.) - strength (14)
vīs, vīs (f) - force, power, violence (14)

4th Declension

córnū, córnūs (n) - horn (20)
cúrsus, cúrsūs (m) - running, race; course (28)
dómī (f) - at home (37)
dómō (f) - from home (37)
dómum (f) - (to) home (37)
dómus, dómūs, dómī (f) - house, home (37)
exércitus, exércitūs (m) - army (32)
frū́ctus, frū́ctūs (m) - fruit; profit, benefit, enjoyment (20)
génū, génūs (n) - knee (20)
mánus, mánūs (f) - hand; handwriting; band (20)
métus, métūs (m) - fear, dread, anxiety (20)
senā́tus, senā́tūs (m) - senate (20)
sḗnsus, sḗnsūs (m) - feeling, sense (20)
spī́ritus, spī́ritūs (m) - breath, breathing; spirit, soul (20)
vérsus, vérsūs (m) - line of verse (20)

5th Declension

díēs, diḗī (m) - day (22)
fídēs, fídeī (f) - faith, trust, trustworthiness, fidelity, promise, guarantee, protection (22)
rēs, réī (f) - thing, matter, property, business, affair (22)
rēs pū́blica, réī pū́blicae (f) - state, commonwealth, republic (22)
spēs, spéī (f) - hope (22)

Indeclinable

níhil - nothing (1)
sátis - enough (5)

Pronouns

áliquis, áliquid - someone, somebody, something (23)
égo, méī - I (11)
hic, haec, hoc - this; the latter; he, she, it, they (9)
ídem, éadem, ídem - the same (11)
ílle, ílla, íllud - that; the former; the famous; he, she, it, they (9)
ípse, ípsa, ípsum - myself, yourself, himself, herself, itself, *etc.,* the very, the actual (13)
is, éa, id - this, that; he, she, it (11)
íste, ísta, ístud - that of yours, that; such (as you have, as you speak of); *sometimes with contemptuous force, e.g.,* that despicable, that wretched (9)
quī, quae, quod - who, which, what, that (17)
quid - what (1)
quídam, quaédam, quíddam - a certain one or thing, someone, something (26)
quis, quid (*after* sī, nisi, nē, num) - anyone, anything, someone, something (33)
quis? quid? - who? whose? whom? what? which? (19)
quísque, quídque, cuiúsque, cuíque - each one, each person, each thing (13)
quísquis, quídquid - whoever, whatever (23)
súī - himself, herself, itself, themselves (13)
tū, túī - you *(sing.)* (11)

Adjectives

1st & 2nd Declension

acérbus, acérba, acérbum - harsh, bitter, grievous (12)

advérsus, advérsa, advérsum - opposite, adverse (34)

aéquus, aéqua, aéquum - level, even; calm; equal, just; favorable (22)

áliī . . . áliī - some . . . others (9)

álius, ália, áliud - other, another (9)

álter, áltera, álterum - the other (of two), second (9)

amī́cus, amī́ca, amī́cum - friendly (11)

antī́quus, antī́qua, antī́quum - ancient, old-time (2)

ásper, áspera, ásperum - rough, harsh (21)

avā́rus, avā́ra, avā́rum - greedy, avaricious (3)

beā́tus, beā́ta, beā́tum - happy, fortunate, blessed (10)

béllus, bélla, béllum - pretty, handsome, charming (4)

bónus, bóna, bónum - good, kind (4)

caécus, caéca, caécum - blind (17)

cándidus, cándida, cándidum - shining, bright, white; beautiful (33)

cā́rus, cā́ra, cā́rum - dear (11)

cértus, cérta, cértum - definite, sure, certain, reliable (19)

cḗterī, cḗterae, cḗtera - the remaining, the rest, the other, all the others (30)

clā́rus, clā́ra, clā́rum - clear, bright; renowned, famous, illustrious (18)

déxter, déxtra, déxtrum - right, right-hand (20)

dígnus, dígna, dígnum (+abl.) - worthy, worthy of (29)

dóctus, dócta, dóctum - taught, learned, skilled (13)

dū́rus, dū́ra, dū́rum - hard, harsh, rough, stern, unfeeling, hardy, difficult (29)

fortūnā́tus, fortūnā́ta, fortūnā́tum - lucky, fortunate, happy (13)

géminus, gémina, géminum - twin (25)

Graécus, Graéca, Graécum - Greek (6)

grā́tus, grā́ta, grā́tum - pleasing, agreeable; grateful (37)

hūmā́nus, hūmā́na, hūmā́num - pertaining to man, human; humane, kind; refined, cultivated (4)

idṓneus, idṓnea, idṓneum - suitable, fit, appropriate (37)

immṓtus, immṓta, immṓtum - unmoved; unchanged; unrelenting (37)

incértus, incérta, incértum - uncertain, unsure, doubtful (22)

īrā́tus, īrā́ta, īrā́tum - angry (35)

iūcúndus, iūcúnda, iūcúndum - pleasant, delightful, agreeable, pleasing (16)

Latī́nus, Latī́na, Latī́num - Latin (22)

lī́ber, lī́bera, lī́berum - free (5)

lóngus, lónga, lóngum - long (16)

magnánimus, magnánima, magnánimum - great-hearted, brave, magnanimous (23)

mágnus, mágna, mágnum - large, great; important (2)

málus, mála, málum - bad, wicked, evil (4)

médius, média, médium - middle; the middle of (22)

mérus, méra, mérum - pure, undiluted (33)

méus, méa, méum - my (2)

míser, mísera, míserum - wretched, miserable, unfortunate (15)

mórtuus, mórtua, mórtuum - dead (28)

múltus, múlta, múltum - much, many (2)

neúter, neútra, neútrum - not either, neither (9)

nóster, nóstra, nóstrum - our, ours (5)

nóvus, nóva, nóvum - new; strange (7)

nū́llus, nū́lla, nū́llum - not any, no, none (9)

párvus, párva, párvum - small, little (4)

paúcī, paúcae, paúca - few, a few (3)

perpétuus, perpétua, perpétuum perpetual, lasting, uninterrupted, continuous (6)

plḗnus, plḗna, plḗnum - full, abundant, generous (6)

prī́mus, prī́ma, prī́mum - first, foremost, chief, principal (27)

pudī́cus, pudī́ca, pudī́cum - modest, chaste (26)

púlcher, púlchra, púlchrum - beautiful, handsome; fine (5)

quántus, quánta, quántum - how large, how great, how much (30)

rīdículus, rīdícula, rīdículum - laughable, ridiculous (30)

Rōmā́nus, Rōmā́na, Rōmā́num - Roman (3)

sálvus, sálva, sálvum - safe, sound (6)

sā́nus, sā́na, sā́num - sound, healthy, sane (5)

secúndus, secúnda, secúndum - second; favorable (6)

siníster, sinístra, sinístrum - left, left-hand; harmful, ill-omened (20)

sṓlus, sṓla, sṓlum - alone, only, the only (9)
stúltus, stúlta, stúltum - foolish (4)
supérbus, supérba, supérbum - arrogant, overbearing, haughty, proud (26)
súperus, súpera, súperum - above, upper (27)
súus, súa, súum - his own, her own, its own, their own (13)
tántus, tánta, tántum - so large, so great, of such a size (29)
tántus . . . quántus - just as much (many) . . . as (30)
tṓtus, tṓta, tṓtum - whole, entire (9)
túus, túa, túum - your *(sing.)* (2)
ū́llus, ū́lla, ū́llum - any (9)
últimus, última, últimum - farthest, extreme; last, final (25)
ū́nus, ū́na, ū́num - one, single, alone (9)
urbā́nus, urbā́na, urbā́num - of the city, urban; urbane, elegant (26)
úter, útra, útrum - either, which (of two) (9)
vḗrus, vḗra, vḗrum - true, real, proper (4)
véster, véstra, véstrum - your *(pl.)* (6)
vī́vus, vī́va, vī́vum - alive, living (30)

3rd Declension

ábsēns, *gen.* abséntis - absent, away (37)
ā́cer, ā́cris, ā́cre - sharp, keen, eager; severe, fierce (16)
brévis, bréve - short, small, brief (16)
céler, céleris, célere - swift, quick, rapid (16)
commū́nis, commū́ne - common, general, of / for the community (20)
diffícilis, diffícile - hard, difficult, troublesome (16)
dī́ligēns, *gen.* dīligéntis - diligent, careful (27)
dissímilis, dissímile - unlike, different (27)
dī́ves, *gen.* dī́vitis *or* dī́tis - rich, wealthy (32)
dúlcis, dúlce - sweet; pleasant, agreeable (16)
fácilis, fácile - easy; agreeable (16)
fḗlīx, *gen.* fēlī́cis - lucky, fortunate, happy (22)
férōx, *gen.* ferṓcis - fierce, savage (25)
fidḗlis, fidḗle - faithful, loyal (25)
fórtis, fórte - strong, brave (16)
grácilis, grácile - slender, thin (27)
grávis, gráve - heavy, weighty; serious, important; severe, grievous (19)
húmilis, húmile - lowly, humble (27)
immortā́lis, immortā́le - not subject to death, immortal (19)
íngēns, *gen.* ingéntis - huge (16)
lévis, léve - light; easy; slight, trivial (17)
máior, máius - greater; older (27)
medíocris, medíocre - ordinary, moderate, mediocre (31)
mortā́lis, mortā́le - mortal (18)
ómnis, ómne - every, all (16)
pār, *gen.* páris (+dat.) - equal, like (32)
paúper, *gen.* paúperis - of small means, poor (32)
pótēns, *gen.* poténtis - able, powerful, mighty, strong (16)
prī́nceps, *gen.* prī́ncipis - chief, foremost (28)
sápiēns, *gen.* sapiéntis - wise, judicious (25)
sénex, *gen.* sénis - old, aged (16)
símilis, símile (+gen. or dat.) - similar (to), like, resembling (27)
suā́vis, suā́ve - sweet (33)
tā́lis, tā́le - such, of such a sort (34)
trī́stis, trī́ste - sad, sorrowful; joyless, grim, severe (26)
túrpis, túrpe - ugly; shameful, base, disgraceful (26)
ū́tilis, ū́tile - useful, advantageous (27)

Indeclinable Adjectives

quot - how many, as many as (27)
sátis - enough, sufficient (5)

Indefinite Adjective

quī́dam, quaédam, quóddam - a certain, some (26)

Interrogative Adjective

quī?, quae?, quod? - what? which? what kind of?; *(sometimes with exclamatory force)* what (a)! what sort of! (19)

Verbs

1st Conjugation

ádiuvō, adiuvā́re, adiū́vī, adiū́tum - to help, aid, assist; to please (4)
ámō, amā́re, amā́vī, amā́tum - to love, like (1)
appéllō, appellā́re, appellā́vī, appellā́tum - to speak to, address (as), call, name (14)
cḗnō, cēnā́re, cēnā́vī, cēnā́tum - to dine (5)

cṓgitō, cōgitā́re, cōgitā́vī, cōgitā́tum- to think, ponder, consider, plan (1)
cōnsérvō, cōnservā́re, cōnservā́vī, cōnservā́tum - to preserve, conserve, maintain (1)
créō, creā́re, creā́vī, creā́tum - to create (12)
cúlpō, culpā́re, culpā́vī, culpā́tum - to blame, censure (5)
cū́rō, cūrā́re, cūrā́vī, cūrā́tum - to care for, attend to; heal, cure; take care (36)
dḗdicō, dēdicā́re, dēdicā́vī, dēdicā́tum - to dedicate (28)
dēléctō, dēlectā́re, dēlectā́vī, dēlectā́tum - to delight, charm, please (19)
dēmṓnstrō, dēmōnstrā́re, dēmōnstrā́vī, dēmōnstrā́tum to point out, show, demonstrate (8)
dēsī́derō, dēsīderā́re, dēsīderā́vī, dēsīderā́tum - to desire, long for, miss (17)
dō, dáre, dédī, dátum - to give, offer (1)
dúbitō, dubitā́re, dubitā́vī, dubitā́tum - to doubt, hesitate (30)
ḗducō, ēducā́re, ēducā́vī, ēducā́tum - to bring up, educate (23)
érrō, errā́re, errā́vī, errā́tum - to wander; err, go astray, make a mistake, be mistaken (1)
exspéctō, exspectā́re, exspectā́vī, exspectā́tum - to look for, expect, await (15)
ímperō, imperā́re, imperā́vī, imperā́tum (+dat.) - to give orders to, command (35)
invī́tō, invītā́re, invītā́vī, invītā́tum - to entertain, invite, summon (26)
iúvō, iuvā́re, iū́vī, iū́tum - to help, aid, assist; to please (4)
labṓrō, labōrā́re, labōrā́vī, labōrā́tum - to labor; be in distress (21)
laúdō, laudā́re, laudā́vī, laudā́tum - to praise (1)
lī́berō, līberā́re, līberā́vī, līberā́tum - to free, liberate (19)
mū́tō, mūtā́re, mūtā́vī, mūtā́tum to change, alter; exchange (14)
nā́rrō, nārrā́re, nārrā́vī, nārrā́tum - to tell, report, narrate (24)
nā́vigō, nāvigā́re, nāvigā́vī, nāvigā́tum - to sail, navigate (17)
nécō, necā́re, necā́vī, necā́tum - to murder, kill (7)
négō, negā́re, negā́vī, negā́tum to deny, say that . . . not (25)
nū́ntiō, nūntiā́re, nūntiā́vī, nūntiā́tum - to announce, report, relate (25)
obléctō, oblectā́re, oblectā́vī, oblectā́tum - to please, amuse, delight; pass time pleasantly (36)
ṓrō, ōrā́re, ōrā́vī, ōrā́tum - to speak, plead; beg, beseech, entreat, pray (36)
párō, parā́re, parā́vī, parā́tum - to prepare, provide; get, obtain (19)
praéstō, praestā́re, praéstitī, praéstitum - to excel; exhibit, show, offer, supply, furnish (28)
próbō, probā́re, probā́vī, probā́tum - to approve, recommend; test (27)
prōnū́ntiō, prōnūntiā́re, prōnūntiā́vī, prōnūntiā́tum - to proclaim, announce; declaim; pronounce (20)
púgnō, pugnā́re, pugnā́vī, pugnā́tum - to fight (29)
pútō, putā́re, putā́vī, putā́tum - to reckon, suppose, judge, think, imagine (25)
récitō, recitā́re, recitā́vī, recitā́tum - to read aloud, recite (17)
récreō, recreā́re, recreā́vī, recreā́tum - to restore, revive; refresh, cheer (36)
recū́sō, recūsā́re, recūsā́vī, recūsā́tum - to refuse (33)
rógō, rogā́re, rogā́vī, rogā́tum - to ask (30)
sátiō, satiā́re, satiā́vī, satiā́tum - to satisfy, sate (3)
serḗnō, serēnā́re, serēnā́vī, serēnā́tum - to make clear, brighten; cheer up, soothe (36)
sérvō, servā́re, servā́vī, servā́tum - to preserve, save, keep, guard (1)
spéctō, spectā́re, spectā́vī, spectā́tum - to look at, see (34)
spḗrō, spērā́re, spērā́vī, spērā́tum - to hope for, hope (25)
stō, stā́re, stétī, státum - to stand, stand still *or* firm (13)
súperō, superā́re, superā́vī, superā́tum - to be above, have the upper hand, surpass; overcome, conquer (5)
tólerō, tolerā́re, tolerā́vī, tolerā́tum - to bear, endure (6)
vī́tō, vītā́re, vītā́vī, vītā́tum - to avoid, shun (14)
vócō, vocā́re, vocā́vī, vocā́tum - to call, summon (1)

2nd Conjugation

aúdeō, audḗre, aúsus sum - to dare (7)

cáreō, carḗre, cáruī, caritū́rum (+abl.) - to be without, be deprived of, want, lack; be free from (20)

contíneō, continḗre, contínuī, conténtum - to hold together, contain, keep, enclose, restrain (21)

dḗbeō, dēbḗre, dḗbuī, dḗbitum - to owe; ought, must, should (1)

dḗleō, dēlḗre, dēlḗvī, dēlḗtum - to destroy, wipe out, erase (17)

dóceō, docḗre, dócuī, dóctum - to teach (8)

dóleō, dolḗre, dóluī, dolitū́rum - to grieve, suffer; hurt, give pain (31)

égeō, egḗre, éguī (+ abl. or gen.) - to need, lack, want (28)

éxpleō, explḗre, explḗvī, explḗtum - to fill, fill up, complete (28)

fóveō, fovḗre, fṓvī, fṓtum - to comfort, nurture, cherish (35)

gaúdeō, gaudḗre, gāvī́sus sum - to be glad, rejoice (23)

hábeō, habḗre, hábuī, hábitum - to have, hold, possess; consider, regard (3)

iáceō, iacḗre, iácuī - to lie; lie prostrate; lie dead (25)

invídeō, invidḗre, invī́dī, invī́sum to be envious; to look at with envy, envy, be jealous of (+dat.) (31)

iúbeō, iubḗre, iússī, iússum - to bid, order, command (21)

máneō, manḗre, mā́nsī, mā́nsum - to remain, stay, stay behind, abide, continue (5)

mísceō, miscḗre, míscuī, míxtum to mix, stir up, disturb (18)

móneō, monḗre, mónuī, mónitum - to remind, advise, warn (1)

móveō, movḗre, mṓvī, mṓtum - to move; arouse, affect (18)

nóceō, nocḗre, nócuī, nócitum (+dat.) - to do harm to, harm, injure (35)

pā́reō, pārḗre, pā́ruī (+dat.) - to be obedient to, obey (35)

páteō, patḗre, pátuī - to be open, lie open; be accessible; be evident (32)

persuā́deō, persuādḗre, persuā́sī, persuā́sum (+dat.) to succeed in urging, persuade, convince (35)

pláceō, placḗre, plácuī, plácitum (+dat.) - to be pleasing to, please (35)

praébeō, praebḗre, praébuī, praébitum - to offer, provide (32)

prohíbeō, prohibḗre, prohíbuī, prohíbitum - to keep (back), prevent, hinder, restrain, prohibit (20)

remáneō, remanḗre, remā́nsī, remā́nsum - to remain, stay, stay behind, abide, continue (5)

respóndeō, respondḗre, respóndī, respṓnsum - to answer (29)

rī́deō, rīdḗre, rī́sī, rī́sum - to laugh, laugh at (24)

sálvē, salvḗte - hello, greetings (1)

sálveō, salvḗre - to be well, be in good health (1)

sédeō, sedḗre, sḗdī, séssum - to sit (34)

sóleō, solḗre, sólitus sum - to be accustomed (37)

stúdeō, studḗre, stúduī (+dat.) - to direct one's zeal to, be eager for, study (35)

subrī́deō, subrīdḗre, subrī́sī, subrī́sum - to smile (down) upon (35)

táceō, tacḗre, tácuī, tácitum - to be silent, leave unmentioned (28)

téneō, tenḗre, ténuī, téntum - to hold, keep, possess; restrain (14)

térreō, terrḗre, térruī, térritum - to frighten, terrify (1)

tímeō, timḗre, tímuī - to fear, be afraid (of) (15)

válē, valḗte - good-bye, farewell (1)

váleō, valḗre, váluī, valitū́rum - to be strong, have power; be well (1)

vídeō, vidḗre, vī́dī, vī́sum - to see; observe, understand (1)

vídeor, vidḗrī, vī́sus sum - to be seen, seem, appear (18)

3rd Conjugation

accḗdō, accḗdere, accéssī, accéssum - to come (to), approach (36)

admíttō, admíttere, admī́sī, admíssum - to admit, receive, let in (17)

ágō, ágere, ḗgī, ā́ctum - to drive, lead, do, act; pass, spend *(life or time)* (8)

álō, álere, áluī, áltum - to nourish, support, sustain, increase; cherish (13)

āmíttō, āmíttere, āmī́sī, āmíssum - to send away; lose, let go (12)

antepṓnō, antepṓnere, antepósuī, antepósitum - to put before, prefer (35)

āvértō, āvértere, āvértī, āvérsum - to turn away, avert (23)
bíbō, bíbere, bíbī - to drink (30)
cádō, cádere, cécidī, cāsū́rum - to fall (12)
cárpō, cárpere, cárpsī, cárptum to harvest, pluck; seize (36)
cḗdō, cḗdere, céssī, céssum - to go, withdraw; yield to, grant, submit (28)
cérnō, cérnere, crḗvī, crḗtum - to distinguish, discern, perceive (22)
cognṓscō, cognṓscere, cognṓvī, cógnitum - to become acquainted with, learn, recognize; know *(in perfect tenses)* (30)
cṓgō, cṓgere, coḗgī, coā́ctum - to drive *or* bring together, force, compel (36)
commíttō, commíttere, commī́sī, commíssum - to entrust, commit (15)
comprehéndō, comprehéndere, comprehéndī, comprehḗnsum - to grasp, seize, arrest; comprehend, understand (30)
cóndō, cóndere, cóndidī, cónditum - to put together *or* into, store; found, establish (29)
cōnsū́mō, cōnsū́mere, cōnsū́mpsī, cōnsū́mptum - to consume, use up (30)
contémnō, contémnere, contémpsī, contémptum - to despise, scorn (36)
conténdō, conténdere, conténdī, conténtum - to strive, struggle, contend; hasten (29)
contúndō, contúndere, cóntudī, contū́sum - to beat, crush, bruise, destroy (36)
crḗdō, crḗdere, crḗdidī, crḗditum to believe, trust (25)
crḗscō, crḗscere, crḗvī, crḗtum - to increase (34)
cúrrō, cúrrere, cucúrrī, cúrsum - to run, rush, move quickly (14)
dēcérnō, dēcérnere, dēcrḗvī, dēcrḗtum - to decide, settle, decree (36)
dēféndō, dēféndere, dēféndī, dēfḗnsum - to ward off; defend, protect (20)
dī́cō, dī́cere, dī́xī, díctum - to say, tell, speak; name, call (10)
dī́ligō, dīlígere, dīlḗxī, dīlḗctum - to esteem, love (13)
discḗdō, discḗdere, discéssī, discéssum - to go away, depart (20)
díscō, díscere, dídicī - to learn (8)
dū́cō, dū́cere, dū́xī, dúctum - to lead; consider, regard; prolong (8)
éxigō, exígere, exḗgī, exā́ctum - to drive out, force out, exact; drive through, complete, perfect (36)
expéllō, expéllere, éxpulī, expúlsum - to drive out, expel, banish (24)
expṓnō, expṓnere, expósuī, expósitum - to set forth, explain, expose (30)
flúō, flúere, flū́xī, flū́xum - to flow (18)
gérō, gérere, géssī, géstum - to carry; carry on, manage, conduct, wage, accomplish, perform (8)
ignṓscō, ignṓscere, ignṓvī, ignṓtum (+dat.) - to grant pardon to, forgive (35)
intéllegō, intellégere, intellḗxī, intellḗctum - to understand (11)
iúngō, iúngere, iū́nxī, iū́nctum - to join (13)
légō, légere, lḗgī, lḗctum - to pick out, choose; read (18)
mínuō, minúere, mínuī, minū́tum - to lessen, diminish (30)
míttō, míttere, mī́sī, míssum - to send, let go (11)
néglegō, neglégere, neglḗxī, neglḗctum - to neglect, disregard (17)
nṓscō, nṓscere, nṓvī, nṓtum - to become acquainted with, learn, recognize; know *(in perfect tenses)* (30)
nū́bō, nū́bere, nū́psī, nū́ptum (+dat.) - to cover, veil; to be married to, marry (35)
óccidō, occídere, óccidī, occā́sum - to fall down; die; set (31)
ópprimō, opprímere, oppréssī, oppréssum - to suppress, overwhelm, overpower, check (23)
osténdō, osténdere, osténdī, osténtum - to exhibit, show, display (23)
párcō, párcere, pepércī, parsū́rum (+dat.) - to be lenient to, spare (35)
péllō, péllere, pépulī, púlsum - to strike, push; drive out, banish (24)
pétō, pétere, petī́vī, petī́tum - to seek, aim at, beg, beseech (23)
pṓnō, pṓnere, pósuī, pósitum - to put, place, set (27)
prémō, prémere, préssī, préssum - to press; press hard, pursue (23)
prōmíttō, prōmíttere, prōmī́sī, prōmíssum - to send forth; promise (32)

quaérō, quaérere, quaesívī, quaesítum - to seek, look for, strive for; ask, inquire, inquire into (24)
régō, régere, réxī, réctum - to rule, guide, direct (16)
relínquō, relínquere, relíquī, relíctum - to leave behind, leave, abandon, desert (21)
requiḗscō, requiḗscere, requiḗvī, requiḗtum - to rest (37)
requírō, requírere, requīsívī, requīsítum - to seek, ask for; miss, need, require (36)
revértō, revértere, revértī, revérsum - turn back (23)
scríbō, scríbere, scrípsī, scríptum to write, compose (8)
súrgō, súrgere, surréxī, surréctum - to get up, arise (29)
tángō, tángere, tétigī, tắctum - to touch (21)
tóllō, tóllere, sústulī, sublắtum - to raise, lift up; take away, remove, destroy (22)
trắdō, trắdere, trắdidī, trắditum to give over, surrender; hand down, transmit, teach (33)
tráhō, tráhere, trắxī, tráctum - to draw, drag; derive, acquire (8)
vértō, vértere, vértī, vérsum - to turn; change (23)
víncō, víncere, vícī, víctum - to conquer, overcome (8)
vívō, vívere, víxī, víctum - to live (10)

3rd Conjugation -iō

accípiō, accípere, accḗpī, accéptum - to take *(to one's self)*, receive, accept (24)
cápiō, cápere, cḗpī, cáptum - to take, capture, seize, get (10)
cúpiō, cúpere, cupívī, cupítum - to desire, wish, long for (17)
ēripiō, ēripere, ēripuī, ēréptum - to snatch away, take away; rescue (22)
excípiō, excípere, excḗpī, excéptum - to take out, except; take, receive, capture (24)
fáciō, fácere, fḗcī, fáctum - to make, do, accomplish (10)
fúgiō, fúgere, fū́gī, fugitū́rum - to flee, hurry away; escape; go into exile; avoid, shun (10)
iáciō, iácere, iḗcī, iáctum - to throw, hurl (15)
incípiō, incípere, incḗpī, incéptum - to begin (17)
interfíciō, interfícere, interfḗcī, interféctum - to kill, murder (37)
patefáciō, patefácere, patefḗcī, patefáctum - to make open, open; disclose, expose (25)
rápiō, rápere, rápuī, ráptum - to seize, snatch, carry away (21)
recípiō, recípere, recḗpī, recéptum - to take back, regain; admit, receive (24)
sápiō, sápere, sapívī - to have good taste; have good sense, be wise (35)
suscípiō, suscípere, suscḗpī, suscéptum - to undertake (25)

4th Conjugation

aúdiō, audíre, audívī, audítum - to hear, listen to (10)
dórmiō, dormíre, dormívī, dormítum - to sleep (31)
invéniō, invenīre, invḗnī, invéntum - to come upon, find (10)
móllio, mollíre, mollívī, mollítum to soften; make calm *or* less hostile (29)
nésciō, nescíre, nescívī, nescítum - to not know, be ignorant (25)
scíō, scíre, scívī, scítum - to know (21)
séntiō, sentíre, sḗnsī, sḗnsum - to feel, perceive, think, experience (11)
sérviō, servíre, servívī, servítum (+dat.) - to be a slave to, serve (35)
véniō, veníre, vḗnī, véntum - to come (10)

Irregular

ábeō, abíre, ábiī, ábitum - to go away, depart, leave (37)
ádeō, adíre, ádiī, áditum - to go to, approach (37)
ádferō, adférre, áttulī, allắtum - to bring to (31)
cṓnferō, cōnférre, cóntulī, collắtum - to bring together, compare; confer, bestow (31)
éō, íre, íī, ítum - to go (37)
éxeō, exíre, éxiī, éxitum - to go out, exit (37)
férō, férre, túlī, lắtum - to bear, carry, bring; suffer, endure, tolerate; say, report (31)
fíō, fíerī, fáctus sum - to occur, happen; become; be made, be done (36)
íneō, iníre, íniī, ínitum - to enter into, begin (37)
mắlō, mắlle, mắluī - to want (something) more, instead; prefer (32)
nṓlō, nṓlle, nṓluī - to not . . . wish, be unwilling (32)
óbeō, obíre, óbiī, óbitum - to go up against, meet; die (37)
ófferō, offérre, óbtulī, oblắtum - to offer (31)

péreō, perī́re, périī, péritum - to pass away, be destroyed, perish (37)
póssum, pósse, pótuī - to be able, can, could, have power (6)
rédeō, redī́re, rédiī, réditum - to go back, return (37)
réferō, reférre, réttulī, relā́tum - to carry back, bring back; repeat, answer, report (31)
sum, ésse, fúī, futū́rum - to be, exist (4)
vólō, vélle, vóluī - to wish, want, be willing, will (32)

Deponent
árbitror, arbitrā́rī, arbitrā́tus sum to judge, think (34)
cṓnor, cōnā́rī, cōnā́tus sum - to try, attempt (34)
ēgrédior, ḗgredī, ēgréssus sum - to go out (34)
fáteor, fatḗrī, fássus sum - to confess, admit (34)
hórtor, hortā́rī, hortā́tus sum - to encourage, urge (34)
lóquor, lóquī, locū́tus sum - to say, speak, tell (34)
mī́ror, mīrā́rī, mīrā́tus sum - to marvel at, admire, wonder (35)
mṓlior, mōlī́rī, mōlī́tus sum - to work at, build, undertake, plan (34)
mórior, mórī, mórtuus sum - to die (34)
nā́scor, nā́scī, nā́tus sum - to be born; spring forth, arrive (34)
pátior, pátī, pássus sum - to suffer, endure; permit (34)
peregrī́nor, peregrīnā́rī, peregrīnā́tus sum - to travel abroad, wander (37)
profícīscor, proficī́scī, proféctus sum - to set out, start (34)
rū́sticor, rūsticā́rī, rūsticā́tus sum to live in the country (34)
séquor, séquī, secū́tus sum - to follow (34)
ū́tor, ū́tī, ū́sus sum (+abl.) - to use; enjoy, experience (34)

Defective
ā́it, ā́iunt - he says, they say, assert (25)
coépī, coepísse, coéptum - began (17)
ínquit - he says *or* said (22)
ṓdī, ōdísse, ōsū́rum - to hate (20)

Impersonal
lícet, licḗre, lícuit (+dat. +infin.) - it is permitted *(for someone to do something),* one may (37)

Adverbs

ánte (+acc.) - before, previously (13)
béne - well, satisfactorily, quite (11)
cíto - quickly (17)
cōtī́diē - daily, every day (36)
crās - tomorrow (5)
cūr - why (18)
déhinc - then, next (25)
deínde - thereupon, next, then (18)
dḗnique - at last, finally, lastly (29)
díū - long, for a long time (12)
étiam - even, also (11)
fórīs - out of doors, outside (37)
fortásse - perhaps (36)
fū́rtim - stealthily, secretly (30)
héri - yesterday (5)
hīc - here (25)
hódiē - today (3)
iam - now, already, soon (19)
íbi - there (6)
íta - so, thus (29)
ítaque - and so, therefore (15)
íterum - again, a second time (21)
mox - soon (30)
nē . . . quídem - not . . . even (29)
nímis, nímium - too, too much, excessively; *(in a positive sense, esp. with adjectives and adverbs)* exceedingly, very (9)
nōn - not (1)
númquam - never (8)
nunc - now, at present (6)
nū́per - recently (12)
ṓlim - once (upon a time), long ago, formerly; some day, in the future (13)
pósteā - afterwards (24)
prī́mō - at first, at the beginning (30)
prṓtinus - immediately (22)
quam - how (16)
quam - than *(after comparatives);* as . . . as possible *(with superlatives)* (26)
quándō - when (5)
quā́rē - because of which thing *(lit.);* therefore, wherefore, why (6)
quídem - indeed, certainly, at least, even (29)
quóndam - formerly, once (22)
quóque - also, too (17)
repénte - suddenly (30)
saépe - often (1)
sátis - enough, sufficiently (5)
sémel - a single time, once, once and for all, simultaneously (31)
sémper - always (3)
sīc - so, thus (29)
súbitō - suddenly (33)
tam - so, to such a degree (29)
tam . . . quam - so . . . as (29)
támen - nevertheless, still (8)
tamquam - as it were, as if, so to speak (29)
tántum - only (26)

tum - then, at that time; thereupon, in the next place (5)
úbi - where, when (6)
últrā - on the other side of, beyond (22)
úmquam - ever, at any time (23)
únde - whence, from what *or* which place, from which, from whom (30)
úsque - all the way, up (to), even (to), continuously, always (31)
vḗrō - in truth, indeed, to be sure, however (29)

Conjunctions

at - but; but, mind you; but, you say (19)
átque, ac - and also, and even, and in fact (21)
aut - or (17)
aut . . . aut - either . . . or (17)
aútem - however; moreover (11)
cum (+indic.) - when (31)
cum (+subj.) - when, since, although (31)
dum - while, as long as, at the same time that; *or* until *(+subjunctive)* (8)
dúmmodo (+subj.) - provided that, so long as (32)
énim - for, in fact, truly (9)
et - and; even (2)
et . . . et - both . . . and (2)
ígitur - therefore, consequently (5)
nam - for (13)
nē - not; in order that . . . not, that . . . not, in order not to (28)
néque, nec - and not, nor (11)
néque . . . néque, nec . . . nec - neither . . . nor (11)
nísi - if . . . not, unless; except (19)
quod - because (11)
quóniam - since, inasmuch as (10)
sed - but (2)
sī - if (1)
ut (+indic.) - as, just as, when (24)
ut (+ subj.) - in order that, so that, that, in order to, so as to, to (28)
útrum . . . an - whether . . . or (30)

Prepositions

ab, ā (+abl.) - away from, from; by (14)
ad (+acc.) - to, up to, near to (8)
ánte (+acc.) - before *(in place or time)*, in front of (13)
ápud (+acc.) - among, in the presence of, at the house of (31)
cóntrā (+acc.) - against (19)
cum (+abl.) - with (10)
dē (+abl.) - down from, from; concerning, about (3)
ex, ē (abl.+) - out of, from, from within; by reason of, on account of ; of *(after cardinal numerals)* (8)
in (+acc.) - into, toward; against (9)
in (+abl.) - in, on (3)
ínter (+acc.) - between, among (15)
per (+acc.) - through; by *(with reflexive pronoun)* (13)
post (+acc.) - after, behind (7)
prae (+abl.) - in front of, before (26)
prō (+abl.) - in front of, before, on behalf of, for the sake of, in return for, instead of, for, as (12)
própter (+acc.) - on account of, because of (5)
síne (+abl.) - without (2)
sub (+abl. w/ verbs of rest *or* +acc. w/ verbs of motion) - under, up under, close to, down to/into, to/at the foot of (7)
trāns (+acc.) - across (14)
últrā (adv. and prep. +acc.) - on the other side of, beyond (22)

Interjections

heu - ah!, alas! (33)
ō - O!, Oh! (2)
vae (often +dat. or acc.) - alas, woe to (34)

Idioms

amā́bō tē - please (1)
grā́tiās ágere (+dat.) - to thank someone; to give thanks to (8)
mḗnsa secúnda (f) - dessert (26)
nōn sṓlum . . . sed étiam - not only . . . but also (9)
poénās dáre - to pay the penalty (2)
sē cōnférre - to go (31)
sī quándō - if ever (5)

Prefix

re-, red- - again, back (24)

Suffixes

-ne – interrogative suffix attached to the first word of a sentence, typically the verb or another word on which the question hinges, to introduce a question whose answer is uncertain (5)
-que - and *(enclitic conjunction; appended to the second of two words to be joined)* (6)
-ve - or (33)

Numerals

Cardinal - ū́nus *to* vīgíntī quī́nque (15)

Ordinal - prī́mus *to* duodécimus (15)

----

céntum - a hundred (15)

mī́lia, mī́lium (n. pl.) - thousands (15)

mī́lle - thousand (15)

Chapter 38

Nouns

1st Declension

adulēscéntia, adulēscéntiae (f) - youth, young manhood; youthfulness (5)
agrícola, agrícolae (m) - farmer (3)
amī́ca, amī́cae (f) - friend (female) (3)
amīcítia, amīcítiae (f) - friendship (10)
ánima, ánimae (f) - air *(breathed by an animal)*, breath; soul, spirit (34)
áqua, áquae (f) - water (14)
Ásia, Ásiae (f) - Asia (12)
Athḗnae, Athēnā́rum (f. pl.) - Athens (37)
cása, cásae (f) - house, cottage, hut (21)
caúsa, caúsae (f) - cause, reason; case, situation (21)
caúsā (abl. + preceding gen.) - for the sake of, on account of (21)
cḗna, cḗnae (f) - dinner (26)
clēméntia, clēméntiae (f) - mildness, gentleness, mercy (16)
cṓpia, cṓpiae (f) - abundance, supply (8)
cṓpiae, cōpiā́rum (f) - supplies, troops, forces (8)
cúlpa, cúlpae (f) - fault, blame (5)
cū́ra, cū́rae (f) - care, attention, caution, anxiety (4)
custṓdia, custṓdiae (f) - protection, custody; guards *(pl.)* (32)
déa, déae (f) - goddess (6)
discípula, discípulae (f) - learner, pupil, student (female) (6)
dīvítiae, dīvitiā́rum (f. pl.) - riches, wealth (13)
fā́bula, fā́bulae (f) - story, tale; play (24)
fā́ma, fā́mae (f) - rumor, report; fame, reputation (2)
família, famíliae (f) - household, family (19)
fḗmina, fḗminae (f) - woman (3)
fenéstra, fenéstrae (f) - window (21)
fī́lia, fī́liae (f) - daughter (3)
fṓrma, fṓrmae (f) - form, shape; beauty (2)
fortū́na, fortū́nae (f) - fortune, luck (2)
glṓria, glṓriae (f) - glory, fame (5)
Graécia, Graéciae (f) - Greece (19)
hásta, hástae (f) - spear (23)
hṓra, hṓrae (f) - hour, time (10)
iā́nua, iā́nuae (f) - door (35)
īnsídiae, īnsidiā́rum (f) - ambush, plot, treachery (6)
ī́nsula, ī́nsulae (f) - island (23)
invídia, invídiae (f) - envy, jealousy, hatred (31)
ī́ra, ī́rae (f) - ire, anger (2)
Itália, Itáliae (f) - Italy (15)
língua, línguae (f) - tongue; language (25)
líttera, lítterae (f) - a letter of the alphabet (7)
lítterae, litterā́rum (f) - a letter (epistle), literature (7)
lū́na, lū́nae (f) - moon (28)
magístra, magístrae (f) - schoolmistress, teacher, mistress (4)
médica, médicae (f) - doctor, physician (female) (12)
memória, memóriae (f) - memory, recollection (15)
mḗnsa, mḗnsae (f) - table; dining; dish, course (26)
móra, mórae (f) - delay (4)
nā́ta, nā́tae (f) - daughter (29)
nātū́ra, nātū́rae (f) - nature (10)
naúta, naútae (m) - sailor (2)
patiéntia, patiéntiae (f) - suffering; patience, endurance (12)
pátria, pátriae (f) - fatherland, native land, (one's) country (2)
pecū́nia, pecū́niae (f) - money (2)
philósopha, philósophae (f) - philosopher (female) (33)
philosóphia, philosóphiae (f) - philosophy (2)
poéna, poénae (f) - penalty, punishment (2)
poḗta, poḗtae (m) - poet (2)
pórta, pórtae (f) - gate, entrance (2)
puélla, puéllae (f) - girl (2)
rēgī́na, rēgī́nae (f) - queen (7)
Rṓma, Rṓmae (f) - Rome (14)
rósa, rósae (f) - rose (2)
sapiéntia, sapiéntiae (f) - wisdom (3)
sátura, sáturae (f) - satire (16)
sciéntia, sciéntiae (f) - knowledge (18)
senténtia, senténtiae (f) - feeling, thought, opinion, vote, sentence (2)
sérva, sérvae (f) - slave (female) (24)
stḗlla, stḗllae (f) - star, planet (28)
Syrācū́sae, Syrācūsā́rum (f. pl.) - Syracuse (37)
térra, térrae (f) - earth, ground, land, country (7)
Trṓia, Trṓiae (f) - Troy (21)
túrba, túrbae (f) - uproar, disturbance; mob, crowd, multitude (14)
vía, víae (f) - way, road, street (10)
vīcī́na, vīcī́nae (f) - neighbor (female) (21)
victṓria, victṓriae (f) - victory (8)

víta, vítae (f) - life; mode of life (2)

2nd Declension

áger, ágrī (m) - field, farm (3)
amícus, amícī (m) - friend (male) (3)
ánimī, animṓrum (m) - high spirits, pride, courage (5)
ánimus, ánimī (m) - soul, spirit, mind (5)
ánnus, ánnī (m) - year (12)
argūméntum, argūméntī (n) - proof, evidence, argument (19)
árma, armṓrum (n. pl.) - arms, weapons (28)
auxílium, auxíliī (n) - aid, help (31)
bā́sium, bā́siī (n) - kiss (4)
béllum, béllī (n) - war (4)
benefícium, benefíciī (n) - benefit, kindness; favor (19)
caélum, caélī (n) - sky, heaven (5)
coniūrā́tī, coniūrātṓrum (m. pl.) - conspirators (20)
cōnsílium, cōnsíliī (n) - plan, purpose, counsel, advice, judgment, wisdom (4)
déus, déī (m) - god (6)
dígitus, dígitī (m) - finger, toe (31)
discípulus, discípulī (m) - learner, pupil, student (male) (6)
dṓnum, dṓnī (n) - gift, present (4)
elephántus, elephántī (m and f) - elephant (31)
équus, équī (m) - horse (23)
exítium, exítiī (n) - destruction, ruin (4)
exsílium, exsíliī (n) - exile, banishment (31)
fáctum, fáctī (n) - deed, act, achievement (13)
fā́tum, fā́tī (n) - fate; death (29)
férrum, férrī (n) - iron; sword (22)
fílius, fíliī (m) - son (3)
fórum, fórī (n) - marketplace, forum (26)
Graécus, Graécī (m) - a Greek (6)
húmus, húmī (f) - ground, earth; soil (37)
impérium, impériī (n) - power to command, supreme power, authority, command, control (24)
ingénium, ingéniī (n) - nature, innate talent (29)
inítium, inítiī (n) - beginning, commencement (33)
iūdícium, iūdíciī (n) - judgment, decision, opinion; trial (19)
libéllus, libéllī (m) - little book (17)
líber, líbrī (m) - book (6)
lóca, locṓrum (n) - places, region (9)
lócī, locṓrum (m) - passages in literature (9)
lócus, lócī (m) - place; passage in literature (9)
lū́dus, lū́dī (m) - game, sport; school (18)
magíster, magístrī (m) - schoolmaster, teacher, master (4)
médicus, médicī (m) - doctor, physician (male) (12)
módus, módī (m) - measure, bound, limit; manner, method, mode, way (22)
mórbus, mórbī (m) - disease, sickness (9)
múndus, múndī (m) - world, universe (21)
númerus, númerī (m) - number (3)
óculus, óculī (m) - eye (4)
ódium, ódiī (n) - hatred (38)
offícium, offíciī (n) - duty, service (4)
ṓsculum, ṓsculī (n) - kiss (29)
ṓtium, ṓtiī (n) - leisure, peace (4)
perfúgium, perfúgiī (n) - refuge, shelter (24)
perículum, perículī (n) - danger, risk (4)
philósophus, philósophī (m) - philosopher (male) (33)
pópulus, pópulī (m) - the people, a people, a nation (3)
praémium, praémiī (n) - reward, prize (35)
prīncípium, prīncípiī (n) - beginning (12)
púer, púerī (m) - boy; boys, children *(pl.)* (3)
remédium, remédiī (n) - cure, remedy (4)
sérvus, sérvī (m) - slave (male) (24)
sígnum, sígnī (n) - sign, signal, indication; seal (13)
sōlā́cium, sōlā́ciī (n) - comfort, relief (24)
sómnus, sómnī (m) - sleep (26)
spéculum, spéculī (n) - mirror (33)
stúdium, stúdiī (n) - eagerness, zeal, pursuit, study (9)
stúltus, stúltī (m) - a fool (4)
súperī, superṓrum (m. pl.) - the gods (27)
tyránnus, tyránnī (m) - absolute ruler, tyrant (6)
vérbum, vérbī (n)- word (5)
vīcī́nus, vīcī́nī (m) - neighbor (male) (21)
vínculum, vínculī (n) - bond, chain, fetter (36)
vī́num, vī́nī (n) - wine (31)
vir, vírī (m) - man, hero (3)
vítium, vítiī (n) - fault, crime, vice (6)
vúlgus, vúlgī (n) - the common people, mob, rabble (21)

3rd Declension

aduléscēns, adulēscéntis (m *or* f) - young man *or* woman (12)
aéstās, aestā́tis (f) - summer (35)
aétās, aetā́tis (f) - period of life, life, age, an age, time (16)
ámor, amṓris (m) - love (7)
árbor, árboris (f) - tree (38)
aúctor, auctṓris (m) - increaser; author, originator (19)
audī́tor, audītṓris (m) - hearer, listener, member of an audience (16)
Caésar, Caésaris (m) - Caesar (12)
cáput, cápitis (n) - head; leader; beginning; life; heading; chapter (11)
cármen, cárminis (n) - song, poem (7)
Carthā́gō, Carthā́ginis (f) - Carthage (24)
Cícerō, Cicerṓnis (m) - (Marcus Tullius) Cicero (8)
cī́vitās, cīvitā́tis (f) - state, citizenship (7)
cṓnsul, cṓnsulis (m) - consul (11)
córpus, córporis (n) - body (7)
cupíditās, cupiditā́tis (f) - desire, longing, passion; cupidity, avarice (10)
cupī́dō, cupī́dinis (f) - desire, compassion (36)
dēlectā́tiō, dēlectātiṓnis (f) - delight, pleasure, enjoyment (27)
dígnitās, dignitā́tis (f) - merit, prestige, dignity (38)
dólor, dolṓris (m) - pain, grief (38)
dux, dúcis (m) - leader, guide; commander, general (23)
flū́men, flū́minis (n) - river (18)
frā́ter, frā́tris (m) - brother (8)
génus, géneris (n) - origin; kind, type, sort, class (18)
hómō, hóminis (m) - human being, man (7)
hónor, honṓris (m) - honor, esteem; public office (30)
imperā́tor, imperātṓris (m) - general, commander-in-chief, emperor (24)
íter, itíneris (n) - journey; route, road (37)
iū́dex, iū́dicis (m) - judge, juror (19)
iūs, iū́ris (n) - right, justice, law (14)
lábor, labṓris (m)- labor, work, toil; a work, production (7)
laus, laúdis (f) - praise, glory, fame (8)
lḗctor, lēctṓris (m) - reader (male) (36)
lḗctrīx, lēctrī́cis (f) - reader (female) (36)
lēx, lḗgis (f) - law, statute (26)
lībértās, lībertā́tis (f) - liberty (8)
lī́men, lī́minis (n) - threshold (26)
lī́tus, lī́toris (n) - shore, coast (23)
lūx, lū́cis (f) - light (26)
maiṓrēs, maiṓrum (m. pl.) - ancestors (27)
mā́ter, mā́tris (f) - mother (12)
mī́les, mī́litis (m) - soldier (23)
mṓrēs, mṓrum (m) - habits, morals, character (7)
mōs, mṓris (m) - habit, custom, manner (7)
nḗmō, nūllī́us, nḗminī, nḗminem, nū́llō, nū́llā (m *or* f) - no one, nobody (11)
népōs, nepṓtis (m) - grandson, descendant (27)
nṓmen, nṓminis (n) - name (7)
occā́siō, occāsiṓnis (f) - occasion, opportunity (28)
ópēs, ópum (f. pl.) - power, resources, wealth (33)
ops, ópis (f) - help, aid (33)
ópus, óperis (n) - a work, task; deed, accomplishment (38)
ōrā́tiō, ōrātiṓnis (f) - speech (38)
ōrā́tor, ōrātṓris (m) - orator, speaker (23)
ōs, ṓris (n) - mouth, face (14)
párēns, paréntis (m *or* f) - parent (28)
páter, pátris (m) - father (12)
paupértās, paupertā́tis (f) - poverty, humble circumstances (32)
pāx, pā́cis (f) - peace (7)
péctus, péctoris (n) - breast, heart (35)
pēs, pédis (m) - lower leg, foot (38)
plēbs, plḗbis (f) - the common people, populace, plebeians (33)
prī́nceps, prī́ncipis (m *or* f) - leader, emperor (28)
próbitās, probitā́tis (f) - uprightness, honesty (18)
rátiō, ratiṓnis (f) - reckoning, account; reason, judgment, consideration; system; manner, method (8)
remíssiō, remissiṓnis (f) - letting go, release; relaxation (34)
rēx, rḗgis (m) - king (7)
rū́mor, rūmṓris (m) - rumor, gossip (31)
rūs, rū́ris (n) - the country, countryside (37)
sacérdōs, sacerdṓtis (m) - priest (23)
sāl, sális (m) - salt; wit (33)
sálūs, salū́tis (f) - health, safety; greeting (21)
sápiēns, sapiéntis (m/f) - a wise man/woman, philosopher (25)
sátor, satṓris (m) - sower, planter; begetter, father; founder (38)
scélus, scéleris (n) - evil deed, crime, sin, wickedness (19)

scríptor, scrīptṓris (m) - writer, author (8)
senéctūs, senectū́tis (f) - old age (10)
sénex, sénis (m) - old man (16)
sérvitūs, servitū́tis (f) - servitude, slavery (20)
sī́dus, sī́deris (n) - constellation, star (29)
sōl, sṓlis (m) - sun (27)
sóror, sorṓris (f) - sister (8)
tempéstās, tempestā́tis (f) - period of time, season; weather, storm (15)
témpus, témporis (n) - time; occasion, opportunity (7)
tímor, timṓris (m) - fear (10)
úxor, uxṓris (f) - wife (7)
vḗritās, vēritā́tis (f) - truth (10)
vésper, vésperis *or* **vésperī (m)** - evening; evening star (28)
vírgō, vírginis (f) - maiden, virgin (7)
vírtūs, virtū́tis (f) - manliness, courage; excellence, character, worth, virtue (7)
volúptās, voluptā́tis (f) - pleasure (10)
vōx, vṓcis (f) - voice, word (34)
vúlnus, vúlneris (n) - wound (24)

3rd Declension I-Stem

ánimal, animā́lis (n) - a living creature, animal (14)
ars, ártis (f) - art, skill (14)
arx, árcis (f) - citadel, stronghold (23)
as, ássis (m) - an as *(a small copper coin)* (31)
aúris, aúris (f) - ear (14)
cī́vis, cī́vis (m *or* **f)** - citizen (14)
fī́nēs, fī́nium (m) - boundaries, territory (21)
fī́nis, fī́nis (m) - end, limit, boundary; purpose (21)
gēns, géntis (f) - clan, race, nation, people (21)
hóstēs, hóstium (m) - the enemy (18)
hóstis, hóstis (m) - an enemy *(of the state)* (18)
ígnis, ígnis (m) - fire (22)
máre, máris (n) - sea (14)
mēns, méntis (f) - mind, thought, intention (16)
moénia, moénium (n. pl.) - walls of a city (29)
mōns, móntis (m) - mountain (20)
mors, mórtis (f) - death (14)
nā́vis, nā́vis (f) - ship, boat (21)
nox, nóctis (f) - night (26)
nū́bēs, nū́bis (f) - cloud (14)
pars, pártis (f) - part, share; direction (14)
urbs, úrbis (f) - city (14)
vī́rēs, vī́rium (f. pl.) - strength (14)
vīs, vīs (f) - force, power, violence (14)

4th Declension

córnū, córnūs (n) - horn (20)
cúrsus, cúrsūs (m) - running, race; course (28)
dómī (f) - at home (37)
dómō (f) - from home (37)
dómum (f) - (to) home (37)
dómus, dómūs, dómī (f) - house, home (37)
exércitus, exércitūs (m) - army (32)
frū́ctus, frū́ctūs (m) - fruit; profit, benefit, enjoyment (20)
génū, génūs (n) - knee (20)
mánus, mánūs (f) - hand; handwriting; band (20)
métus, métūs (m) - fear, dread, anxiety (20)
senā́tus, senā́tūs (m) - senate (20)
sḗnsus, sḗnsūs (m) - feeling, sense (20)
spī́ritus, spī́ritūs (m) - breath, breathing; spirit, soul (20)
vérsus, vérsūs (m) - line of verse (20)

5th Declension

díēs, diḗī (m) - day (22)
fī́dēs, fídeī (f) - faith, trust, trustworthiness, fidelity, promise, guarantee, protection (22)
rēs, réī (f) - thing, matter, property, business, affair (22)
rēs pū́blica, réī pū́blicae (f) - state, commonwealth, republic (22)
spēs, spéī (f) - hope (22)

Indeclinable

níhil - nothing (1)
sátis - enough (5)

Pronouns

áliquis, áliquid - someone, somebody, something (23)
égo, méī - I (11)
hic, haec, hoc - this; the latter; he, she, it, they (9)
ī́dem, éadem, ídem - the same (11)
ílle, ílla, íllud - that; the former; the famous; he, she, it, they (9)
ípse, ípsa, ípsum - myself, yourself, himself, herself, itself, *etc.,* the very, the actual (13)
is, éa, id - this, that; he, she, it (11)
íste, ísta, ístud - that of yours, that; such (as you have, as you speak of); *sometimes with contemptuous force, e.g.,* that despicable, that wretched (9)
quī, quae, quod - who, which, what, that (17)
quid - what (1)

quídam, quaédam, quíddam - a certain one or thing, someone, something (26)
quis, quid (*after* sī, nisi, nē, num) - anyone, anything, someone, something (33)
quis? quid? - who? whose? whom? what? which? (19)
quísque, quídque, cuiúsque, cuíque - each one, each person, each thing (13)
quísquis, quídquid - whoever, whatever (23)
súī - himself, herself, itself, themselves (13)
tū, túī - you *(sing.)* (11)

Adjectives

1st & 2nd Declension

acérbus, acérba, acérbum - harsh, bitter, grievous (12)
advérsus, advérsa, advérsum - opposite, adverse (34)
aéquus, aéqua, aéquum - level, even; calm; equal, just; favorable (22)
áliī . . . áliī - some . . . others (9)
álius, ália, áliud - other, another (9)
álter, áltera, álterum - the other (of two), second (9)
amī́cus, amī́ca, amī́cum - friendly (11)
antī́quus, antī́qua, antī́quum - ancient, old-time (2)
ásper, áspera, ásperum - rough, harsh (21)
avā́rus, avā́ra, avā́rum - greedy, avaricious (3)
beā́tus, beā́ta, beā́tum - happy, fortunate, blessed (10)
béllus, bélla, béllum - pretty, handsome, charming (4)
bónus, bóna, bónum - good, kind (4)
caécus, caéca, caécum - blind (17)
cándidus, cándida, cándidum - shining, bright, white; beautiful (33)
cā́rus, cā́ra, cā́rum - dear (11)
cértus, cérta, cértum - definite, sure, certain, reliable (19)
cḗterī, cḗterae, cḗtera - the remaining, the rest, the other, all the others (30)
clā́rus, clā́ra, clā́rum - clear, bright; renowned, famous, illustrious (18)
déxter, déxtra, déxtrum - right, right-hand (20)
dígnus, dígna, dígnum (+abl.) - worthy, worthy of (29)
dóctus, dócta, dóctum - taught, learned, skilled (13)
dū́rus, dū́ra, dū́rum - hard, harsh, rough, stern, unfeeling, hardy, difficult (29)
fī́rmus, fī́rma, fī́rmum - firm, strong; reliable (38)
fortūnā́tus, fortūnā́ta, fortūnā́tum - lucky, fortunate, happy (13)
géminus, gémina, géminum - twin (25)
Graécus, Graéca, Graécum - Greek (6)
grā́tus, grā́ta, grā́tum - pleasing, agreeable; grateful (37)
hūmā́nus, hūmā́na, hūmā́num - pertaining to man, human; humane, kind; refined, cultivated (4)
idṓneus, idṓnea, idṓneum - suitable, fit, appropriate (37)
immṓtus, immṓta, immṓtum - unmoved; unchanged; unrelenting (37)
incértus, incérta, incértum - uncertain, unsure, doubtful (22)
īnfī́rmus, īnfī́rma, īnfī́rmum - not strong, weak, feeble (38)
īrā́tus, īrā́ta, īrā́tum - angry (35)
iūcúndus, iūcúnda, iūcúndum - pleasant, delightful, agreeable, pleasing (16)
Latī́nus, Latī́na, Latī́num - Latin (22)
lī́ber, lī́bera, lī́berum - free (5)
lóngus, lónga, lóngum - long (16)
magnánimus, magnánima, magnánimum - great-hearted, brave, magnanimous (23)
mágnus, mágna, mágnum - large, great; important (2)
málus, mála, málum - bad, wicked, evil (4)
médius, média, médium - middle; the middle of (22)
mérus, méra, mérum - pure, undiluted (33)
méus, méa, méum - my (2)
míser, mísera, míserum - wretched, miserable, unfortunate (15)
mórtuus, mórtua, mórtuum - dead (28)
múltus, múlta, múltum - much, many (2)
neúter, neútra, neútrum - not either, neither (9)
nóster, nóstra, nóstrum - our, ours (5)
nóvus, nóva, nóvum - new; strange (7)
nū́llus, nū́lla, nū́llum - not any, no, none (9)
párvus, párva, párvum - small, little (4)
paúcī, paúcae, paúca - few, a few (3)
perpétuus, perpétua, perpétuum perpetual, lasting, uninterrupted, continuous (6)
plḗnus, plḗna, plḗnum - full, abundant, generous (6)

prī́mus, prī́ma, prī́mum - first, foremost, chief, principal (27)
prī́stinus, prī́stina, prī́stinum - ancient; former, previous (38)
pudī́cus, pudī́ca, pudī́cum - modest, chaste (26)
púlcher, púlchra, púlchrum - beautiful, handsome; fine (5)
quántus, quánta, quántum - how large, how great, how much (30)
rīdículus, rīdícula, rīdículum - laughable, ridiculous (30)
Rōmā́nus, Rōmā́na, Rōmā́num - Roman (3)
sálvus, sálva, sálvum - safe, sound (6)
sā́nus, sā́na, sā́num - sound, healthy, sane (5)
secúndus, secúnda, secúndum - second; favorable (6)
siníster, sinístra, sinístrum - left, left-hand; harmful, ill-omened (20)
sṓlus, sṓla, sṓlum - alone, only, the only (9)
stúltus, stúlta, stúltum - foolish (4)
supérbus, supérba, supérbum - arrogant, overbearing, haughty, proud (26)
súperus, súpera, súperum - above, upper (27)
súus, súa, súum - his own, her own, its own, their own (13)
tántus, tánta, tántum - so large, so great, of such a size (29)
tántus . . . quántus - just as much (many) . . . as (30)
tṓtus, tṓta, tṓtum - whole, entire (9)
túus, túa, túum - your *(sing.)* (2)
ū́llus, ū́lla, ū́llum - any (9)
últimus, última, últimum - farthest, extreme; last, final (25)
ū́nus, ū́na, ū́num - one, single, alone (9)
urbā́nus, urbā́na, urbā́num - of the city, urban; urbane, elegant (26)
úter, útra, útrum - either, which (of two) (9)
vḗrus, vḗra, vḗrum - true, real, proper (4)
véster, véstra, véstrum - your *(pl.)* (6)
vī́vus, vī́va, vī́vum - alive, living (30)

3rd Declension

ábsēns, ***gen.*** **abséntis** - absent, away (37)
ā́cer, ā́cris, ā́cre - sharp, keen, eager; severe, fierce (16)
brévis, bréve - short, small, brief (16)
céler, céleris, célere - swift, quick, rapid (16)
commū́nis, commū́ne - common, general, of / for the community (20)
diffícilis, diffícile - hard, difficult, troublesome (16)
dī́ligēns, ***gen.*** **dīligéntis** - diligent, careful (27)
dissímilis, dissímile - unlike, different (27)
dī́ves, ***gen.*** **dī́vitis** ***or*** **dī́tis** - rich, wealthy (32)
dúlcis, dúlce - sweet; pleasant, agreeable (16)
fácilis, fácile - easy; agreeable (16)
fḗlīx, ***gen.*** **fēlī́cis** - lucky, fortunate, happy (22)
férōx, ***gen.*** **ferṓcis** - fierce, savage (25)
fidḗlis, fidḗle - faithful, loyal (25)
fórtis, fórte - strong, brave (16)
grácilis, grácile - slender, thin (27)
grávis, gráve - heavy, weighty; serious, important; severe, grievous (19)
húmilis, húmile - lowly, humble (27)
immortā́lis, immortā́le - not subject to death, immortal (19)
íngēns, ***gen.*** **ingéntis** - huge (16)
lévis, léve - light; easy; slight, trivial (17)
máior, máius - greater; older (27)
medíocris, medíocre - ordinary, moderate, mediocre (31)
mīrā́bilis, mīrā́bile - amazing, wondrous, remarkable (38)
mortā́lis, mortā́le - mortal (18)
ómnis, ómne - every, all (16)
pār, ***gen.*** **páris (+dat.)** - equal, like (32)
paúper, ***gen.*** **paúperis** - of small means, poor (32)
pótēns, ***gen.*** **poténtis** - able, powerful, mighty, strong (16)
prī́nceps, ***gen.*** **prī́ncipis** - chief, foremost (28)
sápiēns, ***gen.*** **sapiéntis** - wise, judicious (25)
sénex, ***gen.*** **sénis** - old, aged (16)
símilis, símile (+gen. or dat.) - similar (to), like, resembling (27)
suā́vis, suā́ve - sweet (33)
sublī́mis, sublī́me - elevated, lofty; heroic, noble (38)
tā́lis, tā́le - such, of such a sort (34)
trī́stis, trī́ste - sad, sorrowful; joyless, grim, severe (26)
túrpis, túrpe - ugly; shameful, base, disgraceful (26)
ū́tilis, ū́tile - useful, advantageous (27)

Indeclinable Adjectives

quot - how many, as many as (27)
sátis - enough, sufficient (5)

Indefinite Adjective

quídam, quaédam, quóddam - a certain, some (26)

Interrogative Adjective

quī?, quae?, quod? - what? which? what kind of?; *(sometimes with exclamatory force)* what (a)! what sort of! (19)

Verbs

1st Conjugation

ádiuvō, adiuvā́re, adiū́vī, adiū́tum - to help, aid, assist; to please (4)
ámō, amā́re, amā́vī, amā́tum - to love, like (1)
appéllō, appellā́re, appellā́vī, appellā́tum - to speak to, address (as), call, name (14)
cḗnō, cēnā́re, cēnā́vī, cēnā́tum - to dine (5)
cṓgitō, cōgitā́re, cōgitā́vī, cōgitā́tum- to think, ponder, consider, plan (1)
cōnsérvō, cōnservā́re, cōnservā́vī, cōnservā́tum - to preserve, conserve, maintain (1)
créō, creā́re, creā́vī, creā́tum - to create (12)
cúlpō, culpā́re, culpā́vī, culpā́tum - to blame, censure (5)
cū́rō, cūrā́re, cūrā́vī, cūrā́tum - to care for, attend to; heal, cure; take care (36)
dḗdicō, dēdicā́re, dēdicā́vī, dēdicā́tum - to dedicate (28)
dēléctō, dēlectā́re, dēlectā́vī, dēlectā́tum - to delight, charm, please (19)
dēmṓnstrō, dēmōnstrā́re, dēmōnstrā́vī, dēmōnstrā́tum to point out, show, demonstrate (8)
dēsī́derō, dēsīderā́re, dēsīderā́vī, dēsīderā́tum - to desire, long for, miss (17)
dō, dáre, dédī, dátum - to give, offer (1)
dúbitō, dubitā́re, dubitā́vī, dubitā́tum - to doubt, hesitate (30)
ḗducō, ēducā́re, ēducā́vī, ēducā́tum - to bring up, educate (23)
érrō, errā́re, errā́vī, errā́tum - to wander; err, go astray, make a mistake, be mistaken (1)
exspéctō, exspectā́re, exspectā́vī, exspectā́tum - to look for, expect, await (15)
ímperō, imperā́re, imperā́vī, imperā́tum (+dat.) - to give orders to, command (35)
invī́tō, invītā́re, invītā́vī, invītā́tum - to entertain, invite, summon (26)
iúvō, iuvā́re, iū́vī, iū́tum - to help, aid, assist; to please (4)
labṓrō, labōrā́re, labōrā́vī, labōrā́tum - to labor; be in distress (21)
laúdō, laudā́re, laudā́vī, laudā́tum - to praise (1)
lī́berō, līberā́re, līberā́vī, līberā́tum - to free, liberate (19)
mū́tō, mūtā́re, mūtā́vī, mūtā́tum to change, alter; exchange (14)
nā́rrō, nārrā́re, nārrā́vī, nārrā́tum - to tell, report, narrate (24)
nā́vigō, nāvigā́re, nāvigā́vī, nāvigā́tum - to sail, navigate (17)
nécō, necā́re, necā́vī, necā́tum - to murder, kill (7)
négō, negā́re, negā́vī, negā́tum to deny, say that . . . not (25)
nū́ntiō, nūntiā́re, nūntiā́vī, nūntiā́tum - to announce, report, relate (25)
obléctō, oblectā́re, oblectā́vī, oblectā́tum - to please, amuse, delight; pass time pleasantly (36)
ṓrō, ōrā́re, ōrā́vī, ōrā́tum - to speak, plead; beg, beseech, entreat, pray (36)
párō, parā́re, parā́vī, parā́tum - to prepare, provide; get, obtain (19)
praéstō, praestā́re, praéstitī, praéstitum - to excel; exhibit, show, offer, supply, furnish (28)
próbō, probā́re, probā́vī, probā́tum - to approve, recommend; test (27)
prōnū́ntiō, prōnūntiā́re, prōnūntiā́vī, prōnūntiā́tum - to proclaim, announce; declaim; pronounce (20)
púgnō, pugnā́re, pugnā́vī, pugnā́tum - to fight (29)
pútō, putā́re, putā́vī, putā́tum - to reckon, suppose, judge, think, imagine (25)
récitō, recitā́re, recitā́vī, recitā́tum - to read aloud, recite (17)
récreō, recreā́re, recreā́vī, recreā́tum - to restore, revive; refresh, cheer (36)
recū́sō, recūsā́re, recūsā́vī, recūsā́tum - to refuse (33)
rógō, rogā́re, rogā́vī, rogā́tum - to ask (30)
sátiō, satiā́re, satiā́vī, satiā́tum - to satisfy, sate (3)

serḗnō, serēnā́re, serēnā́vī, serēnā́tum - to make clear, brighten; cheer up, soothe (36)
sérvō, servā́re, servā́vī, servā́tum - to preserve, save, keep, guard (1)
spéctō, spectā́re, spectā́vī, spectā́tum - to look at, see (34)
spḗrō, spērā́re, spērā́vī, spērā́tum - to hope for, hope (25)
stō, stā́re, stétī, státum - to stand, stand still *or* firm (13)
súperō, superā́re, superā́vī, superā́tum - to be above, have the upper hand, surpass; overcome, conquer (5)
tólerō, tolerā́re, tolerā́vī, tolerā́tum - to bear, endure (6)
vī́tō, vītā́re, vītā́vī, vītā́tum - to avoid, shun (14)
vócō, vocā́re, vocā́vī, vocā́tum - to call, summon (1)

2nd Conjugation
aúdeō, audḗre, aúsus sum - to dare (7)
cáreō, carḗre, cáruī, caritū́rum (+abl.) - to be without, be deprived of, want, lack; be free from (20)
contíneō, continḗre, contínuī, conténtum - to hold together, contain, keep, enclose, restrain (21)
dḗbeō, dēbḗre, dḗbuī, dḗbitum - to owe; ought, must, should (1)
dḗleō, dēlḗre, dēlḗvī, dēlḗtum - to destroy, wipe out, erase (17)
dóceō, docḗre, dócuī, dóctum - to teach (8)
dóleō, dolḗre, dóluī, dolitū́rum - to grieve, suffer; hurt, give pain (31)
égeō, egḗre, éguī (+ abl. or gen.) - to need, lack, want (28)
éxpleō, explḗre, explḗvī, explḗtum - to fill, fill up, complete (28)
fóveō, fovḗre, fṓvī, fṓtum - to comfort, nurture, cherish (35)
gaúdeō, gaudḗre, gāvī́sus sum - to be glad, rejoice (23)
hábeō, habḗre, hábuī, hábitum - to have, hold, possess; consider, regard (3)
iáceō, iacḗre, iácuī - to lie; lie prostrate; lie dead (25)
invídeō, invidḗre, invī́dī, invī́sum to be envious; to look at with envy, envy, be jealous of (+dat.) (31)
iúbeō, iubḗre, iússī, iússum - to bid, order, command (21)
máneō, manḗre, mā́nsī, mā́nsum - to remain, stay, stay behind, abide, continue (5)
mísceō, miscḗre, míscuī, míxtum to mix, stir up, disturb (18)
móneō, monḗre, mónuī, mónitum - to remind, advise, warn (1)
móveō, movḗre, mṓvī, mṓtum - to move; arouse, affect (18)
nóceō, nocḗre, nócuī, nócitum (+dat.) - to do harm to, harm, injure (35)
pā́reō, pārḗre, pā́ruī (+dat.) - to be obedient to, obey (35)
páteō, patḗre, pátuī - to be open, lie open; be accessible; be evident (32)
persuā́deō, persuādḗre, persuā́sī, persuā́sum (+dat.) to succeed in urging, persuade, convince (35)
pláceō, placḗre, plácuī, plácitum (+dat.) - to be pleasing to, please (35)
praébeō, praebḗre, praébuī, praébitum - to offer, provide (32)
prohíbeō, prohibḗre, prohíbuī, prohíbitum - to keep (back), prevent, hinder, restrain, prohibit (20)
remáneō, remanḗre, remā́nsī, remā́nsum - to remain, stay, stay behind, abide, continue (5)
respóndeō, respondḗre, respóndī, respṓnsum - to answer (29)
rī́deō, rīdḗre, rī́sī, rī́sum - to laugh, laugh at (24)
sálvē, salvḗte - hello, greetings (1)
sálveō, salvḗre - to be well, be in good health (1)
sédeō, sedḗre, sḗdī, séssum - to sit (34)
sóleō, solḗre, sólitus sum - to be accustomed (37)
stúdeō, studḗre, stúduī (+dat.) - to direct one's zeal to, be eager for, study (35)
subrī́deō, subrīdḗre, subrī́sī, subrī́sum - to smile (down) upon (35)
táceō, tacḗre, tácuī, tácitum - to be silent, leave unmentioned (28)
téneō, tenḗre, ténuī, téntum - to hold, keep, possess; restrain (14)
térreō, terrḗre, térruī, térritum - to frighten, terrify (1)
tímeō, timḗre, tímuī - to fear, be afraid (of) (15)
válē, valḗte - good-bye, farewell (1)
váleō, valḗre, váluī, valitū́rum - to be strong, have power; be well (1)

vídeō, vidḗre, vī́dī, vī́sum - to see; observe, understand (1)
vídeor, vidḗrī, vī́sus sum - to be seen, seem, appear (18)

3rd Conjugation

accḗdō, accḗdere, accéssī, accéssum - to come (to), approach (36)
admíttō, admíttere, admī́sī, admíssum - to admit, receive, let in (17)
ágō, ágere, ḗgī, ā́ctum - to drive, lead, do, act; pass, spend *(life or time)* (8)
álō, álere, áluī, áltum - to nourish, support, sustain, increase; cherish (13)
āmíttō, āmíttere, āmī́sī, āmíssum - to send away; lose, let go (12)
antepṓnō, antepṓnere, antepósuī, antepósitum - to put before, prefer (35)
āvértō, āvértere, āvértī, āvérsum - to turn away, avert (23)
bíbō, bíbere, bíbī - to drink (30)
cádō, cádere, cécidī, cāsū́rum - to fall (12)
cárpō, cárpere, cárpsī, cárptum to harvest, pluck; seize (36)
cḗdō, cḗdere, céssī, céssum - to go, withdraw; yield to, grant, submit (28)
cérnō, cérnere, crḗvī, crḗtum - to distinguish, discern, perceive (22)
cognṓscō, cognṓscere, cognṓvī, cógnitum - to become acquainted with, learn, recognize; know *(in perfect tenses)* (30)
cṓgō, cṓgere, coḗgī, coā́ctum - to drive *or* bring together, force, compel (36)
commíttō, commíttere, commī́sī, commíssum - to entrust, commit (15)
comprehéndō, comprehéndere, comprehéndī, comprehḗnsum - to grasp, seize, arrest; comprehend, understand (30)
cóndō, cóndere, cóndidī, cónditum - to put together *or* into, store; found, establish (29)
cōnsū́mō, cōnsū́mere, cōnsū́mpsī, cōnsū́mptum - to consume, use up (30)
contémnō, contémnere, contémpsī, contémptum - to despise, scorn (36)
conténdō, conténdere, conténdī, conténtum - to strive, struggle, contend; hasten (29)
contúndō, contúndere, cóntudī, contū́sum - to beat, crush, bruise, destroy (36)
crḗdō, crḗdere, crḗdidī, crḗditum to believe, trust (25)
crḗscō, crḗscere, crḗvī, crḗtum - to increase (34)
cúrrō, cúrrere, cucúrrī, cúrsum - to run, rush, move quickly (14)
dēcérnō, dēcérnere, dēcrḗvī, dēcrḗtum - to decide, settle, decree (36)
dēféndō, dēféndere, dēféndī, dēfḗnsum - to ward off; defend, protect (20)
dī́cō, dī́cere, dī́xī, díctum - to say, tell, speak; name, call (10)
dī́ligō, dīlígere, dīléxī, dīlḗctum - to esteem, love (13)
discḗdō, discḗdere, discéssī, discéssum - to go away, depart (20)
díscō, díscere, dídicī - to learn (8)
dū́cō, dū́cere, dū́xī, dúctum - to lead; consider, regard; prolong (8)
éxigō, exígere, exḗgī, exā́ctum - to drive out, force out, exact; drive through, complete, perfect (36)
expéllō, expéllere, éxpulī, expúlsum - to drive out, expel, banish (24)
expṓnō, expṓnere, expósuī, expósitum - to set forth, explain, expose (30)
flúō, flúere, flū́xī, flū́xum - to flow (18)
gérō, gérere, géssī, géstum - to carry; carry on, manage, conduct, wage, accomplish, perform (8)
ignṓscō, ignṓscere, ignṓvī, ignṓtum (+dat.) - to grant pardon to, forgive (35)
intéllegō, intellégere, intellḗxī, intellḗctum - to understand (11)
iúngō, iúngere, iū́nxī, iū́nctum - to join (13)
légō, légere, lḗgī, lḗctum - to pick out, choose; read (18)
métuō, metúere, métuī - to fear, dread; be afraid for (+dat.) (38)
mínuō, minúere, mínuī, minū́tum - to lessen, diminish (30)
míttō, míttere, mī́sī, míssum - to send, let go (11)
néglegō, neglégere, neglḗxī, neglḗctum - to neglect, disregard (17)
nṓscō, nṓscere, nṓvī, nṓtum - to become acquainted with, learn, recognize; know *(in perfect tenses)* (30)
nū́bō, nū́bere, nū́psī, nū́ptum (+dat.) - to cover, veil; to be married to, marry (35)

óccidō, occídere, óccidī, occā́sum - to fall down; die; set (31)

ópprimō, opprímere, oppréssī, oppréssum - to suppress, overwhelm, overpower, check (23)

osténdō, osténdere, osténdī, osténtum - to exhibit, show, display (23)

párcō, párcere, pepércī, parsū́rum (+dat.) - to be lenient to, spare (35)

péllō, péllere, pépulī, púlsum - to strike, push; drive out, banish (24)

pétō, pétere, petī́vī, petī́tum - to seek, aim at, beg, beseech (23)

pṓnō, pṓnere, pósuī, pósitum - to put, place, set (27)

prémō, prémere, préssī, préssum - to press; press hard, pursue (23)

prōmíttō, prōmíttere, prōmī́sī, prōmíssum - to send forth; promise (32)

quaérō, quaérere, quaesī́vī, quaesī́tum - to seek, look for, strive for; ask, inquire, inquire into (24)

recognṓscō, recognṓscere, recognṓvī, recógnitum - to recognize, recollect (38)

régō, régere, rḗxī, rḗctum - to rule, guide, direct (16)

relínquō, relínquere, relī́quī, relíctum - to leave behind, leave, abandon, desert (21)

requiḗscō, requiḗscere, requiḗvī, requiḗtum - to rest (37)

requī́rō, requī́rere, requīsī́vī, requīsī́tum - to seek, ask for; miss, need, require (36)

revértō, revértere, revértī, revérsum - turn back (23)

scrī́bō, scrī́bere, scrī́psī, scrī́ptum to write, compose (8)

súrgō, súrgere, surrḗxī, surrḗctum - to get up, arise (29)

suspéndō, suspéndere, suspéndī, suspḗnsum - to hang up, suspend; interrupt (38)

tángō, tángere, tétigī, tā́ctum - to touch (21)

tóllō, tóllere, sústulī, sublā́tum - to raise, lift up; take away, remove, destroy (22)

trā́dō, trā́dere, trā́didī, trā́ditum to give over, surrender; hand down, transmit, teach (33)

tráhō, tráhere, trā́xī, tráctum - to draw, drag; derive, acquire (8)

vḗndō, vḗndere, vḗndidī, vḗnditum - to sell (38)

vértō, vértere, vértī, vérsum - to turn; change (23)

víncō, víncere, vī́cī, víctum - to conquer, overcome (8)

vī́vō, vī́vere, vī́xī, vī́ctum - to live (10)

3rd Conjugation -iō

accípiō, accípere, accḗpī, accéptum - to take *(to one's self)*, receive, accept (24)

cápiō, cápere, cḗpī, cáptum - to take, capture, seize, get (10)

cúpiō, cúpere, cupī́vī, cupī́tum - to desire, wish, long for (17)

ērípiō, ērípere, ērípuī, ēréptum - to snatch away, take away; rescue (22)

excípiō, excípere, excḗpī, excéptum - to take out, except; take, receive, capture (24)

fáciō, fácere, fḗcī, fáctum - to make, do, accomplish (10)

fúgiō, fúgere, fū́gī, fugitū́rum - to flee, hurry away; escape; go into exile; avoid, shun (10)

iáciō, iácere, iḗcī, iáctum - to throw, hurl (15)

incípiō, incípere, incḗpī, incéptum - to begin (17)

interfíciō, interfícere, interfḗcī, interféctum - to kill, murder (37)

patefáciō, patefácere, patefḗcī, patefáctum - to make open, open; disclose, expose (25)

rápiō, rápere, rápuī, ráptum - to seize, snatch, carry away (21)

recípiō, recípere, recḗpī, recéptum - to take back, regain; admit, receive (24)

sápiō, sápere, sapī́vī - to have good taste; have good sense, be wise (35)

suscípiō, suscípere, suscḗpī, suscéptum - to undertake (25)

4th Conjugation

aúdiō, audī́re, audī́vī, audī́tum - to hear, listen to (10)

dórmiō, dormī́re, dormī́vī, dormī́tum - to sleep (31)

impédiō, impedī́re, impedī́vī, impedī́tum - to impede, hinder, prevent (38)

invéniō, invenī́re, invḗnī, invéntum - to come upon, find (10)

mólliō, mollī́re, mollī́vī, mollī́tum to soften; make calm *or* less hostile (29)

nésciō, nescī́re, nescī́vī, nescī́tum - to not know, be ignorant (25)

scíō, scī́re, scī́vī, scī́tum - to know (21)

séntiō, sentī́re, sḗnsī, sḗnsum - to feel, perceive, think, experience (11)

sérviō, servī́re, servī́vī, servī́tum (+dat.) - to be a slave to, serve (35)
véniō, venī́re, vḗnī, véntum - to come (10)

Irregular

ábeō, abī́re, ábiī, ábitum - to go away, depart, leave (37)
ádeō, adī́re, ádiī, áditum - to go to, approach (37)
ádferō, adférre, áttulī, allā́tum - to bring to (31)
cṓnferō, cōnférre, cóntulī, collā́tum - to bring together, compare; confer, bestow (31)
éō, ī́re, iī, ī́tum - to go (37)
éxeō, exī́re, éxiī, éxitum - to go out, exit (37)
férō, férre, túlī, lā́tum - to bear, carry, bring; suffer, endure, tolerate; say, report (31)
fī́ō, fíerī, fáctus sum - to occur, happen; become; be made, be done (36)
íneō, inī́re, íniī, ínitum - to enter into, begin (37)
mā́lō, mā́lle, mā́luī - to want (something) more, instead; prefer (32)
nṓlō, nṓlle, nṓluī - to not . . . wish, be unwilling (32)
óbeō, obī́re, óbiī, óbitum - to go up against, meet; die (37)
ófferō, offérre, óbtulī, oblā́tum - to offer (31)
péreō, perī́re, périī, péritum - to pass away, be destroyed, perish (37)
póssum, pósse, pótuī - to be able, can, could, have power (6)
rédeō, redī́re, rédiī, réditum - to go back, return (37)
réferō, reférre, réttulī, relā́tum - to carry back, bring back; repeat, answer, report (31)
sum, ésse, fúī, futū́rum - to be, exist (4)
vólō, vélle, vóluī - to wish, want, be willing, will (32)

Deponent

árbitror, arbitrā́rī, arbitrā́tus sum to judge, think (34)
cṓnor, cōnā́rī, cōnā́tus sum - to try, attempt (34)
ēgrédior, ḗgredī, ēgréssus sum - to go out (34)
fáteor, fatḗrī, fássus sum - to confess, admit (34)
hórtor, hortā́rī, hortā́tus sum - to encourage, urge (34)
lóquor, lóquī, locū́tus sum - to say, speak, tell (34)
mī́ror, mīrā́rī, mīrā́tus sum - to marvel at, admire, wonder (35)
mṓlior, mōlī́rī, mōlī́tus sum - to work at, build, undertake, plan (34)
mórior, mórī, mórtuus sum - to die (34)
nā́scor, nā́scī, nā́tus sum - to be born; spring forth, arrive (34)
pátior, pátī, pássus sum - to suffer, endure; permit (34)
peregrī́nor, peregrīnā́rī, peregrīnā́tus sum - to travel abroad, wander (37)
proficī́scor, proficī́scī, proféctus sum - to set out, start (34)
quéror, quérī, quéstus sum - to complain, lament (38)
rū́sticor, rūsticā́rī, rūsticā́tus sum to live in the country (34)
séquor, séquī, secū́tus sum - to follow (34)
ū́tor, ū́tī, ū́sus sum (+abl.) - to use; enjoy, experience (34)

Defective

ā́it, ā́iunt - he says, they say, assert (25)
coépī, coepísse, coéptum - began (17)
ínquit - he says *or* said (22)
ṓdī, ōdísse, ōsū́rum - to hate (20)

Impersonal

lícet, licḗre, lícuit (+dat. +infin.) - it is permitted *(for someone to do something)*, one may (37)

Adverbs

ánte (+acc.) - before, previously (13)
béne - well, satisfactorily, quite (11)
cíto - quickly (17)
cōtī́diē - daily, every day (36)
crās - tomorrow (5)
cūr - why (18)
déhinc - then, next (25)
deínde - thereupon, next, then (18)
dḗnique - at last, finally, lastly (29)
díū - long, for a long time (12)
étiam - even, also (11)
fórīs - out of doors, outside (37)
fortásse - perhaps (36)
fū́rtim - stealthily, secretly (30)
héri - yesterday (5)
hīc - here (25)
hódiē - today (3)
iam - now, already, soon (19)
íbi - there (6)
íta - so, thus (29)
ítaque - and so, therefore (15)
íterum - again, a second time (21)
libénter - with pleasure, gladly (38)

mox - soon (30)
nē . . . quídem - not . . . even (29)
nímis, nímium - too, too much, excessively; *(in a positive sense, esp. with adjectives and adverbs)* exceedingly, very (9)
nōn - not (1)
númquam - never (8)
nunc - now, at present (6)
nū́per - recently (12)
ṓlim - once (upon a time), long ago, formerly; some day, in the future (13)
pósteā - afterwards (24)
prī́mō - at first, at the beginning (30)
prṓtinus - immediately (22)
quam - how (16)
quam - than *(after comparatives)*; as . . . as possible *(with superlatives)* (26)
quándō - when (5)
quā́rē - because of which thing *(lit.)*; therefore, wherefore, why (6)
quídem - indeed, certainly, at least, even (29)
quóndam - formerly, once (22)
quóque - also, too (17)
repénte - suddenly (30)
saépe - often (1)
sátis - enough, sufficiently (5)
sémel - a single time, once, once and for all, simultaneously (31)
sémper - always (3)
sīc - so, thus (29)
súbitō - suddenly (33)
tam - so, to such a degree (29)
tam . . . quam - so . . . as (29)
támen - nevertheless, still (8)
tamquam - as it were, as if, so to speak (29)
tántum - only (26)
tum - then, at that time; thereupon, in the next place (5)
úbi - where, when (6)
últrā - on the other side of, beyond (22)
úmquam - ever, at any time (23)
únde - whence, from what *or* which place, from which, from whom (30)
úsque - all the way, up (to), even (to), continuously, always (31)
vḗrō - in truth, indeed, to be sure, however (29)

Conjunctions

at - but; but, mind you; but, you say (19)
átque, ac - and also, and even, and in fact (21)
aut - or (17)
aut . . . aut - either . . . or (17)
aútem - however; moreover (11)
cum (+indic.) - when (31)
cum (+subj.) - when, since, although (31)
dum - while, as long as, at the same time that; *or* until *(+subjunctive)* (8)
dúmmodo (+subj.) - provided that, so long as (32)
énim - for, in fact, truly (9)
et - and; even (2)
et . . . et - both . . . and (2)
étsī - even if, although (38)
ígitur - therefore, consequently (5)
nam - for (13)
nē - not; in order that . . . not, that . . . not, in order not to (28)
néque, nec - and not, nor (11)
néque . . . néque, nec . . . nec - neither . . . nor (11)
nísi - if . . . not, unless; except (19)
quod - because (11)
quóniam - since, inasmuch as (10)
sed - but (2)
sī - if (1)
ut (+indic.) - as, just as, when (24)
ut (+ subj.) - in order that, so that, that, in order to, so as to, to (28)
útrum . . . an - whether . . . or (30)

Prepositions

ab, ā (+abl.) - away from, from; by (14)
ad (+acc.) - to, up to, near to (8)
ánte (+acc.) - before *(in place or time)*, in front of (13)
ápud (+acc.) - among, in the presence of, at the house of (31)
cóntrā (+acc.) - against (19)
cum (+abl.) - with (10)
dē (+abl.) - down from, from; concerning, about (3)
érga (+acc.) - toward (38)
ex, ē (abl.+) - out of, from, from within; by reason of, on account of; of *(after cardinal numerals)* (8)
in (+acc.) - into, toward; against (9)
in (+abl.) - in, on (3)
ínter (+acc.) - between, among (15)
per (+acc.) - through; by *(with reflexive pronoun)* (13)
post (+acc.) - after, behind (7)
prae (+abl.) - in front of, before (26)
prō (+abl.) - in front of, before, on behalf of, for the sake of, in return for, instead of, for, as (12)
própter (+acc.) - on account of, because of (5)
síne (+abl.) - without (2)
sub (+abl. w/ verbs of rest *or* **+acc. w/ verbs of motion)** - under, up under, close to, down to/into, to/at the foot of (7)

trāns (+acc.) - across (14)
últrā (adv. and prep. +acc.) - on the other side of, beyond (22)

Interjections

heu - ah!, alas! (33)
ō - O!, Oh! (2)
vae (often +dat. or acc.) - alas, woe to (34)

Idioms

amā́bō tē - please (1)
grā́tiās ágere (+dat.) - to thank someone; to give thanks to (8)
mḗnsa secúnda (f) - dessert (26)
nōn sṓlum . . . sed étiam - not only . . . but also (9)
poénās dáre - to pay the penalty (2)
sē cōnférre - to go (31)
sī quándō - if ever (5)

Prefix

re-, red- - again, back (24)

Suffixes

-ne – interrogative suffix attached to the first word of a sentence, typically the verb or another word on which the question hinges, to introduce a question whose answer is uncertain (5)
-que - and *(enclitic conjunction; appended to the second of two words to be joined)* (6)
-ve - or (33)

Numerals

Cardinal - ū́nus *to* vīgíntī quī́nque (15)
Ordinal - prī́mus *to* duodécimus (15)

----

céntum - a hundred (15)
mī́lia, mī́lium (n. pl.) - thousands (15)
mī́lle - thousand (15)

Chapter 39

Nouns

1st Declension

adulēscéntia, adulēscéntiae (f) - youth, young manhood; youthfulness (5)
agrícola, agrícolae (m) - farmer (3)
amíca, amícae (f) - friend (female) (3)
amīcítia, amīcítiae (f) - friendship (10)
ánima, ánimae (f) - air *(breathed by an animal),* breath; soul, spirit (34)
áqua, áquae (f) - water (14)
Ásia, Ásiae (f) - Asia (12)
Athḗnae, Athēnā́rum (f. pl.) - Athens (37)
cása, cásae (f) - house, cottage, hut (21)
caúsa, caúsae (f) - cause, reason; case, situation (21)
caúsā (abl. + preceding gen.) - for the sake of, on account of (21)
cḗna, cḗnae (f) - dinner (26)
clēméntia, clēméntiae (f) - mildness, gentleness, mercy (16)
cṓpia, cṓpiae (f) - abundance, supply (8)
cṓpiae, cōpiā́rum (f) - supplies, troops, forces (8)
cúlpa, cúlpae (f) - fault, blame (5)
cū́ra, cū́rae (f) - care, attention, caution, anxiety (4)
custṓdia, custṓdiae (f) - protection, custody; guards *(pl.)* (32)
déa, déae (f) - goddess (6)
discípula, discípulae (f) - learner, pupil, student (female) (6)
dīvítiae, dīvitiā́rum (f. pl.) - riches, wealth (13)
fā́bula, fā́bulae (f) - story, tale; play (24)
fā́ma, fā́mae (f) - rumor, report; fame, reputation (2)
família, famíliae (f) - household, family (19)
fḗmina, fḗminae (f) - woman (3)
fenéstra, fenéstrae (f) - window (21)
fī́lia, fī́liae (f) - daughter (3)
fṓrma, fṓrmae (f) - form, shape; beauty (2)
fortū́na, fortū́nae (f) - fortune, luck (2)
glṓria, glṓriae (f) - glory, fame (5)
Graécia, Graéciae (f) - Greece (19)
hásta, hástae (f) - spear (23)
hṓra, hṓrae (f) - hour, time (10)
iā́nua, iā́nuae (f) - door (35)
iniū́ria, iniū́riae (f) - injustice, injury, wrong (39)
īnsídiae, īnsidiā́rum (f) - ambush, plot, treachery (6)
ī́nsula, ī́nsulae (f) - island (23)
invídia, invídiae (f) - envy, jealousy, hatred (31)
ī́ra, ī́rae (f) - ire, anger (2)
Itália, Itáliae (f) - Italy (15)
língua, línguae (f) - tongue; language (25)
líttera, lítterae (f) - a letter of the alphabet (7)
lítterae, litterā́rum (f) - a letter (epistle), literature (7)
lū́na, lū́nae (f) - moon (28)
magístra, magístrae (f) - schoolmistress, teacher, mistress (4)
médica, médicae (f) - doctor, physician (female) (12)
memória, memóriae (f) - memory, recollection (15)
mḗnsa, mḗnsae (f) - table; dining; dish, course (26)
móra, mórae (f) - delay (4)
nā́ta, nā́tae (f) - daughter (29)
nātū́ra, nātū́rae (f) - nature (10)
naúta, naútae (m) - sailor (2)
patiéntia, patiéntiae (f) - suffering; patience, endurance (12)
pátria, pátriae (f) - fatherland, native land, (one's) country (2)
pecū́nia, pecū́niae (f) - money (2)
philósopha, philósophae (f) - philosopher (female) (33)
philosóphia, philosóphiae (f) - philosophy (2)
poéna, poénae (f) - penalty, punishment (2)
poḗta, poḗtae (m) - poet (2)
pórta, pórtae (f) - gate, entrance (2)
puélla, puéllae (f) - girl (2)
rēgī́na, rēgī́nae (f) - queen (7)
Rṓma, Rṓmae (f) - Rome (14)
rósa, rósae (f) - rose (2)
sapiéntia, sapiéntiae (f) - wisdom (3)
sátura, sáturae (f) - satire (16)
sciéntia, sciéntiae (f) - knowledge (18)
senténtia, senténtiae (f) - feeling, thought, opinion, vote, sentence (2)
sérva, sérvae (f) - slave (female) (24)
stḗlla, stḗllae (f) - star, planet (28)
Syrācū́sae, Syrācūsā́rum (f. pl.) - Syracuse (37)
térra, térrae (f) - earth, ground, land, country (7)
Trṓia, Trṓiae (f) - Troy (21)
túrba, túrbae (f) - uproar, disturbance; mob, crowd, multitude (14)
vía, víae (f) - way, road, street (10)

vīcī́na, vīcī́nae (f) - neighbor (female) (21)
victṓria, victṓriae (f) - victory (8)
vī́ta, vī́tae (f) - life; mode of life (2)

2nd Declension

aedifícium, aedifíciī (n) - building, structure (39)
áger, ágrī (m) - field, farm (3)
amī́cus, amī́cī (m) - friend (male) (3)
ánimī, animṓrum (m) - high spirits, pride, courage (5)
ánimus, ánimī (m) - soul, spirit, mind (5)
ánnus, ánnī (m) - year (12)
argūméntum, argūméntī (n) - proof, evidence, argument (19)
árma, armṓrum (n. pl.) - arms, weapons (28)
auxílium, auxíliī (n) - aid, help (31)
bā́sium, bā́siī (n) - kiss (4)
béllum, béllī (n) - war (4)
benefícium, benefíciī (n) - benefit, kindness; favor (19)
caélum, caélī (n) - sky, heaven (5)
coniūrā́tī, coniūrātṓrum (m. pl.) - conspirators (20)
cōnsílium, cōnsíliī (n) - plan, purpose, counsel, advice, judgment, wisdom (4)
déus, déī (m) - god (6)
dígitus, dígitī (m) - finger, toe (31)
discípulus, discípulī (m) - learner, pupil, student (male) (6)
dṓnum, dṓnī (n) - gift, present (4)
elephántus, elephántī (m and f) - elephant (31)
équus, équī (m) - horse (23)
exítium, exítiī (n) - destruction, ruin (4)
exsílium, exsíliī (n) - exile, banishment (31)
fáctum, fáctī (n) - deed, act, achievement (13)
fā́tum, fā́tī (n) - fate; death (29)
férrum, férrī (n) - iron; sword (22)
fī́lius, fī́liī (m) - son (3)
fórum, fórī (n) - marketplace, forum (26)
Graécus, Graécī (m) - a Greek (6)
húmus, húmī (f) - ground, earth; soil (37)
impérium, impériī (n) - power to command, supreme power, authority, command, control (24)
ingénium, ingéniī (n) - nature, innate talent (29)
inítium, inítiī (n) - beginning, commencement (33)
iūdícium, iūdíciī (n) - judgment, decision, opinion; trial (19)
libéllus, libéllī (m) - little book (17)
líber, líbrī (m) - book (6)
lóca, locṓrum (n) - places, region (9)
lócī, locṓrum (m) - passages in literature (9)
lócus, lócī (m) - place; passage in literature (9)
lū́dus, lū́dī (m) - game, sport; school (18)
magíster, magístrī (m) - schoolmaster, teacher, master (4)
médicus, médicī (m) - doctor, physician (male) (12)
módus, módī (m) - measure, bound, limit; manner, method, mode, way (22)
mórbus, mórbī (m) - disease, sickness (9)
múndus, múndī (m) - world, universe (21)
númerus, númerī (m) - number (3)
óculus, óculī (m) - eye (4)
ódium, ódiī (n) - hatred (38)
offícium, offíciī (n) - duty, service (4)
ṓsculum, ṓsculī (n) - kiss (29)
ṓtium, ṓtiī (n) - leisure, peace (4)
perfúgium, perfúgiī (n) - refuge, shelter (24)
perī́culum, perī́culī (n) - danger, risk (4)
philósophus, philósophī (m) - philosopher (male) (33)
pópulus, pópulī (m) - the people, a people, a nation (3)
praémium, praémiī (n) - reward, prize (35)
prīncípium, prīncípiī (n) - beginning (12)
púer, púerī (m) - boy; boys, children *(pl.)* (3)
remédium, remédiī (n) - cure, remedy (4)
sérvus, sérvī (m) - slave (male) (24)
sígnum, sígnī (n) - sign, signal, indication; seal (13)
sōlā́cium, sōlā́ciī (n) - comfort, relief (24)
sómnus, sómnī (m) - sleep (26)
spéculum, spéculī (n) - mirror (33)
stúdium, stúdiī (n) - eagerness, zeal, pursuit, study (9)
stúltus, stúltī (m) - a fool (4)
súperī, superṓrum (m. pl.) - the gods (27)
tyránnus, tyránnī (m) - absolute ruler, tyrant (6)
véntus, véntī (m) - wind (39)
vérbum, vérbī (n) - word (5)
vīcī́nus, vīcī́nī (m) - neighbor (male) (21)
vínculum, vínculī (n) - bond, chain, fetter (36)
vī́num, vī́nī (n) - wine (31)
vir, vírī (m) - man, hero (3)
vítium, vítiī (n) - fault, crime, vice (6)
vúlgus, vúlgī (n) - the common people, mob, rabble (21)

3rd Declension

aduléscēns, adulēscéntis (m *or* f) - young man *or* woman (12)
aéstās, aestátis (f) - summer (35)
aétās, aetátis (f) - period of life, life, age, an age, time (16)
ámor, amóris (m) - love (7)
árbor, árboris (f) - tree (38)
aúctor, auctóris (m) - increaser; author, originator (19)
audítor, audītóris (m) - hearer, listener, member of an audience (16)
Caésar, Caésaris (m) - Caesar (12)
cáput, cápitis (n) - head; leader; beginning; life; heading; chapter (11)
cármen, cárminis (n) - song, poem (7)
Carthágō, Carthāginis (f) - Carthage (24)
Cícerō, Cicerónis (m) - (Marcus Tullius) Cicero (8)
cívitās, cīvitátis (f) - state, citizenship (7)
cónsul, cónsulis (m) - consul (11)
córpus, córporis (n) - body (7)
cupíditās, cupiditátis (f) - desire, longing, passion; cupidity, avarice (10)
cupídō, cupídinis (f) - desire, compassion (36)
dēlectátiō, dēlectātiónis (f) - delight, pleasure, enjoyment (27)
dígnitās, dignitátis (f) - merit, prestige, dignity (38)
dólor, dolóris (m) - pain, grief (38)
dux, dúcis (m) - leader, guide; commander, general (23)
flúmen, flúminis (n) - river (18)
fráter, frátris (m) - brother (8)
génus, géneris (n) - origin; kind, type, sort, class (18)
hómō, hóminis (m) - human being, man (7)
hónor, honóris (m) - honor, esteem; public office (30)
imperátor, imperātóris (m) - general, commander-in-chief, emperor (24)
íter, itíneris (n) - journey; route, road (37)
iúdex, iúdicis (m) - judge, juror (19)
iūs, iúris (n) - right, justice, law (14)
lábor, labóris (m)- labor, work, toil; a work, production (7)
laus, laúdis (f) - praise, glory, fame (8)
léctor, lēctóris (m) - reader (male) (36)
léctrīx, lēctrícis (f) - reader (female) (36)
lēx, légis (f) - law, statute (26)
lībértās, lībertátis (f) - liberty (8)
límen, líminis (n) - threshold (26)
lítus, lítoris (n) - shore, coast (23)
lūx, lúcis (f) - light (26)
maiórēs, maiórum (m. pl.) - ancestors (27)
máter, mátris (f) - mother (12)
míles, mílitis (m) - soldier (23)
mórēs, mórum (m) - habits, morals, character (7)
mōs, móris (m) - habit, custom, manner (7)
múlier, mulíeris (f) - woman (39)
némō, nūllíus, néminī, néminem, núllō, núllā (m *or* f) - no one, nobody (11)
népōs, nepótis (m) - grandson, descendant (27)
nómen, nóminis (n) - name (7)
occásiō, occāsiónis (f) - occasion, opportunity (28)
ópēs, ópum (f. pl.) - power, resources, wealth (33)
ops, ópis (f) - help, aid (33)
ópus, óperis (n) - a work, task; deed, accomplishment (38)
ōrátiō, ōrātiónis (f) - speech (38)
ōrátor, ōrātóris (m) - orator, speaker (23)
ōs, óris (n) - mouth, face (14)
párēns, paréntis (m *or* f) - parent (28)
páter, pátris (m) - father (12)
paupértās, paupertátis (f) - poverty, humble circumstances (32)
pāx, pácis (f) - peace (7)
péctus, péctoris (n) - breast, heart (35)
pēs, pédis (m) - lower leg, foot (38)
plēbs, plébis (f) - the common people, populace, plebeians (33)
prínceps, príncipis (m *or* f) - leader, emperor (28)
próbitās, probitátis (f) - uprightness, honesty (18)
rátiō, ratiónis (f) - reckoning, account; reason, judgment, consideration; system; manner, method (8)
remíssiō, remissiónis (f) - letting go, release; relaxation (34)
rēx, régis (m) - king (7)
rúmor, rūmóris (m) - rumor, gossip (31)
rūs, rúris (n) - the country, countryside (37)
sacérdōs, sacerdótis (m) - priest (23)
sāl, sális (m) - salt; wit (33)
sálūs, salútis (f) - health, safety; greeting (21)
sápiēns, sapiéntis (m/f) - a wise man/woman, philosopher (25)
sátor, satóris (m) - sower, planter; begetter, father; founder (38)

scélus, scéleris (n) - evil deed, crime, sin, wickedness (19)
scríptor, scrīptṓris (m) - writer, author (8)
senéctūs, senectū́tis (f) - old age (10)
sénex, sénis (m) - old man (16)
sérvitūs, servitū́tis (f) - servitude, slavery (20)
sī́dus, sī́deris (n) - constellation, star (29)
sōl, sṓlis (m) - sun (27)
sóror, sorṓris (f) - sister (8)
tempéstās, tempestā́tis (f) - period of time, season; weather, storm (15)
témpus, témporis (n) - time; occasion, opportunity (7)
tímor, timṓris (m) - fear (10)
úxor, uxṓris (f) - wife (7)
vḗritās, vēritā́tis (f) - truth (10)
vésper, vésperis *or* **vésperī (m)** - evening; evening star (28)
vírgō, vírginis (f) - maiden, virgin (7)
vírtūs, virtū́tis (f) - manliness, courage; excellence, character, worth, virtue (7)
volúptās, voluptā́tis (f) - pleasure (10)
vōx, vṓcis (f) - voice, word (34)
vúlnus, vúlneris (n) - wound (24)

3rd Declension I-Stem

ánimal, animā́lis (n) - a living creature, animal (14)
ars, ártis (f) - art, skill (14)
arx, árcis (f) - citadel, stronghold (23)
as, ássis (m) - an as *(a small copper coin)* (31)
aúris, aúris (f) - ear (14)
cī́vis, cī́vis (m *or* **f)** - citizen (14)
fī́nēs, fī́nium (m) - boundaries, territory (21)
fī́nis, fī́nis (m) - end, limit, boundary; purpose (21)
gēns, géntis (f) - clan, race, nation, people (21)
hóstēs, hóstium (m) - the enemy (18)
hóstis, hóstis (m) - an enemy *(of the state)* (18)
ígnis, ígnis (m) - fire (22)
máre, máris (n) - sea (14)
mēns, méntis (f) - mind, thought, intention (16)
moénia, moénium (n. pl.) - walls of a city (29)
mōns, móntis (m) - mountain (20)
mors, mórtis (f) - death (14)
nā́vis, nā́vis (f) - ship, boat (21)
nox, nóctis (f) - night (26)
nū́bēs, nū́bis (f) - cloud (14)
pars, pártis (f) - part, share; direction (14)
urbs, úrbis (f) - city (14)
vī́rēs, vī́rium (f. pl.) - strength (14)
vīs, vīs (f) - force, power, violence (14)

4th Declension

córnū, córnūs (n) - horn (20)
cúrsus, cúrsūs (m) - running, race; course (28)
dómī (f) - at home (37)
dómō (f) - from home (37)
dómum (f) - (to) home (37)
dómus, dómūs, dómī (f) - house, home (37)
exércitus, exércitūs (m) - army (32)
frū́ctus, frū́ctūs (m) - fruit; profit, benefit, enjoyment (20)
génū, génūs (n) - knee (20)
mánus, mánūs (f) - hand; handwriting; band (20)
métus, métūs (m) - fear, dread, anxiety (20)
senā́tus, senā́tūs (m) - senate (20)
sḗnsus, sḗnsūs (m) - feeling, sense (20)
spī́ritus, spī́ritūs (m) - breath, breathing; spirit, soul (20)
trā́nsitus, trā́nsitūs (m) - passing over, transit; transition (39)
vérsus, vérsūs (m) - line of verse (20)

5th Declension

dī́ēs, diḗī (m) - day (22)
fī́dēs, fídeī (f) - faith, trust, trustworthiness, fidelity, promise, guarantee, protection (22)
rēs, réī (f) - thing, matter, property, business, affair (22)
rēs pū́blica, réī pū́blicae (f) - state, commonwealth, republic (22)
spēs, spéī (f) - hope (22)

Indeclinable

níhil - nothing (1)
sátis - enough (5)

Pronouns

áliquis, áliquid - someone, somebody, something (23)
égo, méī - I (11)
hic, haec, hoc - this; the latter; he, she, it, they (9)
ī́dem, éadem, ídem - the same (11)
ílle, ílla, íllud - that; the former; the famous; he, she, it, they (9)
ípse, ípsa, ípsum - myself, yourself, himself, herself, itself, *etc.,* the very, the actual (13)
is, éa, id - this, that; he, she, it (11)
íste, ísta, ístud - that of yours, that; such (as you have, as you speak of); *sometimes with contemptuous force, e.g.,* that despicable, that wretched (9)

quī, quae, quod - who, which, what, that (17)
quid - what (1)
quídam, quaédam, quíddam - a certain one or thing, someone, something (26)
quis, quid (*after* sī, nisi, nē, num) - anyone, anything, someone, something (33)
quis? quid? - who? whose? whom? what? which? (19)
quísque, quídque, cuiúsque, cuíque - each one, each person, each thing (13)
quísquis, quídquid - whoever, whatever (23)
súī - himself, herself, itself, themselves (13)
tū, túī - you *(sing.)* (11)

Adjectives

1st & 2nd Declension

acérbus, acérba, acérbum - harsh, bitter, grievous (12)
advérsus, advérsa, advérsum - opposite, adverse (34)
aéquus, aéqua, aéquum - level, even; calm; equal, just; favorable (22)
áliī . . . áliī - some . . . others (9)
álius, ália, áliud - other, another (9)
álter, áltera, álterum - the other (of two), second (9)
amícus, amíca, amícum - friendly (11)
antíquus, antíqua, antíquum - ancient, old-time (2)
ásper, áspera, ásperum - rough, harsh (21)
avā́rus, avā́ra, avā́rum - greedy, avaricious (3)
beā́tus, beā́ta, beā́tum - happy, fortunate, blessed (10)
béllus, bélla, béllum - pretty, handsome, charming (4)
bónus, bóna, bónum - good, kind (4)
caécus, caéca, caécum - blind (17)
cándidus, cándida, cándidum - shining, bright, white; beautiful (33)
cā́rus, cā́ra, cā́rum - dear (11)
cértus, cérta, cértum - definite, sure, certain, reliable (19)
cḗterī, cḗterae, cḗtera - the remaining, the rest, the other, all the others (30)
clā́rus, clā́ra, clā́rum - clear, bright; renowned, famous, illustrious (18)
cúpidus, cúpida, cúpidum - desirous, eager, fond; *or* desirous of, eager for (+gen.) (39)
déxter, déxtra, déxtrum - right, right-hand (20)
dígnus, dígna, dígnum (+abl.) - worthy, worthy of (29)
dóctus, dócta, dóctum - taught, learned, skilled (13)
dū́rus, dū́ra, dū́rum - hard, harsh, rough, stern, unfeeling, hardy, difficult (29)
fī́rmus, fī́rma, fī́rmum - firm, strong; reliable (38)
fortūnā́tus, fortūnā́ta, fortūnā́tum - lucky, fortunate, happy (13)
géminus, gémina, géminum - twin (25)
Graécus, Graéca, Graécum - Greek (6)
grā́tus, grā́ta, grā́tum - pleasing, agreeable; grateful (37)
hūmā́nus, hūmā́na, hūmā́num - pertaining to man, human; humane, kind; refined, cultivated (4)
idṓneus, idṓnea, idṓneum - suitable, fit, appropriate (37)
immṓtus, immṓta, immṓtum - unmoved; unchanged; unrelenting (37)
incértus, incérta, incértum - uncertain, unsure, doubtful (22)
īnfī́rmus, īnfī́rma, īnfī́rmum - not strong, weak, feeble (38)
īrā́tus, īrā́ta, īrā́tum - angry (35)
iūcúndus, iūcúnda, iūcúndum - pleasant, delightful, agreeable, pleasing (16)
Latī́nus, Latī́na, Latī́num - Latin (22)
lī́ber, lī́bera, lī́berum - free (5)
lóngus, lónga, lóngum - long (16)
magnánimus, magnánima, magnánimum - great-hearted, brave, magnanimous (23)
mágnus, mágna, mágnum - large, great; important (2)
málus, mála, málum - bad, wicked, evil (4)
médius, média, médium - middle; the middle of (22)
mérus, méra, mérum - pure, undiluted (33)
méus, méa, méum - my (2)
míser, mísera, míserum - wretched, miserable, unfortunate (15)
mórtuus, mórtua, mórtuum - dead (28)
múltus, múlta, múltum - much, many (2)
neúter, neútra, neútrum - not either, neither (9)
nóster, nóstra, nóstrum - our, ours (5)
nóvus, nóva, nóvum - new; strange (7)
nū́llus, nū́lla, nū́llum - not any, no, none (9)
párvus, párva, párvum - small, little (4)
paúcī, paúcae, paúca - few, a few (3)

perpétuus, perpétua, perpétuum perpetual, lasting, uninterrupted, continuous (6)
plḗnus, plḗna, plḗnum - full, abundant, generous (6)
prī́mus, prī́ma, prī́mum - first, foremost, chief, principal (27)
prī́stinus, prī́stina, prī́stinum - ancient; former, previous (38)
pudī́cus, pudī́ca, pudī́cum - modest, chaste (26)
púlcher, púlchra, púlchrum - beautiful, handsome; fine (5)
quántus, quánta, quántum - how large, how great, how much (30)
rīdículus, rīdícula, rīdículum - laughable, ridiculous (30)
Rōmā́nus, Rōmā́na, Rōmā́num - Roman (3)
sálvus, sálva, sálvum - safe, sound (6)
sā́nus, sā́na, sā́num - sound, healthy, sane (5)
secúndus, secúnda, secúndum - second; favorable (6)
siníster, sinístra, sinístrum - left, left-hand; harmful, ill-omened (20)
sṓlus, sṓla, sṓlum - alone, only, the only (9)
stúltus, stúlta, stúltum - foolish (4)
supérbus, supérba, supérbum - arrogant, overbearing, haughty, proud (26)
súperus, súpera, súperum - above, upper (27)
súus, súa, súum - his own, her own, its own, their own (13)
tántus, tánta, tántum - so large, so great, of such a size (29)
tántus . . . quántus - just as much (many) . . . as (30)
tṓtus, tṓta, tṓtum - whole, entire (9)
túus, túa, túum - your *(sing.)* (2)
ū́llus, ū́lla, ū́llum - any (9)
últimus, última, últimum - farthest, extreme; last, final (25)
ū́nus, ū́na, ū́num - one, single, alone (9)
urbā́nus, urbā́na, urbā́num - of the city, urban; urbane, elegant (26)
úter, útra, útrum - either, which (of two) (9)
vḗrus, vḗra, vḗrum - true, real, proper (4)
véster, véstra, véstrum - your *(pl.)* (6)
vī́vus, vī́va, vī́vum - alive, living (30)

3rd Declension

ábsēns, *gen.* abséntis - absent, away (37)
ā́cer, ā́cris, ā́cre - sharp, keen, eager; severe, fierce (16)
brévis, bréve - short, small, brief (16)
céler, céleris, célere - swift, quick, rapid (16)
commū́nis, commū́ne - common, general, of / for the community (20)
diffícilis, diffícile - hard, difficult, troublesome (16)
dī́ligēns, *gen.* dīligéntis - diligent, careful (27)
dissímilis, dissímile - unlike, different (27)
dī́ves, *gen.* dī́vitis *or* dī́tis - rich, wealthy (32)
dúlcis, dúlce - sweet; pleasant, agreeable (16)
fácilis, fácile - easy; agreeable (16)
fḗlīx, *gen.* fēlī́cis - lucky, fortunate, happy (22)
férōx, *gen.* ferṓcis - fierce, savage (25)
fidḗlis, fidḗle - faithful, loyal (25)
fórtis, fórte - strong, brave (16)
grácilis, grácile - slender, thin (27)
grávis, gráve - heavy, weighty; serious, important; severe, grievous (19)
húmilis, húmile - lowly, humble (27)
immortā́lis, immortā́le - not subject to death, immortal (19)
íngēns, *gen.* ingéntis - huge (16)
lévis, léve - light; easy; slight, trivial (17)
līberā́lis, līberā́le - of, relating to a free person; worthy of a free man, decent, liberal; generous (39)
máior, máius - greater; older (27)
medíocris, medíocre - ordinary, moderate, mediocre (31)
mīrā́bilis, mīrā́bile - amazing, wondrous, remarkable (38)
mortā́lis, mortā́le - mortal (18)
ómnis, ómne - every, all (16)
pār, *gen.* páris (+dat.) - equal, like (32)
paúper, *gen.* paúperis - of small means, poor (32)
pótēns, *gen.* poténtis - able, powerful, mighty, strong (16)
prī́nceps, *gen.* prī́ncipis - chief, foremost (28)
sápiēns, *gen.* sapiéntis - wise, judicious (25)
sénex, *gen.* sénis - old, aged (16)
símilis, símile (+gen. or dat.) - similar (to), like, resembling (27)
suā́vis, suā́ve - sweet (33)

sublímis, sublíme - elevated, lofty; heroic, noble (38)
tális, tále - such, of such a sort (34)
trístis, tríste - sad, sorrowful; joyless, grim, severe (26)
túrpis, túrpe - ugly; shameful, base, disgraceful (26)
útilis, útile - useful, advantageous (27)
vétus, *gen.* **véteris** - old (39)

Indeclinable Adjectives

necésse - necessary, inevitable (39)
quot - how many, as many as (27)
sátis - enough, sufficient (5)

Indefinite Adjective

quídam, quaédam, quóddam - a certain, some (26)

Interrogative Adjective

quī?, quae?, quod? - what? which? what kind of?; *(sometimes with exclamatory force)* what (a)! what sort of! (19)

Verbs

1st Conjugation

ádiuvō, adiuvāre, adiūvī, adiūtum - to help, aid, assist; to please (4)
ámbulō, ambuláre, ambulávī, ambulátum - to walk (39)
ámō, amáre, amávī, amátum - to love, like (1)
appéllō, appelláre, appellávī, appellátum - to speak to, address (as), call, name (14)
cḗnō, cēnáre, cēnávī, cēnátum - to dine (5)
cṓgitō, cōgitáre, cōgitávī, cōgitátum- to think, ponder, consider, plan (1)
cōnsérvō, cōnserváre, cōnservávī, cōnservátum - to preserve, conserve, maintain (1)
créō, creáre, creávī, creátum - to create (12)
cúlpō, culpáre, culpávī, culpátum - to blame, censure (5)
cúrō, cūráre, cūrávī, cūrátum - to care for, attend to; heal, cure; take care (36)
dédicō, dēdicáre, dēdicávī, dēdicátum - to dedicate (28)
dēléctō, dēlectáre, dēlectávī, dēlectátum - to delight, charm, please (19)
dēmṓnstrō, dēmōnstráre, dēmōnstrávī, dēmōnstrátum to point out, show, demonstrate (8)
dēsíderō, dēsīderáre, dēsīderávī, dēsīderátum - to desire, long for, miss (17)
dō, dáre, dédī, dátum - to give, offer (1)
dúbitō, dubitáre, dubitávī, dubitátum - to doubt, hesitate (30)
ḗducō, ēducáre, ēducávī, ēducátum - to bring up, educate (23)
érrō, erráre, errávī, errátum - to wander; err, go astray, make a mistake, be mistaken (1)
exspéctō, exspectáre, exspectávī, exspectátum - to look for, expect, await (15)
ímperō, imperáre, imperávī, imperátum (+dat.) - to give orders to, command (35)
invítō, invītáre, invītávī, invītátum - to entertain, invite, summon (26)
iúvō, iuváre, iūvī, iūtum - to help, aid, assist; to please (4)
labṓrō, labōráre, labōrávī, labōrátum - to labor; be in distress (21)
laúdō, laudáre, laudávī, laudátum - to praise (1)
líberō, līberáre, līberávī, līberátum - to free, liberate (19)
líbō, lībáre, lībávī, lībátum - to pour a libation of, on; pour ritually; sip; touch gently (39)
mútō, mūtáre, mūtávī, mūtátum to change, alter; exchange (14)
nárrō, nārráre, nārrávī, nārrátum - to tell, report, narrate (24)
návigō, nāvigáre, nāvigávī, nāvigátum - to sail, navigate (17)
nécō, necáre, necávī, necátum - to murder, kill (7)
négō, negáre, negávī, negátum to deny, say that . . . not (25)
núntiō, nūntiáre, nūntiávī, nūntiátum - to announce, report, relate (25)
obléctō, oblectáre, oblectávī, oblectátum - to please, amuse, delight; pass time pleasantly (36)
oppúgnō, oppugnáre, oppugnávī, oppugnátum - to fight against, attack, assault, assail (39)
ṓrnō, ōrnáre, ōrnávī, ornátum - to equip, furnish, adorn (39)
ṓrō, ōráre, ōrávī, ōrátum - to speak, plead; beg, beseech, entreat, pray (36)
párō, paráre, parávī, parátum - to prepare, provide; get, obtain (19)
pernóctō, pernoctáre, pernoctávī, pernoctátum - to spend *or* occupy the night (39)

praéstō, praestā́re, praéstitī, praéstitum - to excel; exhibit, show, offer, supply, furnish (28)
próbō, probā́re, probā́vī, probā́tum - to approve, recommend; test (27)
prōnū́ntiō, prōnūntiā́re, prōnūntiā́vī, prōnūntiā́tum - to proclaim, announce; declaim; pronounce (20)
púgnō, pugnā́re, pugnā́vī, pugnā́tum - to fight (29)
pútō, putā́re, putā́vī, putā́tum - to reckon, suppose, judge, think, imagine (25)
récitō, recitā́re, recitā́vī, recitā́tum - to read aloud, recite (17)
récreō, recreā́re, recreā́vī, recreā́tum - to restore, revive; refresh, cheer (36)
recū́sō, recūsā́re, recūsā́vī, recūsā́tum - to refuse (33)
rógō, rogā́re, rogā́vī, rogā́tum - to ask (30)
sátiō, satiā́re, satiā́vī, satiā́tum - to satisfy, sate (3)
serḗnō, serēnā́re, serēnā́vī, serēnā́tum - to make clear, brighten; cheer up, soothe (36)
sérvō, servā́re, servā́vī, servā́tum - to preserve, save, keep, guard (1)
spéctō, spectā́re, spectā́vī, spectā́tum - to look at, see (34)
spḗrō, spērā́re, spērā́vī, spērā́tum - to hope for, hope (25)
stō, stā́re, stétī, státum - to stand, stand still *or* firm (13)
súperō, superā́re, superā́vī, superā́tum - to be above, have the upper hand, surpass; overcome, conquer (5)
tólerō, tolerā́re, tolerā́vī, tolerā́tum - to bear, endure (6)
vī́tō, vītā́re, vītā́vī, vītā́tum - to avoid, shun (14)
vócō, vocā́re, vocā́vī, vocā́tum - to call, summon (1)

2nd Conjugation

aúdeō, audḗre, aúsus sum - to dare (7)
cáreō, carḗre, cáruī, caritū́rum (+abl.) - to be without, be deprived of, want, lack; be free from (20)
contíneō, continḗre, contínuī, conténtum - to hold together, contain, keep, enclose, restrain (21)
dḗbeō, dēbḗre, dḗbuī, dḗbitum - to owe; ought, must, should (1)
dḗleō, dēlḗre, dēlḗvī, dēlḗtum - to destroy, wipe out, erase (17)
dóceō, docḗre, dócuī, dóctum - to teach (8)
dóleō, dolḗre, dóluī, dolitū́rum - to grieve, suffer; hurt, give pain (31)
égeō, egḗre, éguī (+ abl. or gen.) - to need, lack, want (28)
éxpleō, explḗre, explḗvī, explḗtum - to fill, fill up, complete (28)
fóveō, fovḗre, fṓvī, fṓtum - to comfort, nurture, cherish (35)
gaúdeō, gaudḗre, gāvī́sus sum - to be glad, rejoice (23)
hábeō, habḗre, hábuī, hábitum - to have, hold, possess; consider, regard (3)
iáceō, iacḗre, iácuī - to lie; lie prostrate; lie dead (25)
invídeō, invidḗre, invī́dī, invī́sum to be envious; to look at with envy, envy, be jealous of (+dat.) (31)
iúbeō, iubḗre, iússī, iússum - to bid, order, command (21)
máneō, manḗre, mā́nsī, mā́nsum - to remain, stay, stay behind, abide, continue (5)
mísceō, miscḗre, míscuī, míxtum to mix, stir up, disturb (18)
móneō, monḗre, mónuī, mónitum - to remind, advise, warn (1)
móveō, movḗre, mṓvī, mṓtum - to move; arouse, affect (18)
nóceō, nocḗre, nócuī, nócitum (+dat.) - to do harm to, harm, injure (35)
pā́reō, pārḗre, pā́ruī (+dat.) - to be obedient to, obey (35)
páteō, patḗre, pátuī - to be open, lie open; be accessible; be evident (32)
persuā́deō, persuādḗre, persuā́sī, persuā́sum (+dat.) to succeed in urging, persuade, convince (35)
pláceō, placḗre, plácuī, plácitum (+dat.) - to be pleasing to, please (35)
praébeō, praebḗre, praébuī, praébitum - to offer, provide (32)
prohíbeō, prohibḗre, prohíbuī, prohíbitum - to keep (back), prevent, hinder, restrain, prohibit (20)
remáneō, remanḗre, remā́nsī, remā́nsum - to remain, stay, stay behind, abide, continue (5)
respóndeō, respondḗre, respóndī, respṓnsum - to answer (29)
rī́deō, rīdḗre, rī́sī, rī́sum - to laugh, laugh at (24)

sálvē, salvḗte - hello,
greetings (1)
sálveō, salvḗre - to be well,
be in good health (1)
sédeō, sedḗre, sḗdī, séssum -
to sit (34)
sóleō, solḗre, sólitus sum -
to be accustomed (37)
stúdeō, studḗre, stúduī (+dat.) -
to direct one's zeal to,
be eager for, study (35)
subrídeō, subrīdḗre, subrísī,
subrísum - to smile (down)
upon (35)
táceō, tacḗre, tácuī, tácitum -
to be silent,
leave unmentioned (28)
téneō, tenḗre, ténuī, téntum -
to hold, keep, possess;
restrain (14)
térreō, terrḗre, térruī, térritum -
to frighten, terrify (1)
tímeō, timḗre, tímuī - to fear,
be afraid (of) (15)
válē, valḗte - good-bye,
farewell (1)
váleō, valḗre, váluī, valitū́rum -
to be strong, have power;
be well (1)
vídeō, vidḗre, vídī, vísum -
to see; observe,
understand (1)
vídeor, vidḗrī, vísus sum -
to be seen, seem,
appear (18)

3rd Conjugation

accḗdō, accḗdere, accéssī,
accéssum - to come (to),
approach (36)
admíttō, admíttere, admísī,
admíssum - to admit,
receive, let in (17)
ágō, ágere, ḗgī, ā́ctum - to drive,
lead, do, act; pass, spend
(life or time) (8)
álō, álere, áluī, áltum -
to nourish, support, sustain,
increase; cherish (13)
āmíttō, āmíttere, āmísī,
āmíssum - to send away;
lose, let go (12)
antepṓnō, antepṓnere,
antepósuī, antepósitum -
to put before, prefer (35)
āvértō, āvértere, āvértī,
āvérsum - to turn away,
avert (23)
bíbō, bíbere, bíbī - to drink (30)
cádō, cádere, cécidī, cāsū́rum -
to fall (12)
cárpō, cárpere, cárpsī, cárptum
to harvest, pluck; seize (36)
cḗdō, cḗdere, céssī, céssum -
to go, withdraw; yield to,
grant, submit (28)
cérnō, cérnere, crḗvī, crḗtum -
to distinguish, discern,
perceive (22)
cognṓscō, cognṓscere, cognṓvī,
cógnitum -
to become acquainted with,
learn, recognize;
know *(in perfect tenses)* (30)
cṓgō, cṓgere, coḗgī, coā́ctum -
to drive *or* bring together,
force, compel (36)
commíttō, commíttere, commísī,
commíssum - to entrust,
commit (15)
comprehéndō, comprehéndere,
comprehéndī,
comprehḗnsum - to grasp,
seize, arrest; comprehend,
understand (30)
cóndō, cóndere, cóndidī,
cónditum - to put together *or*
into, store; found,
establish (29)
cōnsū́mō, cōnsū́mere,
cōnsū́mpsī, cōnsū́mptum -
to consume, use up (30)
contémnō, contémnere,
contémpsī, contémptum -
to despise, scorn (36)
conténdō, conténdere, conténdī,
conténtum - to strive,
struggle, contend;
hasten (29)
contúndō, contúndere, cóntudī,
contū́sum - to beat, crush,
bruise, destroy (36)
crḗdō, crḗdere, crḗdidī, crḗditum
to believe, trust (25)
crḗscō, crḗscere, crḗvī, crḗtum -
to increase (34)
cúrrō, cúrrere, cucúrrī, cúrsum -
to run, rush,
move quickly (14)
dēcérnō, dēcérnere, dēcrḗvī,
dēcrḗtum - to decide, settle,
decree (36)
dēféndō, dēféndere, dēféndī,
dēfḗnsum - to ward off;
defend, protect (20)
dícō, dícere, díxī, díctum -
to say, tell, speak; name,
call (10)
díligō, dīlígere, dīléxī, dīléctum -
to esteem, love (13)
discḗdō, discḗdere, discéssī,
discéssum - to go away,
depart (20)
díscō, díscere, dídicī -
to learn (8)
dū́cō, dū́cere, dū́xī, dúctum -
to lead; consider, regard;
prolong (8)
éxigō, exígere, exḗgī, exā́ctum -
to drive out, force out, exact;
drive through, complete,
perfect (36)
expéllō, expéllere, éxpulī,
expúlsum - to drive out,
expel, banish (24)
expṓnō, expṓnere, expósuī,
expósitum - to set forth,
explain, expose (30)
flúō, flúere, flū́xī, flū́xum -
to flow (18)
gérō, gérere, géssī, géstum -
to carry; carry on, manage,
conduct, wage, accomplish,
perform (8)

ignṓscō, ignṓscere, ignṓvī, ignṓtum (+dat.) - to grant pardon to, forgive (35)
intéllegō, intellégere, intellḗxī, intellḗctum - to understand (11)
iúngō, iúngere, iū́nxī, iū́nctum - to join (13)
légō, légere, lḗgī, lḗctum - to pick out, choose; read (18)
métuō, metúere, métuī - to fear, dread; be afraid for (+dat.) (38)
mínuō, minúere, mínuī, minū́tum - to lessen, diminish (30)
míttō, míttere, mī́sī, míssum - to send, let go (11)
néglegō, neglégere, neglḗxī, neglḗctum - to neglect, disregard (17)
nṓscō, nṓscere, nṓvī, nṓtum - to become acquainted with, learn, recognize; know *(in perfect tenses)* (30)
nū́bō, nū́bere, nū́psī, nū́ptum (+dat.) - to cover, veil; to be married to, marry (35)
óccidō, occídere, óccidī, occā́sum - to fall down; die; set (31)
ópprimō, opprímere, oppréssī, oppréssum - to suppress, overwhelm, overpower, check (23)
osténdō, osténdere, osténdī, osténtum - to exhibit, show, display (23)
párcō, párcere, pepércī, parsū́rum (+dat.) - to be lenient to, spare (35)
péllō, péllere, pépulī, púlsum - to strike, push; drive out, banish (24)
pétō, pétere, petī́vī, petī́tum - to seek, aim at, beg, beseech (23)
pṓnō, pṓnere, pósuī, pósitum - to put, place, set (27)
prémō, prémere, préssī, préssum - to press; press hard, pursue (23)
prōmíttō, prōmíttere, prōmī́sī, prōmíssum - to send forth; promise (32)
quaérō, quaérere, quaesī́vī, quaesī́tum - to seek, look for, strive for; ask, inquire, inquire into (24)
recognṓscō, recognṓscere, recognṓvī, recógnitum - to recognize, recollect (38)
régō, régere, rḗxī, rḗctum - to rule, guide, direct (16)
relínquō, relínquere, relī́quī, relíctum - to leave behind, leave, abandon, desert (21)
requiḗscō, requiḗscere, requiḗvī, requiḗtum - to rest (37)
requī́rō, requī́rere, requīsī́vī, requīsī́tum - to seek, ask for; miss, need, require (36)
revértō, revértere, revértī, revérsum - turn back (23)
scrī́bō, scrī́bere, scrī́psī, scrī́ptum to write, compose (8)
súrgō, súrgere, surrḗxī, surrḗctum - to get up, arise (29)
suspéndō, suspéndere, suspéndī, suspḗnsum - to hang up, suspend; interrupt (38)
tángō, tángere, tétigī, tā́ctum - to touch (21)
tóllō, tóllere, sústulī, sublā́tum - to raise, lift up; take away, remove, destroy (22)
trā́dō, trā́dere, trā́didī, trā́ditum to give over, surrender; hand down, transmit, teach (33)
tráhō, tráhere, trā́xī, tráctum - to draw, drag; derive, acquire (8)
vḗndō, vḗndere, vḗndidī, vḗnditum - to sell (38)
vértō, vértere, vértī, vérsum - to turn; change (23)
víncō, víncere, vī́cī, víctum - to conquer, overcome (8)
vī́vō, vī́vere, vī́xī, vī́ctum - to live (10)

3rd Conjugation -iō

accípiō, accípere, accḗpī, accéptum - to take *(to one's self)*, receive, accept (24)
cápiō, cápere, cḗpī, cáptum - to take, capture, seize, get (10)
cúpiō, cúpere, cupī́vī, cupī́tum - to desire, wish, long for (17)
ērípiō, ērípere, ērípuī, ēréptum - to snatch away, take away; rescue (22)
excípiō, excípere, excḗpī, excéptum - to take out, except; take, receive, capture (24)
fáciō, fácere, fḗcī, fáctum - to make, do, accomplish (10)
fúgiō, fúgere, fū́gī, fugitū́rum - to flee, hurry away; escape; go into exile; avoid, shun (10)
iáciō, iácere, iḗcī, iáctum - to throw, hurl (15)
incípiō, incípere, incḗpī, incéptum - to begin (17)
interfíciō, interfícere, interfḗcī, interféctum - to kill, murder (37)
patefáciō, patefácere, patefḗcī, patefáctum - to make open, open; disclose, expose (25)
rápiō, rápere, rápuī, ráptum - to seize, snatch, carry away (21)
recípiō, recípere, recḗpī, recéptum - to take back, regain; admit, receive (24)

sápiō, sápere, sapívī - to have good taste; have good sense, be wise (35)
suscípiō, suscípere, suscḗpī, suscéptum - to undertake (25)

4th Conjugation

aúdiō, audī́re, audī́vī, audī́tum - to hear, listen to (10)
dórmiō, dormī́re, dormī́vī, dormī́tum - to sleep (31)
impédiō, impedī́re, impedī́vī, impedī́tum - to impede, hinder, prevent (38)
invéniō, invenī́re, invḗnī, invéntum - to come upon, find (10)
móllio, mollī́re, mollī́vī, mollī́tum to soften; make calm *or* less hostile (29)
nésciō, nescī́re, nescī́vī, nescī́tum - to not know, be ignorant (25)
scíō, scī́re, scī́vī, scī́tum - to know (21)
séntiō, sentī́re, sḗnsī, sḗnsum - to feel, perceive, think, experience (11)
sérviō, servī́re, servī́vī, servī́tum (+dat.) - to be a slave to, serve (35)
véniō, venī́re, vḗnī, véntum - to come (10)

Irregular

ábeō, abī́re, ábiī, ábitum - to go away, depart, leave (37)
ádeō, adī́re, ádiī, áditum - to go to, approach (37)
ádferō, adférre, áttulī, allā́tum - to bring to (31)
cṓnferō, cōnférre, cóntulī, collā́tum - to bring together, compare; confer, bestow (31)
éō, ī́re, íī, ítum - to go (37)
éxeō, exī́re, éxiī, éxitum - to go out, exit (37)
férō, férre, túlī, lā́tum - to bear, carry, bring; suffer, endure, tolerate; say, report (31)
fī́ō, fíerī, fáctus sum - to occur, happen; become; be made, be done (36)
íneō, inī́re, íniī, ínitum - to enter into, begin (37)
mā́lō, mā́lle, mā́luī - to want (something) more, instead; prefer (32)
nṓlō, nṓlle, nṓluī - to not . . . wish, be unwilling (32)
óbeō, obī́re, óbiī, óbitum - to go up against, meet; die (37)
ófferō, offérre, óbtulī, oblā́tum - to offer (31)
péreō, perī́re, périī, péritum - to pass away, be destroyed, perish (37)
póssum, pósse, pótuī - to be able, can, could, have power (6)
rédeō, redī́re, rédiī, réditum - to go back, return (37)
réferō, reférre, réttulī, relā́tum - to carry back, bring back; repeat, answer, report (31)
sum, ésse, fúī, futū́rum - to be, exist (4)
trā́nseō, trānsī́re, trā́nsiī, trā́nsitum - to go across, cross; pass over, ignore (39)
vólō, vélle, vóluī - to wish, want, be willing, will (32)

Deponent

árbitror, arbitrā́rī, arbitrā́tus sum to judge, think (34)
cṓnor, cōnā́rī, cōnā́tus sum - to try, attempt (34)
ēgrédior, égredī, ēgréssus sum - to go out (34)
expérior, experī́rī, expértus sum to try, test; experience (39)
fáteor, fatḗrī, fássus sum - to confess, admit (34)
hórtor, hortā́rī, hortā́tus sum - to encourage, urge (34)
lóquor, lóquī, locū́tus sum - to say, speak, tell (34)
mī́ror, mīrā́rī, mīrā́tus sum - to marvel at, admire, wonder (35)
mṓlior, mōlī́rī, mōlī́tus sum - to work at, build, undertake, plan (34)
mórior, mórī, mórtuus sum - to die (34)
nā́scor, nā́scī, nā́tus sum - to be born; spring forth, arrive (34)
pátior, pátī, pássus sum - to suffer, endure; permit (34)
peregrī́nor, peregrīnā́rī, peregrīnā́tus sum - to travel abroad, wander (37)
profícīscor, profícīscī, proféctus sum - to set out, start (34)
quéror, quérī, quéstus sum - to complain, lament (38)
rū́sticor, rūsticā́rī, rūsticā́tus sum to live in the country (34)
séquor, séquī, secū́tus sum - to follow (34)
ū́tor, ū́tī, ū́sus sum (+abl.) - to use; enjoy, experience (34)

Defective

ā́it, ā́iunt - he says, they say, assert (25)
coépī, coepísse, coéptum - began (17)
ínquit - he says *or* said (22)
ṓdī, ōdísse, ōsū́rum - to hate (20)

Impersonal

lícet, licḗre, lícuit (+dat. +infin.) - it is permitted *(for someone to do something)*, one may (37)

opórtet, oportḗre, opórtuit (+infin.) - it is proper, right, necessary (39)

Adverbs

ánte (+acc.) - before, previously (13)

béne - well, satisfactorily, quite (11)

cíto - quickly (17)

cōtī́diē - daily, every day (36)

crās - tomorrow (5)

cūr - why (18)

déhinc - then, next (25)

deínde - thereupon, next, then (18)

dḗnique - at last, finally, lastly (29)

díū - long, for a long time (12)

étiam - even, also (11)

fórīs - out of doors, outside (37)

fortásse - perhaps (36)

fū́rtim - stealthily, secretly (30)

héri - yesterday (5)

hīc - here (25)

hódiē - today (3)

iam - now, already, soon (19)

íbi - there (6)

íta - so, thus (29)

ítaque - and so, therefore (15)

íterum - again, a second time (21)

libénter - with pleasure, gladly (38)

mox - soon (30)

nē . . . quídem - not . . . even (29)

nímis, nímium - too, too much, excessively; *(in a positive sense, esp. with adjectives and adverbs)* exceedingly, very (9)

nōn - not (1)

númquam - never (8)

nunc - now, at present (6)

nū́per - recently (12)

ṓlim - once (upon a time), long ago, formerly; some day, in the future (13)

póstea - afterwards (24)

prī́mō - at first, at the beginning (30)

prṓtinus - immediately (22)

quam - how (16)

quam - than *(after comparatives);* as . . . as possible *(with superlatives)* (26)

quándō - when (5)

quā́rē - because of which thing *(lit.);* therefore, wherefore, why (6)

quási - as if, as it were (39)

quídem - indeed, certainly, at least, even (29)

quóndam - formerly, once (22)

quóque - also, too (17)

repénte - suddenly (30)

saépe - often (1)

sátis - enough, sufficiently (5)

sémel - a single time, once, once and for all, simultaneously (31)

sémper - always (3)

sīc - so, thus (29)

súbitō - suddenly (33)

tam - so, to such a degree (29)

tam . . . quam - so . . . as (29)

támen - nevertheless, still (8)

tamquam - as it were, as if, so to speak (29)

tántum - only (26)

tum - then, at that time; thereupon, in the next place (5)

úbi - where, when (6)

últrā - on the other side of, beyond (22)

úmquam - ever, at any time (23)

únde - whence, from what *or* which place, from which, from whom (30)

úsque - all the way, up (to), even (to), continuously, always (31)

vḗrō - in truth, indeed, to be sure, however (29)

Conjunctions

at - but; but, mind you; but, you say (19)

átque, ac - and also, and even, and in fact (21)

aut - or (17)

aut . . . aut - either . . . or (17)

aútem - however; moreover (11)

cum (+indic.) - when (31)

cum (+subj.) - when, since, although (31)

dum - while, as long as, at the same time that; *or* until *(+subjunctive)* (8)

dúmmodo (+subj.) - provided that, so long as (32)

énim - for, in fact, truly (9)

et - and; even (2)

et . . . et - both . . . and (2)

étsī - even if, although (38)

ígitur - therefore, consequently (5)

nam - for (13)

nē - not; in order that . . . not, that . . . not, in order not to (28)

néque, nec - and not, nor (11)

néque . . . néque, nec . . . nec - neither . . . nor (11)

nísi - if . . . not, unless; except (19)

quod - because (11)

quóniam - since, inasmuch as (10)

sed - but (2)

sī - if (1)

ut (+indic.) - as, just as, when (24)

ut (+ subj.) - in order that, so that, that, in order to, so as to, to (28)
útrum . . . an - whether . . . or (30)

Prepositions

ab, ā (+abl.) - away from, from; by (14)
ad (+acc.) - to, up to, near to (8)
ánte (+acc.) - before *(in place or time)*, in front of (13)
ápud (+acc.) - among, in the presence of, at the house of (31)
cóntrā (+acc.) - against (19)
cum (+abl.) - with (10)
dē (+abl.) - down from, from; concerning, about (3)
érga (+acc.) - toward (38)
ex, ē (abl.+) - out of, from, from within; by reason of, on account of ; of *(after cardinal numerals)* (8)
in (+acc.) - into, toward; against (9)
in (+abl.) - in, on (3)
ínter (+acc.) - between, among (15)
per (+acc.) - through; by *(with reflexive pronoun)* (13)
post (+acc.) - after, behind (7)
prae (+abl.) - in front of, before (26)
prō (+abl.) - in front of, before, on behalf of, for the sake of, in return for, instead of, for, as (12)
própter (+acc.) - on account of, because of (5)
síne (+abl.) - without (2)
sub (+abl. w/ verbs of rest *or* +acc. w/ verbs of motion) - under, up under, close to, down to/into, to/at the foot of (7)
trāns (+acc.) - across (14)
últrā (adv. and prep. +acc.) - on the other side of, beyond (22)

Interjections

heu - ah!, alas! (33)
ō - O!, Oh! (2)
vae (often +dat. or acc.) - alas, woe to (34)

Idioms

amā́bō tē - please (1)
grā́tiās ágere (+dat.) - to thank someone; to give thanks to (8)
ménsa secúnda (f) - dessert (26)
nōn sṓlum . . . sed étiam - not only . . . but also (9)
poénās dáre - to pay the penalty (2)
sē cōnférre - to go (31)
sī quándō - if ever (5)

Prefix

re-, red- - again, back (24)

Suffixes

-ne – interrogative suffix attached to the first word of a sentence, typically the verb or another word on which the question hinges, to introduce a question whose answer is uncertain (5)
-que - and *(enclitic conjunction; appended to the second of two words to be joined)* (6)
-ve - or (33)

Numerals

Cardinal - ū́nus *to* vīgíntī quī́nque (15)
Ordinal - prī́mus *to* duodécimus (15)

----

céntum - a hundred (15)
mī́lia, mī́lium (n. pl.) - thousands (15)
mī́lle - thousand (15)

Chapter 40

Nouns

1st Declension

adulēscéntia, adulēscéntiae (f) - youth, young manhood; youthfulness (5)
agrícola, agrícolae (m) - farmer (3)
amíca, amícae (f) - friend (female) (3)
amīcítia, amīcítiae (f) - friendship (10)
ánima, ánimae (f) - air *(breathed by an animal),* breath; soul, spirit (34)
áqua, áquae (f) - water (14)
Ásia, Ásiae (f) - Asia (12)
Athḗnae, Athēnā́rum (f. pl.) - Athens (37)
cása, cásae (f) - house, cottage, hut (21)
caúsa, caúsae (f) - cause, reason; case, situation (21)
caúsā (abl. + preceding gen.) - for the sake of, on account of (21)
cḗna, cḗnae (f) - dinner (26)
clēméntia, clēméntiae (f) - mildness, gentleness, mercy (16)
cṓpia, cṓpiae (f) - abundance, supply (8)
cṓpiae, cōpiā́rum (f) - supplies, troops, forces (8)
cúlpa, cúlpae (f) - fault, blame (5)
cū́ra, cū́rae (f) - care, attention, caution, anxiety (4)
custṓdia, custṓdiae (f) - protection, custody; guards *(pl.)* (32)
déa, déae (f) - goddess (6)
discípula, discípulae (f) - learner, pupil, student (female) (6)
dīvítiae, dīvitiā́rum (f. pl.) - riches, wealth (13)
dómina, dóminae (f) - mistress, lady (40)
fā́bula, fā́bulae (f) - story, tale; play (24)
fā́ma, fā́mae (f) - rumor, report; fame, reputation (2)
família, famíliae (f) - household, family (19)
fḗmina, fḗminae (f) - woman (3)
fenéstra, fenéstrae (f) - window (21)
fī́lia, fī́liae (f) - daughter (3)
fṓrma, fṓrmae (f) - form, shape; beauty (2)
fortū́na, fortū́nae (f) - fortune, luck (2)
glṓria, glṓriae (f) - glory, fame (5)
Graécia, Graéciae (f) - Greece (19)
hásta, hástae (f) - spear (23)
hṓra, hṓrae (f) - hour, time (10)
iā́nua, iā́nuae (f) - door (35)
iniū́ria, iniū́riae (f) - injustice, injury, wrong (39)
īnsídiae, īnsidiā́rum (f) - ambush, plot, treachery (6)
ī́nsula, ī́nsulae (f) - island (23)
invídia, invídiae (f) - envy, jealousy, hatred (31)
ī́ra, ī́rae (f) - ire, anger (2)
Itália, Itáliae (f) - Italy (15)
lácrima, lácrimae (f) - tear (40)
língua, línguae (f) - tongue; language (25)
líttera, lítterae (f) - a letter of the alphabet (7)
lítterae, litterā́rum (f) - a letter (epistle), literature (7)
lū́na, lū́nae (f) - moon (28)
magístra, magístrae (f) - schoolmistress, teacher, mistress (4)
médica, médicae (f) - doctor, physician (female) (12)
memória, memóriae (f) - memory, recollection (15)
mḗnsa, mḗnsae (f) - table; dining; dish, course (26)
mḗta, mḗtae (f) - turning point, goal; limit, boundary (40)
móra, mórae (f) - delay (4)
nā́ta, nā́tae (f) - daughter (29)
nātū́ra, nātū́rae (f) - nature (10)
naúta, naútae (m) - sailor (2)
patiéntia, patiéntiae (f) - suffering; patience, endurance (12)
pátria, pátriae (f) - fatherland, native land, (one's) country (2)
pecū́nia, pecū́niae (f) - money (2)
philósopha, philósophae (f) - philosopher (female) (33)
philosóphia, philosóphiae (f) - philosophy (2)
poéna, poénae (f) - penalty, punishment (2)
poḗta, poḗtae (m) - poet (2)
pórta, pórtae (f) - gate, entrance (2)
puélla, puéllae (f) - girl (2)
rēgī́na, rēgī́nae (f) - queen (7)
Rṓma, Rṓmae (f) - Rome (14)
rósa, rósae (f) - rose (2)
sapiéntia, sapiéntiae (f) - wisdom (3)
sátura, sáturae (f) - satire (16)
sciéntia, sciéntiae (f) - knowledge (18)
senténtia, senténtiae (f) - feeling, thought, opinion, vote, sentence (2)
sérva, sérvae (f) - slave (female) (24)
stḗlla, stḗllae (f) - star, planet (28)
Syrācū́sae, Syrācūsā́rum (f. pl.) - Syracuse (37)
térra, térrae (f) - earth, ground, land, country (7)
Trṓia, Trṓiae (f) - Troy (21)

túrba, túrbae (f) - uproar, disturbance; mob, crowd, multitude (14)
vía, víae (f) - way, road, street (10)
vīcína, vīcínae (f) - neighbor (female) (21)
victṓria, victṓriae (f) - victory (8)
víta, vítae (f) - life; mode of life (2)

2nd Declension

aedifícium, aedifíciī (n) - building, structure (39)
áger, ágrī (m) - field, farm (3)
amícus, amícī (m) - friend (male) (3)
ánimī, animṓrum (m) - high spirits, pride, courage (5)
ánimus, ánimī (m) - soul, spirit, mind (5)
ánnus, ánnī (m) - year (12)
argūméntum, argūméntī (n) - proof, evidence, argument (19)
árma, armṓrum (n. pl.) - arms, weapons (28)
auxílium, auxíliī (n) - aid, help (31)
bā́sium, bā́siī (n) - kiss (4)
béllum, béllī (n) - war (4)
benefícium, benefíciī (n) - benefit, kindness; favor (19)
caélum, caélī (n) - sky, heaven (5)
coniūrā́tī, coniūrātṓrum (m. pl.) - conspirators (20)
cōnsílium, cōnsíliī (n) - plan, purpose, counsel, advice, judgment, wisdom (4)
déus, déī (m) - god (6)
dígitus, dígitī (m) - finger, toe (31)
discípulus, discípulī (m) - learner, pupil, student (male) (6)
dóminus, dóminī (m) - master (of a household), lord (40)
dṓnum, dṓnī (n) - gift, present (4)
elephántus, elephántī (m and f) - elephant (31)
équus, équī (m) - horse (23)
exítium, exítiī (n) - destruction, ruin (4)
exsílium, exsíliī (n) - exile, banishment (31)
fáctum, fáctī (n) - deed, act, achievement (13)
fā́tum, fā́tī (n) - fate; death (29)
férrum, férrī (n) - iron; sword (22)
fílius, fíliī (m) - son (3)
fórum, fórī (n) - marketplace, forum (26)
Graécus, Graécī (m) - a Greek (6)
húmus, húmī (f) - ground, earth; soil (37)
impérium, impériī (n) - power to command, supreme power, authority, command, control (24)
ingénium, ingéniī (n) - nature, innate talent (29)
inítium, inítiī (n) - beginning, commencement (33)
iūdícium, iūdíciī (n) - judgment, decision, opinion; trial (19)
libéllus, libéllī (m) - little book (17)
líber, líbrī (m) - book (6)
lóca, locṓrum (n) - places, region (9)
lócī, locṓrum (m) - passages in literature (9)
lócus, lócī (m) - place; passage in literature (9)
lū́dus, lū́dī (m) - game, sport; school (18)
magíster, magístrī (m) - schoolmaster, teacher, master (4)
médicus, médicī (m) - doctor, physician (male) (12)
módus, módī (m) - measure, bound, limit; manner, method, mode, way (22)
monuméntum, monuméntī (n) - monument (40)
mórbus, mórbī (m) - disease, sickness (9)
múndus, múndī (m) - world, universe (21)
nā́sus, nā́sī (m) - nose (40)
númerus, númerī (m) - number (3)
óculus, óculī (m) - eye (4)
ódium, ódiī (n) - hatred (38)
offícium, offíciī (n) - duty, service (4)
ṓsculum, ṓsculī (n) - kiss (29)
ṓtium, ṓtiī (n) - leisure, peace (4)
perfúgium, perfúgiī (n) - refuge, shelter (24)
perículum, perículī (n) - danger, risk (4)
philósophus, philósophī (m) - philosopher (male) (33)
pópulus, pópulī (m) - the people, a people, a nation (3)
praémium, praémiī (n) - reward, prize (35)
prīncípium, prīncípiī (n) - beginning (12)
púer, púerī (m) - boy; boys, children *(pl.)* (3)
remédium, remédiī (n) - cure, remedy (4)
sáxum, sáxī (n) - rock, stone (40)
sérvus, sérvī (m) - slave (male) (24)
sígnum, sígnī (n) - sign, signal, indication; seal (13)
sōlā́cium, sōlā́ciī (n) - comfort, relief (24)
sómnus, sómnī (m) - sleep (26)
spéculum, spéculī (n) - mirror (33)
stúdium, stúdiī (n) - eagerness, zeal, pursuit, study (9)
stúltus, stúltī (m) - a fool (4)
súperī, superṓrum (m. pl.) - the gods (27)

tyránnus, tyránnī (m) - absolute ruler, tyrant (6)
véntus, véntī (m) - wind (39)
vérbum, vérbī (n)- word (5)
vīcī́nus, vīcī́nī (m) - neighbor (male) (21)
vínculum, vínculī (n) - bond, chain, fetter (36)
vī́num, vī́nī (n) - wine (31)
vir, vírī (m) - man, hero (3)
vítium, vítiī (n) - fault, crime, vice (6)
vúlgus, vúlgī (n) - the common people, mob, rabble (21)

3rd Declension

adulḗscēns, adulēscéntis (m *or* f) - young man *or* woman (12)
aes, aéris (n) - bronze (40)
aéstās, aestā́tis (f) - summer (35)
aétās, aetā́tis (f) - period of life, life, age, an age, time (16)
ámor, amṓris (m) - love (7)
árbor, árboris (f) - tree (38)
aúctor, auctṓris (m) - increaser; author, originator (19)
audī́tor, audītṓris (m) - hearer, listener, member of an audience (16)
Caésar, Caésaris (m) - Caesar (12)
cáput, cápitis (n) - head; leader; beginning; life; heading; chapter (11)
cármen, cárminis (n) - song, poem (7)
Carthā́gō, Carthā́ginis (f) - Carthage (24)
Cícerō, Cicerṓnis (m) - (Marcus Tullius) Cicero (8)
cī́vitās, cīvitā́tis (f) - state, citizenship (7)
cṓnsul, cṓnsulis (m) - consul (11)
córpus, córporis (n) - body (7)
cupíditās, cupiditā́tis (f) - desire, longing, passion; cupidity, avarice (10)
cupī́dō, cupī́dinis (f) - desire, compassion (36)
dēlectā́tiō, dēlectātiṓnis (f) - delight, pleasure, enjoyment (27)
dígnitās, dignitā́tis (f) - merit, prestige, dignity (38)
dólor, dolṓris (m) - pain, grief (38)
dux, dúcis (m) - leader, guide; commander, general (23)
flū́men, flū́minis (n) - river (18)
frā́ter, frā́tris (m) - brother (8)
génus, géneris (n) - origin; kind, type, sort, class (18)
hómō, hóminis (m) - human being, man (7)
hónor, honṓris (m) - honor, esteem; public office (30)
imperā́tor, imperātṓris (m) - general, commander-in-chief, emperor (24)
íter, itíneris (n) - journey; route, road (37)
iū́dex, iū́dicis (m) - judge, juror (19)
iūs, iū́ris (n) - right, justice, law (14)
lábor, labṓris (m)- labor, work, toil; a work, production (7)
laus, laúdis (f) - praise, glory, fame (8)
lḗctor, lēctṓris (m) - reader (male) (36)
lḗctrīx, lēctrī́cis (f) - reader (female) (36)
lēx, lḗgis (f) - law, statute (26)
lībértās, lībertā́tis (f) - liberty (8)
lī́men, lī́minis (n) - threshold (26)
lī́tus, lī́toris (n) - shore, coast (23)
lūx, lū́cis (f) - light (26)
maiṓrēs, maiṓrum (m. pl.) - ancestors (27)
mā́ter, mā́tris (f) - mother (12)
mī́les, mī́litis (m) - soldier (23)
mṓrēs, mṓrum (m) - habits, morals, character (7)
mōs, mṓris (m) - habit, custom, manner (7)
múlier, mulíeris (f) - woman (39)
nḗmō, nūllī́us, nḗminī, nḗminem, nū́llō, nū́llā (m *or* f) - no one, nobody (11)
népōs, nepṓtis (m) - grandson, descendant (27)
nṓmen, nṓminis (n) - name (7)
occā́siō, occāsiṓnis (f) - occasion, opportunity (28)
ópēs, ópum (f. pl.) - power, resources, wealth (33)
ops, ópis (f) - help, aid (33)
ópus, óperis (n) - a work, task; deed, accomplishment (38)
ōrā́tiō, ōrātiṓnis (f) - speech (38)
ōrā́tor, ōrātṓris (m) - orator, speaker (23)
ōs, ṓris (n) - mouth, face (14)
párēns, paréntis (m *or* f) - parent (28)
páter, pátris (m) - father (12)
paupértās, paupertā́tis (f) - poverty, humble circumstances (32)
pāx, pā́cis (f) - peace (7)
péctus, péctoris (n) - breast, heart (35)
pēs, pédis (m) - lower leg, foot (38)
plēbs, plḗbis (f) - the common people, populace, plebeians (33)
prī́nceps, prī́ncipis (m *or* f) - leader, emperor (28)
próbitās, probitā́tis (f) - uprightness, honesty (18)
rátiō, ratiṓnis (f) - reckoning, account; reason, judgment, consideration; system; manner, method (8)

remíssiō, remissiṓnis (f) - letting go, release; relaxation (34)
rēx, rḗgis (m) - king (7)
rū́mor, rūmṓris (m) - rumor, gossip (31)
rūs, rū́ris (n) - the country, countryside (37)
sacérdōs, sacerdṓtis (m) - priest (23)
sāl, sális (m) - salt; wit (33)
sálūs, salū́tis (f) - health, safety; greeting (21)
sápiēns, sapiéntis (m/f) - a wise man/woman, philosopher (25)
sátor, satṓris (m) - sower, planter; begetter, father; founder (38)
scélus, scéleris (n) - evil deed, crime, sin, wickedness (19)
scrī́ptor, scrīptṓris (m) - writer, author (8)
senéctūs, senectū́tis (f) - old age (10)
sénex, sénis (m) - old man (16)
sérvitūs, servitū́tis (f) - servitude, slavery (20)
sī́dus, sī́deris (n) - constellation, star (29)
sōl, sṓlis (m) - sun (27)
sóror, sorṓris (f) - sister (8)
tempéstās, tempestā́tis (f) - period of time, season; weather, storm (15)
témpus, témporis (n) - time; occasion, opportunity (7)
tímor, timṓris (m) - fear (10)
úxor, uxṓris (f) - wife (7)
vḗritās, vēritā́tis (f) - truth (10)
vésper, vésperis *or* vésperī (m) - evening; evening star (28)
vírgō, vírginis (f) - maiden, virgin (7)
vírtūs, virtū́tis (f) - manliness, courage; excellence, character, worth, virtue (7)
volúptās, voluptā́tis (f) - pleasure (10)
vōx, vṓcis (f) - voice, word (34)
vúlnus, vúlneris (n) - wound (24)

3rd Declension I-Stem

ánimal, animā́lis (n) - a living creature, animal (14)
ars, ártis (f) - art, skill (14)
arx, árcis (f) - citadel, stronghold (23)
as, ássis (m) - an as *(a small copper coin)* (31)
aúris, aúris (f) - ear (14)
cī́vis, cī́vis (m *or* f) - citizen (14)
fī́nēs, fī́nium (m) - boundaries, territory (21)
fī́nis, fī́nis (m) - end, limit, boundary; purpose (21)
gēns, géntis (f) - clan, race, nation, people (21)
hóstēs, hóstium (m) - the enemy (18)
hóstis, hóstis (m) - an enemy *(of the state)* (18)
ígnis, ígnis (m) - fire (22)
máre, máris (n) - sea (14)
mēns, méntis (f) - mind, thought, intention (16)
moénia, moénium (n. pl.) - walls of a city (29)
mōns, móntis (m) - mountain (20)
mors, mórtis (f) - death (14)
nā́vis, nā́vis (f) - ship, boat (21)
nox, nóctis (f) - night (26)
nū́bēs, nū́bis (f) - cloud (14)
pars, pártis (f) - part, share; direction (14)
urbs, úrbis (f) - city (14)
vī́rēs, vī́rium (f. pl.) - strength (14)
vīs, vīs (f) - force, power, violence (14)

4th Declension

córnū, córnūs (n) - horn (20)
cúrsus, cúrsūs (m) - running, race; course (28)
dómī (f) - at home (37)
dómō (f) - from home (37)
dómum (f) - (to) home (37)
dómus, dómūs, dómī (f) - house, home (37)
exércitus, exércitūs (m) - army (32)
frū́ctus, frū́ctūs (m) - fruit; profit, benefit, enjoyment (20)
génū, génūs (n) - knee (20)
mánus, mánūs (f) - hand; handwriting; band (20)
métus, métūs (m) - fear, dread, anxiety (20)
senā́tus, senā́tūs (m) - senate (20)
sḗnsus, sḗnsūs (m) - feeling, sense (20)
spī́ritus, spī́ritūs (m) - breath, breathing; spirit, soul (20)
trā́nsitus, trā́nsitūs (m) - passing over, transit; transition (39)
vérsus, vérsūs (m) - line of verse (20)
vúltus, vúltūs (m) - countenance, face (40)

5th Declension

díēs, diḗī (m) - day (22)
fídēs, fídeī (f) - faith, trust, trustworthiness, fidelity, promise, guarantee, protection (22)
rēs, réī (f) - thing, matter, property, business, affair (22)
rēs pū́blica, réī pū́blicae (f) - state, commonwealth, republic (22)
spēs, spéī (f) - hope (22)

Indeclinable

níhil - nothing (1)
sátis - enough (5)

Pronouns

áliquis, áliquid - someone, somebody, something (23)
égo, méī - I (11)
hic, haec, hoc - this; the latter; he, she, it, they (9)
ídem, éadem, ídem - the same (11)
ílle, ílla, íllud - that; the former; the famous; he, she, it, they (9)
ípse, ípsa, ípsum - myself, yourself, himself, herself, itself, *etc.,* the very, the actual (13)
is, éa, id - this, that; he, she, it (11)
íste, ísta, ístud - that of yours, that; such (as you have, as you speak of); *sometimes with contemptuous force, e.g.,* that despicable, that wretched (9)
quī, quae, quod - who, which, what, that (17)
quid - what (1)
quídam, quaédam, quíddam - a certain one or thing, someone, something (26)
quis, quid (*after* sī, nisi, nē, num) - anyone, anything, someone, something (33)
quis? quid? - who? whose? whom? what? which? (19)
quísque, quídque, cuiúsque, cuíque - each one, each person, each thing (13)
quísquis, quídquid - whoever, whatever (23)
súī - himself, herself, itself, themselves (13)
tū, túī - you *(sing.)* (11)

Adjectives

1st & 2nd Declension

acérbus, acérba, acérbum - harsh, bitter, grievous (12)
advérsus, advérsa, advérsum - opposite, adverse (34)
aéquus, aéqua, aéquum - level, even; calm; equal, just; favorable (22)
áliī . . . áliī - some . . . others (9)
álius, ália, áliud - other, another (9)
álter, áltera, álterum - the other (of two), second (9)
amícus, amíca, amícum - friendly (11)
antíquus, antíqua, antíquum - ancient, old-time (2)
ásper, áspera, ásperum - rough, harsh (21)
avā́rus, avā́ra, avā́rum - greedy, avaricious (3)
beā́tus, beā́ta, beā́tum - happy, fortunate, blessed (10)
béllus, bélla, béllum - pretty, handsome, charming (4)
bónus, bóna, bónum - good, kind (4)
caécus, caéca, caécum - blind (17)
cándidus, cándida, cándidum - shining, bright, white; beautiful (33)
cā́rus, cā́ra, cā́rum - dear (11)
cértus, cérta, cértum - definite, sure, certain, reliable (19)
cḗterī, cḗterae, cḗtera - the remaining, the rest, the other, all the others (30)
clā́rus, clā́ra, clā́rum - clear, bright; renowned, famous, illustrious (18)
cúpidus, cúpida, cúpidum - desirous, eager, fond; *or* desirous of, eager for (+gen.) (39)
déxter, déxtra, déxtrum - right, right-hand (20)
dígnus, dígna, dígnum (+abl.) - worthy, worthy of (29)
dóctus, dócta, dóctum - taught, learned, skilled (13)
dū́rus, dū́ra, dū́rum - hard, harsh, rough, stern, unfeeling, hardy, difficult (29)
fī́rmus, fī́rma, fī́rmum - firm, strong; reliable (38)
fortūnā́tus, fortūnā́ta, fortūnā́tum - lucky, fortunate, happy (13)
géminus, gémina, géminum - twin (25)
Graécus, Graéca, Graécum - Greek (6)
grā́tus, grā́ta, grā́tum - pleasing, agreeable; grateful (37)
hūmā́nus, hūmā́na, hūmā́num - pertaining to man, human; humane, kind; refined, cultivated (4)
idṓneus, idṓnea, idṓneum - suitable, fit, appropriate (37)
immṓtus, immṓta, immṓtum - unmoved; unchanged; unrelenting (37)
incértus, incérta, incértum - uncertain, unsure, doubtful (22)
īnfī́rmus, īnfī́rma, īnfī́rmum - not strong, weak, feeble (38)
īrā́tus, īrā́ta, īrā́tum - angry (35)
iūcúndus, iūcúnda, iūcúndum - pleasant, delightful, agreeable, pleasing (16)
iū́stus, iū́sta, iū́stum - just, right (40)
Latī́nus, Latī́na, Latī́num - Latin (22)
lī́ber, lī́bera, lī́berum - free (5)
lóngus, lónga, lóngum - long (16)
magnánimus, magnánima, magnánimum - great-hearted, brave, magnanimous (23)
mágnus, mágna, mágnum - large, great; important (2)

málus, mála, málum - bad, wicked, evil (4)
médius, média, médium - middle; the middle of (22)
mérus, méra, mérum - pure, undiluted (33)
méus, méa, méum - my (2)
míser, mísera, míserum - wretched, miserable, unfortunate (15)
mórtuus, mórtua, mórtuum - dead (28)
múltus, múlta, múltum - much, many (2)
neúter, neútra, neútrum - not either, neither (9)
nóster, nóstra, nóstrum - our, ours (5)
nóvus, nóva, nóvum - new; strange (7)
nū́llus, nū́lla, nū́llum - not any, no, none (9)
párvus, párva, párvum - small, little (4)
paúcī, paúcae, paúca - few, a few (3)
perpétuus, perpétua, perpétuum perpetual, lasting, uninterrupted, continuous (6)
plḗnus, plḗna, plḗnum - full, abundant, generous (6)
prī́mus, prī́ma, prī́mum - first, foremost, chief, principal (27)
prī́stinus, prī́stina, prī́stinum - ancient; former, previous (38)
pudī́cus, pudī́ca, pudī́cum - modest, chaste (26)
púlcher, púlchra, púlchrum - beautiful, handsome; fine (5)
quántus, quánta, quántum - how large, how great, how much (30)
rīdículus, rīdícula, rīdículum - laughable, ridiculous (30)

Rōmā́nus, Rōmā́na, Rōmā́num - Roman (3)
sálvus, sálva, sálvum - safe, sound (6)
sā́nus, sā́na, sā́num - sound, healthy, sane (5)
secúndus, secúnda, secúndum - second; favorable (6)
siníster, sinístra, sinístrum - left, left-hand; harmful, ill-omened (20)
sṓlus, sṓla, sṓlum - alone, only, the only (9)
stúltus, stúlta, stúltum - foolish (4)
supérbus, supérba, supérbum - arrogant, overbearing, haughty, proud (26)
súperus, súpera, súperum - above, upper (27)
súus, súa, súum - his own, her own, its own, their own (13)
tántus, tánta, tántum - so large, so great, of such a size (29)
tántus . . . quántus - just as much (many) . . . as (30)
tṓtus, tṓta, tṓtum - whole, entire (9)
túus, túa, túum - your *(sing.)* (2)
ū́llus, ū́lla, ū́llum - any (9)
últimus, última, últimum - farthest, extreme; last, final (25)
ū́nus, ū́na, ū́num - one, single, alone (9)
urbā́nus, urbā́na, urbā́num - of the city, urban; urbane, elegant (26)
úter, útra, útrum - either, which (of two) (9)
vḗrus, vḗra, vḗrum - true, real, proper (4)
véster, véstra, véstrum - your *(pl.)* (6)
vī́vus, vī́va, vī́vum - alive, living (30)

3rd Declension

ábsēns, ***gen.*** **abséntis** - absent, away (37)
ā́cer, ā́cris, ā́cre - sharp, keen, eager; severe, fierce (16)
brévis, bréve - short, small, brief (16)
céler, céleris, célere - swift, quick, rapid (16)
commū́nis, commū́ne - common, general, of / for the community (20)
diffícilis, diffícile - hard, difficult, troublesome (16)
dī́ligēns, ***gen.*** **dīligéntis** - diligent, careful (27)
dissímilis, dissímile - unlike, different (27)
dī́ves, ***gen.*** **dī́vitis** ***or*** **dī́tis** - rich, wealthy (32)
dúlcis, dúlce - sweet; pleasant, agreeable (16)
fácilis, fácile - easy; agreeable (16)
fḗlīx, ***gen.*** **fēlī́cis** - lucky, fortunate, happy (22)
férōx, ***gen.*** **ferṓcis** - fierce, savage (25)
fidḗlis, fidḗle - faithful, loyal (25)
fórtis, fórte - strong, brave (16)
grácilis, grácile - slender, thin (27)
grávis, gráve - heavy, weighty; serious, important; severe, grievous (19)
húmilis, húmile - lowly, humble (27)
immortā́lis, immortā́le - not subject to death, immortal (19)
íngēns, ***gen.*** **ingéntis** - huge (16)
lévis, léve - light; easy; slight, trivial (17)
līberā́lis, līberā́le - of, relating to a free person; worthy of a free man, decent, liberal; generous (39)

máior, máius - greater; older (27)
medíocris, medíocre - ordinary, moderate, mediocre (31)
mīrábilis, mīrábile - amazing, wondrous, remarkable (38)
mortális, mortále - mortal (18)
ómnis, ómne - every, all (16)
pār, ***gen.*** **páris (+dat.)** - equal, like (32)
paúper, ***gen.*** **paúperis** - of small means, poor (32)
pótēns, ***gen.*** **poténtis** - able, powerful, mighty, strong (16)
prínceps, ***gen.*** **príncipis** - chief, foremost (28)
sápiēns, ***gen.*** **sapiéntis** - wise, judicious (25)
sénex, ***gen.*** **sénis** - old, aged (16)
símilis, símile (+gen. or dat.) - similar (to), like, resembling (27)
suávis, suáve - sweet (33)
sublímis, sublíme - elevated, lofty; heroic, noble (38)
tális, tále - such, of such a sort (34)
trístis, tríste - sad, sorrowful; joyless, grim, severe (26)
túrpis, túrpe - ugly; shameful, base, disgraceful (26)
ū́tilis, ū́tile - useful, advantageous (27)
vétus, ***gen.*** **véteris** - old (39)

Indeclinable Adjectives

necésse - necessary, inevitable (39)
quot - how many, as many as (27)
sátis - enough, sufficient (5)
tot - so many, as many (40)
tot...quot - as many...as (40)

Indefinite Adjective

quídam, quaédam, quóddam - a certain, some (26)

Interrogative Adjective

quī?, quae?, quod? - what? which? what kind of?; *(sometimes with exclamatory force)* what (a)! what sort of! (19)

Verbs

1st Conjugation

ádiuvō, adiuváre, adiū́vī, adiū́tum - to help, aid, assist; to please (4)
ámbulō, ambuláre, ambulávī, ambulátum - to walk (39)
ámō, amáre, amávī, amátum - to love, like (1)
appéllō, appelláre, appellávī, appellátum - to speak to, address (as), call, name (14)
cḗnō, cēnáre, cēnávī, cēnátum - to dine (5)
cṓgitō, cōgitáre, cōgitávī, cōgitátum- to think, ponder, consider, plan (1)
cōnsérvō, cōnserváre, cōnservávī, cōnservátum - to preserve, conserve, maintain (1)
créō, creáre, creávī, creátum - to create (12)
cúlpō, culpáre, culpávī, culpátum - to blame, censure (5)
cū́rō, cūráre, cūrávī, cūrátum - to care for, attend to; heal, cure; take care (36)
dḗdicō, dēdicáre, dēdicávī, dēdicátum - to dedicate (28)
dēléctō, dēlectáre, dēlectávī, dēlectátum - to delight, charm, please (19)
dēmṓnstrō, dēmōnstráre, dēmōnstrávī, dēmōnstrátum to point out, show, demonstrate (8)
dēsíderō, dēsīderáre, dēsīderávī, dēsīderátum - to desire, long for, miss (17)
dō, dáre, dédī, dátum - to give, offer (1)
dúbitō, dubitáre, dubitávī, dubitátum - to doubt, hesitate (30)
ḗducō, ēducáre, ēducávī, ēducátum - to bring up, educate (23)
érrō, erráre, errávī, errátum - to wander; err, go astray, make a mistake, be mistaken (1)
éxplicō, explicáre, explicávī, explicátum - to unfold; explain; spread out, deploy (40)
exspéctō, exspectáre, exspectávī, exspectátum - to look for, expect, await (15)
fatī́gō, fatīgáre, fatīgávī, fatīgátum - to weary, tire out (40)
ímperō, imperáre, imperávī, imperátum (+dat.) - to give orders to, command (35)
invī́tō, invītáre, invītávī, invītátum - to entertain, invite, summon (26)
iúvō, iuváre, iū́vī, iū́tum - to help, aid, assist; to please (4)
labṓrō, labōráre, labōrávī, labōrátum - to labor; be in distress (21)
laúdō, laudáre, laudávī, laudátum - to praise (1)
lī́berō, līberáre, līberávī, līberátum - to free, liberate (19)
lī́bō, lībáre, lībávī, lībátum - to pour a libation of, on; pour ritually; sip; touch gently (39)
mū́tō, mūtáre, mūtávī, mūtátum to change, alter; exchange (14)

nā́rrō, nārrā́re, nārrā́vī, nārrā́tum - to tell, report, narrate (24)

nā́vigō, nāvigā́re, nāvigā́vī, nāvigā́tum - to sail, navigate (17)

nécō, necā́re, necā́vī, necā́tum - to murder, kill (7)

négō, negā́re, negā́vī, negā́tum to deny, say that . . . not (25)

nū́ntiō, nūntiā́re, nūntiā́vī, nūntiā́tum - to announce, report, relate (25)

obléctō, oblectā́re, oblectā́vī, oblectā́tum - to please, amuse, delight; pass time pleasantly (36)

oppúgnō, oppugnā́re, oppugnā́vī, oppugnā́tum - to fight against, attack, assault, assail (39)

ṓrnō, ōrnā́re, ōrnā́vī, ornā́tum - to equip, furnish, adorn (39)

ṓrō, ōrā́re, ōrā́vī, ōrā́tum - to speak, plead; beg, beseech, entreat, pray (36)

párō, parā́re, parā́vī, parā́tum - to prepare, provide; get, obtain (19)

pernóctō, pernoctā́re, pernoctā́vī, pernoctā́tum - to spend *or* occupy the night (39)

praéstō, praestā́re, praéstitī, praéstitum - to excel; exhibit, show, offer, supply, furnish (28)

próbō, probā́re, probā́vī, probā́tum - to approve, recommend; test (27)

prōnū́ntiō, prōnūntiā́re, prōnūntiā́vī, prōnūntiā́tum - to proclaim, announce; declaim; pronounce (20)

púgnō, pugnā́re, pugnā́vī, pugnā́tum - to fight (29)

pútō, putā́re, putā́vī, putā́tum - to reckon, suppose, judge, think, imagine (25)

récitō, recitā́re, recitā́vī, recitā́tum - to read aloud, recite (17)

récreō, recreā́re, recreā́vī, recreā́tum - to restore, revive; refresh, cheer (36)

recū́sō, recūsā́re, recūsā́vī, recūsā́tum - to refuse (33)

rógō, rogā́re, rogā́vī, rogā́tum - to ask (30)

sátiō, satiā́re, satiā́vī, satiā́tum - to satisfy, sate (3)

serḗnō, serēnā́re, serēnā́vī, serēnā́tum - to make clear, brighten; cheer up, soothe (36)

sérvō, servā́re, servā́vī, servā́tum - to preserve, save, keep, guard (1)

spéctō, spectā́re, spectā́vī, spectā́tum - to look at, see (34)

spḗrō, spērā́re, spērā́vī, spērā́tum - to hope for, hope (25)

stō, stā́re, stétī, státum - to stand, stand still *or* firm (13)

súperō, superā́re, superā́vī, superā́tum - to be above, have the upper hand, surpass; overcome, conquer (5)

tólerō, tolerā́re, tolerā́vī, tolerā́tum - to bear, endure (6)

vī́tō, vītā́re, vītā́vī, vītā́tum - to avoid, shun (14)

vócō, vocā́re, vocā́vī, vocā́tum - to call, summon (1)

2nd Conjugation

aúdeō, audḗre, aúsus sum - to dare (7)

cáreō, carḗre, cáruī, caritū́rum (+abl.) - to be without, be deprived of, want, lack; be free from (20)

contíneō, continḗre, contínuī, conténtum - to hold together, contain, keep, enclose, restrain (21)

dḗbeō, dēbḗre, dḗbuī, dḗbitum - to owe; ought, must, should (1)

déleō, dēlḗre, dēlḗvī, dēlḗtum - to destroy, wipe out, erase (17)

dóceō, docḗre, dócuī, dóctum - to teach (8)

dóleō, dolḗre, dóluī, dolitū́rum - to grieve, suffer; hurt, give pain (31)

égeō, egḗre, éguī (+ abl. or gen.) - to need, lack, want (28)

éxpleō, explḗre, explḗvī, explḗtum - to fill, fill up, complete (28)

fóveō, fovḗre, fṓvī, fṓtum - to comfort, nurture, cherish (35)

gaúdeō, gaudḗre, gāvī́sus sum - to be glad, rejoice (23)

hábeō, habḗre, hábuī, hábitum - to have, hold, possess; consider, regard (3)

iáceō, iacḗre, iácuī - to lie; lie prostrate; lie dead (25)

invídeō, invidḗre, invī́dī, invī́sum to be envious; to look at with envy, envy, be jealous of (+dat.) (31)

iúbeō, iubḗre, iússī, iússum - to bid, order, command (21)

máneō, manḗre, mā́nsī, mā́nsum - to remain, stay, stay behind, abide, continue (5)

mísceō, miscḗre, míscuī, míxtum to mix, stir up, disturb (18)

móneō, monḗre, mónuī, mónitum - to remind, advise, warn (1)

móveō, movḗre, mṓvī, mṓtum - to move; arouse, affect (18)

nóceō, nocḗre, nócuī, nócitum (+dat.) - to do harm to, harm, injure (35)
pā́reō, pārḗre, pā́ruī (+dat.) - to be obedient to, obey (35)
páteō, patḗre, pátuī - to be open, lie open; be accessible; be evident (32)
persuā́deō, persuādḗre, persuā́sī, persuā́sum (+dat.) to succeed in urging, persuade, convince (35)
pláceō, placḗre, plácuī, plácitum (+dat.) - to be pleasing to, please (35)
praébeō, praebḗre, praébuī, praébitum - to offer, provide (32)
prohíbeō, prohibḗre, prohíbuī, prohíbitum - to keep (back), prevent, hinder, restrain, prohibit (20)
remáneō, remanḗre, remā́nsī, remā́nsum - to remain, stay, stay behind, abide, continue (5)
respóndeō, respondḗre, respóndī, respṓnsum - to answer (29)
rī́deō, rīdḗre, rī́sī, rī́sum - to laugh, laugh at (24)
sálvē, salvḗte - hello, greetings (1)
sálveō, salvḗre - to be well, be in good health (1)
sédeō, sedḗre, sḗdī, séssum - to sit (34)
sóleō, solḗre, sólitus sum - to be accustomed (37)
stúdeō, studḗre, stúduī (+dat.) - to direct one's zeal to, be eager for, study (35)
subrī́deō, subrīdḗre, subrī́sī, subrī́sum - to smile (down) upon (35)
táceō, tacḗre, tácuī, tácitum - to be silent, leave unmentioned (28)
téneō, tenḗre, ténuī, téntum - to hold, keep, possess; restrain (14)
térreō, terrḗre, térruī, térritum - to frighten, terrify (1)
tímeō, timḗre, tímuī - to fear, be afraid (of) (15)
válē, valḗte - good-bye, farewell (1)
váleō, valḗre, váluī, valitū́rum - to be strong, have power; be well (1)
vídeō, vidḗre, vī́dī, vī́sum - to see; observe, understand (1)
vídeor, vidḗrī, vī́sus sum - to be seen, seem, appear (18)

3rd Conjugation

accḗdō, accḗdere, accéssī, accéssum - to come (to), approach (36)
admíttō, admíttere, admī́sī, admíssum - to admit, receive, let in (17)
ágō, ágere, ḗgī, ā́ctum - to drive, lead, do, act; pass, spend *(life or time)* (8)
álō, álere, áluī, áltum - to nourish, support, sustain, increase; cherish (13)
āmíttō, āmíttere, āmī́sī, āmíssum - to send away; lose, let go (12)
antepṓnō, antepṓnere, antepósuī, antepósitum - to put before, prefer (35)
āvértō, āvértere, āvértī, āvérsum - to turn away, avert (23)
bíbō, bíbere, bíbī - to drink (30)
cádō, cádere, cécidī, cāsū́rum - to fall (12)
cárpō, cárpere, cárpsī, cárptum to harvest, pluck; seize (36)
cḗdō, cḗdere, céssī, céssum - to go, withdraw; yield to, grant, submit (28)
cérnō, cérnere, crḗvī, crḗtum - to distinguish, discern, perceive (22)
cognṓscō, cognṓscere, cognṓvī, cógnitum - to become acquainted with, learn, recognize; know *(in perfect tenses)* (30)
cṓgō, cṓgere, coḗgī, coā́ctum - to drive *or* bring together, force, compel (36)
commíttō, commíttere, commī́sī, commíssum - to entrust, commit (15)
comprehéndō, comprehéndere, comprehéndī, comprehḗnsum - to grasp, seize, arrest; comprehend, understand (30)
cóndō, cóndere, cóndidī, cónditum - to put together *or* into, store; found, establish (29)
cōnsū́mō, cōnsū́mere, cōnsū́mpsī, cōnsū́mptum - to consume, use up (30)
contémnō, contémnere, contémpsī, contémptum - to despise, scorn (36)
conténdō, conténdere, conténdī, conténtum - to strive, struggle, contend; hasten (29)
contúndō, contúndere, cóntudī, contū́sum - to beat, crush, bruise, destroy (36)
crḗdō, crḗdere, crḗdidī, crḗditum to believe, trust (25)
crḗscō, crḗscere, crḗvī, crḗtum - to increase (34)
cúrrō, cúrrere, cucúrrī, cúrsum - to run, rush, move quickly (14)
dēcérnō, dēcérnere, dēcrḗvī, dēcrḗtum - to decide, settle, decree (36)
dēféndō, dēféndere, dēféndī, dēfḗnsum - to ward off; defend, protect (20)

dī́cō, dī́cere, dī́xī, díctum - to say, tell, speak; name, call (10)
dī́ligō, dīlígere, dīlḗxī, dīlḗctum - to esteem, love (13)
discḗdō, discḗdere, discéssī, discéssum - to go away, depart (20)
dī́scō, dī́scere, dídicī - to learn (8)
dū́cō, dū́cere, dū́xī, dúctum - to lead; consider, regard; prolong (8)
éxigō, exígere, exḗgī, exā́ctum - to drive out, force out, exact; drive through, complete, perfect (36)
expéllō, expéllere, éxpulī, expúlsum - to drive out, expel, banish (24)
expṓnō, expṓnere, expósuī, expósitum - to set forth, explain, expose (30)
flúō, flúere, flū́xī, flū́xum - to flow (18)
gérō, gérere, géssī, géstum - to carry; carry on, manage, conduct, wage, accomplish, perform (8)
ignṓscō, ignṓscere, ignṓvī, ignṓtum (+dat.) - to grant pardon to, forgive (35)
intéllegō, intellégere, intellḗxī, intellḗctum - to understand (11)
iúngō, iúngere, iū́nxī, iū́nctum - to join (13)
légō, légere, lḗgī, lḗctum - to pick out, choose; read (18)
métuō, metúere, métuī - to fear, dread; be afraid for (+dat.) (38)
mínuō, minúere, mínuī, minū́tum - to lessen, diminish (30)
míttō, míttere, mī́sī, míssum - to send, let go (11)
néglegō, neglégere, neglḗxī, neglḗctum - to neglect, disregard (17)
nṓscō, nṓscere, nṓvī, nṓtum - to become acquainted with, learn, recognize; know *(in perfect tenses)* (30)
nū́bō, nū́bere, nū́psī, nū́ptum (+dat.) - to cover, veil; to be married to, marry (35)
óccidō, occídere, óccidī, occā́sum - to fall down; die; set (31)
ópprimō, opprímere, oppréssī, oppréssum - to suppress, overwhelm, overpower, check (23)
osténdō, osténdere, osténdī, osténtum - to exhibit, show, display (23)
párcō, párcere, pepércī, parsū́rum (+dat.) - to be lenient to, spare (35)
péllō, péllere, pépulī, púlsum - to strike, push; drive out, banish (24)
pétō, pétere, petī́vī, petī́tum - to seek, aim at, beg, beseech (23)
pṓnō, pṓnere, pósuī, pósitum - to put, place, set (27)
prémō, prémere, préssī, préssum - to press; press hard, pursue (23)
prōmíttō, prōmíttere, prōmī́sī, prōmíssum - to send forth; promise (32)
quaérō, quaérere, quaesī́vī, quaesī́tum - to seek, look for, strive for; ask, inquire, inquire into (24)
recognṓscō, recognṓscere, recognṓvī, recógnitum - to recognize, recollect (38)
régō, régere, rḗxī, rḗctum - to rule, guide, direct (16)
relínquō, relínquere, relī́quī, relíctum - to leave behind, leave, abandon, desert (21)
requiḗscō, requiḗscere, requiḗvī, requiḗtum - to rest (37)
requī́rō, requī́rere, requīsī́vī, requīsī́tum - to seek, ask for; miss, need, require (36)
revértō, revértere, revértī, revérsum - turn back (23)
scrī́bō, scrī́bere, scrī́psī, scrī́ptum to write, compose (8)
súrgō, súrgere, surrḗxī, surrḗctum - to get up, arise (29)
suspéndō, suspéndere, suspéndī, suspḗnsum - to hang up, suspend; interrupt (38)
tángō, tángere, tétigī, tā́ctum - to touch (21)
tóllō, tóllere, sústulī, sublā́tum - to raise, lift up; take away, remove, destroy (22)
trā́dō, trā́dere, trā́didī, trā́ditum to give over, surrender; hand down, transmit, teach (33)
tráhō, tráhere, trā́xī, tráctum - to draw, drag; derive, acquire (8)
vḗndō, vḗndere, vḗndidī, vḗnditum - to sell (38)
vértō, vértere, vértī, vérsum - to turn; change (23)
víncō, víncere, vī́cī, víctum - to conquer, overcome (8)
vī́vō, vī́vere, vī́xī, vī́ctum - to live (10)

3rd Conjugation -iō

accípiō, accípere, accḗpī, accéptum - to take *(to one's self)*, receive, accept (24)
cápiō, cápere, cḗpī, cáptum - to take, capture, seize, get (10)
cúpiō, cúpere, cupī́vī, cupī́tum - to desire, wish, long for (17)

ērípiō, ērípere, ērípuī, ēréptum - to snatch away, take away; rescue (22)
excípiō, excípere, excḗpī, excéptum - to take out, except; take, receive, capture (24)
fáciō, fácere, fḗcī, fáctum - to make, do, accomplish (10)
fúgiō, fúgere, fū́gī, fugitū́rum - to flee, hurry away; escape; go into exile; avoid, shun (10)
iáciō, iácere, iḗcī, iáctum - to throw, hurl (15)
incípiō, incípere, incḗpī, incéptum - to begin (17)
interfíciō, interfícere, interfḗcī, interféctum - to kill, murder (37)
patefáciō, patefácere, patefḗcī, patefáctum - to make open, open; disclose, expose (25)
rápiō, rápere, rápuī, ráptum - to seize, snatch, carry away (21)
recípiō, recípere, recḗpī, recéptum - to take back, regain; admit, receive (24)
sápiō, sápere, sapī́vī - to have good taste; have good sense, be wise (35)
suscípiō, suscípere, suscḗpī, suscéptum - to undertake (25)

4th Conjugation

aúdiō, audī́re, audī́vī, audī́tum - to hear, listen to (10)
dórmiō, dormī́re, dormī́vī, dormī́tum - to sleep (31)
impédiō, impedī́re, impedī́vī, impedī́tum - to impede, hinder, prevent (38)
invéniō, invenī́re, invḗnī, invéntum - to come upon, find (10)
mólliō, mollī́re, mollī́vī, mollī́tum to soften; make calm *or* less hostile (29)
nésciō, nescī́re, nescī́vī, nescī́tum - to not know, be ignorant (25)
repériō, reperī́re, répperī, repértum - to find, discover, learn; get (40)
scíō, scī́re, scī́vī, scī́tum - to know (21)
séntiō, sentī́re, sḗnsī, sḗnsum - to feel, perceive, think, experience (11)
sérviō, servī́re, servī́vī, servī́tum (+dat.) - to be a slave to, serve (35)
véniō, venī́re, vḗnī, véntum - to come (10)

Irregular

ábeō, abī́re, ábiī, ábitum - to go away, depart, leave (37)
ádeō, adī́re, ádiī, áditum - to go to, approach (37)
ádferō, adférre, áttulī, allā́tum - to bring to (31)
cṓnferō, cōnférre, cóntulī, collā́tum - to bring together, compare; confer, bestow (31)
éō, ī́re, íī, ítum - to go (37)
éxeō, exī́re, éxiī, éxitum - to go out, exit (37)
férō, férre, túlī, lā́tum - to bear, carry, bring; suffer, endure, tolerate; say, report (31)
fī́ō, fíerī, fáctus sum - to occur, happen; become; be made, be done (36)
íneō, inī́re, íniī, ínitum - to enter into, begin (37)
mā́lō, mā́lle, mā́luī - to want (something) more, instead; prefer (32)
nṓlō, nṓlle, nṓluī - to not . . . wish, be unwilling (32)
óbeō, obī́re, óbiī, óbitum - to go up against, meet; die (37)
ófferō, offérre, óbtulī, oblā́tum - to offer (31)
péreō, perī́re, périī, péritum - to pass away, be destroyed, perish (37)
póssum, pósse, pótuī - to be able, can, could, have power (6)
rédeō, redī́re, rédiī, réditum - to go back, return (37)
réferō, reférre, réttulī, relā́tum - to carry back, bring back; repeat, answer, report (31)
sum, ésse, fúī, futū́rum - to be, exist (4)
trā́nseō, trānsī́re, trā́nsiī, trā́nsitum - to go across, cross; pass over, ignore (39)
vólō, vélle, vóluī - to wish, want, be willing, will (32)

Deponent

árbitror, arbitrā́rī, arbitrā́tus sum to judge, think (34)
cṓnor, cōnā́rī, cōnā́tus sum - to try, attempt (34)
ēgrédior, ḗgredī, ēgréssus sum - to go out (34)
expérior, experī́rī, expértus sum to try, test; experience (39)
fáteor, fatḗrī, fássus sum - to confess, admit (34)
for, fā́rī, fā́tus sum - to speak (prophetically), talk, foretell (40)
hórtor, hortā́rī, hortā́tus sum - to encourage, urge (34)
lóquor, lóquī, locū́tus sum - to say, speak, tell (34)
mī́ror, mīrā́rī, mīrā́tus sum - to marvel at, admire, wonder (35)
mṓlior, mōlī́rī, mōlī́tus sum - to work at, build, undertake, plan (34)

mórior, mórī, mórtuus sum - to die (34)
nā́scor, nā́scī, nā́tus sum - to be born; spring forth, arrive (34)
opī́nor, opīnā́rī, opīnā́tus sum - to suppose (40)
pátior, pátī, pássus sum - to suffer, endure; permit (34)
peregrī́nor, peregrīnā́rī, peregrīnā́tus sum - to travel abroad, wander (37)
proficī́scor, proficī́scī, proféctus sum - to set out, start (34)
quéror, quérī, quéstus sum - to complain, lament (38)
rū́sticor, rūsticā́rī, rūsticā́tus sum to live in the country (34)
séquor, séquī, secū́tus sum - to follow (34)
ū́tor, ū́tī, ū́sus sum (+abl.) - to use; enjoy, experience (34)
véreor, verḗrī, véritus sum - to show reverence for, respect; be afraid of, fear (40)

Defective

ā́it, ā́iunt - he says, they say, assert (25)
coépī, coepísse, coéptum - began (17)
ínquit - he says *or* said (22)
ṓdī, ōdísse, ōsū́rum - to hate (20)

Impersonal

lícet, licḗre, lícuit (+dat. +infin.) - it is permitted *(for someone to do something)*, one may (37)
opórtet, oportḗre, opórtuit (+infin.) - it is proper, right, necessary (39)

Adverbs

ánte (+acc.) - before, previously (13)
béne - well, satisfactorily, quite (11)
cíto - quickly (17)
cōtī́diē - daily, every day (36)
crās - tomorrow (5)
cūr - why (18)
déhinc - then, next (25)
deínde - thereupon, next, then (18)
dḗnique - at last, finally, lastly (29)
díū - long, for a long time (12)
étiam - even, also (11)
fóris - out of doors, outside (37)
fortásse - perhaps (36)
fū́rtim - stealthily, secretly (30)
héri - yesterday (5)
hīc - here (25)
hódiē - today (3)
iam - now, already, soon (19)
íbi - there (6)
íta - so, thus (29)
ítaque - and so, therefore (15)
íterum - again, a second time (21)
libénter - with pleasure, gladly (38)
mox - soon (30)
nē . . . quídem - not . . . even (29)
nímis, nímium - too, too much, excessively; *(in a positive sense, esp. with adjectives and adverbs)* exceedingly, very (9)
nōn - not (1)
nṓnne - introduces questions expecting the answer "yes" (40)
num - 1. introduces direct questions which expect the answer "no"
2. introduces indirect questions and means *whether* (40)
númquam - never (8)
nunc - now, at present (6)
nū́per - recently (12)
ṓlim - once (upon a time), long ago, formerly; some day, in the future (13)
omnī́nō - wholly, entirely, altogether; *(with negatives)* at all (40)
pósteā - afterwards (24)
postrḗmum - after all, finally; for the last time (40)
prī́mō - at first, at the beginning (30)
prṓtinus - immediately (22)
quam - how (16)
quam - than *(after comparatives)*; as . . . as possible *(with superlatives)* (26)
quándō - when (5)
quā́rē - because of which thing *(lit.)*; therefore, wherefore, why (6)
quási - as if, as it were (39)
quídem - indeed, certainly, at least, even (29)
quīn - indeed, in fact, furthermore (40)
quóndam - formerly, once (22)
quóque - also, too (17)
repénte - suddenly (30)
saépe - often (1)
sátis - enough, sufficiently (5)
sémel - a single time, once, once and for all, simultaneously (31)
sémper - always (3)
sīc - so, thus (29)
súbitō - suddenly (33)
tam - so, to such a degree (29)
tam . . . quam - so . . . as (29)
támen - nevertheless, still (8)
tamquam - as it were, as if, so to speak (29)
tántum - only (26)
tum - then, at that time; thereupon, in the next place (5)
úbi - where, when (6)

últrā - on the other side of, beyond (22)
úmquam - ever, at any time (23)
únde - whence, from what *or* which place, from which, from whom (30)
úsque - all the way, up (to), even (to), continuously, always (31)
vḗrō - in truth, indeed, to be sure, however (29)

Conjunctions

at - but; but, mind you; but, you say (19)
átque, ac - and also, and even, and in fact (21)
aut - or (17)
aut . . . aut - either . . . or (17)
aútem - however; moreover (11)
cum (+indic.) - when (31)
cum (+subj.) - when, since, although (31)
dum - while, as long as, at the same time that; *or* until *(+subjunctive)* (8)
dúmmodo (+subj.) - provided that, so long as (32)
énim - for, in fact, truly (9)
et - and; even (2)
et . . . et - both . . . and (2)
étsī - even if, although (38)
ígitur - therefore, consequently (5)
nam - for (13)
nē - not; in order that . . . not, that . . . not, in order not to (28)
néque, nec - and not, nor (11)
néque . . . néque, nec . . . nec - neither . . . nor (11)
nísi - if . . . not, unless; except (19)
quod - because (11)
quóniam - since, inasmuch as (10)
sed - but (2)
sī - if (1)
ut (+indic.) - as, just as, when (24)
ut (+ subj.) - in order that, so that, that, in order to, so as to, to (28)
útrum . . . an - whether . . . or (30)

Prepositions

ab, ā (+abl.) - away from, from; by (14)
ad (+acc.) - to, up to, near to (8)
ánte (+acc.) - before *(in place or time)*, in front of (13)
ápud (+acc.) - among, in the presence of, at the house of (31)
cóntrā (+acc.) - against (19)
cum (+abl.) - with (10)
dē (+abl.) - down from, from; concerning, about (3)
érga (+acc.) - toward (38)
ex, ē (abl.+) - out of, from, from within; by reason of, on account of; of *(after cardinal numerals)* (8)
in (+acc.) - into, toward; against (9)
in (+abl.) - in, on (3)
ínter (+acc.) - between, among (15)
per (+acc.) - through; by *(with reflexive pronoun)* (13)
post (+acc.) - after, behind (7)
prae (+abl.) - in front of, before (26)
praéter (+acc.) - besides, except; beyond, past (40)
prō (+abl.) - in front of, before, on behalf of, for the sake of, in return for, instead of, for, as (12)
própter (+acc.) - on account of, because of (5)
síne (+abl.) - without (2)
sub (+abl. w/ verbs of rest *or* +acc. w/ verbs of motion) - under, up under, close to, down to/into, to/at the foot of (7)
trāns (+acc.) - across (14)
últrā (adv. and prep. +acc.) - on the other side of, beyond (22)

Interjections

heu - ah!, alas! (33)
ō - O!, Oh! (2)
vae (often +dat. or acc.) - alas, woe to (34)

Idioms

amā́bō tē - please (1)
grā́tiās ágere (+dat.) - to thank someone; to give thanks to (8)
mḗnsa secúnda (f) - dessert (26)
nōn sṓlum . . . sed étiam - not only . . . but also (9)
poénās dáre - to pay the penalty (2)
sē cōnférre - to go (31)
sī quándō - if ever (5)

Prefix

re-, red- - again, back (24)

Suffixes

-ne – interrogative suffix attached to the first word of a sentence, typically the verb or another word on which the question hinges, to introduce a question whose answer is uncertain (5)
-que - and *(enclitic conjunction; appended to the second of two words to be joined)* (6)
-ve - or (33)

Numerals

Cardinal - ū́nus *to* vīgíntī quī́nque (15)

Ordinal - prī́mus *to* duodécimus (15)

----

céntum - a hundred (15)

mī́lia, mī́lium (n. pl.) - thousands (15)

mī́lle - thousand (15)

WHEELOCKIANA

READINGS FROM WHEELOCK'S LATIN

Mark Robert Miner (readings and performances)
and Richard A. LaFleur (producer)

This 4-CD audio package has recitation in restored classical pronunciation of all vocabulary and paradigms in *Wheelock's Latin,* as well as dramatic readings of *Sententiae Antiquae* and narrative passages, and brief representative selections from the *Loci Antiqui.* Students who hear Latin correctly pronounced have an edge in memorization; and listening to dramatic readings increases aural skills. Listening while reading silently helps increase retention during review of sentences and longer passages.

Running Time: 280 minutes (4 CDs) + 8 pp. booklet (2006)
Audio CDs + booklet , ISBN 978-0-86516-638-7

38 LATIN STORIES

Anne H. Groton and James M. May

Originally designed as a supplement to the Latin course by F. M. Wheelock, this book is well suited for use in any introductory or review course. All the stories are based on actual Latin literature, simplified at first and made gradually more complex. Students will learn how classical Latin was really written as they become familiar with the works of the great Latin authors. The Teacher's Guide contains literal translations of all the stories.

> I would enthusiastically recommend *38 Latin Stories* to all those who teach elementary Latin via Wheelock . . .
>
> –Richard A. LaFleur
>
> Anyone looking for an easy reader to augment a conventional Latin course could well consider this book.
>
> –Ian Pratt, *JACT,* England
>
> Excellent . . . it improved my students' reading ability and also gave the opportunity to talk about Roman culture
>
> –Robert Brown, Vassar College

Student Text: vi + 104 pp. (5th edition, 1995, revised 2004)
6" x 9" Paperback, ISBN 978-0-86516-289-1
Teacher's Guide: vi + 26 (2004) 6" x 9" Paperback, ISBN 978-0-86516-591-5

BOLCHAZY CARDUCCI PUBLISHERS, INC.
WWW.BOLCHAZY.COM